D0845168

butterflyfishes
of the world

a monograph of the family chaetodontidae

by dr. warren e. burgess

Cover: *Chaetodon trifasciatus, Chaetodon xanthurus,* and *Chaetodon auriga.* A Colour Library International Photo.

Frontispiece: *Chaetodon semilarvatus*

All black and white photos are by the author, unless credited otherwise.

© 1978 by T.F.H. Publications, Inc. Ltd.

ISBN 0-87666-470-2

Distributed in the U.S.A. by T.F.H. Publications, Inc., 211 West Sylvania Avenue, P.O. Box 27, Neptune City, N.J. 07753; in England by T.F.H. (Gt. Britain) Ltd., 13 Nutley Lane, Reigate, Surrey; in Canada to the book store and library trade by Clarke, Irwin & Company, Clarwin House, 791 St. Clair Avenue West, Toronto 10, Ontario; in Canada to the pet trade by Rolf C. Hagen Ltd., 3225 Sartelon Street, Montreal 382, Quebec; in Southeast Asia by Y.W. Ong, 9 Lorong 36 Geylang, Singapore 14; in Australia and the south Pacific by Pet Imports Pty. Ltd., P.O. Box 149, Brookvale 2100, N.S.W., Australia. Published by T.F.H. Publications, Inc. Ltd.,

This book is dedicated to my wife Lourdes without whose love and understanding this work would have been impossible.

Table of Contents

This book represents a dissertation presented to the faculty of the University of Hawaii, Honolulu, Hawaii, in partial fulfillment of the requirements for the degree of Doctor of Philosophy. The information presented here was freely available in manuscript form for a period of more than ten years, and I thank my colleagues who generously withheld publishing any parts of my study until the publication of this book. The classification used here is basically the same as that of the early drafts, but where recent publications changed the status of a species a footnote has been added. My thanks also to colleagues who have helped me keep up to date with the latest papers since I left the campus of the University of Hawaii with its magnificent library facilities.

Chaetodon rainfordi.
Photo by Allan Power

Introduction

Butterflyfishes are among the most popular of reef fishes. Their striking color patterns and flitting type movements over the reef are reminiscent of the insects for which they are so aptly named. Scientists and laymen alike have been attracted to these colorful fishes and the volume of information published on them is enormous. Unfortunately much of the information is inaccurate and, although most ichthyologists have believed the classification of these fishes to be relatively stable, this study has revealed a surprising number of systematic problems, the solutions of which necessitate many changes in nomenclature.

The last major revision of the butterflyfishes was made by E. Ahl in 1923. It was relatively complete for that period of time but lack of extensive museum material and published information greatly restricted the import of that work. On completion of some preliminary investigations in 1960, I found a number of errors in Ahl's work, decided a modern revision was necessary, and began to study the butterflyfishes and angelfishes. The problem of amassing enough specimens and literature for as complete a work as the present one has been facilitated by modern modes of communication and transportation. Well over 30,000 specimens of butterflyfishes and angelfishes from all over the world have been examined during my investigations and in that time I have also gathered more than 1,000 references dealing with these fishes.

Butterflyfishes and angelfishes have generally been considered subfamilies of the family Chaetodontidae. In the present study they are considered as separate families and substantial evidence is presented supporting the elevation of the angelfishes to family level (Pomacanthidae).

One hundred and fourteen species of butterflyfishes, in ten genera, are recognized in the present work. The largest genus, *Chaetodon*, is subdivided into thirteen subgenera.

Published information on the behavior and ecology of the family is summarized and additional information from personal observations is presented. Much more data are needed on the biology of these fishes, however. It is hoped that this study will generate more interest in the group, making possible a greater understanding of the butterflyfishes and their role on the coral reefs of the world.

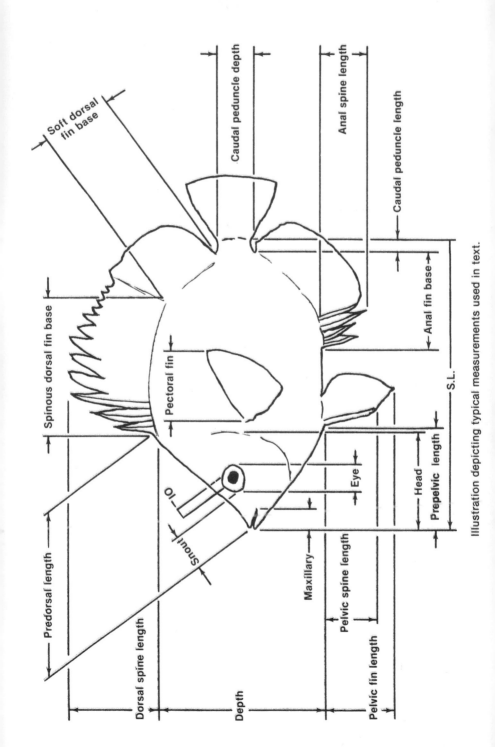

Illustration depicting typical measurements used in text.

Methods and Materials

More than two thousand specimens of butterflyfishes were used for detailed measurements and counts. These are listed under the material examined section of each species account. Many additional specimens were more briefly surveyed for variations in color pattern, anomalies, ontogenetic changes, locality data, geographic variations, etc.; the latter are not listed in the material examined section.

Material used in dissections and osteological studies came mainly from the Hawaiian Islands, Johnston Atoll, and the Marshall Islands.

In the summer of 1968 the following institutions were visited for the purpose of examining the pomacanthids and chaetodontids, and specimens were generously loaned for further study. All specimens on the shelves at that time were examined. Abbreviations that follow the institution names are used in the material examined sections: California Academy of Sciences (CAS); Stanford University (now housed at CAS) (SU); United States National Museum of Natural History (USNM); Academy of Natural Sciences, Philadelphia (ANSP); Museum of Comparative Zoology, Harvard University (MCZ); and the American Museum of Natural History (AMNH). In addition the collections of the Bernice P. Bishop Museum (BPBM), Hawaii Institute of Marine Biology (HIMB), University of Hawaii Department of Zoology (UH), National Marine Fisheries Service, Miami (NMFS-M), National Marine Fisheries Service, Honolulu (NMFS-H), Eniwetok Marine Biological Laboratory (EMBL), and the University of Miami Rosenstiel School of Marine and Atmospheric Sciences (UMML) were studied.

Foreign museums visited included the Australian Museum, Sydney (AMS), Philippine National Museum, Manila (PNP), Zoologischen Staatssammlung, Munchen (SMM), Senckenberg Museum u. Forschungs-Institut, Frankfurt a. Main (SMF), and the British Museum (Natural History), London (BMNH).

Loans of specimens, in addition to those listed above, were made by the Smithsonian Oceanographic Sorting Center (these specimens are now housed at the USNM) (SOSC); Scripps Institution of Oceanography (SIO); Los Angeles County Museum (LACM); Field Museum of Natural History, Chicago (FMNH); British Museum (Natural History) (BMNH);

11

Museum National d'Histoire Naturelle, Paris (MNHN); J.L.B. Smith Institute of Ichthyology, Grahamstown (JLBS); Australian Museum, Sydney (AMS); Western Australian Museum, Perth (WAM); Natur-museum u. Forschungs-Institut "Senckenberg" (SMF); and Rijksmuseum van Natuurlijke Historie (RMNH).

A number of specimens were personally collected and others were given to me by individuals. These have been deposited in museums, mostly BPBM and USNM, and are listed in the material examined sections under the abbreviation (WEB).

Specimens used for measurements and counts and listed in the material examined sections are abbreviated by listing only the number of specimens and the range of standard lengths in millimeters (for example, three specimens of standard length ranging from 72 to 130 mm would be written (3: 72-130)). These specimens are also listed in the tables of proportional measurements after their specific size ranges.

Measurements were made with the aid of dial calipers and recorded to the nearest tenth of a millimeter. The standard methods of Hubbs and Lagler (1958) were employed in making the measurements. Some of the measurements, however, need qualification:

Depth: vertically from pelvic fin base to base of dorsal fin.

Head: from tip of snout to posterior edge of opercular bone.

Eye: horizontal diameter of bony orbit.

Snout: anterior edge of bony orbit to tip of snout.

Pectoral fin length: from upper point of insertion of pectoral fin to tip of longest ray.

Interorbital width: least width of bony interorbital.

Prepelvic fin length: from tip of lower jaw to base of pelvic spine.

The measurement of body depth is difficult to obtain because scales obscure the juncture of body and dorsal fin. Some authors, such as Ahl (1923), have preferred not to use this measurement due to its unreliability. Since it is useful, particularly in the separation of subgenera, it has been included in this monograph. A fairly precise measurement can be obtained by one of two methods: (1) hold the specimen up to a strong light so that the bases of the spines can be seen; (2) move the spines laterally to see where the point of flexion, and hence the base of the spines, is located. Fin spine lengths can be obtained using these same methods.

The head measurement was taken to the bony edge of the opercle rather than the posterior edge of the opercular membrane because the membrane is often damaged and distorted on preserved material. In addition, the larval (tholichthys) plates (see fig. 10A) that are still present in prejuvenile and juvenile specimens interfered with this measurement.

The last dorsal fin ray is normally split to its base. Upon dissection it can be seen to have a single basal element. This split ray is therefore considered as one ray. A similar situation exists in the last ray of the anal fin. All pectoral fin elements were counted except the uppermost short element.

Cleared and stained skeleton of a juvenile *Chaetodon vagabundus*. Prepared and photographed by Glen S. Axelrod.

Scales were counted along the lateral line to a point near the last ray of the dorsal fin on a level with the upper edge of the caudal peduncle in those specimens with an incomplete lateral line. Scales were counted to the base of the caudal fin in those specimens with a complete lateral line. Scales above the lateral line were counted from the base of the first dorsal fin spine diagonally downward and backward to the lateral line. Small scales at the base of the spine were excluded from the count. Scales below the lateral line were counted from the base of the first anal fin spine diagonally upward and forward to the lateral line. Small scales at the base of the anal fin spine were not included. In several species (e.g. *Chaetodon triangulum*, *C. mertensii*, etc.) the pattern of the scales made this count difficult, for the scales follow a curved path to the lateral line instead of a straight one.

Skeletal material was prepared using two methods: (1) boiling to obtain disarticulated bones (2) using dermestid beetle colonies to obtain articulated skeletons.

The synonymy for each species includes only the following: (1) original descriptions; (2) synonyms; (3) all known misidentifications; (4) references which are pertinent to the discussion or which include important descriptions or illustrations. Subsequent correct identifications of either the original name or synonyms are not included. References in which the identification is uncertain (checklists, etc) are also not included. All references included in the bibliography were checked for possible inclusion in a synonymy.

The table of proportional measurements for each species is designed to show any ontogenetic changes that may occur. The tables are divided into three columns which represent, as far as can be determined, juvenile, mid-sized (subadult), and adult specimens. The figures used in the diagnoses and discussion of the species are all from the adult column unless otherwise specified. The descriptions were based entirely on the specimens seen; comparisons with the literature, if there are discrepancies, are noted in the text.

All black and white photographs were taken by the author. The color photos were obtained from various sources and were selected to depict life colors for each species, habitat, behavioral sequences, or other aspects of the butterflyfishes pertinent to this study.

Standardization of common names in fishes is desirable. Below the scientific name of each species in the description will be the preferred common name. These have been derived from sources such as the American Fisheries Society Common Names List (1970), faunal reports, current usage, etc. Additional common names, when they have been used extensively in addition to the preferred name, are included in parentheses in the same place.

Historical Review

Although Linnaeus' *Systema Naturae* (1758) marks the official starting point in zoological nomenclature it is useful to mention here a few works published previous to that time which had some influence on the systematic status of the chaetodontids. Since Linnaeus gave the briefest of descriptions, it is necessary to refer to pre-Linnaean publications at times to determine the correct identity of a species.

The first, and perhaps most important of these, was Artedi's *Ichthyologia* (1738). It was in this volume, under order Acanthopterygii, that the generic name *Chaetodon* was first used. Four species were listed in the third section, *Genera Piscium*, under the generic name *Chaetodon;* two of these are acanthurids and two pomacanthids. In the fourth section, *Synonymia Nominum Piscium*, ten species were included. The last two of these were chaetodontids, *Heniochus acuminatus* and *Chaetodon striatus.* The fifth section, *Descriptiones Specierum Piscium* contained the descriptions of these two species. Linnaeus referred frequently to the *Ichthyologia* in this *Systema Naturae*. Artedi probably aided in the preparation of the fish section of the *Systema*. Linnaeus' *Museum Adolphi Frederici* (1754) gave illustrations of some of the chaetodontids and is very helpful in their identification.

The *Historia Piscium Naturalis* (Klein, 1740-1744) must also be mentioned since it later influenced Bleeker (1868) to make changes in the nomenclature of the chaetodontids. Klein's genera were used in a post-Linnaean dictionary called "Neuer Schauplatz" (1775) and therefore came under consideration as valid names. Klein introduced the generic names *Tetragonoptrus* (not to be confused with *Tetragonopterus*, a genus applied to the characins), *Platiglossus*, and *Rhombotides*, all three of which contained species that are now considered as belonging in the family Chaetodontidae. Only the first-named genus, however, was later classified under the family name Chaetodontidae. Linnaeus made no reference to Klein's work.

In post-Linnaean literature, another pertinent publication, this one referred to in the *Systema Naturae*, was Seba's *Thesaurus Naturae* (1758). The plates were better than those of Linnaeus (1754) and more complete descriptions of each species were given.

In Linnaeus (1758) the genus *Chaetodon* was placed in the third division of the Pisces, the Thoracici (ventral fins below pectorals). Of the twenty species listed, only six were true chaetodontids; another two were pomacanthids. The remaining species were a mixture of fishes now recognized as acanthurids, pomacentrids, ephippids, and zanclids.

Very few changes were made in the chaetodontid classification, except for the addition of new species, until 1775, when Forsskal treated the genus. His subdivisions of the genus *Chaetodon* included *Chaetodon*, "Abu-defduf" and *Acanthurus*; the last name, however, was previously listed under the headings of new genera and included the species numbered 88-91. These species were all referred to as *Chaetodon* in the section giving species descriptions. The three sub-divisions of *Chaetodon* have been accepted as genera, thus the restriction of the genus *Chaetodon* had begun.

More species were added to the genus *Chaetodon* by Bloch (*Naturgeschichte der auslandischen Fische*, 1787-1793). He did not follow Forsskal (1775) and included acanthurids, pomacentrids, and even carangids in his genus *Chaetodon*. The illustrations were highly stylized but recognizable, and the descriptions were usually adequate. Further species were added and some editing of Bloch's work was accomplished by Schneider (Bloch and Schneider, *Systema Ichthyologia*, 1801).

Lacepede (*Histoire Naturelle des Poissons* IV, 1803) made a significant advance in the division of the genus *Chaetodon*. His most important changes with respect to the chaetodontids were the establishment of the genera *Pomacanthus* and *Holacanthus*. This, in combination with the removal of many non-chaetodontid and pomacanthid genera, reduced the genus to a group of species not unlike the concept of the family Chaetodontidae of today.

Cuvier (1817) erected the genus *Heniochus* and separated some longsnouted species into a grouping which he called 'Les Chelmons.' This name was in the vernacular, a matter which caused a great deal of confusion when both Cloquet and Oken latinized it at approximately the same time. A full discussion of this problem is given in the remarks section of genus *Chelmon*.

Cuvier's second edition of the *Regne Animal* (1829) included only one small change, a new subgenus, *Taurichthys*, of the genus *Heniochus*.

Cuvier, in Cuvier and Valenciennes (*Histoire Naturelle des Poissons* VII, 1831), attempted to include every known species of chaetodontid under their family heading Squamipennes. The family Squamipennes, placed in the order Acanthopterygiens, included those fishes which had the rayed portions of the dorsal and anal fins covered with scales. Among the present-day families included were the Ephippidae, Pomacanthidae, Pempheridae, Toxotidae, Scatophagidae, and Psettidae.

Swainson (*The Natural History of Fishes* . . ., 1839) added the genus *Rabdophorus* as well as the pomacanthid genus *Genicanthus* and the scorpidid genus *Microcanthus* to the Chaetodontidae.

Chaetodon striatus as illustrated in Evermann and Marsh (1902).

New species were constantly being added to the chaetodontids as the voyages of exploration and trade missions brought back specimens to the museums.

A small paper by Guichenot was published in 1848 in which he described the genus *Megaprotodon*.

At this time Bleeker commenced the publication of the results of his research on fishes in the East Indies. In the next twenty to thirty years he described many new species of butterflyfishes from the rich fauna of that area. His more than 500 papers were to be the basis of Weber and de Beaufort's *Fishes of the Indo-Australian Archipelago*.

Cantor (1849) proposed the genus *Diphreutes* to replace *Heniochus* Cuvier, supposedly preoccupied by *Henioche* Hubner, 1816 (Lepidoptera).

After removing such genera as *Psettus* and *Platax*, Gunther (*Catalogue of the Acanthopterygian Fishes of the British Museum* II, 1860) divided the family Squamipennes into three groups, Chaetodontina, Scorpedina, and Toxotina. These three groups have been raised to family level since that time. Within the Chaetodontina he included the true chaetodontids along with other genera of the families Pomacanthidae, Scatophagidae, Ephippidae, etc. The chaetodontid genera were *Chaetodon*, *Chelmo* (= *Chelmon*), and *Heniochus*.

Kaup's *Ueber die Chaetodontidae* appeared in the same year as Gunther's Catalogue (volume II). Kaup, however, restricted his treatment to the Chaetodontidae, dividing it into five subfamilies: (a) Dipterodontinae (*Dipterodon, Pimelepterus*); (b) Drepaninae (*Ephippus, Drepane, Scatophagus*); (c) Henjochinae (*Therapaina, Chelmon, Henjochus, Zanclus*); (d) Chaetodontinae (*Citharoedus, Coradion, Eteira, Chaetodon, Linophora*); (e) Psettinae (*Holacanthus, Pomacanthus, Centropyge, Platax, Psettus*). Although some of the genera he described are valid today, his system of classification of the group never gained acceptance.

The first American influence on the classification of the chaetodontids came when Gill (1861) tried to replace the name *Chaetodon* with *Sarothrodus*. He reasoned that Artedi's (1738) genus *Chaetodon* contained none of the species then regarded as true chaetodontids. A year later Gill (1862) established the genus name *Prognathodes* on the basis of a species he separated from the genus *Chelmon*.

Gunther (1868) described a rather peculiar-looking species with bony plates covering the head for which he erected a new genus, *Tholichthys*. This turned out to be a larval stage of a known species of *Chaetodon*. The name "tholichthys" has since been used for the larval stage of all butterfly-fishes much as "leptocephalus" has been used for eels, "acronurus" for acanthurids, etc.

Bleeker (1868), using the same arguments as Gill (1861), substituted *Tetragonoptrus* Klein for the name *Chaetodon*. He went further on this line of thought by stating (1876) that the first species mentioned by Artedi (1738) was one that belonged in the genus *Pomacanthus* as restricted by Cuvier (1831). He suggested the substitution of the generic name *Tetragonoptrus* for what was considered the genus *Chaetodon*, and *Chaetodon* as a substitute for the genus *Pomacanthus*. Although *Tetragonoptrus* appeared in many of his papers in this sense, he later reverted to the use of *Pomacanthus* rather than *Chaetodon* for the angelfishes.

In 1874 Bleeker added another genus, *Parachaetodon*, to the Chaetodontidae. In his *Systema Percarum Revisum* (1876) he described several more: *Hemitaurichthys, Chelmonops, Chaetodontops, Lepidochaetodon, Oxychaetodon*, and *Gonochaetodon*. Descriptions of these genera were repeated in his paper on the subfamily Taurichthyiformes (1876). A year later a second paper on the chaetodontids was published (*Revision des especes insulindiennes de la famille des Chetodontoides*, 1877). Volume IX of the *Atlas Ichthyologique*, a compendium of his work in the East Indies, which included the chaetodontids, appeared in 1877. Bleeker divided the Chaetodontidae into subfamilies as follows: (a) Taurichthyiformes (*Chelmon, Prognathodes, Taurichthys, Hemitaurichthys, Coradion, Tetragonoptrus, Chaetodon, Megaprotodon*); (b) Holacanthiformes (*Chaetodontoplus, Holacanthus, Acanthochaetodon*); (c) Plataciformes (*Platax*); (d) Zancliformes (*Zanclus*); (e) Pimelepteriformes (*Pimelepterus*); (f) Proteracanthiformes (*Proteracanthus*); (g) Chaetodipteriformes (*Harpochirus, Ilarches*); and (h) Scatophagiformes (*Scatophagus*).

Gill (1862) included the ephippids under the family Chaetodontidae but later (1873) separated them and considered them as two families. In 1883, on the basis of osteological research, he was convinced that they were definitely distinct, though closely related families.

Klunzinger (1870) distinguished two groups, the Chaetodontini and Drepanini and subsequently (1884) three subfamilies, Chaetodontinae, Holacanthinae, and Drepaninae. In his 1884 paper he proposed *Anisochaetodon* as a substitute name for *Linophora* Kaup and *Oxychaetodon* Bleeker. *Anisochaetodon* has been used by some authors (Weber and de Beaufort, 1936; Munro, 1967) but generally is considered as a synonym of *Linophora*, here considered a subgenus of the genus *Chaetodon*.

Jordan and Evermann (1898) raised Cuvier's Squamipennes to subordinal status under the Acanthopteri. Four families were included: Chaetodontidae, Ephippidae, Zanclidae, and Teuthididae. The chaetodontids contained the genera *Prognathodes*, *Forcipiger*, *Chaetodon*, *Pomacanthus*, *Holacanthus*, and *Angelichthys*. A new genus, *Forcipiger*, was based on a species originally placed in the genus *Chelmon*. The suborder Squamipennes was distinguished from the suborder Percoidea by having the posttemporal bone typically co-ossified with the skull, and 24 or fewer vertebrae. The relationships with other families included the Carangidae on the one hand and certain percoids on the other. In addition, Jordan and Evermann stated that the plectognaths were derived from the Squamipinnes, saying (p. 1666), "This relationship is shown in the osteology (the reduced post-temporal and the coalesced bones of the jaws, in the great development of the pubic bone, in the restriction of the gill openings and in the character of the scales, especially the armature of the tail.)" The family Chaetodontidae was divided into two subfamilies, Chaetodontinae and Pomacanthinae, the former containing the genera *Prognathodes*, *Forcipiger*, and *Chaetodon*.

Jordan and Fowler's *Review of the Chaetodontidae and related families of fishes found in the waters of Japan* (1902) still maintained two subfamilies; their Chaetodontinae included *Chaetodon*, *Coradion*, *Microcanthus*, and *Heniochus*.

Boulenger (1904) placed the family Chaetodontidae in his division Perciformes. He included additional genera such as *Ephippus*, *Parapsettus*, *Scatophagus*, *Platax*, *Holacanthus*, and *Pomacanthus* along with the usual genera *Chaetodon*, *Chelmo*, and *Heniochus*. *Drepane* was placed in a separate family, the Drepanidae.

Regan (1913), in his classification of the percoid fishes, listed families as the Ephippidae (*Ephippus*, *Platax*, *Parapsettus*), Drepanidae (*Drepane*), Scatophagidae (*Scatophagus*), and Chaetodontidae (*Chaetodon*, *Chelmo*, *Heniochus*, *Holacanthus*, and *Pomacanthus*).

Boulenger (1922) placed the chaetodontids in the suborder Acanthopterygii in the division Perciformes but did not conform to the ideas of Regan and kept the same genera in his family Chaetodontidae. He again maintained that there was a close relationship between the Scorpididae

Chaetodon ephippium

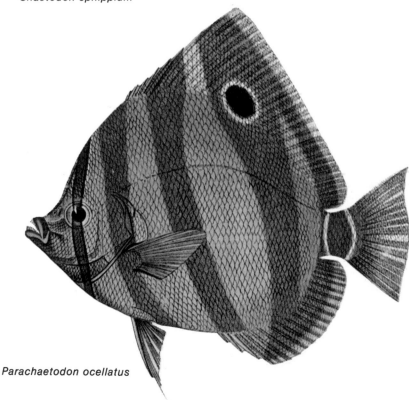

Parachaetodon ocellatus

20

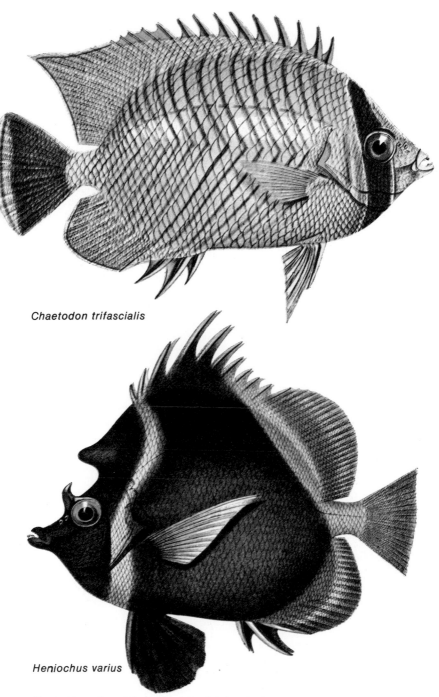

Chaetodon trifascialis

Heniochus varius

Illustrations from Bleeker's *Atlas Ichthyologique* (1877).

and the Chaetodontidae.

Meanwhile, other genera were being added to the family Chaetodontidae. Franz (1910) described *Osteochromis*, thinking that it belonged to the family Pomacentridae. It was actually a tholichthys-stage of a chaetodont. *Vinculum* was described by McCulloch (1914) based on *Chaetodon sexfasciatus* Richardson. *Tifia* and *Loa* were described in 1922, the former by Jordan and Jordan, the latter by D. S. Jordan. A year later D. S. Jordan replaced the preoccupied name *Loa* with *Roa*.

Jordan (1923) still employed the suborder Squamipennes. The characteristics were: posttemporal firmly attached to the skull, the interspaces between the three forks being filled by bone, gill openings restricted to the sides, and rayed parts of the fins usually scaled. He placed many of the other families thus far associated with the Chaetodontidae in the Ephippiformes (i.e. Scorpididae, Monodactylidae, Ephippidae, Drepanidae, and Platacidae). The family Scatophagidae was placed with the chaetodontids in the Squamipennes. Jordan (*Fishes*, 1924) used Squamipennes as a chapter heading but did not give it any other significance. He suggested a possible relationship between the Antigoniidae and Chaetodontidae, as well as the formerly proposed relationship of the scorpidids with the chaetodontids. His work on fossils suggested to him a relationship between the Pygaeidae, Chaetodontidae, and Acanthuridae.

In 1923 a complete revision of the subfamily Chaetodontinae by E. Ahl appeared. Ahl included in the broad family Chaetodontidae several other presumably allied groups. This was the most comprehensive work on the chaetodontids thus far and he characterized the family as follows: body deep, compressed; dorsal and anal fins covered with scales (at least their soft parts); 3-4 anal spines; mouth small, terminal, more or less protrusible; maxillary border with rows of small, bristle- or brush-shaped teeth; no incisors or canines; palatines usually toothless; high occipital process; 23-24 vertebrae, etc. In addition, all members of the family were supposed to have tholichthys larvae. Six subfamilies were included under the family Chaetodontidae: Chaetodontinae (*Chaetodon, Coradion, Hemitaurichthys, Heniochus, Microcanthus, Vinculum, Parachaetodon, Chelmonops, Chelmon, Prognathodes, Forcipiger*); Holacanthinae (*Holacanthus, Acanthochaetodon, Chaetodontoplus, Angelichthys, Pomacanthus*); Scatophaginae (*Scatophagus*); Ephippinae (*Ephippus*); Platacinae (*Platax*); and Drepaninae (*Drepane*).

Starks (1926) studied the ethmoid region of these fishes and found a definite relationship between the chaetodontids (especially the pomacanthid genera) and the drepanids. He also mentioned that the posttemporal bone, which had previously been used as a prominent character in distinguishing these groups, had beeen overemphasized. Starks found that within the family Chaetodontidae there was a complete gradation from the forms with a well-developed lower limb of the posttemporal bone to those with no lower limb at all. In addition, there was a complete transition from those forms with complete co-ossification to those with the loosely attached condition of the attachment of the posttemporal bone to the cranium.

Schmidt and Lindberg (1930) described a new genus, *Paracanthochaetodon*. This was later found to be based on a tholichthys stage of *Chaetodon modestus*.

In a comprehensive study of fish skulls, Gregory (1933) agreed that there was a close relationship between the Chaetodontidae and Scorpididae. The genus *Scorpis*, according to him, formed a good base for the chaetodontid series. He referred to Starks (1926) in regard to the relationship between the chaetodontids and drepanids. He also regarded the differences between acanthurids and plectognaths as being of lesser magnitude than that between the chaetodontids and acanthurids.

Weber and de Beaufort (1936) divided the family Chaetodontidae into seven subfamilies: Scatophaginae (*Scatophagus*); Chaetodontinae (*Forcipiger, Chelmon, Microcanthus, Hemitaurichthys, Coradion, Parachaetodon, Heniochus, Gonochaetodon, Megaprotodon, Chaetodon, Anisochaetodon*); Pomacanthinae (*Chaetodontoplus, Pomacanthus, Euxiphipops, Genicanthus, Holacanthus, Pygoplites, Centropyge*); Zanclinae; Ephippinae; Drepaninae; and Platacinae. Each of these subfamilies has been raised to family status at one time or another. Toxotidae, Monodactylidae, and Pempheridae were listed as separate families in the suborder Percoidea, division Perciformes.

Berg (1940) applied uniform endings to the higher categories of fishes and changed the name of the order to Perciformes. The families he recognized conformed to those used in Regan's classification.

Schultz and Dunkle *in* Schultz and Stern (1948) included three subfamilies within the Chaetodontidae: Chaetodontinae, Pomacanthinae, and Ephippinae. The Platacidae, however, remained as a family.

Woods and Schultz *in* Schultz *et al* (1953) placed the Chaetodontidae in the suborder Percomorphina. It was divided into the same two subfamilies (Chaetodontinae and Pomacanthinae) as many others had done. In this work, differences in color were considered as an important taxonomic tool. Those authors who had disregarded the basic color pattern (i.e., Fraser-Brunner, 1933; Weber and de Beaufort, 1936, etc.) had synonymized several nominal species (now considered valid) into single "catch-all species" in several instances (*Chaetodon collare*, for example, in Weber and de Beaufort became a resting place for several species, as did *Centropyge bispinosus* in Fraser-Brunner).

Fowler (1953) classified the chaetodontids into two superfamilies, Monodactylicae and Chaetodonticae. The former included families Monodactylidae, Platacidae, Ephippidae, and Drepanidae. The latter contained Scatophagidae, Chaetodontidae, and Pomacanthidae. He further divided the family Chaetodontidae into subfamilies and tribes as follows: subfamily Chaetodontinae with tribes Chaetodontini (*Chaetodon, Parachaetodon*), Heniochini (*Heniochus, Taurichthys*), and Microcanthini (*Microcanthus, Hemitaurichthys, Coradion*), and subfamily Chel-

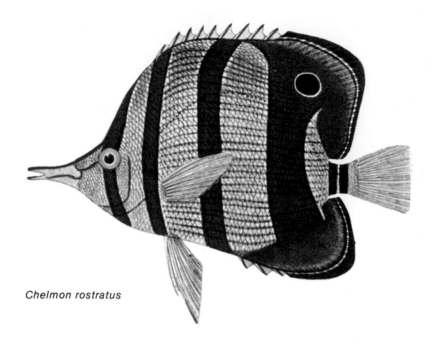

Chelmon rostratus

Forcipiger flavissimus

Chaetodon trifasciatus

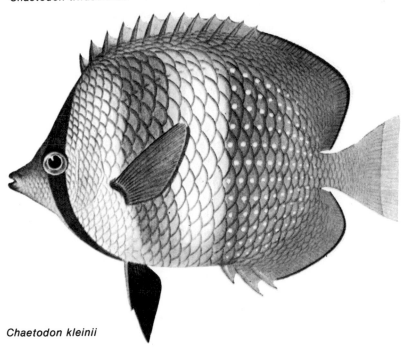

Chaetodon kleinii

Illustrations from Herre and Montalban (1927).

25

moninae with a single tribe Chelmonini (*Forcipiger, Chelmon*).

Norman, in his *Draft Synopsis* . . . (1957), followed Ahl (1923) and divided the family Chaetodontidae into Chaetodontinae and Pomacanthinae, but regarded the Scatophagidae, Drepanidae, and Chaetodipteridae as separate families.

J.L.B. Smith consistently utilized the family designations Chaetodontidae and Pomacanthidae. In a 1955 paper he stated that the angelfishes should be raised to family rank on the basis of the head armature (large preopercular spine).

Marshall (1964) included five subfamilies in the family Chaetodontidae; Scatophaginae, Chaetodontinae, Pomacanthinae, Drepaninae, and Platacinae.

Nalbant described a new genus of butterflyfishes (*Bauchotia*) in 1965 but later considered it as a subgenus of *Prognathodes* (Nalbant, 1971).

Greenwood *et al* (1966) included the angelfishes within the Chaetodontidae.

The following major faunal works also contributed to the systematics of chaetodontids and were important to my preparation of the systematic section: Jordan and Seale (1906), Samoa; Herre and Montalban (1927), Philippine Islands; Fowler (1928, etc.), Oceania; Fowler and Bean (1929), Philippine Islands and adjacent seas; Fowler (1936), West Africa; Longley and Hildebrand (1941), Tortugas, Florida; Aoyagi (1948), Japan; Schultz (1943), Phoenix and Samoan Islands; Schultz *et al* (1953), Marshall and Marianas Islands; Fowler (1953), China; Smith (1953), South Africa; Harry (1953), Tuamotu Archipelago; Baschieri-Salvadori (1953), Red Sea; Randall (1955), Gilbert Islands; Munro (1955), Ceylon; Gosline and Brock (1960), Hawaiian Islands; Wang and Fang (1962), South China; Smith and Smith (1963), Seychelles; Rofen (1963), Gulf of Thailand; Taylor (1964), Arnhem Land, Northern Australia; Marshall (1964), Great Barrier Reef, Queensland, Australia; Cervigon (1966), Venezuela; Munro (1967), New Guinea; Randall (1968), Caribbean Sea; Bohlke and Chaplin (1968), Bahama Islands.

Associated Families

The family Scatophagidae has been placed near the family Chaetodontidae in almost all modern classifications. Scatophagids are similar to chaetodontids in having small ctenoid scales, scales extending onto the soft dorsal and anal fins, a small mouth with setiform teeth, gill membranes united to the isthmus, axillary process at the base of the pelvic spines, six to seven branchiostegals, posttemporal solidly united to the skull, and the larvae going through a tholichthys-type larval stage. They differ from the chaetodontids in having 16 branched caudal fin rays instead of 15; in having $11+12=23$ vertebrae; the teeth, although setiform, are tricuspid; and there is a procumbent spine before the dorsal fin. The scatophagids, in addition to these differences, differ from pomacanthids in lacking the strong preopercular spine as well as the spination of the lachrymal and interopercle and in possessing an axillary scale and tholichthys-like larva (compiled from Norman, 1957; Weber and de Beaufort, 1936; Fowler, 1953; Herre and Montalban, 1927; and personal observations). The Scatophagidae, therefore, appear to be more closely related to the Chaetodontidae than the Pomacanthidae. The gas bladder of the scatophagids is simple, without projecting horns, resembling neither butterflyfishes nor angelfishes. Chaetodontids, by the way, are almost always found on coral reefs, in pure marine water. Scatophagids are almost never found on reefs, occurring instead in brackish water. They are always shoaling fish.

Munro (1964) proposed a new family, Rhinoprenidae, with a single genus *Rhinoprenes*, which he considered closely allied to the Scatophagidae. Among the common characters given were the procumbent spine before the dorsal fin and the tricuspid teeth. Differences mentioned included three anal spines (scatophagids have four), filamentous extensions of certain rays of the dorsal, pectoral, and pelvic fins, and the peculiar bluntly rounded, projecting snout. Greenwood *et al* (1966) place the Rhinoprenidae between the Scatophagidae and Chaetodontidae in their classification. Without having seen specimens of these fishes I would hesitate to assign this family to any particular position in a classification. The developmental pattern of the rhinoprenids should also be known before placing them between two families known to have a tholichthys

Scatophagus argus, family Scatophagidae. Photo by H.J. Richter.

Microcanthus strigatus, family Kyphosidae (incl. Scorpididae). Photo by K.H. Choo.

Histiopterus acutirostris, family Pentacerotidae. Photo by Wade Doak.

Enoplosus armatus, family Enoplosidae. Photo by Dr. Herbert R. Axelrod.

larva. For the time being I will follow Munro in placing this family near the Scatophagidae.

The Scorpididae have been considered as closely related to the chaetodontids based on similarities between the scorpidids and genera *Microcanthus* and *Vinculum* of the chaetodontids. Fraser-Brunner (1945) removed the genus *Microcanthus* from the chaetodontids and placed it in the family Scorpididae on the basis of such characters as gill membranes being free from the isthmus, the scaly sheath of the dorsal fin being a true sheath, lack of a tholichthys larva, and the ribs being attached directly to the centra above and behind the parapophysis. The genus *Vinculum* is removed from the family Chaetodontidae and placed in the family Scorpididae for reasons similar to those of Fraser-Brunner for *Microcanthus* (Burgess, MS).

The family Scorpididae, however, closely resembles some chaetodontids, particularly the chaetodontid genus *Hemitaurichthys*, on the basis of mouth structure, small numerous scales, and a complete lateral line. Greenwood *et al* (1966) placed the family Scorpididae within the family Kyphosidae, a move with which I concur. Further study on these groups is indicated.

The Pentacerotidae (Histiopteridae) is also normally placed in the vicinity of the family Chaetodontidae. The genus *Histiopterus* has representatives whose appearance is very suggestive of the chaetodontid genus *Heniochus*, at least superficially. Pentacerotids are too poorly known, however, to be able to place them anywhere in a classification system with any degree of certainty. Until further studies are made I would prefer to leave them near the chaetodontids.

The Australian family Enoplosidae appears to be related to the Pentacerotidae, and most authors place the two families close together.

The family Ephippidae (including Platacidae and Drepanidae) has always been considered close to the Chaetodontidae. The comparisons that have been made (Starks, 1926, 1930—ethmoid region and shoulder girdle; Cockerell, 1915—scales; etc.) always indicate that ephippids and pomacanthids are more similar to each other than ephippids are to chaetodontids. In separating the pomacanthids from the chaetodontids the ephippids would therefore be placed close to the angelfishes.

Families that have been considered closely related to the Chaetodontidae (*sensu lato*) can, at least tentatively, be aligned with either the Chaetodontidae on the one hand or the Pomacanthidae on the other. Further studies on the osteology of these families should be made and their position more firmly established.

Ecology and Behavior

RELATIONSHIP TO CORALS

Butterflyfishes are primarily reef fishes, and their distribution closely coincides with the limits of coral growth in regard to both their northern and southern extent as well as the depths to which they penetrate. Ahl (1923) believed that one would find butterflyfishes on every coral reef. If none were found it would simply be a matter of poor collecting. He may be correct in this assumption since, as far as is known, butterflyfishes have been found on every well-explored coral reef.

A few shallow-water species are found beyond the limits of coral reef growth. *Chelmonops truncatus* for instance, although its northern limits of distribution are within the fringes of the coral reef zone, is found primarily along the southern coast of Australia. *Amphichaetodon melbae* from San Felix Island off the coast of Chile and *A. howensis* from New South Wales, Lord Howe Island, and northern New Zealand can also be considered temperate species.

This correlation between butterflyfishes and coral reefs in regard to their distribution may be due to one or more of the following factors. The coral serves as both a hiding place for small invertebrates that form part of the diet of butterflyfishes and as a food source itself (Hobson, 1972, personal observations). The coral reef is so constructed as to provide good protection for extremely compressed fishes such as butterflyfishes; more will be said about this in the section on anatomy of the butterflyfishes. The physical requisites (salinity, temperature, etc.) of both corals and butterflyfishes may be similar.

TEMPERATURE AND DEPTH

Butterflyfishes are tropical fishes occurring almost entirely within the 21°C isotherms of the northern hemisphere summer (July) and southern hemisphere summer (January). Within these isotherms the majority of species are found in shallow waters. A few are found in comparatively deeper water (i.e. greater than 30 meters) and are rarely seen in waters shallower than this. The seven species of *Chaetodon* comprising the subgenus *Prognathodes* are normally found at depths ranging from 30 to 60 meters where temperatures encountered may reach or surpass the lower

Stand of coral on outer edge of reef at Johnston Atoll. Sheltering among the branches of coral are *Forcipiger longirostris*, *Chaetodon trifascialis*, *Chaetodon unimaculatus*, and *Chaetodon multicinctus*. Above the coral individuals of a species of *Dascyllus* and *Acanthurus achilles* can be seen.

A pair of *Chaetodon plebeius* feeding among a heavy coral growth on the Great Barrier Reef. Photo by Walter Deas.

Chaetodon dichrous feeding on the surface fauna of an old shipwreck. Notice the raised dorsal fin spines as it feeds. Photo by Ken Jourdan.

Chaetodon sedentarius, a member of the *miliaris* species group from the Tropical Western Atlantic. Photo by Dr. Herbert R. Axelrod.

limits tolerated by shallow-water species. The *Chaetodon miliaris* group, a circumtropical complex of six species (*Chaetodon miliaris,* C. *dolosus,* C. *assarius,* C. *guentheri,* C. *sanctaehelenae,* and C. *sedentarius*), has a similar 30- to 60-meter depth range with two known exceptions: *Chaetodon miliaris* from the Hawaiian Islands and C. *sanctaehelenae* from St. Helena and Ascension Islands in the middle Atlantic. *Chaetodon miliaris* has an extremely wide depth range, from shallow water (including tide pools when considering juveniles) to over 200 meters (Brock and Chamberlain, 1965). *Chaetodon sanctaehelenae,* endemic to islands on the edge of the tropical zone, has been reported only from shallow water (Cunningham, 1910). Juveniles of some of the species included in the *miliaris*-group are common in shallow water even though the adults are more or less restricted to deeper water. *Chaetodon dolosus* is an example of this type (Smith, 1966).

The species complex comprised of *Chaetodon modestus,* C. *jayakari,* and C. *excelsa* provides an example of an interesting distributional pattern between closely related species with respect to depth. *Chaetodon modestus,* common around the subtropical islands off southern Japan and the southern China coast, is found in shallow water (although the extent of its depth range is still not precisely known). *Chaetodon jayakari,* from the waters off India, Sri Lanka, and vicinity, and *Chaetodon excelsa,* from the Hawaiian Islands, are both essentially deep-water butterflyfish species (Norman, 1939; Jordan, 1922).

Butterflyfishes have been reported from depths greater than 200 meters (Strasburg, 1959). The ultimate depth limit is still uncertain principally due to (1) inadequate collections in the butterflyfish-type habitat between the 200 meter level and trawling operations in deep water of over 1,000 meters and (2) lack of suitable habitats beyond 200 meters in many areas.

SALINITY

Butterflyfishes are usually thought to be stenohaline, with narrow tolerance limits, but the salinity tolerances of chaetodontids are not precisely known. It is probable that most butterflyfishes are stenohaline, but this is not necessarily true for every species. There are many records of species being captured in brackish water areas such as estuaries (ex. *Chelmon rostratus*, *Chaetodon oxycephalus*, *C. rafflesi*, and *C. marleyi*).

Juveniles of many species of butterflyfishes are found in tide pools. In some of these tide pools extreme conditions of temperature and salinity occur. It is quite possible that butterflyfishes may only enter pools that do not regularly become isolated and where normal inshore conditions persist through the low tide cycle, or the length of time that elapses before these areas are flushed by incoming tides is too short to cause any serious damage to the fishes. But it is quite possible that the young butterflyfishes have to withstand, at least temporarily, adverse conditions.

It is difficult to maintain many species of butterflyfishes in captivity due to susceptibility to infections, inability to provide natural food, etc. Even so, some experimental work was attempted in an effort to ascertain what tolerance these fishes had to higher than normal salinity values. Juveniles of *Chaetodon miliaris* were maintained in a 100-gallon closed-system aquarium at the Hawaii Institute of Marine Biology. Aeration and filtration (undergravel type) were provided. Natural evaporation was intentionally allowed to occur over an eight-week period, causing a salinity increase. The salinity rose to a value of 42 o/oo without any noticeable effect on the fishes' behavior. No changes in the amount of food eaten or movements about the tank were observed. Problems with the air system necessitated the termination of the experiment. Attempts to keep adults of this or other species of butterflyfishes in a similar aquarium were not successful.

FOOD AND FEEDING

Observations on butterflyfishes in their natural habitats and studies on the stomach contents of these fishes have indicated that butterflyfishes eat small invertebrates, including coral polyps and planktonic copepods, and at least some of them browse on algae (Hiatt and Strasburg, 1960; Hobson, 1974; Reese, 1975; personal observations).

Hiatt and Strasburg (1960) examined the stomach contents of seven species of butterflyfishes in the Marshall Islands and observed feeding habits in the field of these and other species. The butterflyfishes examined were species with wide Indo-Pacific distribution, but at the same time

Chaetodon rainfordi in a typical habitat on the Great Barrier Reef of Australia. Photo by Allan Power.

Two closely related species of butterflyfish, *Chaetodon rainfordi* and *C. aureofasciatus,* on the Great Barrier Reef. Photo by Dr. E. Reese.

A juvenile *Chaetodon rainfordi* (note caudal peduncle band) and a pair of *C. plebeius* among several species of coral. Photo by Dr. Walter A. Stark II.

Chaetodon citrinellus was classified by Hiatt and Strasburg as an omnivore.
Photo by W. Hoppe.

they were almost always found in close proximity to coral reefs. On the
basis of their studies, Hiatt and Strasburg classified some of the butterflyfishes as omnivores and others as carnivores. *Chaetodon citrinellus*, *C.*
ephippium, and *C. vagabundus* were classified by them as omnivores,
with a "strong predilection for browsing and grazing off polyps of coral as
well as algal filaments." *Chaetodon auriga* was found to be a less selective
omnivore, although polychaetes comprised the bulk of its diet. *Chaetodon*
(Megaprotodon) trifascialis was categorized as a carnivore. All specimens
with food still remaining in their stomachs "contained only coral polyps
with no skeletal material admixed." They therefore did not, as in the case
of the parrotfishes (family Scaridae), break off pieces of coral which were
crushed in the pharyngeal mill and ultimately passed out with the feces.

Hobson (1974) reported on the feeding habits of 13 species of butterflyfishes found on the Kona coast of Hawaii. His findings agreed for the
most part with those of Hiatt and Strasburg, i.e. a predominance of predation on corals (and other coelenterates), crustaceans, and other invertebrates. *Chaetodon ornatissimus* and *C. multicinctus* were more specifically feeding on the coral polyps themselves (mostly of the genera *Porites*
and *Pocillopora* in the case of *C. multicinctus*), with *C. unimaculatus* and
C. quadrimaculatus consuming other invertebrates along with the corals.

The two closely related species of the genus *Forcipiger* were found to
have some differences in their diet, at least in the procurement of the ani-

mals. *Forcipiger flavissimus*, with a more forceps-like mouth at the end of its elongate snout, tore pieces off larger benthic animals, whereas *F. longirostris*, with a pipette-like or eyedropper-shaped mouth opening, took entire animals.

Although *Chaetodon miliaris* is generally a benthic feeder in shallow water, it is often found in deeper water in large aggregations hovering in "curtains" extending from the bottom to near the surface. These were thought to be feeding aggregations, the food consumed being plankton (Brock, personal communication). Hobson (1974) opined that not only *Chaetodon miliaris* but *C. kleinii* (his *C. corallicola*), *Hemitaurichthys thompsoni*, and *H. polylepis* were plankton feeders, all but *C. kleinii* rising above the substrate a distance in fairly large aggregations. *C. kleinii* remained fairly close to the reef (within one meter) and supplemented its diet with benthic organisms, particularly amphipods and hydroids. *Hemitaurichthys polylepis* was also seen to feed on alcyonarians and other bottom invertebrates (Hobson, 1974).

Chaetodon auriga and *C. fremblii* were more generalized omnivores, feeding on a wide variety of benthic organisms.

It is especially interesting to note that all reports of chaetodontid activities indicated that they are diurnal predators. Hobson (1974), however, observed that *C. lunula* occurred in large aggregations during the day, these breaking up at night into solitary individuals or small groups of two or three, apparently for feeding. The diet was also unusual, consisting mainly of opisthobranch mollusks with other mollusks (gastropods) as a supplemental item.

Reese (1975) observed 20 species of butterflyfishes in the field, characterizing their pairing behavior, territoriality, and feeding behavior. Sixteen of the 20 species were considered, at least in part, coral-feeding (those which fed on living coral), nine of the 16 also being classified as omnivorous (fed indiscriminately on many available kinds of food). Three other species, *Chaetodon auriga*, *C. lineolatus*, and "probably" *C. lunula*, were difficult to assign to particular categories because of differences in behavior correlated with different ecological settings but were classified as probably opportunistic omnivores. The feeding behavior of the twentieth species, *C. melannotus*, was not observed.

From these observations on butterflyfishes in their natural habitat it appears that they find their food mainly by sight. It follows that the vast majority of butterflyfishes are diurnal feeders. Night dives were made in Hawaii and the Marshall Islands to determine the activities of the butterflyfishes at that time. All chaetodontids seen during these dives were resting quietly near the bottom in a stupor in nighttime color patterns (see below). They could easily be netted at this time and in some cases could be picked up by hand.

The butterflyfishes therefore can be classified into several different categories depending upon feeding habits, effectively reducing the competition in this group of fishes.

Habitat characteristic of that in which butterflyfishes may be found. Seen here is *Chaetodon ornatissimus*. Photo by Dr. Gerald R. Allen.

There are plankton feeders adapted for picking small animals, usually copepods, from the water column. These species occur in rather large aggregations, often forming a wall or curtain of fish from the surface to near the bottom. Some species, such as *C. kleinii*, combine this particulate plankton feeding with selection of small benthic animals and usually remain close to the shelter of the reef.

Certain butterflyfishes feed strictly on living corals without supplementing their diet with any other invertebrates. Even these coral feeders may not be in strict competition with each other since one species may feed on a certain species of coral and another species on a different species of coral. *C. trifascialis* feeds exclusively on *Acropora*, for instance, whereas *C. trifasciatus* appears to favor *Pocillopora* and *C. multicinctus* feeds mainly on *Porites* (Hobson, 1974; Reese, 1975).

Of the more generalized invertebrate feeders, some species feed on the small organisms whereas others tear bits and pieces from the larger benthic animals. The two species of *Forcipiger* are good examples of this type. In addition the elongate snouts enable them to tap a source of food unavailable to the shorter snouted generalized feeding forms such as *C. auriga*.

Chaetodon unimaculatus adults have a very strong robust snout and mouth, which enables them to tear off relatively large pieces of soft corals, a food source apparently not utilized by other butterflyfishes (Reese, personal communication).

Chaetodon lunula, on the other hand, may be a nocturnal feeder, preying upon nudibranchs and other organisms that come out from shelter after dark (Hobson, 1974).

Finally, although nothing is known about the feeding habits of relatively deep-water species, they are physically out of direct competition with the shallow-water butterflyfishes. *C. falcifer*, one of the deep-water forms is suspected to feed on tube feet of sea urchins and other echinoderms as well as on crustaceans (Fitch and Lavenburg, 1975).

Therefore, although butterflyfishes may be common reef inhabitants and apparently highly competitive for the invertebrate food supply of the reef, they may be utilizing different prey organisms and reducing the competition to relatively low levels.

I have observed butterflyfishes in their natural habitat on the reefs of southern Florida, the Hawaiian Islands, Johnston Island, the Marshall Islands, the Great Barrier Reef of Australia, Tahiti, Fiji, and the Philippine Islands. Most of the species could be seen moving around the various sections of the reef "inspecting" here and there a particular coral growth and occasionally picking at something on the surface of the coral head. The butterflyfishes in these apparent feeding movements do not necessarily remain upright. They will follow the contour of the coral at least to a vertical (head down) position if not beyond it to a nearly upside down position. Suyehiro (1942) claimed *Chaetodon modestus* would lie on its side and eat. This is certainly true of other butterflyfishes as well, but they

The elongated snout of *Forcipiger flavissimus* enables it to reach into the coral interstices for food. Photo by H. Hansen.

are definitely not restricted to a sideways feeding posture. I have seen *Chaetodon modestus* feeding in an upright position in an aquarium. *Forcipiger flavissimus* will frequent caves where it can be found upside down orienting to the surface of the ceiling while feeding. There seems to be no apparent stress to maintain this position, it being quite "natural" to this species.

The butterflyfishes are, then, acrobatic in their feeding habits, assuming the position that will enable them to get the best angle of attack in relation to the food selected, whether it be on its side, head down, or even upside down.

Occasionally butterflyfishes will eat food items not easily accessible to them under normal circumstances. While diving in Hawaii, I at times disturbed pomacentrid nests, causing the guarding parent to flee from it, at least a short distance. Among the fishes that moved in to devour the unguarded eggs were the butterflyfishes *Chaetodon miliaris, C. fremblii,* and *C. lunula.*

Experiments were conducted in an attempt to determine if coral polyps were, in fact, eaten and what species of coral was preferred.

Hiatt and Strasburg (1960) placed several individuals of *Chaetodon auriga* and *C. citrinellus* in an aquarium and supplied them with live coral. These fishes were observed feeding on the coral polyps and in time left white patches where the coral was completely cleaned. The use of the produced snout was also observed, as these fishes thrust them into the

Anemones occasionally form part of the diet of butterflyfishes. Here an individual of *Chaetodon lunula* is seen nipping at the anemone, apparently immune or not bothered by the nematocysts. Photos by Glen S. Axelrod.

Chaetodon ornatissimus, one of the short-snouted butterflyfishes, feeding on a coral *(Porites).* Photo by Dr. Gerald R. Allen.

Chaetodon miliaris, C. multicinctus, and *C. fremblii* feeding on a sea urchin that was broken open. Photo by Scott Johnson.

crevices and interstices in the coral. I made similar observations on these and other species of butterflyfishes (*Chaetodon lunula, C. kleinii, C. ornatissimus,* and *C. trifasciatus*) at the Eniwetok Marine Biological Laboratory and the Hawaii Institute of Marine Biology. The coral pieces which were put into the aquarium also included other invertebrates and algae. Once the disturbance of placing the coral in the aquarium passed, the butterflyfishes flocked around the coral and began feeding, some on the other invertebrates or algae, but most on the coral polyps. The corals were eventually almost entirely cleaned in this manner. With proper lighting, the actual feeding on the polyps could be seen. In many instances the feeding motion was accompanied by a sideways jerk of the head as the polyp was removed by the fish.

The coral experiment was carried one step further at the Hawaii Institute of Marine Biology. Additional species of butterflyfishes (*Heniochus acuminatus, Chaetodon miliaris, C. fremblii,* and *C. multicinctus*) were present. Three different genera of corals were introduced into the aquarium at the same time: *Montipora, Porites,* and *Pocillopora.* This was repeated twice a week for three months. Observations were made to determine which genus of coral was approached first for feeding. Each time coral was introduced the position of the different species was changed so that location in the aquarium was not a factor. Invariably *Montipora* was approached first, *Pocillopora* second, and *Porites* last. Since all three corals were easily available to the butterflyfishes in their natural habitat, this appeared to be a definite preference for one genus over another. On one occasion *Dendrophyllia* was made available to the fishes, but it was not touched. Possibly the bright orange color of the large polyps of this coral advertise a distasteful quality, or perhaps the polyps were too big.

The mouths of chaetodontids are small, without exception, and the teeth are slender, curved, and numerous. The arrangement of the teeth may differ slightly from group to group, but basically the size of the mouth and the type of teeth are similar throughout the family. What does differ remarkably is the various prolongations of the snout. In *Forcipiger* and *Chelmon* this prolongation is carried out to the greatest degree and enables them to reach into the crevices and interstices of coral (Hobson, 1974). Prolonged snouts also appear in other families of fishes (for example Labridae, Cirrhitidae, etc.), possibly a similar adaptation to crevice-type feeding.

Several species of butterflyfishes were dissected in an attempt to determine general anatomy, sex, and stomach contents. According to Hiatt and Strasburg (1960) and Suyehiro (1942) the stomach of many species of butterflyfishes is "Y"-shaped, thick-walled, and the intestine long and coiled. In general the length of the intestine is correlated with the particular diet of the fish. A short intestine is usually found in fishes which are carnivorous, i.e. feeding mainly on fishes and/or other animals, whereas a long intestine, variously coiled, is more usually associated

An aggregation or school of *Hemitaurichthys zoster* feeding on the planktonic animals in the water columns above the reef. Photo by Dr. W. Klausewitz.

with vegetarians or mud eaters. The long intestine of the butterflyfishes, not so long as in many of the herbivorous fishes, seems to corroborate the findings that they are in many cases omnivorous, with vegetable matter composing part of their diet. A thick-walled stomach also may indicate a diet at least partly vegetable. The thickness of the stomach walls in butterflyfishes in no way approaches the special adaptation found in the mullets or shad, which resembles the gizzard of a fowl. But not all of the butterflyfishes possess thick-walled stomachs. In the species found around the Hawaiian Islands that I have dissected, at least two, *Chaetodon miliaris* and *Hemitaurichthys polylepis*, had thin-walled stomachs. This might be interpreted as an adaptation associated with the plankton-feeding behavior of these species.

CLEANING BEHAVIOR

Juveniles of many species of butterflyfishes have been observed removing parasites from other fishes. It is believed that the bulk of their food is obtained from other sources and that parasite-picking behavior is only exhibited on occasion. Among the species personally observed cleaning other fishes were juveniles of *Chaetodon auriga, C. lunula, C. fremblii, C. kleinii, C. unimaculatus, C. capistratus, C. multicinctus, C. ocellatus,* and *Heniochus acuminatus.* Observations were made in the field as well as on fishes confined in aquaria. In some instances, when fishes from

47

Chaetodon kleinii feeding on the biocover of a dead bivalve. Photo by Heiko Bleher.

Opposite: *Chelmon rostratus* picking at a dead bivalve. Photo by Dr. Teh.

Chetodon melapterus feeding on frozen aquarium food that was placed on a piece of coral. This is an excellent way to start difficult species on aquarium type foods. Photo by Dr. Warren E. Burgess.

both the Atlantic and Pacific Oceans were kept in the same aquarium, butterflyfishes were seen picking parasites from fishes from not only the same ocean where they were found, but from the other ocean as well. This action does not seem to be unique to butterflyfishes, as other cleaner fishes were also observed ignoring geographical distribution in regard to their cleaning habits.

This cleaning behavior is not restricted to the juvenile butterflyfishes. Randall (personal communication) observed *Heniochus acuminatus* and *Chaetodon miliaris* adults participating in cleaning activity, and I have seen adult *Chaetodon kleinii* pick parasites off a large carangid. *Pseudochaetodon nigrirostris* is well known for its parasite-picking habits (Hobson, 1955) and has been given the colloquial name "El Barbero" in reference to their "grooming" behavior. They maintain regular cleaning stations much like the cleaner wrasses of the genus *Labroides*. *Labroides* is a genus of small wrasses whose parasite-picking behavior has been well publicized. They remain in one particular spot on the reef and service fishes that stop there. It is even reported that the same fishes return to the same spot and have their parasites removed periodically. *Labroides*, in contrast to the butterflyfishes, is quite dependent upon parasites for food. *Pseudochaetodon nigrirostris* are usually found in aggregations unlike the more solitary wrasse. Juvenile butterflyfishes do not maintain a particular cleaning station although they may occupy a certain territory on the reef for a time.

Chaetodon collare being cleaned by the cleaner wrasse, *Labroides dimidiatus*. Photo by H. Hansen.

"El Barbero", *Pseudochaetodon nigrirostris,* is one of the butterflyfishes that clean even when adult. Because of this action it has received its common name. Photo by Dr. E. Hobson.

Butterflyfishes will present themselves for cleaning to other cleaners on the reef, even to members of their own species. The posturing of butterflyfishes when they are host fishes, i.e. those being cleaned, is similar to that of other fishes. They spread their fins, elevate the operculum, and remain as motionless as possible while positioning themselves with head up or down at an angle. My limited observation of this behavior suggests that *Chaetodon lunula* and *C. trifasciatus* orient themselves with their head angled downward, whereas *C. miliaris, C. citrinellus,* and *Heniochus acuminatus* assume a head-up position.

There appear to be several different types of cleaners acceptable to the butterflyfishes. I have observed them posturing before *Labroides phthirophagus* (Hawaiian cleaner wrasse) as well as the cleaning shrimps *Stenopus hispidus* and *Lysmata grabhami.* A preference may be shown, however, although the observations on parasite-picker selection were made in aquaria. *Chaetodon lunula* ignored *Labroides* and always postured before *Lysmata* when both cleaners were present. Any attempted approach by *Labroides* was met by a sudden chasing by *C. lunula,* but this butterflyfish would remain posturing before the shrimp even while the shrimp was occupied with other fishes. Perhaps the suggested nocturnal feeding of *C. lunula* (Hobson, 1974) is connected with this preference. Juveniles of other fishes, such as *Bodianus,* were usually accepted, and conspecific juvenile butterflyfishes would take turns cleaning each other.

Juvenile *Heniochus acuminatus* feeding on a suspended clump of freeze-dried Tubifex worms. Photo by J.A. Lomas.

"Tame" butterflyfishes, *Chaetodon ulietensis* and *C. auriga,* taking food from the fingers of a diver in Bora Bora. Photo by Dr. Gerald R. Allen.

The short-snouted Chaetodon meyeri feeding on coral of the genus *Porites*.
Photo by Rodney Jonklaas.

PAIRING BEHAVIOR

Butterflyfishes occur either as individuals, as pairs strongly or loosely bound together, as small groups of three or more, and as relatively large aggregations (Hobson, 1974; Reese, 1975; personal observation). This social behavior is currently under study by Dr. E. Reese of the University of Hawaii.

Perhaps the most interesting of these groupings is the formation of pairs. Many species of butterflyfishes are normally found in their natural habitat as pairs (Reese, 1975; Hobson, 1974; personal observations). It is suspected that these pairs are male-female pairs, formed early in life, that stay together for purposes of spawning. The actual time of pair formation is not precisely known, although it would be logical if this event took place at the time of sexual maturity. My observations on *Chaetodon trifasciatus* indicate that juveniles are almost always solitary individuals maintaining a small territory in living coral heads. Pair formation occurs (at least pairs were observed) when individuals reach about three-fourths their adult size. It is not known if sexual maturity is reached at this size. Pairs of *Chaetodon trifasciatus* have strong bonds and are not easily separated. I have observed *Chaetodon ornatissimus*, another species with strong pair bonds, at Johnston Atoll, where one of the pairs studied was formed by individuals only three to four inches in length. Only one individual of the pair was captured, and subsequent examination proved it was not sexually mature. The question still remains unanswered, then, as to when or how the pairs are formed.

Chaetodon trifasciatus is almost always found as pairs when adult. Juveniles are more likely to be solitary. Photo by Dr. E. Reese.

Heniochus acuminatus forms feeding aggregations. Photo by Dr. W. Klausewitz (Maldive Islands).

Strong pair bonds have been observed by Reese (1975) in *Chaetodon trifasciatus*, *C. baronessa* (his *triangulum*), *C. unimaculatus*, *C. vagabundus*, *C. ornatissimus*, *C. multicinctus*, *C. punctatofasciatus*, and *C. ephippium*, and by Doak (1972) in *Amphichaetodon howensis*. Weakly paired species included *C. citrinellus*, *C. quadrimaculatus* and *C. reticulatus* (Reese, 1975).

Other species of butterflyfishes normally form schools or large aggregations. Some of these aggregations are definitely the feeding type mentioned above, while others may involve spawning, although modes of spawning of butterflyfishes have not been confirmed. Some species of the genera *Hemitaurichthys* and *Heniochus* are reported to form large aggregations, possibly for feeding (Klausewitz, personal communication; Hobson, 1974). *Heniochus pleurotaenia* was seen to hover over large coral heads much like the pomacentrid *Dascyllus* (Klausewitz, personal communication), and *H. acuminatus* was observed and photographed in the Hawaiian Islands in large schools (Wass, personal communication). *Heniochus varius*, the Pacific Ocean counterpart of the Indian Ocean *H. pleurotaenia*, has been regarded as a solitary species (DeWitt, MS), and I have seen *H. chrysostomus* only as pairs. The aggregations of all these species mentioned here seem to occur near the bottom, but they extend into open water to quite an extent.

A two photo sequence in which a butterflyfish, *Chelmon rostratus*, approaches a cleaning station and is cleaned by a shrimp, *Lysmata grabhami*. The long white antennae is not only characteristic of this cleaner shrimp but also of another well-known cleaning shrimp *Stenopus hispidus*. Colour Library International photos.

Other species of butterflyfishes form smaller groups which are more or less closely tied to the bottom. *Chaetodon auriga* was seen in Johnston Atoll and the Hawaiian Islands in small groups of up to 30 individuals, although juveniles in both areas were almost always solitary. They would move as a group from coral head to coral head across open sandy areas, dispersing at each stop to feed. An individual *Chaetodon ephippium* was occasionally seen mixed in with these *C. auriga*. Adult pairs of *C. auriga* occurred more frequently at Eniwetok, Marshall Islands than in the Hawaiian Islands or at Johnston Atoll. At Johnston Atoll, juveniles of *C. ephippium* occurred as solitary individuals, whereas the adults were mostly seen in pairs. One large coral head housed seven *C. ephippium* juveniles of different sizes, each maintaining a small but discrete territory.

There are species of butterflyfishes that appear individually, pairing apparently only at spawning time. *Chaetodon trifascialis* is very territorial as an adult, usually residing between the plate-like branches of the coral *Acropora* (Reese, 1975; personal observation). At Johnston and Eniwetok atolls the adults could be found, one per head of coral, in almost every area visited. Newly transformed individuals (still with tholichthys plates) of less than 20 mm standard length were seen in the same type habitat, but with as many as seven or eight fish per colony. Half-grown *C. trifascialis* occurred in groups of two or three to a branch. It is possible that these fishes become more territorial with age so that, perhaps as a result of a dominant fish driving away weaker individuals, a section of *Acropora* would eventually have only one left. Predation may also be a major factor in the reduction of numbers.

AGGRESSIVE BEHAVIOR

Butterflyfishes would not be regarded, in the sense of a predator, as aggressive fishes. They are quite defenseless in terms of teeth or armor. They will flee danger if possible, disappearing into one of the small openings of the reef. The deepness of their bodies, further enlarged when the spines are raised, makes predation on these fishes more difficult (Gosline, personal communication).

When flight is not possible and the butterflyfish is exposed to danger from predators or aggressors (including conspecifics), it must rely on a defensive stance which brings into play the anatomical features that it possesses. Normally butterflyfishes will face the danger, head lowered like a bull about to charge and the spines of the dorsal fin fully erect. The attacker is thus presented with an array of pointed spines which it has to get past before it can arrive at the more vulnerable parts. If this aggressor moves about to circumvent the spines, the butterflyfish constantly adjusts its position so that the spines are always properly oriented. I have seen damselfishes, small non-piscivorous reef fishes, approach butterflyfishes and elicit this type of behavior pattern from them. The damsels would bite at the spine tips, but the encounter usually ended at that.

When two butterflyfishes show aggression toward each other, both

The basic defensive posture, head lowered with dorsal fin spines erect, is exhibited by this *Chelmon rostratus*. Photo by H. Hansen.

assume the above-mentioned position. In this head-down-fins-raised position, they circle each other until one of the antagonists folds its spines back, signaling the end of the encounter. This "defeated" individual usually flees, being pursued by the "victor."

In addition to the head-down posture, a butterflyfish will sometimes, when presented with this same posture, respond by oscillatory movements of its body directed toward the opponent. This wagging movement is found in many other fishes and is probably best known in the Cichlidae, a family of freshwater fishes. It has been suggested that this motion in the cichlids is a test of strength. It probably has a similar function in the butterflyfishes. Mutual body wagging, in contrast to mutual head down positions, has not been observed.

Other aggressive actions were personally observed in some butterflyfishes. At times an individual would position its body at right angles to the opponent, its fins fully extended. This position was usually stiffly maintained and some vibrations, not wagging, were evident. On other occasions the two antagonists, after a frontal encounter, would lock jaws (also well known behavioral action of cichlids and other fishes) and twist to the side or circle each other. These jaw-locks are always of short duration, a well known matter of seconds.

Heniochus species, with some general anatomical differences from other chaetodontid genera, show some modification of aggressive behavior. Their first three dorsal spines are very short with the fourth

An individual of *Chaetodon leucopleura* is approached by a cleaner wrasse, *Labroides dimidiatus*. In the upper photo it touches the butterflyfish near the gills and in the lower photo it is allowed to enter and search this highly sensitive area. Photos by H. Hansen.

A view from behind showing the gill cover opened to allow the cleaner to enter and remove parasites. Photo by H. Hansen.

Butterflyfishes will accept many different cleaners. This *Chaetodon sedentarius* is being cleaned by a juvenile French angelfish, *Pomacanthus paru.* Photo by Klaus Paysan.

long and produced into a filament in some species. In addition, there is a bony protuberance or spine in the supraorbital area and, in some species, a bony projection on the nape. The usual spine-raising of the other butterflyfishes would not suffice for these species, the short spines offering little protection. The act of dipping the head down is still exhibited by species of *Heniochus*, but with the protuberances or 'horns' facing the aggressor. Zumpe (1965) described how, in *Heniochus*, the two opponents would assume the head down position with dorsal spines erect and then butt each other in the region of the horns. *Heniochus acuminatus*, the species she studied, has less well developed horns than most other species of the genus. The butting, she states, would continue until one individual would turn and flee. In species of *Heniochus* which have better developed horns, such as *Heniochus varius*, the fish would have to incline their bodies laterally to provide the most advantageous contact.

The above mentioned behavioral postures were observed in a long-snouted butterflyfish (*Chelmon rostratus*) by Zumpe (1964) along with the following additional postures. Two conspecifics would orient to each other in a head-to-tail position and then swim quickly around each other. She called this action circling or carousel-swimming. A second pattern observed in *Chelmon rostratus* was ramming, wherein one individual actually rams the other on its side. True bites, as occurs in cichlids, were not observed in the butterflyfishes.

These behavior patterns observed by Zumpe (1964) were not restricted to *Heniochus acuminatus* and *Chelmon rostratus* but were seen in all the chaetodontids studied by her, including several species of *Chaetodon*. The actions were used in the establishment of peck orders in *Heniochus* and *Chelmon* (Zumpe, 1964). The individuals engaged in trials of strength without much actual combat until the dominant and subordinate rankings were established.

In nature, probably the most aggressive displays in butterflyfishes will be seen in defense of their territories (Reese, 1974). When the territory of a butterflyfish is violated by another conspecific, the defender will normally make a quick pass at the invader, chasing it from the territory. This action is rapid and decisive in strongly territorial species such as *Chaetodon trifascialis*. Other species, less defensive when guarding a territory, will exhibit a weaker response, often allowing another to cross (but not stop in) the territory. When the conspecific enters the territory of another, the owner of the territory will swim rapidly at the intruder with its fins folded. As it nears its opponent, it will turn sideways, exhibiting a lateral display with fins spread, and then swim rapidly back to its original position. This entire sequence is repeated if the intruder remains in the territory. An encounter at the edge of the territory occurs when the intruder persists in remaining. This consists of frontal or lateral displays while the two opponents move back and forth across the boundary. They may also engage in a zigzag chase along the edge of the territory.

The territory defended may be directly concerned with feeding. For example, the food of *C. trifascialis* is the coral *Acropora*, and the territory defended is a stand of *Acropora* (Reese, 1974).

SPAWNING

Spawning has never been reported from field observations for any species of chaetodontid. Lorenz (personal communication) stated that *Chaetodon kleinii* spawned in captivity. He described the sequence as cichlid-like, with the pair moving over a flat surface, the female slightly in advance, laying eggs. The eggs did not adhere to the substrate but floated freely toward the surface. Lorenz believed this behavior is a hold-over from substrate spawning. Pairing behavior seems to indicate that spawning is accomplished in many species of chaetodontids through single male-female pairs. Whether these pairs spawn in nature as Lorenz has observed in aquaria is still an open question.

In their natural habitat the pairs may not be so closely tied to sub-strate contact as he observed in *Chaetodon kleinii*. With some species forming moderate to large aggregations, it is possible that aggregate school-type spawning in open water might occur. Wass (personal communication) observed *Hemitaurichthys polylepis* (a schooling species) in Hawaii in which a part of the white area on the side of the fishes was a violet or purplish color. Because of the actions of this group of fishes and the color change, Wass surmised that it might be a spawning or pre-spawning event.

Whatever spawning method or methods occur, the eggs released are small, numerous (3000-4000 according to my estimate of gonad content), and pelagic.

The time of spawning of chaetodontids is not known. In Hawaii, from early February to early March *Chaetodon miliaris* do not enter the fish traps set in Kaneohe Bay (Zukeran, personal communication). They are caught in fairly large numbers before and after this time. I suspect that this absence in the traps is related to spawning since investigations of the gonads in January revealed that there were several ripe females and nearly ripe males. The females were not running ripe, but the eggs were comparatively large, nearly 1 mm in diameter. No ripe individuals were detected among 25 specimens of *Chaetodon miliaris* examined in April.

Aside from ripeness of specimens, further indications that the dis-appearance from the traps coincide with spawning can be seen in the appearance of the juveniles. *Chaetodon miliaris* juveniles are common on the reefs, some still with tholichthys plates, throughout the month of May. This would indicate about a three-month pelagic period of develop-ment for *Chaetodon miliaris*. The size at metamorphosis for this species is about 32-36 mm standard length.

Not only *Chaetodon miliaris* juveniles but those of almost all Hawaiian species of butterflyfishes are abundant from June through September; they were conspicuously absent from the same areas during the winter according to diving observations. *Chaetodon trifasciatus* juveniles

A small group of *Chaetodon ulietensis* on a New Caledonian reef. Some species of butterflyfishes do form small groups like this. Photo by Piere Laboute.

A pair of *Chaetodon paucifasciatus* in the Red Sea. Pairs usually relatively close together. Photo by K. Probst.

Forcipiger longirostris. This close swimming pair was photographed at a depth of 30 feet at Euston Reef, Great Barrier Reef by Dr. Gerald R. Allen.

were occasionally found throughout the year, although present in greater numbers in the summer.

These data indicate that in Hawaii butterflyfishes probably spawn during the winter, with larvae arriving inshore in the spring and early summer.

PREDATORS

Butterflyfishes fall prey to many of the same predators as other reef fishes. Moray eels, snappers, scorpionfishes, groupers, etc. all take their toll of the adults and juveniles. Butterflyfishes would appear to fall easy prey to night-hunting predators such as morays since they are comatose during the evening hours. A specimen of *Forcipiger flavissimus* was found among the stomach contents of a tiger shark in the Hawaiian Islands (Allen, personal communication).

Butterflyfish larvae, on the other hand, are frequently found among stomach contents of large pelagic fishes. The major predators appear to be tunas and dolphins (*Coryphaena*). I have examined tuna stomachs from the Caribbean, eastern United States, and the Gulf of Guinea (East Africa) and found larval chaetodontids to be well represented among the stomach contents from all areas. Reintjes and King (1953) examined stomachs from yellowfin tuna, and King and Ikehara (1956) examined them from both bigeye and yellowfin tuna of the Central Pacific. In both instances larval chaetodontids were common. I also examined the collection of fishes from stomachs of tuna under the care of Dr. Brian Rothschild, formerly of the Bureau of Commercial Fisheries (now National Marine Fisheries Service) in Honolulu. Chaetodontid larvae were present, taken from stomachs of tuna captured near the Line Islands and Samoa.

The occasional specimens of *Coryphaena* that I was able to examine for stomach contents in the Caribbean area had eaten chaetodontid larvae, but these larvae turned up less frequently than in tuna stomachs. In an *Alepisaurus* stomach one butterflyfish larva was found.

The pelagic larvae of the butterflyfish are probably subject to predation by other open-water predators, but fewer data are available on the dietary habits of those fishes than on the commercially important species like tuna.

In the Maldive Islands the native fishermen use small chaetodonts 4-8 cm standard length as bait to attract and hold schooling tuna (Axelrod, personal communication).

PARASITES AND DISEASES

A complete survey of the parasites of butterflyfishes was not made. However, several adult specimens of *Chaetodon lunula, C. auriga, C. miliaris,* and *C. fremblii* from Hawaiian waters were examined for ecto- and endo-parasites. This survey revealed that the dinoflagellate *Amblyoodinium* was the most prevalent parasite infecting these species. Gill flukes and parasitic copepods were not uncommon. Occasional specimens of acanthocephalans were found in the stomach and intestinal tract. Yamagouti (1963) reported several species of parasitic copepods and branchiurans on various species of *Chaetodon*.

Larval butterflyfishes were occasionally, sometimes often, infested with the hydroid *Hydrichthys*. Those collected by the National Marine Fisheries Service on cruise TC-32 were heavily infected by this parasite. Other larval fishes collected in the same trawls were similarly infected, including the manini (*Acanthurus triostegus sandvicensis*) previously reported on by Randall (1961). In many instances the chaetodontid larvae were so heavily covered by *Hydrichthys* that their swimming ability must have been greatly impaired. Newly transformed *Chaetodon miliaris* showed occasional light infections by the *Hydrichthys*. It is not known what effect this has on the fishes, i.e. whether it is temporary or fatal. Randall (1961) stated that *Hydrichthys* on the manini (*A. triostegus*) regresses quickly during early benthic life. There is also a possibility that cleaner fishes will remove this parasite from the newly transformed juveniles. No live fishes so infected were ever available for experimentation along these lines.

White-spot disease, probably caused by the ciliate parasite *Cryptocaryon irritans*, was occasionally seen on larvae and adults in the field. When these fishes were placed in aquaria the disease spread quickly and was difficult to control.

Chaetodon auriga was used as one of the exerimental animals in testing for causes and cures of the disease Dr. Earl Herald called the "Kaneohe Crud." Most of the fishes that succumbed to this disease were collected at Kaneohe Bay, Oahu. Photo by H. Hansen.

At Johnston Atoll a pair of *Chaetodon ephippium* was seen and photographed. This species also appeared as small groups and even as individuals mixed in with the groups of *C. auriga* in the same vicinity. Photo by Dr. Warren E.
Burgess.

Adult butterflyfishes from Kaneohe Bay had a much higher death rate when kept in captivity than similar species from other parts of Oahu (the late Dr. Earl S. Herald of the Steinhart Aquarium, personal communication; Mr. William P. Braker of the Shedd Aquarium, personal communication; personal observations). The staff of the Steinhart Aquarium had not yet found the specific cause of the disease at the time of this writing.

Tests were run on *Chaetodon auriga* from Kaneohe Bay in an attempt to gain more information about this disease. Three fully grown specimens of *Chaetodon auriga* were placed in a circulating water aquarium of 100-gallon capacity at the Hawaii Institute of Marine Biology, Kaneohe Bay, Hawaii. Water was pumped in from Kaneohe Bay, the origin of the butterflyfishes. Three other individuals of this butterflyfish caught at the same time and same place were placed in an identical tank but the system was closed. Airstones and undergravel filters were provided for both tanks. One milliliter of a 2 % copper sulphate solution was added per gallon to the closed system only. The dosage was repeated in one week. Within seven to ten days the specimens in the aquarium with the system open to Kaneohe Bay water were dead. The symptoms were as follows: (1) they stopped eating after three days; (2) within a week they became lethargic and remained at the bottom of the tank, usually in a corner; and (3) red areas appeared at the base of the fins, the fish dying soon afterward. Examination of the specimens showed no indication of the cause of death. The *Chaetodon auriga* in the aquarium with copper sulphate were still alive two weeks after the start of the test and were apparently normal. The tanks were cleaned and the test repeated with new fishes; the closed system tank now became the open system tank and vice versa. The result was the same, with the open system fish dying in about the same length of time as the previous trio. Those fish in the closed system lived well beyond the time of death of the open system fish. However, when this system was opened these fish also died within a week to ten days. The copper solution was added to both tanks in a third experiment to see if an initial introduction made any difference. Two of the test individuals died as before, and a third survived for two weeks but then died. Although the particular cause of this disease was not traced, at least some means of control is indicated by these experiments.

Color and Pattern

The color and color patterns of butterflyfishes, and reef fishes in general, have been subjects of many controversial discussions. At present there is still no truly acceptable theory as to the function of these patterns. The patterns of butterflyfishes remain fixed as adults (except day/night in a few species), and the colors are changeable only to a very slight degree (usually fading) except in a limited number of species. One of these species is *Forcipiger longirostris,* which may vary in color from bright butter yellow to dark brownish-black.

The variety of designs exhibited by butterflyfishes is probably significant as recognition devices for conspecifics and other fishes. Species recognition on a coral reef where there are many species of brightly colored and patterned fishes including other butterflyfishes should be of considerable importance whether it be for territory recognition and/or spawning or other reasons. Species such as *Chaetodon aureofasciatus* and *C. rainfordi* are very similar in shape and coloration, particularly in the head region. In pattern, however, the body of *C. aureofasciatus* is plain whereas that of *C. rainfordi* is barred, both species being basically colored in shades of yellows and orange. Since these species are sympatric over part of their ranges, recognition would be very important to prevent wasteful spawning mix-ups and hybridization.

Bright colors of reef fishes often advertise some disagreeable aspect of the fishes. Gosline (personal communication) believes the color patterns of butterflyfishes may function as a warning device. The deep body and spiny nature of these fishes make them difficult to eat, especially in conjunction with their behavior toward aggressors. Advertising such difficulty in obtaining a meal would seem to benefit both predator and prey alike.

It also has been reported that the bright colors and patterns of butterflyfishes act as a sort of protective coloration in the myriad of colors of the coral reef. In my experience in diving for these fishes and observing their behavior, I find that their patterns and color make them more obvious rather than less conspicuous. In most instances butterflyfishes are easily spotted on the reef. As is the case with many other species of fishes, butterflyfishes are less colorful in temperate waters. In Easter Island, St. Helena

This species is also encountered as pairs as seen here. Photo by Rodney Jonklass.

Opposite:
Hemitaurichthys zoster moving as a school over the reef using the sharp branching corals for shelter. Photo by Dr. Herbert R. Axelrod.

and Ascension Island, temperate Japan, etc., where there are fewer species of chaetodontids, the patterns are usually more simple and the colors more drab. In such cases there probably is less selection pressure for complicated designs or bright colors.

There is general agreement that the eyeband, found in most species of butterflyfishes, is protective in function, obliterating the outline of the eye. The "eyespot" in the dorsal fin of many juvenile and adult chaetodontids is supposed to function as a false eye which directs the attacker's attention toward it rather than to the vulnerable eye. One hypothesis proposes that the fishes swim backward in stress situations, giving this posterior spot an apparent anterior position. Once the attacker moves toward the eyespot, the butterflyfish reverses direction and escapes in a forward direction. The extra fraction of a second gained by the confusion of the attacker may be the difference between escape or capture. I have never seen this behavior in adult butterflyfishes under any circumstances, but have seen it in juveniles of not only butterflyfishes but acanthurids as well. The acanthurids had no dorsal fin spots. Many juvenile butterflyfishes have a dorsal spot that is lost with age (*Chaetodon lunula*, *C. adiergastos*, *C. auripes*, etc.), whereas other species retain it throughout life (for example, *Coradion chrysozonus*, *Chaetodon assarius*, *C. auriga*, etc.).

Night coloration in butterflyfishes, in at least several species, differs but slightly from daytime patterns (Hobson, 1974), with the basic species

Chaetodon capistratus has a spot in the posterior portion of its body which has often been referred to as a "false eyespot". Photo by W. Hoppe.

At night some butterflyfishes change color. Most often light areas will become darker and dark areas become grayer. This is *Pseudochaetodon nigrirostris* photographed at night by Dr. E. Hobson.

recognition pattern always easily recognizable. At night several species (i.e. *Chaetodon paucifasciatus*) have a dark spot in the dorsal fin which is absent during the day. In other species the night pattern is one in which the dorsal half of the body becomes very dark with the exception of two white or light spots aligned horizontally on the side. *Chaetodon quadrimaculatus* is one species in which this night pattern appears to have become fixed as a diurnal pattern. The two light spots have been observed as night patterns in several species (*Chaetodon trifascialis, C. citrinellus, C. melannotus*, etc.) of different subgenera. *Hemitaurichthys polylepis* exhibits the darkening of the body, but with only a single light spot in the upper center of its body (Hobson, 1974). The significance of these night-time patterns is not known. Butterflyfishes are particularly vulnerable at night while sleeping as they are only partially protected by coral, and the night pattern may serve in some way to distract predators from these fishes. Freshly captured butterflyfishes will often show night-time color patterns. If they are placed in aquaria or returned to their natural environment, they will quickly revert to normal coloration. The night pattern therefore appears to be identical with a stress or fright display.

Certain groups of species of butterflyfishes have some aspects of color pattern in common. These species complexes will be more fully discussed in the systematic section, but some mention should be made of these patterns here. In my estimation these patterns are significant in delimiting species groups. Ahl (1921) referred to the "spotted-*Chaetodon*" complex,

Chaetodon trifascialis adult patrolling the perimeter of its territory. The territory often is a single stand of coral such as shown here. Photo by Dr. Gerald R. Allen.

If another *C. trifascialis* approaches it is immediately chased from the territory. Photo by Dr. Warren E. Burgess.

Chaetodon semilarvatus is another of those species that form both pairs and small groups. Photo by K. Probst.

Chaetodon auriga is commonly found in small aggregations as this one. On occasion a *C. ephippium* will join the group as it moves from one feeding area to another. Photo by Dr. Warren E. Burgess.

which was characterized by a yellowish to white background or body color overlaid with dark spots, one per scale, usually in rows following the pattern of the scale rows. The confusion as to the identity of these spotted butterflyfishes was considerable, and even now one or two nominal species were not readily identifiable (mainly due to lack of material or insufficient description). Among the spotted *Chaetodon* species are *C. miliaris, C. citrinellus, C. assarius, C. guentheri, C. dolosus,* etc.

In another group of butterflyfishes there is a tendency for the posterior part of the body to be colored differently from the remaining portion. This posterior color (usually dark) is often found in combination with a chevron pattern as in *Chaetodon mertensi* or *C. larvatus*. In one species, *C. trifascialis*, the posterior black area shrinks with age until the adult displays none of this color. The dark posterior color is not confined to this group but transcends some of the non-closely related non-chevron subgenera. In these species (i.e. *C. decussatus* and *C. dolosus*), however, the dark posterior area is not confined to a limited portion of the body as in the above groups. The chevron pattern may vary, becoming a checkerboard pattern in some species, but the chevron pattern is still visible.

The eyeband of butterflyfishes is quite variable among the different species. There are eyebands that are dark-bordered, others light-bordered. Some eyebands are light-centered, others dark-centered. The width varies individually as well as between species groups, and many

The chevron pattern is found in this *Chaetodon larvatus* as well as a posterior area which is dark in color. Photo by G. Marcuse.

variations may be found in a single subgenus. Certain groups undergo changes with age in eyeband development, but they will be discussed below under juvenile-adult variations.

At least one specific aspect of the color pattern can be found in closely related genera of butterflyfishes as well as in some species of the large genus *Chaetodon*. This is the presence of an interorbital stripe. This stripe extends from the nape or between the eyes to the tip of the snout. Such species as *Chelmon rostratus*, *Coradion chrysozonus*, and *Chaetodon modestus* possess this type of stripe. They also have in common a barred pattern in which the bars are yellow to orange on a background of white to yellow. Another species complex exhibits the interorbital stripe but not the barred pattern. This includes such species as *Chaetodon aya*, *Chaetodon falcifer*, and *Chaetodon aculeatus*. These have in common a dark band usually following the base of the dorsal fin.

Other pattern similarities are present among the chaetodontids, but these are covered in the systematic discussions and need not be treated here.

The changes of color pattern of butterflyfishes from juvenile to adult have caused many problems in the systematics of these fishes. Countless synonyms have resulted from the naming of various developmental stages of chaetodontids. There are several basic pattern changes that occur with growth, and once these are recognized the problem of matching juveniles with adults becomes much simplified.

Juveniles of many species of butterflyfishes have a dark spot (usually black, sometimes ocellated) in the dorsal fin near the angle of the fin. The spot gradually fades with growth, and by the time the fish reaches adulthood it is absent. Species of the subgenus *Chaetodontops* exhibit this change; *Chelmon marginalis* and *Coradion altivelis* are examples from different genera. *Chaetodon auriga* and certain other species retain the spot throughout life, and at least one species, *Chaetodon paucifasciatus*, has the spot as an adult only at certain times.

A second change common to many butterflyfishes is the loss with age of a dark band (usually black, sometimes margined with a lighter color) around the caudal peduncle of juveniles. Examples of species exhibiting this changing pattern are *Chaetodon ephippium*, *C. xanthocephalus*, *C. semeion*, *C. lineolatus*, *C. wiebeli*, and *C. aureofasciatus*. In addition, *Chaetodon aureofasciatus* has a large lateral body spot that also disappears at about the same rate as the caudal peduncle band. Again there are species of chaetodontids that retain a caudal peduncle band throughout life.

The eyeband, as mentioned above, is quite variable, not only from species to species, but from young to adult. Some species lack eyebands in all stages of life (i.e. *Chaetodon fremblii*, *C. dichrous*, *C. hemichrysus*). Two others, *Chaetodon ephippium* and *C. xanthocephalus*, have them as juveniles only. In these species the eyeband is normal in juveniles but becomes reduced in length and width with age. By the time they become

An aggressive stance with head down and fins raised is exhibited by *Heniochus acuminatus.* Photo by K. Paysan.

The same aggressive behavior is often displayed in *Heniochus varius* but the horns and frontal hump are much more developed and can probably cause much more damage. Photo by Dr. Gerald R. Allen.

At the first sign of trouble the dorsal fin spines are raised as in this *Chaetodon bennetti*. As the danger approaches the butterflyfish will dart in among the coral branches, stop, turn, and raise the spines again. Photo by Michio Goto, Marine Life Documents.

The characteristic head-down fin-raised position is exhibited by this *Chaetodon austriacus*. Photo by Dr. Victor G. Springer.

subadults there are only dark lines through the eyes, extending only for short distances above and below the rim of the orbit. Several species of butterflyfishes have a normally shaped eyeband as juveniles, but with age the upper section on the nape becomes separated into a hoof- or horse-shoe-shaped marking. This occurs in species of the *C. mertensi* group, in *Chaetodon adiergastos*, *C. oxycephalus*, etc. Incomplete separation, in which the hoof-shaped marking is still connected by a dark area to the eyeband, can be found in the *punctatofasciatus*-group and *C. lineolatus*. This marking, often accented by a partial or complete white border, may have some significance in the frontal display exhibited by the chaetodontids. Other variations in eyebands exist but usually are species specific. These are described under the species accounts.

The caudal fin color pattern changes in many species from juvenile to adult. Normally the juvenile will possess a dusky or black crossband near the base of the fin, the outer two-thirds being hyaline. With age the band increases in width, becomes darker, and progresses toward the outer section of the fin, the hyaline portion becoming reduced to a narrow edge. The basal portion of the caudal fin usually retains color of some sort.

Very few species of butterflyfishes undergo a complete color change from juvenile to adult so that the two are so different as to be almost unrecognizable as the same species. One of those species which does change drastically with age is *Chaetodon lunula*.

Many species undergo almost no change at all when progressing from juvenile to adult. Species of the *Chaetodon miliaris* group, *C. aya* group, and most non-*Chaetodon* species all have color patterns as juveniles which are almost identical to those of the adults.

Heniochus chrysostomus, in contrast to the species of *Coradion* and *Chelmon* that lose dorsal fin spots, is a non-*Chaetodon* species that has a black spot in the anal fin of juveniles. It is contained within a blackish or dark brownish band that extends into the anal fin and is usually obscured by it. On some preserved specimens there is a hint of a white ring around the spot, thereby making it more visible. This species could easily pass for one in which no changes occur with age.

The color pattern is quite useful in determining species identification, and photographs of each species, including juveniles, have been presented whenever possible.

Larvae

All chaetodontids have a tholichthys larva. It differs from most other larvae in possessing bony armor surrounding the head. Only one other family (Scatophagidae) is presently known to have a tholichthys-like larvae.

Early tholichthys larvae are not much different from those nearing metamorphosis. They have small dorsal spines, and the pelvic spines are hidden under a ventral bony projection. The postlarvae still retain the bony plates, but the dorsal and pelvic spines are more highly developed. The ventral bony extension is much reduced, the upper plates less so. The extension of these spines from the dorsal and ventrolateral edges of these fishes decreases the ability of another fish to swallow it (Gosline, personal communication).

Tholichthys larvae from the following genera were studied: *Chaetodon*, *Heniochus*, *Chelmon*, *Hemitaurichthys*, *Forcipiger*, and *Pseudochaetodon*. All are basically similar but do exhibit generic (and subgeneric) differences. The most unusual tholichthys of *Chaetodon meyeri* and *C. ornatissimus* was mentioned earlier. It has the usual head armature but in addition possesses a bony projection or horn above each eye directed forward. In the early larvae the horns are thick and straight, but in the postlarvae they become more slender and curved. It was thought that these horns identified the larvae as belonging to the genus *Heniochus*, which has supraorbital horns as adults, but this is not so. The larvae are quickly recognized as not belonging to genus *Heniochus* since they possess an incomplete lateral line (that of *Heniochus* is complete). The dorsal and pelvic spines of this type larva are not so developed as in other species of chaetodontids. Perhaps the horns act as a compensatory mechanism for the protection of the larvae. Specimens of this horned type of larva have been captured in mid-water trawls and night-light stations at the surface as well as in tuna and *Alepisaurus* stomachs (personal observations). Newly metamorphosed hornless individuals were captured of the same size as larvae possessing the horns. It is difficult to imagine horns of such size being absorbed so rapidly by the early juvenile. Perhaps the horns are simply discarded rather than absorbed as are the head plates. The head plates remain for at least several weeks after metamorphosis but gradually shrink and disappear. They are transparent in juveniles so that the body color can be seen through them.

Chaetodon auriga parasitized by one of the highly modified copepods. Photo by Walter Deas.

Chaetodon excelsa parasitized by *Hydrichthys.* This specimen was captured nightlighting. Photo by Dr.John E. Randall.

Chaetodon auriga with a dorsal fin spot typical of most of its range. Photo by Walter Deas.

The spotless variey of *Chaetodon auriga* is commonly found in the Red Sea but may turn up on occasion elsewhere. Photo by Helmut Debelius.

The unusual *tholichthys* larva found in the subgenus *Citharoedus* of the genus *Chaetodon*. Photo by Fujio Yasuda.

A second unusual tholichthys form is that of the genus *Forcipiger*. This larva was first illustrated by Kendall and Goldsborough (1911). Randall (1961) suspected that the ragged edge of the dorsal plate extension was the result of a piece being broken off. I have seen several specimens of *Forcipiger* larvae of both species, and all have this ragged edge to the upper plate. It appears to be the normal condition for this type larva. The plates of the early larva extend in the same planes as the dorsal and anal spines and hide them from view.

The pelagic postlarva of butterflyfishes is silvery in color, similar to many other pelagic larvae of reef-type fishes. The change from this pelagic coloration to the color pattern of the juvenile occurs within a relatively short time. Specimens of *Chaetodon lunula*, *C. auriga*, *C. fremblii*, and *C. miliaris* caught while night-lighting transformed into the juvenile phase within a matter of minutes. The longest period of time observed for this change required about 30 minutes. One individual of *Chaetodon kleinii* made the transformation similar to the others, but a slight silvery sheen was present for about three weeks. I have never seen a regression to the pelagic coloration once the color metamorphosis has taken place.

The bony head plates were visible on all individuals at the time of metamorphosis but, being transparent, were difficult to see. The progressive resorption of these plates was closely followed until they were no longer visible. The plates disappeared completely in about one month although the length of time was apparently species specific.

The size at the time of metamorphosis varies greatly from species to species. Species of the genera *Forcipiger* and *Hemitaurichthys* have the largest tholichthys larvae, being up to 60 mm standard length at the time of metamorphosis. On the other hand, *Chaetodon trifascialis*, *C. octofasciatus*, and *Chelmon rostratus* are among those species with the smallest larvae at the time of metamorphosis. They are 9-18 mm standard length.

Anatomical Features Used in the Systematic Section

The anatomical features used by systematists in apportioning the various genera and species to their assumed correct position in relationship to each other may differ from one group of fishes to the next. The characteristics of the butterflyfishes are not necessarily the same as those that would be important in divisions of other families such as the angelfishes, damselfishes, surgeonfishes, etc. For example, the length of the snout is very useful as an identification feature of the butterflyfishes but of little significance in the angelfishes. The discussion that follows, therefore, deals with features which, although not peculiar to the chaetodontids, are important for their identification.

BODY SHAPE

Butterflyfishes are deep-bodied, highly compressed fishes that are able to maneuver between the branches or plates of certain corals with apparent ease. The actual shape of the body, when considered without snout or fins, is not especially variable among species; the vast majority of species have oval bodies. Only a few might be considered as deviating from this general plan, but there are always a number of intergrades from one shape to another, so none can be considered as extreme. The rounded-oval species (*Parachaetodon ocellatus*, *Chaetodon triangulum*, *C. adiergastos*, etc.), having body depths in relationship to standard length of 1.3-1.5, and, of course, the almost circular *Chaetodon aureofasciatus*, *C. rainfordi*, etc., with a body depth of 1.2 in the standard length, are at one end of the spectrum. *Chaetodon trifascialis*, with a body depth of 2.2 in relation to its standard length, is at the other. It is of interest to note that two presumably closely related species, *Chaetodon triangulum* and *C. trifascialis*, should be so very different in body shape.

SNOUT LENGTH

Snout lengths vary considerably among the butterflyfishes, and one can find almost all gradations from the one extreme, *Forcipiger*, to the other, *Parachaetodon*. But, although some species of *Chaetodon* (i.e.

Chaetodon trifasciatus trifasciatus (notice orange caudal peduncle) and *Chaetodon plebeius* (lacking the blue lateral blotch). Photo by R. Jonklaas.

Opposite:
Chaetodon plebeius- aberrant color form or hybrid between *C. plebeius* and *C. zanzibariensis.* Photo by R. Jonklaas at Sri Lanka.

One of the more complicated adult patterns is shown in this *Chaetodon flavirostris.* This is also the only species in the genus *Chaetodon* to exhibit a prominent nuchal hump. A Colour Library International photo.

The produced snout of this *Chaetodon aculeatus* differs from the produced snout in genera such as *Chelmon* and *Forcipiger*. Photo by H. Hansen.

Chaetodon aculeatus, C. falcula, etc.) have a rather produced snout, they differ from those of *Forcipiger* and *Chelmon*. In *Chaetodon* the extension of the snout is more like an extension of the head and the snout is robust, unlike the situation in *Forcipiger* and *Chelmon* in which the elongate snouts are slender and tubular, rather distinct from the rest of the head.

The relationship of snout length to body depth varies greatly within the family Chaetodontidae. The chaetodontid snout reaches its greatest development in *Forcipiger* (1.1-1.5 in body depth) and *Chelmon* (3.0-3.1 in body depth), and is least developed in the genus *Parachaetodon* and subgenera *Corallochaetodon, Citharoedus*, and *Discochaetodon* of the genus *Chaetodon. Parachaetodon* has a snout length which is contained 8.0-9.0 times in the body depth.

FINS (SHAPE, LENGTH, SPINES, ETC.)

The shape of the spinous portion of the dorsal fin of the genus *Chaetodon* varies from subgenus to subgenus. In most species the spines increase gradually in height posteriorly until the fifth to seventh spines, which are longest, and then decrease in height until the last or maintain an even height until the end of the spinous portion of the dorsal fin. Each spine is neither much longer nor shorter than the adjacent one, giving the spinous portion of the fin a gently curved appearance. A variation of this pattern occurs in some species (i.e. *C. pelewensis, C. kleinii, C. litus*, etc.) in which the first or first and second dorsal fin spines are extremely short, the succeeding spines as above. Characteristic of the subgenera *Progna-thodes* and *Roa* is a more or less triangular-shaped spinous dorsal fin in which the third to fifth spines are noticeably longer than all other spines. No other subgenera have this type of spinous dorsal fin shape, although the subgenus *Rhombochaetodon* may approach it somewhat. Other genera, however, such as *Forcipiger, Amphichaetodon*, etc., also have a triangular shape to the spinous dorsal fin. In the genus *Heniochus* an extreme development of the triangular-shaped fin is present in which the fourth dorsal fin spine is elongated. In some species the spine is prolonged into a filament at times as long or longer than the length of the fish. Juve-niles of almost all chaetodontid species have a triangular-shaped dorsal fin, as do most larvae.

Only one subgenus of *Chaetodon, Gonochaetodon*, appears to have the dorsal spines progressively longer, i.e. first shortest, last longest. *Para-chaetodon, Chelmonops, Chelmon*, and *Coradion* have this graduated-type fin, although the last two genera contain species without a strictly elevated fin. In these species the posterior spines are more level or of similar height, not increasingly noticeably in height.

The number of dorsal fin spines varies from a low of six (*Parachae-todon*) to highs of fifteen or sixteen (*Chaetodon blackburnii, Hemitaur-ichthys multispinus*). The vast majority of species, regardless of genus, have eleven to fourteen dorsal fin spines, the low numbers being excep-tional (91 species have 12, 13, or 14 spines).

The soft or rayed portion of the dorsal fin varies as much as or more than the spinous portion. There are two common shapes, one evenly rounded or nearly so, in which the contour of the fin continues as a smooth arc from the end of the spinous portion to the last rays of the fin, and the other with some of the rays just beyond the center of the rayed portion of the fin longer than the others, producing an angle (i.e. *Chaeto-don rafflesi, C. vagabundus*).

Some species of the subgenus *Rabdophorus* have one or more rays extended into a filament. This filament begins as a short spike on the periphery of the fin and increases in length as the fish grows (e.g. in *Chae-todon auriga*). *Chaetodon ephippium* and *C. semeion* are the only other species with a dorsal fin filament.

A soft dorsal fin in which the hind edge is vertically oriented, or nearly so, is present in many species. Along with several subgenera of the genus *Chaetodon* (namely *Prognathodes, Roa*, and *Gonochaetodon*), other genera possess this character (*Forcipiger, Coradion, Chelmon*, and *Amphichaetodon*). *Chaetodon trifascialis* has a sharp angle in the soft dorsal fin, the posterior edge sloping back toward the body of the fish rather than straight down, and *Parachaetodon ocellatus*, with an elevated dorsal fin, has an "S"-shaped or sigmoid trailing edge to its dorsal fin. *Chelmonops truncatus* has a soft dorsal fin similar to that of *Chaetodon trifascialis* when young, but the rays at the angle become elongate with age forming an extension of the fin (not a filament like those mentioned

A juvenile *Chaetodon austriacus* from the Red Sea. The characteristic black anal fin is noticeable even at this small size. Photo by H. Debelius.

Chaetodon meyeri is a member of the subgenus *Citharoedus*. Its pattern of black lines on a white and yellow background is easily recognized. Photo by R. Jonklaas.

Chaetodon ornatissimus is also a member of the subgenus *Citharoedus*. The body pattern of orange lines differs from that of *meyeri* but the head pattern is very much alike. Photo by Dr. Warren E. Burgess.

The dorsal fin extension in this *Chaetodon ephippium* is just beginning to develop. Signs of maturing are also seen in the color pattern (losing of eye band and caudal peduncle band). Photo by G. Marcuse.

above). Other variations occur in the rayed portion of the dorsal fin. These can be seen in the photographs of the species in the systematic portion of this study.

The anal fin, other than complementing the shape of the dorsal fin, has fewer variations. Most are rounded. A few species possess angular anal fins, such as the subgenus *Rhombochaetodon* and genus *Heniochus*. Others have a more vertical edge, continuing the effect of the dorsal fin, such as the subgenera *Roa* and *Prognathodes* and the genera *Forcipiger* and *Amphichaetodon*. Again, *Chaetodon trifascialis* has an angular anal fin, and *Chelmonops truncatus* has a fin in which the rays are extended (like its dorsal fin).

The anal fin spines contribute little to the diagnosis of the genera but are of some use for subgenera of *Chaetodon*. In *Prognathodes* and *Roa* the middle (of three) anal fin spine is significantly stronger and longer than the other two, extending beyond the edge of the fin a significant distance. Normally this spine is only slightly longer and stronger than the third, and the difference between these two types of spines is easily seen. In fact, many species have the third spine subequal to the second, although it normally is not as strong. The first anal fin spine may be only slightly shorter or significantly shorter than the second anal fin spine.

Most chaetodontids have a total of three anal spines like many percoid families, but some have more. Typically *Chaetodon plebeius* has four anal fin spines, *C. trifascialis* mostly four but occasionally five, and *Hemi-*

taurichthys multispinus has five. The extra anal fin spines characterize species but do not seem to be diagnostic for other categories. Like extra dorsal fin spines (see *Hemitaurichthys multispinus* and *Chaetodon blackburni*), the extra anal fin spines appear in scattered genera and subgenera, not exhibiting any particular pattern. Occasionally even one of the normally three-spined species will turn up with four, or even five, anal fin spines, indicating that this might be a tendency for the family in general.

The pectoral, pelvic, and caudal fins are not so variable as the dorsal and anal fins but nevertheless show some differences. The pectoral fins of almost all species of butterflyfishes are of normal length and shape when compared to other types of fishes. Only two genera, *Forcipiger* and *Hemitaurichthys*, possess pectoral fins that may be considered modified from this general design. In both of these genera the pectoral fins are elongate, about 2.5-3.0 in standard length, when compared with those of the other species, usually 3.5-4.5 in standard length. In addition, the pectoral fins of species of *Forcipiger* are pointed at the tips with the posterior edge "S"-shaped or sigmoid, giving the fin a falcate configuration, whereas the pectorals of *Hemitaurichthys* approach this design but cannot be considered truly falcate. The pectoral fins of almost all species are unpigmented hyaline or only slightly colored.

Pelvic fins vary in length from one group to another although the shape is very uniform. The first ray is elongate and curled downward, away from the body, at the tip. Although the pelvic fins decrease proportionately in length with age, some species retain an elongated fin, i.e. extending beyond the first spine of the anal fin as adults (for example all species of *Chelmon*). In most other species the pelvic fins are short, not reaching the anal opening. Species of the genus *Heniochus* have notably strong, flat pelvic fin spines, in contrast to the more slender spines of most other species, and the rayed portion is short, fan-like in shape and dark brown to black in color.

The shape of the caudal fin is also comparatively uniform throughout the family. Normally it is truncate-rounded (basically truncate, but with the posterior edge forming an arc or curve from angle to angle). There is a true truncate-shaped caudal fin present in some species (e.g. *Chaetodon trifascialis*) as well as a fin shape in which the upper rays are slightly prolonged (e.g. species of *Forcipiger*).

Although many species of butterflyfishes have the caudal fin extending well beyond the posterior edges of the dorsal and anal fins, others do not. A number of species have the dorsal and anal fins extending to the halfway to three-fourths point of the caudal fin and a few even further. The subgenus *Corallochaetodon* contains species in which the dorsal and anal fins extend to or nearly to the edge of the caudal fin so that, when extended, the three fins form an almost continuous line. The color pattern continues uninterrupted from fin to fin to enhance the appearance. In the previously mentioned type (dorsal and anal fins not reaching end of

Night color pattern of *Heniochus intermedius* with darkening of light areas between dark bands. Photo by H. Debelius.

Opposite:
Chaetodon lineolatus has an unusual eyebar and a pattern of thin vertical lines. Upper photo by Walter Deas at night (apparently this fish is awake and is not displaying the night pattern however).

Night pattern of *Chaetodon vagabundus.* The typical daytime pattern is not much changed although a large dark blotch is now evident. Lower photo by Allan Power.

caudal) some of the species have the color pattern continued from the dorsal fin across the caudal fin and onto the anal fin, but not as smoothly as in the species of *Corallochaetodon.*

LATERAL LINE

Probably one of the more variable characters of butterflyfishes, and one that is useful in diagnosing both genera and subgenera, is the shape and extent of the lateral line. The lateral line extends either to the base of the caudal fin (all genera except *Chaetodon* and *Parachaetodon*) or stops at about the base of the last rays of the dorsal fin (*Chaetodon* and *Parachaetodon*). In some instances the lateral line terminates somewhat earlier, ending high on the body near the bases of the first soft rays of the dorsal fin. This condition most often occurs in the subgenus *Corallochaetodon.* Also present in some specimens, but quite unusual, is the splitting of the lateral line into two or more branches. This branching usually appears on either side of the specimen, the opposite side being normal.

The lateral line varies in shape from a low, smooth arc to a high, peaked one, as well as having angular configurations. Most species have a lateral line in which the central portion lies fairly high on the body, is flat, and the angle at the posterior end of the flat portion is slightly higher than that of the anterior end of the flat portion. Variations of this shape are found in the genera *Heniochus* and *Hemitaurichthys,* where the flat portion is more or less level, and in the subgenus *Citharoedus,* where the posterior angle is noticeably higher than in most species. The lateral line of the genus *Coradion* rises to a single elevated peak, lacking the flat section. Smooth (without angles), low lateral lines are present in subgenera such as *Megaprotodon. Gonochaetodon,* and *Discochaetodon,* with species of the subgenus *Tetrachaetodon* and genus *Parachaetodon* approaching this shape.

The shape of the lateral line is subject to anomalies much as is its extent. In several specimens the lateral line is seen to wander irregularly across the body (though mostly in the direction of the normal lateral line shape), sometimes on one side only, sometimes on both sides. In other examples the lateral line is barely discernible in part or completely or is marked only by pits rather than the usual tubes through the scales.

SCALES

The shape, size, and pattern of the scales are other characters that can be used for distinguishing genera and subgenera, although previous workers in this family laid too much emphasis on scale patterns. The shape of the exposed portions of butterflyfish scales varies from vertically elongate with a rounded edge to angular and rhomboidal. Most species have scales that are rounded (not elongate) to angular, sometimes with the rounded type changing to the angular type toward the posterior end of the fish (subgenus *Chaetodon*). Elongate-rounded scales are found in species of the subgenus *Corallochaetodon,* and rounded (but not elongate) scales are present in species of the subgenus *Tetrachaetodon*. Those subgenera with rhomboidal scales usually also have them arranged in a chevron pattern, as can be seen in the subgenera *Rhombochaetodon*, *Megaprotodon*, and *Gonochaetodon*.

The most common scale pattern is one in which the scales are arranged in ascending rows from the lower anterior to the upper posterior end of the body. The pattern is most pronounced, i.e. the rows are more steeply angled, in the upper part of the body, the rows becoming more horizontal in the lower part. *Chaetodon auripes* has most of the scale rows on the side of the body below the lateral line horizontal, whereas in most species the horizontal rows are relegated to the extreme lower part of the body. The problem with using scale patterns is that two workers looking at the same species could easily discern different patterns.

Scale size does not differ significantly from one species to the next, except for a few species, but does differ from one part of the body to another. Scales on the side of the body are largest, those on the head, chest, and posterior end of the body (including the caudal peduncle) are generally smaller, and those on the fins are extremely small. Actual scale sizes between species are reflected by the number of scales in a lateral series (or parallel to the lateral line). This scale count may be as low as the 20's (i.e. *Chaetodon trifascialis*) in species with larger scales to as high as 80 or more (*Forcipiger*, *Hemitaurichthys*) in smaller-scaled species. A species with an average number of scales would have a count between 30 and 50.

One character involved with the placement of scales which has not been considered until now is the extent of the scaly "sheath" covering the dorsal fin spines. Actually a true sheath is not fully formed since the skin in which the scales are embedded is adherent to the dorsal spines and stretches upward as the spines are raised. The sheath starts near the bases of the anterior dorsal fin spines and progressively covers more of each succeeding spine until the last, which is normally almost entirely hidden. In most species the sheath reaches to the midpoint of the middle dorsal fin spines, a condition which I refer to in the species descriptions as "normal." A "low" sheath is one in which the anterior and middle dorsal fin spines are relatively free of scales, the sheath covering only the very bases of the spines and the scaly covering increasing in height sharply near the posterior spines so that the last spine is almost hidden (i.e. subgenera *Roa* and *Prognathodes*). A high sheath is one in which the scales reach half or more of the height of the spines well before the middle spines (*Coradion*). An anal spine sheath is present but is too variable to use for purposes of identification.

TEETH

The name "chaetodon" means "bristle-teeth" (*Chaetos* = bristle, *dont* = teeth), a name which describes well the type of teeth found in this family. All species of butterflyfishes have similar teeth, that is, slender,

Night patterns of two species of the subgenus *Citharoedus, Chaetodon ornatissimus* (above) and *C. meyeri.* (below) Photos by Scott Johnson.

Night patterns for *Chaetodon fremblii* (above) and *Chaetodon ephippium* (below). Photos by Scott Johnson.

Patterns exhibited by the rows of teeth in the various butterflyfishes. (1) series of discrete rows, (2) series of bands, (3) a single anterior band.

long, flattened, and slightly curved at their tips. These teeth are apparently well suited for scraping and nipping at the small invertebrates or algae that form the bulk of the chaetodontid diet.

Evidently not noticed (or considered important) by most workers in this family is the arrangement of these teeth in the jaws. There are three basic patterns of tooth arrangement in these fishes: (1) series of discrete rows, (2) series of bands, or (3) a single anterior band.

The first of these types is the most common. The teeth are arranged single-file in rows, there being about four to ten rows in each jaw. The rows are separated by enough space to make counting them relatively easy, although displacement of individual teeth may cause some confusion.

The second type of arrangement is present in species of *Chelmon* and consists of rows of teeth grouped into bands; these bands are distinctly separated from one another. Usually only a few rows of teeth (three or four) make up a band and only a few bands are found in each jaw.

The third type of tooth arrangement, seen in species of the subgenus *Corallochaetodon* for example, is simply a group of rows combined to form a single anterior band in each jaw. The number of rows cannot easily be discerned due to displacement of teeth, but it is estimated to be between two and five.

LACHRYMAL

The shape of the lachrymal bone varies from short to elongate (usually dependent upon the length of the snout), rounded to angular, smooth to serrate or toothed, and scaled to naked. The subgenus *Corallochaetodon*, for example, has species with the lachrymal bone short and rounded, almost completely hidden by scales. This condition is approached by the subgenus *Tetrachaetodon*, although the lachrymal in that group is only partially hidden by scales. *Amphichaetodon* is partially distinguishable from *Pseudochaetodon* by having a serrate and scaled lachrymal, as compared to that of *Pseudochaetodon* which is smooth-edged and not scaled.

The identification of genera and subgenera then is dependent upon combinations of characters, each genus or subgenus requiring a number of characters to distinguish it from other genera or subgenera.

SYSTEMATIC SECTION

Family Chaetodontidae

Body strongly compressed, usually deep, oval to orbicular or sub-rhomboidal (exclusive of fins); dorsal fin continuous or with slight notch; no procumbent spine preceding dorsal fin; head about as high as long; snout, at times, slightly to greatly prolonged; mouth small, terminal, protractile, gape not extending to anterior rim of orbit; teeth setiform, curved, slightly flattened, usually arranged in (1) individual rows across jaws, (2) groups of rows (bands), or (3) a single anterior band of indistinguishable rows; vomer and palatines without teeth; maxillary bone twisted; preoperculum smooth to denticulate, never with a strong spine at angle; lachrymal smooth to serrate; gill membranes narrowly attached to isthmus.

Scales ctenoid, small to large, rounded to angular in shape, and arranged in various patterns on sides; scales smaller on head, vertical fins, chest, and usually posterior end of body; base of dorsal spines covered with scales to various heights; soft portions of dorsal and anal fins scaled almost to their distal borders; axillary scaly process present at base of pelvic spine; lateral line variously arched, ending either (1) in vicinity of last rays of dorsal fin or (2) continuing to base of caudal fin. Dorsal fin spines VI-XVI, dorsal fin soft rays 15-30; anal fin spines III-V (usually III); anal fin soft rays 14-23; gill rakers short, usually 9-25 in number; pseudobranchiae present; 6-7 branchiostegal rays; branched caudal rays normally 15.

Gut repeatedly coiled, caecae not numerous; vertebrae $11+13=24$; gas bladder with anterior portion divided or with two projecting horns; ribs with distal portions expanded antero-posteriorly; supraoccipital crest with dorsal end bifurcate to accept first predorsal element.

Tholichthys larval stage present.

GENERIC CLASSIFICATION

The family Chaetodontidae is a family which contains a great number of very similar species and only a few seemingly divergent ones. This has caused many problems in its division into genera and subgenera. Because of the nature of the problems and the complexity of the species groups, the chaetodontids would lend themselves to cladistic computer analysis. A more thorough study of the generic and subgeneric limits using osteology and other features is in progress.

Chaetodon kleinii has an unusual light area behind the shoulder region in addition to the broad light band through the pectoral region. Photo by Walter Deas.

Opposite·

A few butterflyfishes, such as this *Chaetodon kleinii* and the species shown below *(Chaetodon semeion),* exhibit a distinct bluish color in the interorbital region. Photo above by Allan Power, photo below by Roger Steene.

The development of generic divisions which followed the restriction of the family is summarized in the section *Historical Review*.

The classification proposed on the following pages is to a large extent in agreement with previous workers such as Weber and de Beaufort (1936). The major differences appear in the status of the various groups that have been considered subgenera by some authors but genera by others.

Ahl (1923) was the first worker since Bleeker to revise the Chaetodontidae (his Chaetodontinae). He recognized eleven genera, one of which (*Microcanthus*) has been referred to the family Scorpididae (Kyphosidae) by Fraser-Brunner (1945). I refer a second genus of those he listed (*Vinculum*) to the Kyphosidae as well. *Prognathodes*, which Ahl and most authors have regarded as a genus, is considered as a subgenus of *Chaetodon* in this study. The remaining eight genera, except for some additions or corrections of the species included, remain the same.

Since Ahl (1923), few genera have been proposed for the family Chaetodontidae. Schmidt and Lindberg (1930) erected the genus *Paracanthochaetodon*, but the type-species belongs in the subgenus *Roa* (which predates *Paracanthochaetodon*) of the genus *Chaetodon*.

Bauchotia, the only other genus to be described since Ahl's revision, was proposed by Nalbant (1965), who later (1971) relegated his own genus to the synonymy of *Prognathodes*. In this later paper Nalbant also proposed two new subgenera of the genus *Chaetodon*, *Discochaetodon* and *Exornator*. One of these (*Discochaetodon*) I am using in this work; the other (*Exornator*) I relegate to the synonymy of the subgenus *Chaetodon*.

Only one other subgenus, *Tetrachaetodon* Weber and de Beaufort, 1936, was proposed since 1923. It is also used as a valid subgenus in the present study.

Basically, the ten chaetodontid genera can be divided into two groups, those with complete lateral lines and those with incomplete or abbreviated lateral lines, *Chaetodon* and *Parachaetodon*.

The sole feature which, in fact, unites all 90 species of the genus *Chaetodon* is the reduced lateral line, an advanced or specialized condition over the complete lateral line exhibited by eight of the nine other genera, the ninth seemingly derived from a *Chaetodon*-like ancestor. It is assumed that a reduced lateral line occurred only once, but if this can not be confirmed, and if there are indications that a reduced lateral line occurred more than once, then some subgenera of *Chaetodon* might have to be elevated to genera and some realignment of genera would necessarily occur.

Parachaetodon is unique in possessing only six dorsal fin spines, fewer than in any other genus of chaetodontid (five fewer than in any species of the genus *Chaetodon*). It appears to be an offshoot of the basic chaetodontid line but resembles, superficially at least, the genus *Coradion*.

Coradion along with *Chelmon* and *Chelmonops* form a group of similar genera characterized by their low dorsal fin spine count (VIII-XI), by their dorsal spines generally increasing in height posteriorly (last spine longest), their scales numbering between 45 and 55 in the lateral line, and a color pattern which normally consists of vertical bars of yellow to brownish-orange with an ocellus included in the last bar of the dorsal fin and a stripe from nape to snout. The differences between these genera consist of variations in the prolongation of the snout, the shape of the fins, and the number of dorsal fin spines. They bear a resemblance to the subgenus *Roa*, particularly the *modestus*-group.

Two genera which hitherto had not been considered closely related are *Forcipiger* and *Hemitaurichthys*. Although their general appearance is quite different (*Forcipiger* for example has a very elongate, tubular snout whereas *Hemitaurichthys* has a normal, short snout), if other characters are selected they indicate that the two genera are basically related. Common to both *Forcipiger* and *Hemitaurichthys* are a high number of scales, 68-83, in the lateral line, elongate falcate or falcate-like pectoral fins, and the ability to darken all or part of their bodies (exclusive of the darkening for night patterns), characters which are found nowhere else in the family Chaetodontidae. Other similarities involve the shape of the lateral line and certain meristics. Both genera have complete lateral lines. The tholichthys stages are quite different, that of *Forcipiger* being highly modified, that of *Hemitaurichthys* being relatively normal.

The systematic position of *Chaetodon nigrirostris* was discussed by Hubbs (1958), who eventually, but hesitantly, placed it in the genus *Heniochus*. His hesitation was well founded since this species, with a complete lateral line, shares characters with both *Chaetodon* and *Heniochus*. I have erected a new genus, *Pseudochaetodon*, for this species and consider it intermediate between *Chaetodon* and *Heniochus*.

The other new genus, *Amphichaetodon*, has a low scaly sheath to the dorsal spines similar to that of *Forcipiger* and *Hemitaurichthys* and a serrated or toothed lachrymal bone, characters which would tend to place it in the vicinity of subgenus *Prognathodes*.

The subgenera of *Chaetodon* are treated in the systematic section under that genus.

The genera are easily characterized by external features which are summarized in Table 1 and may be identified by using the following key.

Key to the Genera of the Family Chaetodontidae

1. Lateral line incomplete, ending in vicinity of last rays of dorsal fin . . . 2
   Lateral line complete, ending at base of caudal fin 3
2. Dorsal spines VI . . . .*Parachaetodon*
   Dorsal spines X to XVI. . . . .*Chaetodon*
3. Fourth dorsal spine elongate to filamentous; supraorbital of adults with spines or horns; nape of adults usually with hump or strong bony projection . . . .*Heniochus*

One of the most common color combinations in the butterflyfishes is white, yellow and black as can be seen on these two pages. Above and below can be seen *Chaetodon falcula* in which the black markings (aside from the eye band and caudal peduncle band) are two wedge-shaped triangles along the back. Photos by R. Jonklaas.

Chaetodon oxycephalus and *C. lineolatus* have very similar patterns. A close look will reveal that the eye band is broken in the upper fish *(C. oxycephalus)* but not so in the lower one *(C. lineolatus)*. Photo above by Dr. Herbert R. Axelrod; photo below by Dr. Gerald R. Allen.

Fourth dorsal spine normal or only slightly elongate; no horns on supraorbital; normally no hump or projection at nape (one or two species may have slight prominence or hump on nape but fourth dorsal spine normal) 4

4. More than 65 scales in lateral line; pectoral fins elongate, falcate 5
   Less than 60 scales in lateral line; pectoral fins not elongate, rounded
  6

5. Snout elongate, tubular . . . . *Forcipiger*
   Snout not elongate, not tubular . . . . *Hemitaurichthys*

6. Normally VIII to XI dorsal spines 7
   Normally XII dorsal spines 9

7. Dorsal spines XI; snout moderately projecting, not tubular . . . .
   . . . . *Chelmonops*
   Dorsal spines VIII to X; snout either not projecting or, when projecting, tubular 8

8. Snout short, not tubular . . . . *Coradion*
   Snout elongate, tubular . . . . *Chelmon*

9. Lachrymal serrate or toothed, scaled over most of its surface; scale covering of dorsal spines low; body depth 1.7-1.8 in standard length; dorsal fin XII, 21-22; anal fin III, 16 . . . . *Amphichaetodon*
   Lachrymal smooth-edged, almost devoid of scales; scale covering of dorsal spines normal; body depth 1.4-1.5 in standard length, dorsal fin XII, 24; anal fin III, 19 . . . . *Pseudochaetodon*

Genera of Chaetodontidae

Parachaetodon   Chaetodon   Chaetodon   Heniochus

Forcipiger   Hemitaurichthys   Chelmonops

Coradion   Chelmon   Amphichaetodon   Pseudochaetodon

TABLE I
Characters of Genera of the Family Chaetodontidae

Lateral Line	Snout	Dorsal Spines	Pectoral Sheath	Fin Shape	Lachrymal	L.L. Scales	Teeth	Genera
incomplete	moderate to short	XI-XVI various	various	normal	various	22-55	rows or anterior bands	*Chaetodon*
incomplete	short, 2.8-3.8 in H.L.	VI, increasing in height	high	normal	scaled, smooth, short	40-43	rows	*Parachaetodon*
complete	short, 3.0-3.5 in H.L.	XII, 4th longest, tri-angular	normal	normal	scaleless, smooth, moderate	52-63	rows	*Pseudochaetodon*
complete	moderate, 2.5-4.5 in H.L.	XI-XII 4th very elongate	high	moderately long	partly scaled, rounded	40-60	rows	*Heniochus*
complete	moderate, 2.4-3.3 in H.L.	XII, Triangular	low	normal	scaled, toothed, moderate	47-55	rows	*Amphichaetodon*
complete	short, 2.5-3.6 in H.L.	XII-XVI, rounded	low	very long, falcate	rounded, short, partly scaled	70-90	rows	*Hemitaurichthys*
complete	prolonged, 1.2-2.1 in depth of body	XI-XII, deeply incised	very low	very long, falcate	long, smooth, partly scaled	66-80	rows	*Forcipiger*
complete	elongate, 2.4-4.9 in depth of body	IX, increasing in height	normal	normal	scaleless, moderate	45-55	bands	*Chelmon*
complete	long, 3.2-4.3 in depth of body	XI, increasing	normal	normal	scaleless, smooth, serrate ant.	51-56	bands	*Chelmonops*
complete	short, 5.9-7.9 in depth of body	VIII-X, increasing	normal	normal	scaled, smooth	43-52	hidden, modified	*Coradion*

Species of the genus *Heniochus* have similar patterns. Compare the pattern of *Heniochus acuminatus* above with that of *Heniochus chrysostomus* (below). Photo of *H. acuminatus* by R. Jonklaas; photo of *H. chrysostomus* by Allan Power.

Many of the butterflyfishes (including those in several different genera) have snout stripes. In this species it is yellow in color but may darken to brown depending upon mood. Photo by Allan Power.

Genus CHELMON Cloquet

Chelmon Cloquet, 1817: p. 369 (type-species *Chaetodon rostratus* Linnaeus, 1758, by subsequent designation of Bleeker, 1876, p. 4; based on Cuvier, 1817, "Les Chelmons" vernacular).

Chelmo Oken, 1817: p. 1269 (based on Cuvier, 1817, "Les Chelmons" vernacular). *Nomen nudum.*

Chelmo Schinz, 1822: p. 532 (based on Cuvier, 1817, "Les Chelmons" vernacular, and takes the same type-species as *Chelmon* Cloquet, *Chaetodon rostratus* Linnaeus).

Chelmonus Jarocki, 1822: p. 260 (based on Cuvier, 1817, "Les Chelmons" vernacular, and takes the same type-species as *Chelmon* Cloquet, *Chaetodon rostratus* Linnaeus).

Diagnosis.—Lateral line complete, forming a moderately high arc across body; snout projecting, tubular, 2.4 to 4.9 in body depth; IX dorsal fin spines, usually increasing in length posteriorly; soft portion of dorsal and anal fins not drawn out into a point; teeth in rows arranged in several bands in each jaw.

Description.—Body oval to rounded, dorsal outline (exclusive of dorsal fin) arched; snout prolonged, tubular, 2.4-4.9 in body depth, prolongation of snout due to extension of premaxillary and mandibular bones; mouth small, gape horizontal; teeth arranged in bands composed of several rows; palate toothless; lachrymal rounded, moderately short, serrate at anterior end; preopercle obtuse-angled, lightly serrate to toothed (particularly at angle); supraorbital toothed.

Dorsal fin continuous, with IX spines increasing in length posteriorly; first few dorsal fin soft rays continue increase; posterior edges of dorsal and anal fins rays vertical; dorsal and anal fins without sharp angle or prolongation of soft rays as in *Chelmonops*. Anal spines strong, third longest, slightly longer than second; first about half length of second. Dorsal fin with approximately 26-31 soft rays, anal fin with 17-21 soft rays; angle of dorsal and anal fins occurs at fourth to seventh rays; pectoral fin normal; pelvic fins long, first ray extending to level of first anal fin ray or beyond; caudal fin truncate or rounded; spinous dorsal fin base shorter than that of soft portion.

Lateral line complete, describing moderately high arc which follows contour of back and which becomes horizontal at caudal peduncle and ends at base of caudal fin; scales moderate to small, 45-55 in longitudinal series; scales arranged in horizontal rows on lower half of body and ascending rows in upper portion; scale covering of dorsal spines normal, extending to middle of fourth spine and almost completely covering last one.

Juveniles resemble adults although some color pattern changes occur with growth in one of the species. Proportional changes are included in tables for each species.

Color usually yellowish or white with orange or brown bars; median head stripe present; dorsal fin spot or ocellus present (in *C. marginalis* only in young stages).

Indian Ocean from African coast to East Indies, and western Pacific Ocean from southern Japan to Australia. All three species occur in Australian waters.

The three species are readily distinguishable by the characters given in the key below.

Key to the Species of the Genus Chelmon (Adults)

1. Snout short, 2.6-3.0 in head length, 4.8-4.9 in body depth; central body bar broad, brownish in alcohol; pelvic fins black; anterior profile gibbous; D.IX, 26 (-30 lit). . . . . *Chelmon muelleri*
   Snout longer, 1.7-2.1 in head length, 2.4-3.4 in body depth; central body bar not broad, light with dark borders or absent; barred pattern continued onto pelvic fin, part grayish to white, part yellowish or hyaline; anterior profile not gibbous 2
2. Central body bar absent; spot in soft portion of dorsal fin normally faint, nonocellated; snout 3.1-3.4 in body depth; interorbital width 4.4-4.8 in head length; caudal peduncle depth 8.5-9.1 in standard length; D. IX, 30-31 . . . . *C. marginalis*
   Central body bar evident, black bordered; spot in dorsal fin obvious, ocellated; snout 2.4-3.1 in body depth; interorbital width 5.0-5.9 in head length; caudal peduncle depth 9.1-11.3 in standard length; D. IX, 28-29 . . . . *C. rostratus*

Remarks.—There has been much controversy as to the correct author of the name of this genus. Cuvier, in his *Regne Animal* (1817) separated a group of species from the genus *Chaetodon* and distinguished them by their having an elongate snout forming a narrow beak. He bestowed upon them the name "Les Chelmons," which is a vernacular name. The question then arises, who was the first to latinize Cuvier's name?

Oken (1817) has been credited with giving Latin equivalents to many of the Cuvierian names in *Isis*, as have Bosc and Cloquet in their respective dictionaries of natural history. Although Bosc did not include *Chelmon*, both Oken and Cloquet did, giving the latinized names *Chelmo* and *Chelmon* respectively. Both referred to Cuvier's work. Both of the above works were dated 1817 in the volumes pertaining to this genus, and more research was necessary in order to determine the exact month of publication. To additionally confuse the issue, there is a possibility that one or both of the authors had access to Cuvier's manuscript and may have preceded Cuvier in publication (Whitley, 1935). The dates of publication of Cuvier's *Regne Animal* are not precisely known (Whitehead, 1967). In dealing with the taxonomic problem of *Curimata* Walbaum, Taylor (1964) provided the date for Oken's section 148 (*Chelmo* occurs under the

Chaetodon auriga, similar to *C. vagabundus* and its close relatives, has a pattern in which the body striping meets at right angles above the shoulder. Photo by Dr. Warren E. Burgess.

heading "Cuvier's System" on the page preceding that of *Curimata*) as probably "in August or later," 1817. He also gives December 1818 as the publication date for volume 12 of Cloquet's *Dictionnaire des Sciences Naturelles.* Since Whitley (1935) gives January 1817 as the publication date for volume 3 of Cloquet's work, it follows that the volume in question, 8, was published in the interim. But the exact date is still unknown since the volumes were obviously not published with reasonable periodicity.

Whitley also refers to Mr. T. Iredale, who, after seeing Oken's *Isis,* informed him that Oken's names are all *nomina nuda.* In the case of *Curimata,* Opinion 772 (*Bull. Zool. Nomen.*, 1966, vol. 23, part 1, pp. 41-45), the Secretary's Note which accompanied Voting Paper (65) 28 stated in part, "In summary, *Curimatus* Oken cannot be placed on the Official List, as requested, because it is a *nomen nudum.*" Since the problem with *Chelmon,* which involves Cuvier and Oken, is very similar to the above, it is also probable that *Chelmo* Oken should be considered as a *nomen nudum. Chelmon* Cloquet should then be accepted as the valid name.

CHELMON ROSTRATUS (Linnaeus)

Chaetodon rostratus Linnaeus, 1758: p. 273 (type locality "Habitat in Indiis").

Chaetodon enceladus Shaw & Nodder, 1791: (pages not numbered) pl. 67 (type locality India).

Chelmon rostratus, Bennett, 1830: p. 689 (new combination; Sumatra).

Chaetodon rostratus, Cuvier, 1831: p. 87 (Java; placed under heading "Chelmons").

Chelmo rostratus, Valenciennes, 1839: pl. 40, fig. 1-1a (no locality).

Chelmon lol Thiolliere, 1857: p. 444 (used in synonymy of *Chelmon rostratus*; based on Montrouzier manuscript; type locality Woodlark Island).

Chelmon rostratus marginalis (not *Chelmon marginalis* Richardson), Marshall, 1965: p. 248, pl. 34 (Great Barrier Reef, Queensland, Australia).

Diagnosis.—D. IX, 28-30 (one with 31); A. III, 19-21 (one with 18); pectoral rays 14 or 15 (occasionally 16 on one side); L.l. scales 48-55 (usually 50-51); snout elongate, 2.4-3.1 in body depth; interorbital width 5.0-5.9 in head length; depth of caudal peduncle 9.1-11.3 in S.L.; spinous portion of dorsal fin base shorter (4.0-4.3 in S.L.) than that of soft portion (2.4-2.8 in S.L.); central body bar present in adult as well as juvenile stages, orange with dark borders; dorsal fin ocellus present in all stages; caudal peduncle band dark colored.

Closely related to *C. marginalis* but distinguishable from that species by color pattern and number of dorsal fin rays (fewer in *C. rostratus*).

Chelmon rostratus (Linnaeus). 113 mm S.L. Queensland, Australia.

Ratios	Standard Length (mm)		
	20-45(7)	46-75(5)	above 75(22)
Depth/S.L.	1.4-1.8	1.5-1.7	1.5-2.0
Head/S.L.	2.0-2.4	2.3-2.4	2.2-2.5
Eye/Head	3.5-4.1	3.7-4.3	4.0-5.8
Snout/Head	2.1-2.4	2.0-2.3	1.7-2.1
Snout/Depth	2.7-3.1	2.9-3.1	2.4-3.1
Interorb. W./Head	4.2-4.5	4.4-4.9	5.0-5.9
Maxillary L./Head	2.6-3.1	2.4-2.8	2.4-2.7
Caud. Ped./S.L.	9.0-9.3	9.1-9.7	9.1-11.3
Pect. Fin L./S.L.	3.3-3.9	3.3-3.8	3.7-4.4
Pelvic Sp. L./S.L.	3.3-4.8	3.7-4.2	4.1-5.3
Predorsal L./S.L.	1.7-2.0	1.7-1.8	1.7-1.9
Prepelvic L./S.L.	2.0-2.2	2.0-2.2	2.0-2.3
Dorsal Sp. No. 1/S.L.	11.3-17.4	16.5 (1)	12.7-19.0
Dorsal Sp. No. 2/S.L.	6.2-9.0	8.7 "	8.3-14.5
Dorsal Sp. No. 3/S.L.	4.3-4.7	5.8 "	5.9-9.1
Dorsal Sp. No. 4/S.L.	3.4-4.3	4.7 "	4.5-7.8
Anal Sp. No. 1/S.L.	7.3-10.1	9.5 "	8.5-12.9
Anal Sp. No. 2/S.L.	4.2-4.4	4.8 "	4.7-6.8
Anal Sp. No. 3/S.L.	4.0-4.4	4.1 "	4.1-6.4

Chelmon rostratus showing the banded pattern on the sides and on the snout.

Opposite:
Chelmon rostratus adult. The middle body bar and the eye spot in the dorsal fin are retained. Photo by Dr. D. Terver, Nancy, Aquarium.

Chelmon rostratus. Typical pattern from the Philippines and surrounding area. Photo by Earl Kennedy

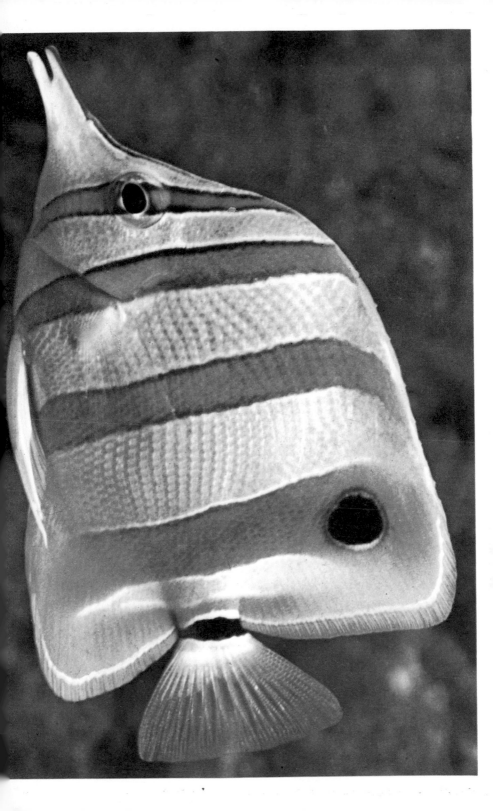

Chelmon rostratus growth stages (26 mm S.L., 36 mm S.L., and adult of 79 mm S.L.) Singapore.

Chelmon marginalis lacks the central body bar and dorsal ocellus and has a light colored bar on the caudal peduncle. Juvenile *C. rostratus* have a wider central body bar than juveniles of *C. marginalis*.

Meristics.—D. IX, 28-30 (one with 31); A. III, 19-21 (one with 18); pectoral rays 14 to 15 (two with 14/16); L.l. scales 48-55 (usually 50-51); L.l. pores 43-46; scales above L.l. 8-11; scales below L.l. 19-24 (usually 20-21); gill rakers 13-17 (at times middle rakers are missing, leaving 4 above angle and 4 below).

Description.—Predorsal contour straight to slightly convex from first dorsal fin spine to just below level of eyes, concave thereafter; snout elongate, tubular, 2.4-3.1 in body depth; rows of teeth grouped into bands; snout length greater than depth of caudal peduncle, which is greater than eye diameter; eye diameter greater than interorbital width.

Dorsal fin spines increasing in length posteriorly although last four or five only slightly longer; pelvic fins long, reaching base of third anal fin ray or beyond; base of spinous portion of dorsal fin shorter (4.0-4.3 in S.L.) than that of soft portion (2.4-2.8 in S.L.).

Anal fin spines partially covered by scales, first spine only at base, second half-covered, and third almost entirely hidden.

Juveniles resemble adults. Ontogenetic changes are included in table of proportional measurements; color pattern of juvenile not significantly different from that of adult.

Color Pattern.—Median stripe present on snout, extending from nape just above eye level to tip of snout, dark-bordered to tip of lachrymal and solid colored from there to tip of snout; eyebands connected at nape; light portion of bar which passes through pectoral fin base includes pelvic fin base, the dark borders of this bar crossing ventral portion of fish anterior and posterior (often faded) to pelvic fin insertion; middle body bar originates at seventh to ninth dorsal fin spines and connects across ventral portion of body; submarginal dark line continues from soft dorsal and anal fins along edges of scaly portions of spines.

Remarks.—*Chelmon rostratus* is a very distinctive and therefore easily recognized species. This may have considerably reduced any systematic problems associated with it. Of the nominal species, Shaw and Nodder's *Chaetodon enceladus* was simply a substitute name for *Chelmon rostratus*, these authors deeming the latter name "insufficiently distinctive of the species."

Chelmon lol had been placed in the synonymy of species of *Forcipiger* by several authors (Fowler and Bean, 1929; Weber & de Beaufort, 1936; and Randall, 1961). Thiolliere (1857), however, placed the name "*Chelmon lol*, mss", in parenthesis after the name *Chelmon rostratus* and referred to a figure of *C. lol* comparable to figure 202 of Bloch (1787). This figure is undoubtedly that of *Chelmon rostratus* and not a species of *Forcipiger*. Thiolliere also compared his figure with one from Valenciennes (1835), mentioning the dorsal ocellus and vertical bands of yellow bordered with black.

Chelmon rostratus. Photo by H. Hansen.

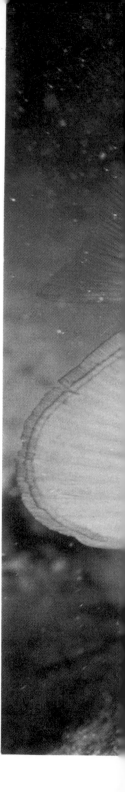

Chelmon marginalis, juvenile. Note dorsal ocellus and lateral bands. Photo by Roger Steene.
Chelmon marginalis, subadult. Both lateral band and dorsal fin spot are weaker. Photo by Walter Deas.

Chelmon marginalis, subadult. Lateral band is much weaker; caudal peduncle band is noticeably light centered. Photo by Allan Power.

The specimens I have been able to examine are primarily from two areas, the South China Sea (Thailand, Singapore, and the Philippine Islands) and Australia (coast of Queensland). During this examination certain variations or differences were noted to exist between specimens from the two sampling areas. In the Australian specimens the white area anterior to the caudal peduncle and posterior to the last body bar is significantly smaller than that of the Philippine or Thailand specimens, and the dorsal and anal fins are more covered with yellow. The Australian sample also showed a trend to a slightly higher mean number of soft dorsal fin rays, anal fin rays, lateral line scales, and scales above the lateral line. The overlap is considerable, so more specimens are needed (especially from intermediate areas) to ascertain whether or not they can be regarded as subspecies or part of a cline.

Chelmon rostratus had gained early fame as the fish that could shoot insects from the air (Schlosser, 1763, 1777). Weber & de Beaufort (1936) dealt with the history of this claim, and the reader is referred to their explanation.

Chelmon rostratus has been reported as being moderately abundant in the Gulf of Thailand along rocky shores and coral reefs; there they are considered of little economic importance and are used primarily for fish meal, duck food, and fertilizer (Rofen, 1963). Cantor (1849) had previously referred to this species from Malaya as being "considered excellent by the natives, and eaten both fresh and dried."

Distribution.—The range of *Chelmon rostratus* is the largest of the genus. It occurs on the northern coast of Australia, New Guinea, Solomon Islands, throughout the East Indies and the Philippine Islands northward to the coast of Southeast Asia including the Malay Peninsula and Archipelago to Sri Lanka and India, and from there extending to Mauritius and the African coast.

Material Examined.—(34 spec.: 14-151 mm S.L.) USNM Acc. 267599 (9: 52-114), One Tree Island, Queensland, Australia; USNM 150666 (1:14), Philippines; CAS 20008 (9: 24-86), Singapore; CAS 37641 (5: 78-111), west side of Gulf of Thailand; CAS 37642 (6: 129-151), Gulf of Thailand; AMS IB.8169 (2: 30-34), Heron Island, Queensland; MCZ 36946 (1: 108), Gladstone, Queensland; BPBM uncat. (1: 56), Heron Island, Queensland.

CHELMON MARGINALIS Richardson
Willemawillum
(Bocuroo)

Chelmon marginalis Richardson, 1842: p. 29 (type locality Port Essington, Australia).

Chelmo tricinctus Castelnau, 1876: p. 14 (type locality Port Darwin, Northern Territory, Australia). Macleay, 1880: p. 392 (Port Darwin, Northern Territory, Australia).

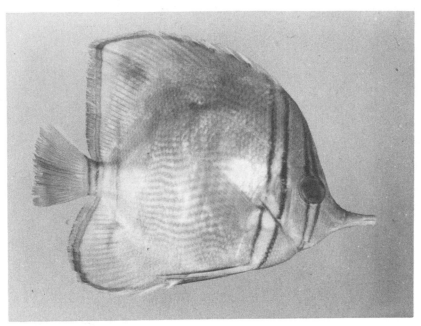

Chelmon marginalis Richardson. 85 mm S.L. Yirrkala, Northern Territory, Australia.

Chelmon rostratus marginalis Ahl, 1923: p. 14 (treated as subspecies; west coast of Australia).
Chelmon rostratus (not of Linnaeus), Taylor, 1964: p. 238 (Arnhem Land, Northern Territory, Australia).

Diagnosis.—D. IX (one with X), 29-33 (usually 30-31); A. III, 21-22; pectoral rays 15 (one with 14, one with 16 on one side); L.l. scales 46-57 (usually 46-50); snout elongate, 3.1-3.4 in body depth; interorbital width 4.4-4.8 in head length; depth of caudal peduncle 8.5-9.1 in S.L.; spinous portion of dorsal fin base shorter (3.7-3.8 in S.L.) than that of soft portion (2.3-2.4 in S.L.); central body bar absent in adults; dorsal fin spot unocellated, reduced and eventually absent in adults.

Close to *Chelmon rostratus* but differing as noted under that species.

Meristics.—D. IX (one with X), 29-33 (usually 30-31); A. III, 21-22; pectoral rays 15 (one with 14, one with 16 on one side); L.l. scales 46-57 (usually 46-50); scales above L.l. 10-12; scales below L.l. 21-26 (usually 22-23); gill rakers 13-16.

Description.—Predorsal contour approximately straight until level of nostrils, then concave; snout elongate, tubular, 3.1-3.4 in body depth; rows of teeth grouped into bands; snout length greater than depth of caudal peduncle, which is greater than eye diameter; eye diameter greater than interorbital width.

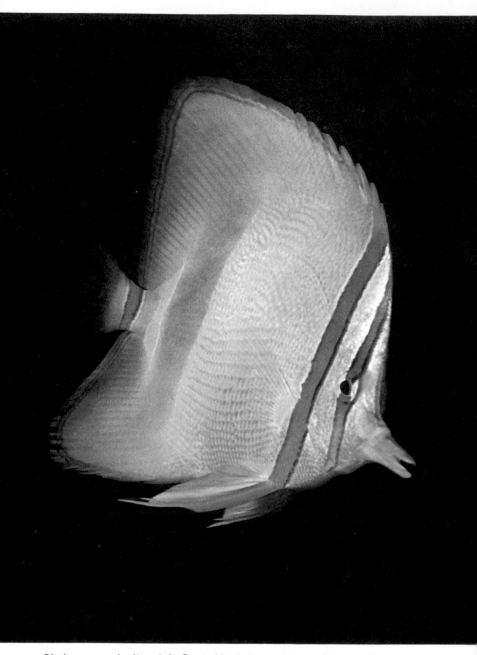

Chelmon marginalis, adult. Central body bar and dorsal fin spot are complete-ly gone. Photo by N. Coleman, Dampier Archipelago, Western Australia.

Chelmon marginalis (above and below) in its natural habitat. Note the orange peduncle bands. Photos by Dr. Gerald R. Allen at Dampier Archipelago, Western Australia.

Ratios	Standard Length (mm)		
	20-45(3)	46-75(5)	above 75(5)
Depth/S.L...............	1.6-1.7	1.6-1.7	1.5-1.7
Head/S.L...............	2.3-2.6	2.4-2.5	2.4-2.5
Eye/Head...............	3.2-3.7	3.9-4.4	4.0-4.5
Snout/Head............	2.3-2.4	2.1-2.2	2.0-2.1
Snout/Depth...........	3.6	3.0-3.2	3.1-3.4
Interorb. W./Head......	4.0	4.3-4.7	4.4-4.8
Maxillary L./Head......	3.1	2.6-3.0	2.5-2.7
Caud. Ped./S.L.........	8.7-9.2	8.2-9.6	8.5-9.1
Pect. Fin L./S.L........	3.3-3.7	3.5-3.8	3.6-3.9
Pelvic Sp. L./S.L........	4.2-4.3	4.3-4.9	4.4-4.8
Predorsal L./S.L........	1.8-1.9	1.9	1.8-1.9
Prepelvic L./S.L........	2.2 (1)	2.0-2.3	2.2-2.3
Dorsal Sp. No. 1/S.L.....	12.8 "	11.5-14.3	12.4-15.3
Dorsal Sp. No. 2/S.L.....	6.5 "	6.5-8.3	7.9-8.4
Dorsal Sp. No. 3/S.L.....	4.6 "	4.8-6.0	5.9-6.8
Dorsal Sp. No. 4/S.L.....	4.0 "	4.2-5.0	4.4-4.8
Anal Sp. No. 1/S.L......	11.0 "	8.9-10.5	9.4-11.1
Anal Sp. No. 2/S.L......	5.7 "	4.6-4.9	4.6-5.0
Anal Sp. No. 3/S.L......	4.9 "	4.1-4.9	4.1-4.7

Dorsal fin spines increase in length posteriorly, the increments quite small between the posterior spines; pelvic fins long, extending to bases of anal fin rays; base of spinous portion of dorsal fin shorter (3.7-3.8 in S.L.) than that of soft portion (2.3-2.4 in S.L.).

First two anal fin spines relatively free from scaly covering, third covered from half to four-fifths of its length.

Juveniles resemble adults, but some color changes occur.

Color Pattern.—Median snout stripe present, extending from eye level or above to tip of snout, dark bordered to end of lachrymal, solid brownish from there to tip of snout; eyebands faintly connected at nape; first body bar includes first two dorsal fin spines and continues across ventral part of body at pelvic fin insertion; central body bar absent in adults; pelvic fins banded, corresponding to body pattern, a brownish stripe following course of second pelvic fin ray and bases of third through fifth rays so that when fin is spread this stripe is more or less continuous with brown posterior border of body band; band surrounding caudal peduncle light with dark borders (in contrast with *C. rostratus* and *C. muelleri,* in which it is dark); dorsal fin spot variable from distinct to absent, more or less absent in larger specimens.

There are several changes in color pattern from the juvenile to adult stages. The smallest specimens have the full number of bars, including the central body bar which, when compared with that of similar sized *C. rostratus*, is narrower; caudal peduncle band is solid brownish (dark color); an ocellus in the soft dorsal fin (somewhat higher in position than in

Chelmon marginalis, growth series. Left 15 and 31 mm S.L., below 56 mm S.L., far below 81 mm S.L. Yirrkalla, Northern Territory, Australia.

Chelmon muelleri. The short snout and dark bands easily distinguish this species from the others. Photo by Dr. Herbert R. Axelrod.

Chelmonops trun-catus, adult about 12 inches in length. Photo by Walter Deas

Chelmon muelleri. Although easily distinquishable from *Chelmonops trun-catus* as adults, the juveniles are quite similar. Photo by Roger Steene.

C. rostratus). As the fish grows, the central body bar becomes paler and a more diffuse brown, eventually disappearing altogether; the caudal peduncle band becomes lighter in the central region, becoming a light band with dark borders; the ocellus in the dorsal fin becomes a simple black spot which eventually fades and disappears.

These changes occur at an early age. A specimen of 32 mm S.L. has the above-described juvenile coloration, but one of 43 mm is nearing the complete adult pattern. In the latter specimen the dorsal fin spot is present but unocellated, the caudal peduncle band is light-centered, and the central body bar is reduced to a scarcely visible grayish-brown bar. The exact size of transformation cannot be determined because it depends on age, not necessarily on size, and occurs over a period of time, being a gradual change and not an abrupt one. The fish might have a certain amount of control over the color pattern, such as being able to cause the dorsal spot to become paler or darker, perhaps in fright or as a night pattern.

Remarks.—Distributional patterns indicate that *Chelmon marginalis* could be sympatric with both *C. rostratus* and *C. muelleri* in Northern Territory, Australia.

Chelmon tricinctus Castelnau does not appear to be distinct from *C. marginalis*. The main differences noted are the lack of the posterior body bar and horizontal stripes following the scale rows. M. Bauchot kindly sent me a photograph of the holotype of *Chelmo tricinctus*, and it appears to agree closely with *C. marginalis*. The light center of the caudal peduncle band is present, and the central body bar and dorsal fin spot are both absent. The posterior body bar and the stripes following the scale rows are generally pale in preserved specimens when compared to the anterior bar. This apparently accounts for the lack of the posterior body bar in the holotype of *C. tricinctus*. The stripes along the scale rows are evident in the photograph.

According to Macleay (1878) specimens of this species were very abundant around Port Darwin.

Richardson (1842) stated that this species "frequents shallow rocky places and sandy beaches in all the bays of Port Essington." He mentions that the aboriginal name of this fish is "willemawillum." Taylor (1964) added another native name, "bocuroo."

Distribution.—Northern and western Australia. In the Northern Territory, specifically from Arnhem Land, Port Darwin, and Port Essington; on the west coast from Point Quobba and the Swan River (Perth). It has not been reported east of the Torres Straits.

Material Examined.—(13 spec.: 15-93 mm S.L.) USNM 173532 (7: 15-85), Yirrkalla, Northern Territory, Australia; USNM 173530 (1: 43), Groote Eyelandt, Northern Territory, Australia; USNM 173531 (1: 93), Northern Territory, Australia; USNM 173529 (1: 85), Darwin, Northern Territory, Australia; WAM P8328-8330 (3: 66-70), Point Quobba (42 miles north of Carnarvon), Western Australia, Australia.

Chelmon muelleri (Klunzinger). 81 mm S.L. Townsville, Queensland, Australia.

CHELMON MUELLERI (Klunzinger)
Blackfin coralfish

Chelmo Mülleri Klunzinger, 1879: p. 361 (type locality not stated (Port Denison according to McCulloch, 1929)).
Chelmon mülleri, McCulloch, 1916: p. 193, pl. LV, fig. 2 (near Bowen, Queensland, Australia).
Chelmon Mülleri, Ahl, 1923: p. 14 (first good description; Port Darwin).

Diagnosis.—D. IX-X (lit. IX), 26-30; A. III, 18 (-21 lit.); pectoral rays 15; L.1 scales 49-50; snout moderate, tubular, 4.8-4.9 in body depth; interorbital width 3.8-4.4 in head length; depth of caudal peduncle 8.4-8.9 in S.L.; spinous portion of dorsal fin shorter (3.5-3.6 in S.L.) than that of soft portion (2.4-2.8 in S.L.); body bars solid brown; pelvic fins black; dorsal fin spot present, dorsal and anal fins with light borders.

Easily distinguishable from both *C. marginalis* and *C. rostratus* by color pattern (body bars dark; pelvic fins dark), snout length, and gibbous nape.

Juvenile *Chelmonops truncatus* about 3 inches total length, from Geographe Bay, Western Australia. Photo by Dr. Gerald R. Allen.

Subadult *Chelmonops truncatus* about 6 inches total length, from Geographe Bay, Western Australia. Photo by Dr. Gerald R. Allen.

Adult *Chelmonops truncatus.* Photo by Walter Deas.

Ratios	Standard Length (mm)		
	20-45	46-75	above 75(2)
Depth/S.L.	---	---	1.6
Head/S.L.	---	---	2.6-2.9
Eye/Head	---	---	3.0-3.9
Snout/Head	---	---	2.6-3.0
Snout/Depth	---	---	4.8-4.9
Interorb. W./Head.	---	---	3.8-4.4
Maxillary L./Head.	---	---	3.0
Caud. Ped./S.L.	---	---	8.4-8.9
Pect. Fin L./S.L.	---	---	3.2-3.3
Pelvic Fin L./S.L.	---	---	4.6-4.7
Predorsal L./S.L.	---	---	1.9-2.1
Prepelvic L./S.L.	---	---	2.1-2.4
Dorsal Sp. No. 1/S.L.	---	---	11.5-16.2
Dorsal Sp. No. 2/S.L.	---	---	6.4 (1)
Dorsal Sp. No. 3/S.L.	---	---	4.4 "
Dorsal Sp. No. 4/S.L.	---	---	3.9-4.3
Anal Sp. No. 1/S.L.	---	---	8.1 (1)
Anal Sp. No. 2/S.L.	---	---	4.4 "
Anal Sp. No. 3/S.L.	---	---	4.5 "

Meristics.—D. IX-X (lit. IX), 26-30; A. III, 18 (-21 lit.); pectoral rays 15; L.l. scales 49-50; scales above L.l. 11-12; scales below L.l. 22-23; gill rakers 11-12.

Description.—Predorsal contour gibbous, a slight hump at nape, concave below level of eye; snout moderate, tubular, 4.8-4.9 in body depth; rows of teeth grouped into five to eight bands in each jaw; snout length equal to eye diameter, both greater than depth of caudal peduncle, which is greater than interorbital width.

Dorsal fin spines increase in length posteriorly, last longest, first two relatively short; pelvic fins long, reaching to base of first anal fin ray; base of spinous portion of dorsal fin shorter (3.5-3.6 in S.L.) than that of soft portion (2.4-2.8 in S.L.).

First two anal fin spines relatively free of scales, third almost completely covered.

Juveniles not seen.

Color Pattern.—Dark bordered eyebands connected at nape; bar from first dorsal fin spines to pelvic fins connecting across chest, dark-bordered; middle body bar not dark bordered, originating at bases of seventh to ninth dorsal fin spines and connecting across abdomen; posterior body bar starts from fifth to about thirteenth dorsal fin rays and crosses body to second to about twelfth anal fin rays; dark band encircles caudal peduncle; median snout stripe present, dark, extending from nape to tip of snout; dark spot or ocellus included in posterior body bar in soft dorsal fin.

Remarks.—The dorsal fin in one specimen had ten spines, one more than that normally attributed to this species. The soft dorsal fin also had one less ray, an occurrence not uncommon in other species of butterflyfishes.

There seems to be little agreement as to whether *Chelmon muelleri* (Klunzinger) is a species, subspecies, or merely a synonym of the widely distributed and well known *C. rostratus*. Thus, Fowler and Bean (1929) state that it does not appear to be different from *C. rostratus* and place it in synonymy with that species. Ahl (1923) lists it as a valid species (while relegating *C. marginalis* to subspecific level), whereas Whitley (1932a) recognizes only two Australian forms, *Chelmon rostratus mülleri* and *C. r. marginalis* from northeastern Australia and western and northwestern Australia respectively. Weber & de Beaufort (1936), in a note after their treatment of *C. rostratus*, indicate they believe both *C. marginalis* and *C. Mülleri* are doubtful as to their specific status. They cite Fowler & Bean, Whitley, and, erroneously, Ahl as regarding these latter species as subspecies or synonyms of *C. rostratus*. Marshall (1965) apparently followed Whitley and included *Chelmon rostratus mülleri* and *C. r. marginalis* in his book, presenting a key distinguishing the two and a short description and color plate of the latter. The color plate of Marshall cannot be of *Chelmon rostratus marginalis* (or *C. marginalis*), however, due to the presence of a dark bordered central body bar which *C. marginalis* lacks, and the solid, dark-colored caudal peduncle band which in *C. marginalis* is pale or cream colored. The species represented apparently is *Chelmon rostratus*. *Chelmon muelleri* appears to occur in northern parts of Australia and would therefore be sympatric with *C. marginalis*. It is also very possible that all three species of *Chelmon* occur in northern Australia.

Because *C. muelleri* is sympatric with *C. rostratus* on the coast of Queensland and with *C. marginalis* (and perhaps also *C. rostratus*) in northern Australia, and because the fish are easily distinguishable by the conspicuously shorter snout and other proportions, and by color pattern, from other species of this genus, it should be regarded as a valid species.

The record by McCulloch (1916) gives the depth of capture as 16 fathoms, a considerable but not extreme depth for these fishes. The greatest size recorded was 133 mm long (McCulloch, 1916).

The discrepancy in counts between the two descriptions (Klunzinger, 1879; McCulloch, 1916) cannot be resolved at this time. The specimens I have seen have lower counts than given in either paper but are more similar to those presented by McCulloch (1916). The snout length in proportion to the head length indicates that the snout may be still shorter than indicated in my specimens. I get 2.6 and 3.0 as indices as compared to McCulloch's 2.3 and Klunzinger's 2.5. These differences in proportions and the meristic differences may be due to variations within the species or differences in methods of counting and measurement.

Juvenile *Coradion chrysozonus* from Northwest Cape, Western Australia.
Photo by Dr. Gerald R. Allen.

A pair of *Coradion chrysozonus* feeding on the reef. Photo by Walter Deas.

Coradion chrysozonus adult. Note the rounded fins and distinctly ocellated spot in the dorsal fin. Photo by Walter Deas.

Coradion altivelis. In this specimen the spot in the dorsal fin is in the process of fading. Photo by Walter Deas.

Distribution.—Queensland and Northern Territory, Australia, possibly also reaching western New Guinea and Misol. The original description by Klunzinger (1879) makes no mention of locality. Other chaetodontids mentioned on the preceding and following pages of his paper were mainly from Port Darwin. Ahl (1923), basing his description completely on Klunzinger, gave Port Darwin as the type locality. McCulloch (1929) listed *Chelmon mülleri* and gave, after the original description citation, "No locality (= Port Denison)." Port Denison is very near Bowen, Queensland, where he reported on four specimens 113-133 mm long (McCulloch, 1916). In the British Museum (Natural History) there is a specimen of *Chelmon muelleri* listed as from "W. of Torres St."

Material Examined.—(2 spec.: 81-102 mm S.L.) AMS IB.5456 (1:81), Townsville, Queensland, Australia; BMNH uncatalogued (1: 102), West of Torres Straits.

Genus CHELMONOPS Bleeker

Chelmonops Bleeker, 1876: p. 4 (=311) (type-species *Chaetodon truncatus* Kner by original designation).

Diagnosis.—Lateral line complete, forming a moderately high. arc across body; snout somewhat projecting, not tubular, 3.2-4.3 in body depth; XI dorsal fin spines, increasing in length posteriorly; soft portion of dorsal and anal fins with first few rays extended in adults; rows of teeth arranged in about nine bands in each jaw.

Description.—Body oval; snout moderately projecting, 3.2-4.3 in body depth; mouth small, gape horizontal; rows of teeth grouped into about nine bands in each jaw; predorsal contour relatively straight from first dorsal fin spine to level of nostrils, where it becomes concave; preopercle approximately right-angled, serrate; supraorbital with spines or teeth; lachrymal long, smooth to denticulate; snout length greater than depth of caudal peduncle, which is greater than interorbital width; interorbital width greater than or equal to eye diameter.

Dorsal fin continuous, with XI strong spines increasing in length posteriorly, last longest; posterior edges of soft dorsal and anal fins vertical; adults with soft dorsal and, to a lesser extent, anal fin extended at their angle by the prolongation of several rays; anal fin spines strong, also increasing in length posteriorly; pectoral fins moderately long, 3.5-4.1 in S.L.; pelvic fins long, reaching base of third anal fin spine; caudal fin truncate, base of spinous portion of dorsal fin slightly shorter than or equal to base of soft portion (2.9-3.3 and 2.7-3.0 in S.L. respectively).

Lateral line complete, describing a high arc to the posterior edge of the last dark body bar, where it turns abruptly toward the caudal peduncle and eventually ends at the base of the caudal fin; scales of body medium sized, smaller on head, chest, caudal peduncle, and portions of soft dorsal and anal fins; scale covering of dorsal fin spines normal, reaching about halfway up fifth spine and almost completely covering last spine; first two anal fin spines relatively free from scales, third almost completely covered.

Juveniles undergo some proportional changes and color changes with growth.

Five vertical bars present, three on body, one on caudal peduncle, the fifth being the eyeband; median snout stripe present.

Only one species recognized, found along the southwestern, southern, and eastern coasts of Australia in cool water.

Remarks.—*Chelmonops* is most closely related to the genus *Chelmon* Cloquet. It is distinguished from that genus by the eleven dorsal fin spines (species of *Chelmon* have nine, although one specimen of *C. muelleri* had ten) and the more robust, somewhat shorter snout (species of *Chelmon* have more slender, tubular, and, except for *Chelmon muelleri*, much longer snouts). The eyeband in *Chelmonops* is broader than in *Chelmon* and the bars are dark brown to black (in species of *Chelmon*, except for *C. muelleri*, they are orange). The soft dorsal and anal fins are never prolonged into a point in *Chelmon* as they are in *Chelmonops*. *Chelmonops* also grows to a much larger size than does *Chelmon*.

Chelmonops may be connected to the genus *Chelmon* through *Chelmon muelleri*. *Chelmonops truncatus* and *Chelmon muelleri* both have the rather short snout and dark bars. Juveniles of *Chelmonops truncatus* do not have the extensions of the dorsal and anal fins and the two species appear more similar. However, they are still separable by dorsal fin spine number, robustness of the snout, predorsal contour, and color pattern.

Chelmonops appears to be a cool water replacement of species of the genus *Chelmon*. The generic ranges overlap at Queensland, Australia, which is more tropical in nature than the rest of the range of *Chelmonops*, but there *Chelmonops* is usually found in deep water. The records from Western Australia are too sparse to determine if any overlap with *Chelmon marginalis* exists on that coastline.

CHELMONOPS TRUNCATUS (Kner).
Truncate coralfish

Chaetodon truncatus Kner, 1859: p. 442, pl. 2 (type locality Sydney, New South Wales, Australia).

Chelmo truncatus, Gunther, 1860: p. 516 (after Kner; new combination).

Chelmo trochilus Gunther, 1874: p. 368 (type locality "Australia," purchased (New South Wales according to McCulloch, 1929)).

Chelmonops truncatus, Bleeker, 1876: p. 4 (=311) (new combination). Ahl, 1923: p. 16 (no locality).

Chelmonops trochilus, Ahl, 1923: p. 17, pl. 1, fig. 2 (Sydney, Australia; new combination).

Fully adult *Coradion altivelis* with spot completely gone. Photo by Walter Deas.

Chelmonops truncatus (Kner). 138 mm S.L. Southeastern Queensland, Australia.

Ratios	Standard Length (mm)		
	20-45(1)	46-75	above 75(4)
Depth/S.L.	1.6	---	1.8-2.0
Head/S.L.	2.4	---	2.9-3.0
Eye/Head	3.3	---	3.8-4.5
Snout/Head	2.4	---	2.2-2.6
Snout/Depth	3.6	---	3.2-4.3
Interorb. W./Head	4.6	---	3.8-4.2
Maxillary L./Head	4.0	---	3.3-3.7
Caud. Ped./S.L.	7.9	---	9.0-9.2
Pect. Fin L./S.L.	3.7	---	3.5-4.1
Pelvic Sp. L./S.L.	3.7	---	4.4-5.2
Predorsal L./S.L.	1.9	---	2.1-2.2
Prepelvic L./S.L.	2.0	---	2.3-2.4
Dorsal Sp. No. 1/S.L.	11.6	---	19.1-26.9
Dorsal Sp. No. 2/S.L.	6.2	---	12.9-17.4
Dorsal Sp. No. 3/S.L.	4.3	---	9.0-14.1
Dorsal Sp. No. 4/S.L.	3.6	---	6.6-10.2
Anal Sp. No. 1/S.L.	8.0	---	11.5-15.8
Anal Sp. No. 2/S.L.	5.5	---	6.3-8.1
Anal Sp. No. 3/S.L.	4.2	---	4.7-5.8

Diagnosis.—D. XI, 26-27; A. III, 19; pectoral rays 14 (one with 14/15; one with 15/16); L.l. scales 51-56; snout prolonged, robust, not tubular, 3.2-4.3 in body depth; dorsal spines increase in length posteriorly, last longest; dorsal fin with extension at angle due to prolongation of several dorsal fin rays; anal fin prolonged but less so than dorsal fin rays; dark vertical bars cross head, body, and caudal peduncle; median snout stripe present.

Meristics.—D. XI, 26-27; A. III, 19; pectoral rays 14 (one with 14/15; one with 15/16); L.l. scales 51-56; scales above L.l. 9-12; scales below L.l. 26-31; gill rakers not known.

Description.—Since the genus *Chelmonops* is monotypic, much of the description given under the genus description is not repeated here.

Dorsal fin spines strong, gradually increasing in length until the last, dorsal fin rays continuing this increase until the angle of the fin where they are prolonged; anal fin spines also gradually increasing in length posteriorly, last longest, first about half length of second, which is about two-thirds length of third; anal fin also produced at angle as adult; base of spinous portion of dorsal fin shorter or about equal to base of soft portion (2.9-3.3 and 2.7-3.0 in S.L. respectively).

Juveniles lack prolongation of dorsal and anal fins. Their fins are rounded at the angles and the posterior edge is vertical, similar to species of *Chelmon*.

Chelmonops truncatus, juvenile. 44.2 mm S.L. Western Australia, Australia.

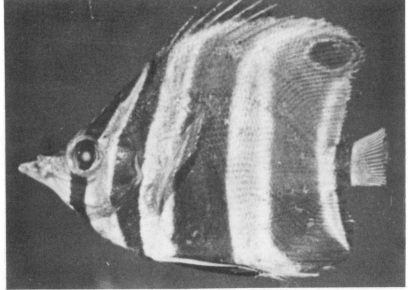

Coradion altivelis juvenile. The high fin is already beginning to become noticeable. Photo by Yasuda and Hiyama.

Adult *Coradion altivelis* in its natural habitat. Note solid dark caudal peduncle band. Photo by Allan Power.

Coradion melanopus subadult. This species has two ocellated spots as compared with one or none in the other species. Photo by Aaron Norman.

Coradion melanopus adult. The second dorsal fin spine membrane in species of *Coradion* (plus others) is black. Photo by Roger Steene.

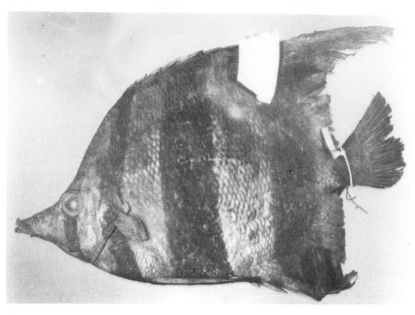

Chelmonops truncatus adult, 183 mm S.L. with dorsal and anal fins extended.

Color Pattern.—Eyebands joined at nape but not ventrally; dark median stripe present on interorbital area from just below nape to tip of snout, from nape to edge of lachrymal light brown with dark brown edges, and from lachrymal to tip of snout solid brown; faint whitish border to entire stripe; body bars connect ventrally; dark spot in posterior body bar variable from ocellated spot in small specimens to absent in large individuals, having been lost in the dark color of the bar; middle body bar originating at dorsal fin spines seven to eight and including anus by an extension of the dark color; posterior body bar connected with band at border of anal fin but only slightly connected with band at edge of dorsal fin; pelvic fins with outer third dark brown, inner portion dusky yellow; area between pelvic insertions white.

A juvenile (44 mm S.L.) had a distinct ocellus in the soft dorsal fin. With increase in age, this ocellus becomes less distinct and eventually is lost in the dark color of the last body bar. In this small specimen the last body bar just barely included the ocellus, having a narrow dark extension on the outside of the white ring separating this from the white or silvery body color. There was a distinct gap between this and the dark edge of the dorsal fin; a narrower gap appeared between the lower end of this bar and the dark edge of the anal fin. The bar was thus completely surrounded by white or silvery color. The pelvic fins were black except for the spine and a very small portion of the base, which were white.

Remarks.—There does not seem to be any substantial differences between *Chelmonops truncatus* and *C. trochilus*. In the original description (Kner, 1859), fewer scales were indicated than later reported for *C. trochilus* (43-44 in the former, 54-55 in the latter species). In five specimens, my counts range from 51-56, agreeing more closely with that of *C. trochilus*. However, additional counts using several methods of counting indicated that the possibility of obtaining lower counts could be due to differing methods rather than a true difference in the number of scales.

This is one of the cooler-water species of chaetodontids, occurring in southern Australian waters. It extends northward into Queensland but apparently only in deep water (trawl record of a specimen from Queensland was 29-30 fathoms). This species is most abundant around New South Wales (Scott, 1962). Its range extends out from there in both directions around the Australian coastline, becoming rarer with distance.

Distribution.—Western Australia south of Geraldton, along the southern coast of the continent, around New South Wales, and up the eastern coast to Queensland. The record from Lord Howe Island by Waite (1900) was emended by him a few years later (Waite 1903) under his description of *Chaetodon howensis*.

Material Examined.—(5 spec.: 44-183 mm S.L.) AMS IB.8174 (1:138), southeast Queensland, Australia; AMS IB.8172 (1:44, dried), off Perth, Western Australia, Australia; SU 104070 (1: 183), New Castle, Western Australia, Australia; USNM 47914 (1: 161), Port Jackson, New South Wales, Australia; USNM 47872 (formerly AMS 1.3446) (1: 143), Port Jackson, New South Wales, Australia.

Genus CORADION Kaup

Coradion Kaup, 1860: pp. 137, 146 (type-species *Chaetodon chrysozonus* Cuvier by subsequent designation of Bleeker, 1876, pl. 312).

Diagnosis.—Lateral line complete, forming a high arc on body; snout relatively short, 2.9-3.8 in head length, 5.9-7.9 in body depth; dorsal spines VIII-X; teeth barely visible, hidden by thick, swollen, pleated lips.

Description.—Body rounded, deep, depth 1.3-1.5 in standard length; predorsal contour approximately straight to level of nostrils then slightly concave; teeth scarcely visible, hidden by thick, swollen, pleated lips; palate toothless; preopercle right-angled, a slight posterior extension an angle, serrate; supraorbital smooth to spiny; lachrymal usually smooth-edged, long, scaled; opercular membranes united across throat, those of branchiostegals broadly attached to isthmus.

Dorsal fin continuous, with VIII to X spines, either increasing in height until last spine or middle spines longest; dorsal and anal fins rounded, bluntly rounded, or squarish, posterior edges always vertical; spinous dorsal fin base shorter than that of soft portion; anal fin spines increasing in height posteriorly; pectoral fins normal, of moderate length;

Forcipiger flavissimus juvenile. Even at this size the fins are developed and the snout is quite elongated. Photo by Dr. Herbert R. Axelrod.

Typical color pattern of *Forcipiger flavissimus*. Note also the gape of the mouth (a characteristic of this species). Photo by Allan Power.

An unusual head pattern for *Forcipiger flavissimus*. The area between the eye and shoulder is usually solid black. Photo by Walter Deas.

Normal swimming of *Forcipiger flavissimus* with dorsal and anal fins folded back. The spines held erect (see opposite) is usually a threat or defensive action. Photo by Dr. Gerald R. Allen.

pelvic fins long, reaching at least to base of second anal fin spine; pelvic spine strong, flattened; caudal fin truncate.

Lateral line complete, rising in a high arc, following contour of back, reaching peak below last spines or first soft rays of dorsal fin, becoming horizontal on caudal peduncle, and ending at base of caudal fin; scales moderate, rounded, in horizontal series below lateral line and ascending series above and immediately below it; 43 to 52 scales in lateral line; scale covering of dorsal and anal fin normal, extending from base of first dorsal spine to cover 4/5 of last spine; scales cover base of first anal spine, half of second, and ½ to ¾ or more of third.

Very small juveniles not seen, smallest specimen (47 mm S.L.) similar in proportions, etc. to adult.

Color pattern consists of vertical bars of orange to brown-orange, the first divided into two portions above pectoral fins but united below; median snout stripe present; ocellus or black spot usually present in soft dorsal fin sometime during life, absent in adult *Coradion altivelis.*

East Indies, north to southern Japan, south to Australia, and east to Palau, western Caroline Islands, New Guinea, and Bismarck Archipelago.

Three species recognized, none exceeding 120 mm S.L., distinguished by the following key:

Key to the Species of the Genus Coradion (Adults)

1. D. VIII, 31-32; soft dorsal elevated; median snout stripe ending at upper lip; eyebands not continuous on isthmus; dorsal ocellus absent (sometimes faded spot evident); never an ocellus in anal fin
   . . . . *Coradion altivelis*
   D. IX or X; less than 30 rays in soft dorsal fin. .2
2. D. IX, 28-29; soft dorsal fin rounded, not elevated; median snout stripe not continuous on chin as stripe, although spot or blotch may be present; eyebands joined at isthmus and extend toward, but do not reach, insertion of pelvic fins; dorsal fin always with ocellated spot; anal fin without ocellated spot . . . .*C. chrysozonus*
   D. X, 24-27 (usually 25); soft dorsal fin squarish in shape; median snout stripe continuous on chin; eyebands not continuous on isthmus; both dorsal and anal fins with well developed ocellus . . . .
   . . . .*C. melanopus*

Remarks.—The peculiarities of the lips suggest a different mode of feeding than in other chaetodontids. Weber (1913) suggested that the phylogenetic position of *Coradion* is not unlike that of *Cheiloprion* of the damselfishes (family Pomacentridae), which has a similarly structured mouth, and that the food of both should be similar.

The closest relatives of genus *Coradion* appear to be species of the genera *Chelmon* and *Chelmonops* on the one hand and *Chaetodon modestus* and its related species in the genus *Chaetodon* on the other. All these species possess vertical banding in common along with a black membrane or flap on the second dorsal spine. In general aspect they all appear quite similar.

Species that previously were erroneously included in this genus are *Coradion desmotes* Jordan & Fowler (= *Chaetodon modestus*), *Coradion modestus* Snyder (= *Chaetodon modestus*), *Coradion Bennettii* Kaup (= *Chaetodon bennetti*), and *Chaetodon festivus* Desjardins (= *nomen dubium*).

CORADION ALTIVELIS McCulloch
High-finned coralfish

Chaetodon chrysozonus (not of Cuvier), Kner, 1865: p. 101
(in part; description included this species; Java).

Coradion altivelis McCulloch, 1916: p. 191, pl. 56, fig. 1
(type locality Wide Bay, Queensland, Australia).

Coradion fulvocinctus Tanaka, 1918: p. 223 (type locality Kii, Wakayama Pref., Japan). Kamohara, 1935: 732
(broadened Tanaka's original description; Okinoshima Suyaki, Tosa Pref., Japan).

Coradion chrysozonus, Ahl, 1923: p. 40 (in part; new combination; after Kner).

Coradion altivelis McCulloch. 91.3 mm S.L. Heron Island, Australia.

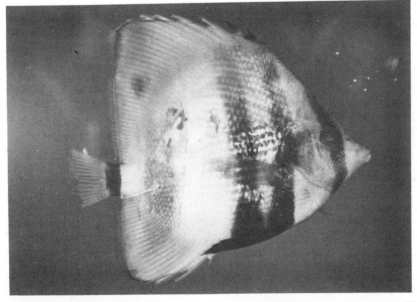

Forcipiger longirostris in its dark phase. This 5-inch individual was photographed by Dr. Gerald R. Allen at Kona, Hawaii.

Although most of the fish is dark, some yellow areas are still evident in this *Forcipiger longirostris.* Photo by Dr. Gerald R. Allen.

Forcipiger longirostris in its yellow phase. This color pattern is almost identical to that of *F. flavissimus* (which does not have a dark phase). Photo by James H. O'Neill.

The snout of *Forcipiger longirostris* is quite elongate compared to *F. flavissimus* and its gape is much smaller. Photo by Dr. Gerald R. Allen.

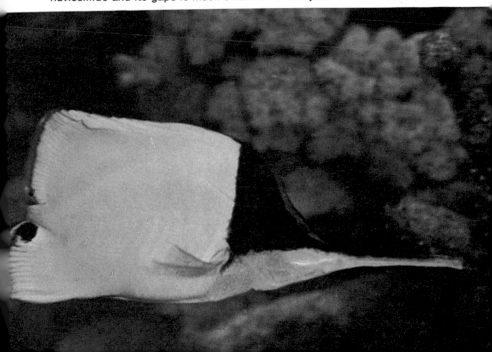

Ratios	Standard Length (mm)		
	20-50	51-89	above 90(1)
Depth/S.L.............	---	---	1.4
Head/S.L..............	---	---	3.0
Eye/Head	---	---	3.3
Snout/Head	---	---	3.1
Interorb. W./Head......	---	---	3.6
Maxillary L./Head......	---	---	4.4
Caud. Ped./S.L.........	---	---	8.5
Pect. Fin L./S.L........	---	---	3.4
Pelvic Sp. L./S.L........	---	---	3.7
Predorsal L./S.L........	---	---	1.8
Prepelvic L./S.L........	---	---	2.3
Dorsal Sp. No. 1/S.L.....	---	---	19.8
Dorsal Sp. No. 2/S.L.....	---	---	9.8
Dorsal Sp. No. 3/S.L.....	---	---	5.7
Dorsal Sp. No. 4/S.L.....	---	---	4.2
Dorsal Sp. No. 5/S.L.....	---	---	3.3
Dorsal Sp. No. 6/S.L.....	---	---	2.9
Anal Sp. No. 1/S.L......	---	---	12.7
Anal Sp. No. 2/S.L......	---	---	5.4
Anal Sp. No. 3/S.L......	---	---	4.1

Diagnosis.—D. VIII, 31-33 (mostly 32); A. III, 20-22; pectoral rays 14; L.l. scales 49-50; dorsal fin very elevated, posterior border vertical; dorsal fin spines increase in length posteriorly, last longest, first few dorsal fin rays continuing this increase; eyeband not continued on isthmus; median snout stripe extends from upper lip to level of nostrils; spot in dorsal fin present in juveniles, faded in subadults, and absent in adults.

Meristics.—D. VIII, 31-33 (mostly 32); A. III, 20-22 (mostly 20); pectoral rays 14; L.l. scales 49-50; scales above L.l. 10-11; scales below L.l. 22-23; gill rakers 11.

Description.—Predorsal contour straight, sloping at an angle of 50-55° from the horizontal; supraorbital serrate to spiny; tip of snout scaleless, scales starting at level of nostrils; caudal peduncle depth greater than snout length, which is greater than eye diameter; eye diameter greater than interorbital width.

Dorsal fin with VIII spines, gradually increasing in length posteriorly; soft rays continue this increase until the third ray; resulting soft dorsal fin very elevated, longest dorsal fin ray 2.3 in S.L.; pectoral fins normal, reaching level of about second anal fin spine; pelvic fins long, reaching base of third anal fin spine; base of spinous portion of dorsal fin only one-half or less (4.7 in S.L.) that of soft portion (2.1 in S.L.).

Juveniles not examined, but a photograph of a juvenile from Japan by Yasuda shows the characteristic high dorsal fin and proportions similar to those of the adult.

Color Pattern.—Median snout stripe present, extending from level of nostrils to upper lip; eyebands joined at nape, ending at lower edge of interopercle; membrane flap between second and third dorsal fin spines black; anterior arm of first body bar originates at first two or three dorsal fin spines, posterior arm at fifth through eighth dorsal fin spines; posterior body bar originates at eighth to twenty-third dorsal fin rays and terminates at sixth to seventeenth or eighteenth anal fin rays; dorsal fin spot, when present, extends from about tenth to sixteenth rays.

A juvenile specimen from Japan is similarly colored but with some exceptions. Median snout stripe extending to eye level and above. A large ocellus is present in the dorsal fin (eleventh to seventeenth rays, McCulloch, 1916), black, ringed with bluish-white and with an exterior black line as a border (from color slide of juvenile specimen in an aquarium).

Remarks.—*Coradion altivelis* is a poorly known species. It is usually relegated to the synonymy of *C. chrysozonus* or considered an Australian endemic. It is here considered a valid species, with its range recorded as far north as Japan. Kner (1865) noticed the differences between several specimens of *Coradion* collected at Java. He explained the differences away as a combination of variation and sexual dimorphism. It is evident he had a mixture of at least two of the species treated here and possibly all three. He mentions two specimens which have the dorsal fin ocellus, which is absent in a third. He notices that the median snout stripe in some specimens reaches to the nostrils, whereas in others to the level of the eyes; the posterior body bar was in varying intensities (not a good species character); the eyeband reached only to the interopercle in one specimen while crossing the isthmus almost to the pelvic fins in others; and finally, the posterior edge of the dorsal fin rounded in some and almost vertical in another. His "males" apparently are *Coradion chrysozonus*, his "female" *C. altivelis*.

Although the description was brief and not as complete as would be desired, *Coradion fulvocinctus* Tanaka seems to be a synonym of *C. altivelis*. The dorsal fin of that species had IX spines and 31 rays, a combination of meristic characters that does not place it definitely with any species. A second specimen with VIII dorsal fin spines agrees with *C. altivelis*. Tanaka also mentions the high anterior rays of the dorsal and anal fins and the posterior edges being perpendicular with the body.

Kamohara (1935), in describing a new collection of *Coradion fulvocinctus*, gives the counts as D. VIII (no IX), 31-32; A. III, 20; scales 55. He did not mention the presence of a dorsal spot.

Finally, a photograph of a juvenile *Coradion fulvocinctus* shows a fish extremely close to *C. altivelis* in coloration and form. The dorsal ocellus is present, but this is apparently normal for juveniles of this species, the ocellus disappearing with age. McCulloch (1916) and Marshall (1964)

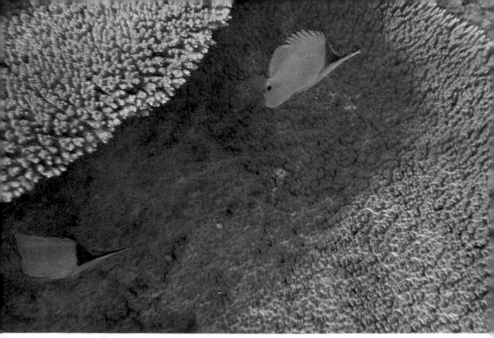

A pair of *Forcipiger longirostris* among the coral at Johnston Atoll. Note the extended spines of the one out in the light. Photo by Dr. Warren E. Burgess.

Forcipiger flavissimus has crossed the East Pacific Barrier to the western coast of Mexico. Photo of a specimen by Alex Kerstitch at Cabo San Lucas, Baja California, Mexico.

Hemitaurichthys polylepis is most commonly found in large aggregations such as this one. Note the dark heads. Photo by Roger Steene.

Hemitaurichthys polylepis may exhibit a very dark head or a yellow one. These individuals are somewhere in-between. Photo by Paul Allen.

indicated that the young had a large ocellus in the soft dorsal fin. With specimens occurring in Japan (Tanaka, 1918; Kamohara, 1935), Java (Kner, 1865), and Australia (McCulloch, 1916) the range can be seen to be continuous or nearly so from Japan to Australia. Perhaps with a better understanding of the differences between the species new records will now come to light.

This species appears to be sympatric, at least in the East Indies region, with the two other species of *Coradion*.

Distribution.—From southern Japan through the East Indies to northern and northeastern Australia.

Material Examined.—(1 spec.: 91 mm S.L.) AMS IB.7667 (1: 91), Heron Island, Queensland, Australia.

The holotype (AMS E.1506) and paratypes (AMS I.10963) were examined and additional counts made.

CORADION MELANOPUS (Cuvier)
Two-spot coralfish

Chaetodon melanopus Cuvier, 1831: p. 84 (type locality Moluccas).

Tetragonoptrus melanopus, Bleeker, 1865: p. 282 (Amboina).

Coradion melanopus, Bleeker, 1877a: p. 39 (Amboina, Ceram). Bleeker, 1877b: p. 26, pl. 375 (=13), fig. 4 (erroneously marked as fig. 1; Amboina, Ceram).

Diagnosis.—D. X, 24-27; A. III, 17-18; pectoral rays 14 (one with 15/15, two with 14/15); L.l. scales 43-47; dorsal fin squarish, posterior edge vertical; fourth to fifth dorsal spine longest; eye band not continued on isthmus; median snout stripe extends from about level of eyes to upper lip and continues on lower lip to chin; ocellus present in anal fin as well as in dorsal fin.

Meristics.—D. X, 24-27; A. III, 17-18; pectoral rays 14 (one with 15/15, two with 14/15); L.l. scales 43-47; scales above L.l. 9; scales below L.l. 21-22; gill rakers 10 or 11.

Description.—Predorsal contour straight or slightly gibbous, sloping at an angle of about 50-55° from the horizontal; supraorbital spiny; snout length greater than or equal to depth of caudal peduncle, which is greater than eye diameter; eye diameter greater than interorbital width.

Dorsal fin with X spines, increasing rapidly in length until fourth or fifth, then decreasing in length gradually until the last; soft portion of dorsal fin roughly square, sixth to eighth ray longest, 3.4 in S.L.; anal fin with second spine little shorter than third, first about two-thirds second; pectoral fin reaching to level of first anal fin spine; pelvic fins long, reaching to level of anterior anal fin ray bases; base of spinous portion of dorsal fin about three-fourths (approximately 3.3 in S.L.) of length of soft portion (2.5-2.6 in S.L.).

Coradion melanopus (Cuvier). 75mm S.L. Ceram, East Indies.

Ratios	20-50	Standard Length (mm) 51-89(4)	above 89(2)
Depth/S.L.	---	1.3-1.4	1.4
Head/S.L.	---	2.8-3.1	3.0-3.1
Eye/Head	---	3.1-3.5	3.2-3.4
Snout/Head	---	2.7-2.9	2.9
Interorb. W./Head	---	3.5-3.8	3.4-3.7
Maxillary L./Head	---	4.5-5.3	4.8-4.9
Caud. Ped./S.L.	---	8.6-9.1	8.0-8.3
Pect. Fin L./S.L.	---	3.1-3.3	3.1-3.4
Pelvic Sp. L./S.L.	---	3.7-4.1	4.0-4.3
Predorsal L./S.L.	---	1.7-1.8	1.9
Prepelvic L./S.L.	---	2.2-2.3	2.1-2.3
Dorsal Sp. No. 1/S.L.	---	8.9-11.0	10.1-10.2
Dorsal Sp. No. 2/S.L.	---	4.7-5.9	5.4-5.7
Dorsal Sp. No. 3/S.L.	---	3.2-4.1	3.7-3.8
Dorsal Sp. No. 4/S.L.	---	2.7-3.4	3.1-3.2
Dorsal Sp. No. 5/S.L.	---	2.7-3.1	3.0-3.2
Dorsal Sp. No. 6/S.L.	---	2.8-3.1	3.0-3.2
Anal Sp. No. 1/S.L.	---	6.7-7.7	7.3-8.2
Anal Sp. No. 2/S.L.	---	3.6-3.8	4.1-4.4
Anal Sp. No. 3/S.L.	---	3.4-3.6	3.7-4.2

*Hemitaurichthys
polylepis* in a
defensive stance
with spines
spread. Photo by
Michio Goto from
Marine Life
Documents.

Hemitaurichthys polylepis does not do well in aquaria. Perhaps they will settle down if several individuals were kept together. Photo by Dr. D. Terver,
Nancy Aquarium, France.

The dark headed phase (above) and the all yellow phase (below) of *Hemitaurichthys polylepis.* The specimen above also has an indication of a dark spot in the dorsal fin. Photo above by Dr. Gerald R. Allen, photo below by Dr. Herbert R. Axelrod.

Juveniles not seen. Smallest specimen (74 mm S.L.) not differing from larger ones.

Color Pattern.—Median snout stripe extending from eye level or above to tip of upper lip, then continues on the lower lip and chin as a broad band; upper portion of snout stripe is a brown band or a lighter band with dark borders above the nostrils; eyebands joined at nape, upper portion brown or light brown with dark edges; anterior arm of split body bar extends from about first three or four dorsal fin spines, posterior arm from about fifth through ninth dorsal fin spines; the combined bar continues around abdomen and pelvic fin base; posterior body bar originates from bases of seventh to fourteenth dorsal soft rays; caudal peduncle band narrow, solid brown, not bulging in middle; dorsal ocellus extends from fourth to ninth soft rays, anal fin ocellus more or less centrally located in fin, extending from third to sixth rays; anal fin ocellus barely included in body bar, the ring extending beyond it slightly; dorsal ocellus, ring included, extends into bar only for one-third of its diameter; membrane flap of second dorsal fin spine black.

Remarks.—*Coradion melanopus* is a poorly known species. It is quite distinct, however, from the other two species of the genus. The original description of Cuvier (1831) refers to the second ocellus and the ten dorsal fin spines characteristic of this species. Specimens of *C. melanopus* are very similar to the color plate in Bleeker's *Atlas Ichthyologique* (1877); Fig. 4 of Bleeker is actually *C. melanopus* although the legend of the plate calls it figure 1. Figure 1 is *Chaetodon trifascialis* (formerly *Megaprotodon strigangulus*). Fowler & Bean (1929) include this apparent switch in their synonymy as *Megaprotodon strigangulus* (not Gmelin). Kner (1865) may have included this species in his synonymy, but from his description it appears that only the other two species were at hand. It does seem that all three species are present in the East Indies.

Coradion melanopus is the most restricted species in distribution if current records are accurate.

The largest size recorded is about 118 mm standard length.

The variations discussed under this species appear to be well within the normal variation for the species. The lack of pearly scales may be due to preservation as are, in part, the different aspect of the bordered or non-bordered eyebands and snout stripes.

Chaetodon festivus of Desjardins (1836) is insufficiently described to properly place it with any species. The twelve dorsal fin spines recorded by Desjardins are not in agreement with the count for *C. melanopus*. The two ocelli of course do agree. Of the species of chaetodontids along the African coast that reach Madagascar (and probably also to Mauritius), the only one that is generally orbicular or round and has a dorsal ocellus is *Chaetodon marleyi*. But *C. marleyi*, although it does have two ocelli at one stage of its life history, has them both in the dorsal fin, and it has XI dorsal fin spines, not XII. There were no specimens of *Chaetodon festivus* in the Paris Museum (Bauchot, personal communication), although the holotype of *Chaetodon chrysurus* Desjardins, described in the same paper, was found. *Chaetodon festivus* cannot at present be placed in its proper position (it may in fact not even be a chaetodontid) and must be considered a *nomen dubium*. *Coradion merlangus* listed by Bleeker (1879) is most likely a poorly interpreted version of a hand-written "*melanopus.*"

Distribution.—East Indies to New Guinea and the Bismarck Archipelago.

Material Examined.—(6 spec.: 75-94 mm S.L.) RMNH 5469 (1: 87), East Indies; RMNH 5798 (2: 83-93), East Indies; RMNH 14395 (1: 94), Ambon; RMNH 14396 (1: 87), East Indies; RMNH 14397 (1: 75), Ceram.

CORADION CHRYSOZONUS (Cuvier)
Golden-girdled coralfish

Chaetodon chrysozonus Cuvier, 1831: p. 82 (type locality Java).

Chaetodon labiatus Cuvier, 1831: p. 83 (type locality Java).

Chaetodon guttatus (not of Bloch) Gray, 1854: p. 71 (type locality Indian Ocean).

Coradion chrysozonus, Kaup, 1860: p. 146 (Java). Ahl, 1923: p. 40 (in part; Java).

Tetragonoptrus chrysozonus, Bleeker, 1865: p. 286 (Amboina).

Chaetodon chrysozonus, Kner, 1865: p. 101 (in part; Java).

Coradion chrysozonus (Cuvier). 115 mm S.L. Malakal, Palau Islands.

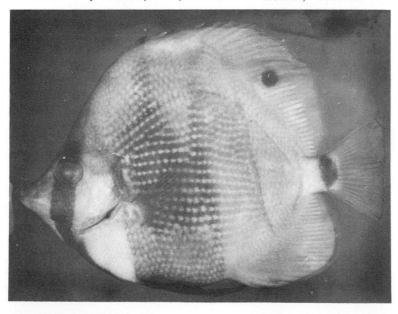

Hemitaurichthys zoster from the Maldive Islands. Photo by Dr. Herbert R. Axelrod.

The pattern of *Hemitaurichthys zoster* is different from that of *H. polylepis* and the two are easily distinguished. Photo by H. Hansen.

A young *Hemitaurichthys zoster*. Juveniles look very much like the adults. Photo by D.L. Savitt and R.B. Silver.

Ratios	Standard Length (mm) 20-50(1)	51-89(8)	above 89(4)
Depth/S.L.............	1.4	1.3-1.5	1.4-1.5
Head/S.L..............	3.0	2.9-3.0	3.0
Eye/Head.............	2.6	3.0-3.2	3.1-3.8
Snout/Head...........	4.1	2.9-3.6	3.0-3.8
Interorb. W./Head......	3.1	3.2-3.4	3.4-3.5
Maxillary L./Head......	4.6	4.2-4.9	4.0-6.2
Caud. Ped./S.L....'.....	8.2	7.7-8.5	8.5-8.9
Pect. Fin L./S.L........	3.1	3.4-3.8	3.6-4.1
Pelvic Sp. L./S.L........	3.6	3.4-4.1	3.9-4.8
Predorsal L./S.L........	1.8	1.7-1.9	1.8-2.0
Prepelvic L./S.L........	2.2	2.1-2.3	2.2-2.5
Dorsal Sp. No. 1/S.L.....	11.4	10.1-14.9	13.9-18.0
Dorsal Sp. No. 2/S.L.....	6.3	6.9-9.4	8.7-12.2
Dorsal Sp. No. 3/S.L.....	4.6	4.0-6.0	6.8-7.4
Dorsal Sp. No. 4/S.L.....	3.4	3.6-4.9	5.6-6.9
Anal Sp. No. 1/S.L......	7.3	8.1-9.9	10.3-12.2
Anal Sp. No. 2/S.L......	4.7	4.5-5.2	6.0-6.9
Anal Sp. No. 3/S.L......	4.4	3.9-4.8	5.1-6.4

Diagnosis.—D. IX, 28-30 (usually 28-29); A. III, 19-21 (usually 20); pectoral rays 15 (one with 16, one with 15/16); L.l. scales 48-52; dorsal fin rounded; sixth or seventh dorsal fin spine longest, posterior spines approximately equal; eyebands joined at isthmus and extending toward pelvic fins (but do not reach them); median snout stripe present, extending from eye level to tip of snout, not continued below on chin; dorsal fin ocellus well-developed at all ages, none in anal fin.

Meristics.—D. IX, 28-29 (one with 30); A. III, 20 (one with 19, another with 21); pectoral rays 15 (one with 16, one with 15/16); L.l. scales 48-52; scales above L.l. 9-10; scales below L.l. 20-24; gill rakers 9.

Description.—Predorsal contour approximately straight, slightly convex at nape, concave below eye level; slope angle of predorsal contour 50-55° from horizontal; supraorbital smooth to slightly toothed; depth of caudal peduncle greater than snout length, which is greater than or equal to eye diameter; eye diameter greater than interorbital width.

Dorsal fin with IX spines, increasing in length until the sixth or seventh, then leveling off, the posterior spines of equal length or slightly longer; soft portion of dorsal fin distinctly rounded, last portion of fin edge, however, vertical; longest ray of dorsal fin about 3.6 in S.L.; third anal fin spine only slightly longer than second, first about half to two-thirds second; pectoral fins reaching level of anus or slightly beyond; pelvic fins long, reaching at least to second anal fin ray; base of spinous portion of dorsal fin about half length of soft portion (3.8-4.0 in S.L. as compared to 2.0 in S.L.).

Juveniles (smallest specimen examined was 47 mm S.L.) were very much like adults. No specific differences could be seen between them and the adults.

Color Pattern.—Median snout stripe present, extending from nape or about upper eye level to tip of snout; chin may or may not have spot or blotch, but never has a continuous stripe; eyebands joined at nape and isthmus, forming a complete band around head, lower portion extending on isthmus part way toward pelvic insertion; anterior arm of split body bar originating from first two dorsal fin spines, posterior arm at about fourth to sixth or seventh dorsal fin spines; posterior bar extends from about seventh to twenty-first dorsal fin soft rays to eighth to fifteenth anal fin soft rays; caudal peduncle band wider at center than top or bottom, almost spot-like; in larger specimens band almost separated into distinct lateral spots, in smaller ones more or less band-like; caudal peduncle band light-bordered; dorsal fin ocellus located in soft dorsal fin from about eighth to thirteenth rays.

Remarks.—*Coradion chrysozonus* is the most common and consequently best known of the species of *Coradion*. It apparently reaches the western coast of Australia but has not yet been reported from the Great Barrier Reef area on the eastern Australian coast. All three species appear to be sympatric in the East Indies and all three have specifically been reported from Java. *Coradion chrysozonus* was reported from western Java in the Indian Ocean but apparently has not crossed the Andaman Sea to Sri Lanka or India.

The pearly spots on the scales which induced Cuvier (1831) to give two separate names, *Chaetodon chrysozonus* and *C. labiatus*, to this species seem to be an overlay pattern, variable and subject to changes and fading depending upon condition of specimens and method of preservation. *Chaetodon enneacanthus* was mentioned by Cuvier (1831) as the name he intended for the species, but in deference to Kuhl and van Hasselt, who supplied the specimens of this species, he retained their name, *Chaetodon chrysozonus*. Bleeker (1877) and Fowler & Bean (1929) included *C. enneacanthus* in their synonymies while Weber & de Beaufort (1936) and Ahl (1923) omitted it.

Chaetodon guttatus Gray (1854) is included on the basis of photographs of the holotype and an illustration of that specimen kindly supplied by Mr. Alwyne Wheeler of the British Museum (Natural History).

Ahl (1923) had two 6 mm specimens which he suggested might be *Coradion chrysozonus*, but due to their size he could not be absolutely certain. They were captured in the brackish water of a river mouth in New Pomerania.

This species is common in Malaya, occasionally appearing in the market (J.S. Scott, 1959).

Distribution.—East Indies north to China, south to western Australia,

Hemitaurichthys multispinus, 148 mm S.L., from Pitcairn Island. Photo by Dr. J.R. Randall.

This *Hemitaurichthys thompsoni* was spotted among a school of surgeon-fishes and photographed by Dr. Gerald R. Allen.

Photos of *Hemitaurichthys thompsoni* (some 5 inches long) from Kona, Hawaii at a depth of 30 feet by Dr. Gerald R. Allen.

east to the Philippine Islands, New Guinea, Bismarck Archipelago, and western Caroline Islands, and west to western Java.

Material Examined.—(13 spec.: 47-114 mm S.L.) USNM 182904 (1: 88), Philippine Islands; USNM 182084 and 182088 (6: 47-93), Philippine Islands; CAS 37694 (2: 57-59), Gulf of Thailand; CAS 37643 (2: 98-111), Gulf of Thailand; CAS 37644 (1: 114), Gulf of Thailand; WAM P.5654 (1: 62), Western Australia, Australia.

Genus FORCIPIGER Jordan and McGregor

Forcipiger Jordan & McGregor, in Jordan and Evermann, 1898: p. 1671 (type-species *Chelmon longirostris* Cuvier and Valenciennes [=*F. flavissimus*, type-species misidentified] by original designation).

Diagnosis.—Body rhomboid-oval; snout elongate, tube-like, contained 1.1-2.1 times in body depth; lateral line complete; pectoral and pelvic fins elongate, extending beyond origin of anal fin in adults; fourth dorsal spine not extraordinarily elongate; D. XI-XII, 22-27; A. III, 17-20; pectoral fin 14-15; scales small, 66-80 in lateral line.

Description.—Body compressed, rhomboid-oval; predorsal contour concave; snout elongate, 1.1-2.1 in body depth; mouth opening small, located at tip of elongate snout; preopercle denticulate to serrate, particularly at angle, which is obtuse.

Dorsal fin continuous, XI-XII (occasionally X or XIII) long, strong spines; these spines increasing in height rapidly until fourth or fifth, those more posteriorly decreasing in height until last; soft rayed portion of dorsal fin with posterior border almost vertical; anal fin spines long and strong, the first half or slightly more than half length of second, which is slightly shorter than third; soft rayed portion of anal fin with posterior border almost vertical, the angle at about fourth or fifth ray; caudal fin truncate but with upper rays extended; pectoral and pelvic fins elongate, reaching to or beyond last anal fin spine; pectoral fins falcate.

Lateral line complete, describing a high arc following dorsal contour of body, becoming horizontal on caudal peduncle, and ending at base of caudal fin; scales very small, rounded, minute on head and vertical fins; dorsal and anal fin almost entirely covered with these very small scales; 66-80 scales in the lateral line; body scales in horizontal series pattern; spines of dorsal fin relatively free from scale covering, the scale very low at anterior end of fin and reaching only to halfway mark or less of last dorsal spine; interspinal membranes deeply incised at least anteriorly; anal spines also relatively free from scales, the third spine only about one-third covered.

Juveniles similar to adults except for some proportional changes.

Color very similar in the two species although one has a dark brown phase which the other lacks. Normally yellow with upper section of head dark gray to black, lower portion white; anal fin with large black spot covering last few rays.

Widely distributed from the western Mexican coast and the offshore islands of the East Pacific to the east coast of Africa and the Red Sea; occurs northward to southern Japan and southward to the Great Barrier Reef of Australia.

Two species recognized, distinguishable by the following key:

Key to the Species of the Genus Forcipiger

1a. Dorsal fin spines XII; lateral line scales 74-80; snout 1.6-2.1 in body depth; mouth opening normal, approximately 10.0-14.2 in body depth . . . .*Forcipiger flavissimus*

1b. Dorsal fin spines XI; lateral line scales 66-75; snout 1.1-1.5 in body depth; mouth opening very small, the snout almost appearing as a simple tube, 20.0-50.0 in body depth . . . .*Forcipiger longirostris*

Remarks.—*Forcipiger* is probably the most distinctive of all chaetodontid genera. The elongate snout is only comparable to that of the genus *Chelmon*. It is easily distinguishable from *Chelmon* by its elongate and falcate pectoral fins (in *Chelmon* they are normal), by the number of dorsal fin spines (XI-XII in *Forcipiger;* VIII-IX in *Chelmon*), by the shape of the spinous dorsal fin, by the smaller and more numerous scales in *Forcipiger* (66-80 lateral line scales as compared with 45-55 in *Chelmon*), by the extent of the scales covering the dorsal spines (low in *Forcipiger*, moderate to high in *Chelmon*), by the shape of the soft dorsal and anal fins, and by color pattern.

By virtue of the elongate snouts of both *Forcipiger* and *Chelmon*, these genera are usually considered closely related. The many other characters that differentiate these genera (including larval stages which are now under study) indicate that the lengthening of the snout which occurred several times in the history of the chaetodontids, was independently evolved in these two genera and that the relationship is not as close as expected.

The descriptions of the new genus *Forcipiger* and the new species *F. flavissimus* appeared twice, once in Jordan and Evermann (1898), the second in Jordan and McGregor (1899), almost simultaneously. In the former work the following appeared, "*Forcipiger*, Jordan & McGregor, new genus (*longirostris*)." The latter work had, "Type *Chelmon longirostris* Cuvier and Valenciennes."

A juvenile *Heniochus acuminatus* with a well developed fourth dorsal spine and a solid yellow area adjacent to the posterior black band. Photo by Dr. Herbert R. Axelrod.

A pair of *Heniochus acuminatus* one-half mile south of Kealoha Point, Hawaii. Photographed at a depth of 50 feet by Paul Allen.

An adult *Heniochus acuminatus* still with a well developed fourth dorsal fin spine. Note the white space between the yellow fins and posterior dark band. Photo by Walter Deas.

FORCIPIGER LONGIROSTRIS (Broussonet)
Black long-nosed butterflyfish

Chaetodon longirostris Broussonet, 1782: p. 6, fig. 7 (type locality Sandwich Islands = Hawaiian Islands). Bonnaterre, 1788: p. 86, pl. 47, fig. 176 (Pacific Ocean). Gmelin, 1789: p. 1264 (Pacific Ocean). Walbaum, 1792: p. 438 (on Broussonet). Bloch & Schneider, 1801: p. 321 (Pacific Ocean).

Forcipiger longirostris, Fowler & Bean, 1929: p. 45 (in part; Philippine Islands).

Forcipiger cyrano Randall, 1961: p. 58, fig. 5 and 6C (type locality Celebes).

Forcipiger inornatus Randall, 1961: p. 58, fig. 4 and 6B (type locality Keahe Point, Oahu, Hawaiian Islands).

Diagnosis.—D. XI, 24-27 (rarely 27); A. III, 17-20 (rarely 27); pectoral rays 14 or 15 (three with 14/15, one with 15/16); L.l. scales 66-75; snout extremely elongate, 1.1-1.5 in body depth; mouth opening very small, gape about 20-50 times in body depth; dark color phase present.

Closely related to *F. flavissimus* and often confused with that species, but has XI dorsal fin spines (*F. flavissimus* has XII), a longer snout (*F.*

Forcipiger longirostris (Broussonet). 154 mm S.L. Comoro Islands.

Ratios	Standard Length (mm)		
	40-69(1)	70-99	above 100 (12)
Depth/S.L.	1.9	---	2.1-2.5
Head/S.L.	2.6	---	1.9-2.2
Eye/Head	4.3	---	5.8-7.4
Snout/Head	2.1	---	1.4-1.7
Snout/Depth.	2.9	---	1.1-1.5
Gape/Depth	---	---	19.2-49.6
Maxillary/Depth	5.0	---	1.3-2.2
Maxillary/Head	3.7	---	1.6-2.0
Interorb. W./Head.	4.5	---	7.2-8.9
Caud. Ped./S.L.	12.0	---	13.0-16.5
Pect. Fin L./S.L.	3.7	---	2.6-3.2
Pelvic Sp. L./S.L.	5.3	---	5.4-6.4
Predorsal L./S.L.	2.2	---	1.8-2.0
Prepelvic L./S.L.	2.1	---	1.7-2.0
Dorsal Sp. No. 1/S.L.	13.4	---	13.4-25.2
Dorsal Sp. No. 2/S.L.	5.7	---	8.7-13.9
Dorsal Sp. No. 3/S.L.	3.1	---	4.0-5.4
Dorsal Sp. No. 4/S.L.	---	---	3.5-4.5
Dorsal Sp. No. 5/S.L.	---	---	3.7-4.5
Anal Sp. No. 1/S.L.	9.0	---	9.2-11.7
Anal Sp. No. 2/S.L.	5.1	---	4.9-6.1
Anal Sp. No. 3/S.L.	4.5	---	4.4-5.9

flavissimus snout is 1.6-2.1 in body depth) and a smaller mouth opening (gape of *F. flavissimus* 10-14 times in body depth).

Meristics.—D. XI, 24-27 (rarely 27); A. III, 17-20 (rarely 17); pectoral rays 14 or 15 (three with 14/15, one with 15/16); L.l. scales 66-75; scales above L.l. 10-12; scales below L.l. 26-30; gill rakers 15-18.

Description.—Snout exceptionally elongate, 1.1-1.5 in body depth; gape extremely small, restricted to the very tip of the snout, 20-50 in body depth, snout appearing somewhat like an eyedropper; teeth long, slender, about 3 rows in jaw; lachrymal elongate, smooth to weakly serrate; snout length much greater than eye diameter, which is greater than depth of caudal peduncle; depth of caudal peduncle greater than interorbital width.

Dorsal fin with XI long, strong spines, fourth or fifth longest; base of spinous portion of dorsal fin longer (2.9-3.6 in S.L.) than that of soft portion (4.1-4.6 in S.L.).

Scales small, 66-75 in lateral line.

Juveniles resemble adults.

A 2-inch juvenile *Heniochus acuminatus* from Makua, Oahu, Hawaii. Photo by Dr. Gerald R. Allen at 30 feet deep.

A group of small (3-inch) individuals of *Heniochus acuminatus* from Eilat, Red Sea. Photo by Dr. Gerald R. Allen.

Two small individuals of *Heniochus acuminatus* from Hawaii. Photo by Dr. Herbert R. Axelrod.

Color Pattern.—This species is notable in having two distinct color patterns. The first is almost identical to that of *Forcipiger flavissimus* and is the more common. The dark triangular section on the head connects with the one from the opposite side at the nape but is separate from just below nape to near end of lachrymal, connecting again at the end of the lachrymal; the area between these dark sections is light, but within this light zone is a narrow median brown stripe that extends from just above eye level to the tip of the lachrymal; a brown stripe of varying intensity and length (usually not long) extends along the upper part of the snout; the eyes may be entirely enclosed in the brown zones or the upper and lower edges may be in contact with the lighter colors.

The second color pattern is almost uniformly dark brown, with the caudal fin dusky, edges of dorsal and anal fins hyaline and a light streak passing through dorsal and anal fins in a vertical direction. Portions of the color pattern (anal fin spot and triangle on head) can often be seen through the dark color.

Remarks.—The specimen used by Broussonet (1782) in his description of *Forcipiger longirostris* was, unfortunately, the rarer of the two species. Although two specimens were mentioned (Broussonet, 1782; Jordan and Evermann, 1905) from the Hawaiian Islands and the Society Islands, the description and figure is undoubtedly that of the longer snouted form. This was discovered and confirmed by Wheeler (1964), who saw the type specimen of Broussonet's species in the British Museum. It was indeed the longer snouted species. The search for the type was prompted by Randall's (1961) description of two new species of *Forcipiger*, *F. inornatus* and *F. cyrano*, both long-snouted forms, the former dark colored and the latter the normal yellow pattern. Wheeler (1964) suggested that *F. cyrano* be placed in synonymy under *F. longirostris* and that the species long regarded as *F. longirostris* take the next available name (see *F. flavissimus*). Caldwell and Randall (1970) reviewed the problem and added the dark form, *F. inornatus*, to the synonymy of *F. longirostris* based on further investigation of additional specimens.

The new specimens showed no gaps in the meristics between Randall's two species as he had previously indicated. In addition, the dark form was reported to change color from dark to yellow, the pattern eventually being identical to that of *F. longirostris* (as currently accepted). It has been personally observed that the brown form does change to the light form. The instance observed took place in a pet shop over a period of about one month and took place in two ill-defined steps. The first was a change in color from brown to dirty yellow that took two to three days to accomplish. This color remained for quite some time, and it was doubtful whether the final change could or would occur. During the fourth week, however, the final color change did take place and the specimen could not be distinguished (by color) from the 'normal' yellow specimens. Since the change was observed in a captive specimen in an aquarium, no additional explanation can be added about this change. In the natural habitat a

Forcipiger longirostris, dark phase. 147.3 mm S.L. from the Comoro Islands.

specimen in the middle color phase was seen and photographed by Richard Wass, confirming that the change apparently also occurs in nature. No instance of a reverse color change, that from yellow to dark, has been recorded.

Brown specimens were examined by the author and found to consist of both sexes. A pair of brown forms was speared by two skin divers from the University of Hawaii, one being male and one female.

Uses of the extraordinarily long snout have, as yet, not been observed, but the differences in snout length and gape size between the two species of *Forcipiger* may prove to be ecological, food size and food capturing, devices. Randall (1961) investigated the food of the different forms then available to him. He found the brown specimens' stomach contents consisted mainly of caridean shrimps; those of the yellow forms from the Solomon Islands contained mysid shrimps and a crab megalops.

Distribution.—The exact distribution is not known since the species has until recently been confused and combined with the following species. It has been recognized from the Hawaiian Islands, Tuamotus, Solomon Islands, Philippine Islands, East Indies, Comoro Islands, Marshall Islands, Wake Island, and Christmas Island.

Material Examined.—(13 spec.: 66-176 mm S.L.) BPBM 4211 (2: 147-176), Wake Island; BPBM 6240 (1: 112), Eniwetok, Marshall Islands; USNM 181372 (1: 102), Philippine Islands; USNM 181373 (1: 140) Celebes; SOSC Anton Bruun Cr. 9 Sta. HA-14 (4: 134-153), Comoro Islands; NMFS-H HMS Cr. 47 Sta. 2 (1: 66), midwater trawl, Hawaiian Islands; WEB (3: 130-150), Hawaiian Islands.

Heniochus chrysostomus adult.

Opposite:
Young *Heniochus chrysostomus*. The small dark spot in the anal fin is usually hidden by the dark band. Photo by Dr. Shih-chieh Shen.

FORCIPIGER FLAVISSIMUS Jordan & McGregor
Long-nosed butterflyfish
(Lauwiliwili; Forceps Fish)

Chaetodon longirostris (not of Broussonet), Cuvier, 1831: p. 89, pl. 175 (Mauritius).

Chelmo longirostris (not of Broussonet), Gunther, 1860: p. 38 (Ile de France to Polynesia, Amboina).

Prognathodes longirostris (not of Broussonet), Bleeker, 1877: p. 23, pl. 366, fig. 5 (Ternate, Amboina, Ceram, Nussalaut, Banda).

Forcipiger flavissimus Jordan & McGregor *in* Jordan & Evermann, 1898: p. 1671 (type locality Clarion and Socorro Islands).

Forcipiger longirostris (not of Broussonet), Fowler, 1900: p. 512 (Hawaiian Islands). Ahl, 1923: p. 8 (Matupi, New Guinea, Mauritius, Ralum, Tsingtau, Mysol, Jaluit). Fowler & Bean (in part), 1929: p. 45 (Philippine Islands).

Diagnosis.—D. XII (an aberrant specimen had XIII), 22-24 (the aberrant specimen had 19); A. III, 17-18; pectoral rays 15; L.l. scales 74-80; snout very elongate, 1.6-2.1 in body depth; mouth opening forceps-like, 10.1-14.2 in body depth; no dark color phase known.

Forcipiger flavissimus Jordan and McGregor. 124 mm S.L. Enewetak, Marshall Islands.

Ratios	Standard Length (mm)		
	40-69(2)	70-99(3)	above 99(19)
Depth/S.L.	2.2-2.4	2.2-2.3	1.9-2.4
Head/S.L.	2.2-2.5	2.4	2.2-2.4
Eye/Head	4.2-4.5	4.2-4.3	4.6-6.4
Snout/Head	1.8-2.0	1.8-1.9	1.6-1.8
Snout/Depth	1.8-2.1	1.9-2.1	1.6-2.1
Gape/Depth	---	11.7	10.1-14.2
Maxillary/Depth	2.5-3.8	2.8-2.9	2.2-2.8
Maxillary/Head	2.5	---	2.4-2.5
Interorb. W./Head.	4.4-6.5	5.8-6.3	5.7-6.7
Caud. Ped./S.L.	11.6-13.8	12.4-13.0	11.8-14.6
Pect. Fin L./S.L.	2.3-4.0	2.5-2.7	2.3-3.0
Pelvic Sp. L./S.L.	4.6-4.8	5.1-5.5	4.9-6.4
Predorsal L./S.L.	2.1-2.3	2.2	1.8-2.4
Prepelvic L./S.L.	1.9-2.2	2.0-2.1	1.7-2.1
Dorsal Sp. No. 1/S.L.	9.9-10.9	12.4-15.0	10.3-17.8
Dorsal Sp. No. 2/S.L.	4.7-5.1	6.0-6.9	5.1-9.6
Dorsal Sp. No. 3/S.L.	3.6-3.9	4.4-4.5	3.9-5.9
Dorsal Sp. No. 4/S.L.	3.0	3.7-3.8	3.0-5.0
Dorsal Sp. No. 5/S.L.	3.0	---	3.0-4.0
Anal Sp. No. 1/S.L.	7.3-7.9	7.9-9.1	7.3-11.4
Anal Sp. No. 2/S.L.	4.1-5.4	5.3-5.4	4.1-6.3
Anal Sp. No. 3/S.L.	3.5-5.5	4.2-4.5	3.5-5.0

Meristics.—D. XII (one aberrant specimen had XIII), 22-24 (the aberrant specimen had 19); A. III, 17-18; pectoral fin 15 (one had 14 on one side; two specimens had 16); L.l. scales 74-80; scales above L.l. 11-14; scales below L.l. 27-34 (usually 28-30); gill rakers 12-16.

Description.—Snout elongate, 1.6-2.1 in body depth; snout length greater than eye diameter, which is greater than caudal peduncle depth; depth of caudal peduncle greater than interorbital width; lachrymal extremely wide, smooth to weakly serrate; gape normal, 10.1-14.2 in body depth; teeth long, slender, arranged in about 13-15 rows in each jaw.

Dorsal fin with XII spines, fourth or fifth longest; base of spinous portion of dorsal fin longer (2.9-3.2 in standard length) than that of soft portion (4.0-4.7 in standard length).

Scales small, 74-80 in lateral line.

Juveniles similar to adults.

Color Pattern.—Identical to the yellow phase of *F. longirostris*. This species has never been reported to have the dark phase of *Forcipiger longirostris*.

Heniochus intermedius adult with well developed horns.

Heniochus intermedius juveniles. The fourth dorsal fin spine is well developed but the horns have not yet made their apearance. (upper fish, facing front, is *Heniochus acuminatus* juvenile). Photo by Klaus Paysan.

Heniochus intermedius is very similar in appearance to *H. acuminatus*. Very little is known about their habits. Photo by Walter Deas at Sha'ab Rumi.

A pair of *Heniochus intermedius* from Wingate Reef. These specimens have much more yellow than most others. Photo by Walter Deas.

Remarks.—Since Wheeler (1964) rediscovered the type specimen of *F. longirostris* (Broussonet), he suggested the species usually referred to as *F. longirostris* take the next available name indicated in Randall's synonymy (1961), *Chelmon lol* (Thiolliere, 1857). According to the description in Thiolliere's paper, *Chelmon lol* is a true *Chelmon* and should be placed in the synonymy of *Chelmon rostratus*. Fowler and Bean (1929) included *Chelmon lol* with *Forcipiger longirostris*, an error apparently copied by Weber and de Beaufort (1936), as eventually did Randall (1964). With *Chelmon lol* unavailable, the next name that can be used is *Forcipiger flavissimus* Jordan and McGregor. I have examined the type specimens and topotypes of *F. flavissimus* and found that, although larger than specimens from other areas, they do not differ in any other way.

This species is much more common than the previously described species. It has been known as *F. longirostris* at least since Cuvier's description in 1831. Most of the citations in the literature of *Forcipiger longirostris* are in reality *F. flavissimus* or a combination of both species. Misidentifications are too many to list, so almost all have been omitted from the synonymy. However, all citations that are identifiable as actually being *F. longirostris* are included in the synonymy, the remainder most probably being *F. flavissimus*. The photographs and descriptions herein are enough to determine the proper identity of any adequately described specimens of *Forcipiger*.

Jordan and McGregor apparently placed their description of the genus *Forcipiger* and their new species *F. flavissimus* in two different publications at approximately the same time. It appears that the description included in Jordan and Evermann appeared in 1898, whereas that in the *Fisheries Bulletin* is cited as 1899. Both descriptions, however, refer to their taxa as new genus and species.

Forcipiger flavissimus is not uncommon throughout its range, which is considerable. In fact, the range of this species is the largest of any species within the family Chaetodontidae.

Specialized tholichthys larva of *Forcipiger.*

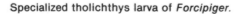

Forcipiger flavissimus. Photo by Hilmar Hansen.

Randall (1961) reported on the stomach contents of two specimens from San Lucas Canyon, Baja California. The larger specimen's stomach contained mysid shrimps, fish eggs, barnacle cirri, and tips of sabellid worm tentacles; the smaller specimen's stomach contained several polychaete worms and numerous tips of sabellid worm tentacles.

This species is occasionally seen inverted on roofs of caves. At night it assumes this position and turns neutral gray (Jonklaas, personal communication).

The largest size reported or measured is 161 mm standard length.

Distribution.—Widely distributed throughout the Pacific and Indian Oceans; from the west coast of Mexico and the offshore islands of the tropical eastern Pacific to the east coast of Africa; Easter Island to Australia as far south as Sydney and northward to Osaka in southern Japan; Red Sea and southward at least to Durban, South Africa. Most of the tropical islands in the Pacific and Indian Oceans are included in its range.

Material Examined.—(24 spec. 60-161 mm S.L.) BPBM 4208 (5: 107-140), Hawaiian Islands; WEB (7: 74-117), Hawaiian Islands; WEB (1: 114), Tahiti, Society Islands; NMFS-H TC32 Sta. 1C (1: 60) (tholichthys), Hawaiian Islands; BPBM (uncatalogued) (1: 125), Eniwetok, Marshall Islands; USNM 8528 (2: 81-119) Socorro Island (paratypes of *Forcipiger flavissimus*); Su. 5709 (1: 161), Clarion Island (holotype of *Forcipiger flavissimus*); CAS 1034-1036 (3: 144-158), Clarion Island; SOSC Anton Bruun Cr. 9, HA-14 (1: 67) Comoro Islands.

Heniochus monoceros juvenile from the area around Taiwan. Photo by Dr. Shih-chieh Shen.

Heniochus monoceros adult with well developed frontal protuberance and strong (but short) horns. Photo by Bill Wood.

The "mask" of *Heniochus monoceros* is distinctive and can be used for identification purposes. Photo by Yasuda and Hiyama.

Adult *Heniochus monoceros* on the reef at Fujikawa, Enewetak. Photo by Scott Johnson.

Genus HEMITAURICHTHYS Bleeker

Hemitaurichthys Bleeker, 1876: p. 304 (type-species *Chaetodon polylepis* Bleeker, 1857 by original designation).

Diagnosis.—Lateral line complete; snout short, 2.5-3.6 in head length; scales along lateral line 70 to 90; fourth dorsal fin spine not extraordinarily elongate; pectoral and pelvic fins elongate; dorsal fin formula XII-XVI, 18-27, anal fin III-V, 15-21; gill rakers 14-20.

Description.—Body oval; snout short, 2.5-3.6 in head length, pointed; gape horizontal; teeth normal, in four to seven closely set rows (may be bunched into a single narrow band) in each jaw; preopercle right-angled, serrate, a slight notch above the angle which is extended posteriorly slightly; supraorbital finely denticulate to toothed; lachrymal rounded, short, scaled.

Dorsal and anal fins rounded posteriorly; first dorsal fin spine relatively short, included up to 25 times in standard length; succeeding dorsal fin spines progressively longer until the seventh, after which they are approximately equal in length or shorter by small increments until the last; last anal spine longest; pectoral fins long, included 2.6-3.0 times in standard length; pelvic fins moderate to long, extending in adults to base of last spine or first rays of anal fin; caudal fin truncate to lunate, upper lobe sometimes longer than lower lobe; dorsal fin continuous, first rays not longer than last spines; spinous portion of dorsal fin longer (2.3-2.5 in standard length) than soft rayed portion (2.9-4.1 in standard length).

Lateral line complete, in the shape of a moderately high arc following the curvature of the back as far as the caudal peduncle, upon which it extends horizontally to base of caudal fin rays; scales small, rounded, 70 to 90 in lateral line, 60 to 75 in a horizontal series; scales smaller around periphery of body and on cheek, minute on rest of head and on fins; dorsal fin spines relatively free from scaly covering, which begins at about base of third to fifth spines and extends upward posteriorly to cover half to three-quarters of last spine; last anal spine about half covered by scales; soft rayed portions of both fins covered by minute scales almost to their tips.

Juveniles not adequately known. The smallest specimens found are described under *Hemitaurichthys thompsoni*. Juveniles are apparently similar to the adults except for variations in color in some species.

Color patterns are simple combinations of brown, yellow and white. *Hemitaurichthys polylepis* has the ability to vary its color pattern to some extent (see discussion of that species for details).

Indian and Pacific Oceans, one species reaching the Hawaiian Islands; Japan to northern Australia. Not recorded from the Red Sea.

Four species are recognized, easily distinguishable by color and meristics in the following key.

Key to the Species of the Genus Hemitaurichthys

1. Uniformly dark brownish, center of body not white 2
   Not uniformly dark brownish, center of body white 3
2. Dorsal fin XVI, 18-20; anal fin V, 15 . . . . *Hemitaurichthys multispinus*
   Dorsal fin XII, 26; anal fin III, 20-21 . . . . *H. thompsoni*
3. Posterior portion of body from about level of first anal fin spine dark
   brown; anterior portion of body from vertical through insertion of
   pectoral fin dark brown; central portion of body white . . . *H. zoster*
   Central and posterior portion of body white except for soft dorsal fin,
   anal fin, and triangular section on upper anterior portion of body;
   head and throat to pelvic fins yellow, dusky yellow, or brown . . . .
   . . . . *H. polylepis*

Remarks.—The four species of *Hemitaurichthys* are superficially very
similar except for color pattern, by which two species can easily be identified. The other two species are similar in color (dark brown) but have a
considerable gap in the number of dorsal and anal spines and rays. *Hemitaurichthys multispinus*, with several more spines in both dorsal and anal
fins than the other three species, also has fewer rays, making the total
element count of both fins comparable to the others. Species with more
than three anal spines are found in genus *Chaetodon* as well, and species
with a normal complement of three anal fin spines have occasionally produced specimens with four or more, so this phenomenon is not extraordinary enough to erect a new genus for *H. multispinus*, although it
deserves subgeneric recognition.

HEMITAURICHTHYS ZOSTER (Bennett)
Brown-and-white butterflyfish

Chaetodon zoster Bennett, 1831: p. 61 (type locality Mauritius).
Hemitaurichthys zoster, Bleeker, 1879: p. 14 (new combination; Mauritius). Ahl, 1923: p. 38, pl. 2, fig. 7 (Mauritius).
Tetragonoptrus zoster, Bleeker, 1879: p. 14 (new combination; Mauritius).

Diagnosis.—D. XII, 24-26 (usually 25); A. III, 21; pectoral rays 17 (one
with 17/18); L.l. scales 69-73; dark brown with broad white band in
center of body from fifth to ninth dorsal fin spines to area between pelvic
base and first anal fin spine base.
   Very close to *H. polylepis* of the Pacific but easily distinguishable
from that species by color pattern.
   Meristics.—D. XII, 24-26 (usually 25); A. III, 21; pectoral rays 17 (one
with 17/18); L.l. scales 69-73; L.l. pores 68-72; scales above L.l. 14-15;
scales below L.l. 33-37; gill rakers 14-17

Adult *Heniochus singularius* in a photo tank. Photo by Dr. Warren E. Burgess in the Philippines.

Below:
Adult *Heniochus singularius* on the reef. There is a second individual of the pair immediately behind the first one. Photo by Roger Steene.

Juvenile *Heniochus singularius* from the Philippine Islands. Photo by Dr. Warren E. Burgess.

A subadult *Heniochus singularius*. The facial pattern is similar to that of *H. monoceros* but with a little practice the two species can easily be differentiated. Photo by Yasuda and Hiyama.

Hemitaurichthys zoster (Bennett) 109 mm S.L. Maldive Islands.

		Standard Length (mm)	
Ratios	**20-60**	**61-90(2)**	**above 90(5)**
Depth/S.L.	---	1.5-1.6	1.5-1.6
Head/S.L.	---	3.0-3.4	3.4-3.5
Eye/Head	---	2.7-2.8	2.7-3.2
Snout/Head	---	3.6-3.9	3.0-3.6
Interorb. W./Head	---	2.9-3.0	2.4-2.9
Maxillary L./Head	---	4.3-4.8	4.0-5.3
Caud. Ped./S.L.	---	8.7-9.2	8.1-9.0
Pect. Fin L./S.L.	---	2.6-2.8	2.6-2.9
Pelvic Sp. L./S.L.	---	4.2-5.3	4.5-5.0
Predorsal L./S.L.	---	2.2-2.5	2.4-2.6
Prepelvic L./S.L.	---	2.2-2.4	2.3-2.4
Dorsal Sp. No. 1/S.L.	---	11.0-13.6	11.7-15.0
Dorsal Sp. No. 2/S.L.	---	6.6-8.0	6.8-10.2
Dorsal Sp. No. 3/S.L.	---	4.8-5.9	4.8-8.0
Dorsal Sp. No. 4/S.L.	---	4.1-4.9	4.0-6.0
Dorsal Sp. No. 5/S.L.	---	3.7-4.4	3.5-4.4
Dorsal Sp. No. 6/S.L.	---	3.6-4.6	3.5-4.3
Anal Sp. No. 1/S.L.	---	6.9-10.4	7.5-9.8
Anal Sp. No. 2/S.L.	---	4.5-5.7	4.4-5.6
Anal Sp. No. 3/S.L.	---	3.7-4.8	4.0-4.8

Description.—Predorsal contour approximately straight, a slight hump at nape; teeth small, slender, in four to seven rows in each jaw; caudal peduncle depth greater than interorbital width, which is greater than eye diameter; eye diameter greater than snout length.

Anal spines graduated, third longest, first less than half length of second; longest ray of pelvic fins reaching to bases of first few anal fin rays; base of spinous portion of dorsal fin longer (2.3-3.7 in standard length) than that of soft portion (2.8-3.0 in standard length).

Scales covering dorsal spines start along bases of fifth or sixth spines, increasing posteriorly until last spine is half to three-fourths covered; scale covering of anal fin spines reaches about to midpoint of third anal spine.

No juveniles of this species were seen. The form and color pattern of the smallest known specimens closely resemble that of the adult.

Color Pattern.—Whitish area extends from the fourth or fifth dorsal spine to ninth to eleventh and ventrally between pelvic fin base and first spine of anal fin.

Remarks.—Although it is quite difficult to distinguish this species from *Hemitaurichthys polylepis* by meristic or proportional characteristics, it is readily distinguishable by color and color pattern. In addition, *Hemitaurichthys zoster* appears to be restricted to the Indian Ocean, whereas *H. polylepis* is found in the Pacific Ocean.

Bleeker (1876) was the first to synonymize his *H. polylepis* with the earlier *H. zoster*, but he did so hesitantly on the basis of the written description of Bennett (1831), having seen no specimen of that species. It appears that most authors who combined the two species had seen only one and were therefore unable to make a proper comparison. Ahl (1923), with both forms in his possession, accepted them as being clearly distinct.

Underwater photographs of *H. zoster* always show it as a schooling species. This agrees with the known habits of the other species in this genus.

Distribution.—Indian Ocean: Maldive Islands, Seychelles, Aldabra and Comoro Islands, Mauritius, and east coast of Africa.

Material Examined.—(7 spec.: 76-148 mm S.L.) MCZ 5755 (1: 148), Mauritius; ANSP 108368 and 108575 (2: 132-138), Seychelle Islands; FMNH 72979 and 73966 (3: 76-109), Maldive Islands; SOSC Antor Bruun Sta. HA-14 (1: 97), Comoro Islands.

HEMITAURICHTHYS POLYLEPIS (Bleeker)
Shy butterflyfish
(Brushytooth butterflyfish)

Chaetodon polylepis Bleeker, 1857: p. 54 (type locality Amboina).

Tetragonoptrus polylepis, Bleeker, 1863: p. 270 (Amboina).

Hemitaurichthys polylepis, Bleeker, 1876: p. 304 (new com-

Adult *Heniocnus pleurotaenia*. The frontal protuberance is well developed but the fourth dorsal fin spine is relatively shorter than in most species of *Heniochus* except *H. varius*. Photo by Dr. Herbert R. Axelrod.

Opposite:
Juvenile *Heniochus pleurotaenia*. Even at this size the light area in the body is evident. Photo by K. Paysan.

bination; Amboina and Timor). Ahl, 1923: p. 37 (Amboina, Timor, and New Guinea).

Hemitaurichthys zoster (not of Bennett), Fowler & Bean, 1929: p. 142 (Philippine Islands). Gosline & Brock, 1960: p. 198 (Hawaiian Islands). Kamohara, 1964: p. 5 (Japan).

Diagnosis.—D. XII, 23-26 (usually 24-25); A. III, 20-21; pectoral rays 16-18 (mostly 17, one with 16, two with 17/18); L.l. scales 68-74; mostly white, dorsal and anal fins plus triangular patch from about first seven dorsal fin spines to pectoral fin base yellow; head yellow but can turn dark brown.

Similar to *H. zoster*, with which it has often been confused and synonymized, but easily distinguishable by color pattern.

Meristics.—D. XII, 23-26 (usually 24 or 25); A. III, 20-21; pectoral rays 16-18 (mostly 17, one with 16, two with 17/18); L.l. scales 68-74; scales above L.l. 12-16; scales below L.l. 31-37; gill rakers 15-17.

Description.—Predorsal contour approximately straight; teeth in about four to six tightly packed rows in each jaw; interorbital width greater than or equal to caudal peduncle depth, which is greater than snout length; snout length greater than or equal to eye diameter.

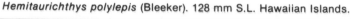

Hemitaurichthys polylepis (Bleeker). 128 mm S.L. Hawaiian Islands.

Ratios	20-60	Standard Length (mm) 61-90(5)	above 90(12)
Depth/S.L............	---	1.4-1.6	1.4-1.6
Head/S.L.............	---	3.0-3.1	3.0-3.5
Eye/Head	---	2.8-3.0	2.7-3.2
Snout/Head	---	3.1-3.4	2.8-3.6
Interorb. W./Head......	---	2.9-3.1	2.3-2.9
Maxillary L./Head......	---	5.1-5.8	4.5-5.8
Caud. Ped./S.L........	---	8.0-8.9	8.5-9.5
Pect. Fin L./S.L........	---	2.5-2.9	2.6-3.0
Pelvic Sp. L./S.L........	---	5.1-5.4	4.2-5.1
Predorsal L./S.L........	---	2.3-2.4	2.4
Prepelvic L./S.L........	---	2.3	2.2-2.4
Dorsal Sp. No. 1/S.L.....	---	11.8-16.6	11.9-17.9
Dorsal Sp. No. 2/S.L.....	---	7.4-8.5	8.3-10.6
Dorsal Sp. No. 3/S.L.....	---	6.3-6.7	6.2-8.5
Dorsal Sp. No. 4/S.L.....	---	5.8-6.1	5.1-5.9
Dorsal Sp. No. 5/S.L.....	---	---	4.9
Dorsal Sp. No. 6/S.L.....	---	---	4.7
Anal Sp. No. 1/S.L......	---	8.1-10.3	7.8-9.6
Anal Sp. No. 2/S.L.......	---	5.7-7.6	4.6-5.8
Anal Sp. No. 3/S.L......	---	5.6-6.1	3.9-5.8

Pelvic fins long, extending at least to bases of anal fin spines in adults; base of spinous portion of dorsal fin longer (about 2.2-2.4 in standard length) than that of soft portion (about 2.9 in standard length).

Scaled portion of dorsal spines low, not evident until fourth to fifth spines, then gradually increasing until last spine is two-thirds to three-fourths covered; scale covering of anal spines moderate, the last spine approximately half-covered.

No juvenile specimens of this species were found. The form and color pattern of the smallest known specimens closely resemble that of the adult.

Color Pattern.—No ocular band present; white or grayish area of body extends part way into dorsal fin and includes caudal peduncle and chest; head variable in color depending upon condition of specimen at time of preservation (see below).

Remarks.—*Hemitaurichthys polylepis* appears quite distinct from the other three species in the genus *Hemitaurichthys*. All reports of *Hemitaurichthys zoster* from the Pacific Ocean that I have seen can be referred to the synonymy of *H. polylepis*. These are too numerous to be included in the above synonymy, and until a substantiated record of *H. zoster* (Bennett) is found, it can be assumed that the species is restricted to the

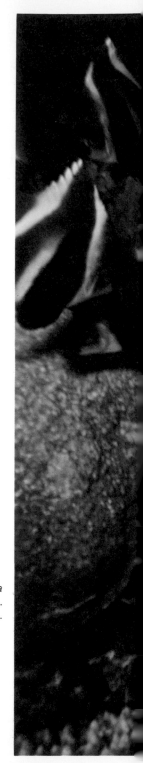

A school of *Heniochus pleurotaenia* on a reef off the Maldive Islands. Photo by R. Jonklaas.

Indian Ocean. *Hemitaurichthys polylepis* is found in the East Indies, whereas it seems that *H. zoster* is not. It is not known whether there is a zone of sympatry in the western part of the East Indies. *Hemitaurichthys polylepis* has recently been discovered by Dr. R. Wass and Dr. G. Allen in Eniwetok, Marshall Islands (personal communication).

Hemitaurichthys polylepis is not uncommon in the Hawaiian Islands, forming schools of various sizes in water normally 40 feet or more deep.

The color change in this species is restricted to the head region as noted above in the section on color pattern. All underwater photographs seen of this species showed a dark brown head color. Aquarium specimens almost always had a bright yellow head, the color continuous with the yellow triangular section of the upper anterior portion of the body. No explanation of the use of this ability to change color has yet been advanced.

Wass (personal communication) reported *Hemitaurichthys polylepis* in nature with a distinct violet to lavender color in the white area of the upper portion of the body between the yellow areas. Whether this is an indication of a distinct breeding color pattern is not known.

Distribution.—Widespread throughout the central and western Pacific Ocean and East Indies from the Hawaiian and Society Islands to the western part of the Java Sea and to Sumatra. It extends south to the Great Barrier Reef and the Australian coast as far south as Ballina. Also recorded from Darwin, Northern Territory, Australia. In the north it extends past Taiwan and the Ryukyu Islands to southern Japan as far as Tokyo and Noto Pena. Also recorded from Korea.

Material Examined.—(17 spec.: 62-127 mm S.L.) BPBM 6112 (4: 104-108), Tahiti, Society Islands; BPBM 4198 (2: 104-112), Hawaiian Islands; WEB (1: 127), Hawaiian Islands; CAS 37695, (1: 75), Hawaiian Islands; CAS Reg. 37645 (2: 106-107), Takaroa, Tuamotu Islands; CAS 37646 (1: 75), Moorea; CAS 37647 (2: 66-67), Ifaluk, Caroline Islands; CAS 37648 (2: 62-67), Ifaluk, Caroline Islands; CAS 37649 (1: 100), Western Caroline Islands; CAS Sta. 37650 (1: 102), Palau Islands.

HEMITAURICHTHYS THOMPSONI Fowler
Thompson's butterflyfish

Hemitaurichthys thompsoni Fowler, 1923: p. 384 (type locality Honolulu, Oahu, Hawaiian Islands).

Diagnosis.—D. XII, 25-27 (usually 26); A. III, 20-21; pectoral rays 18 (one with 17/17); L.l. scales 76-87; color overall brown to dark brown, no white area in central portion of body.

Similar in color to *Hemitaurichthys multispinus* but differs from that species in meristics and proportional measurements (see diagnosis of *H. multispinus*). *Hemitaurichthys thompsoni* can be distinguished from

Hemitaurichthys thompsoni Fowler. 122 mm S.L. Johnston Atoll.

Ratios	Standard Length (mm)		
	20-60(1)	61-90(1)	above 90(6)
Depth/S.L..............	1.7	1.6	1.7-1.9
Head/S.L..............	3.0	3.3	3.2-3.6
Eye/Head	3.3	3.3	2.7-3.6
Snout/Head	3.0	3.0	2.5-3.1
Interorb. W./Head......	2.8	2.8	2.7-3.3
Maxillary L./Head......	4.6	4.5	4.3-5.0
Caud. Ped./S.L.........	8.0	8.3	8.9-9.9
Pect. Fin L./S.L........	3.3	3.3	2.6-3.0
Pelvic Sp. L./S.L........	4.0	5.9	5.1-5.8
Predorsal L./S.L........	2.6	2.7	2.4-2.8
Prepelvic L./S.L........	2.5	2.5	2.3-2.6
Dorsal Sp. No. 1/S.L.....	9.5	21.0	18.3-24.7
Dorsal Sp. No. 2/S.L.....	5.9	8.6	11.5-13.5
Dorsal Sp. No. 3/S.L.....	4.8	6.7	8.5-10.7
Dorsal Sp. No. 4/S.L.....	4.3	5.7	7.1-9.2
Dorsal Sp. No. 5/S.L.....	4.0	5.2	5.1-6.7
Dorsal Sp. No. 6/S.L.....	3.7	5.0	5.0-5.9
Anal Sp. No. 1/S.L......	7.8	10.5	9.0-11.8
Anal Sp. No. 2/S.L......	5.1	7.3	7.2-9.0
Anal Sp. No. 3/S.L......	4.1	5.5	5.8-7.6

Heniochus varius juvenile. Even at this size the frontal gibbosity is somewhat developed. Photo by Yasuda and Hiyama.

Below:
Heniochus varius subadult photographed by Dr. Gerald R. Allen at a depth of 10 feet on the Great Barrier Reef, Australia.

Heniochus varius adult with well developed horns and frontal protuberance but not as developed as they will be.

Hemitaurichthy thompsoni juvenile or postlarva with dark dorsal fin spots. 94 mm S.L. Johnston Atoll.

both *H. polylepis* and *H. zoster* by meristics and proportional measurements. *Hemitaurichthys thompsoni* normally has 26 dorsal soft rays whereas the other two species have 24 or 25 rays, although the extreme ranges of all three species overlap. Similarly, *H. thompsoni* has 18 pectoral fin rays compared to 17 in the other two species (*H. polylepis* had 18 pectoral fin rays in four of the seventeen specimens counted.) Scale counts are higher for *H. thompsoni*, ranging from 76-87 compared with 68-74 for the other two in lateral line scales and 16-19/38-42 compared with 12-16/31-37 for scales above and below the lateral line. *Hemitaurichthys thompsoni* is also less deep-bodied, 1.7-1.9 in standard length compared to 1.4-1.6 in standard length in the other two, and has a relatively shorter pelvic fin spine, 5.1-5.8 in standard length compared to 4.2-5.1 in standard length for *H. polylepis* and *H. zoster*.

Meristics.—D. XII, 25-27 (usually 26); A. III, 20-21; pectoral rays 18 (one with 17); L.l. scales 76-87; scales above L.l. 16-19; scales below L.l. 38-42; gill rakers 14-17.

Description.—Predorsal contour usually with a hump or protuberance at the nape; teeth small, slender, in one or two rows in each jaw; snout length greater than depth of caudal peduncle, which is greater than interorbital width; interorbital width greater than eye diameter.

Anal spines graduated, second shorter than third, first about two-thirds of second; longest ray of pelvic fin reaching to about second anal fin ray base; base of spinous portion of dorsal fin longer (approximately 2.4 in standard length) than base of soft portion (approximately 3.0 in standard length).

Scale covering of dorsal spines low, starting at about first to third dorsal spine base and gradually increasing in height until the last spine is about three-fourths covered; third anal spine one-fourth to one-half covered by scales.

This is the only species of *Hemitaurichthys* in which juvenile specimens were found. They were lighter in color (in alcohol) than the adults. Basically they are light brown, the edges of the dorsal, anal, and pelvic fins blackish. Lips brownish-black. Not included in adult specimens but prominent in the 90 mm specimen and all smaller individuals are three blackish spots in the dorsal fin. The first spot is located on the scaly sheath of the seventh and eighth dorsal fin spines, the second on or just behind the last dorsal fin spine and covering the middle portions of the first dorsal soft rays, and the third spot, which is somewhat smaller, is located on the tenth to fourteenth dorsal fin rays.

Color Pattern.—No eyeband present. Color more or less uniformly brown in alcohol.

Remarks.—The color changes exhibited by *Forcipiger longirostris* caused concern as to whether or not this type change could occur in *Hemitaurichthys thompsoni*. The ability to change color is evident in another species of *Hemitaurichthys, H. polylepis,* but only in the head region. The possibility that *H. thompsoni* is a dark phase of *H. polylepis* seems to be precluded by the meristic differences between these species (see diagnoses of these species). In addition, no underlying pattern 'shows through' the dark brown color of *H. thompsoni* as it does in the dark phase of *Forcipiger longirostris.*

The lighter color of the smaller specimens is either a juvenile or pelagic larval coloration. The 61 mm specimen was taken by a Nanaimo Mark IV midwater trawl fishing at 300 meters depth.

Brock, et al (1965) indicated that *Hemitaurichthys thompsoni* was usually found in fairly large schools at Johnston Atoll. Randall (personal communication) found this species in similar numbers on his trip to the same area. In one week of diving in the waters of Johnston Atoll where *H. thompsoni* was reported abundant, only a single specimen was seen and photographed by Dr. Gerald R. Allen and myself. Dr. Allen spotted it schooling with dark-colored acanthurids, and it was very difficult to distinguish from them.

Distribution.—Almost all specimens captured were taken in the Hawaiian Islands and Johnston Atoll. A single specimen was captured by midwater trawl near Manihiki of the Tokelau Islands.

Juvenile *Parachaetodon ocellatus* appear very similar to adults. Photo by F. Earl Kennedy.

Parachaetodon ocellatus subadult. Photo by Dr. Herbert R. Axelrod.

Parachaetodon ocellatus, subadult. Note the darker color of the banding. Photo by Dr. Fujio Yasuda.

Adult *Parachaetodon ocellatus* with sigmoid shaped trailing edge of dorsal fin. Photo by a 6 inch individual by Dr. Gerald R. Allen.

Material Examined.—(8 spec.: 61-166 mm S.L.) BPBM 3390 (1: 122), (holotype), Hawaiian Islands; BPBM 6193 (1: 122), Johnston Atoll; BPBM 8942 (1: 90), Johnston Atoll; WEB (2: 102-121), Johnston Atoll; USNM 165446 (2: 146-166), Hawaiian Islands; NMFS (formerly POFI) CHG-89 Sta. 18 (1: 61), 11°55'S 162°22.3'W (300 meters deep).

HEMITAURICHTHYS MULTISPINUS Burgess & Randall, NEW SPECIES *
Spiny butterflyfish

Diagnosis.—D. XV-XVI (mostly XVI), 18-20; A. V, 15; pectoral rays 17-18; color overall dark, no white area in center of body.

Resembles *Hemitaurichthys thompsoni* in color, but differs from that and all other species of *Hemitaurichthys* by the high number of dorsal and anal spines.

Meristics.—D. XV-XVI (mostly XVI), 18-20; A. V, 15; pectoral rays 17-18 (two with 17/18); L.l. scales 80-90 (mostly 88-90); scales above L.l. 16-19; scales below L.l. 34-41; gill rakers 18-21 (usually 20).

Description.—Predorsal contour almost straight, a slight convexity at nape; teeth small, slender, in one or two rows in each jaw; interorbital width greater than depth of caudal peduncle, which is greater than eye diameter; eye diameter greater than snout length.

Fourth to eighth dorsal fin spines longest; last anal spine longest; pelvic fin rays moderate to short, usually not reaching anus; base of

Hemitaurichthys multispinus Burgess and Randall. 148 mm S.L. Pitcairn Island. Photo by Dr. John E. Randall.

*Completed manuscript sent to Dr. Randall in Summer, 1974 for joint publication.

| | | Standard Length (mm) | |
Ratios	20-60	61-90	above 90(11)
Depth/S.L............	---	---	2.1-2.3
Head/S.L.............	---	---	3.3-3.8
Eye/Head............	---	---	2.9-3.4
Snout/Head..........	---	---	2.9-3.4
Interorb. W./Head......	---	---	2.8-3.1
Maxillary L./Head......	---	---	3.9-4.5
Caud. Ped./S.L.........	---	---	9.8-11.2
Pect. Fin L./S.L........	---	---	2.7-3.0
Pelvic Sp. L./S.L........	---	---	6.0-6.5
Predorsal L./S.L........	---	---	2.6-2.9
Prepelvic L./S.L........	---	---	2.4-2.7
Dorsal Sp. No. 1/S.L.....	---	---	16.3-21.6
Dorsal Sp. No. 2/S.L.....	---	---	11.7-14.7
Dorsal Sp. No. 3/S.L.....	---	---	7.8-10.1
Dorsal Sp. No. 4/S.L.....	---	---	6.6-8.4
Dorsal Sp. No. 5/S.L.....	---	---	6.6-8.2
Dorsal Sp. No. 6/S.L.....	---	---	6.8-7.8
Anal Sp. No. 1/S.L......	---	---	14.0-16.0
Anal Sp. No. 2/S.L......	---	---	8.3-10.4
Anal Sp. No. 3/S.L......	---	---	6.1-8.0
Anal Sp. No. 4/S.L.......	---	---	5.8-6.6
Anal Sp. No. 5/S.L......	---	---	5.3-6.2

spinous part of dorsal fin longer (about 2.4-2.5 in standard length than that of the soft portion (3.5-4.1 in standard length)).

Scale covering of dorsal spines low to moderate, starting at about third spine and gradually increasing in height to last spine, which is mostly covered; base of third anal spine, half of fourth, and three-fourths of fifth anal spine covered with scales.

Juveniles not known.

Color Pattern.—Eyeband absent. Color more or less uniformly brown in alcohol.

Remarks.—*Hemitaurichthys multispinus* can easily be mistaken for *H. thompsoni* at first glance. Upon closer scrutiny however, differences that can easily separate them become evident. The most obvious, aside from color, is the difference in dorsal and anal fin spine counts. Proportions as well separate them. Depth of *H. thompsoni* is 1.7-1.9, that of *H. multispinus* is 2.1-2.3. The pelvic fins are short in *multispinus* compared to the more elongate fins of *Hemitaurichthys thompsoni*. The steeper, more gibbous predorsal profile of *thompsoni* contrasts with the almost straight one of *multispinus*.

Pseudochaetodon nigrirostris from the Gulf of California. The head mask is quite distinctive. Photo by Ken Lucas at the Steinhart Aquarium.

Pseudochaetodon nigrirostris of about 6 inches length. Photo by Dr. Gerald R. Allen.

"El Barbero", *Pseudochaetodon nigrirostris,* in its natural habitat at Cabo San Lucas, Baja California. Photo by Alex Kerstitch at 30 feet.

This species is typically a *Hemitaurichthys* in all its characters except two, the many spined dorsal and anal fins and the relative shortness of the pectoral fin, neither deemed great enough to warrant erection of a new genus but enough to warrant a subgenus which is called:

Hemitaurichthys (*Acanthotaurichthys*) Burgess, **new subgenus** (type by monotypy and original designation: *H. multispinus* Burgess and Randall).

Distribution.—Known only from Pitcairn Island, Pacific Ocean.

Material Examined.—(11 spec.: 136-162 mm S.L.) BPBM 13225 (1: 145), Pitcairn Is. (holotype); BPBM 13222 (2: 138-159), Pitcairn Is. (paratypes); BPBM 13327 (8: 136-162), Pitcairn Is. (paratypes).

Genus HENIOCHUS Cuvier

Heniochus Cuvier, 1817: p. 335 (type-species *Chaetodon macrolepidotus* Linnaeus 1758, by subsequent designation of Jordan and Evermann 1917, p. 105). Non *Henioche* Hubner 1816, Lepidoptera.

Taurichthys Cuvier, 1829: p. 192 (type-species *Taurichthys varius* Cuvier 1829, by subsequent designation of Bleeker 1876, p. 304).

Diphreutes Cantor, 1849: p. 1141 (substitute name for *Heniochus* Cuvier, presumed preoccupied by *Henioche* Hubner, and therefore taking the same type-species, *Chaetodon macrolepidotus* Linnaeus 1758).

Diagnosis.—Lateral line complete; fourth dorsal fin spine elongate, at times filamentous and approaching or exceeding length of body; bony projection at supraorbital (in *Heniochus acuminatus* relatively small and appearing in only largest specimens); bony projection at nape (greatly developed in some species, poorly developed in others); D. XI-XII; usually brown or black bands on light background.

Description.—Dorsal outline elevated; predorsal contour various depending on extent of development of bony protuberances at supraorbital and nape; supraorbital projection in form of short spike to more complicated structures resembling antlers (these "horns" are absent in juveniles and may not appear in some species until animal reaches considerable size); bony projection at nape variously developed, almost absent in some cases (i.e. *H. acuminatus*) or highly developed in others (i.e. *H. varius*); lachrymal rounded, moderately long, completely scaled; preopercle approximately right-angled, angle slightly extended, smooth to lightly serrate; snout moderate, 2.4-4.5 in head length, pointed; teeth in spaced rows in jaws.

Lateral line complete, describing moderately high arc, descending to caudal peduncle where it becomes horizontal and ends at base of caudal fin; scales moderate; scaly portion of dorsal fin high, covering approximately three-fourths of each spine except elongated fourth spine; anal spine scales reaching to midpoint of third spine; soft portions of dorsal and anal fins with scales covering only half of fins.

First two dorsal spines very short, up to 32 in standard length for first, 28 for second; fourth spine very elongate, sometimes filamentous and longer than body length, up to 0.6 compared to standard length; succeeding spines decreasing in height posteriorly, last shorter than, equal to, or longer than (depending on species) next to last; soft portion of dorsal fin with anterior soft rays more elevated than posterior spines, creating a slightly notched fin; anal fin with second spine longest; soft portions of dorsal and anal fins rounded; pectoral fins moderate to long, 2.2-3.9 in standard length, pointed, reaching to middle soft rays of anal fin; pelvic fins rounded, spine flattened, reaching as far as anal spines; caudal fin truncate, edge rounded; base of spinous portion of dorsal fin equal to or slightly longer than base of soft portion.

D. XI-XII, 21-28; A. III, 17-19; L.l. scales 40-60; scales above L.l. 9-12; scales below L.l. 21-27.

Usually brown or black bands against a light background; dorsal and anal yellow or greenish; pelvic fins always deep brown or black; pectoral fins yellow or hyaline.

Widely distributed from the Hawaiian Islands to the eastern coast of Africa and Red Sea, and from Japan to Australia.

Extending from shallow water, including tide pools, to depths exceeding 200 meters.

Seven species are recognized, distinguished by the following key:

Key to the Species of the Genus Heniochus (Adults)

1. First dark band includes eyes as well as pectoral and pelvic fins . . . . . .
   . . . . *Heniochus chrysostomus*
   First dark band does not include eyes but does include pectoral and
   pelvic fins 2
2. Dark band includes pectoral and pelvic fins and first three spines of
   dorsal fin 3
   Dark band which includes pelvic and pectoral fins can include one or
   more dorsal fin spines but always posterior to first three 5
3. Dark band which passes through eye extends below to edge of interopercle; a black band encircles snout; a white streak crosses under
   chin . . . . *H. singularius*
   Dark band which passes through eye does not continue below it to
   interopercle; no black band encircling snout; no white streak
   crossing under chin (entire area below level of eye whitish) 4
4. Dark band which includes pectoral and pelvic fins just reaches posterior edge of orbit; dark band which crosses body from anal fin
   ends at base of elongate (fourth) dorsal spine; both body bands

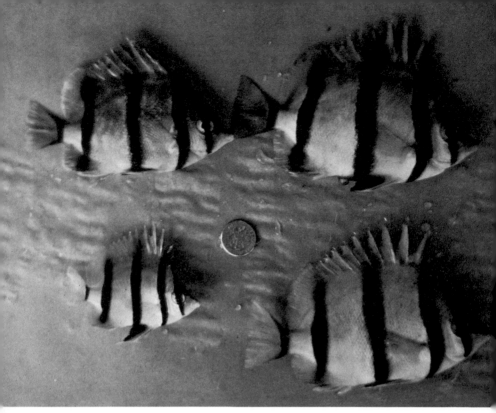

Amphichaetodon melbae from San Felix Island, juvenile and adults. Photo by Wayne J. Baldwin.

Amphichaetodon howensis subadults. North Rock, Lord Howe Island, at 100 feet. Photo by Walter Deas.

An adult pair of Amphichaetodon howensis from New Zealand. Photo by Wade Doak.

fading perceptibly upon nearing dorsal fin base; prominent "horns" present .... *H. intermedius*

Dark band which includes pectoral and pelvic fins separated from orbit by a white band; dark band which crosses body from anal fin continues into spinous dorsal fin at about sixth to ninth dorsal spines, not at base of fourth; both body bands continue into spinous dorsal fin and include some dorsal spines; horns only evident in larger specimens and never well developed ...... *H. acuminatus*

5. Dark band which includes pectoral and pelvic fins does not include elongate (fourth) dorsal fin spine .... *H. monoceros*

Dark band which includes pectoral and pelvic fins includes elongate (fourth) dorsal fin spine 6

6. Body bands merge at central part of body so that entire body from insertion of pelvic fins to end of anal fin is uniformly dark colored .... *H. varius*

Body bands merging only in upper part of body, leaving a white triangular space in mid-ventral portion of body ..... *H. pleurotaenia*

Heniochus acuminatus juveniles, one with yellow of dorsal fin adjacent to black band, the other with white intervening. Photo by Klaus Paysan.

Remarks.—Species contained in the genus *Heniochus* form a very closely allied group. They are all very similar in appearance and differ in assorted characters as mentioned in the key above. *Heniochus* is easily distinguishable from other genera of chaetodontids by the elongation of the fourth dorsal fin spine, color pattern, and by the extraordinary development of the projections on the nape and supraorbital area.

Cuvier (1829) erected the genus *Taurichthys* on the basis of the above mentioned projections as typified by *Heniochus varius* and other minor features. Although *H. varius* has extremely well developed projections, it does not diverge enough from other species of the genus to warrant placing it in a separate genus.

Cantor (1849) was of the opinion that *Henioche* Hubner 1816 (Lepidoptera) invalidated the genus *Heniochus* by virtue of preoccupation and proposed the new generic name *Diphreutes*. But according to the rules of nomenclature, *Henioche* Hubner does not preclude the use of *Heniochus* because there is a difference of one or more letters. *Heniochus* is therefore the valid name for the genus.

HENIOCHUS ACUMINATUS (Linnaeus)
Pennant coralfish
(Coachman; featherfin coralfish; threadbacked coralfish; wimpelfische)

Chaetodon acuminatus Linnaeus, 1758: p. 272 (type locality "Indiis").

Chaetodon macrolepidotus Linnaeus, 1758: p. 274 (type locality "Habitat in Indiis").

Chaetodon bifasciatus Shaw, 1803: p. 342 (type locality Indian Seas).

Heniochus acuminatus, Cuvier, 1831: p. 98 (on Linnaeus; new combination). Klausewitz, 1969: p. 59 (various localities).

Heniochus macrolepidotus, Cuvier, 1831: p. 93 (Mauritius, Pondicherry, Celebes, New Guinea). Ahl, 1923: p. 33.

Diphreutes macrolepidotus, Cantor, 1849: p. 114 (Penang, Singapore, Malay Peninsula; new combination).

Chaetodon mycteryzans Gray, 1854: p. 76 (type locality East Indies according to McCulloch, 1929).

Taurichthys macrolepidotus, Bleeker, 1878: p. 29, pl. 367, fig. 1 (East Indies, Philippines, New Guinea; new combination).

Heniochus diphreutes Jordan, 1903: p. 694, fig. 3 (type locality Nagasaki, Japan).

Diagnosis.—D. XI-XII, 22-26; A. III, 17-19; pectoral rays 16, occasionally 17; L.l. scales 48-57; fourth dorsal fin spine greatly elongate, filamen-

Juvenile *Amphichaetodon howensis* from Seal Rocks, New South Wales. Photo of a 40 mm S.L. individual by Rudie Kuiter.

Adult *Amphichaetodon howensis* photographed at a depth of 80 feet at Lord Howe Island by Dr. Gerald R. Allen.

Juvenile *Chaetodon falcifer*. Photo by Al Engasser.

Adult *Chaetodon falcifer* in natural habitat. Photo at Cabo San Lucas Canyon, Baja California by Alex Kerstitch at a depth of 250 feet.

Heniochus acuminatus (Linnaeus). 97 mm S.L. Nosse-Be, Madagascar.

Ratios	Standard Length (mm)		
	20-50(8)	51-80(2)	above 80(19)
Depth/S.L.	1.5-1.8	1.4	1.3-1.5
Head/S.L.	2.4-2.8	2.6-2.9	2.8-3.1
Eye/Head	2.3-3.2	2.7-2.9	2.8-3.6
Snout/Head	2.9-3.7	3.0-3.7	2.6-3.8
Interorb. W./Head.	2.9-3.9	2.9-3.4	2.7-3.4
Maxillary L./Head.	4.4-5.7	4.4	4.0-5.7
Caud. Ped./S.L.	7.9-9.5	8.3-8.4	7.9-8.8
Pect. Fin L./S.L.	2.6-3.4	2.7-3.5	2.8-3.9
Pelvic Sp. L./S.L.	3.1-4.6	3.4	3.5-4.4
Predorsal L./S.L.	1.8-2.3	1.9	1.7-2.2
Prepelvic L./S.L.	2.0-2.2	2.0-2.2	2.1-2.4
Dorsal Sp. No. 1/S.L.	12.8-18.1	13.5-14.8	14.1-24.5
Dorsal Sp. No. 2/S.L.	7.3-10.4	8.1-8.9	9.2-18.1
Dorsal Sp. No. 3/S.L.	3.6-4.6	3.9-4.6	4.5-8.7
Dorsal Sp. No. 4/S.L.	0.9-1.9	0.7-0.8	0.6-1.1
Dorsal Sp. No. 5/S.L.	4.3	2.9	3.3-4.3
Anal Sp. No. 1/S.L.	7.9-10.5	6.2-8.8	7.6-11.3
Anal Sp. No. 2/S.L.	4.2-5.3	3.8-4.4	4.0-5.8
Anal Sp. No. 3/S.L.	4.4-5.7	3.8-4.2	3.9-6.6

tous, often exceeding length of body; eyeband reduced to dark bar across interorbital, not extending below eye; first dark band includes first three dorsal spines, pectoral base, and pelvic fin base; horns small.

Close to *H. intermedius* of the Red Sea and Gulf of Aden, both having the fourth spine exceeding body length and similar color patterns. *Heniochus intermedius* differs from *H. acuminatus* in having well developed horns and having the first dark band more anterior, touching or even including posterior rim of orbit.

Meristics.—D. XI-XII, 22-26; A. III, 17-19; pectoral rays 16-17 (usually 16; two with 16/17, one with 16/15); L.l. scales 48-57; scales above L.l. 11-13; scales below L.l. 23-28; gill rakers 13-18.

Description.—Predorsal contour with slight convexity at nape and concavity at interorbital; usually a small prominence at nape, and a small stout spine at supraorbital in larger specimens; preopercle right-angled, edge smooth or lightly serrate; snout pointed, 2.6-3.8 in head length; teeth in about 10 spaced rows in each jaw; lachrymal moderate, rounded, no spines along edge; caudal peduncle depth greater than snout, which is greater than interorbital width, interorbital width greater than eye diameter in Indian Ocean specimens; caudal peduncle depth greater than interorbital width, which is greater than or equal to eye diameter, eye diameter greater than snout length in Pacific Ocean specimens.

Fourth dorsal spine greatly elongate, filamentous, often longer than body length (0.6-1.9 in standard length); succeeding spines shorter, the last spine slightly longer than next to last; soft dorsal fin rounded, first rays longer than last dorsal spines, creating a notched effect in the dorsal fin; second anal spine about equal to third, the first half or a little more than half of second; anal fin with rounded angle, posterior edge sloping back toward anterior part of caudal peduncle; base of spinous portion of dorsal fin equal to base of soft portion (both 2.4-2.6 in standard length); pectoral fins moderately long, 3.0-3.9 in standard length; pelvic fins moderately long, reaching to base of anal fin spines.

Peak of lateral line flattened, flat part reaching from level of seventh to last dorsal fin spines, posterior section descending parallel to dorsal fin base, becoming horizontal on caudal peduncle and ending at base of caudal fin; scale covering of dorsal spines reaches midpoint of third, lower portion of fourth (due to its size), and covering succeeding spines almost entirely; scales of anal fin reaching to halfway to three-fourths of third spine; scales cover to 80% of length of soft rays.

Juveniles similar to adults in form and color.

Color Pattern.—Dark bar crosses interorbital from one eye to the other, not continued below eye; snout with dark blotch from nostrils to lips, not reaching lower edge of lachrymal; first dark band connecting with one opposite across pelvic fin base and abdomen; posteriorly this band may or may not connect with dark anal spines; this latter dark area of spines may or may not connect with next body band around edge of anal fin; second band includes portion of fifth and sixth dorsal spines and most of seventh to ninth spines.

Chaetodon falcifer adult. Photo by Alex Kerstitch.

Chaetodon marcellae from Ghana. Photo by Roger Lubbock.

Chaetodon marcellae in natural habitat. Photo at the Cape Verde Islands by H. Debelius.

Heniochus acuminatus adult showing development of small horns, typical for this species. Photo by Walter Deas.

Remarks—*Heniochus acuminatus* is probably the commonest, most widely distributed, yet most complex of any of the species of the genus *Heniochus*.

There are indications that the widely distributed species has become differentiated in various parts of its range. My first indication of this was when I discovered that the juveniles examined from the Hawaiian Islands and Japan appeared to have transformed from the larval state at a larger size than those from Tahiti, Australia, and the Philippines (no information was available on the Indian Ocean specimens). The body bars were also found to be different distances apart when specimens from these geographic areas were compared. According to J. Allen (personal communication), who has followed up on this distinction between populations, there are two distianct species, *H. acuminatus*, characterized in part by having XI dorsal fin spines, and *H. diphreutes*, characterized in part by having XII dorsal fin spines. For convenience these forms will be referred to as the XI and XII spined forms. The XII spined form occupies scattered geographic localities, the XI spined form a more tropical Indo-Pacific distribution. According to my records the XI and XII spined forms co-exist in several localities: Hawaiian Islands, Japan, and Sri Lanka, and J. Allen (personal communication) informs me that southeast and southwest Australia and southeast Africa can be added to this pattern. Klausewitz (1969) adds the northern Red Sea to the list. One cannot avoid noticing that the common denominator for all these areas save one (Sri Lanka) is cooler water. The distribution of the XII spined form lies entirely north of 20° N latitude and entirely south of 20°S latitude. It remained to check the Sri Lanka collecting data to see that the XII spined specimens were taken from deep water trawl hauls—again cooler water.

But the species is still more complex. As a matter of course the tooth rows of a few individuals were checked during my examination of the specimens at various museums. I found that in the Pacific Ocean samples the XI spined forms had about 4-6 discrete rows of teeth; the XII spined forms had a bunch of anterior teeth composed of about 3-4 rows. To complicate matters, the Indian Ocean specimens I examined (XI spined forms from Sri Lanka) had 10 discrete rows of teeth.

A detailed analysis of the various populations including many specimens from each locality is needed before the problems of this complex species are unraveled.

Unfortunately, there was an error in the original description of *Chaetodon acuminatus* Linnaeus. The spinous dorsal fin count was given as three instead of the actual XI or XII. Many authors preferred to use *Heniochus macrolepidotus* instead of *H. acuminatus* for this reason. In the synonymy of *Chaetodon acuminatus* Linnaeus, however, was a reference to a figure in Linnaeus' *Mus. Ad. Frid.* (1754). The figure clearly showed more than three dorsal spines and was undoubtedly that of *H. acuminatus*. The error is usually explained by saying that the "1" of the number 13 was omitted in printing. Thirteen is too many spines for this species, but it certainly is closer to the true number than three. If *Heniochus acuminatus* turns out to be a complex of species the first problem would be to determine the identities of the various nominal species, *H. macrolepidotus*, *H. bifasciatus*, *H. mycteryzans*, and finally *H. diphreutes*.

In the Hawaiian Islands (a subtropical area with little coral) *Heniochus acuminatus* is a schooling species normally found in waters greater than 12 meters deep (to over 150 meters). Juveniles were commonly found in shallower water (3 meters or so) in the summer months. At Enewetak (a tropical atoll with an abundance of coral) a solitary adult was found in 2 meters of water associated with an isolated coral head only 2-3 meters in diameter. However, large schools of this same species were seen in the deepor parts of the lagoon, possibly feeding aggregations similar to those in Hawaii.

Chaetodon aculeatus in its natural habitat. The dark dorsal area blends in with the background disrupting the outline of the fish. Photo by Dr. P. Colin in the Bahamas.

Chaetodon aculeatus in an aquarium. The strong second anal spine is quite noticeable. Photo by Aaron Norman.

Chaetodon dichrous has an unusual pattern of dark and light, almost opposite that of *C. aculeatus.* Photo by Ken Jourdan.

The triangular dorsal fin is easily discernible in this *Chaetodon dichrous.* Photo by Ken Jourdan.

Heniochus acuminatus can be trapped and is found in fish markets in Malaya (J.S. Scott 1959), Thailand (Rofen 1963), Philippines, and Hawaii (personal observation). They are apparently not highly regarded as food, and the prices are quite low.

Distribution.—Widely distributed in the Pacific and Indian Oceans from the Hawaiian and Society Islands to Japan, Indonesia, and Australia. It crosses the Indian Ocean to the African coast as far south as Durban and extends north to the Red Sea.

Material Examined.—(29 spec.: 27-200 mm S.L.) HIMB (1: 115), Oahu, Hawaiian Islands; WEB (14: 45-108), Oahu, Hawaiian Islands; WEB night light stations (4: 27-46), Oahu, Hawaiian Islands; SU 7247 (1: 42), Nagasaki, Japan (type of *Heniochus diphreutes* Jordan); SOSC HA 67-18 (1: 53), Chagas Archipelago, Indian Ocean; SOSC 532 FCH 69-215 (1: 192), Colombo, Sri Lanka; Yasuda (Univ. of Tokyo) (1: 38), Japan; SOSC Anton Bruun Cr. I Sta. 28A (2: 175-200), Andaman Islands; SOSC HA 67-17 (3: 126-137), Diego Garcia Archipelago, Indian Ocean; Smith-Vaniz 69-81 (1: 158), Sri Lanka.

HENIOCHUS CHRYSOSTOMUS Cuvier
Threeband pennant coralfish

Heniochus chrysostomus Cuvier, 1831: p. 99 (type locality Tahiti; on Parkinson manuscript).

Heniochus melanistion Bleeker, 1854: p. 98 (type locality Banda, East Indies).

Heniochus drepanoides Thiolliere, 1857: p. 166 (type locality Woodlark Island, Solomon Islands).

Heniochus chrysostoma, Gunther, 1860: p. 41 (East Indian Archipelago (Otaheite?)).

Diphreutes chrysostomus, Bleeker, 1865: p. 180 (Ceram, East Indies; new combination).

Taurichthys chrysostomus, Bleeker, 1877: p. 29, pl. 366, fig. 2.

Heniochus permutatus (not of Cuvier), Jordan & Seale, 1906: p. 346 (Samoa). Herre, 1936: p. 233 (Philippine Islands). Weber & de Beaufort, 1936: p. 40. Woods *in* Schultz, et al, 1953: p. 576, pl. 49B (Marshall Islands).

Chaetodon teatae Curtiss, 1938: p. 118 (type locality Tahiti).

Taurichthys permutatus (not of Cuvier), Fowler, 1944: p. 172, fig. 13.

Diagnosis.—D. XI, I or XII, I (usually XI, I), 21-22; A. III, 17-18; pectoral rays 16; L.l. scales 57-61; anterior dark band extends from nape to ventral fins, including eyes, pectoral bases, and pelvic base.

Heniochus chrysostomus Cuvier. 90 mm S.L. Vanikoro, Solomon Islands.

| Ratios | Standard Length (mm) | | |
	20-50(6)	51-90(6)	above 90(8)
Depth/S.L.............	1.6-1.9	1.4-1.6	1.4-1.6
Head/S.L..............	2.6-2.9	2.8-3.0	2.8-3.2
Eye/Head	2.7-3.2	2.5-2.9	2.5-3.0
Snout/Head	2.7-2.9	3.1-3.9	3.1-3.9
Interorb. W./Head......	3.5-4.0	3.0-3.5	2.5-3.1
Maxillary L./Head......	4.2-5.2	4.9-5.9	5.0-5.7
Caud. Ped./S.L.........	9.8-10.3	8.7-9.4	8.8-9.6
Pect. Fin L./S.L........	2.5-2.6	2.5-2.7	2.5-2.8
Pelvic Sp. L./S.L........	3.5-4.8	3.8-4.3	4.0-4.8
Predorsal L./S.L........	2.2-2.5	2.0-2.1	1.9-2.1
Prepelvic L./S.L........	2.2-2.4	2.3-2.4	2.3-2.5
Dorsal Sp. No. 1/S.L.....	15.0-19.0	10.9-15.1	15.4-17.7
Dorsal Sp. No. 2/S.L.....	8.5-9.5	9.0-11.6	11.6-15.5
Dorsal Sp. No. 3/S.L.....	4.3-5.0	4.3-5.6	5.8-7.4
Dorsal Sp. No. 4/S.L.....	0.9-1.0	1.3-1.4	1.3-2.4
Anal Sp. No. 1/S.L......	7.5-10.2	6.6-7.7	7.1-13.3
Anal Sp. No. 2/S.L......	4.5-6.8	3.8-4.5	4.2-4.9
Anal Sp. No. 3/S.L......	3.8-4.7	3.6-4.2	4.1-5.1

Chaetodon aya is rarely photographed at all and apparently never in its natural habitat. The two photographs here are perhaps among the few to show this species in its natural colors. Photos by Dr. George C. Miller.

Chaetodon guyanensis is even rarer in photographs. Here the pattern can be compared with that of its closest relative, *C. aya* (opposite). Photos by Dan Halliday.

Meristics.—D. XI, I (two with XII, I), 21-22; A. III, 17-18; pectoral fin 16; L.l. scales 57-61; scales above L.l. 11-12; scales below L.l. 23-25; gill rakers 22-23 (-26).

Description.—Predorsal contour with hump at nape and small to moderate supraorbital process; preopercle right-angled, smooth to moderately serrate, sometimes spiny at angle; snout pointed, 3.1-3.9 in head length; teeth in about 11 rows in each jaw, spaced; lachrymal smooth, rounded, short; eye diameter greater than interorbital width, which is greater than caudal peduncle depth; caudal peduncle depth greater than snout length.

Fourth dorsal fin spine elongate, 1.3-2.4 in standard length; first two dorsal spines small, last spine slightly longer than penultimate spine; soft portion of dorsal fin rounded, first rays longer than last spines, giving fin a notched appearance; second and third anal fin spines about equal, first approximately half second; second anal spine more robust than third; anal fin with rounded angle, posterior edge approximately vertical or sloping back toward anterior edge of caudal peduncle; base of spinous portion of dorsal fin slightly longer (2.2-2.3 in S.L.) than that of soft portion (2.7-2.9 in S.L.); pectoral fins moderate, 2.5-2.8 in S.L.; pelvic fins long, reaching base of second anal fin spine.

Lateral line describing moderately high arc across body; scales at base of dorsal fin spines cover about three-fourths of the shorter spines and about one-third of the elongate fourth spine; scales of anal spines reaching just over half length of third spine.

Juveniles without hump at nape; horns appear at about 70 mm S.L.; predorsal concave; fourth dorsal spine proportionally longer than that of adult (0.9-1.0 in S.L.); anal fin more angular and more elongate; snout longer, 2.7-2.9 in head length as compared to 3.1-3.9 in adults.

Color Pattern.—Median stripe on interorbital originates at nape or slightly above level of eyes and ends at tip of upper lip; anterior band continuous across nape and abdomen; pelvic fins black.

Color of juvenile specimens similar, but the anterior and second bands are closer together at the dorsal fin; a black ocellated (although light ring may be obscure) spot in anal fin, included in the dark brown of the band (and sometimes obscured by it) from the eighth to eleventh dorsal fin rays.

According to Steindachner (1893) a yellow ring surrounds the black spot in the anal fin of juveniles.

Remarks.—*Heniochus chrysostomus* and *H. permutatus* are two names which have been used interchangeably since they were both described by Cuvier in 1831. *Heniochus permutatus* was poorly described, reference being made to a reverse of the black and white bands from the pattern of *H. macrolepidotus* (= *H. acuminatus*). Bauchot (1963) discussed the situation and concluded that the specimen described was in reality *H. monoceros*. She goes on to say, "Puisque le specimen du British, 'type-presume' de *Heniochus permutatus*, est en realite un *H. monoceros*, il serait preferable comme l'a fait Ahl (1923) de rehabiliter l'espece *H. chrysostomus* et

*Heniochus
chrysostomus*
juvenile, 41 mm S.L.,
Tahiti, Society Islands.

de designer un neotype." Therefore, according to Ahl and Bauchot the name of this species is *H. chrysostomus.*

The characteristic horns appear at about 70 to 80 mm standard length. They become developed to some extent but never equal those of *H. varius.* Either a single spike, a compound spike, or two or three individual spikes may be evident.

This species seems restricted to the Pacific Ocean, although there are some questionable records from Madras, India and Madagascar.

This is the only species of *Heniochus* known that has a difference in the juvenile coloration. It is difficult to theorize about the possible usefulness of the anal fin spot, especially since it is included in a dark stripe and may not be easily visible. In life, however, it sometimes is ocellated with a white or yellow ring, thus providing a contrast with the background. It is also interesting to note that the eye in this species is included in a dark background.

Heniochus chrysostomus is usually found in pairs on the reef, secluded under ledges or in caves. Harry (1953) observed them swimming upside down on the ceiling of caves or overhanging coral shelves. Randall (1953) found the young in tide pools on the outer reef flat in the Gilbert Islands. Harry (1953) reports this species always in schools, seldom swimming individually.

239

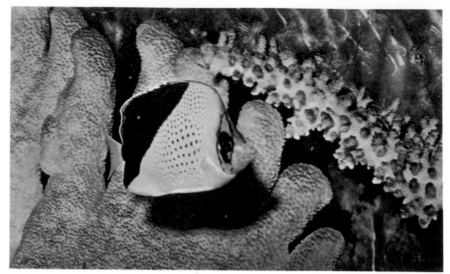

Chaetodon tinkeri with dorsal fin folded. Photo by Dr. Herbert R. Axelrod.

Chaetodon tinkeri with dorsal fin expanded in threat posture. Photo by Dr. D. Terver, Nancy Aquarium, France.

Chaetodon tinkeri does well in aquaria, perhaps because in its deep water habitat it is less dependent upon living coral for sustenance. Photo by Dr. Herbert R. Axelrod.

Chaetodon tinkeri caught at a depth of 180 feet in the Hawaiian Islands. Photographed at Steinhart Aquarium by Ken Lucas.

Distribution.—Islands of the Pacific Ocean with the exception of the Hawaiian Islands; Ryukyu Islands through East Indies to Queensland, Australia; Melanesia. Day (1878) reported this species from Madras, India, but it may have been a case of misidentification.

Material Examined.—(20 spec.: 36-124 mm S.L.) NMFS-H (1: 87), Samoa; BPBM 6057 (3: 102-116), Tahiti; CAS 37736 (4: 82-124), Bora Bora, Society Islands; CAS 37737 (2: 73-82), Yap I., Western Caroline Islands; CAS 37738 (1: 45), Iwayama Bay, Palau Islands; CAS 37739 (1: 40), Ifaluk, Caroline Islands; AMS IB. 8170 (1: 36), Heron Islands, Queensland; Yasuda (Univ. of Tokyo) (1: 47), Japan; SOSC te Vega-308 (2: 58-77), Tonga Islands; SOSC Te Vega-247 (2: 114-116), Bougainville, Solomon Islands; SIO 61-83-32A (2: 40-41), Tahiti.

HENIOCHUS INTERMEDIUS Steindachner
Red Sea bannerfish

Heniochus intermedius Steindachner, 1893: p. 222, pl. 2, fig. 2 (type locality Red Sea at Suez).

Heniochus macrolepidotus (not of Linnaeus), Ruppell, 1835: p. 36 (Red Sea). Klunzinger, 1870: p. 784 (Red Sea). Klunzinger, 1884: p. 58, pl. 8, fig. 3 (Red Sea). Boulenger, 1887: p. 657 (Red Sea). Regan, 1905: p. 330 (Red Sea). Zugmeyer, 1913: p. 11 (Red Sea).

Heniochus acuminatus (not of Linnaeus), Baschieri-Salvatore, 1954: p. 97, pl. 5, fig.·2 (Red Sea).

Diagnosis.—D. XI, 25-26; A. III, 17-18; anal rays 15 (one with 16); L.l. scales 48-53; anterior dark band extends from nape below first dorsal spines, close behind eye and touching posterior rim of orbit, across posterior part of operculum, pectoral base to pelvic base.

Close to *Heniochus acuminatus*, but separable from that species by the position of the first bar. In *H. intermedius* it passes close to and even touches the posterior rium of the orbit, while in *H. acuminatus* it passes the orbit at a short distance, the white clearly evident in this space. The origin of the second bar is more anterior in *H. intermedius* (includes the fourth spine base) and terminates further back on the anal fin, including only the last few spines. The notched eye tubercles are outwardly directed as in *H. chrysostomus*, better developed and developing earlier in *H. intermedius* than in *H. acuminatus*.

Meristics.—D. XI, 25-26; A. III, 17-18; pectoral rays 15 (one with 16); L.l. scales 48-53; L.l. pores 46-52; scales above L.l. 9-10; scales below L.l. 21-24; gill rakers 14-16.

Description.—Predorsal contour concave, with slight hump at nape; strong bilobed horns developing early over supraorbital; preopercle right-angled, lightly serrate, a slight extension at the angle; snout pointed, 3.2-3.5 in head length; teeth in about 7-9 rows in each jaw; caudal

Heniochus intermedius Steindachner. 120 mm S.L. Red Sea.

Ratios	20-50(1)	Standard Length (mm) 51-90	above 90(3)
Depth/S.L..............	1.4	---	1.3-1.4
Head/S.L..............	2.6	---	2.9-3.0
Eye/Head	2.8	..	2.8-2.9
Snout/Head	3.0	---	3.2-3.5
Interorb. W./Head......	4.1	---	3.1-3.5
Maxillary L./Head......	4.5	---	3.9-5.0
Caud. Ped./S.L.........	8.5	---	8.1-8.3
Pect. Fin L./S.L........	2.8	---	3.1-3.7
Pelvic Sp. L./S.L........	3.6	---	4.4-4.7
Predorsal L./S.L........	2.0	---	1.7-1.8
Prepelvic L./S.L........	2.2	---	2.1-2.2
Dorsal Sp. No. 1/S.L.....	11.0	---	12.0-13.2
Dorsal Sp. No. 2/S.L.....	6.2	---	7.4-9.3
Dorsal Sp. No. 3/S.L.....	3.5	---	4.1-5.0
Dorsal Sp. No. 4/S.L.....	0.69	---	0.9-1.5
Anal Sp. No. 1/S.L......	6.1	---	7.1-7.9
Anal Sp. No. 2/S.L......	3.6	---	4.6-4.9
Anal Sp. No. 3/S.L......	3.4	---	4.2-4.7

Chaetodon burgessi seems to share color pattern elements with both *C. tinkeri* from Hawaii and *C. mitratus* from the Indian Ocean. Photo by Roger Lubbock.

Chaetodon declevis is very close to *C. tinkeri* but can be distinguished from that species by color. Photo by Dr. John E. Randall.

Above and below. Adult and juvenile *Chaetodon mitratus*. Although described from specimens in the Western Indian Ocean these specimens were collected in the Eastern Indian Ocean. Photos by Dr. Wm. Smith-Vaniz.

Heniochus intermedius, juvenile, 45.8 mm S.L. Gold Mohur Bay.

peduncle depth greater than eye diameter, which is greater than inter-orbital width; interorbital width greater than snout length.

Fourth dorsal fin spine greatly elongate, filamentous, 0.9-1.5 in standard length, first two spines relatively short, last equal to or slightly longer than penultimate; soft dorsal fin rounded, first rays longer than last dorsal spines, giving the fin a slight notch at the juncture; anal spines strong, second strongest, third spine equal to or slightly longer than second (but more slender); soft portion of anal fin with a blunt angle, posterior edge straight; base of spinous portion of dorsal fin shorter (2.6 in S.L.) than that of soft portion (2.7 in S.L.); pectoral fins moderate (3.7 in S.L.); pelvic fins long, reaching base of anal fin spines; caudal fin truncate.

Lateral line describing a moderately high arc, its peak somewhat flattened at level of eighth spine to third or fourth soft ray of dorsal fin; scales on dorsal spines covering about half of second spine, somewhat less than half of third, a third or less of fourth, and most of remaining spines; scales covering about three-fourths of third spine of anal fin.

Juveniles similar to adults but without supraorbital process; fourth dorsal spine filamentous, elongate, 0.7 in S.L.; color pattern similar to adult.

Color Pattern.—Snout, interorbital area, and nape all dark, merging with first bar; area around nostrils light; some areas around nape lighter; ventral edge of body dark to past anus and including anal fin spines; posterior rays of anal fin dark or entire fin light colored; second dark bar originating at base of sixth through last dorsal fin spine bases.

Color of juvenile similar to adult.

Remarks.—The confusion with *Heniochus acuminatus* is understandable, as these two species are very similar. They can be separated as described under the diagnosis section and in the key. Most of the Red Sea records for *Heniochus acuminatus* can be ascribed to this species. Dr. W. Klausewitz has a record for *H. acuminatus* in the Red Sea, so the two species occur sympatrically in that area.

These two species have the longest fourth dorsal fin spine of the genus *Heniochus*. It is usually longer than the standard length in adult animals. *Heniochus intermedius* also has a well developed supraorbital spine or horn, much better developed and appearing earlier in life than in *H. acuminatus*.

Heniochus intermedius is restricted to the Red Sea. It is apparently abundant below the reef slope and in deeper rock formations. It is found along the entire coast of coral and is common in both the northern and southern sectors (Baschieri-Salvatore 1954).

Normally this species is found in pairs or as isolated individuals and rarely as small groups. The largest seen was 153 mm standard length (Baschieri-Salvatore 1954).

Distribution.—Endemic to the Red Sea and Gulf of Aden.

Material Examined.—(4 spec.: 47-123 mm S.L.) BPBM uncatalogued (2: 111-120), Massaua, Red Sea (gift of Dr. W. Klausewitz to the B.P. Bishop Museum); SOSC Anton Bruun Sta. FT-26 (1: 47), Aden; BPBM 10512 (1: 123), Red Sea.

HENIOCHUS MONOCEROS Cuvier
Masked bannerfish
(Unicorn pennant coralfish)

Heniochus permutatus Cuvier, 1831: p. 99 (no locality; from Broussonet manuscript).

Heniochus monoceros Cuvier, 1831: p. 100, pl. 176 (type locality Mauritius).

Heniochus macrolepidotus (not of Linnaeus), Brevoort, 1856: p. 267 (Seas of Japan; juvenile).

Taurichthys monoceros, Bleeker, 1877: p. 28, pl. 365, fig. 3 (new combination). Fowler, 1953: p. 51, fig. 106 (China, Ryukyu Islands).

Heniochus singularius (not of Smith & Radcliffe), Watanabe, 1949: p. 38 (Zamami, Ryukyu Islands).

Diagnosis.—D. XII, 24-27 (usually 25); A. III, (17) 18-19; pectoral rays (16) 17; L.l. scales 58-64; body bar which includes pectoral base narrows above lateral line and includes only fifth and sixth dorsal spines; face from anterior dorsal fin spines to chin dark.

Chaetodon modestus juvenile (about 30 mm S.L.). Photo by Dr. Warren E. Burgess.

Opposite: *Chaetodon modestus* adult. Photo by Dr. Fujio Yasuda.

Chaetodon jayakari is the least well known of this species group. Photo by Dr. Loren P. Woods.

Heniochus monoceros Cuvier. 110 mm S.L. Enewetak, Marshall Islands.

Ratios	Standard Length (mm)		
	20-40(1)	41-80(12)	81 and above (6)
Depth/S.L.............	1.7	1.5-1.7	1.4-1.6
Head/S.L.............	2.5	2.6-2.8	2.7-3.1
Eye/Head.............	3.0	2.5-2.9	2.8-3.2
Snout/Head...........	3.3	2.9-3.6	3.1-4.5
Interorb. W./Head......	3.9	3.5-3.8	3.4-3.6
Maxillary L./Head......	5.4	4.1-5.8	4.2-4.8
Caud. Ped./S.L........	9.6	8.6-9.5	8.2-9.1
Pect. Fin L./S.L........	2.9	2.7-3.0	2.9-3.4
Pelvic Sp. L./S.L........	3.9	3.4-4.2	4.1-4.6
Predorsal L./S.L........	1.8	1.7-1.9	1.8-1.9
Prepelvic L./S.L........	2.1	2.2-2.5	2.3-2.6
Dorsal Sp. No. 1/S.L....	26.7	13.0-26.2	17.5-22.8
Dorsal Sp. No. 2/S.L....	13.3	9.4-14.3	11.4-14.0
Dorsal Sp. No. 3/S.L....	6.0	4.4-6.9	5.8-8.0
Dorsal Sp. No. 4/S.L....	1.2	1.2-2.3	1.5-1.7
Anal Sp. No. 1/S.L......	8.1	7.2-9.4	8.3-11.7
Anal Sp. No. 2/S.L......	4.2	3.5-4.6	4.7-5.4
Anal Sp. No. 3/S.L......	3.7	3.2-3.9	3.8-4.8

Meristics.—D. XII, 24-27 (usually 25); A. III, 18-19 (one with 17); pectoral rays 17 (four with a 17/16 combination, one with 16/16); L.l. scales 58-64; L.l. pores 55-61; scales above L.l. 9-10; scales below L.l. 23-26; gill rakers 13-19.

Description.—Predorsal contour modified by a strong, projecting hump at nape; horn present in larger specimens at supraorbital, usually simple, short, but strong; preopercle right-angled, angle rounded, slightly serrate to smooth; snout 3.1-4.5 in head; teeth in 8-9 rows in each jaw; eye diameter greater than snout length, which is greater than or equal to depth of caudal peduncle; caudal peduncle depth greater than interorbital width.

Fourth dorsal fin spine long, flexible, 1.5-1.6 in standard length, succeeding spines gradually shorter, the last two approximately equal; first rays of soft dorsal longer than last spine but not enough to create a noticeable notch; first anal spine about half length of second which is slightly shorter than third; soft portion of anal fin with blunt angle, the posterior edge angling back toward anterior edge of caudal peduncle; base of spinous portion of dorsal fin longer (2.6-2.7 in standard length) than soft portion (2.7-3.3 in S.L.); pelvic fins moderate, reaching base of first anal fin spine; caudal fin truncate.

Lateral line describing moderately high arc, flattened at about seventh to last dorsal fin spine bases; scale covering of dorsal spines extending to cover over half of third, a moderate portion of elongate fourth, and at least three-fourths of succeeding spines; anal spines covered by scales to one-third to half of second and almost all of third.

Juveniles similar to adults but without predorsal prominences; fourth dorsal fin spine proportionately longer than that of adult.

Color Pattern.—Face and nape various shades of brown; eyeband evident, crossing interorbital and continuing below eye (this area may extend upward and backward from the posterior corner of the orbit); snout stripe including part of upper lip and reaching to interorbital space; first body bar from fifth to seventh dorsal fin spines; posterior bar starts from below last spines of dorsal fin; scales with centers lighter than edges, giving appearance of horizontal dotted lines on body.

Juvenile color pattern very much like that of the adult, easily recognizable as *Heniochus monoceros*.

Remarks.—It is this species that Bauchot reports (1963) was seen by Cuvier and described under the name *Heniochus permutatus*. The description by Cuvier is very incomplete, and positive identification cannot be made. I have seen the specimens referred to in the British Museum and agree with Bauchot's identification.

Heniochus monoceros is very close to *H. singularius*, both having similar development of the nape area and reasonably similar color patterns. The origin of the first body bar in *H. monoceros*, however, is behind the fourth dorsal spine whereas that of *H. singularius* is anterior to it. The white areas around the snout of *H. singularius* are helpful in iden-

Chaetodon nippon adult. Photographed by Dr. Gerald R. Allen at Miyake Jima, Japan at 10 meters depth.

Chaetodon nippon juvenile. Photo by Dr. Fujio Yasuda.

Above and Below: *Chaetodon excelsa* from the Hawaiian Islands. This species occurs in very deep water and is rarely seen alive. Photo above by Dr. John E. Randall; Photo below by Dr. Thomas Clark.

Heniochus monoceros juvenile. 52 mm S.L. Philippine Islands.

tification, but the corresponding areas in *H. monoceros*, although brownish, are also lighter than the surrounding areas.

This species is never reported as common, although it occupies a wide range.

The listing of *Loa excelsa* (= *Chaetodon excelsa*) in the synonymy of this species by Weber & de Beaufort (1936) certainly is incorrect. Authors (i.e. Klausewitz, 1969) following this synonymy have attributed *Heniochus monoceros* as occurring at the Hawaiian Islands. Specimens of only one species of *Heniochus*, *H. acuminatus*, are presently available from the Hawaiian Islands. Sight records from two sources have been made of a possible new species of *Heniochus*. They are deep water (about 200 meters) observations, but no specimens or clear photographs have been obtained.

A 132 mm specimen with a prominent nape protuberance as well as horns has been reported from Minecoy Island (Indian Ocean) by Jones and Kumaran (1967).

Brevoort (1856) reported on a specimen, although very small, with the head pattern and first band position similar to that of *Heniochus monoceros*. Brevoort noted the entire snout as black, but the illustration shows a larger proportion of black as in *H. monoceros*.

Distribution.—Widespread throughout the Pacific and Indian Oceans. It occurs from the Marshall, Marianas, and Caroline Islands, the Society Islands across the Pacific Ocean to Indonesia, north to China, and south to New Guinea. It crosses the Indian Ocean to the Maldives, Mauritius, Aldabra, and to the coast of Africa. It has not been reported from the Hawaiian Islands or the Red Sea.

Material Examined.—(19 spec.: 37-139 mm S.L.) CAS 37651, (2: 67-

81), Palau Islands; CAS 37652 (1: 70), Marianas Islands; CAS 37653 (1: 50), Yap I., Western Caroline Islands; CAS 37654 (1: 37), Palau Islands; CAS 37655 (3: 43-57) Palau Islands; CAS 37656, (1: 114), Yap I., Western Caroline Islands; CAS 37700 (1: 111), Cook Islands; CAS 37657 (1: 90), Yap I., Western Caroline Islands; CAS 37658, (1: 76), Yap I., Western Caroline Islands; CAS 37659 (1: 79), Yap I., Western Caroline Islands; CAS 37660 (1: 65), Palau Islands; CAS 37661 (1: 49), Yap I., Western Caroline Islands; EMBL (1: 111), Eniwetok, Marshall Islands; Yasuda (Univ. of Tokyo) (1: 52), Japan; SOSC HA 67-62 (1: 139), Aldabra Atoll, Indian Ocean; CAS 37701 (1: 43), Koror I., Palau Islands.

HENIOCHUS SINGULARIUS Smith & Radcliffe
Philippine pennant coralfish
(Singular bannerfish)

Heniochus singularius Smith & Radcliffe, 1911: p. 321, fig. 2 (type locality Alibijaban Island, Ragay Gulf, Luzon, Philippines).

Heniochus monoceros, (not of Cuvier) Delsman & Hardenberg, 1934: (see col. pl. 371).

Taurichthys singularius, Fowler, 1953: p. 52, fig. 107 (China, Suowan, Formosa; new combination).

Heniochus singularius Smith & Radcliffe. 133 mm S.L. Yap Island.

Subadult *Chaetodon argentatus*. Photo by Dr. Fujio Yasuda.

Chaetodon argentatus, 80 mm S.L., from Onna, Okinawa. Photo by Dr. John E. Randall.

When swimming the dorsal fin is folded back and the propulsion is mainly furnished by the posterior section of the body and the caudal fin. Photo by M. Goto, Marine Life Documents.

Although similar to the other species of the subgenus, *Chaetodon argentatus* lacks the yellow color encountered there. Photo by K.H. Choo.

		Standard Length (mm)	
Ratios	20-50	51-80	above 80(9)
Depth/S.L.............	1.6	---	1.5-1.6
Head/S.L..............	2.8	---	3.3-3.5
Eye/Head	2.5	---	3.2-3.9
Snout/Head	3.2	---	2.5-4.3
Interorb. W./Head......	3.3	---	3.0-3.2
Maxillary/Head	5.1	---	4.7-8.3
Caud. Ped./S.L.........	9.3	---	8.3-9.5
Pect. Fin./S.L..........	2.7	---	3.2-3.8
Pelvic Spine/S.L........	3.4	---	4.0-5.0
Predorsal L./S.L........	2.0	---	1.9-2.1
Prepelvic L./S.L........	2.5	---	2.4-2.6
Dorsal Sp. No. 1/S.L.....	12.3	---	17.0-32.5
Dorsal Sp. No. 2/S.L.....	7.6	---	11.7-28.3
Dorsal Sp. No. 3/S.L.....	3.8	---	7.8-11.7
Dorsal Sp. No. 4/S.L.....	2.0	---	1.7-2.4
Anal Sp. No. 1/S.L......	6.4	---	9.9-13.2
Anal Sp. No. 2/S.L......	3.4	---	4.9-6.2
Anal Sp. No. 3/S.L......	3.3	---	4.4-8.7

Diagnosis.—D. XI-XII, 25-27 (usually 25); A. III, 17-18; pectoral rays 17 (occasionally 16 or 16/17); L.l. scales 53-64; anterior dark body bar covers posterior edge of operculum; eyeband present, extending to lower edge of interopercle, a white streak forming anterior border; anterior body bar including first three dorsal fin spines; most of anal fin dark colored.

Meristics.—D. XI-XII, 25-27 (usually 25); A. III, 17-18; pectoral rays 17 (occasionally 16 or 17/16); L.l. scales 53-64; L.l. pores 51-60; scales above L.l. 10-11 (one with 12); scales below L.l. 24-28; gill rakers 13-14.

Description.—Predorsal contour modified by a strong projecting bump at nape; horns present in adult specimens and usually simple, short spikes projecting from the supraorbital; preopercle right-angled, smooth or lightly serrate; snout 2.5-4.3 in head length; lips fleshy, teeth almost hidden (similar to teeth of *Coradion*); caudal peduncle depth greater than snout length, which is greater than interorbital width; interorbital width greater than eye diameter.

Fourth dorsal spine elongate, 1.7-2.4 in standard length; last dorsal fin spine equal to or slightly longer than next to last spine; first few dorsal fin rays about equal to last dorsal fin spines so no notch evident; first anal spine about half length of second, which is subequal to the third; soft part of anal fin angled, sometimes pointed, the posterior edge slanting anteriorly; base of spinous part of dorsal fin shorter (2.4-2.9 in S.L.) than that of soft portion (2.4-2.6 in S.L.); pectoral fins long, 3.2-3.8 in standard length; pelvic fins short, reaching only to area immediately preceding anus; caudal fin truncate.

Lateral line with flattened peak extending from seventh to last dorsal fin spine; dorsal spine scale covering high, to half of third spine, base or more of fourth, and most of succeeding spines; anal spine covering reaches to midpoint of third spine.

Juveniles similar to adults. Nape gibbous instead of bump being present.

Color Pattern.—Snout stripe present, broad, brownish (including lips except extreme tip of lips white); white band before eyeband continuous around snout and reaches bony projections over eyes; eyebands connected ventrally; light area at mid-body originating at about fifth to seventh dorsal fin spines; light centers to scales giving appearance of horizontal lines, though in light area of body some have dark centers, a reverse color.

Juvenile pattern similar to that of adults.

Remarks.—Very similar to *Heniochus monoceros*. *Heniochus singularius* is limited in distribution, occurring in the East Indies and nearby island groups. It is a poorly known species and may eventually be discovered in other areas.

Several authors (Herre & Montalban, 1927; Weber & de Beaufort, 1936; and Klausewitz, 1969) cite closeness to *Heniochus varius*. The projections (horns) on the snout are similar to *H. varius* and the color approaches it, but the similarity between this species and *H. monoceros* is

Heniochus singularius juvenile, 50 mm S.L. Yap Island.

Chaetodon xanthurus is relatively common in the Philippine Islands. Photo by Dr. Fujio Yasuda.

The pattern of *Chaetodon xanthurus* resembles its close relatives on the following pages except it has a crosshatching that they lack. Photo by K.H. Choo.

Chaetodon xanthurus, natural habitat. Photo by M. Goto, Marine Life Documents.

Juvenile *Chaetodon xanthurus.* Photo by F. Earl Kennedy.

Adult *Chaetodon xanthurus.* Photo by Dr. D. Terver, Nancy Aquarium, France.

even more striking. The counts seems to support this stand, *H. monoceros* and *H. singularius* having composite counts of D. XII, 24-27; anal III, 17-19; pectoral 17 (16); whereas *H. varius* has D. XI, 22-24; anal III, 17-18; pectoral 14.

Distribution.—Indonesia, Ryukyu Islands to the Philippine Islands and Java. This species extends into the Indian Ocean to the Nicobar Islands and into the Caroline Islands of the Pacific Ocean.

Material Examined.—(10 spec.: 49-186 mm S.L.) USNM 182418-182423 (6: 139-183), Philippine Islands; USNM 67354 (1: 186), Philippine Islands (holotype); CAS 37702 (1: 133), Yap I., Western Caroline Islands; CAS 37703 (1: 49), Yap I., Western Caroline Islands; SU 13519 (1: 186), Philippine Islands.

HENIOCHUS PLEUROTAENIA Ahl
Indian Ocean bannerfish

Heniochus varius, (not of Cuvier) Kner, 1865: p. 103 (no locality).

Heniochus pleurotaenia Ahl, 1923: p. 24 (type locality Padang).

Diagnosis.—D. X, I, 23-25; A. III, 17-18; pectoral rays (14) 15; L.l. 56-59; light colored triangular area from abdomen to just above middle of body, not reaching above lateral line to dorsal fin base.

Very closely related to *Heniochus varius* but distinguishable by color pattern. *Heniochus pleurotaenia* has the above-mentioned light body area

Heniochus pleurotaenia Ahl. 74 mm S.L. Sri Lanka.

Ratios	Standard Length (mm)		
	20-59(1)	60-89(3)	above 89(1)
Depth/S.L.	1.6	1.4-1.6	1.4
Head/S.L.	2.8	2.9-3.1	3.0
Eye/Head	2.6	2.6-2.7	2.8
Snout/Head	2.8	2.7-3.2	2.7
Interob. W./Head.	3.8	3.6-3.8	.2
Maxillary/Head	5.2	4.8-5.8	4.5
Caud. Ped./S.L.	8.9	8.4-9.1	9.0
Pect. Fin/S.L.	2.2	2.3-2.7	2.6
Pelvic Spine/S.L.	4.3	4.2-4.4	4.6
Predorsal L./S.L.	2.0	1.9-2.0	1.8
Prepelvic L./S.L.	2.4	2.5	2.5
Dorsal Sp. No. 1/S.L.	15.2	16.5-19.0	17.0
Dorsal Sp. No. 2/S.L.	8.5	8.4-12.7	9.4
Dorsal Sp. No. 3/S.L.	4-2	4.9-6.1	5.6
Dorsal Sp. No. 4/S.L.	1.7	2.0-2.1	2.3
Anal Sp. No. 1/S.L.	7.5	7.9-9.5	7.1
Anal Sp. No. 2/S.L.	3.9	3.9-4.1	4.1
Anal Sp. No. 3/S.L.	3.4	3.8-4.0	4.1

whereas *H. varius* has the body center very dark-colored.

Meristics.—D. X, I, 23-25; A. III, 17-18; pectoral rays 15 (two with 15/14); L.l. scales 55-59; L.l. pores 54-59; scales above L.l. 12-13; scales below L.l. 24-27; gill rakers 15-24.

Description.—Predorsal contour with a prominent bony protuberance at nape and a strong horn above each orbit; preopercle with slight extension of angle, edge serrate; snout about 2.7 in head length; three to four rows of teeth in each jaw; eye diameter greater than snout length, which is greater than depth of caudal peduncle; caudal peduncle greater than interorbital width.

Fourth dorsal fin spine elongate, about 2.3 in standard length; last dorsal spine slightly longer than penultimate; first few dorsal fin soft rays longer than last spines, the fin therefore slightly notched; soft anal fin with blunt angle; second anal fin slightly longer than third; base of spinous portion of dorsal fin longer (2.5-2.6 in S.L.) than that of soft portion (2.6-2.9 in S.L.); pectoral fin normal to slightly elongate; pelvic fins long, reaching to base of anal spines.

Lateral line as in other species of *Heniochus*; scale covering of dorsal spines high, reaching to two-thirds or three-fourths of fifth dorsal spine; scales cover about three-fourths of third anal spine.

Juveniles with proportionately longer fourth dorsal spine, no horns, and less of a prominence on nape.

Chaetodon mertensii juvenile and adult showing very little change in color pattern. Photo by Dr. Warren E. Burgess.

Chaetodon mertensii from Australia (Sydney) was described there under the name *C. dixoni*. Photo by Rudie Kuiter.

Chaetodon mertensii in its natural habitat. The "mate" of the pair should not be far away. Photo by Dwayne Reed in Fiji.

Heniochus pleurotaenia 43.2 mm S.L. Djakarta, Java.

Color Pattern.—Snout and interorbital area to origin of dorsal fin dark colored; dark body color starts from about fourth dorsal spine; chest white; narrow horizontal lines or rows of dots following lower scale rows; first three dorsal spines white, next several bicolored brown and white.

Juveniles similar to adults in coloration.

Remarks.—Closely related to *Heniochus varius* and most likely a geographic replacement of that species.

Normally occurring in large schools over the reef, *Heniochus pleurotaenia* presents a vivid picture.

Further discussion of the *Heniochus pleurotaenia-H. varius* complex is given under the latter species.

Distribution.—Indian Ocean, possibly reaching to the East .Indies. Most records are from the area around India and Sri Lanka to the west coast of Sumatra.

Material Examined.—(5 spec.: 43-110 mm S.L.) SMF (3: 68-79), Sri Lanka; SMF (1: 110), Padang, Sumatra (lectotype); SMF 3828 (1: 43), Djakarta, Java.

HENIOCHUS VARIUS (Cuvier)
Sea bull
(Brown notch-head; horned pennant coralfish)

Taurichthys varius Cuvier, 1829: p. 192 (type locality East Indies; on Renard, 1718).

Taurichthys viridis Cuvier, 1829: p. 192 (type locality East Indies; on figures of Ruysch, Renard, and Valentyn). Cuvier, 1831: p. 114 (Amboina).

Heniochus varius, Gunther, 1860: p. 41 (Molucca Sea and Amboina; new combination).

Diphreutes varius, Bleeker, 1865: p. 182-3 (Ceram; new combination).

Diphreutes viridis, Bleeker, 1865: p. 283 (Amboina; new combination).

Taurichthys Bleekeri Castelnau, 1875: p. 15 (type locality Cape York, Queensland).

Heniochus (*Taurichthys*) *varius*, Steindachner, 1900: p. 420 (Ternate).

Heniochus varius 113 mm S.L. Guam.

Diagnosis.—D. XI, 22-24 (usually 23-24); A. III, 17-18; pectoral rays 14-15 (two with 14/15); L.l. scales 55-65; dark brown except for white band from predorsal area to chest and another from posterior dorsal fin spines to caudal peduncle.

Chaetodon madagascariensis subadult. The eyeband was connected with the nape spot at an earlier age. Photo by Dr. Herbert

Chaetodon madagascariensis in its natural habitat. Photo by Dr. Herbert R. Axelrod in the Maldives.

As with other members of this subgenus, *Chaetodon madagascariensis* commonly occurs as pairs. Photo by R. Jonklass.

Ratios	Standard Length (mm)		
	20-50(2)	51-90(6)	above 90(8)
Depth/S.L.	1.5-1.7	1.3-1.5	1.4-1.5
Head/S.L.	2.8-2.9	2.7-3.0	2.9-3.3
Eye/Head	2.6-2.9	2.5-2.9	2.6-3.1
Snout/Head	2.6-3.4	2.9-3.6	2.9-3.5
Interorb. W./Head	3.5-3.6	2.9-3.4	2.5-3.1
Maxillary/Head	4.2-4.4	4.8-5.9	5.4-6.7
Caud. Ped./S.L.	8.0-8.1	8.6-9.0	8.2-9.1
Pect. Fin/S.L.	2.1-2.9	1.9-2.3	2.2-2.5
Pelvic Spine/S.L.	3.0-4.0	3.5-3.8	3.7-4.7
Predorsal L./S.L.	1.9-2.1	1.8-1.9	1.7-2.0
Prepelvic L./S.L.	2.2-2.4	2.3-2.5	2.3-2.7
Dorsal Sp. No. 1/S.L.	15.3-18.3	11.3-14.8	14.1-21.7
Dorsal Sp. No. 2/S.L.	8.2-8.7	6.6-10.2	8.1-13.3
Dorsal Sp. No. 3/S.L.	3.6-4.1	3.4-4.2	4.0-5.5
Dorsal Sp. No. 4/S.L.	1.5-1.7	1.5-1.9	2.0-2.7
Anal Sp. No. 1/S.L.	7.3-8.5	6.1-8.4	6.7-10.5
Anal Sp. No. 2/S.L.	4.3-4.6	3.5-4.6	4.1-5.0
Anal Sp. No. 3/S.L.	4.2-40	3.3-4.8	3.8-5.8

Very close to *H. pleurotaenia*, but lacks the white area from center of body to abdomen.

Meristics.—D. XI, 23-24 (occasionally 22); A. III, 17-18; pectoral rays 14-15 (two 14/15); L.l. scales 55-65; L.l. pores 52-62; scales above L.l. 11-13; scales below L.l. 21-24; gill rakers 15-22.

Description.—Predorsal profile highly modified by the presence of a strongly projecting bump at nape and highly developed horns above each supraorbital (horns are variously modified into straight spikes, curved horns, or bifurcate antler-like structures); preopercle as in other species of genus, angle serrate; lachrymal smooth; snout 2.9-3.5 in head length; five to seven rows of teeth in each jaw; interorbital width greater than depth of caudal peduncle, which is greater than or equal to eye diameter; eye diameter greater than snout length.

Fourth dorsal fin spine elongate, 2.2-2.7 in standard length; last dorsal fin spine equal to or slightly longer than next to last spine; first few dorsal fin rays longer than last dorsal fin spines, giving fin a notched appearance; anal fin with rounded angle; second anal spine longest, but only slightly longer than third; base of spinous portion of dorsal fin slightly longer than or equal to (2.5-2.7 in S.L.) that of soft portion (2.7-2.9 in S.L.); pectoral fins long, 2.2-2.5 in S.L., pointed, and reaching to level of middle anal fin rays; pelvic fins moderately long, reaching to level of second anal fin spine.

Heniochus varius subadult with horns and hump established but not greatly enlarged yet. Photo by H. Hansen.

Lateral line describing a moderately high, smooth arc; scaly portion of dorsal fin high, covering about three-fourths of succeeding spines after fifth; anal scale covering half of third spine.

Juveniles without horns or prominent bump at nape, although the

Juvenile *Chaetodon paucifasciatus* with eyeband and nape spot just separating. Note also dorsal fin spot. Photo by H. Debelius.

Chaetodon paucifasciatus adults with eyeband and nape spot separate. The dorsal fin spot shows up most often at night. Photo by Dr. Gerald R. Allen.

Pair of *Chaetodon paucifasciatus* in natural habitat. Photo by Walter Deas.

area may be gibbous; fourth dorsal spine proportionally longer in juveniles, only 1.5 in S.L. compared with 2.0-2.7 in adults. Anal fin spines possibly more angular in juveniles.

Color Pattern.—Anterior band includes first three dorsal fin spines; lower portion of body darker than upper; light lines cross body horizontally; edge of anal fin white.

Color of juveniles similar to that of adults.

Remarks.—A great deal of comment has been offered to contrast the species *Heniochus varius* and *H. monoceros*. This does not seem to be a problem as they are quite distinct and maintain their identities although sympatric over a wide portion of their range. The question as to the specific status of *H. pleurotaenia* has also been raised. This is more of a problem. As with some other chaetodontid species, there is a Pacific Ocean form (*H. varius*) and an Indian Ocean form (*H. pleurotaenia*). The point of juncture seems to be the Indo-Australian Archipelago. Klausewitz (1969) thinks that they might be sympatric around Sumatra and Java. The record from Djakarta (Batavia) of *H. pleurotaenia* possibly is a specimen obtained from the market as was the Weber and de Beaufort (1936) specimen. These specimens could easily have been caught on the Indian Ocean side of Java. The question of sympatry must remain open until collection data is obtained from that area. It must be determined whether these species are (1) sympatric or (2) whether there are any intermediates as Weber (1936, p. 45) maintains. Until such a time I follow Klausewitz, who has done more extensive work on these two species, and call them both distinct species.

The relative sizes of the horns and their significance in sexual recognition (males with larger horns, females with smaller ones) have been referred to by several authors. The validity of this idea has not been proved, and more study on the growth patterns of the horns and the relative sizes in the two sexes will have to be made.

Taurichthys Bleekeri Castelnau appears to be a synonym of *H. varius*. In Castelnau's synonym "*T. varius?*" was given. In a note on p. 15, he says, "I believe this fish to form a distinct species that I propose calling *Taurichthys Bleekeri.*" The (?) that was added was due to his having only a single specimen, incomplete because of broken dorsal fin spines.

Distribution.—Pacific Ocean islands from at least Samoa to the East Indies. It reaches north from the East Indies to southern Japan and south to the coast of Australia (Queensland). It also has been reported from the Maldives.

Material Examined.—(16 spec.: 37-121 mm S.L.) BPBM 10049 (1: 119), Ishigaki, Ryukyu Islands; BPBM (uncatalogued) Snyder Coll. #2 (1: 83), Efate, New Hebrides; Yasuda, (Univ. of Tokyo) (1: 37), Japan(?); CAS 37662 (2: 66-88), Palau Islands; CAS 37704 (1: 64), Palau I.,; CAS 37663, CAS 37664, CAS 37665, CAS 37666, CAS 37667, CAS 37668, CAS 37669, (8: 73-121), Palau Islands; CAS 37670 (1: 120), Palau Islands; WEB (1: 38), Onotoa.

Genus PARACHAETODON Bleeker

Parachaetodon Bleeker 1874: p. 371 (type-species *Chaetodon oligacanthus* Bleeker 1845, by original designation).

Diagnosis.—Lateral line incomplete; snout short, 2.8-3.8 in head length; six dorsal fin spines, increasing in height posteriorly; first two dorsal fin soft rays continuing this increase to form pointed elevation of fin; teeth normal, in rows.

Description.—Body rounded, moderately deep, depth 1.3-1.4 in standard length; snout short, 2.8-3.8 in head length; predorsal and prepelvic contours meeting at snout at an obtuse angle; gape of mouth oblique; teeth normal, arranged in separate rows; preopercle finely serrate, right-angled; lachrymal smooth.

D. VI, increasing in height posteriorly, *Platax*-like; first two dorsal fin soft rays continuing this increase, forming an elevated, pointed fin; anal fin less deep, more rounded; anal spines increase in height posteriorly; first anal fin rays slightly longer than the spines; caudal fin truncate; pectoral fins short, 3.6-4.6 in standard length; pelvic fins long, reaching anal fin base; spinous dorsal fin base only one-third to one-fourth base of soft portion.

Lateral line incomplete, in the form of a low arc crossing body, ending near bases of last dorsal fin rays; scales rounded, moderate to small, 40-43 in lateral line; scaled portion of dorsal and anal fins high, covering a great percentage of every spine.

Juveniles similar to adults in shape and coloration.

Color pattern consists of orange to brownish dark edged bars on lighter body, blackish band or spot on caudal peduncle, and black spot (sometimes obscured) in dorsal fin.

Distribution of genus from southern China to Australia, and Melanesia to Sri Lanka.

A single species recognized.

Remarks.—*Parachaetodon* is distinctive in two ways. It is the chaetodontid genus with the fewest dorsal fin spines (VI) and the only genus besides the genus *Chaetodon* with an incomplete lateral line.

The elevated dorsal fin prompted Cuvier (1831) to describe the single species under the genus *Platax*, which is distinguished by having few dorsal spines and elevated dorsal and anal fins.

PARACHAETODON OCELLATUS (Cuvier)
False batfish
(Ocellated coral fish)

Platax ocellatus Cuvier, 1831: p. 229 (no type locality, Zoological Society of London Collection).
Chaetodon oligacanthus Bleeker, 1850: p. 16 (type locality Batavia).

Juvenile *Chaetodon trifascialis* with broad band of black in posterior section of body and fins. Photo by F. Earl Kennedy.

Slightly larger individual of *C. trifascialis* in which dark portion has spread out on caudal fin but has diminished in size in anal fin. Photo by Dr. Fujio Yasuda.

The next step in the growth series is the disappearance of the black in the anal fin and the shrinking of it in the dorsal fin. Photo by M. Goto, Marine Life Documents.

Chaetodon trifascialis nearing adult stage has very little dark area remaining on its dorsal fin. Photo by W. Deas.

Sarothrodus oligacanthus, Bleeker, 1863: p. 156 (Sindang-ole).

Tetragonoptrus oligacanthus, Bleeker, 1863: p. 234 (Ternate).

Parachaetodon ocellatus, Bleeker, 1877: p. 24, pl. 377, fig. 4 (Pinang, Singapore, Bintang, Banka, Java, Celebes, Halmahera, Ternate, Buru, Amboina, Ceram, Waigu, Philippines; new combination).

Chaetodon Townleyi De Vis, 1885: p. 454 (type locality Moreton Bay, Queensland, Australia).

Chaetodon ocellatus (not of Bloch), Day, 1889: p. 10 (India).

Chaetodon occellatus (not of Bloch), Seale, 1910: p. 283 (Borneo: misspelling of *ocellatus*).

Diagnosis.—D. VI (rarely VII), 28-30 (normally 28-29); A. III, 18-20 (usually 19); pectoral rays 14-15 (three with 14/15, two with 13/14); L.l. scales 39-46; dorsal fin spines ascending in height from front to rear, first two dorsal fin rays continuing this progression, the resulting fin elevated and pointed; three dark bordered bars crossing body in addition to dark bordered eyeband and caudal peduncle band (light bordered); blackish spot (sometimes obscured) included in dorsal fin in third bar of body.

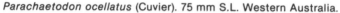

Parachaetodon ocellatus (Cuvier). 75 mm S.L. Western Australia.

Ratios	Standard Length (mm)		
	20-40	41-60(1)	above 60(22)
Depth/S.L.............	---	1.3	1.3-1.4
Head/S.L..............	---	3.3	2.9-3.4
Eye/Head	---	2.7	2.8-3.6
Snout/Head	---	3.8	2.8-3.8
Interorbital/Head	---	2.8	3.8-4.6
Maxillary/Head	---	5.0	3.5-5.5
Caud. Ped./S.L.........	---	7.2	7.2-8.3
Pect. Fin/S.L...........	---	3.6	3.8-4.6
Pelvic Spine/S.L........	---	4.0	3.9-4.8
Predorsal L./S.L........	---	1.8	1.9-2.2
Prepelvic L./S.L........	---	2.2	2.3-2.6
Dorsal Sp. No. 1/S.L.....	---	42.0	20.5-50.5
Dorsal Sp. No. 2/S.L.....	---	40.7	14.0-36.0
Dorsal Sp. No. 3/S.L.....	---	15.7	13.2-24.5
Dorsal Sp. No. 4/S.L.....	---	9.7	8.1-18.0
Anal Sp. No. 1/S.L......	---	10.6	15.6-29.7
Anal Sp. No. 2/S.L......	---	7.7	9.2-14.7
Anal Sp. No, 3/S.L......	---	7.3	7.2-11.5

Meristics.—D. VI (rarely VII), 28-30 (normally 28 or 29); A. III, 18-20 (usually 19); pectoral fin 14-15 (three specimens with a combination of 14/15 rays, two with 13/14); L.l. 39-46, pores 34-44; scales above L.l. 14-16; scales below L.l. 22-30 (usually 24-27); gill rakers 11-20 (usually 16-19).

Description.—Predorsal contour approximately straight from nape to tip of snout, ventral contour from tip of lower jaw to pelvic fin insertion rounded; these contours meet at mouth in an obtuse angle; about 10 or 11 rows of teeth in each jaw; preopercle smooth to lightly denticulate, right-angled; depth of caudal peduncle greater than interorbital width, which is greater than eye diameter; eye diameter greater than snout length.

D. VI, increasing rapidly in height from front to rear; first two dorsal fin soft rays continuing this increase; dorsal fin thus elevated, pointed at second dorsal soft ray; anal fin with spines graduated, last longest, first soft rays longer than last spine; anal fin rounded, posterior section similar to posterior section of soft dorsal fin; caudal fin truncate, upper and lower lobes sometimes slightly extended; pectoral fin short, 3.8 to 4.6 in standard length; pelvic fins long, reaching bases of anterior soft anal fin rays; spinous dorsal fin base much shorter (5.8-7.4 in standard length) than base of soft portion (1.6-1.7 in standard length).

Lateral line in form of very low arc across body, center of arc well below sixth or seventh soft dorsal fin rays.

Chaetodon trifascialis showing night or fright coloration. These light areas appear in other species as well. Photo by Michio Goto, Marine Life Documents.

Normal adult *Chaetodon trifascialis* with fins folded for faster swimming. Break in pattern lines above midside represent track of lateral line. Photo by Dr. Gerald R. Allen.

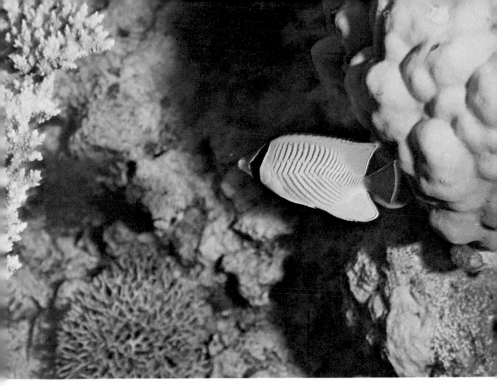

Natural habitat of *Chaetodon trifascialis*, Red Sea. Photo by N. Schuch.

Fully mature *Chaetodon trifascialis* from Taiwan. Photo by Dr. Shih-chieh Shen of a 92mm S.L. specimen.

Juveniles similar to adults in form and color pattern. At most soft dorsal fin more rounded and snout possibly more projecting than in adults.

Color Pattern.—Median snout stripe present, extending from just below nape to tip of snout, dark bordered; eyebands joined at nape and on chest before pelvic insertion; middle of body stripe extends from about fifth or sixth dorsal fin spines to second and third anal fin spines. (One specimen from Thailand had almost entire caudal fin black, though other specimens in same collection had normally colored fins.)

Juveniles may have more of a bulging caudal peduncle band, the connections above and below narrower than in adults.

Remarks.—Due to the unusual shape of this species as compared to other butterflyfishes, Cuvier (1831) originally described it under the genus *Platax*. This prevented the forming of a primary homonym as a species had been described under the name *Chaetodon ocellatus* by Bloch (1787). In several instances these names have been confused and the original description cited for this species was the one by Bloch. Fowler and Bean (1929) had the proper citation (*Platax ocellatus*), but Fowler (1938) indicated he had found an earlier description by Bloch and changed his synonymy accordingly.

As late as 1963, Rofen cited Bloch's *Chaetodon ocellatus* as the original description. Gunther (1860) recognized that a species described as *Chaetodon oligacanthus* by Bleeker (1850) was the same as *Platax ocellatus* Cuvier. He objected to changing *Platax ocellatus* to *Chaetodon ocellatus* as more than one or "another" species had already been described under that name and this would effectively have created a secondary junior homonym. He used *Chaetodon oligacanthus*, which was apparently accepted since the name *Chaetodon ocellatus* as applied to this species does not appear in any of the papers of the various authors of that day that I have been able to find.

Bleeker (1874) erected the genus *Parachaetodon*, naming his *Chaetodon oligacanthus* the type-species. In 1876 Bleeker changed his type-species from *Chaetodon oligacanthus* to *Parachaetodon ocellatus*, recognizing that *Parachaetodon ocellatus* = *Platax ocellatus* = *Chaetodon oligacanthus*. *Chaetodon oligacanthus* was still used in a few papers (Day, 1878; Macleay, 1878, 1880; Klunzinger, 1880; and Duncker, 1904), but almost all authors since then have used *Parachaetodon ocellatus*.

With this almost universal acceptance of *Parachaetodon ocellatus*, the virtual lack of use of *Chaetodon ocellatus* as applied to this species, and the apparent stability of the genus *Parachaetodon* which would preclude its being placed in synonymy with the genus *Chaetodon*, it seems best to retain the name *Parachaetodon ocellatus*. It should be noted that Seale (1910) did use the name *Chaetodon occellatus* (sic) for this species.

It appears that, with Bleeker synonymizing his own species (*Chaetodon oligacanthus*) with *Platax ocellatus* as *Parachaetodon ocellatus*, and with McCulloch (1916) referring to Ogilby as having examined the type of

Parachaetodon ocellatus. Photo by Miloslav Kocar.

Chaetodon townleyi De Vis and finding it identical with *Parachaetodon ocellatus*, there is but a single species. In comparing specimens from Thailand and with those from Western Australia, I find very little difference. The counts of the dorsal, anal, and pectoral fin rays, in only two specimens from Western Australia, are within the range I find in the Thailand specimens but, as in *Chelmon rostratus*, they fall to one side of the mode. There are too few specimens to indicate if this is a true difference or other phenomenon.

The black portion
of the dorsal and
anal fins
resembles that of
a subadult
*Chaetodon
trifascialis,* and
the chevron pat-
tern as well is
similar.
Photo by W. Hoppe.

Chaetodon larvatus has often been referred to as *Gonochaetodon larvatus.*

Natural habitat of *Chaetodon larvatus* at Wingate Reef, Red Sea. This species is also commonly paired as seen here. Photo by W. Deas.

Parachaetodon ocellatus has a wide depth range, being collected in shallow water as well as depths of at least 120 feet (McCulloch, 1916).

Distribution.—From southern China and the Philippine Islands throughout the East Indies to Australia as far south as Sidney on the east coast and Houtman's Abrolhos on the west coast; the islands of Melanesia as far as the Fiji Islands; and the Indian Ocean at least to Sri Lanka and India.

The records of Fowler (1938) from Christmas Island (Line Islands), Tahiti and Huahine (Society Islands), are based on his identification of tholichthys larvae and are not reliable.

Material Examined.—(23 spec.: 42-125 mm S.L.) CAS 37671 (1: 42), Gulf of Thailand; CAS 37673 (9: 80-94), Gulf of Thailand; CAS 37672 (4: 115-125), Mae Hat Bay, Thailand; CAS 37674 (6: 91-108), Samet Island, Thailand; WAM P13803 and P13804 (2: 72-75), Western Australia; SOSC 5th Thai Danish Exped. Sta. 10 (1: 92), Thailand.

Genus AMPHICHAETODON Burgess
NEW GENUS

Type-species.—*Amphichaetodon melbae* Burgess   by original designation.

Diagnosis.—Lateral line complete; fourth dorsal fin spine not greatly elongate; no horns present; XII dorsal fin spines; less than 60 lateral line scales; lachrymal serrate or toothed, scaled over most of its surface; scale covering of dorsal spines low; body depth 1.7-1.9.

Description.—Body oval to squarish, moderately deep (1.7-1.9 in S.L.), compressed; predorsal contour relatively straight, slight convexity in front of dorsal fin and concavity at level of nostrils; snout moderately projecting, 2.4-3.3 in head length; preopercle serrate to spinous, angle slightly projecting; lachrymal serrate to spinous, scaled to tip (bare patch around nostrils); supraorbital serrate; mouth small, terminal, gape horizontal; teeth normal, in 10 to 11 rows in each jaw.

Dorsal with XII very long, strong spines, fourth or fifth longest; first three dorsal spines increase rapidly in height until the fourth then decrease gradually after fifth until the last; rayed portion of dorsal fin slightly higher at first soft rays than last spines of dorsal fin, the fin rounded and the posterior margin almost vertical; anal fin with second spine long and strong, first spine half or slightly more than half second, and third spine slightly shorter than second (but more slender); rayed portion of anal fin with its posterior edge approximately vertical; caudal fin truncate-rounded; pectoral fins normal, rounded; pelvic fins long, extending to origin of anal fin; spinous portion of dorsal fin longer (2.3-2.4 in S.L.) than that of soft portion (3.5-3.6 in S.L.).

Lateral line complete, describing a low arc, about four or five rows of scales separating it from dorsal fin base at high point of arc, and ending at base of caudal fin; scales moderate, rounded, aligned in a pattern of almost vertical rows (slanting slightly to posterior) and of strongly slanting rows from upper anterior to lower posterior at about 45° angle; scales on head, chest, caudal peduncle, and scaly portions of dorsal and anal fins smaller than body scales; scale covering of dorsal fin spines low, leaving much of spines exposed (similar to that of *Forcipiger*); scale covering originates at base of first dorsal fin spine and increases in height until last spine is about half covered; anal spine scaly covering also low, starting from base of first spine but reaching only to midpoint of third anal fin spine; soft portions of both fins covered almost to the tips of every ray.

Color yellowish to silvery with black stripes, one on snout, one through eye, one across opercle from dorsal to pelvic fins, another in center of body, one from soft dorsal to soft anal fins, and one across caudal fin at its base.

Distribution.—Tasman Sea (New South Wales, Australia, Lord Howe Island, New Zealand) and San Felix Islands off the coast of Chile.

Two species are recognized and can be distinguished by the following key:

Key to the Species of the Genus Amphichaetodon

1a. Vertical black bars broad, much greater than eye diameter.........
...............................*Amphichaetodon howensis*
1b. Vertical black bars narrow, less than eye diameter in width ....
....*A. melbae*

Remarks.—This genus is composed of only two species, *Amphichaetodon howensis* and *A. melbae*, closely related and very similar in appearance but from opposite sides of the southern Pacific Ocean. In spite of expeditions and collections in intermediate areas, no specimens of any similar species have been captured.

Both species lie outside the tropical zone proper and are therefore more tolerant of cooler waters, being among the few chaetodontids to do so.

The genus *Amphichaetodon* apparently has affinities to *Chelmonops*, another Australian genus of butterflyfishes, but differs in the number of spines in the dorsal fin, shape of the dorsal fin, extension of the snout, etc. *Amphichaetodon howensis* has at times been placed in genus *Chelmonops*.

AMPHICHAETODON HOWENSIS (Waite)
Broad-barred butterflyfish

Chaetodon howensis Waite, 1903: p. 33, fig. 2 (type locality Lord Howe Island).

This individual of *Chaetodon baronessa* has abnormal pattern below the midside of the body, a not very unusual event. Photo by Roger Steene.

A fully adult *Chaetodon triangulum* with the specific marking at the base and edge of the caudal fin. Photo by Dr. Herbert R. Axelrod, Maldive Islands.

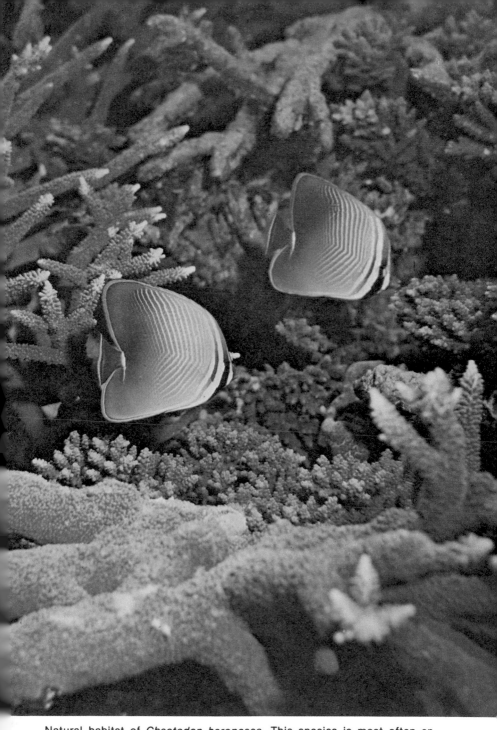

Natural habitat of *Chaetodon baronessa.* This species is most often encountered in pairs. Photo by W. Deas at Heron Island.

Amphichaetodon howensis (Waite). 140 mm S.L. Lord Howe Island.

		Standard Length (mm)	
Ratios	**20-60**	**61-90**	**above 90(2)**
Depth/S.L................	---	---	1.7-1.9
Head/S.L..............	---	---	3.0-3.2
Eye/Head ....:........	---	---	3.2
Snout/Head	---	---	2.4-2.9
Interorb. W./Head......	---	---	3.1-3.5
Maxillary/Head	---	---	4.1-4.2
Caud. Ped./S.L.........	---	---	8.4-8.8
Pect. Fin/S.L...........	---	---	3.4-4.1
Pelvic Spine/S.L........	---	---	4.2-4.9
Predorsal L./S.L........	---	---	2.1
Prepelvic L./S.L........	---	---	2.4
Dorsal Sp. No. 1/S.L.....	---	---	10.7-13.8
Dorsal Sp. No. 2/S.L.....	---	---	6.0-7.8
Dorsal Sp. No. 3/S.L.....	---	---	4.1-4.8
Dorsal Sp. No. 4/S.L.....	---	---	3.4-3.7
Anal Sp. No. 1/S.L.......	---	---	8.7-10.8
Anal Sp. No. 2/S.L.......	---	---	4.9-5.4
Anal Sp. No. 3/S.L.......	---	---	4.5-5.0

Diagnosis.—D. XII, 22-23; A. III, 16; pectoral rays 15; L.l. scales 47-50; dark bars broad, wider than light interspaces, and wider than eye diameter.

This species is very close to *Amphichaetodon melbae* but easily distinguishable by the width of the dark bars.

Meristics.—D. XII, 22-23; A. III, 16; pectoral rays 15; L.l. scales 47-50; L.l. pores 44-50; scales above L.l. 12-13; scales below L.l. 29-31; gill rakers 15.

Description.—As in genus. Teeth in 9-12 rows in each jaw.

Juveniles similar to adults.

Color Pattern.—Snout stripe present originating above level of eye and ending at lips, triangular in shape, widest at lips; eyeband continuous across nape; first dark bar includes first two dorsal fin spines and joins opposite bar across chest broadly; central bar originates at sixth to eighth dorsal fin spines and is continuous around abdomen; pelvic fin pale at its base, dark brown remainder (spine and first ray light).

Remarks.—This species is uncommon in collections, probably due to its restricted range and relatively deep normal depth of capture. The record from continental Australia was from 75 fathoms. It apparently reaches shallow water in some instances, as a photograph of it taken by a diver appeared in a diving magazine (*DIVE*, 1970, vol. 9, no. 1, p. 22). It is the only butterflyfish recorded from New Zealand.

Distribution.—Lord Howe Island; southern New South Wales (new record); New Zealand.

Material Examined.—(2 spec.: 117 and 140 mm S.L.) AMS I. 4124 (1: 140), Lord Howe Island; AMS (uncat.), (1: 117), Woolagang, Australia. (Note: Holotype, AMS I. 4361, seen).

AMPHICHAETODON MELBAE Burgess & Caldwell, NEW SPECIES
Narrow-barred butterflyfish

Diagnosis.—D. XII (XIII), (21) 22-23; A. III (IV), 16-17; pectoral rays 15-16 (usually 15); lateral line scales 48-55; dark bars of sides narrow, much narrower than light interspaces, and equal to or narrower than eye diameter.

This species is closely related to *Amphichaetodon howensis* but is easily distinguished from that species by the width of the dark bars.

Meristics.—D. XII (one obviously aberrant specimen had thirteen dorsal fin spines, but the additional spine was much shorter than the others and located between the spinous and soft portions), 22-23 (a single specimen had 21); A. III (one specimen had an extra spine but again was obviously aberrant), 16-17; pectoral fin 15 (two with 16 and one with 15/16); L.l. scales 48-55; scales above L.l. 12-14; scales below L.l. 26-31; gill rakers about 17.

Chaetodon baronessa juvenile. The head and body pattern are established by this stage, the fin pattern will soon follow. Photo by Allan Power.

Chaetodon baronessa feeding on a species of *Acropora*. Photo by Dr. Gerald R. Allen at Euston Reef, Great Barrier Reef.

Juvenile *Chaetodon baronessa* (older than specimen opposite). Photo by F. Earl Kennedy.

Subadult *Chaetodon baronessa* with fully developed color pattern. Photo by Allan Power.

Amphichaetodon melbae Burgess and Caldwell. 110 mm S.L. San Felix Islands, Chile. Photo by Dr. David G. Caldwell.

Ratios	Standard Length (mm)		
	20-60(3)	61-90(4)	above 90(10)
Depth/S.L..............	1.7-1.8	1.7-1.9	1.7-1.9
Head/S.L..............	2.8-3.0	2.9-3.1	3.0-3.2
Eye/Head.............	2.7-2.8	2.8-3.1	2.7-3.2
Snout/Head...........	2.9	2.7-3.0	2.7-3.3
Interorb. W./Head.....	3.5-3.8	3.4-3.7	3.3-3.7
Maxillary/Head........	3.7-4.0	3.7-3.9	3.8-4.1
Caud. Ped./S.L.........	8.5-8.9	8.7-9.5	8.5-9.4
Pect. Fin./S.L.........	3.0-3.2	3.1-3.5	3.0-3.7
Pelvic Spine/S.L........	3.7-3.9	4.0-4.4	4.0-5.0
Predorsal L./S.L........	2.1	2.1-2.2	2.2-2.4
Prepelvic L./S.L........	2.2-2.4	2.3-2.4	2.4-2.5
Dorsal Sp. No. 1/S.L....	9.4-9.9	9.4-13.0	10.1-12.4
Dorsal Sp. No. 2/S.L....	5.0-5.4	5.4-7.9	4.7-7.1
Dorsal Sp. No. 3/S.L....	3.4-3.6	3.5-4.5	3.7-4.7
Dorsal Sp. No. 4/S.L....	2.9-3.2	3.0-3.5	3.0-3.9
Anal Sp. No. 1/S.L.......	6.4-6.7	6.8-8.2	7.0-8.5
Anal Sp. No. 2/S.L.......	3.6-4.1	3.8-4.4	4.1-5.0
Anal Sp. No. 3/S.L.......	3.8-4.1	4.1-4.4	4.3-5.1

Description.—As for genus. 8-9 rows of teeth in each jaw. Juveniles similar to adults.

Color Pattern.—Snout stripe present, triangular in shape, from above eye level to lips; eyeband narrowly connected on nape, widens gradually to eye; first body bar originates at first and part of second dorsal fin spines, and connects with opposite bar across chest as a narrow band (perhaps even interrupted in some specimens); central body bar starts at seventh to eighth, sixth to seventh, or sixth to eighth dorsal spines, also connecting ventrally; dark caudal fin marking extends along upper and lower edges of fin to varying degrees; pelvic fins dark, except for base which is pale; spine and first pelvic ray pale; width of bars variable, but widest bar contained at least twice in pale space in front of it.

Color in life silvery, yellowish above lateral line; bars black; upper half of dorsal fin spines yellow; soft portions of dorsal fin, entire anal fin, caudal fin, and perhaps chin or lips, yellow; pelvic fins black and white; pectoral fins hyaline.

Amphichaetodon melbae adults, subadult and juveniles. Photo by Dr. David G. Caldwell.

295

Chaetodon bennettii, juvenile with almost identical color pattern as adult. Photo by Dr. Warren E. Burgess in the Philippines.

Chaetodon bennettii adult showing clearly lateral ocellated spot. Pale area also present in upper segment of eye band. Photo by Ken Lucas, Steinhart Aquarium.

Night coloration of *Chaetodon bennettii*. Photo by Scott Johnson, Enewetak.

Adult *Chaetodon bennettii* with lateral spot mostly obscured by lateral blotch. Photo by Rodney Jonklaas, Sri Lanka.

Remarks.—Additional counts provided by Dr. David Caldwell make the total number of specimens used for computation of meristics 54. These counts are very similar to those of *Amphichaetodon howensis* and, in fact, the two species cannot be separated on this basis, at least until additional specimens of *howensis* become available. It is quite possible that *melbae* is only a subspecies of *howensis*, but due to the obvious differences in color pattern, and since color pattern appears to be a useful tool for diagnosis, this species will be considered valid at this time. The apparent geographic separation also seems to confirm this opinion.

The specimens were captured at a depth of 30-40 feet.

Distribution.—Known only from the San Felix Islands off the coast of Chile.

Material Examined.—(21 spec.: 55-110mm S.L.) SIO65-629 (1:110), Isla San Felix, off Chile (HOLOTYPE); SIO65-626 and SIO65-629 (20:55-106), Isla San Felix (PARATYPES).

Genus PSEUDOCHAETODON Burgess,
NEW GENUS

Type-species.—*Sarothrodus nigrirostris* Gill, 1863, by original designation and monotypy.

Diagnosis.—Lateral line complete; D. XII, fourth spine not exceedingly elongate; body depth 1.4-1.5 in S.L.; snout moderate, 3.0-3.5 in head length; scaled portion of dorsal spines moderate, reaching about half-way up middle dorsal spines; scales 55-60 in lateral line; edge of lachrymal smooth to lightly denticulate; lachrymal almost devoid of scales.

Description.—Body rounded, deep, depth 1.4-1.5 in S.L.; predorsal contour relatively straight, a slight concavity at level of nostrils; snout pointed, 3.0-3.5 in head length; gape horizontal; teeth in regular rows; preopercle approximately right-angled, serrate, a slight projection at the angle; lachrymal not scaled anterior to level of nostrils, its edge smooth to lightly denticulate; supraorbital lightly serrate.

D. XII, spines increasing in height until third or fourth, then decreasing gradually until last; soft dorsal fin rounded, first rays slightly longer than last spines; anal fin spines strong, second longest, only slightly longer than third, first about two-thirds of second; soft anal fin rounded; caudal truncate; pelvic fins moderately long, reaching anal spine bases; pectoral fins moderately long, reaching anal spine bases and 2.9-3.9 in S.L.; spinous portion of dorsal fin slightly longer than soft portion.

Lateral line complete, ascending to about level of sixth dorsal spine base, relatively flat from sixth to tenth dorsal spine bases, then descending parallel to soft dorsal base and ending at base of caudal fin; scales moderate, arranged in horizontal rows on lower portions of body, ascending rows on upper portion; scale covering of dorsal fin normal, reaching mid-point at about fifth or sixth dorsal spines.

Juveniles vary little from adults.

Confined to the eastern tropical Pacific.

Only one species recognized.

Remarks.—This species has been a puzzle to ichthyologists for quite some time. It has most of the characteristics of the genus *Chaetodon* but differs strikingly from it by possessing a complete lateral line. Hubbs and Rechnitzer (1958) discussed this problem and came to the conclusion that it did not fit well into any known genus of chaetodontids. They, with much reservation, tentatively placed it in the genus *Heniochus* by virtue of the slightly elongate fourth dorsal fin spine and the complete lateral line. They pointed out that it did not have the extremely elongate fourth dorsal fin spine so characteristic of the species of the genus *Heniochus* nor did it possess the supraorbital horns or protuberances on the nape of that genus.

Pseudochaetodon differs from *Heniochus* by the lack of the elongate fourth dorsal fin spine at some stage in its life history, by the normal sheath compared to the high one in *Heniochus*, by the shorter pectoral fin and by the scaleless, smooth, moderately long lachrymal compared to the partly scaled, rounded lachrymal of *Heniochus*. The color patterns of the species of *Heniochus* are very similar and differ from that of *Pseudochaetodon*.

The lachrymal of the genus *Pseudochaetodon* is relatively smooth edged and almost devoid of scales, that of *Amphichaetodon* along with the first and possibly second orbital bones is very spiny and almost entirely covered with scales; the scale covering of the spinous dorsal fin of the genus *Pseudochaetodon* is higher, covering a good portion of the last spine, whereas in *Amphichaetodon* it is lower, covering only about half of the last spine; the spinous dorsal base is almost equal to the soft portion in *Pseudochaetodon* but is somewhat longer in *Amphichaetodon*; the scale rows below the middle of the body are horizontally arranged in *Pseudo-chaetodon* and slanting in *Amphichaetodon*; the shape of the pelvic fins is different, being more elongate and pointed in *Pseudochaetodon*; the pre-opercle is less spiny in *Pseudochaetodon*; and the body is proportionately deeper and rounder in *Pseudochaetodon* (depth about 1.4 in *Pseudochae-todon* and 1.7-1.9 in *Amphichaetodon*).

Pseudochaetodon is distinguishable from *Forcipiger* and *Chelmon* by snout length, from *Chelmonops* by dorsal fin spine number and shape of dorsal fin, and from *Hemitaurichthys* by shape of the dorsal fin and size of scales as well as number of scales. It is similar in general shape to *Cora-dion* but differs in dorsal spine number, pectoral fin length and shape, lateral line shape, and shape of the spinous portion of the dorsal fin, as well as color pattern.

Chaetodon zanzibariensis with relatively small lateral spot and obvious horizontal lines on body. Photo by Roger Lubbock.

Subadult *Chaetodon speculum* with larger spot and less noticeable lines on the body. Photo by Dr. Warren E. Burgess, Philippines.

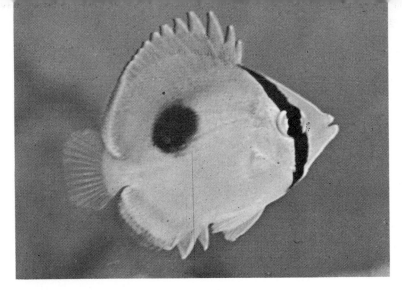

Juvenile *Chaetodon speculum*. Photo by F. Earl Kennedy.

Chaetodon speculum adult, with weak connection of eyebands at nape. Photo by Dr. Gerald R. Allen, Great Barrier Reef of Australia.

PSEUDOCHAETODON NIGRIROSTRIS (Gill)
Black-nosed butterflyfish

Sarothrodus nigrirostris Gill, 1863: p. 243 (type locality Cape San Lucas, Lower California).

Chaetodon nigrirostris, Jordan & Gilbert, 1882: p. 365 (Cape San Lucas; new combination).

Heniochus nigrirostris, Hubbs & Rechnitzer, 1958: p. 296 (new combination).

Pseudochaetodon nigrirostris. Photo by Aaron Norman.

Diagnosis.—D. (XI) XII, 24-25 (usually 24); A. III, 18-20 (usually 19); pectoral rays 16; L.l. scales 52-63; nape area from origin of dorsal fin to nostrils and posterior edge of eye dark colored; snout dark, lips light; broad band from mid-dorsal spines to lower edge of caudal peduncle following base of dorsal fin; complete lateral line.

Meristics.—D. XII (one with XI), 24-25 (usually 24); A. III, 18-20 (usually 19); pectoral rays 16; L.l. scales 52-63; L.l. pores 52-62; scales above L.l. 10-12; scales below L.l. 23-26; gill rakers 16-20.

Ratios	Standard length (mm)		
	20-50(1)	51-89(8)	above 89(5)
Depth/S.L.	1.5	1.4-1.5	1.4
Head/S.L.	2.7	2.8-2.9	2.8-3.0
Eye/Head	3.1	2.9-3.1	3.0-3.6
Snout/Head	2.7	2.8-3.3	3.0-3.5
Interorb. W./Head	3.4	3.1-3.6	3.0-3.2
Maxillary/Head	5.6	4.5-5.9	4.5-5.1
Caud. Ped./S.L.	8.4	8.0-8.9	8.2-8.6
Pect. Fin/S.L.	3.0	2.7-3.1	2.9-3.9
Pelvic Spine/S.L.	3.9	3.8-4.4	4.2-5.1
Predorsal L./S.L.	1.9	1.8-1.9	1.9-2.0
Prepelvic L./S.L.	1.9	2.0-2.2	2.2-2.3
Dorsal Sp. No. 1/S.L.	9.4	9.5-15.4	14.0-22.2
Dorsal Sp. No. 2/S.L.	4.7	5.1-7.0	6.5-8.5
Dorsal Sp. No. 3/S.L.	2.9	3.0-4.2	3.9-5.3
Dorsal Sp. No. 4/S.L.	2.8	2.6-3.7	3.6-3.9
Anal Sp. No. 1/S.L.	6.0	6.1-6.8	6.7-7.9
Anal Sp. No. 2/S.L.	4.2	4.3-4.8	4.3-5.0
Anal Sp. No. 3/S.L.	5.3	5.0-6.2	4.9-5.4

Description.—As in genus.

Specimens as small as 49 mm S.L. were very much like the adult specimens except for slight differences in color pattern.

Color Pattern.—Dark triangular nape patch extending from origin of dorsal fin to level of nostrils, last section from just above eyes to nostrils slightly lighter except for semilunar area above each eye and encircling eye; snout blackish, lips tan; white stripe originating from first two dorsal fin spines; posterior band from base of fifth dorsal fin spine through last spine across base of dorsal fin, half on fin half on body; each scale on body with light center and brownish edge.

In specimens approximating 70-75 mm S.L. the color pattern is similar except that the dark area on the pectorals reaches only three-fourths of way to the lower edge of pectoral base and the posterior stripe reaches to the base of the anal fin. In a smaller specimen of about 50 mm S.L. the posterior band reaches into the anal fin; a dark line is evident in the anal fin and a white one in the dorsal fin. The 70 mm specimen has the black between the eyes not extending between the interorbital space, it being simply two black blotches above the eye. Dark opercular margin is continued across, or nearly so, the base of the pectoral fin.

In young specimen the black margin of opercle, the bar above and behind upper angle of gill opening, and the black base of the pectoral fins are all united into one broad bar.

Remarks.—According to Gill (1862) the lateral line scale count was 44.

Late tholichthys stage of *Chaetodon plebeius*. Except for lateral spot and minor details, color pattern resembles adult. Photo by Allan Power, New Hebrides.

Subadult *Chaetodon plebeius* with lateral spot blurred but caudal fin pattern still not developed. Photo by Dr. Herbert R. Axelrod.

Day (above) and night (below) patterns in adult *Chaetodon plebeius*.
Photo by Michio Goto, Marine Life Documents.

I have examined the type and obtained a count of from 54 to 56 scales.

Hobson (1968) observed the night coloration of this species. The dark stripe along the base of the dorsal fin disappears except for black on the caudal peduncle and adjacent dorsal rays. "A dark smudge appears on the side edges coinciding with interior of where black mark disappears and edge of light stripe behind head. Noticeable are horizontal lines probably there during day as well."

Distribution.—Eastern Pacific Ocean from Baja California to Panama and the offshore islands (Cocos I., Revilla Gigedo, and Galapagos Is.). Probably also at Clipperton Island.

Material Examined.—(14 spec.: 50-131 mm S.L.) USNM 3667 (1: 51), Cape San Lucas (second specimen of type material also noted) (type); USNM 1514 and 1515 (2: 101-102), Socorro I., Revilla Gigedo Is.; USNM Acc. 1964: VII: 9 (1: 112), Baja California; CAS 23730 (1: 81), Santa Cruz I., Galapagos; CAS 37696 (1: 55), Revilla Gigedo Is.; CAS 37698 (1: 50), Mazatlan, Mexico; CAS 37699 (4: 58-131), Sinaloa, Mexico; BPBM (uncatalogued) (1: 113), Gulf of California.

Genus CHAETODON Linnaeus

Chaetodon Linnaeus, 1758: p. 272 (type-species *Chaetodon capistratus* Linnaeus, 1758, by subsequent designation of Jordan and Gilbert, 1883, p. 614). *Ex.* Artedi, 1738: *Ichth., Gen. XXXVI*, p. 51.

Tetragonoptrus Klein, 1776: p. 153 (type-species *Chaetodon striatus* Linnaeus, 1758, by subsequent designation of Bleeker, 1876, p. 305).

Rabdophorus Swainson, 1839: pp. 170, 211 (type-species *Chaetodon ephippium* Cuvier, 1831, by monotypy).

Megaprotodon Guichenot, 1848: p. 12 = "Megaprotodon" *vernacular*, index p. 378 = *Megaprotodon* (type-species *Chaetodon bifascialis* Cuvier, 1831, by monotypy).

Citharoedus Kaup, 1860: pp. 136 and 141 (type-species *Chaetodon meyeri* Schneider, 1801, by subsequent designation of Bleeker, 1876, p. 305).

Eteira Kaup, 1860: p. 136 and 147 (type-species *Chaetodon triangularis* Ruppell, 1828, by subsequent designation of Jordan, 1919, p. 297).

Linophora Kaup, 1860: p. 137 and 155 (type-species *Chaetodon auriga* Forsskal, 1775, by subsequent designation of Bleeker, 1876, p. 306).

Sarothrodus Gill, 1861: p. 99 (substitute name for *Chaetodon* Linnaeus, 1758, and therefore taking the same type-species, *Chaetodon capistratus* Linnaeus, 1758).

Prognathodes Gill, 1863: p. 238 (type-species *Chelmo pelta* Gunther, 1860, by monotypy).

Tholichthys Gunther, 1868: p. 457 (type-species *Tholichthys osseus* Gunther, 1868, by monotypy). Larval form; assignment uncertain.

Hemichaetodon Bleeker, 1876: p. 305 (type-species *Chaetodon capistratus* Linnaeus, 1758, by original designation).

Chaetodontops Bleeker, 1876: p. 305 (type-species *Chaetodon collaris* Bloch, 1787, by original designation).

Lepidochaetodon Bleeker, 1876: p. 306 (type-species *Chaetodon unimaculatus* Bloch, 1787, by original designation).

Oxychaetodon Bleeker, 1876: p. 306 (type-species *Chaetodon lineolatus* Cuvier, 1831, by original designation).

Gonochaetodon Bleeker, 1876: p. 306 (type-species *Chaetodon triangulum* Cuvier, 1831, by original designation).

Anisochaetodon Klunzinger, 1884: p. 54 (type-species *Chaetodon auriga* Forsskal, 1775, by subsequent designation of Jordan, 1920: p. 429).

Osteochromis Franz, 1910: p. 52 (type-species *Osteochromis larvatus* Franz, 1910, by monotypy). Larval stage, originally placed in family Pomacentridae; not assignable with certainty to any *Chaetodon* species.

Tifia Jordan and Jordan, 1922: p. 60 (type-species *Chaetodon corallicola* Snyder, 1904, by original designation).

Loa Jordan, 1922: p. 652, fig. 6 (type-species *Loa excelsa* Jordan, 1922, by original designation).

Roa Jordan, 1923: p. 63 (substitute name for *Loa* Jordan 1922, preoccupied, and therefore taking the same type-species, *Loa excelsa* Jordan 1922).

Paracanthochaetodon Schmidt and Lindberg, 1930: p. 469 (type-species *Paracanthochaetodon modestus* Schmidt and Lindberg, 1930, by original designation).

Tetrachaetodon Weber and de Beaufort, 1936: pp. 53, 56, and 59 (as a subgenus of *Chaetodon;* type-species *Chaetodon plebeius* Cuvier, 1831, by original designation).

Bauchotia Nalbant, 1965: p. 585 (type-species *Chaetodon marcellae* Poll, 1950, by original designation).

Exornator Nalbant, 1971: 215 (type-species *Chaetodon punctatofasciatus* Cuvier, 1831, by original designation; described as a subgenus).

Discochaetodon Nalbant, 1971: 222 (type-species *Chaetodon octofasciatus* Bloch, 1787, by original designation; described as a subgenus).

Chaetodon austriacus adult. The interorbital pattern often varies from this simple lined pattern to more complex geometric figures. Photo by Dr. Gerald R. Allen, Eilat, Red Sea.

Pair of *Chaetodon austriacus* in their natural habitat. This species is commonly found in close contact on the reef. Photo by Dr. Gerald R. Allen at Eilat, Red Sea.

Chaetodon austriacus has solid black anal and caudal fins but a mostly white dorsal fin. Photo by Norbert Schuch in the Red Sea.

A pair of *Chaetodon austriacus* in the company of an angelfish, *Pygoplites diacanthus.* Photo by W. Deas, Sanganeb Reef, Red Sea.

Diagnosis.—Lateral line incomplete, ending in area of last rays of dorsal fin; XI to XVI spines in dorsal fin; base of spinous dorsal fin equal to or longer than that of soft dorsal; scales rounded or angular, less than 55 in lateral line.

Description.—Body oval, orbicular or subrhomboid; snout short to moderate; teeth in rows across jaws or as group of indistinguishable rows at tip of jaw; preopercle right- or obtuse-angled, variously toothed or entire; lachrymal smooth to serrate, partially hidden or exposed.

Dorsal fin with spines graduated or triangular, third to fifth spine longest (not greatly elongate as in genus *Heniochus*); dorsal fin continuous or notched; base of spinous portion of dorsal fin equal to or longer than that of soft portion; anal fin with second spine equal to or much greater than third; pectoral fins moderate; pelvic fins moderate to elongate, sometimes extending to base of anal fin rays.

Lateral line incomplete, reaching only to vicinity of last dorsal fin rays (and in some cases only to early dorsal rays); scales rounded or angular; scaly portion of dorsal fin low to high.

D. XI-XVI, 15-30; A. III-IV, 14-27; lateral line scales 22-55; scales above L.l. 4-14; scales below L.l. 9-30.

Color pattern various, often changing from juvenile to adult.

Widely distributed around the world. Circumtropical, normally found within the 70°F isotherm. Occasionally straying into temperate regions, particularly during summer months, but apparently not maintaining any breeding populations there.

Extending from shallow water (at times even a few inches) to over 600 feet.

A large genus of 90 species contained in 13 subgenera.

Diagnoses of the Subgenera of Chaetodon

1. Subgenus *Prognathodes* Gill

   Body subrhomboidal to oval; spinous dorsal fin triangular, third or fourth spine longest; second anal fin spine usually significantly longer than third; dorsal fin notched; posterior edges of dorsal and anal fins vertical or nearly so; snout projecting, 2.1-3.0 in head length; eyeband absent or angled anteriorly below eye; scaly sheath of dorsal spines low; D. XIII, 18-21; A. III, 15 or 16. (6 species.)

2. Subgenus *Roa* Jordan

   Body subrhomboidal to oval; spinous dorsal fin triangular, third or fourth spine longest; second anal fin spine usually significantly longer than third; posterior edges of dorsal and anal fins vertical or nearly so; snout pointed, 2.7-3.7 in head length; eyeband normally vertical below eye; scaly sheath of dorsal spines low; D. XIII, 19-22; A. III, 16. (8 species.)

3. Subgenus *Rhombochaetodon* Burgess

Body oval; spinous dorsal fin rounded, approaching triangular; soft portion rounded; anal fin angular; snout pointed, 2.6-3.2 in head length; L.l. in low arc; scales rhomboidal, in chevron pattern; D. XIII, 20-23; A. III, 16-17. (5 species.)

4. Subgenus *Megaprotodon* Guichenot

Body elongate-oval; spinous dorsal fin rounded, fifth spine longest; soft portion pointed; anal fin pointed; L.l. in low arc; scales rhomboidal, in chevron pattern; D. XIV, 15; A. IV, 15. (1 species.)

5. Subgenus *Gonochaetodon* Bleeker

Body deep, rounded; dorsal fin high; dorsal spines increase in length posteriorly, last longest; L.l. in moderate, smooth arc; lachrymal free, smooth; scales rhomboidal, in chevron pattern; eyeband with accessory bands on either side; D. XI, 24-25; A. III, 20-22. (3 species.)

6. Subgenus *Tetrachaetodon* Weber and de Beaufort

Body elongate-oval; dorsal spines graduated; dorsal and anal fins with rounded angles; snout short, blunt, 3.0-4.0 in head length; L.l. a low arc; scales rounded; lachrymal partly hidden by scales; base of spinous dorsal fin about twice base of soft portion; D. XIV, 16-17; A. III-IV, 15-16. (4 species.)

7. Subgenus *Corallochaetodon* Burgess

Body elongate-oval; spinous dorsal fin evenly graduated; dorsal and anal fins with rounded angles; snout short, 3.1-4.1 in head length; teeth grouped in indistinguishable rows in front of each jaw; lachrymal almost completely hidden by scales; L.l. in high, angular arc; scales vertically elongate; eyeband with additional band on each side; D. XIII, 20-21; A. III, 19. (3 species.)

8. Subgenus *Citharoedus* Kaup

Body rounded to oval; dorsal spines evenly graduated; dorsal and anal fins with blunt angles; snout short, blunt, 3.0-4.0 in head length; eyeband with additional stripes before and behind; L.l. high and angular; teeth in undefined rows in front of jaws; specialized tholichthys larva present, with supraorbital bony "horns;" D. XII, 23-28; A. III, 19-23. (3 species.)

9. Subgenus *Chaetodontops* Bleeker

Body oval; dorsal and anal fins with blunt angles; snout short, 2.8-3.5 in head length; L.l. in high angular arc; scales rounded; lachrymal free, rounded; teeth normal; D. XII, 23-26; A. III, 17-22; juveniles with dorsal spot; usually yellow with brown and black markings. (8 species.)

10. Subgenus *Rabdophorus* Swainson

Body oval; dorsal and anal fins with blunt angles (dorsal at times

Chaetodon trifasciatus lunulatus juvenile with somewhat different color pattern when compared with the adults. The single eyeband and posterior body and fin pattern are most obvious. Photo by K.H. Choo, Taiwan.

Adult *Chaetodon trifasciatus lunulatus* with full pattern. Photo by Dr. Herbert R. Axelrod at Marau, Solomon Islands.

Chaetodon trifasciatus lunulatus in its natural habitat. Daytime coloration.
Photo by Allan Power.

Chaetodon trifasciatus lunulatus in its natural habitat. Nighttime coloration.
Photo by Roy O'Conner, Great Barrier Reef.

with a filament); L.l. with a high angle; scales angular; lachrymal free, smooth; snout pointed, slightly projecting, 1.9-2.8 in head length; D. XII-XIV, 20-25; A. III, 19-22. (16 species.)

11. Subgenus *Lepidochaetodon* Bleeker

Body oval to rounded; dorsal and anal fins rounded; snout short, robust, 2.5-3.2 in head length; L.l. a high, smooth arc; lachrymal partly hidden by scales; teeth in rows, outer row stronger than inner rows; black spot on side astride lateral line; D. XIII, 21-23; A. III, 19. (1 species.)

12. Subgenus *Discochaetodon* Nalbant

Body rounded, almost circular; dorsal and anal fins strongly rounded; L.l. in low, smooth arc; snout short, 2.8-4.5 in head length; lachrymal restricted; scales rounded; D. XI (one species with XII), 19-22; A. III, 16-18. (4 species.)

13. Subgenus *Chaetodon* Linnaeus

Body oval; dorsal and anal fins with blunt angle; snout pointed, short, 2.7-3.3 in head length; lachrymal free, smooth; L.l. a high arc; scales mixed, rounded to angular; D. XI-XIV, 18-25; A. III, 16-19. (28 species.)

Subgenus PROGNATHODES Gill

Prognathodes Gill, 1862: p. 316 (type-species *Chelmo pelta* Gunther, 1860, by original designation).
Bauchotia Nalbant, 1965: pp. 584-589 (type-species *Chaetodon marcellae* Poll, 1950, by original designation).

Diagnosis.—Dorsal fin triangular, third or fourth spine longest; slight notch from spinous dorsal to soft portion; scaly sheath very low, leaving most spines free; second anal spine usually long, strong; snout projecting, 2.1-3.0 in head length; scales large; D. XIII, 18-21; A. III, 15 or 16; scales in L.l. 38-40.

Description.—Body oval to squarish or trapezoidal; predorsal contour straight, becoming concave at level of nostrils; snout moderately project- ing, 2.1-3.0 in head length; mouth small, gape horizontal; teeth in spaced rows in each jaw; preopercle right-angled, serrate to relatively smooth, angle slightly extended; supraorbital smooth to lightly serrate; lachrymal serrate in larger specimens.

Spinous dorsal fin triangular in shape, the apex being the tip of the third or fourth spine; dorsal spines long, strong, the notches between the first four or five spines deep, leaving the first six spines relatively free from each other; succeeding dorsal spines progressively shorter, the anterior rays longer than the last spines, creating a 'step' or notch in the fin; soft portion of dorsal and anal fins rounded but with posterior edge vertical or nearly so; base of spinous portion of dorsal fin about double that of soft

314

portion (2.0-2.4 in S.L. as compared to 3.7-4.3 respectively); second anal spine usually long and strong, 3.5-5.0 in standard length; pectorals normal; pelvic fins moderate to long, reaching at least to anal opening and possibly to anal fin base; caudal fin truncate.

Lateral line incomplete, describing a relatively high arc, broadly flattened on top, ending at base of last rays of dorsal fin; scales moderately large, 38-40 in lateral line; scaly sheath of dorsal fin very low, originating at base of first spine but remaining near base of dorsal fin until about sixth to ninth spines, then covering more of each succeeding spine until ½ to ¾ of last spine is hidden; scaly sheath of anal spines also low, not reaching midpoint of third spine; first rays of anal fin relatively free of scales near their ends, the succeeding ones covered nearly to their tips.

Usually XIII dorsal fin spines though occasionally XII or XIV , and 18-21 rays; anal fin III, 14-16 (but usually 15 or 16) rays; lateral line scales 35-41 (normally 38-40); gill rakers 15-18 (4 or 5 + 11-13).

Juveniles essentially like adults in color and form.

Color patterns variable, usually combinations of yellow or white background with dark brown to black markings; eyeband either absent (as in *C. dichrous*) or narrowing considerably below eye and angled forward toward end of lachrymal or chin; median snout stripe usually present.

Distributed throughout the Caribbean, eastern Pacific Ocean, Ascension and St. Helena Islands in the central Atlantic Ocean, and western tropical Africa.

Most species of this subgenus are normally found at greater depths than most other chaetodontids.

Six species recognized, differentiated in the following key.

Key to the Species of the Subgenus Prognathodes

1. Snout moderately long, 2.1-2.3 in head length; body nearly uniformly colored, lighter below; eyeband orange in life, bordered with dark, passing forward below eye, ending on upper portion of the snout . . . . *Chaetodon aculeatus* (Trop. W. Atlantic)

   Snout shorter, more than 2.4 in head length; bicolored dark and light or with black bands variously positioned on body; eyeband absent, black with light borders, or black above eye, orange below it 2

2. Body bicolored, lower half and upper anterior portion dark, upper posterior area including caudal fin and part of caudal peduncle white, no ocular band . . . . *C. dichrous* (St. Helena and Ascension Islands, Central Atlantic)

   Body white to yellow, crossed by dark bands; ocular band present . . . 3

3. Black band on side in form of scythe-shaped mark, the angle directed upward, one arm crossing opercle, the other crossing body and ending in middle part of anal fin; outer rays of caudal fin black;

Chaetodon trifasciatus trifasciatus from the Indian Ocean with its orange peduncle and caudal fin base. Photo by Dr. Herbert R. Axelrod.

Chaetodon trifasciatus trifasciatus in captivity. The orange base of the caudal fin and peduncle is weak but noticeable. Photo by Klaus Paysan.

Juvenile *Chaetodon melapterus* in an aquarium. The dorsal fin and especially the anal fin are already darkening. Photo of an individual from the Gulf of Oman by Aaron Norman.

A similar sized juvenile *Chaetodon austriacus* with dark anal fin, light dorsal fin and lighter body color. Photo by H. Debelius, Red Sea.

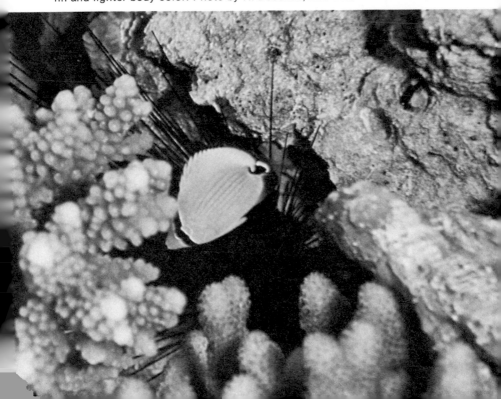

eyeband dark above eye, orange below it, extending toward upper
part of snout after leaving lower edge of orbit . . . .
. . . . *C. falcifer* (E. Pacific)
Black bands not scythe-shaped; caudal fin uniformly colored; eyeband
directed toward chin from lower edge of orbit 4
4. Single vertical black band from last spines of dorsal fin to middle of
anal fin . . . . *C. marcellae* (W. Africa)
Black oblique band or bands crossing body at an angle from spinous
dorsal fin toward anal fin 5
5. Single black oblique band from middle spines of dorsal fin to midportion of anal fin ending well before angle of fin. . . . .
. . . . *C. aya* (Trop. W. Atlantic)
Black oblique band from middle dorsal spines to tip of angle of anal
fin; second black band along base of soft dorsal fin . . . .
. . . . *C. guyanensis* (Trop. W. Atlantic)

CHAETODON ACULEATUS (Poey)
Poey's butterflyfish

Chelmo aculeatus Poey, 1860: p. 202 (type locality Matan-
zas, Cuba).

Chelmo pelta Gunther, 1860: p. 38 (type locality "Hab.
_____?").

Prognathodes aculeatus, Poey, 1868: p. 354 (Cuba). Hubbs,
1963: p. 166.

Chaetodon unicolor Sauvage, 1880: p. 222 (type locality
Martinique).

Chaetodon sp. Zaneveld *in* Collins, 1956 (Netherlands West
Indies).

Diagnosis.—D. XIII, 18-19 (usually 18); A. III, 14-16 (usually 15); pectoral rays 13 (one with 12/13, one with 13/14); L.l. scales 39-43; eye 3.3-
3.7 in head length; snout 2.2-2.3 in head length; color white below, becoming tan to brownish above, without dark crossbars; eyeband light
with dark borders.

Meristics.—D. XIII, 18-19 (usually 18); A. III, 14-16 (usually 15); pectoral rays 13 (one with 12/13, one with 13/14); L.l. scales 39-43; L.l.
pores 24-29; scales above L.l. 8-9; scales below L.l. 19-21 (usually 20); gill
rakers 17-20.

Description.—Snout pointed, somewhat produced, 2.2-2.3 in head
length; preopercle approximately right-angled, a slight concavity above
angle, lightly serrated; lachrymal elongate, smooth to partly toothed;
teeth in spaced rows, 8-10 in upper jaw, about 10-11 in lower jaw; first
row of teeth in upper jaw longer than succeeding rows; snout length
much longer than eye diameter, which is longer than depth of caudal

Chaetodon aculeatus (Poey). 63 mm S.L. St. Thomas, Virgin Islands.

| | | Standard Length (mm) | |
Ratios	20-40	41-60(6)	above 60(3)
Depth/S.L.	---	1.7-1.9	1.8
Head/S.L.	---	2.5-2.7	2.6
Eye/Head	---	3.3-3.7	3.4
Snout/Head	---	2.1-2.3	2.3
Interorb. W./Head.	---	4.1-4.3	4.1
Maxillary/Head	---	3.2-3.8	3.6
Caud. Ped./S.L.	---	9.5-11.5	10.1
Pect. Fin/S.L.	---	3.5-4.0	3.6
Pelvic Sp./S.L.	---	4.0-4.3	4.3
Predorsal L./S.L.	---	2.0-2.1	2.0
Prepelvic L./S.L.	---	2.1-2.2	2.0
Dorsal Sp. No. 1/S.L. . . . . :	---	11.0-12.0	10.7
Dorsal Sp. No. 2/S.L.	---	4.9-6.0	6.3
Dorsal Sp. No. 3/S.L.	---	3.1-3.5	3.8
Dorsal Sp. No. 4/S.L.	---	3.0-3.4	3.4
Dorsal Sp. No. 5/S.L.	---	3.4-3.5	3.5
Anal Sp. No. 1/S.L.	---	6.6-7.9	6.6
Anal Sp. No. 2/S.L.	---	3.7-4.4	3.9
Anal Sp. No. 3/S.L.	---	3.4-4.4	4.3

Adult *Chaetodon melapterus* in its natural habitat, the coral reef. Photo by N. Schuch.

Chaetodon melapterus with vertical fins black and more orange-colored body than the other two species. Photo by H. Debelius, Djibouti.

Chaetodon melapterus, as with other members of the subgenus, is almost always found as pairs. Photo by Norbert Schuch.

peduncle; depth of caudal peduncle equal to or greater than interorbital width.

Spinous portion of dorsal fin triangular in shape, fourth spine longest, forming apex; second anal fin spine long, strong, first half of second, third slightly longer than second but not as strong; pelvic fins long, extending to base of third anal fin spine; base of spinous portion of dorsal fin longer (2.2-2.6 in S.L.) than that of soft portion (4.0-4.7 in S.L.).

Lateral line as described under *C. guyanensis*; scales moderate, 39-43 in L.l.; scaly covering of dorsal spines very low, starting to increase in height only at level of sixth or seventh spine but covering most of last spine; anal spines relatively free from scale covering, third above half covered.

Juveniles resemble adults in color and form.

Color Pattern.—Pale centered, brownish gray (in alcohol) bordered line between eyes from nape to snout, solid dark brown on extension of snout; eyeband lightly colored with dark borders from just anterior to first dorsal fin spine to eye, then continuing forward to end at upper edge of lachrymal below the median snout stripe; pelvic fins clear or white on outer half, dusky or brownish on inner half; rayed portions of dorsal and anal fins with submarginal dark brown line.

Remarks.—This is a case in which a species was named twice within a short period of time. Poey's name, *Chelmo aculeatus*, was published in July 1860. Gunther's name, *Chelmo pelta*, was published a few months later, September 1860.

The extension of the snout caused this species to be relegated to a separate genus, *Prognathodes*. It is my contention that this snout extension has occurred on several occasions in different lines in this family as a specialized adaptation to feeding. When compared to the truly long-snouted genera *Chelmon* and *Forcipiger*, the snout of *Chaetodon aculeatus* appears rather insignificant. In addition, there is almost a continuous gradation of snout length:standard length within this subgenus, *C. aya* with 2.4-3.0 and *C. falcifer* with 2.4-2.6 coming closest to the 2.2-2.3 of *C. aculeatus*. Other species of the genus *Chaetodon* have snout as long or longer than that of *C. aculeatus* (*C. falcula*, 1.9-2.2; *C. oxycephalus*, 2.2-2.5, *C. mesoleucos*, 2.3-2.4, etc.). Other characteristics of this species decidedly place it within the group discussed rather than as a separate genus.

No specimen has been reported of greater size than 71 mm standard length.

Chaetodon aculeatus normally inhabits moderate to deep water, being most abundant at 15-55 meters. It reaches greater depths, the deepest recorded being 91 meters at Northwest Slope, Saba Bank (Hubbs, 1963). It is occasionally found in shallower water of less than a meter (Randall, personal communication).

Its elongate snout is apparently a modification to select small invertebrates from the crevices of corals and among other normally inaccessible places such as between the spines of sea urchins. It has been reported as one of the butterflyfishes that does not pick parasites (Böhlke and Chaplin, 1968).

Distribution.—From the islands of the northern coast of South America through the Caribbean Island arc to southern Florida and the Bahama Islands.

Material Examined.—(9 spec.: 44-68 mm S.L.) SIO 59-54 (3: 58-63), St. Thomas, Virgin Islands; ANSP 83649 (1: 68), Havana, Cuba; ANSP 94893 (1: 44), Bahama Islands; ANSP 102343 (1: 59), Grand Cayman Island; MCZ 16253 (1: 59), Havana, Cuba (labeled "type of *Chelmo aculeatus* Poey"); NMFS-M SB 5187 (1: 50), Dominican Republic.

CHAETODON MARCELLAE Poll
French butterflyfish

Chaetodon marcellae Poll, 1950: p. 2, fig. 1 (type locality 3°57½'S, 10°36½'E (near Point Noir)).

Chaetodon altipinnis Cadenat, 1950 (1951): p. 239, fig. 174 (type locality Senegal)

Chaetodon marcellae Poll. 91 mm S.L. Senegal. (Syntype of *C. altipinnis* Cadenat).

Chaetodon reticulatus juvenile with color pattern very similar to that of the adult. Photo by Dr. Fujio Yasuda.

Adult *Chaetodon reticulatus* with characteristic "mailed" pattern and red trailing edge of anal fin. Photo by Roger Steene.

Above and below. *Chaetodon reticulatus* in its natural habitat, plenty of coral to eat and clean, clear water. Photo above by W. Deas; photo below by Paul Allen, Hawaii.

| | | Standard Length (mm) | |
Ratios	20-40	41-60(1)	above 60(3)
Depth/S.L.	---	1.7	1.6-1.7
Head/S.L.	---	2.6	2.6-2.8
Eye/Head	---	3.4	3.5-3.7
Snout/Head	---	2.6	2.5-2.7
Interorb./Head	---	4.4	3.9-4.3
Maxillary/Head	---	3.8	3.6-4.0
Caud. Ped./S.L.	---	8.7	8.9-9.3
Pect. Fin/S.L.	---	3.8	3.5-4.0
Pelvic Sp./S.L.	---	4.3	3.9-4.6
Predorsal L./S.L.	---	2.1	2.1-2.3
Prepelvic L./S.L.	---	2.1	2.1-2.2
Dorsal Sp. No. 1/S.L. . . .	---	11.2	9.2-11.6
Dorsal Sp. No. 2/S.L. . . .	---	3.9	4.9-4.8
Dorsal Sp. No. 3/S.L. . . .	---	2.9	2.9-3.8
Dorsal Sp. No. 4/S.L. . . .	---	2.8	2.9-3.6
Dorsal Sp. No. 5/S.L. . . .	---	3.2	3.1-3.8
Anal Sp. No. 1/S.L.	---	6.4	7.3-7.9
Anal Sp. No. 2/S.L.	---	3.9	3.8-4.4
Anal Sp. No. 3/S.L.	---	4.0	4.4-5.0

Diagnosis.—D. XIII, 19; A. III, 15; pectoral rays 14 (one with 13); L.l. scales 42-44; eye 3.5-3.7 in head length; snout 2.5-2.7 in head length; a single nearly vertical dark band extends from last dorsal fin spines and first rays to middle of anal fin.

Meristics.—D. XIII, 19-20; A. III, 15-16 pectoral rays 14 (one with 13; one with 13 on one side); L.l. 39-44; L.l. pores 31-33; scales in longitudinal series 34 (Poll); scales above L.l. 10-11·(8 Poll); scales below L.l. 21-23; gill rakers 13-14.

Description.—Snout pointed, slightly produced, 2.5-2.7 in head length; preopercle lightly serrate, right-angled, the angle slightly produced; lachrymal long, smooth, supraorbital smooth; cleithrum toothed; teeth in spaced rows, about 11 in lower jaw and 8 or 9 in upper jaw; snout length greater than depth of caudal peduncle, which is greater than eye diameter; eye diameter greater than interorbital width.

Dorsal spines long and strong, fourth longest and forming the apex of the spinous dorsal fin triangle; second anal spine longest, first about half second, third a little shorter than second; base of spinous portion of dorsal fin shorter (2.2 in S.L.) than that of soft portion (3.4-3.5 in S.L.); pelvic fins moderate, extending to the anus.

Lateral line follows same pattern as described under *Chaetodon guyanensis*; scales moderate to large on body (central and anterior); scale covering of dorsal spines starts increasing at about the sixth dorsal fin spine, increasing in height until it covers ½ to ¾ of the last spine; anal fin scales cover only leading edge of half of third anal fin spine.

No juveniles were seen, but it is expected they closely resemble the adult in both color and form. Medium size specimens had the pelvic fin rays reaching as far as the first anal ray.

Color Pattern.—Median snout stripe present from just above eye level to and including upper lip.

Color of living specimens silvery white with yellowish reflections on sides; band blackish (bordered with pale color); head yellow, lighter below; base of pectoral yellow; bases of soft dorsal and anal fins pale orange, remainder yellowish; ventral fins yellow; pectorals hyaline to whitish; caudal hyaline to dusky.

Remarks.—The two nominal species *C. marcellae* and *C. altipinnis* were described almost simultaneously. The former was published in November of 1950, the latter, although also marked 1950, was not published until 1951.

Chaetodon marcellae is also one of the deeper-living species of *Chaetodon*, being found in depths from 35 meters to 140 meters. However, Mr. H. Debelius photographed it at 12 meters depth in the Cape Verde Islands (personal communication).

The type was taken on a sandy brown mud bottom.

Attains a size of about 100 mm S.L.

Distribution.—Tropical West Africa from 4° S (25 miles WSW of Pointe de Banda) to as far north as Cape Verde, Senegal.

Material Examined.—(4 spec.: 48-96 mm S.L.) MHNH 1111, 1114, and 1144 (4: 48-96), Senegal (syntypes of *Chaetodon altipinnis* Cadenat).

CHAETODON AYA Jordan
Bank butterflyfish

Chaetodon aya Jordan, 1886: p. 225 (type locality snapper banks near Pensacola, Florida, "spewed up" by a red snapper (*Lutjanus aya*)).

Chaetodon eques Steindachner, 1903: p. 18, fig. 1 (type locality Yucatan coast).

Diagnosis.—D. XIII, 18-19; A. III, 15; pect. 13; L.l. scales 37-40; eye 3.2-3.8 in head length; snout 2.4-3.0; broad oblique band from middle dorsal spines to middle of anal fin, but not reaching edge of fin.

Closely related to *Chaetodon guyanensis* but lacks the second dark band at the base of the soft dorsal fin and has 13 pectoral rays compared with 14 of *C. guyanensis*. Other differences are discussed under *C. guyanensis*.

Meristics.—D. XIII (one with XII, two with XIV), 17-20 (rarely 17 or 20); A. III, 14-16 (rarely 14); pectoral fin 13 (one with 12/13, another with 13/14, a third with 13/15); L.l. scales 35-41 (usually 37-40); scales

Chaetodon ornatissimus adult in captivity. The head has a complicated striped pattern similar in some respects to that of the subgenus *Corallochaetodon.* Photo by Dr. Fujio Yasuda.

Opposite:

Chaetodon ornatissimus adult. Photo by Allan Power.

Chaetodon ornatissimus juvenile. Color pattern is almost fully developed in this young individual. Photo by K.H. Choo, Taiwan.

Chaetodon aya Jordan. 70 mm S.L. Florida (trawled south of Tortugas).

Ratios	Standard Length (mm)		
	20-40(3)	41-60(1)	above 60(18)
Depth/S.L.............	1.7-1.9	1.8	1.5-1.9
Head/S.L..............	2.4-2.6	2.8	2.6-2.9
Eye/Head	3.2-3.4	3.1	3.2-3.8
Snout/Head	2.7-2.9	3.0	2.3-3.0
Interorb./Head	3.5-4.2	3.8	3.0-4.1
Maxillary/Head	2.9-3.3	4.2	3.5-4.3
Caud. Ped./S.L.........	8.5-9.7	9.2	8.6-9.8
Pect. Fin/S.L..........	4.1-4.5	3.4	3.4-4.3
Pelvic Sp./S.L.........	3.6-3.8	3.6	3.5-4.4
Predorsal L./S.L........	2.0	2.2	2.0-2.3
Prepelvic L./S.L........	2.2-2.3	2.3	2.1-2.3
Dorsal Sp. No. 1/S.L.....	7.7-11.1	8.7	7.1-12.6
Dorsal Sp. No. 2/S.L.....	3.4-3.8	3.6	3.5-5.1
Dorsal Sp. No. 3/S.L.....	2.2	2.6	2.3-2.9
Dorsal Sp. No. 4/S.L.....	2.5-2.9	2.9	2.4-3.5
Anal Sp. No. 1/S.L......	6.5-7.8	6.4	5.1-8.0
Anal Sp. No. 2/S.L......	3.9-4.1	3.9	3.4-4.4
Anal Sp. No. 3/S.L......	4.5-4.6	4.4	3.9-5.0

above L.l. 9-10 (occasionally 8); scales below L.l. 16-20; gill rakers 15-21 (usually 18-20).

Description.—Snout pointed, slightly produced, 2.4-3.0 in head length; preopercle right-angled, angle slightly extended, edge lightly serrated; supraorbital smooth to serrate; lachrymal elongate, scaled, serrated in larger specimens; teeth in spaced rows, about 7-9 in upper jaw, 5-7 in lower jaw; snout length greater than caudal peduncle depth, which is greater than eye diameter; eye diameter greater than interorbital width.

Third dorsal spine longest, forming apex of spinous dorsal fin triangle; second anal spine long, strong, first spine half or slightly less than second, third shorter than second; base of spinous portion of dorsal fin longer (2.2-2.3 in S.L.) than that of soft portion (4.0-4.3 in S.L.); pelvic fins long, extending to base of first anal spine in larger specimens.

Lateral line as in *Chaetodon guyanensis*, the posterior turn downward occurring below the ninth to twelfth dorsal spine bases; scales moderate to large, in horizontal series below lateral line and ascending series above it (following rise of anterior portion of lateral line); scaly portion of dorsal spines starts increasing at about sixth or seventh spine until the last spine, which is about ¾ hidden; anal scale covering barely reaching midpoint of third spine.

Juveniles similar in color and form to adults.

Color Pattern.—Median snout stripe present, originates at nape and extends to tip of upper lip but does not continue below eye, though less prominent to area of chin; posterior broad band originates at the sixth to tenth dorsal fin spines.

Remarks.—Hubbs (1963) has covered *Chaetodon aya* in detail so that much of the data need not be repeated here.

Normally found in deeper water, from about 35-150 meters depending upon location. Apparently most common on, if not restricted to, the shelf areas.

Jordan (1886) gives XII dorsal spines; I count XIII in the type.

Chaetodon eques is undoubtedly a synonym of this species.

Chaetodon aya and *C. guyanensis* appear to be replacement species, *aya* being found in the northern range and on shelf areas, whereas *guyanensis* follows the island arc toward the south.

Largest size recorded is 112 mm standard length.

Distribution.—Tropical western Atlantic: Campeche Banks, Yucatan Peninsula, Gulf of Mexico, Florida, and north to Cape Hatteras.

Material Examined.—(22 spec.: 29-105 mm S.L.) USNM 3747 (1: 29), near Pensacola, Florida (holotype); USNM 159269 (2: 81-94), Pensacola, Florida; USNM 31893 (1: 82), Gulf of Mexico; USNM 58637 (1: 90), Gulf coast of Florida; USNM 196437 (1: 62), Florida Straits; USNM 196859 (2: 98 each), off South Carolina; USNM 196436 (3: 67-105), off Vero Beach, Florida; USNM 190361 (1: 84), off North Carolina; USNM 159269 (2: 80-95), 29°56.5'N-87°03'W; USNM 196439 (1: 69), off South Carolina; USNM 116850 (7: 32-82), Florida and south of Tortugas.

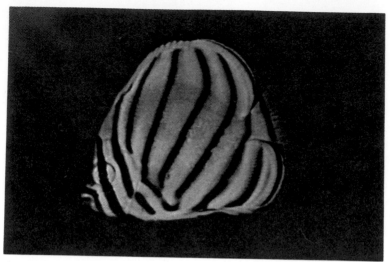

Chaetodon meyeri juvenile. The pattern is very similar to that of juvenile *C. ornatissimus* although the color is different. Photo by F. Earl Kennedy.

Chaetodon meyeri adult. The curving lines of black are distinctive. Photo by Dr. Herbert R. Axelrod in the Maldives.

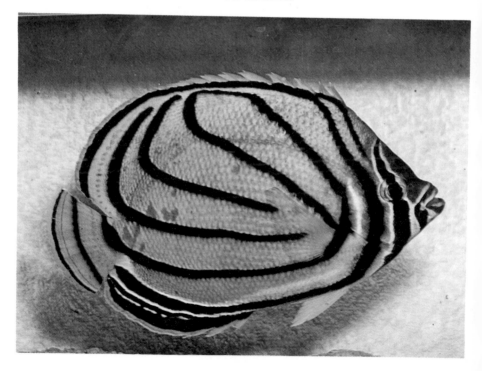

Chaetodon meyeri.

CHAETODON GUYANENSIS Durand
Guyana butterflyfish

Chaetodon guyanensis Durand, 1960: p. 209 (type locality Guyane).

Chaetodon goniodes Woods, "1960" (Jan. 19, 1961): p. 417-420 (type locality Mona Passage off western Puerto Rico).

Chaetodon guyanensis Durand. 87 mm S.L. Guyane (52°34′W 6°35′N). (Syntype.)

Diagnosis.—D. XIII, 19; A. III, 15; pectoral rays 14 (2 with 13); L.l. scales 37-41; eye 2.9-3.2 in head length; snout 2.7-2.8 in head length; broad dark band from middle dorsal fin spines to angle of anal fin, second dark band along tips of posterior dorsal spines and middle to base of soft portion of dorsal fin.

Very closely related to *Chaetodon aya* but differing in color pattern as indicated in the key; in addition *C. guyanensis* has the eyeband and diagonal band of body in closer proximity (less than 1 eye diameter) than *C. aya* (more than two eye diameters) at dorsal fin base; *C. guyanensis* normally has 14 pectoral rays to 13 for *C. aya*; eye larger in *C. guyanensis* (2.9-3.2 in head length) than in *C. aya* (3.2-3.8).

Ratios	Standard Length (mm)		
	20-40	41-60	above 60(3)
Depth/S.L.............	---	---	1.6-1.8
Head/S.L..............	---	---	2.7-2.8
Eye/Head.............	---	---	2.9-3.2
Snout/Head	---	---	2.7-2.8
Interorb. W./Head......	---	---	3.1-3.6
Maxillary:Head	---	---	3.6-3.7
Caud. Ped./S.L.........	---	---	9.6-10.0
Pect. Fin/S.L...........	---	---	3.6-3.9
Pelvic Sp./S.L..........	---	---	4.2-5.1
Predorsal L./S.L........	---	---	2.1-2.2
Prepelvic L./S.L........	---	---	2.2-2.3
Dorsal Sp. No. 1/S.L.....	---	---	9.4-10.9
Dorsal Sp. No. 2/S.L.....	---	---	4.3-5.1
Dorsal Sp. No. 3/S.L.....	---	---	3.1-3.3
Dorsal Sp. No. 4/S.L.....	---	---	3.2-3.4
Anal Sp. No. 1/S.L......	---	---	7.3-7.9
Anal Sp. No. 2/S.L......	---	---	4.0-4.4
Anal Sp. No. 3/S.L......	---	---	4.7-5.9

Meristics.—D. XIII, 19; A. III, 15; pectoral rays 14 (2 with 13 on one side only); L.l. scales 37-41; L.l. pores 29-34; scales above L.l. 9-11; scales below L.l. 15-18; gill rakers 16-17; scales in lateral series 34 (Woods) or 40 (Durand).

Description.—Snout pointed, slightly produced, 2.7-2.8 in head length; preopercle approximately right-angled, lightly serrated (more so at angle), a slight projection at angle; subopercle and interopercle serrate; lachrymal (preorbital) serrate, particularly anteriorly; supraorbital (dorsal orbital bony rim) "with fine serrae on anterior portion" (Woods, "1960"); teeth in regularly spaced rows, about seven in upper jaw and eight in lower; snout length greater than eye diameter, which is greater than interorbital width; interorbital width greater than depth of caudal peduncle.

Third dorsal spine longest, forming apex of triangle, first spine less than ½ second; anal spines strong, second longest, third somewhat shorter than second, first about half second; base of spinous dorsal fin longer (2.2-2.4 in S.L.) than base of soft portion (3.6-3.9 in S.L.); anal fin angle at about middle rays; pelvic fin moderate, longest rays reaching anal opening.

Lateral line ascends at about 30° angle until level of fifth to sixth dorsal fin spines, flattens out to an angle of 6°-15° until last dorsal fin spines, there descending along base of rayed portion and ending near the base of the last dorsal rays; scales moderate to large on anterior sides of

Chaetodon lunula juvenile pattern. This species undergoes very great changes from juvenile to adult. Photo by Dr. Fujio Yasuda.

Juvenile *Chaetodon lunula* in their natural habitat. Photo by James H. O'Neill, Hawaii.

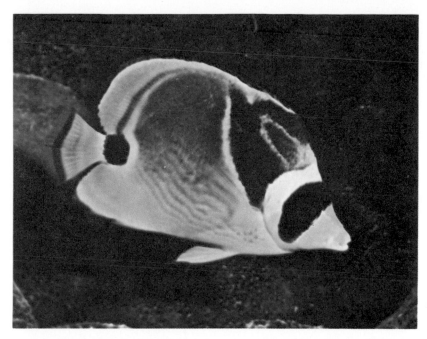

Chaetodon lunula in its natural habitat. The adult pattern is evident. Photo by Dr. Gerald R. Allen, Hawaii.

Chaetodon lunula subadult with adult pattern visible but not strong and juvenile dorsal spot considerably faded. Photo by K.H. Choo, Taiwan.

body; scaly covering of dorsal spines covers up to ¾ of last spine; anal spines have what may be true sheath covering bases of first two anal fin spines and reaching middle of third; first ray of anal fin lacks scales from midpoint outward, rest of dorsal and anal rays covered with small adherent scales almost to their tips.

No juveniles were seen, but it is expected that they closely resemble the adult in both color and form.

Color Pattern.—Median snout stripe present, extending from a short distance above the eyes down to and including upper lip; eyebands joined at nape, extending obliquely forward below eye; pelvic fins have the spine and first ray lightly colored, the remaining rays strongly tinted with black, particularly at the outer edges.

Remarks.—Consistent with the subgenus, this species was named twice within a short period of time. *Chaetodon guyanensis* Durand was published just a few months previous to *C. goniodes* Woods.

Chaetodon guyanensis appears to be restricted to the islands of the Caribbean and the northern coast of South America, whereas the closely related *C. aya* is found only around the Campeche Banks, Yucatan Peninsula, Gulf of Mexico, and Florida to Cape Hatteras.

It is a deeper water species found in water to at least 750 feet. The type specimen of *C. goniodes* was taken in 125 fathoms (750').

Largest recorded size is 95 mm standard length.

Distribution.—Antilles and northern South America; recorded from Puerto Rico, Barbados, Guyana.

Material Examined.—(3 spec.: 82-94 mm S.L.) MHNH 60-271 and 60-272 (2: 82-87), Guyane (syntypes); USNM 186318 (1: 94), west of Puerto Rico, 18°26'N, 67°11'W (holotype of *Chaetodon goniodes*).

CHAETODON FALCIFER Hubbs & Rechnitzer
Scythe-marked butterflyfish

Chaetodon falcifer Hubbs and Rechnitzer, 1958: p. 275, fig. 1 and 2 (type locality Guadalupe Island, Baja California).

Diagnosis.—D. XII, 19-20 (usually 20); A. III, 14-16; pectoral rays 13-14 (usually 14); L.l. scales 45-56; eye 3.7-4.4 in head; snout 2.4-2.6 in head length; falcate black band from lower opercle to below fourth dorsal fin spine and then to middle of anal fin.

Meristics.—D. XII, 19-20 (usually 20); A. III, 14-16; pectoral rays 13-14 (usually 14); L.l. scales 45-56; scales above L.l. 13 or 14; scales below L.l. 24 (one with 26); gill rakers 15 or 16.

Description.—Snout pointed, somewhat produced, 2.4-2.6 in head length; preopercle right-angled, serrate, the angle slightly produced; lachrymal serrate, scaled in larger specimens; supraorbital serrate; teeth in spaced rows, 18 or more in upper jaw, 17 or more in lower jaw; snout

Chaetodon falcifer Hubbs and Rechnitzer. 136 mm S.L. San Benito Island, Baja California.

Ratios	Standard Length (mm)		
	2o-40	41-60	above 60(4)
Depth/S.L.	---	---	1.8-1.9
Head/S.L.	---	---	2.8-3.0
Eye/S.L.	---	---	3.3-4.4
Snout/Head	---	---	2.4-2.7
Interorb. W./Head.	---	---	4.0-4.4
Maxillary/Head	---	---	3.3-3.5
Caud. Ped./S.L.	---	---	9.4-10.3
Pect. Fin/S.L.	---	---	3.4-4.0
Pelvic Sp./S.L.	---	---	3.5-4.4
Predorsal L./S.L.	---	---	2.3-2.4
Prepelvic L./S.L.	---	---	2.4-2.5
Dorsal Sp. No. 1/S.L.	---	---	6.4-10.3
Dorsal Sp. No. 2/S.L.	---	---	3.0-5.4
Dorsal Sp. No. 3/S.L.	---	---	2.3-4.4
Dorsal Sp. No. 4/S.L.	---	---	3.0-3.8
Dorsal Sp. No. 5/S.L.	---	---	3.3-4.0
Anal Sp. No. 1/S.L.	---	---	5.7-9.5
Anal Sp. No. 2/S.L.	---	---	3.2-5.0
Anal Sp. No. 3/S.L.	---	---	4.0-5.3

A group of adult *Chaetodon lunula* in their natural habitat. Photographed by
Paul Allen, Hawaii.

Chaetodon lunula, adult color and pattern. Compare this photo with the one
on the opposite page of *C. fasciatus* with which it is almost always confused.
Photo by Ken Lucas, Steinhart Aquarium.

Chaetodon fasciatus juvenile in its natural habitat in the Red Sea. Photo by H. Debelius, Red Sea.

Chaetodon fasciatus adult. Similar to *C. lunula,* this species goes through some changes in pattern from juvenile to adult. Photo by Dr. Gerald R. Allen, Eilat, Red Sea.

length greater than caudal peduncle depth, which is greater than eye diameter; eye diameter greater than interorbital width.

Third or fourth dorsal spine longest, forming apex; second anal fin spine longest and strongest, first between half and three-fourths second, third shorter than second; anal rays slightly thickened; base of spinous portion of dorsal fin longer (2.1-2.3 in S.L.) than that of soft portion (3.7-3.9 in S.L.); caudal fin truncate but with upper rays slightly extended; pelvic fins moderate, reaching a point between anus and base of first anal fin spine.

Lateral line as in *Chaetodon guyanensis*, the flexures at about the sixth and twelfth dorsal fin spines; scales moderate to small, 45-56 in lateral line; scale series in horizontal rows below lateral line, ascending rows above it; scale covering of dorsal spines starts increase in height at about fifth or sixth dorsal spine, reaching only to a little more than ⅓ of last spine; soft portions of dorsal and anal fin covered about halfway with small scales; scale covering reaches only a little above ⅓ of third anal spine.

Juveniles similar to adult in form and color.

Color Pattern.—Median interorbital stripe present from nape to end of upper lip; eyeband extends forward below eye to edge of lachrymal; scythe-shaped mark ends at about fourth anal fin ray; membranes of the third and fourth dorsal spines light, remainder—as are spines—black.

Remarks.—*Chaetodon falcifer* is a strikingly patterned species only recently described (1958). New records are still being added (Freihofer, 1966), and the full extent of the range of this species is perhaps not completely known. The lack of records from coastal areas at the time of his report prompted Freihofer to suggest that better deeper water collections be made along the mainland coast to determine whether *C. falcifer* is an insular form. More recent sightings and collections have been made, at least one from La Jolla, California (Kiwala and McConnaughey, 1971). *Chaetodon guyanensis* similarly is a relatively poorly known species whose records suggest it may be exclusively insular.

Chaetodon falcifer has been found in waters varying from 40-175 feet deep.

The counts and color variation of *Chaetodon falcifer* from the Galapagos Islands do not seem to be enough to warrant species status for that area. My counts on the Mexican island material seem to be intermediate or even closer to Freihofer's counts. Perhaps this is just a variation due to methods of the examiners rather than in the specimens themselves. A photograph of a Mexican area *C. falcifer* shows a very high scythe-mark reaching the base of the dorsal fin. The color photograph did not show any white bordering to the upper edge of the scythe-shaped mark.

Distribution.—Eastern Pacific Ocean: Galapagos Islands, Cape San Lucas, Guadalupe Island, West San Benito Island, Santa Cataline Island, and La Jolla, California.

Material Examined.—(4 spec.: 73-152 mm S.L.) SIO 59-46, (2 (male and female): 102-137), San Benito Islands, Baja California Norte; SIO 63-162 (1: 73), Cabo San Lucas, Baja California Sur; SIO 67-162 (1: 152), Guadalupe Island, Baja California Norte.

CHAETODON DICHROUS Gunther
Bicolored butterflyfish

Chaetodon dichrous Gunther, 1869: p. 239, pl. 16 (type locality St. Helena).

Chaetodon dichrous Gunther. 100 mm S.L. James Bay, St. Helena.

Diagnosis.—D. XII, 19; A. III, 15; pectoral rays 14; L.l. scales 43; eye 3.2 in head; snout 2.9 in head; bicolored, mostly dark brown except for upper posterior quadrant of body, most of caudal peduncle and caudal fin; no eyeband.

Meristics.—D. XII, 19; A. III, 15; pectoral rays 14; L.l. scales 43; scales above L.l. 11; scales below L.l. 21; gill rakers 15.

Description.—Snout pointed, slightly produced, 2.9 in head length; preopercle right-angled, lightly serrate, the angle slightly produced; lachrymal toothed; supraorbital very slightly serrate; teeth in spaced rows, 11 or 12 in upper jaw, about 9 rows in lower jaw; snout length greater than depth of caudal peduncle, which is greater than eye diameter; eye diameter greater than interorbital width.

Chaetodon fasciatus in its natural habitat in the Red Sea. Photo above by Norbert Schuch; photo below by W.Deas at Sanganeb Reef.

A pair of Chaetodon fasciatus on a Red Sea coral reef. Photo by L. Sillner.

Ratios	Standard Length (mm)		
	20-40	41-60	above 60 (1)
Depth/S.L.............	---	---	1.7
Head/S.L..............	---	---	2.9
Eye/S.L..............	---	---	3.2
Snout/Head	---	---	2.9
Interorb. W./Head......	---	---	3.5
Maxillary/Head	---	---	3.9
Caud. Ped./S.L........	---	---	8.6
Pect. Fin/S.L..........	---	---	3.7
Pelvic Sp./S.L.........	---	---	4.3
Predorsal L./S.L........	---	---	2.3
Prepelvic L./S.L........	---	---	2.3
Dorsal Sp. No. 1/S.L.....	---	---	10.6
Dorsal Sp. No. 2/S.L.....	---	---	6.6
Dorsal Sp. No. 3/S.L.....	---	---	3.0
Dorsal Sp. No. 4/S.L.....	---	---	3.4
Anal Sp. No. 1/S.L.......	---	---	9.0
Anal Sp. No. 2/S.L.......	---	---	3.9
Anal Sp. No. 3/S.L.......	---	---	5.1

Third dorsal spine longest, forming apex; second anal spine long, strong, first about half or less of second, third spine somewhat shorter than second; base of spinous portion of dorsal fin longer (2.4 in S.L.) than that of soft portion (3.8 in S.L.); pelvic fins long, extending to base of second anal spine; pelvic spine flattened, blade-like.

Lateral line similar to that described under *Chaetodon guyanensis;* scales moderate, about 43 in L.l.; scales in horizontal series below L.l. and ascending series above it; scaly covering of dorsal spines remaining low until ninth spine, increasing posteriorly until last spine is more than ¾ covered; scale covering of anal fin extending only a short distance above base of third spine.

Juvenile specimens not seen but are expected to be similar to adult in color and form.

Color Pattern.—Dividing line between two colors at about third dorsal spine; pelvic fins dark brown; pectoral fins hyaline but with brownish lines marking edges of rays; dorsal spines dusky green-gray.

Remarks.—Although primarily a deep, cool water species, *Chaetodon dichrous* occurs in water as shallow as 3-5 meters at St. Helenae (the cooler of the two islands). The depth range was reported to be 3-30 m with the greater part of the population at the deeper end of the range, (Jourdan, pers. comm.). Large numbers were captured at 100 m depth west of Point Catherine, Ascension (Cadenat & Marachal, 1963).

Neither Hubbs (1963) nor Nalbant (1965) included this species in their treatments of the species included in this subgenus.

Distribution.—Mid-Atlantic Ocean: islands of Saint Helena and Ascension.

Material Examined.—(1 spec.: 100 mm S.L.) BMNH 1969-3-10-5 (1: 100), St. Helena.

Subgenus ROA Jordan

Loa Jordan, 1922: p. 652, fig. 6 (type-species *Loa excelsa* Jordan, 1922, by original designation).

Roa Jordan, 1923: p. 63 (substitute name for *Loa* Jordan, 1922, preoccupied, and therefore taking the same type-species, *Loa excelsa* Jordan, 1922).

Paracanthochaetodon Schmidt & Lindberg, 1930: p. 469 (type-species *Paracanthochaetodon modestus* Schmidt & Lindberg, 1930, by original designation).

Diagnosis.—Body subrhomboidal to oval; dorsal fin triangular; third to fifth spine longest; second anal fin spine normally significantly longer than third; posterior edges of dorsal and anal fins vertical or nearly so; scaly sheath of dorsal spines moderately low.

Description.—Body subrhomboidal to oval; predorsal contour straight, concave at level of nostrils; snout moderate, 2.7-3.6 in head length; mouth small; teeth in spaced rows in jaws; preopercle right-angled, serrate to relatively smooth; supraorbital smooth; lachrymal smooth.

Spinous dorsal fin triangular in shape, apex at third to fifth spine; dorsal spines long, strong, the notches between the first four or five deep, leaving them relatively free; no noticeable notch between spinous and soft portions; rayed portion of dorsal fin rounded, the posterior edges approaching vertical; base of spinous portion of dorsal fin longer to near equal (2.0-2.7 in standard length) than that of soft portion (2.9-3.7 in standard length); second anal spine long, strong, 3.2 to 5.9 in S.L.; pectoral fins normal; pelvic fins short to long; caudal fin truncate.

Lateral line describing a relatively high arc, flat on top; scales moderate, 35-49 in lateral line; scaly "sheath" of dorsal spines moderately low, reaching midpoint only of latter spines; scale covering of anal spines extending only to midpoint of third spine.

D. XI-XIII, 19-23; A. III, 15-18; pectoral rays 14; L.l. scales 35-59; scales above L.l. 7-12; scales below L.l. 15-27; gill rakers 13-20.

Color usually white to yellow or light brown with either broad yellow to orange-brown bars or posterior dark brown to black diagonal band including soft portion of dorsal fin and portion of anal fin; spot present in soft dorsal at some time in life history of some of the species (*Chaetodon modestus* complex).

Chaetodon flavirostris undergoes very great changes from juvenile to adult as most species in this subgenus do. A very small juvenile (above) shows a distinct dorsal fin spot, whereas a slightly older individual (below) has already lost it. Photo above by W. Deas, New South Wales; photo below by Dr. Herbert R. Axelrod, Marau, Solomon Islands.

Chaetodon flavirostris has a very complicated pattern, especially in the head region. Photo by W. Deas, Great Barrier Reef.

Chaetodon flavirostris are commonly found as paired individuals, but the pair bond is less strong than in other species and the mate may be out of sight for short intervals. Photo by W. Deas, Great Barrier Reef.

Juveniles, as far as known, similar to adults in both form and color. Median snout stripe usually present.

Distribution of subgenus from Hawaiian Islands to southern Japan to the Palau Islands and the Philippines; East Indies (at least northern part) to Cocos-Keeling and Mauritius; Sri Lanka and India, Gulf of Oman, Gulf of Aden, and southern Arabia.

This subgenus is composed of mostly deeper water species (greater than 100 feet), although *Chaetodon modestus*, for one, reaches shallow water.

Eight species are currently recognized as distinguished by the following key.

Key to the Species of Subgenus Roa

1. Dorsal fin XIII (occasionally XII or XIV), 18-21; scales above L.l. 6-10, scales below L.l. 12-20 (*tinkeri* complex) 2

   Dorsal fin XI (occasionally XII), 21-23; scales above L.l. 11-13, scales below L.l. 21-24 (*modestus* complex) 6

2. Dark area at posterior part of body includes soft dorsal fin and posterior part of anal fin 3

   Dark area at posterior part of body does not include soft dorsal fin nor any part of anal fin; color pattern of double slanting bars connected at base of anterior dorsal fin spines but separate posteriorly....

   .... *Chaetodon mitratus* (Mauritius and Cocos-Keeling)

3. Dark posterior area including most of dorsal fin, extending from third or fourth spine to middle of anal fin; scales below L.l. about 12-16

   4

   Dark posterior area including most of soft portion of dorsal fin but little of spiny part, extends from posterior spines to middle of anal fin; scales below L.l. about 20...............................

   .... *C. nippon* (Japan to Philippine Islands)

4. Dark bar present from nape to behind pectoral fin ....

   .... *C. burgessi* (Palau Islands)

   No dark bar from nape to behind pectoral fin 5

5. Posterior dark area black in life; pelvic fins whitish ....

   .... *C. tinkeri* (Hawaii)

   Posterior dark area brown in life, caudal peduncle and adjacent area black; pelvic fins yellowish .... *C. declevis* (Marquesas)

6. Body bars dark edged; head 2.8-3.2 in standard length 7

   Body bars not dark edged; head 2.6 in standard length; caudal peduncle 8.5-9.0 in S.L. .... *C. jayakari* (Indian Ocean)

7. Spot in dorsal fin round; body bars more parallel; eye 2.9-3.2 in head; second anal spine 4.3-5.9 in standard length ....

   .... *C. modestus* (Japan to East Indies)

   Spot in dorsal fin oval to teardrop-shaped; body bars converging

toward dorsal fin; eye 2.5-2.6 in head length; second anal spine
3.0-3.2 in standard length .... *C. excelsa* (Hawaii and Guam)

Remarks.—Although the subgenus *Roa* can roughly be divided into
two groups, the division is not great enough so that these groups can be
considered subgenera by themselves. *Chaetodon nippon*, for instance, has
a spot in the dorsal fin (at least as a juvenile) like members of the *modestus*
complex, but thirteen dorsal fin spines like those of the *tinkeri* complex.
The posterior dark area is closer to vertical as in the *modestus* complex,
but the species lacks the anterior band of that group. In addition the
counts, if not absolutely overlapping, are continuous between the two
groups.

    Chaetodon excelsa and *C. modestus* have, at various times, been
placed in different genera such as *Coradion* and *Heniochus*. Both of these
genera have complete lateral lines, however, whereas the species in subgenus *Roa* have not. *Loa* (replaced by *Roa*) and *Paracanthochaetodon*
were described on juvenile specimens apparently recently metamorphosed from the tholichthys larva. Nalbant (1971), apparently unaware
that *Chaetodon excelsa* was closely related to *C. modestus*, chose *Paracanthochaetodon* to represent this subgenus.

CHAETODON MODESTUS Schlegel
Japanese golden-barred butterflyfish
(Brown-banded butterflyfish)

Chaetodon modestus Schlegel, *in* Temminck & Schlegel,
    1842: p. 80, pl. 4, fig. 2 (type locality Nagasaki).
Chaetodon ocellatus (not of Bloch), Gray, 1854: p. 68.
Coradion desmotes Jordan & Fowler, 1902: p. 539, fig. 5
    (type locality Nagasaki). Smith & Pope, 1908: p. 480
    (Urado).
Coradion modestus, Snyder, 1912: p. 422 (new combina-
    tion). Jordan & Hubbs, 1925: pp. 93-346 (Osaka Mar-
    ket, Toba Market, Fukui (Nonaku)).
Coradion modestum, Jordan, Tanaka, & Snyder, 1913: p.
    211, fig. 153 (Nagasaki, Misaki, Sigami).
Paracanthochaetodon modestus, Schmidt and Lindberg,
    1930: p. 468 (Tsuruga, Japan, new combination, genus
    based on tholichthys).
Chaetodon desmotes, Fowler, 1953: p. 59 (China; Hong
    Kong, Canton Foo Chow).

Diagnosis.—D. XI, 20-23 (usually 22-23); A. III, 16-19 (usually 17-18);
pectoral rays 13-15 (usually 14); L.l. scales 41-49; closely related to *Chaetodon jayakari* and *C. excelsa* but differing from these species in depth of
caudal peduncle (*modestus* 7.2-8.3, *jayakari* 8.5-9.0, *excelsa* 9.1-9.4), and

A pair of *Chaetodon semilarvatus* in their natural habitat in the Red Sea.
Photo by Dr. Gerald R. Allen, Eilat.

Chaetodon semilarvatus is quite strikingly colored with its red lines across a
yellow body and blueish eye patch.

Chaetodon semilarvatus is one of the more disc-shaped members of the genus *Chaetodon*. Photo by Guy Van Den Bossche.

Chaetodon semilarvatus, adult. Juveniles are similar but have a dark band surrounding the caudal peduncle and a more normal eye band. The changes are therefore less drastic than in the previous species. Photo by Dr. Herbert R. Axelrod.

Chaetodon modestus Schlegel. 68 mm S.L. Hong Kong.

Ratios	Standard Length (mm)		
	20-49(4)	50-79(7)	above 79(11)
Depth/S.L.	1.5-1.7	1.5-1.6	1.3-1.5
Head/S.L.	2.1-2.7	2.7-3.0	2.0-3.2
Eye/Head	2.4-3.3	2.8-3.0	2.9-3.2
Snout/Head	3.0-3.7	2.8-3.3	2.7-3.6
Interorb. W./Head	3.2-3.6	3.1-3.8	2.9-3.7
Maxillary/Head	4.1-4.9	3.7-4.7	3.8-4.8
Caud. Ped./S.L.	6.9-8.8	7.4-8.3	7.2-8.3
Pect. Fin./S.L.	2.9-3.5	3.2-3.8	3.5-4.1
Pelvic Spine/S.L.	2.8-4.5	3.8-4.7	3.9-4.5
Predorsal L./S.L.	1.7-2.0	1.9-2.1	1.9-2.0
Prepelvic L./S.L.	2.0-2.2	2.1-2.4	2.2-2.4
Dorsal Sp. No. 1/S.L.	8.6-11.2	10.1-14.2	10.3-14.2
Dorsal Sp. No. 2/S.L.	3.5-5.8	4.7-5.9	4.8-6.6
Dorsal Sp. No. 3/S.L.	3.2-4.0	3.3-4.0	3.4-4.7
Dorsal Sp. No. 4/S.L.	2.1-3.6	2.9-3.9	3.1-4.3
Anal Sp. No. 1/S.L.	6.3-10.4	6.6-9.1	7.6-11.1
Anal Sp. No. 2/S.L.	3.1-5.4	4.0-4.9	4.3-5.9
Anal Sp. No. 3/S.L.	3.6-5.8	4.1-5.3	4.6-5.9

in having a rounded dorsal fin spot in comparison to the oval or teardrop-shaped spot of the other two; *modestus* is further distinguished from the more closely related *jayakari* by head length (*modestus* 2.9-3.2, *jayakari* 2.6) and possibly by second anal spine length (*modestus* 4.3-5.9, *jayakari* 3.8-4.7) and pectoral fin length (*modestus* 3.5-4.1, *jayakari* 3.3-3.7); the dark bars are closer together at the dorsal fin in *jayakari* and *excelsa* than in *modestus*. Further differences between *modestus* and *excelsa* will be given under the latter species.

Meristics.—D. XI, 20-23 (usually 21-23); A. III, 16-19 (usually 17 or 18); pectoral rays 14 (8 with 14/15, one with 13/14, one with 13/13, and one with 15/15); L.l. scales 41-49; L.l. pores 36-45; scales above L.l. 11-13; scales below L.l. 24-27; gill rakers 13-18.

Description.—Mouth moderate, gape horizontal to slightly oblique; teeth in about 9 rows in each jaw; preopercle crenulate; lachrymal smooth; supraorbital smooth; caudal peduncle greater than eye diameter, which equals snout length; snout length and eye diameter greater than interorbital width.

Fourth dorsal spine longest; second anal spine longest, slightly longer than third spine, first half or slightly more than half second; first dorsal fin rays about equal or slightly longer than last dorsal fin spines; anal fin rounded; posterior edges of dorsal and anal fins near vertical; pelvic fins long, reaching base of first anal fin spine; base of spinous portion of dorsal fin longer (2.6-2.7 in S.L.) than that of soft portion (2.9-3.0).

Chaetodon modestus Schlegel. 40 mm S.L. Hong Kong.

Chaetodon adiergastos, small juvenile. Eye spot in dorsal fin and complete eye band are present. Photo by Dr. Fujio Yasuda.

Chaetodon adiergastos, subadult. Dorsal spot is gone and eyeband has changed into a nape spot and eye patch. Photo by K.H. Choo, Taiwan.

Chaetodon adiergastos, intermediate form between juvenile and adult. The eye band is barely connected by a dark area and the dorsal fin spot has faded perceptibly. Photo by Dr. Gerald R. Allen, Dampier Archipelago, Western Australia.

Adult *Chaetodon adiergastos.* In addition to other pattern characteristics, the dark lines on the sides are strongly ascending posteriorly. Photo by Dr. Fujio Yasuda.

Peak of lateral line at about last spine and first rays of dorsal fin; scaly covering of dorsal spines low, nearing midpoint of last spine; anal spine covering reaching midpoint of third spine.

Juveniles similar to adults.

Color Pattern.—Bars edged with darker color though this edging is sometimes very obscure or even absent; first bar originates at third through sixth dorsal fin spines and connects across abdomen; anterior edge (dark stripe) of posterior bar from tenth dorsal fin spine to base of third or fourth anal fin ray (and across anal fin); caudal peduncle light, base of caudal fin with dark bar; pelvic fins dusky, nearing blackish at edges, spine yellowish; eyebands join at nape; median snout stripe present from lower part of nape to tip of upper lip; eyeband and snout stripe may be dark bordered; dorsal spot ocellated; flap of second dorsal spine black. Juvenile color pattern similar to that of adults.

Remarks.—The similarity of this species to *Coradion chrysozonus* and its allied species prompted Jordan and Fowler (1902) as well as subsequent authors to place it in genus *Coradion*. The lateral line ending near the last rays of the dorsal fin in *Chaetodon modestus*, however, places this species outside genus *Coradion*, in which the lateral line ends near the base of the caudal fin. The genus *Paracanthochaetodon* was based on a larval or newly transformed specimen of *Chaetodon modestus*.

The closeness of *Chaetodon modestus* to *C. jayakari* is noted under the diagnosis. The question again arises as to whether or not to place *jayakari* as a subspecies of *C. modestus*. With only three specimens of *C. jayakari* measured, concrete evidence cannot be given as to whether or not this might be the case. Indications from the three specimens are that they have tenable differences (i.e. head size, caudal peduncle depth, etc.) from *C. modestus*. *Chaetodon excelsa* is discussed under that species.

Chaetodon modestus appears regularly in Japanese collections and apparently is not rare. It frequents shallow water at times but may extend to deeper water, although adequate records are absent.

Distribution.—Southern Japan to the East Indies and Philippine Islands.

Material Examined.—(22 spec.: 27-106 mm S.L.) USNM 86510 (1: 27), China; CAS 37675, CAS 37676, CAS 37677, CAS 37678, CAS 37740, CAS 37679, and CAS 37741 (17: 36-104), Hong Kong; USNM 59696 (1: 106), Urado, Japan; USNM 94786 (1: 80), Hainan, China; USNM 87037 (1: 49), Foochow, China; SU 7192 (1: 95) Nagasaki, Japan (holotype of *Coradion desmotes*).

CHAETODON JAYAKARI Norman
Indian golden-barred butterflyfish

Chaetodon jayakari Norman, 1939: p. 63, text fig. 21 (type locality Muscat, Gulf of Oman).

Coradion jayakari, Kotthaus, 1976: p. 45-61, pl. 378.

Chaetodon jayakari Norman. 93 mm S.L. Somali Coast, Africa.

Ratios	Standard Length (mm)		
	20-49	50-79	above 79(3)
Depth/S.L.	---	---	1.5-1.6
Head/S.L.	---	---	2.6
Eye/S.L.	---	---	3.0-3.3
Snout/Head	---	---	3.1-3.4
Interorb. W./Head	---	---	3.4-3.8
Maxillary/Head	---	---	3.8-4.3
Caud. Ped./S.L.	---	---	8.5-9.0
Pect. Fin/S.L.	---	---	3.2-3.7
Pelvic Sp./S.L.	---	---	3.8-4.0
Predorsal L./S.L.	---	---	2.0
Prepelvic L./S.L.	---	---	2.3
Dorsal Sp. No. 1/S.L.	---	---	11.2-11.9
Dorsal Sp. No. 2/S.L.	---	---	5.0-5.5
Dorsal Sp. No. 3/S.L.	---	---	3.3-3.7
Dorsal Sp. No. 4/S.L.	---	---	3.0-3.5
Anal Sp. No. 1/S.L.	---	---	6.9-10.3
Anal Sp. No. 2/S.L.	---	---	3.8-4.7
Anal Sp. No. 3/S.L.	---	---	4.5-4.9

Chaetodon auripes newly metamorphosed tholichthys. Photo by Dr. Fujio Yasuda.

Chaetodon auripes juvenile with dorsal fin spot. Photo by Dr. Fujio Yasuda.

Chaetodon auripes adult. Photo by Michio Goto.

Chaetodon auripes in its natural habitat exhibiting its nighttime pattern. Photo by Michio Goto, Marine Life Documents.

Chaetodon auripes adult, daytime color pattern. The lines on the body are horizontal in contrast to its closest relatives where they are inclined. Photo by Dr. Fujio Yasuda.

Diagnosis.—D. XI, 21-22; A. III, 16-18; pectoral rays 14; L.l. scales 37-45; closely related to *Chaetodon modestus* and *C. excelsa* but differing as noted under those species, i.e. head length 2.6, depth of caudal peduncle 8.5-9.0, second anal spine 3.8-4.7, and dark bars close together near dorsal fin.

Meristics.—Dorsal fin XI, 21-22; A. III, 16-18; pectoral rays 14 (one with 13/13); L.l. scales 37-45; L.l. pores 40-42; scales above L.l. 11-12; scales below L.l. 22-24; gill rakers 15-17.

Description.—Predorsal contour convex at nape, concave above eyes; mouth moderate, gape horizontal to slightly oblique; teeth in about 9-10 rows in each jaw; preopercle right-angled serrate, a slight extension at angle; lachrymal and supraorbital smooth; eye diameter greater than snout length, which equals or is greater than depth of caudal peduncle; caudal peduncle greater than interorbital width.

Fourth or fifth dorsal spines longest; second anal spine longest, slightly longer than third, first half length of second; first dorsal rays equal to or slightly longer than last spines; anal fin rounded; dorsal and anal fins posterior edges vertical or nearly so; base of spinous portion of dorsal fin longer (2.5-2.7 in S.L.) than soft portion (3.0-3.2 in S.L.); pelvic fins long, reaching level of first anal fin spine base.

Peak of lateral line below last spine and first rays of dorsal fin; scaly covering of dorsal spines low, reaching midpoint of eighth or ninth spines; anal spine scale covering reaching midpoint of third spine.

Juveniles not seen.

Color Pattern.—First body bar from third to sixth or seventh dorsal spines; second bar from tenth dorsal spine to angle of fin to rayed portion of anal fin; eyebands join at nape; medial brown stripe on interorbital from nape to tip of upper lip; black spot in dorsal fin ocellated; membrane of second dorsal spine black; pelvic fins dark.

Juveniles not known but should conform to the pattern of *Chaetodon modestus*.

Color of living animals not specifically known. A 35 mm slide of a freshly caught specimen taken by Dr. Loren P. Woods indicated the body was white, bars olive-brown. No dark borders to the bars evident. Dorsal spot and second dorsal spine membrane black; lower end of second body bar darker than upper portion; white stripe bordering second body bar posteriorly on dorsal and anal fins; edges of dorsal and anal fins hyaline; caudal fin yellow; caudal peduncle white; pelvic fins dark brown; eyeband similar in color to body bars; medial snout bar not visible but should be color of eyeband; snout tip dusky; horizontal lines of a slightly darker color than bars on body following scale rows (visible only within bands).

Remarks.—A poorly known species from rather deep water along the southern Arabian to Indian coastline. With further collections it is expected the range will be extended to the western edge of the Malay Archipelago. This is the Indian Ocean replacement species of *Chaetodon modestus*.

The dark edges of the body stripes in *Chaetodon modestus* may or may not be permanent parts of the color pattern and should not be relied upon too greatly as a field character, at least until more specimens of *C. jayakari* can be collected, including the smaller stages. The proportional differences used in the diagnosis have served in recognition of these species on all specimens collected to date.

Depth of capture ranged from 70 to 274 meters.

Norman's (1939) difference in eye size, fewer scales, and size of dorsal spot may or may not be real. When I measured eye size I obtained 3.0-3.3 in head length for *Chaetodon jayakari* and 2.9-3.2 in head length for *C. modestus*. L.l. scales were 40-42 for *C. jayakari* and 41-49 for *C. modestus*. The dorsal spot appears more elongate or oblong in *C. jayakari* than in *C. modestus*. The dorsal spines appear similar.

Distribution.—Indian Ocean from Gulf of Oman (Muscat), Gulf of Aden, and the south Arabian coast to off Quilon, southern India (9°00'N, 75°55'E).

Material Examined.—(3 spec.: 83-94 mm S.L.) FMNH 70233 (1: 94), southern Arabia; SOSC Anton Bruun Sta. 463 (1: 93), Somali coast, northern Africa (Gulf of Aden); BMNH 1939-5-24-960-2 (1: 83), Gulf of Aden.

CHAETODON EXCELSA (Jordan)
Hawaiian gold-barred butterflyfish

Loa excelsa Jordan, 1922: p. 652, fig. 6 (type locality Hawaiian Islands). Jordan and Jordan, 1922: p. 61, fig. 6 (Hawaiian Islands).

Roa excelsa, Jordan, 1923: p. 63 (Hawaiian Islands; *Loa* preoccupied).

Heniochus excelsa, Gosline, 1965: p. 198 (Hawaiian Islands; new combination).

Diagnosis.—D. XI, 21-22; A. III, 17; pectoral rays 14; lateral line scales 37-43; closely related to the two previously described species, *Chaetodon modestus* and *C. jayakari*, but differing from them in depth of caudal peduncle (*excelsa* 9.1-9.4, *modestus* 7.2-8.3, *jayakari* 8.5-9.0), second anal spine length (*excelsa* 3.0-3.2, *modestus* 4.3-5.9, *jayakari* 3.8-4.7), pectoral fin length (*excelsa* 2.9-3.1, *modestus* 3.5-4.1, *jayakari* 3.2-3.7), eye diameter (*excelsa* 2.5-2.6, *modestus* 2.9-3.2, *jayakari* 3.0-3.3), fourth dorsal spine length (*excelsa* 2.5-2.6, *modestus* 3.1-4.3, *jayakari* 3.0-3.5), and pelvic spine length (*excelsa* 3.6-3.8, *modestus* 3.9-4.5, *jayakari* 3.4-3.8).

Meristics.—D. XI, 21-22; A. III, 17; pectoral rays 14; L.l. scales 37-43; L.l. pores 36-42; scales above L.l. 11-13; scales below L.l. 20-22; gill rakers about 16.

Description.—Predorsal contour relatively straight, a slight hump

Chaetodon wiebeli late juvenile. In this specimen the eyeband is in the process of separating into an eyeband and a nape blotch. Photo by Dr. Fujio Yasuda.

A slightly older individual of *Chaetodon wiebeli* in which the separation is almost complete. The band about the caudal peduncle has almost disappeared. Photo by K.H. Choo, Taiwan.

Chaetodon wiebeli, adult. Photo by Dr. Shih- chieh Shen, Taiwan.

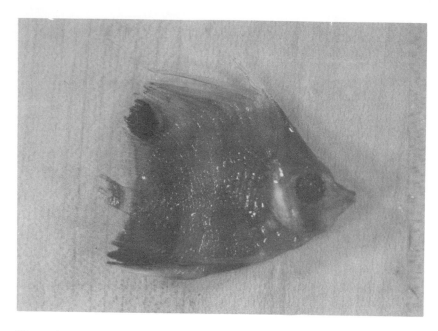

Chaetodon excelsa Jordan. 41 mm S.L. Hawaiian Islands (Holotype of *Loa excelsa*).

Ratios	Standard Length (mm)		
	20-49(2)	50-79(4)	above 79(1)
Depth/S.L.	1.5	1.5-1.6	1.5
Head/S.L.	2.6	2.8-2.9	3.0
Eye/Head	2.6	2.5-2.7	2.5
Snout/Head	3.0	2.9-3.3	3.0
Interorb. W./Head.	3.5	3.4-3.6	3.1
Maxillary/Head	---	3.9-4.8	4.4
Caud. Ped./S.L.	8.2	8.7-9.4	9.1
Pect. Fin./S.L.	3.0	2.9-3.1	3.0
Pelvic Spine/S.L.	2.8-3.2	3.3-3.6	3.8
Predorsal L./S.L.	1.9	1.9-2.1	2.0
Prepelvic L./S.L.	2.1	2.2-2.4	2.4
Dorsal Sp. No. 1/S.L.	10.4	8.6-11.0	10.4
Dorsal Sp. No. 2/S.L.	3.5	3.1-4.5	4.9
Dorsal Sp. No. 3/S.L.	1.7	2.2-2.5	2.6
Dorsal Sp. No. 4/S.L.	2.1	2.5-2.6	3.1(Bkn)
Anal Sp. No. 1/S.L.	6.3	6.3-7.1	6.7
Anal Sp. No. 2/S.L.	3.1	3.0-3.1	3.2
Anal Sp. No. 3/S.L.	3.6	3.5-3.9	4.3

noticeable at nape and a concavity at level of nostrils; preopercle right-angled, a slight projection at angle, edge lightly serrate; lachrymal with light serrations; supraorbital toothed; teeth in about 9 spaced rows in jaws; eye diameter greater than snout length, which is greater than both interorbital width and depth of caudal peduncle, which are equal.

Third dorsal fin spine longest; second anal fin spine longest; posterior edges of dorsal and anal fins nearly vertical; spinous dorsal fin base longer (2.5-2.7 in standard length) than that of soft portion (3.0-3.2 in S.L.).

Lateral line peak under last dorsal fin spines; scaly covering low.

Color Pattern.—Body bars dark bordered, first bar from first and or second dorsal fin spines to sixth or seventh spines, second from ninth spine to near posterior edge of fin; dark streak across base of caudal fin; eye-bands united anterior to first dorsal fin spine; dark ocellated spot extending from second to seventh dorsal fin ray.

Remarks.—The recent rediscovery of *Chaetodon excelsa* by Dr. Thomas Clark and Dr. John E. Randall has added much information to the understanding of this species. Until then the species was recorded from Hawaiian waters on the basis of two specimens, the first being the holotype. The second specimen, also a postlarval or prejuvenile, was discovered by Dr. Gerald R. Allen. It was taken by a Cobb midwater trawl off the leeward coast of Oahu set at 16-26 meters from 1946 to 0146 hours on July 13, 1967. Color notes were taken by Dr. Allen as follows: Body white, banded with brassy; dorsal and anal spines yellow, the yellow of the dorsal fin interrupted between the sixth and eighth spines by white color; pelvic fins yellow; vertical fins hyaline; black ocellated spot present between third and ninth rays of dorsal fin; head silvery white; indication of ocular band but weak; lower lip black; median interorbital stripe present. This specimen was apparently nearing time for metamorphosis and possibly was heading inshore at the time of capture. The latest specimens were trawled in deep water, re-confirming that this is indeed a deep-water butterflyfish. The specimen from Hawaii was trawled in 80 fathoms and those from Guam in 94 fathoms. On the basis of these recent specimens, up to 95 mm standard length, comparison between this and the two previously described species can be more confidently made.

The possibility of *Chaetodon excelsa* being identical with one or both of the other two species no longer exists. It of course may be considered as a subspecies by some, but there are now not enough comparative data to base a decision upon.

Distribution.—Once thought to be endemic to the Hawaiian Islands, this species has recently been discovered at Guam. Due to its deep-water habitat, it may still be found in other tropical Pacific localities.

Material Examined.—(7 spec.: 34-94 mm S.L.) USNM 84094 (1: 41), Hawaiian Islands (holotype of *Loa excelsa*); BPBM (uncatalogued) (1: 34), Hawaiian Islands; BPBM 10868 (1: 95.4), Hawaiian Islands; BPBM (1: 72), Hawaiian Islands; BPBM 11600 (3: 69-76), Guam, Marianas Islands.

Chaetodon ephippium, newly metamorphosed tholichthys. Even at this size the large black blotch is present. Photo by Dr. Fujio Yasuda.

Chaetodon ephippium juvenile. Blotch is well defined and the caudal peduncle and eye bands are both present. Photo by F. Earl Kennedy.

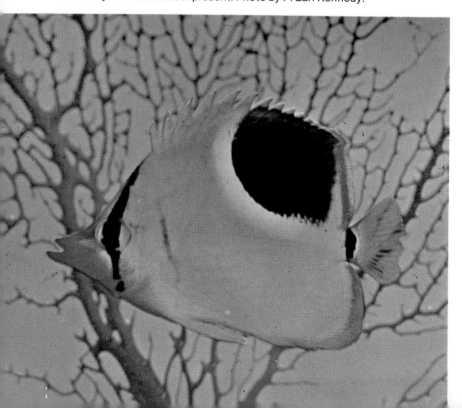

Chaetodon ephip-pium adult with well-developed dorsal fin fila-ment. The eye band has been slow to disappear however. Photo by W. Deas, Great Barrier Reef.

Chaetodon ephippium lacking eye and peduncle bands but the dorsal fila-ment is still small. Photo by Allan Power, New Hebrides.

CHAETODON TINKERI Schultz
Tinker's butterflyfish

Chaetodon tinkeri Schultz, 1951: p. 485, pl. 15A (type locality Oahu, Hawaiian Islands).

Chaetodon tinkeri Schultz. 109 mm S.L. (female). Hawaiian Islands.

Diagnosis.—D. XIII-XIV, 19-21; A. III, 16 (-17); pectoral rays 14; L.l. scales 38-42; closely related to *Chaetodon declevis* but distinguishable from that species by color pattern (*tinkeri* black posteriorly, *declevis* brownish) and possibly eye diameter (*declevis* 2.5-3.0, *tinkeri* 2.9-3.2); also related to *C. mitratus* and *C. burgessi* but lacks the second black band of those species.

Meristics.—D. XIII (one with XIV), 19-21; A. III, 16 (one with 17); pectoral rays 14 (two with 15/14); L.l. scales 38-42; L.l. pores 36-41; scales above L.l. 8-10 (normally 9); scales below L.l. 15-16; gill rakers 16-17.

Description.—Predorsal contour slightly convex at nape, concave at level of nostrils; snout short, pointed, 2.7-3.5 in head length; mouth small, gape horizontal to slightly oblique; teeth in 7 rows in each jaw;

		Standard Length (mm)	
Ratios	20-49	50-79	above 79(7)
Depth/S.L.	---	---	1.5-1.7
Head/S.L.	---	---	3.3-3.7
Eye/Head	---	---	2.9-3.2
Snout/Head	---	---	2.7-3.5
Interorb. W./Head.	---	---	2.5-3.2
Maxillary/Head	---	---	3.4-4.6
Caud. Ped./S.L.	---	---	9.1-10.0
Pect. Fin/S.L.	---	---	2.8-3.7
Pelvic Sp./S.L.	---	---	3.9-4.3
Predorsal L./S.L.	---	---	2.2-2.4
Prepelvic L./S.L.	---	---	2.2-2.5
Dorsal Sp. No. 1/S.L.	---	---	8.7-13.0
Dorsal Sp. No. 2/S.L.	---	---	4.7-6.7
Dorsal Sp. No. 3/S.L.	---	---	3.1-3.7
Dorsal Sp. No. 4/S.L.	---	---	3.0-3.4
Anal Sp. No. 1/S.L.	---	---	7.7-9.5
Anal Sp. No. 2/S.L.	---	---	3.2-3.7
Anal Sp. No. 3/S.L.	---	---	3.7-4.3

preopercle obtuse-angled, rounded, crenulate; lachrymal and supraorbital smooth; caudal peduncle depth greater than snout length, which is greater than eye diameter; eye diameter greater than interorbital width.

Fourth dorsal fin spine longest, first short, 8.7 to 13.0 in standard length; soft dorsal rounded, both posterior edges of both dorsal and anal fins near vertical; second anal spine long, strong, 3.2-3.7 in S.L., first spine small, between a third and a half of second; base of spinous portion of dorsal fin longer (2.0-2.1 in S.L.) than that of soft portion (3.0-3.4 in S.L.); pelvic fins moderate to short, reaching just short of or just past anus.

Lateral line with anterior angle at fifth dorsal spine base, posterior (higher angle) at twelfth (10-12); scaly portion of dorsal spines low, reaching midpoint of sixth or seventh spine, last almost completely covered (first five spines in true sheath?); anal spine covering reaching a third of third spine.

Juveniles not known. It is expected that they resemble adults as do others in this subgenus.

Color Pattern.—Dark portion of body extends from base of fourth dorsal spine (spine incl.) to base of tenth anal ray; eyeband close to diameter of eye, sometimes wider, sometimes narrower, separated from one of opposite side by a narrow space (in one specimen it was joined and extended toward and reached first dorsal spine); white to yellowish mark on

Chaetodon xanthocephalus, small juvenile with strong eyeband and caudal peduncle band (like *C. ephippium* juveniles.) Photo by Aaron Norman.

Chaetodon xanthocephalus larger individual with more adult fin pattern but still with the eye and peduncle bands. Photo by Dr. Herbert R. Axelrod.

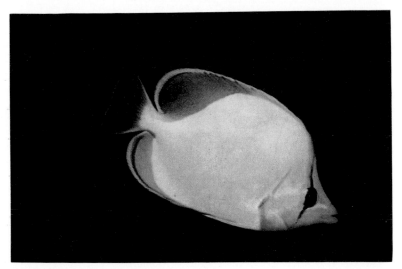

Chaetodon xanthocephalus subadult. The eyeband is very reduced and the caudal peduncle band is absent. Photo by K. Knaack.

Chaetodon xanthocephalus adult. Darkening of most of body is fright pattern. Photo by Dr. Herbert R. Axelrod, Maldives.

upper snout squarish to "H-"shaped with two legs almost reaching the eyes; chin light grayish; interorbital dusky; each scale with dusky spot in center, larger above lateral line (above L.l. generally darkish and without spots); spots form horizontal lines along scale rows below L.l.; pelvic fins body color.

Remarks.—*Chaetodon tinkeri* is an endemic Hawaiian species of butterflyfish rarely found in water less than 90 feet deep.

The pair of *C. tinkeri* speared by Dr. John E. Randall was a male-female pair. The male lacked the light stripe (orange in life) of the soft dorsal fin. On the basis of a single pair it cannot be stated for certain whether this is a sexually dimorphic character.

Juvenile specimens thus far have not been found although SCUBA dives in the area where adults were located were made several times.

In addition to the other characters given to distinguish *Chaetodon tinkeri* and *C. nippon*, the second anal spines can be seen to be longer in *C. tinkeri* (3.2-3.7 in S.L. vs 5.1-5.3 in *C. nippon*).

Distribution.—Endemic to the Hawaiian Islands.

Material Examined.—(7 spec.: 99-114 mm S.L.) USNM 111976 (1: 114), Nanakuli, Oahu, Hawaiian Islands (holotype); USNM 111977 (2: 99-109), Nanakuli, Hawaiian Islands (paratypes); HIMB 68-43 (1: 109), Moku Manu, Oahu, Hawaiian Islands; BPBM 6012 (1: 113), Waianae, Oahu, Hawaiian Islands; BPBM (uncatalogued) (2: 100-105), South Point, Hawaii, Hawaiian Islands.

CHAETODON MITRATUS Gunther
Black and yellow butterflyfish

Chaetodon mitratus Gunther, 1860: p. 16. (No type locality ("Probably from Dr. Janvier's collection, who collected at the Mauritius"—Gunther)).

Diagnosis.—D. XIII, 18-20; A. III, 14-15 (usually 15); L.l. scales 30-38; close to *Chaetodon burgessi* but differs from that species by color pattern, *mitratus* having light colored dorsal (except 3-7 D. spines) and anal fins and the nape bar extending to anal fin base, *burgessi* having a mostly blackish dorsal fin and half of anal fin, and the nape bar extending only to about pectoral fin base.

Meristics.—D. XIII, 18-20; A. III, 14-15 (usually 15); pectoral rays 14 (one with 13); L.l. scales 30-38; scales above L.l. 7-8; scales below L.l. 13-14; gill rakers 18.

Description.—Snout pointed, 2.6-3.0 in standard length; preopercle approximately right-angled, the angle slightly produced; snout length greater than eye diameter, which is greater than interorbital width and depth of caudal peduncle, which are approximately equal.

Fourth dorsal spine longest, 3.5-4.1 in standard length; second anal spine longest and strongest, 3.3-4.0 in standard length (approximately

Chaetodon mitratus Gunther. 72.7 mm S.L. Photo by Dr. W. Smith-Vaniz.

Ratios	Standard Length (mm)			(Holotype) (Stuffed)
	20-40	41-60(1)	above 60(3)	
Depth/S.L.	---	1.7	1.8-1.9	(1.7)
Head/S.L.	---	2.8	3.0	(3.1)
Eye/Head	---	2.7	3.0-3.2	(3.1)
Snout/Head	---	3.3	2.7-3.0	(2.6)
Interorb. W./Head....	---	3.5	3.6-3.7	(3.3)
Maxillary/Head	---	4.1	4.0-4.5	(---)
Caud. Ped./S.L.	---	10.4	10.4-11.0	(10.6)
Pect. Fin./S.L.	---	3.3	3.7-3.8	(---)
Pelvic Spine/S.L.	---	3.9	4.1	(---)
Predorsal L./S.L.	---	2.4	2.4	(2.4)
Prepelvic L./S.L.	---	2.3	2.6-2.7	(2.2)
Dorsal Sp. No. 1/S.L. ..	---	10.4	9.1-9.6	(11.4)
Dorsal Sp. No. 2/S.L. ..	---	4.0	3.6-5.0	(5.9)
Dorsal Sp. No. 3/S.L. ..	---	3.0	3.7-3.8	(4.8)
Dorsal Sp. No. 4/S.L. ..	---	3.0	3.5-3.6	(4.1)
Anal Sp. No. 1/S.L.	---	x	7.2-8.8	(8.7)
Anal Sp. No. 2/S.L.	---	3.0	3.3-3.4	(4.0)
Anal Sp. No. 3/S.L.	---	3.4	3.6	(4.3)

Chaetodon auriga, newly metamorphosed tholichthys. The color pattern already is complete enough for identification. Photo by Dr. Warren E. Burgess, Hawaii.

Chaetodon auriga juvenile. The pattern is well developed but the dorsal filament is not evident. Photo by K.H. Choo, Taiwan.

Chaetodon auriga photographed at night. Photo by Michio Goto, Marine Life Documents.

Chaetodon auriga adult with well developed filament. Photo by Dr. Gerald R. Allen, Hawaii.

equal to fourth dorsal spine); base of spinous portion of dorsal fin longer (1.9-2.2 in standard length) than that of soft portion (3.6-3.8 in standard length); pectoral and pelvic fins normal; caudal fin truncate.

Lateral line with flexures in vicinity of sixth and twelfth dorsal fin spines; scales moderate, 30-38 in lateral line; scales at base of dorsal spines relatively low; scales covering anal spines to about one-third of third spine.

Color Pattern.—Ocular band crosses interorbital as broad dark band; below eyes it extends as dark-margined light band almost to edge of preopercle; dark dorsal band includes dorsal spines 3-5 from about bases of fith dorsal spine on.

Juveniles similar to adults.

Remarks.—Very little is known about *Chaetodon mitratus*. A single specimen of doubtful locality was known until recently when three more were collected at Cocos-Keeling Island. The type specimen itself is not in good condition, but the rediscovery of the species and the closely related *Chaetodon burgessi* made it possible to place *mitratus* in its proper taxonomic position.

Distribution.—Mauritius; Cocos-Keeling Is., E. Indian Ocean.

Material Examined.—(4: spec.: 51-91mm S.L.) BM(NH) (1: 91) holotype, no locality (probably Mauritius), stuffed; ANSP 128355, 128304, and 128305 (3: 51-77) Cocos-Keeling Island.

CHAETODON BURGESSI Allen and Starck
Burgess' butterflyfish

Chaetodon burgessi Allen and Starck, 1973: p. 17, fig. 1 (type locality Bairakaserv I., Ngemelis Islands, Palau Group).

Diagnosis.—D. XIII, 18-19; A. III, 15-16; pectoral fin 15? (possibly 14 by my way of counting); L.1 scales 35-37; closely related to *Chaetodon mitratus*, *C. tinkeri* and *C. declevis*, but distinguishable from those species by color pattern, *mitratus* with light colored dorsal and anal fins and nape bar extending almost to anal fin base, *burgessi* with almost completely dark dorsal fin and half dark anal fin and with nape bar extending only to behind pectoral fin, *tinkeri* and *declevis* both lacking the dark bar from predorsal area to behind pectoral fins.

Meristics.—D. XIII, 18-19; A. III, 15-16; pectoral fin 15? (probably 14 according to my method of counting); L.l. scales 35-37; scales above L.l. about 8; scales below L.l. about 15; gill rakers 17-20.

Description.—The following description is based on that of Allen and Starck (1973) and the photographs of this species. Predorsal contour straight, slightly concave at level of nostrils; snout short, 2.7 in head length, pointed; mouth small, gape horizontal to slightly oblique; preopercle right to slightly obtuse-angled, finely denticulate; teeth "in several

Chaetodon burgessi Allen and Starck. 80.4 mm S.L. Palau Islands. Photo by Allen & Starck.

		Standard Length (mm)	
Ratios	20-49	41-60(2)	above 60(1)
Depth/S.L.............	---	1.7	1.6
Head/S.L......	---	2.8-2.9	2.9
Eye/Head.............	---	3.1-3.3	3.2
Snout/Head...........	---	2.9-3.1	2.7
Interorb. W./Head......	---	4.3-4.4	3.8
Maxillary/Head........	---	---	4.3
Caud. Ped./S.L.........	---	10.2-10.4	9.8
Pect. Fin./S.L..........	---	3.4	3.6
Pelvic Spine/S.L........	---	3.8-4.0	4.2
Predorsal L./S.L........	---	2.2-2.4	2.3
Prepelvic L./S.L........	---	2.3-2.4	2.4
Dorsal Sp. No. 1/S.L.....	---	11.0-12.7	12.5
Dorsal Sp. No. 2/S.L.....	---	4.6-4.7	5.2
Dorsal Sp. No. 3/S.L.....	---	3.3	3.8
Anal Sp. No. 1/S.L.......	---	7.1-8.5	9.3
Anal Sp. No. 2/S.L.......	---	3.3-3.5	3.4
Anal Sp. No. 3/S.L........	---	3.7-3.8	4.2

Chaetodon auriga from the Red Sea without the black spot in the dorsal fin. Photo by Dr. D. Terver, Nancy Aquarium.

Chaetodon auriga in its natural habitat in the Red Sea. Neither of these individuals (above or below) have the dorsal spot. Photo above by Dr. Gerald R. Allen, Eilat; photo below by W. Deas, Wingate Reef.

rows;" caudal peduncle depth greater than interorbital width, which is greater than eye diameter; eye diameter greater than snout length.

Third or fourth dorsal fin spine longest, first relatively short, 12.5 in standard length; soft dorsal fin rounded; posterior edges of dorsal and anal fins near vertical; second anal fin spine strong, 3.4 in standard length, first about half second; pelvic fins moderate, almost reaching anal opening.

Lateral line as in *Chaetodon tinkeri*; scaly sheath low, anterior spines mostly free; anal spine sheath also low.

Juveniles not known. It is expected that they resemble adults.

Color Pattern.—Eyeband extends from interorbital region, where it is continuous with one from other side, to lower edge of preopercle; anterior bar connected across nape broadly; dividing line of the dark and light colors extending from fourth dorsal fin spine base to distal portion of second anal fin ray; each scale of lower sides with grayish spots (black in life) arranged in rows; pelvic fins body color.

Remarks.—According to Allen and Starck (1973) the type specimens were captured in an area characterized by a sheer vertical wall starting at a depth of about two meters and descending to 150 meters or more. Eight pairs were observed at depths ranging between 40 and 80 meters. This area had a rich growth of black coral (*Antipathes*).

The data for this species agree very well with other species in the *tinkeri*-complex. The discovery of most of the species in this group in recent times can probably be explained by their deep-water habitats.

Distribution.—Known only from the Palau Islands.

Material Examined.—No specimens were examined personally.

CHAETODON DECLEVIS Burgess and Randall, NEW SPECIES *
Marquesas butterflyfish

Diagnosis.—D. XII-XIII, 18-21; A. III, 15-16; pectoral rays 14; L.l. scales 37-41; very closely related to *Chaetodon tinkeri* but distinguishable from that species by color pattern as follows: posterior dark area of *declevis* brown in life except caudal peduncle and adjacent area of body, which are black; dividing line of dark and light areas starts from base of third dorsal fin spine and extends to include last few rays of anal fin; pelvic fins yellowish; posterior dark area of *tinkeri* black, dividing line extends from base of fourth spine to include almost half of anal fin; pelvic fins white; eye diameter may be different.

Meristics.—D. XII-XIII, 18-21; A. III, 15-16; pectoral rays 14; L.l. scales 37-41; scales above L.l. 6-7; scales below L.l. 12-14; gill rakers 17-19.

Description.—Predorsal contour slightly convex at nape, concave at level of nostrils; snout short, pointed, 3.0-3.5 in head length; mouth small, gape horizontal to slightly oblique; teeth in 6-8 rows in each jaw;

*Completed manuscript sent to Dr. Randall in Summer, 1974 for joint publication.

| | Standard Length (mm) | | |
Ratios	20-49	50-79	above 79(6)
Depth/S.L............	---	---	1.7-1.8
Head/S.L.............	---	---	3.3-3.5
Eye/Head	---	---	2.5-2.8
Snout/Head	---	---	3.0-3.5
Interorb. W./Head......	---	---	3.0-3.4
Maxillary/Head	---	---	3.8-4.1
Caud. Ped./S.L.........	---	---	9.5-11.0
Pect. Fin/S.L...........	---	---	3.3-3.8
Pelvic Sp./S.L..........	---	---	3.8-4.2
Predorsal L./S.L........	---	---	2.4-2.6
Prepelvic L./S.L........	---	---	2.5-2.6
Dorsal Sp. No. 1/S.L.....	---	---	7.2-9.8
Dorsal Sp. No. 2/S.L.....	---	---	4.3-5.8
Dorsal Sp. No. 3/S.L.....	---	---	3.2-3.6
Dorsal Sp. No. 4/S.L.....	---	---	3.1-3.5
Dorsal Sp. No. 5/S.L.....	---	---	3.6-3.9
Anal Sp. No. 1/S.L.......	---	---	6.3-8.0
Anal Sp. No. 2/S.L.......	---	---	3.2-3.6
Anal Sp. No. 3/S.L.......	---	---	3.5-4.1

preopercle obtuse to right-angled, rounded, crenulate on edge; lachrymal and supraorbital smooth; eye diameter greater than depth of caudal peduncle, which is greater than interorbital width; interorbital width greater than snout length.

Fourth dorsal spine longest, first short, 7.2-9.8 in standard length; soft dorsal fin rounded, both posterior edges of dorsal and anal fins near vertical; second anal spine long, strong, 3.2-3.6 in standard length, first about one-third to one-half of length of second; base of spinous portion of dorsal fin longer (2.1-2.3 in S.L.) than that of soft portion (3.1-3.4 in S.L.); pelvic fins moderate to short, barely reaching anal opening.

Lateral line as in *Chaetodon tinkeri*; sheath low, reaching midpoint of about eighth spine; anal spine sheath also low, reaching up to a third of third spine.

Juveniles not known. It is expected they resemble adults as do others in this subgenus.

Color Pattern.—Dark portion of body extends from base of third to fourth dorsal fin spine (including third spine) to base of about thirteenth ray of anal fin; eyeband narrower than eye, not connected above; area above upper lip yellowish with yellow lines extending to nostrils; face and interorbital dusky; each scale with dark spot at base, larger anteriorly just below lateral line, arranged in horizontal rows following scale pattern; pelvic fins body color.

Chaetodon semeion, late juvenile. Dorsal and anal fins are just developing their pattern and the caudal peduncle band is still evident as a spot. Photo by Dr. Fujio Yasuda, Japan.

Opposite:
Chaetodon semeion adult. Photo by Dr. Shih-chieh Shen.

Chaetodon semeion subadult. The pattern is complete and the dorsal fin filament is beginning to develop. Photo by Rodney Jonklaas, Sri Lanka.

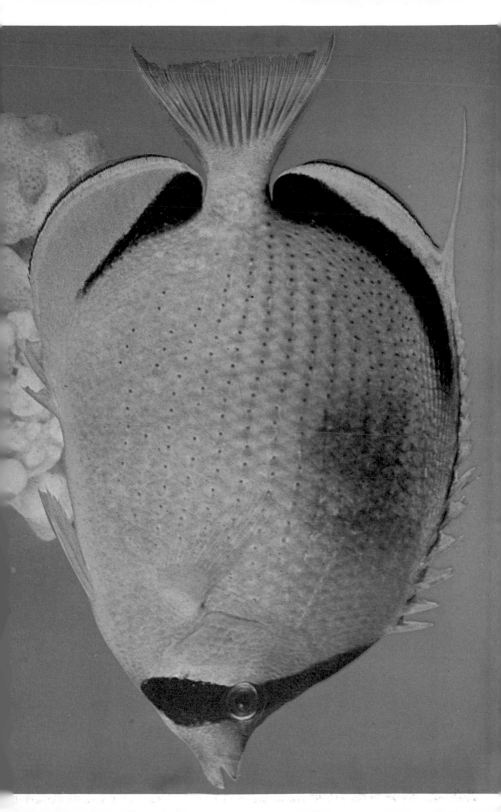

Dark portion of body light in alcohol, yellow on extremities of fins; dorsal fin with submarginal black line, outside of which is hyaline or white; blackish caudal area not connected above on peduncle but is united below.

Remarks.—Although very similar to *Chaetodon tinkeri*, this species is separable by elements of the color pattern. In addition the eye diameter is different (*declevis* 2.5-2.8 in head, *tinkeri* 2.9-3.2 in head) and possibly the predorsal and prepelvic ratios (*declevis* 2.4-2.6 and 2.5-2.6 respectively, *tinkeri* 2.2-2.4 and 2.2-2.5 respectively).

This species was taken by Dr. Randall at depths of 75-100 feet.

Distribution.—Known only from the Marquesas Islands. The specimens were taken at Fatu Hiva.

Material Examined.—(6 spec.: 85-95mm S.L.) BPBM 11734 (1: 92), BPBM 11733 (2: 87-95), BPBM 11777 (3: 85-95), Fatu Hiva, Marquesas.

CHAETODON NIPPON Doderlein
Blackloin butterflyfish
(Japanese butterflyfish)

Chaetodon nippon Doderlein, *in* Steindachner & Doderlein, 1884: p. 23, pl. 4, fig. 2 (type locality Tokyo).

Chaetodon carens Seale, 1910: p. 115, pl. 1, fig. 1 (type locality Bantayan Island, Phil.). Herre & Montalban 1927: p. 55, pl. 15, fig. 2.

Chaetodon decipiens Ahl, 1923: p. 79 (on *C. nippon* Jordan & Fowler, 1902; Totomi Bay and Misaki, Japan).

Chaetodon nippon Doderlein. 117 mm S.L. Misaki, Japan.

Ratios	Standard Length (mm)		
	20-49	50-79(4)	above 79(4)
Depth/S.L.	---	1.6-1.7	1.7-1.8
Head/S.L.	---	3.2-3.3	3.4-3.5
Eye/Head	---	2.5-2.9	3.0-3.1
Snout/Head	---	3.1-3.6	2.8-3.1
Interorb. W./Head.	---	2.9-3.3	2.7-3.2
Maxillary/Head	---	4.3-5.0	4.3-5.7
Caud. Ped./S.L.	---	8.5-9.6	9.5-10.4
Pect. Fin./S.L.	---	3.5-3.7	3.8-4.1
Pelvic Spine/S.L.	---	4.6-4.9	4.7-5.3
Predorsal L./S.L.	---	2.3-2.5	2.4-2.6
Prepelvic L./S.L.	---	2.2-2.3	2.2-2.4
Dorsal Sp. No. 1/S.L.	---	10.6-13.8	12.1-17.0
Dorsal Sp. No. 2/S.L.	---	4.9-6.7	6.4-8.2
Dorsal Sp. No. 3/S.L.	---	3.3-5.0	4.8-6.0
Dorsal Sp. No. 4/S.L.	---	3.5-4.9	4.4-5.6
Anal Sp. No. 1/S.L.	---	6.5-7.9	8.3-9.2
Anal Sp. No. 2/S.L.	---	4.4-4.8	5.1-5.3
Anal Sp. No. 3/S.L.	---	4.5-5.4	5.4-5.9

Diagnosis.—D. XII-XIII, 18-20 (usually 19); A. III, 15-17 (usually 16); pectoral rays 14; L.l. scales 38-41; dark area of body extending from last dorsal spines to last anal spine, including rayed portions of both fins; eyeband absent in adults; second anal spine 5.1-5.3 in S.L., shorter than closest relative, *Chaetodon tinkeri*, in which it is 3.2-3.7.

Meristics.—D. XIII (one with XII), 18-20 (usually 19); A. III, 15-17 (usually 16); pectoral rays 14; L.l. scales 38-41; L.l. pores 35-39; scales above L.l. 8-10; scales below L.l. 19-21; gill rakers 16-20.

Description.—Predorsal contour straight; snout short, 2.8-3.1 in head length; gape horizontal to slightly oblique; teeth in 7 rows in each jaw; preopercle edge rounded, crenulate to lightly serrate; lachrymal smooth, partially covered by scales; supraorbital smooth; interorbital width equal to or greater than depth of caudal peduncle, which is equal to or greater than eye diameter; eye diameter equal to or greater than snout length.

Fourth to fifth dorsal spine longest; second anal spine longer than third but not excessively so, first slightly more than half second; posterior edges of dorsal and anal fins near vertical; base of spinous portion of dorsal fin longer (2.1-2.3 in S.L.) than that of soft portion (3.6-3.7 in S.L.); pelvic fins short, not reaching level of anus.

Lateral line in moderate arc, highest point at base of posterior dorsal spines; scales mostly rounded though some angular; scaly covering of dorsal spines reaching midpoint of sixth or seventh dorsal spines; anal scale covering reaching midpoint of third spine.

Chaetodon lineolatus newly metamorphosed tholichthys. The characteristic pattern is already evident in this tiny individual. Photo by Allan Power, New Hebrides.

Chaetodon lineolatus late juvenile. The pattern is well-developed and the snout has become somewhat longer. Photo by K.H. Choo, Taiwan.

Chaetodon lineolatus adult. This species is one of the largest in the genus *Chaetodon.* Photo by Dr. Shih-chieh Shen, Taiwan.

Chaetodon lineolatus in its natural habitat. Usually more than one individual will be seen at any time. Photo by Norbert Schuch.

Juveniles similar to adults. The snout is a little more pointed and the soft dorsal and anal fins slightly more angular.

Color Pattern.—Dark posterior area extends from ninth dorsal spine to last anal spine (base of ninth anal ray to tip of first anal ray); submarginal dark line in dorsal and anal rayed portion of fins; ocular band absent; flaps of dorsal spines dark; lips dark brown.

Juveniles diverge slightly from adult color pattern. An eyeband is present, extending from nape to at least lower edge of preopercle (and probably extending to lower edge of interopercle); eyeband widest at eye but not as wide as eye, and is joined at nape by one from opposite side; edges of eyeband not sharply defined. A large dark spot present in soft dorsal fin at about the angle, almost as deep as the fin itself. Caudal fin about two-thirds hyaline compared with just small part of edge in adults.

Remarks.—I have examined the specimens in the USNM type section listed as *Chaetodon decipiens* Ahl (one specimen is labelled *C. nippon* #50902) from Totomi Bay, Japan, as well as the specimens from Misaki, Japan in the collection formerly housed at Stanford University. The description of these last specimens by Jordan and Fowler (1902) as *C. nippon* Doderlein was used by Ahl as the basis of his new species *C. decipiens*. In comparing them with the original description I find no basis upon which to retain the nominal species *Chaetodon decipiens*. *Chaetodon carens* Seale 1910 is without doubt this species.

Apparently not a shallow water species though some specimens may be taken in shoreline waters.

Distribution.—Philippine Islands to Japan and Korea.

Material Examined.—(8 spec.: 60-121 mm S.L.) USNM 50802 (3: 70-102), Totomi Bay, Japan (types of *C. decipiens*); SU 7244 (5: 60-121), Misaki, Japan (types of *C. decipiens*).

RHOMBOCHAETODON Burgess,
NEW SUBGENUS

Type-species.—*Chaetodon mertensii* Cuvier, 1831, by original designation.

Diagnosis.—Scales large, rhomboidal, in rows following a chevron-like pattern, steeply ascending above midpoint of body, descending obliquely posteriorly in the lower portion; D. XIII, 20-23; A. III, 16-17; pectoral fin 14; L.l. scales 32-43; soft dorsal fin rounded, anal angular.

Description.—Body oval; snout short, pointed, 2.4-3.5 in head length; predorsal contour straight or slightly convex at nape, a concavity at level of nostrils; gape horizontal to slightly oblique; teeth in spaced rows; preopercle right-angled to slightly obtuse, lightly serrate; lachrymal and supraorbital smooth.

Fourth or fifth dorsal fin spine longest, first relatively short, 8.7-17.4 in standard length; dorsal fin continuous, no notch between soft and spinous portions; spinous dorsal fin base longer (1.9-2.5 in S.L.) than that of soft portion (2.7-3.4 in S.L.); pelvic fins short to moderate, not reaching base of anal fin; pectoral fins normal; caudal fin truncate to rounded; second and third anal spines subequal, first half or less of second.

Lateral line crosses body in moderate arc which is flattened on top but usually slightly higher at its posterior flexure, which occurs at about the level of the eleventh or twelfth spine of the dorsal fin, the posterior portion of the line heading directly toward the base of the last rays of dorsal fin where it ends; scales large, rhomboidal, in pattern following chevron color pattern; scales smaller posteriorly on body; scaly portion of dorsal fin normal, covering most of last spine and about half of middle spines.

Juveniles similar to adults in both color pattern and form.

Color pattern consists of either chevrons or reticulated pattern outlining scale rows of body; posteriorly an abrupt change of color, usually to yellow or yellow orange but also to red or black; dark mark usually present on nape above eyeband; eyeband narrow or reduced, dark spot sometimes evident in dorsal fin.

Found only in the Pacific and Indian Oceans (including Red Sea).

Five species are recognized, distinguished by the following key.

Key to the Species of the Subgenus Rhombochaetodon

1. Posterior body band black; eyeband reduced to dark marking above eyes; pattern on sides reticulations (S. Japan to Philippine Is.).....
. . . .*Chaetodon argentatus*
Posterior body band yellow to reddish; eyeband present, narrow, light or dark bordered or both; pattern on sides chevrons or reticulations
. 2

2. Body pattern consisting of reticulations, each scale being completely edged with dark; posterior band not reaching dorsal spines (Philippine Is.) . . . .*C. xanthurus*
Body pattern consisting of chevrons; posterior band extending forward to include at least part of last dorsal spines. 3

3. Eyeband connected on interorbital; dark mark on nape reduced to smudge, indistinct, without white border (Pacific Ocean) . . . .
. . . .*C. mertensii*
Eyeband not connected on nape or interorbital; nape mark distinct, horseshoe-shaped, with white border, at least on upper edge 4

4. Mark on nape bordered with white only on upper edge; posterior body band yellow in life (light colored in alcohol), lower end extending to angle of anal fin (Indian Ocean) . . . .*C. madagascariensis*
Mark on nape usually completely surrounded by white line; posterior body band brick red to vermilion in life (grayish to dark brownish

Chaetodon oxycephalus in its natural habitat. Photographed by Dr. Herbert R. Axelrod in the Maldives.

Chaetodon oxycephalus has a more limited distribution than its sister species, *C. lineolatus.* Photo by Roger Steene.

Chaetodon oxycephalus is very similar in pattern to *C. lineolatus* but has a different eyeband pattern. Photo by Allan Power.

in alcohol), lower end curved past angle of anal fin and ending at
tip of eighth ray (Red Sea) .... *C. paucifasciatus*
   Remarks.—The species of this subgenus are somewhat separated geographically: *C. argentatus*—southern Japan to the Philippines; *C. xanthurus*—Philippines; *C. mertensii*—Pacific; *C. madagascariensis*—Indian
Ocean; and *C. paucifasciatus*—Red Sea and parts of Indian Ocean. There
are areas of sympatry, however, *C. argentatus* with *C. xanthurus* in the
Philippines and with *C. mertensii* in southern Japan, and *C. madagascariensis* with *C. paucifasciatus* in the northwestern corner of the Indian
Ocean. It is also possible that *C. xanthurus* and *C. mertensii* are sympatric around the Philippines or East Indies. I have not seen *C. mertensii*
in the Philippines, where *C. xanthurus* is moderately common.
   Rhombochaetodon is named after a distinguishing characteristic of
this subgenus, the rhomboidal shape of the scales.

CHAETODON MERTENSII Cuvier
Mertens butterflyfish

   Chaetodon Mertensii Cuvier, 1831: p. 47 (no locality, on
      figure of Mertens, naturalist on Russian Expedition of
      Captain Lutken).
   Citharoedus Mertensi, Kaup, 1860: p. 143 (no locality—
      on Cuvier, 1831).
   Chaetodon dixoni Regan, 1904: p. 276, fig. (type locality
      New Hebrides). Whitley, 1964: p. 152 (as *C. dixsoni*,
      sic., Coral Sea).

Chaetodon mertensii Cuvier. 86 mm S.L. Enewetak, Marshall Islands.

Ratios	Standard Length (mm)		
	10-30	31-60(1)	above 60(19)
Depth/S.L.	---	1.7	1.7-1.8
Head/S.L.	---	3.1	3.1-3.7
Eye/Head	---	3.1	2.7-3.1
Snout/Head	---	3.0	2.6-3.5
Interorb. W./Head	---	4.0	3.2-4.2
Maxillary/Head	---	5.1	3.8-4.8
Caud. Ped./S.L.	---	10.1	9.9-10.7
Pect. Fin/S.L.	---	3.5	3.2-3.8
Pelvic Sp./S.L.	---	4.6	4.1-4.8
Predorsal L./S.L.	---	2.4	2.3-2.6
Prepelvic L./S.L.	---	2.3	2.3-2.7
Dorsal Sp. No. 1/S.L.	---	12.3	8.7-14.7
Dorsal Sp. No. 2/S.L.	---	6.0	4.9-8.3
Dorsal Sp. No. 3/S.L.	---	4.9	3.9-6.4
Dorsal Sp. No. 4/S.L.	---	4.8	3.5-6.0
Dorsal Sp. No. 5/S.L.	---	---	3.6-4.1
Anal Sp. No. 1/S.L.	---	10.3	8.0-11.0
Anal Sp. No. 2/S.L.	---	4.5	3.6-4.5
Anal Sp. No. 3/S.L.	---	4.5	3.4-4.8

Diagnosis.—D. XII-XIV (usually XIII), 21-23 (usually 22); A. III, 16 or 17 (usually 17); mark on nape reduced to dark blotch or smudge, indistinct; eyeband connected across nape in adults; posterior yellow area from 11th to 13th dorsal spine tip to angle of anal fin.

Meristics.—D. XIII (occasionally XII or XIV), 21 to 23 (usually 22); A. III, 16 or 17 (usually 17); pectoral rays 14 (one with 15/15, one with 14/15); L.l. scales 35-43; L.l. pores 30-41; scales above L.l. 4-7; scales below L.l. 12-16; gill rakers 19-21 (one with 16).

Description.—Snout pointed, 2.6-3.5 in head length; predorsal contour approximately straight until level of nostrils, then concave; gape of mouth horizontal; teeth in spaced rows, 6-7 rows in upper jaw and 6-7 in lower jaw; preopercle angle slightly obtuse; preopercle slightly dentate; eye diameter greater than or equal to snout length, which is greater than or equal to depth of caudal peduncle; caudal peduncle greater than interorbital width.

Fourth or fifth dorsal spine longest; base of spinous portion of dorsal fin longer (2.3-2.5 in S.L.) than that of soft portion (3.2-3.4 in S.L.); pelvic fins moderate. reaching area between anus and first anal spine.

Lateral line reaches highest point under 11th dorsal fin spine; scales in series following chevrons; scaly portion of dorsal spines increasing evenly until last spine, which is mostly hidden; scales covering anal spines reach just above midpoint of third anal spine.

Above and below. *Chaetodon falcula* is the Indian Ocean replacement species for the Pacific *Chaetodon ulietensis*. Photo above by Klaus Paysan; photo below by Dr. D. Terver, Nancy Aquarium, France.

Opposite:

Chaetodon falcula. Photo by Dr. Herbert R. Axelrod, Maldives.

Juveniles similar to adults in both form and color.

Color Pattern.—Ocular band connected across nape area, faded below eye, but extends to lower edge of interopercle; nape, snout, and interorbital dusky; a dark, indistinct smudge just anterior to dorsal fin; posterior yellow area starts at tip of 11th to 13th dorsal fin spines and crosses body to angle of anal fin; pelvic fins dusky.

Eyeband of juvenile possibly comparatively wider than adult band just above eye. Connection with nape blotch not evident.

Remarks.—There appears to be no concrete differences between *Chaetodon mertensii* and *C. dixoni*. The holotype of *dixoni*, AMS IB. 4905, is no different from other specimens of *C. mertensii* from different locations.

Chaetodon mertensii is the Pacific Ocean representative of this group. It is not known whether this species and *C. xanthurus* are sympatric in the area of the East Indies.

Distribution.—Pacific Ocean from the Tuamotu and Society Islands to Japan and the Great Barrier Reef of Australia. Possibly also from the Philippine Islands and East Indies, but confusion with *Chaetodon xanthurus* prevents positive identification of records in these areas.

Material Examined.—(21 spec.: 47-92 mm S.L.) BPBM 5862 (1: 92), Tahiti; BPBM 6246 (7: 78-89), Eniwetok, Marshall Islands; CAS 37680, (1: 82), Moorea; CAS 37681 (1: 90), Tahiti; CAS 37682 and CAS 37683 (3: 62-75), Ifaluk, Caroline Islands; CAS 37684 (1: 74), Palau Islands; CAS 37685 (1: 71), Tahiti; CAS 7047 (1: 56), Tahiti; WEB)(1: 47), Eniwetok, Marshall Islands; SOSC Te Vega Sta. 308 (4: 62-71), Tonga Islands.

CHAETODON MADAGASCARIENSIS Ahl
Indian Ocean chevron butterflyfish

Chaetodon chrysurus Desjardins, 1833: p. 117 (preoccupied by *Chaetodon chrysurus* Schneider, 1801, a pomacanthid; type locality Mauritius).

Chaetodon mertensii (not of Cuvier), Day, 1875: p. 105, pl. 27, fig. 2 (India).

Chaetodon [*Tetragonoptrus*] *xanthurus* (not of Bleeker), Sauvage, 1891: p. 261, pl. 29, fig. 1 (Madagascar).

Chaetodon chrysurus (not of Schneider), Day, 1889: p. 6 (India). Ahl, 1923: p. 161 (Mauritius).

Chaetodon chrysurus madagascariensis Ahl, 1923: p. 162 (type locality Madagascar).

Diagnosis.—D. XIII, 20-21; A. III, 16-17; eyeband does not join at nape; horseshoe-shaped spot on nape distinct above, where there is white border, but indistinct below and without border; posterior yellow area starts at tips of 12th or 13th dorsal fin tip spine and crosses to angle of anal fin.

Chaetodon madagascariensis Ahl. 94.2 mm S.L. Seychelles Islands, Indian Ocean.

Ratios	Standard Length (mm)		
	10-30	31-60	above 60(4)
Depth/S.L.	---	---	1.7-1.8
Head/S.L.	---	---	3.4-3.5
Eye/Head	---	---	2.7-3.0
Snout/Head	---	---	2.7-3.2
Interorb. W./Head	---	---	3.1-3.5
Maxillary/Head	---	---	3.9-4.4
Caud. Ped./S.L.	---	---	9.0-9.9
Pect. Fin/S.L.	---	---	3.5-3.9
Pelvic Sp./S.L.	---	---	4.3-5.5
Predorsal L./S.L.	---	---	2.5-2.7
Prepelvic L./S.L.	---	---	2.5-2.6
Dorsal Sp. No. 1/S.L.	---	---	10.5-13.0
Dorsal Sp. No. 2/S.L.	---	---	6.4-7.7
Dorsal Sp. No. 3/S.L.	---	---	5,0-6.1
Dorsal Sp. No. 4/S.L.	---	---	4.4-5.1
Dorsal Sp. No. 5/S.L.	---	---	4.0-4.8
Anal Sp. No. 1/S.L.	---	---	8.4-9.5
Anal Sp. No. 2/S.L.	---	---	4.1-4.2
Anal Sp. No. 3/S.L.	---	---	3.6-4.0

Chaetodon ulietensis juvenile. The pattern is very similar to that of the adult. Photo by F. Earl Kennedy, Philippines.

Chaetodon ulietensis subadult. Photo by Dr. Fujio Yasuda.

Chaetodon ulietensis in its natural habitat. Often several individuals are seen rather than a single pair. Photo by Dr. Warren E. Burgess, Enewetak.

Chaetodon ulietensis adult. There is a light area in the upper part of the eye band but this rarely separates into a nape spot. Photo by K.H. Choo, Taiwan.

Meristics.—D. XIII, 20-21; A. III, 16 or 17; pectoral rays 14 (one with 15/14); L.l. scales 34-41; L.l. pores 31-38; scales above L.l. 5-7; scales below L.l. 13-15; gill rakers 17-19.

Description.—Snout pointed, 2.7-3.2 in head length; predorsal contour slightly convex at nape, concave at level of nostrils, straight in between; gape oblique; teeth in spaced rows, 6-8 in each jaw; preopercle approximately right-angled to slightly obtuse, slightly dentate; depth of caudal peduncle greater than eye diameter, which is approximately equal to snout length; snout length greater than interorbital width.

Fifth dorsal spine longest; base of spinous portion of dorsal fin longer (2.0-2.2 in S.L.) than that of soft portion (2.9-3.4 in S.L.); pelvic fins moderately short, reaching only to anus.

Lateral line reaches highest point at about twelfth dorsal spine; scales large, rhomboidal, in series following chevron pattern; scaly portion of dorsal spines covers most of last spine, that of anal spines reaches past midpoint of third spine.

Juveniles similar to adults in both form and color.

Color Pattern.—Head dusky; horseshoe-shaped spot on nape blackish, edged above only with white, indistinct below; eyebands not joined above; posterior yellowish area starts from tip of 12th or 13th spine and base of 3rd or 4th ray, crosses body to end at angle of anal fin (fourth or fifth ray tip) after crossing base at about tenth ray; dusky spot in soft dorsal sometimes present, usually about 3rd to 8th rays.

Remarks.—*Chaetodon madagascariensis* is the Indian Ocean representative of the chevroned-species complex. It has been recorded mostly under the name of *Chaetodon chrysurus* Desjardins, but unfortunately *C. chrysurus* is preoccupied by *C. chrysurus* Schneider, a pomacanthid.

Distribution.—Indian Ocean from African coast and its offshore islands to Sri Lanka and Cocos-Keeling.

Material Examined.—(4 spec.: 76-94 mm S.L.) ANSP 108551 and 108589 (2: 76-94), Seychelles; SOSC Anton Bruun HA-14 (1: 84), Comoro Islands; SOSC Anton Bruun HA-11 (1: 84), Comoro Islands.

CHAETODON PAUCIFASCIATUS Ahl
Red Sea chevron butterflyfish

Chaetodon guttatissimus (not of Bennett), Klunzinger, 1870: p. 780 (Red Sea).

Chaetodon mertensii (not of Cuvier), Klunzinger, 1884: p. 57 (Red Sea).

Chaetodon chrysurus paucifasciatus Ahl, 1923: p. 162 (type locality Kosier, Red Sea).

Chaetodon chrysurus paucifasciatus, Baschieri-Salvatore, 1954: p. 91, pl. 2, fig. 4 (Red Sea).

Diagnosis.—D. XII-XIV (usually XIII), 20-23 (usually 21-22); A. III, 15-18 (usually 16-17); black mark on nape completely enclosed in white

Chaetodon paucifasciatus Ahl. 80 mm S.L. Red Sea.

| Ratios | Standard Length (mm) | | |
	10-30	31-60	above 60(12)
Depth/S.L.............	---	---	1.5-1.7
Head/S.L..............	---	---	3.4-3.8
Eye/Head	---	---	3.2-3.5
Snout/Head	---	---	2.8-3.1
Interorb. W./Head......	---	---	3.0-3.5
Maxillary/Head	---	---	3.7-4.8
Caud. Ped./S.L........	---	---	9.1-10.2
Pect. Fin/S.L..........	---	---	3.6-4.3
Pelvic Sp./S.L.........	---	---	4.6-5.2
Predorsal L./S.L.......	---	---	2.5-2.8
Prepelvic L./S.L.......	---	---	2.4-2.7
Dorsal Sp. No. 1/S.L....	---	---	12.6-15.0
Dorsal Sp. No. 2/S.L....	---	---	7.5-8.8
Dorsal Sp. No. 3/S.L....	---	---	5.6-7.0
Dorsal Sp. No. 4/S.L....	---	---	4.7-6.5
Dorsal Sp. No. 5/S.L....	---	---	4.7-5.9
Anal Sp. No. 1/S.L......	---	---	8.9-10.5
Anal Sp. No. 2/S.L......	---	---	4.3-5.1
Anal Sp. No. 3/S.L......	---	---	4.0-5.0

Chaetodon collare juvenile. Photo by Aaron Norman.

Chaetodon collare adult. Photo by Dr. D. Terver, Nancy Aquarium, France.

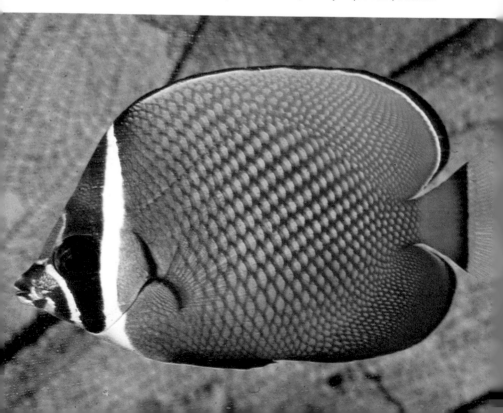

Chaetodon nigropunctatus juvenile. Photo by Roger Lubbock, Das I., Arabian Gulf.

Chaetodon nigropunctatus adult. Photo by Dr. Gerald R. Allen at Muscat, Oman.

border; eyeband not connected above; posterior portion of body brick red, not yellow or yellowish, from tips of last two dorsal fin spines to anal fin ray eight, past angle; eyeband orange with narrow dark borders in turn bordered with white.

Meristics.—D. XIII (occasionally XII or XIV), 20-23, (usually 21 or 22); A. III, 15-18 (usually 16 or 17); pectoral rays 14 (one with 13/14, one with 15/14); L.l. scales 36-40; L.l. pores 31-37; scales above L.l. 4-5 (usually 4); scales below L.l. 11-13 (usually 12); gill rakers 16-19.

Description.—Snout pointed, 2.8-3.1 in head length; predorsal contour slightly convex at nape, concave at nostrils, straight in between; gape slightly oblique; teeth in spaced rows, 6-7 in upper jaw, 6-7 rows in lower jaw; preopercle right-angled to slightly obtuse, smooth to lightly serrate; depth of caudal peduncle greater than snout length, which is greater than interorbital width; interorbital width equal to eye diameter.

Fourth or fifth dorsal spine longest; base of spinous portion of dorsal fin longer (1.9-2.1 in S.L.) than that of soft portion (2.7-3.1 in S.L.); pelvic fins moderately short, extending just to anus or short of it.

Lateral line as in other members of this subgenus; scales in series following chevron pattern; scaly covering of dorsal spines reaching almost to tip of last spine; that of anal fin covers ¾ or more of third spine.

Juveniles similar to adults in both form and color.

Color Pattern.—Horseshoe-shaped mark on nape edges with white (lower edge may be faded); eyeband not connected above, orange with dark lines as borders, which are in turn bordered with light; top of snout dusky; posterior brick red color starts from tips of last two dorsal spines and crosses body to end on line from base of twelfth ray to tip of eighth ray, past angle; a dusky spot in dorsal fin from about third to tenth dorsal ray which can appear dark, faded, or entirely absent.

Remarks.—Apparently sympatric on the East African coast with *C. madagascariensis*. Very similar to other chevroned species, but differing remarkably in color.

Distribution.—As far as known, confined to the Red Sea and East Africa records.

Material Examined.—(12 spec.: 72-99 mm S.L.) USNM 191663 (10: 72-99), Red Sea; CAS 37705 (2: 73-84), Eylath, Red Sea.

CHAETODON XANTHURUS Bleeker
Philippine chevron butterflyfish
(Netted butterflyfish)

Chaetodon xanthurus Bleeker, 1857: p. 53 (type locality Amboina).

Tetragonoptrus (*Linophora*) *mertensi* (not of Cuvier), Bleeker, 1877: p. 50, pl. 378, fig. 3.

Chaetodon chrysurus xanturus Ahl, 1923: p. 163 (Misspelling of *xanthurus*).

Chaetodon chrysurus (not of Schneider), Herre and Montal-
   ban, 1927: p. 35, pl. 8, fig. 1 (Puerto Galera, Mindoro,
   Philippine Islands).
Chaetodon mertensi (not of Cuvier), Fowler and Bean,
   1929: p. 127 (Philippine Islands).
Anisochaetodon (*Linophora*) *chrysurus* (not of Schneider),
   Watanabe, 1959: p. 36, fig. 2 (Okinawa).

Chaetodon xanthurus Bleeker. 84 mm S.L. Philippine Islands.

Diagnosis.—D. XII-XIV (usually XIII), 20-23 (usually 21); A. III, (15)
16-17; eyeband not joining above on nape, completely surrounded by
white line; scales completely edged with dark lines giving reticulated pattern on body; posterior yellow area curved backward at the upper end,
completely bypassing any of the dorsal spines.

Meristics.—D. XIII (occasionally XII or XIV), 20-23 (usually 21); A.
III, 16-17 (one with 15); pectoral fin 14 (occasionally 13, two with 13/
14); L.l. scales 32-39; L.l. pores 29-37; scales above L.l. 4 or 5; scales
below L.l. 11 or 12; gill rakers 16-19.

Description.—Snout pointed, 2.4-3.2 in head length; predorsal contour
slightly convex at nape, concave above nostrils, in between straight, gape

407

Chaetodon rafflesi juvenile with a prominent "half-spot" in the dorsal fin. Photo by Allan Power, New Hebrides.

Chaetodon rafflest subadult with basic adult color pattern well developed. Photo by K.H. Choo, Taiwan.

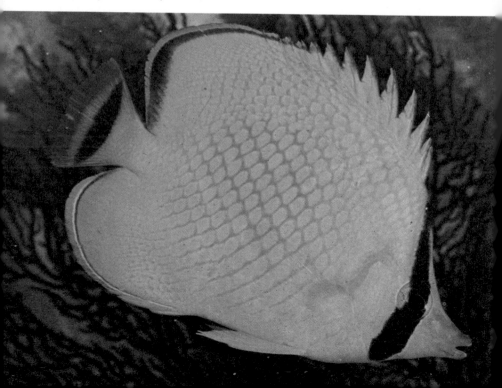

Chaetodon rafflesi in its natural habitat. Photo by Scott Johnson, Enewetak.

Chaetodon rafflesi adult. The dorsal fin band is usually a dark black. Photo by Dr. Fujio Yasuda, Japan.

Ratios	Standard Length (mm)		
	10-30	31-60	above 60(38)
Depth/S.L.	---	---	1.6-1.8
Head/S.L.	---	---	3.2-3.6
Eye/Head	---	---	2.5-3.3
Snout/Head	---	---	2.4-3.2
Interorb. W./Head.	---	---	3.0-3.5
Maxillary/Head	---	---	3.9-5.3
Caud. Ped./S.L.	---	---	9.2-10.2
Pect. Fin/S.L.	---	---	3.2-3.8
Pelvic Sp./S.L.	---	---	4.3-5.1
Predorsal L./S.L.	---	---	2.3-2.6
Prepelvic L./S.L.	---	---	2.4-2.7
Dorsal Sp. No. 1/S.L.	---	---	10.1-12.9
Dorsal Sp. No. 2/S.L.	---	---	6.1-8.3
Dorsal Sp. No. 3/S.L.	---	---	4.9-5.8
Dorsal Sp. No. 4/S.L.	---	---	3.9-5.5
Dorsal Sp. No. 5/S.L.	---	---	3.7-6.0
Anal Sp. No. 1/S.L.	---	---	7.7-10.4
Anal Sp. No. 2/S.L.	---	---	3.9-4.5
Anal Sp. No. 3/S.L.	---	---	3.6-5.0

slightly oblique; teeth in spaced rows, 7-8 in each jaw; preopercle slightly obtuse-angled, lightly toothed to smooth; snout length greater than caudal peduncle depth, which is greater than eye diameter; eye diameter greater than interorbital width.

Fourth dorsal spine longest; base of spinous dorsal fin longer (2.1-2.4 in S.L.) than that of soft portion (3.0-3.2 in S.L.); pelvic fins moderate, reaching to anal opening or slightly beyond.

Lateral line as in other species of this subgenus; scales rhomboidal, large, following angles of chevrons; scaly covering of dorsal fin including almost all of 8th and 9th and succeeding spines; anal spines covered with scales so that ½ to ¾ of the 3rd spine is covered.

Juveniles similar to adult in form as well as color pattern.

Color Pattern.—Posterior yellow area starts at tip of sixth or seventh dorsal rays, crosses body to base of anal fin at 12th to 13th ray and across anal fin to tip of fifth ray (at angle); eyebands do not meet at nape; well-developed horseshoe-shaped mark on nape white bordered.

Eyeband approaching nape mark in smaller specimens and may connect with it in small juveniles.

Remarks.—There has been a great deal of confusion about this species, and it has been variously identified as *C. mertensii* or *C. chrysurus* (= *C. madagascariensis*). However, *C. xanthurus* is quite distinct from those species. The color pattern of cross-hatching most closely resembles that of *C. argentatus*.

Distribution.—Not well defined because of the confusion in the literature with other chevroned species. Definitely known from the East Indies, Philippines, and Okinawa.

Material Examined.—(38 spec.: 65-86 mm S.L.) USNM 181110-181134 (37: 65-86), Philippine Islands; SU 29897 (1: 84), Philippine Islands.

CHAETODON ARGENTATUS Smith and Radcliffe
Three-band butterflyfish
(Silver and black butterflyfish)

Chaetodon argentatus Smith and Radcliffe, 1911: p. 319, fig. 1 (type locality Agojo Point, Southern Luzon, Philippines).

Oxychaetodon falcula (not of Bloch), Fowler, 1946: p. 138 (Riu Kiu Islands).

Chaetodon (Linophora) argentatus, Fowler, 1953: p. 41, fig. 101 (China, Kominato, Amami-Oshima, Itoman, Formosa, Yaeyama, Riu Kiu).

Diagnosis.—D. XIII (XIV), 21-22 (one with 24); A. III, 16 (rarely 15); eyeband reduced to dark markings above eyes, not evident below orbit; scales outlined with black, no chevrons; posterior band black, not yellowish.

Chaetodon argentatus Smith and Radcliffe. 80 mm S.L. Palau Islands.

411

Chaetodon vagabundus, newly transformed. The color pattern at this stage is very similar to that of *C. auriga.* Photo by Glenn S. Axelrod, East Africa.

Chaetodon vagabundus. Typical juvenile with remnant of a dorsal spot but dark posterior band present. Photo by Dr. Warren E. Burgess, Philippines.

Chaetodon vagabundus subadult. Caudal fin pattern still not as far out as in full adult. Photo by K.H. Choo, Taiwan.

Chaetodon vagabundus, adult. Typical pattern. Photo by Dr. John E. Randall of a 113 mm S.L. specimen from Tahiti.

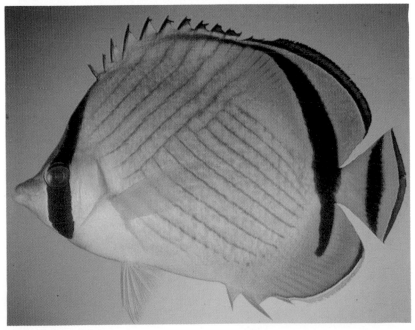

Ratios	Standard Length (mm)		
	10-30	31-60(3)	above 60(5)
Depth/S.L...............	---	1.8-1.9	1.7-1.9
Head/S.L................	---	3.0-3.3	3.2-3.5
Eye/Head...............	---	2.8-3.1	2.9-3.3
Snout/Head.............	---	2.9-3.9	2.7-3.0
Interorb. W./Head......	---	3.2-3.5	3.3-3.6
Maxillary/Head.........	---	3.8-5.3	4.3-5.8
Caud. Ped./S.L.........	---	8.6-9.5	9.0-10.3
Pect. Fin./S.L..........	---	3.3-3.9	3.7-4.3
Pelvic Spine/S.L........	---	4.1-4.5	4.6-5.3
Predorsal L./S.L........	---	2.2-2.4	2.4-2.6
Prepelvic L./S.L........	---	2.3-2.5	2.3-2.6
Dorsal Sp. No. 1/S.L.....	---	11.8-13.7	11.1-17.4
Dorsal Sp. No. 2/S.L.....	---	5.9-6.4	6.8-10.0
Dorsal Sp. No. 3/S.L.....	---	4.4-4.8	4.9-7.0
Dorsal Sp. No. 4/S.L.....	---	3.8-4.1	4.4-6.0
Dorsal Sp. No. 5/S.L.....	---	3.9-4.1	4.2-5.6
Anal Sp. No. 1/S.L.......	---	8.5-10.3	8.8-12.9
Anal Sp. No. 2/S.L.......	---	4.5-5.4	4.4-5.3
Anal Sp. No. 3/S.L.......	---	4.2-4.4	4.6-5.3

Meristics.—D. XIII (one with XIV), 21-22 (one with 24); A. III, 16 (rarely 15); pectoral rays 14-15 (one with 13/13, one with 13/14); L.l. scales 35-39; L.l. pores 34-38; scales above lateral line 5 (-6); scales below L.l. 11 (-12); gill rakers 22-23.

Description.—Snout pointed, 2.8 in head length; predorsal contour straight, slightly concave at level of nostrils; gape approximately horizontal; teeth in spaced rows, 4-5 in upper jaw, 5-6 in lower jaw; preopercle slightly toothed; snout length greater than depth of caudal peduncle, which is greater than eye diameter; eye diameter greater than interorbital width.

Fifth dorsal spine longest; spinous portion of dorsal fin longer (2.1-2.2 in S.L.) than that of soft portion (3.0-3.2 in S.L.); pelvic fins short, failing to reach level of anal opening.

Lateral line flexures at approximately sixth and twelfth dorsal spine levels; L.l. about four scale rows distant from base of dorsal fin; scales on body large, rhomboidal, smaller posteriorly; scaly sheath of dorsal spines reaches to about 5/6 of last spine, that of anal spines covers ⅔ of last spine.

Juveniles similar to adults in both color and form.

Color Pattern.—Chest to anal spine without dark markings; eyeband reduced to a bar across interorbital space, partially or completely separated from orbit by narrow light gap; upper edge of orbit with dark mark; large dark blotch connects across nape at first dorsal spines; upper part of snout dusky; upper and lower edges of caudal fin dark to base of fin.

Remarks.—Except for the misidentification by Fowler (1946), there seems to be no problem with this very distinct species.

Distribution.—This species was described from the Philippine Islands but apparently is more common northward in China, Ryu Kyu Islands, and southern Japan. It has not been recorded from any other adjacent areas.

Material Examined.—(8 spec.: 50-80 mm S.L.) USNM 196652 (1: 80), Amami Islands; USNM 67353 (2: 67-80), Philippines (syntypes); BPBM 7260 (1: 80), Riu Kiu Islands; Yasuda (Univ. of Tokyo) (4: 50-69), southern Japan (?).

Subgenus MEGAPROTODON Guichenot

Megaprotodon Guichenot, 1848: p. 12 = "Megaprotodon" *vernacular*, index p. 378 = *Megaprotodon*. (Type-species *Chaetodon bifascialis* Cuvier, 1831, by monotypy.)

Eteira Kaup, 1860: pp. 136 and 147. (Type-species *Chaetodon triangularis* Ruppell, 1828, by subsequent designation of Jordan, 1919: p. 297.)

Diagnosis.—Body elongate-oval, depth 1.7-2.2 in S.L.; scales large, rhomboidal, in rows following chevron-like pattern; L.l. in low arc; IV anal spines; dorsal fin with XIV spines; dorsal and anal fins with 15 rays.

Description.—Body elongate-oval; snout short, pointed, 2.8-3.4 in head length; predorsal contour straight to slightly convex; gape oblique; mouth small; preopercle right-angled, angle extended slightly, serrate; supraorbital smooth to lightly serrate; lachrymal smooth.

Dorsal spines strong, graduated, middle spines (eighth to tenth) longest; later spines leveling out and becoming shorter until last; four anal spines; dorsal and anal fins with posterior edges vertical when spread; spinous dorsal fin base more than twice base of soft portion; pectoral fins normal; pelvic fins short, at most reaching anus; caudal fin truncate.

Lateral line describing a very low, flat arc; scales large, rhomboidal, in a pattern following the chevrons; scaly portion of dorsal spines moderately low, reaching midpoint at about seventh or eighth spine (and covering almost all of last spine).

Juveniles differ from adults in color pattern and slightly in proportions.

Color pattern basically light with multiple chevrons directed forward, following scale rows.

A single species recognized.

Remarks.—*Megaprotodon* has often been used as a generic name, but it is my contention that it should not have that status. The differences between other subgenera of genus *Chaetodon* are no less distinctive than those between *Megaprotodon* and those subgenera.

Chaetodon decussatus is very similar to *C. vagabundus* but is characterized by a broad dark area in the posterior part of the body and fins. Photo by Aaron Norman.

Chaetodon vagabundus pictus has black dorsal fin spine edges in contrast to *C. v. vagabundus* where they are mostly white. Photo by Dr. Gerald R. Allen, Muscat, Oman.

Chaetodon decussatus. Photo by Dr. Herbert R. Axelrod, Maldives.

CHAETODON TRIFASCIALIS Quoy & Gaimard
Chevron butterflyfish
(V-lined butterflyfish)

Chaetodon stringuli Gmelin, 1789: p. 1269 (on Broussonet MS; a plural name and a *nomen nudum*, so non-
admissible).

Chaetodon trifascialis Quoy & Gaimard, 1825: p. 379, pl.
62, fig. 5 (type locality Guam). Colloquial name = Chetodon Taunay.

Chaetodon triangularis Ruppell, 1828: p. 42, pl. 9, fig. 3
(type locality Red Sea).

Chaetodon bifascialis Cuvier, 1829: p. 190 (on *C. trifascialis* Quoy & Gaimard).

Chaetodon bifascialis Cuvier, 1831: p. 48 (redescription; on
Chetodon Taunay, pl. 62, fig. 5 = *C. trifascialis* Q. &
G., pl. 42, fig. 5).

Chaetodon strigangulus Cuvier, 1831: p. 42, pl. 172 (ex
Solander MS; Otaiti).

Chaetodon triangulum (not of Cuvier p. 34), Cuvier, p. 44
(cited by Cuvier as Reinhardt name; Java).

Chaetodon Leachii Cuvier, 1831: p. 49 (no locality).

Megaprotodon bifascialis, Guichenot, 1848: p. 12 (new
combination).

Megaprotodon leachii, Guichenot, 1848: p. 12 (new combination).

Eteira triangularis, Kaup, 1860: p. 147 (new combination).

Eteira Taunayi Kaup, 1860: p. 148 (on Quoy & Gaimard,
1825).

Eteira Leachii, Kaup, 1860: 149 (new combination).

Sarothrodus strigangulus, Bleeker, 1863: p. 156 (Halmahera; new combination).

Tetragonoptrus strigangulus, Bleeker, 1863: p. 282 (new
combination).

Megaprotodon strigangulus, Bleeker, 1877: p. 54, pl. 375,
fig. 1 (note captions are reversed, fig. 4 being *Coradion
melanopus*).

Chaetodon (Megaprotodon) strigangulus, Klunzinger, 1884;
p. 56 (Red Sea).

Chaetodon trifasciatis (not of Park), Seale, 1901: p. 102
(misspelling of *trifascialis*; juvenile, Guam).

Megaprotodon trifascialis, Jordan & Seale, 1906: p. 336,
pl. 50, fig. 1 (Samoa).

Chaetodon tearlachi Curtiss, 1938: p. 117 (type locality
Tahiti near Tautira).

Chaetodon trifascialis Quoy and Gaimard. 108 mm S.L. Teavaraa Pass, Tahiti.

Ratios	Standard Length (mm)		
	10-49(10)	50-89(19)	above 89(16)
Depth/S.L.	1.7-2.2	1.8-2.1	1.7-2.2
Head/S.L.	2.1-3.0	2.9-3.6	3.3-3.6
Eye/Head	2.0-2.9	2.6-3.1	2.8-3.4
Snout/Head	2.8-5.7	2.7-3.4	2.8-3.4
Interorb. W./Head.	1.8-3.1	2.5-2.9	2.3-2.8
Maxillary/Head	3.7-4.6	3.7-5.1	3.8-4.7
Caud. Ped./S.L.	6.8-11.1	8.2-9.3	7.9-9.6
Pect. Fin./S.L.	3.5-4.2	3.5-4.3	3.9-4.5
Pelvic Spine/S.L.	3.7-5.0	4.4-5.7	5.1-6.1
Predorsal L./S.L.	1.6-2.3	2.3-2.7	2.5-2.7
Prepelvic L./S.L.	2.1-2.6	2.3-2.8	2.5-2.9
Dorsal Sp. No. 1/S.L.	7.1-13.1	9.4-12.7	10.2-14.7
Dorsal Sp. No. 2/S.L.	5.5-10.0	6.9-11.1	8.9-12.2
Dorsal Sp. No. 3/S.L.	4.4-7.5	5.3-9.4	6.4-10.9
Dorsal Sp. No. 4/S.L.	3.9-6.1	4.3-7.9	5.4-10.0
Anal Sp. No. 1/S.L.	6.2-11.1	5.9-8.0	7.0-13.1
Anal Sp. No. 2/S.L.	4.0-10.1	4.0-5.7	4.4-7.7
Anal Sp. No. 3/S.L.	4.1-9.6	3.9-6.0	4.4-5.9
Anal Sp. No. 4/S.L.	4.1-7.2	4.0-6.5	4.3-5.7

Chaetodon mesoleucos is an oddly patterned butterflyfish with a weak eye-band. In this subadult it is still very evident. Photo by G. Marcuse.

Chaetodon mesoleucos in its natural habitat in the Red Sea. Photo by W. Deas, Sha'ab Rami, Red Sea.

Chaetodon leucopleura being cleaned by a cleaner wrasse, *Labroides dimidiatus.* Photo by H. Hansen.

Subadult *Chaetodon leucopleura* in captivity. Pattern is typical of the adult. Photo by Roger Lubbock.

Diagnosis.—D. XIII-XV, 14-16 (usually 15); A. IV (V), 13-15 (usually 15); pectoral rays 14; L.l. scales 22-29 (usually 24-26); body elongate, depth 1.7-2.2 in standard length; anteriorly directed chevrons on sides; posterior portion of body black in juveniles, dark area decreasing in size with growth.

Meristics.—D. XIV (two with XIII, three with XV), 14-16 (mostly 15); A. IV (one with V), 15 (one with 13, three with 14); pectoral rays 14 (one with 14/15, one with 13/15); L.l. scales 22-29 (usually 24-26); L.l. pores 20-29 (usually 20-25); scales above L.l. 4-6; scales below L.l. 16-19; gill rakers 23-27 (usually 23 or 24).

Description.—Teeth in bunched rows at end of each jaw; preopercle toothed around entire length, teeth on angle larger, pleated; caudal peduncle depth greater than interorbital width, which is greater than snout length and eye diameter, the latter two being equal.

Dorsal spines strong, eighth to tenth longest; third anal spine longest, second and fourth subequal, first not much smaller than second; dorsal fin pointed, anal fin angular, squarish; pectoral fins short, at most reaching anus; base of spinous portion of dorsal fin more than twice length of soft portion (1.8-2.1 in S.L. and 4.2-5.1 in S.L. respectively).

Scales large, rhomboidal; lateral line a low arc; scaly portion of dorsal spines moderately low, reaching midpoint at about seventh or eighth spine, and covering almost all of last spine; anal scale sheath covering about a third of third spine and near three-fourths of fourth; vertical fins covered with very small scales almost to their tips.

Juveniles similar to adults but with the dorsal fin less pointed and more squarish to rounded; anal fin more rounded; pelvic fins proportionately longer than in adult.

Color Pattern.—Eyeband bordered with light streak on each side, connected with opposite one on throat and faintly connected or not at nape; pelvic fins yellowish; light streaks extend along upper and lower edges of caudal fin; face dusky.

The color pattern changes with growth, which accounts for many of the synonyms. The juvenile coloration (of a specimen 19 mm S.L.) includes the chevrons of the adult; eyeband connects broadly in front of dorsal fin and again at throat, forming continuous band around head; base of caudal fin yellow, a brown line crossing the fin at its center or even closer to the peduncle, outer portion hyaline; posterior end of body, including soft portions of dorsal and anal fins and half of caudal peduncle, dark brown with light yellow anterior border; pectoral and pelvic fins light yellow to hyaline; edges of dorsal and anal fins narrowly light colored; eyeband still with light borders.

In a 45 mm specimen the pattern is similar but with the following changes. The eyeband is losing its dorsal connection; brown line of caudal fin about three-fourths of way toward posterior end; dorsal fin becoming more pointed; and dark posterior area becoming smaller, particularly on anal fin. By 55 mm the dark areas of dorsal fin reach only to point of the

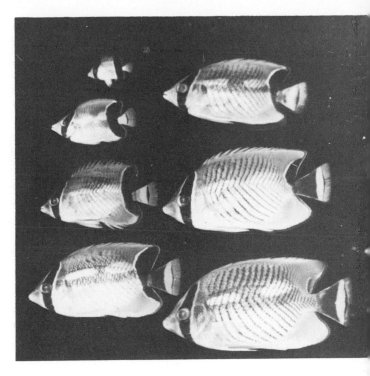

Series of specimens of *Chaetodon trifascialis* showing changes which occur with growth.

angle, those on anal fin reduced to a semicircular area at its posterior edge, still connected across caudal peduncle; caudal peduncle starting to gain some dark color at its base.

A 64 mm S.L. specimen has a large dark area and a lens-shaped yellow area on caudal fin, nearing coloration of adult; a remnant of the dark posterior area appears as a semi-circular spot on the lower portion of the posterior edge of the dorsal fin. By 70 mm S.L. the adult color pattern is usually present.

Remarks.—With Gmelin's name *striganguli* a *nomen nudum* as well as a plural noun, it is unacceptable under the present rules of nomenclature. The next available name is *Chaetodon trifascialis* Quoy & Gaimard (1825). It is one of the juvenile forms that caused confusion in this species.

This species is quite widespread and usually found in areas where there is the flat plate-like *Acropora* coral. Its somewhat elongate body is well adapted to its hiding places between the flat 'shelves' of this coral. It has only recently been found in Hawaii, the first specimens being adults trapped in Kaneohe Bay, Oahu, by Lester Zukeran, the last a juvenile collected by hand net in the same area. Baschieri-Salvatore (1954), who found it in the Red Sea, said it was present in the rich underparts of madreporarian corals at depths of one to three meters. Harry (1953) at Raroia found it in lagoons on coral heads and shore reefs, but rather uncommon, usually only scattered individuals.

Chaetodon gardneri has a pattern very similar to that of its closest relatives, *C. selene* and *C. leucopleura*. Photo by Rodney Jonklaas, Sri Lanka.

A juvenile or subadult *Chaetodon gardneri* in captivity. Photo by Roger Lubbock.

Chaetodon gardneri in its natural habitat in Sri Lanka. Photo by Rodney Jonklaas.

Chaetodon trifascialis is closely related to the other chevroned species, subgenera *Rhombochaetodon* and *Gonochaetodon*. Its four anal spines are shared, however, by only one other —apparently unrelated— species, *Chaetodon plebeius*. The dark area of the juvenile shows a similar pattern to such species as *Chaetodon argentatus* and *C. larvatus*. The dark posterior areas of *C. fremblii*, etc. may or may not be related.

The often seen pattern of grayish with two elongate, white, oval spots on the upper side of the body is shown both under stress and at night.

Seale (1901) reported on two species, *Chaetodon strigangulus* and *C. trifasciatus*. Both are *Chaetodon trifascialis*, his first specimen being an adult, his second a juvenile of *C. trifascialis* (misspelled as *trifasciatis*).

Gunther (1860) described the air bladder as having two sections, a larger posterior and smaller anterior, the anterior one bearing two small processes.

Distribution.—Widespread in the Pacific and Indian Oceans. From the eastern coast of Africa and the Red Sea to Australia, Japan, and central and western Pacific Islands including the Hawaiian Islands.

Material Examined.—(45 spec.: 11-134 mm S.L.) HIMB (1: 112), Palmyra Island; WEB (11: 37-134), Tahiti; WEB (4: 62-87), Heron Island, Queensland, Australia; BPBM 6045 (1: 25), Johnston Island; WEB (3: 11-39), Eniwetok, Marshall Islands; EMBL (12: 17-94), Eniwetok, Marshall Islands; SOSC Te Vega (4: 55-94), Thailand; SOSC HA 67-18, HA 67-7, HA 67-3, HA 67-8 (4: 54-104), Chagas Archipelago, Indian Ocean; SOSC HA 67-55, HA 67-61, HA 67-65 (4: 78-109), Aldabra Atoll, Indian Ocean; BPBM (uncatalogued) (1: 91), Oahu, Hawaiian Islands.

Subgenus GONOCHAETODON Bleeker

Gonochaetodon Bleeker, 1876: p. 306. (Type-species *Chaetodon triangulum* Cuvier, 1831, by original designation).

Diagnosis.—Body rounded, deep, depth 1.3-1.5 in standard length; scales angular, arranged in chevron pattern; lateral line moderate to low; dorsal spines increasing in height posteriorly, last longest; dorsal fin high; D. XI, 24-25; A. III, 20-22; pectoral 14-15; L.l. scales 24-37.

Description.—Body round, deep, depth 1.3-1.5 in standard length; snout short, pointed, 2.8-3.9 in head length; predorsal contour approximately straight until level of nostrils; mouth small, gape oblique; teeth in a few bunched rows at tips of jaws; preopercle right-angled to slightly obtuse, the angle rounded, serrate, or crenulate; supraorbital smooth to lightly serrate, lachrymal smooth.

Dorsal spines increase in length from front to rear, last longest; anterior dorsal rays continue this increase, the total fin quite high; dorsal and anal fins rounded, posterior edges slanting back toward caudal peduncle; anal fin smaller than dorsal fin; base of spinous portion of dorsal fin about equal to base of soft portion; pectoral fins normal; pelvic fins long, reaching base of first or second anal fin spine; caudal fin truncate to slightly rounded.

Lateral line describing a moderately low arc across body; scales moderate, rhomboid to rounded, in series following chevron pattern; scale covering of dorsal spines of normal height, reaching to midpoint of fifth or sixth and most of last dorsal spines (80-90% of last).

Juveniles similar to adults.

Color pattern of distinct chevrons on body; eyeband present or not as adult.

Western Pacific (from about Fiji Islands) to East Indies, Japan, Australia, and across the Indian Ocean to Sri Lanka, Gulf of Aden, and Red Sea.

Three species are presently recognized, as distinguished by the following key.

Key to the Species of the Subgenus Gonochaetodon

1. Eyeband absent in adults; large black area including most of soft portion of dorsal fin, sharply separated from body color by white stripe; L.l. scales 31-37 (Red Sea) . . . . *Chaetodon larvatus*
   Eyeband present, usually with additional bands on either side; no large posterior black area as above; L.l. scales 22-32 2
2. Boomerang-shaped light marking on caudal fin in addition to vertical light stripe near edge; anterior chevrons with light areas wider, up to twice dark areas (Indian Ocean) . . . . *C. triangulum*
   Caudal fin dark except for vertical light stripe near edge; anterior chevrons about equal width (Pacific Ocean) . . . . *C. baronessa*

Remarks.—This distinctive subgenus appears to occur mainly along continental coastlines, although extending throughout the western Pacific Islands to Fiji.

CHAETODON TRIANGULUM Cuvier
Triangle butterflyfish

Chaetodon triangulum Cuvier, 1831: p. 44 (type locality Batavia; ex. Kuhl & Van Hasselt MS).

Citharoedus triangulum, Kaup, 1860: p. 143 (Java, Africa; new combination).

Tetragonoptrus (*Gonochaetodon*) *triangulum*, Bleeker, 1877: p. 53, pl. 374, fig. 1 (figure is *C. triangulum*; East Indies; new combination).

Gonochaetodon baronessa, (not of Cuvier), Klausewitz, 1955: p. 315, fig. 4 (Java Sea near Djakarta).

Chaetodon selene subadult. Photographed in the Philippines by Dr. Warren E. Burgess.

Adult *Chaetodon selene*. Photo by Dr. Norbert Rau, Philippines.

Above and below. Young *Chaetodon selene* in their natural habitat in the Philippine Islands. Both photos by Roger Lubbock.

Chaetodon triangulum Cuvier. 80 mm S.L. Mentawai Islands (off west coast of Sumatra).

Ratios	Standard Length (mm)		
	20-49(1)	50-79(3)	above 79(5)
Depth/S.L.	1.6	1.4-1.5	1.4-1.5
Head/S.L.	2.8	3.1-3.2	3.2-3.4
Eye/Head	2.9	3.0	2.6-3.2
Snout/Head	2.9	2.8-3.0	2.9-3.6
Interorb. W./Head.	2.9	2.8-3.2	2.7-2.9
Maxillary/Head	4.2	3.6-4.1	3.7-4.4
Caud. Ped./S.L.	9.2	7.8-8.3	7.8-8.6
Pect. Fin/S.L.	3.4	3.4-3.5	3.3-3.5
Pelvic Sp./S.L.	4.4	4.5-4.9	4.2-4.8
Predorsal L./S.L.	2.1	2.1-2.2	2.1-2.3
Prepelvic L./S.L.	2.3	2.6-2.7	2.5-2.7
Dorsal Sp. No. 1/S.L.	8.9	7.9-8.6	7.4-8.6
Dorsal Sp. No. 2/S.L.	6.0	6.7-7.8	6.8-7.9
Dorsal Sp. No. 3/S.L.	4.2	5.0-6.0	5.4-6.3
Dorsal Sp. No. 4/S.L.	3.4	4.2	4.5-5.1
Anal Sp. No. 1/S.L.	6.4	6.2-6.8	6.8-7.7
Anal Sp. No. 2/S.L.	5.1	4.3-4.6	4.1-5.0
Anal Sp. No. 3/S.L.	5.3	3.7-4.0	3.4-4.8

Diagnosis.—D. XI (one with XII), 23-26 (usually 24 or 25); A. III, 20-21; pectoral rays 14; L.l. scales 25-33; very close to *Chaetodon baronessa*, but with boomerang-shaped white marking on caudal fin (absent in other two species); anterior light chevrons normally wider (up to twice) than dark chevrons.

Meristics.—D. XI (one with XII), 23-26 (usually 24 or 25); A. III, 20 or 21; pectoral rays 14 (one with 13/14); L.l. scales 25-33; L.l. pores 14-26 (usually 18-20); scales above L.l. 6-8; scales below L.l. 19-23; gill rakers 21-28.

Description.—Teeth in bunched rows at end of jaws; caudal peduncle depth greater than interorbital width; interorbital width greater than eye diameter and snout length, which are equal.

Last dorsal spine longest; second dorsal spine at times smaller than first, otherwise dorsal spines graduated from first to last; first dorsal rays longer than last spines, increasing height of fin, sixth to seventh rays longest; resulting dorsal fin high; anal spines graduated, last longest, first about two-thirds of second; base of spinous portion of dorsal fin equal to base of soft portion, both 2.3-2.6 in standard length; pelvic fins moderately long, barely reaching base of first anal spine.

Lateral line low, high point well below dorsal fin base, ending near 19th or 20th ray, which may vary, but lateral line usually ends far above caudal peduncle; anal spine scale covering more than half of last spine.

Juveniles similar to adults.

Color Pattern.—Edge of dorsal fin black; submarginal dark line in dorsal fin extending forward to 6th or 7th spine; anal fin with clear edge; snout dark, the dark color extends down to anterior edge of interopercle and up onto nape above eyes and is darker bordered; eyeband dark bordered, originating from first and second dorsal fin spines; eyebands join broadly at nape and chest, extending to area between pelvic fins, fading abruptly; pelvic fins light, spines lighter.

Juveniles (from a 27.5 mm S.L. specimen from Sri Lanka) with body chevrons similar to adults; eyeband same, but anterior and posterior bands much lighter; light stripe behind posterior light brown band from base of pectoral fin to behind pelvics following abdomen to first anal spine; outer half of caudal fin hyaline, a lens-shaped dark marking light-bordered on both sides; brown inside inner light border fading to lighter brown of body color; anal fin with hyaline border, dark submarginal band fading into brown of fin color; dorsal fin with light edge and dark submarginal band; no trace of light streak crossing caudal peduncle into anal fin.

Remarks.—*Chaetodon triangulum* is a species which has a close relative in the Pacific Ocean, *C. baronessa*. The question of whether this represents a pair of species or subspecies is difficult to answer. The answer will lie in the East Indies where the two come together. It is not certain whether these two species are sympatric, but in all the material seen there were no intermediates. This could mean a sharp line of demarcation

Chaetodon unimaculatus unimaculatus juvenile from Hawaii with teardrop-shaped lateral spot. Photo by Douglas Faulkner.

Chaetodon u. unimaculatus adult. Photo by Dr. Gerald R. Allen, Hawaii.

Young *Chaetodon u. unimaculatus* from Taiwan. The lateral spot is less tear-drop shaped. Photo by K.H. Choo.

Chaetodon u. unimaculatus adult with heavy snout. Photo by Dr. Gerald R. Allen, Great Barrier Reef, Australia.

somewhere in the East Indies, possibly along the Indo-Australian archipelago, or an area of sympatry in which the two forms do not mix. Bleeker (1877) collected intensively in this area and had both forms, based on the figure included being that of *Chaetodon triangulum* and his statement that some of his examples had the triangle in the caudal fin. These of course may have been collected in the Indian Ocean, as *triangulum* has been taken from the offshore island of Mentawai a short distance from Sumatra. The color pattern of the adult easily separates the two, and the possibility or even probability of sympatry leads me to regard them as good species.

Klausewitz (1955) notes that Cuvier (1831) described both species (*triangulum* and *baronessa*). He thinks these species synonymous and uses the name *C. baronessa* since Bleeker (1851) was the first reviser and used that name in preference to *C. triangulum*.

Distribution.—Indian Ocean from west coast of Indo-Australian Archipelago (Mentawai Island) to Sri Lanka and eastern Africa.

Material Examined.—(9 spec.: 28-92 mm S.L.) MCZ 41724 (1: 28), Colombo, Sri Lanka; FMNH 73968 and 73974 (2: 90-92), Maldive Islands; SOSC Te Vega Sta. 104 and 112 (2: 75-80), Mentawai Island, Indonesia; SOSC Te Vega Sta. 71 (4: 73-90), Pulo Jarak, Indonesia.

CHAETODON BARONESSA Cuvier
Baroness butterflyfish

Chaetodon baronessa Cuvier, 1831: p. 45 (no locality; on Vlaming).

Sarothrodus baronessa, Bleeker, 1863: p. 234 (Ternate, new combination).

Chaetodon triangulum (not of Cuvier), Steindachner, 1900: p. 420 (Ternate).

Gonochaetodon triangulum (not of Cuvier), Jordan & Seale, 1907: p. 33. Jordan & Richardson, 1908: p. 269 (Philippines). McCulloch, 1929: p. 247.

Chaetodon triangulum baronessa, Ahl, 1923: p. 175, pl. 2, fig. 11 (Padang, Sipora, Sumatra; new combination).

Chaetodon (Gonochaetodon) triangulum (not of Cuvier), Herre & Montalban, 1927: p. 26, pl. 5, fig. 1 (Philippines).

Gonochaetodon baronessa, Fowler, 1927: p. 286 (Philippines; new combination).

Diagnosis.—D. XI-XII (usually XI), 23-26 (usually 25); A. III, 20-22; pectoral rays 14 (13); L.l. scales 24-30 (usually 26-28); close to *Chaetodon triangulum*, but without light boomerang-shaped marking on caudal fin; light and dark chevrons on anterior portion of body of equal width.

Chaetodon baronessa Cuvier. 59 mm S.L. Vanikoro Island, Solomons.

Ratios	Standard Length (mm)		
	20-49(1)	50-79(16)	above 79(8)
Depth/S.L.	1.5	1.3-1.4	1.2-1.4
Head/S.L.	3.1	3.0-3.2	3.1-3.4
Eye/Head	2.7	2.5-3.3	2.8-3.3
Snout/Head	3.3	2.7-4.3	2.8-3.6
Interorb. W./Head.	2.9	2.6-3.0	2.5-2.8
Maxillary/Head	3.6	3.6-4.9	3.5-4.5
Caud. Ped./S.L.	8.3	7.9-8.9	8.1-9.0
Pect. Fin/S.L.	3.2	3.0-3.6	3.3-3.7
Pelvic Sp./S.L.	4.5	4.0-5.1	4.3-5.0
Predorsal L./S.L.	2.1	2.0-2.1	2.1-2.3
Prepelvic L./S.L.	2.4	2.4-2.6	2.4-2.7
Dorsal Sp. No. 1/S.L.	---	7.4-10.7	7.8-12.2
Dorsal Sp. No. 2/S.L.	---	6.9-10.3	7.3-10.6
Dorsal Sp. No. 3/S.L.	---	5.2-7.6	7.1-8.9
Dorsal Sp. No. 4/S.L.	---	4.4-6.8	4.8-6.7
Anal Sp. No. 1/S.L.	---	6.2-7.9	6.6-8.5
Anal Sp. No. 2/S.L.	---	4.8-5.9	5.0-5.9
Anal Sp. No. 3/S.L.	---	4.5-6.3	4.6-5.8

Chaetodon u. unimaculatus pair in their natural habitat. The coral is a species of *Acropora.* Photo by M. Goto, Marine Life Documents.

Chaetodon u. unimaculatus from Hawaii. Photo by Ken Lucas, Steinhart Aquarium.

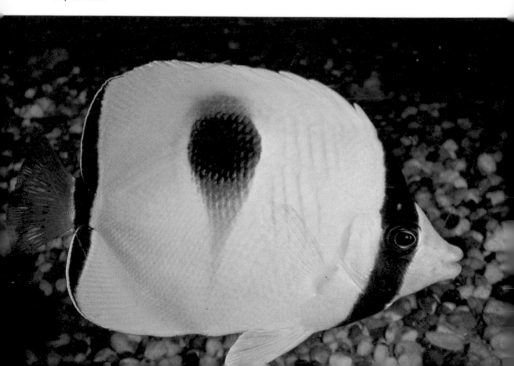

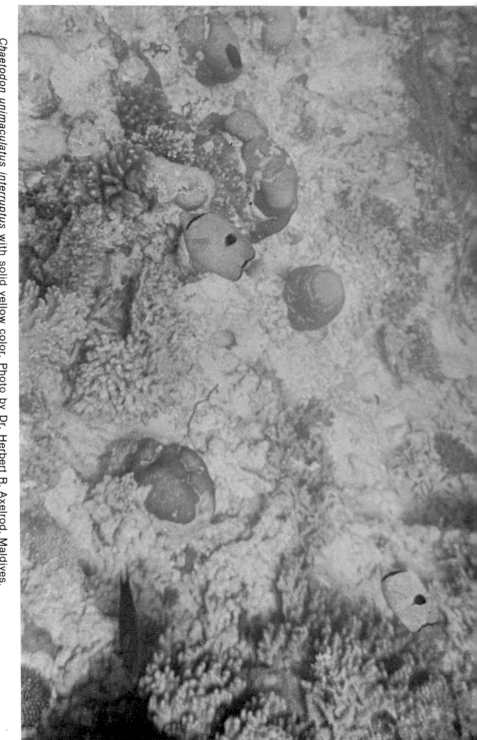

Chaetodon unimaculatus interruptus with solid yellow color. Photo by Dr. Herbert R. Axelrod, Maldives.

Meristics.—D. XI (two with XII), 23-26 (usually 25); A. III, 20-22; pectoral rays 14 (one with 13/13, three with 13/14, one with 15/14); L.l. scales 24-30 (usually 26-28); L.l. pores 16-23; scales above L.l. 6-10 (usually 7 or 8); scales below L.l. 19-21; gill rakers 22-27.

Description.—Teeth in group of rows (4?) at tip of jaws; caudal peduncle depth greater than interorbital width, which is greater than eye diameter and snout, eye diameter and snout being equal.

Last dorsal spine longest, first dorsal rays continuing this increase, fifth or sixth rays longest; anal spines strong, second and third about equal, first slightly shorter; base of spinous portion of dorsal fin approximately equal to that of soft portion, both 2.5-2.8 in standard length; pelvic fins long, reaching to level of second anal fin spine.

Lateral line ending near bases of soft dorsal fin rays a short distance above caudal peduncle (the extent of lateral line varies but rarely reaches last rays of dorsal fin); dorsal fin scales reach halfway up on fifth spine; anal spine scale covering to about three-fourths of third spine.

Color Pattern.—Very fine dark edge to dorsal and anal fins; snout dark from anterior edge of interopercle to nape well above eye level, darker bordered, lips pale; eyeband dark bordered, connected at nape (peak of the dark snout band reaches this connection); eyeband wider below eye, not dark bordered there, joins at isthmus and extends to pelvic fins where it fades abruptly and continues as a lighter color on the pelvic fins; pelvic fins white; dark smudge on upper base of pectoral fin.

Juveniles are similar to those of *Chaetodon triangulum*. Only one specimen was seen, 25 mm S.L., quite faded, from the Solomon Islands. Noticeably different is the caudal fin. Half of it is hyaline, then a dark band, then a white "V"-shaped marking.

Remarks.—*Chaetodon baronessa* is the Pacific Ocean representative of the subgenus *Gonochaetodon*. As stated under *Chaetodon triangulum*, there is some doubt as to the extent of the species in the East Indies, and it is not known whether these two closely related species are sympatric. The juveniles seem very close and no particular differences can be found. However, the material available is not good and only one juvenile of each species was available, that of *C. baronessa* very faded. The width of the chevrons, which Ahl (1923) uses as a distinction between these two forms, is not wholly reliable, which can readily be seen by comparison of photographs.

The records of *Chaetodon triangulum* from the Pacific Ocean, as far as I can determine, in actuality all belong to *C. baronessa*, and most have been eliminated from the above synonymy. Munro (1967) uses an illustration of *Gonochaetodon triangulum* instead of one of *G. baronessa*, probably a carry over from his book on fishes of Ceylon (1955).

Distribution.—East Indies, Philippines, China, Japan, south to Queensland and eastward to the Fiji Islands; Palau Islands; New Guinea.

Material Examined.—(25 spec.: 45-98 mm S.L.) CAS 37686, 37687, 37688, 37689, 37690, 37691, 37692 (15: 57-85), Palau Islands; CAS 37693

(1: 98), Gulf of Thailand; USNM 169766 (5: 52-84), New Georgia, Solomon Islands; USNM 169855 (1: 25), New Georgia, Solomon Islands; AMS IB 8171 (1: 86), Heron Island, Queensland; SOSC Te Vega Cr. 6 Sta. 236 (2: 45-62), Rabaul, New Britain.

CHAETODON LARVATUS Cuvier
Masked butterflyfish

Chaetodon larvatus Cuvier, 1831: p. 45 (type locality Red Sea; ex Ehrenberg MS).

Chaetodon karraf Cuvier, 1831: p. 46 (type locality Red Sea; on an illustration by Ehrenberg MS; juvenile of 1 inch).

Chaetodon triangulum var. *larvatus*, Bleeker, 1877: p. 54 (Red Sea).

Chaetodon (Anisochaetodon) larvatus, Klunzinger, 1884: p. 57 (Red Sea).

Chaetodon (Anisochaetodon) triangulum var. *karraf*, Klunzinger, 1884: p. 57 (Red Sea).

Chaetodon larvatus var. *karraf*, Ahl, 1923: p. 177 (Red Sea).

Chaetdodon larvatus Cuvier. 75 mm S.L. Red Sea.

439

Chaetodon octofasciatus juvenile with double striped pattern. Stripes are normal distance apart. Photo by Roger Lubbock.

Chaetodon octofasciatus juvenile with stripes closer together. Photo by F. Earl Kennedy, Philippines.

Chaetodon octofasciatus in its natural habitat. Photo by Dr. Walter A. Starck II, Palau.

Chaetodon octofasciatus adult. The stripes are further apart than in the other Individuals pictured on these pages. Photo by Walter A. Starck II, Palau.

| | | Standard Length (mm) | |
Ratios	20-49(6)	50-79(5)	above 79(3)
Depth/S.L............	1.5	1.4-1.5	1.4-1.5
Head/S.L..............	2.6-3.0	3.2-3.5	3.7
Eye/Head............	2.4-2.9	2.6-2.9	2.8-2.9
Snout/Head...........	3.1-3.4	3.3-4.1	3.1-3.9
Interorb. W./Head......	2.9-3.1	2.2-2.6	2.4-2.5
Maxillary/Head........	3.2-4.6	4.1-5.5	4.3-5.5
Caud. Ped./S.L.........	7.5-8.4	7.8-8.3	8.0-8.8
Pect. Fin./S.L..........	3.3-3.5	3.8-4.5	4.1
Pelvic Spine/S.L........	4.0-4.7	4.7-5.5	4.9
Predorsal L./S.L........	2.0-2.3	2.0-2.3	2.2
Prepelvic L./S.L........	2.2-2.4	2.5-2.6	2.8
Dorsal Sp. No. 1/S.L.....	7.7-10.0	9.2-14.4	10.2-11.7
Dorsal Sp. No. 2/S.L.....	4.9-8.2	7.6-10.8	8.8-11.2
Dorsal Sp. No. 3/S.L.....	4.3-5.7	5.5-8.4	7.9
Dorsal Sp. No. 4/S.L.....	3.5-4.1	5.0-6.6	7.4
Anal Sp. No. 1/S.L......	5.7-7.4	7.3-9.6	8.3-9.8
Anal Sp. No. 2/S.L......	4.4-4.9	4.8-5.6	5.0-5.6
Anal Sp. No. 3/S.L......	4.1-4.7	4.3-5.7	4.7-5.3

Diagnosis.—D. XI-XII (mostly XI), 23-26 (mostly 24-25); A. III (20) 21-22; pectoral rays 14-15; L.l. scales 31-37; similar in form to *Chaetodon triangulum* and *C. baronessa* but with eyeband absent in adults, large black area including most of soft portion of dorsal fin sharply separated from body color by white stripe, and higher number of L.l. scales (other two species average 22-32 L.l. scales).

Meristics.—D. XI-XII (mostly XI), 23-26 (usually 24 or 25); A. III, 21-22 (one with 20); pectoral rays 14 or 15 (one with 15/14, one with 13/14); L.l. scales 31-37; L.l. pores 22-28; scales above L.l. 7-10; scales below L.l. 19-24, usually 21-22; gill rakers 18-22.

Description.—Teeth in group of rows in anterior of jaws; caudal peduncle depth greater than or equal to interorbital width; interorbital width greater than eye diameter, which is greater than snout length.

Last dorsal spine longest, first dorsal rays longer until sixth or seventh rays, which are longest; anal spines also graduated, last longest, first about half length of second; base of spinous portion of dorsal fin about equal to that of soft portion, both 2.5-2.8 in standard length; pelvic fins long, reaching base of first anal spine.

Lateral line describing low arc across body, ending high above caudal peduncle at about middle of soft portion of dorsal fin base; scales of dorsal fin spines reaching midpoint of about sixth spine; anal spine scale covering extending to midpoint of third spine.

Chaetodon larvatus 40.3 and 26.9 mm S.L. Gold Mohur Bay.

Color Pattern.—No ocular band; head dark, including nape to first dorsal fin spine base and breast to origin of pelvic fins (opercle excluded); dark spot (indefinite) at upper corner of head color before first dorsal spine; white line bordering head color; edges of dorsal and anal fins white, submarginal black line present; caudal fin edge hyaline, submarginal white line and black lines present; upper and lower edges of caudal fin white.

Juveniles similar but with slightly different color pattern. In specimens of 28-38 mm standard length, chevrons are present as well as posterior black area. This posterior black area is less defined and smaller in area, reaching from the angle of dorsal fin past the anterior end of caudal peduncle a short distance into the anal fin. The white anterior border is present only in front of the caudal peduncle. Base of caudal fin dark, the light stripe is at the center of the fin, the clear portion beyond that equal to half the fin. Edges of dorsal and anal fins white with submarginal dark line. Posterior border of head color similar to that of adults, but the snout and face have become much lighter, leaving the dark area in the form of an eyeband (although the anterior border is somewhat indefinite). The smallest specimen has a more differentiated eyeband which joins at the nape and again on the chest. This specimen is about 1-3/8 inches total length compared with the one-inch type of *Chaetodon karraf*.

Juvenile *Chaetodon rainfordi* with dark band around caudal peduncle. Photo by Allan Power.

Young *Chaetodon rainfordi* in captivity. Caudal peduncle bar has become weaker. Photo by Roger Steene.

Chaetodon rainfordi subadult. This species occurs in areas with living coral, one of the items of its diet. Photo by Allan Power.

Adult *Chaetodon rainfordi* lacks the caudal peduncle bar. Photo 60 feet deep by W. Deas at Heron Island, Great Barrier Reef.

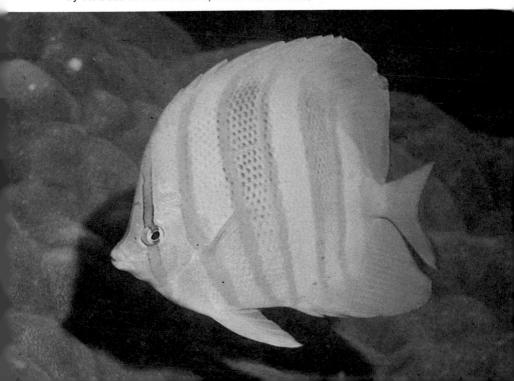

Remarks.—As far as I can determine, all accounts of the species or variety called *karraf* are of juvenile specimens about an inch long. The description of the above juveniles indicates that the eyeband, which is relied upon to separate the two forms, is present in the juveniles. *Chaetodon larvatus* is known from both the Red Sea and Gulf of Aden, so Fraser-Brunner's (1949) suggestion that the two might be geographic forms is not upheld.

The dark posterior area, the chevron pattern, and the shape and disposition of the scales indicate the relationship of this species to the other chevroned species.

Distribution.—Red Sea and Gulf of Aden.

Material Examined.—(14 spec.: 27-92 mm S.L.) AMNH 9457 (2: 88-92), Red Sea; BPBM 7849 (6: 63-80), Red Sea; SOSC Anton Bruun Cruise #9, Sta. FT-26 (6: 27-40), Gold Mohur Bay, Aden.

Subgenus TETRACHAETODON Weber and de Beaufort

Tetrachaetodon Weber and de Beaufort, 1936: pp. 53, 56, and 59. (Type-species *Chaetodon plebeius* Cuvier 1831, by original designation.)

Diagnosis.—Body elongate-oval; dorsal spines graduated, no spines exceptionally long; dorsal and anal fins with rounded angle; snout short, blunt, 3.0-4.0 in head length; lateral line in low arc; scales rounded; lachrymal partly hidden by scales; base of spinous dorsal fin about twice base of soft portion; D. XIV, 16-18; A. III-IV, 15-16.

Description.—D. XIV (rarely XIII or XV), 15-19 (usually 16-18); A. III or IV (IV in *Chaetodon plebeius* only), 14-17 (usually 15 or 16); pectoral fin rays 14-16; L.l. scales 35-42; scales above L.l. 5-12 (usually 6-7 or 9-11); scales below L.l. 13-20 (usually 14-15 or 18-20); gill rakers 15-24.

Body oval to elongate-oval; snout short, blunt, 3.0-4.0 in head length; predorsal profile straight to slightly convex; lateral line describing a low arc to base of last rays of dorsal fin; scales moderate, rounded to slightly angular, in horizontal series below lateral line and slightly ascending series above lateral line; dorsal and anal fins symmetrical, with rounded angles posteriorly; caudal fin truncate to slightly convex; pelvic fins moderately short to short, normally not reaching anal opening in adult; mouth small, gape horizontal to slightly oblique, teeth in 8-12 spaced rows in each jaw (first few rows more compact); preopercle obtuse to right-angled, usually serrate; lachrymal short, rounded, lower edge usually serrate or toothed, posterior edge partly hidden by scales; vertical fins almost entirely covered by small scales; scales covering dorsal spines moderate, extending from base of first spine to cover almost all of last.

Color yellow to yellow-orange with darker horizontal lines on sides following scale rows; dark spot on side, lateral line passing through it about one-third of way from upper edge (this spot may be somewhat faded in *Chaetodon plebeius*); eyeband narrower than eye, darker on nape, bordered by white or bluish white stripes.

Juveniles similar to adults. Pelvic fins extend further posteriorly than those of adults, reaching level of anal spines; longest dorsal spine may be third, fourth or fifth; hyaline section of caudal fin broader.

Tropical Pacific and Indian Oceans.

Four species presently included in this subgenus as distinguished by the following key.

Key to the Species of the Subgenus Tetrachaetodon

1. Four anal spines; spot on side elongate-oval, blue in life (often faded); ocellated spot on caudal peduncle (Indo-Pacific) . . . .
. . . . *Chaetodon plebeius*

   Three anal spines; spot on side round to oval, black in life; no ocellus on caudal peduncle 2

2. Spot on side ocellated (may be obscured by dark area surrounding spot); two lines on side (blue in life), one above pectoral fin, one below it, converging at or near origin of lateral line (Indo-Pacific) . . . . *C. bennetti*

   Spot on side never ocellated; no converging lines on sides. 3

3. Pectoral fin with 14 rays; lateral spot large (nearly size of head); horizontal dusky lines on sides following scale rows at juncture of scales, i.e. between the rows (western Pacific) . . . . *C. speculum*

   Pectoral fin with 15 rays; lateral spot smaller, distinctly less than head length; horizontal lines on sides following scale rows but passing through center of scales (western Indian Ocean) . . . .
. . . . *C. zanzibariensis*

Remarks.—Although the subgenus was erected for a single species, *Chaetodon plebeius*, and based mainly on that species having four anal spines, it shares most other characteristics with the three other species I have included with it. The multi-spined condition occurs several times in different species which are unrelated, and I do not believe a separate subgenus should be considered on the basis of spine number alone.

CHAETODON PLEBEIUS Cuvier
Blue-blotched butterflyfish
(Blue-spot butterflyfish)

Chaetodon plebeji Gmelin, 1788: p. 1269, footnote (after Broussonet MS; *nomen nudum;* no locality).

Chaetodon plebeius Cuvier, 1831: p. 68 (type locality Mer du Sud; after Broussonet MS).

447

Juvenile *Chaetodon aureofasciatus* among the tips of the coral *Acropora*.
Photo by Roger Steene.

Juvenile *Chaetodon aureofasciatus* with the normally white body and band
around the caudal peduncle. Photo by Roger Steene.

Chaetodon aureofasciatus adult, lacking caudal peduncle band and with a grayish body. Photo by Allan Power.

Adult *Chaetodon aureofasciatus* among a similar species of *Acropora*. Photo by Dr. Gerald R. Allen, Great Barrier Reef.

Chaetodon cordiformis Thiolliere *in* Montrouzier, 1856: p. 443 (type locality Woodlark Island).
Chaetodon plebejus, Gunther, 1860: p. 5 (South Sea).
Eteira plebejus, Kaup, 1860: p. 149 (South Seas; new combination).
Megaprotodon maculiceps Ogilby, 1910: p. 14 (type locality Moreton Bay, Queensland).
Chaetodon maculiceps, Ahl, 1923: p. 54 (Moreton Bay; new combination).
Megaprotodon plebeius, Fowler, 1928: p. 256 (India, Queensland, Polynesia, Melanesia; new combination).
Chaetodon (Tetrachaetodon) plebeius, Weber and de Beaufort, 1936: p. 56, fig. 18 (New Guinea, Andamans, Formosa, Philippine Islands, Sue Is., Torres Straits, Queensland, Fiji).
Tetrachaetodon plebeius, Whitley, 1961: pp. 60-65 (New Caledonia; new combination).

Diagnosis.—D. XIII-XV (usually XIV), 16-18 (usually 17); A. IV (rarely V), 14-16 (usually 15); pectoral rays 15 (14); distinguished from all other species of chaetodonts by its indefinite elongate lateral spot (blue in life but may fade in preservative) and black spot (usually ocellated) on the anterior portion of the caudal peduncle.

Similar in aspect to the species of subgenus *Corallochaetodon* but easily distinguished by color pattern and four anal spines.

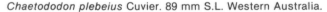

Chaetododon plebeius Cuvier. 89 mm S.L. Western Australia.

| | | Standard Length (mm) | |
Ratios	10-39(2)	40-69(10)	above 69(13)
Depth/S.L.............	1.6-1.7	1.7-1.9	1.7-1.9
Head/S.L.............	3.0	3.1-3.5	3.2-3.6
Eye/Head	2.5-2.8	2.6-3.0	2.7-3.1
Snout/Head	3.2-4.2	2.8-3.5	2.7-4.1
Interorb. W./Head......	2.6-2.7	2.5-2.9	2.4-2.7
Maxillary/Head	4.5-4.8	3.3-5.7	3.7-5.9
Caud. Ped./S.L........	8.7-9.4	8.6-9.7	8.7-10.0
Pect. Fin/S.L..........	3.5-3.6	3.5-4.4	3.5-4.1
Pelvic Sp./S.L.........	4.1-4.3	4.0-4.9	4.4-5.3
Predorsal L./S.L........	2.2-2.3	2.3-2.5	2.3-2.7
Prepelvic L./S.L........	2.3-2.5	2.2-2.6	2.5-2.8
Dorsal Sp. No. 1/S.L.....	9.2-10.3	8.2-12.0	9.9-14.4
Dorsal Sp. No. 2/S.L.....	5.6-6.3	5.7-9.1	6.5-10.7
Dorsal Sp. No. 3/S.L.....	4.1-4.6	4.4-5.8	4.9-8.2
Dorsal Sp. No. 4/S.L.....	3.7-4.3	3.5-4.7	4.1-6.6
Dorsal Sp. No. 5/S.L.....	3.5	3.5-3.9	4.0-5.3
Dorsal Sp. No. 6/S.L.....	3.4	3.3-4.2	4.0-5.5
Anal Sp. No. 1/S.L......	7.0-7.1	6.1-7.8	6.4-9.1
Anal Sp. No. 2/S.L......	4.7-5.1	4.1-4.7	4.3-5.2
Anal Sp. No. 3/S.L......	5.3-5.6	4.1-5.3	4.6-5.8
Anal Sp. No. 4/S.L......	5.5-7.4	4.5-6.3	4.8-6.9

Meristics.—D. XIV (rarely XIII or XV), 16-18 (usually 17); A. IV (rarely V), 14-16 (usually 15); pectoral fin 15 (one with 14/14, one with 15/16, one with 12/15); L.l. scales 36-41; L.l. pores 33-41; scales above L.l. 5-8; scales below L.l. 13-17; gill rakers 19-24.

Description.—Body elongate-oval; dorsal spines moderately long, evenly graduated, fourth to sixth longest; second anal spine longest, third and fourth approximately equal, first two-thirds of second and slightly shorter than last two; dorsal fin angle at about tenth or eleventh ray, anal fin angle at ninth ray; pelvic fins moderately short, barely reaching or just short of anal opening; base of spinous dorsal fin about twice that of soft portion (2.2 and 4.4 in standard length respectively).

Preopercle obtuse-angled to right-angled, serrate; supraorbital smooth to slightly toothed; lachrymal short, smooth to lightly serrate on lower edge; teeth in eight rows in each jaw, the anterior rows closer together; interorbital greater than caudal peduncle; caudal peduncle greater than or equal to eye, eye greater than snout.

Lateral line four to five rows of scales distant from dorsal fin base; scales reach midpoint of third anal spine and cover about three-fourths of fourth.

Chaetodon tricinctus. Photographed off Philip Point, Lord Howe Island by W. Deas, about 50 feet deep.

Young *Chaetodon tricinctus* in captivity. Photo by Roger Steene.

Chaetodon tricinctus photographed in only six feet of water, Lord Howe Island. Photo by Dr. Gerald R. Allen.

Color Pattern.—Lateral spot about one-third above lateral line, often faded; lateral stripes narrow below lateral line, passing through centers of scales, those above lateral line wider; eyeband dark on nape, not connecting with band from opposite side.

Juveniles similar in color pattern to the adults; eyebands connected on nape and extend onto isthmus; caudal peduncle spot more centrally located and possibly connected above and/or below to form a true band; hyaline posterior section of caudal fin wider.

Remarks.—Gmelin (1788) first used the name *Chaetodon plebeji* based on a Broussonet manuscript. However, the name is a *nomen nudum* which cannot be accepted under the Rules of Nomenclature.

There seems to be no question that *Chaetodon maculiceps* is a synonym of this species.

An association with *Chaetodon trifascialis* due to the four anal spines seems to be unwarranted when additional features are compared.

The similarity to the *Chaetodon trifasciatus* group may also be superficial, the contour of the lateral line, teeth, and squamation being some features to separate these species-groups.

Distribution.—Tropical Pacific and Indian Oceans. East Indies and Philippine Islands north to China and southern Japan (Osaka); south to the Great Barrier Reef of Australia, Brisbane, Western Australia (Abrolhos); east to include Melanesia (New Caledonia, Fiji); west across the Indian Ocean (Andaman Islands, Dar-es-Salaam).

Material Examined.—(25 spec.: 38-107 mm S.L.) USNM Acc. 285012 (7: 57-87), Heron Island, Queensland, Australia; USNM 181223-181228 (6: 68-107), Philippine Islands; WAM P13727-8 (2: 50-89), Rat I., Abrolhos, Western Australia, Australia; AMS IB. 8173 (2: 39-47), Heron Island, Queensland, Australia; CAS 37768 (3: 52-63), Fiji Islands; CAS 7013 (1: 89), Tahiti, Society Islands; CAS 7033 (1: 73), Fiji Islands; WEB (3: 38-82), Heron Island, Queensland, Australia).

CHAETODON SPECULUM Cuvier
Mirror butterflyfish
(Oval-spot coral fish)

Chaetodon speculum Cuvier, 1831: p. 73 (type locality Batavia; after figure in Kuhl and van Hasselt MS).

Chaetodon spilopleura Cuvier, 1831: p. 74 (type locality Moluccas; after figure in Reinwardt MS).

Citharoedus speculum, Kaup, 1860: p. 145 (Java; new combination).

Tetragonoptrus speculum, Bleeker, 1865: p. 189 (Ceram; new combination).

Tetragonoptrus (Rabdophorus) speculum, Bleeker, 1877: p. 34 (Java (Batavia), Bawean, Amboina, Ceram, Banda).

Chaetodon ocellifer Franz, 1910: p. 49, pl. V, fig. 35 (type locality Nagasaki, Japan; juvenile).
Chaetodon (Rabdophorus) speculum, Weber and de Beaufort, 1936: p. 64 (various localities).

Chaetodon speculum Cuvier. 88 mm S.L. Heron Island, Queensland, Australia.

Diagnosis.—D. XIV, 17-18 (usually 17); A. III, 15-16 (usually 16); pectoral rays 14 (13); close to *Chaetodon zanzibariensis*, but differs in having the lateral spot much larger (about ⅔ head size); *C. speculum* has 14 pectoral fin rays as compared with 15 for *C. zanzibariensis*.

Meristics.—D. XIV, 17-18 (usually 17); A. III, 15-16 (usually 16); pectoral fin 14 (one with 13/13, five with 15/14); L.l. scales 37-42 (usually 39 or 40); L.l. pores 33-39; scales above L.l. 9-12 (usually 10 or 11); scales below L.l. 18-20; gill rakers 17-22.

Description.—Body elongate-oval; dorsal spines evenly graduated, fifth to seventh longest; second and third anal spines about equal (second often slightly longer), first about two-thirds second; pelvic fins moderate to short, barely reaching anal opening in adult; base of spinous portion of

Chaetodon hoefleri feeding on the biocover of a wooden beam. The interorbital stripe can be plainly seen on the facing specimen. Photo by Roger Lubbock at Ghana.

Compare
*Chaetodon
hoefleri* in this
photo with *C.
marleyi,* its
closest relative,
below. Photo by
Roger Lubbock,
Ghana.

Chaetodon marleyi in captivity. Aside from the dorsal fin color there are subtle differences in the bars between this species and *C. hoefleri.* Photo by Gerald R. Shaeffer.

Ratios	10-39(1)	Standard Length (mm) 40-69(14)	above 69 (11)
Depth/S.L.............	1.4	1.4-1.6	1.4-1.6
Head/S.L..............	2.5	2.8-3.4	3.3-3.6
Eye/Head.............	2.6	2.5-2.9	2.7-3.3
Snout/Head...........	4.4	2.6-3.9	3.0-4.2
Interorb. W./Head......	2.1	2.4-2.9	2.4-2.7
Maxillary/Head........	---	3.7-5.7	3.6-4.9
Caud. Ped./S.L........	7.7	8.1-9.0	8.0-8.8
Pect. Fin/S.L..........	3.7	3.4-4.1	3.6-4.2
Pelvic Sp./S.L.........	4.7	4.1-4.8	4.4-5.3
Predorsal L./S.L.......	1.9	2.2-2.4	2.3-2.6
Prepelvic L./S.L.......	2.1	2.2-2.6	2.4-2.6
Dorsal Sp. No. 1/S.L....	7.7	9.2-13.4	9.2-13.2
Dorsal Sp. No. 2/S.L....	5.3	5.3-8.4	7.2-9.2
Dorsal Sp. No. 3/S.L....	3.9	4.0-5.7	4.4-6.7
Dorsal Sp. No. 4/S.L....	3.5	3.6-4.5	3.5-5.0
Dorsal Sp. No. 5/S.L....	---	3.3-3.6	3.6-4.3
Dorsal Sp. No. 6/S.L....	---	3.4-3.5	3.6-4.2
Anal Sp. No. 1/S.L.....	7.4	6.2-8.0	6.0-7.6
Anal Sp. No. 2/S.L.....	6.4	4.3-5.3	4.2-5.2
Anal Sp. No. 3/S.L.....	6.4	4.3-6.4	4.5-6.0

dorsal fin twice or more than twice that of soft portion (1.9-2.0 and 3.8-4.6 in standard length, respectively).

Preopercle obtuse to right-angled, lightly serrate to toothed, an indentation above the angle; supraorbital toothed; lachrymal short, rounded, serrate on lower edge; teeth in about 8-10 rows in lower jaw and 8-12 rows in upper jaw, the first 4 or 5 rows more compact; caudal peduncle greater than or equal to interorbital width; interorbital width greater than eye and eye greater than snout.

Lateral line 5 to 6 scale rows distant from dorsal fin base; scales reach to about midpoint of third anal spine.

Color Pattern.—Dark spot extends from level of fourth dorsal fin spine to about fifth dorsal fin ray; in alcohol eyeband brown, bordered by a darker brown; eyeband continuous across nape and isthmus, forming a complete band around head; dark horizontal lines on body along juncture of scale rows (not through their centers as in *Chaetodon zanzibariensis*).

Juvenile color pattern similar to that of adult. In smallest specimens (20 mm) there is a dark edge on the anal fin. It is no longer evident in the preserved specimens of 40 mm S.L.

Remarks.—The three specimens (lectotype, RMNH 498, and two paratypes, RMNH 497 and 500) sent to the Leiden Museum by Reinwardt are thought to be those used by Kuhl and van Hasselt for their description and illustration upon which Cuvier based his description (Boeseman *in* Bauchot, 1963).

Chaetodon speculum is closely related to *C. zanzibariensis* but differs from that species as indicated in the diagnosis above.

The black edge to the anal fin in the smallest juveniles (about 20 mm S.L.) has been noted in specimens from Australia, Palau, and the Philippines. It appears to be an ontogenetic rather than a geographic characteristic. At this size the tholichthys characters are still evident.

Reese (1974) observed *Chaetodon speculum* at Heron Island in areas of wave action, moving over the reef flat at high tide. Two fish were seen in the same general area but did not form a close relationship like that of the truly paired species. He classifies them as solitary or loosely paired resident species. I have observed this species in the Philippines in a shallow protected bay. They behaved as true pairs and remained close together most of the time. Feeding was similar to other species, moving over the reef and stopping now and then to pick at the coral. It is not known for sure whether the coral polyps were taken or the associated invertebrates.

Distribution.—Western Pacific Ocean from southern Japan (Osaka, Nagasaki) and the Ryukyu Islands to Taiwan, Pescadores Islands, Philippine Islands, East Indies, Western Caroline Islands, Palau Islands, New

Chaetodon speculum on the Great Barrier Reef. The anal fin has a dark edge in this individual. Photo by Dr. E. Reese.

Chaetodon humeralis from the East Pacific. Photo by Dr. Herbert R. Axelrod.

Chaetodon humeralis in its natural habitat. Photo by Alex Kerstitch 50 feet deep off Guyamas, Mexico.

Chaetodon robustus has been commonly referred to as *C. luciae,* which, it turns out, is a later name. Photo by Roger Lubbock, Ghana.

Guinea, Bismarck Archipelago, New Caledonia, and Tonga (new record). Australia from the Great Barrier Reef to Western Australia (Abrolhos).

Material Examined.—(26 spec.: 19-104 mm S.L.) USNM Acc. 285012 (4: 50-88), Heron Island, Queensland, Australia; AMS IB. 8168 (1: 59), Heron Island, Queensland, Australia; CAS 37769 (8: 42-63), Iwayama Bay, Palau Islands; CAS 37770 (2: 65-90), Palau Islands; CAS 37771 (2: 84-95), Palau Islands; CAS 37772 (1: 103), Yap I., Western Caroline Islands; CAS 37773 (1: 94), Palau Islands; CAS 37774 (2: 19-62), Koror I., Palau Islands; CAS 37775 (1: 90), Palau Islands; BPBM (uncatalogued) (1: 57), Tonga Islands; WEB (2: 61-88), Heron Island, Queensland, Australia; SOSC VGS 68-16 (1: 104), Taiwan.

CHAETODON ZANZIBARIENSIS Playfair
Zanzibar butterflyfish

Chaetodon spilopleura (not of Cuvier) Kaup, 1860: p. 145 (Mozambique).
Chaetodon zanzibariensis Playfair, 1866: p. 33, pl. 6, fig. 1 (type locality Zanzibar).

Diagnosis.—D. XIII-XV (usually 14), 15-19 (usually 16-17); A. III, 15-17 (rarely 17); pectoral rays 15; resembles *Chaetodon speculum* but

Chaetodon zanzibariensis Playfair. 93 mm S.L. Seychelles Islands, Indian Ocean.

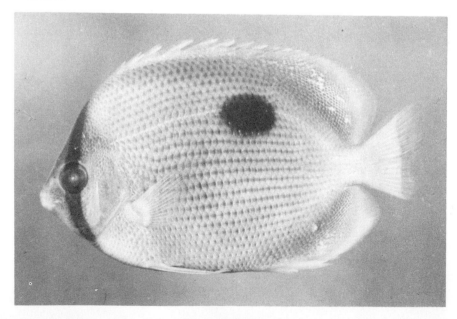

Ratios	Standard Length (mm)		
	10-39(3)	50-69(5)	above 69(8)
Depth/S.L............	1.5-1.6	1.4-1.7	1.5-1.7
Head/S.L.............	2.9-3.0	3.0-3.5	3.3-3.6
Eye/Head	2.6-2.8	2.6-2.9	3.0-3.3
Snout/Head	3.2-4.1	2.9-3.5	3.0-3.8
Interorb. W./Head......	2.4-2.7	2.5-2.6	2.4-2.6
Maxillary/Head	4.3-5.6	3.5-4.3	3.8-4.5
Caud. Ped./S.L........	7.9-8.4	7.9-8.8	8.1-8.9
Pect. Fin/S.L..........	3.2-3.8	3.4-4.2	3.5-3.9
Pelvic Sp./S.L.........	4.2	4.2-4.6	4.6-5.2
Predorsal L./S.L........	2.2	2.3-2.4	2.4-2.5
Prepelvic L./S.L........	2.2-2.4	2.4-2.5	2.6-2.7
Dorsal Sp. No. 1/S.L.....	7.8-13.5	9.7-11.1	11.4-13.7
Dorsal Sp. No. 2/S.L.....	5.6-6.7	6.1-7.0	7.9-9.8
Dorsal Sp. No. 3/S.L.....	4.0-4.6	4.5-5.0	5.9-7.2
Dorsal Sp. No. 4/S.L.....	3.7-4.5	3.6-4.4	5.1-5.4
Dorsal Sp. No. 5/S.L.....	3.5-4.5	3.4-4.0	4.8-5.0
Dorsal Sp. No. 6/S.L.....	3.6	3.7-4.3	5.0-5.1
Anal Sp. No. 1/S.L......	6.3-7.0	5.7-6.2	6.9-7.6
Anal Sp. No. 2/S.L......	4.3-4.7	4.1-4.6	4.6-4.8
Anal Sp. No. 3/S.L......	5.0-5.6	4.1-5.2	4.8-5.2

has 15 pectoral fin rays as compared to 14 for that species; possesses a much smaller lateral spot than *C. speculum*, and the horizontal lines on the body pass through the center of each scale (in *C. speculum* they pass between the scale rows).

Meristics.—D. XIV (one with XV, two with XIII), 15-19 (usually 16 or 17); A. III, 15-17 (usually 15 or 16); pectoral rays 15 (two with 14 on one side, 1 with 16 on one side); L.l. scales 37-43; L.l. pores 33-42; scales above L.l. 9-12 (usually 9 or 10); scales below L.l. 18-20 (rarely 20); gill rakers 19-23.

Description.—Body elongate-oval; dorsal spines evenly graduated, fourth or fifth longest; second and third anal spines about equal (second often slightly longer), first about two-thirds second; pelvic fins moderate to short, short of or barely reaching anal opening in adult; base of spinous portion of dorsal fin about twice that of soft portion (1.9-2.2 and 3.8-4.2 in S.L. respectively).

Preopercle obtuse to right-angled, lightly serrate to toothed; supraorbital smooth to toothed; lachrymal smooth to serrate on lower edge, short, rounded; teeth in about 9 or 10 rows in each jaw.

Lateral line about 6 scale rows distant from the base of the dorsal fin; scales reach to about midpoint of third anal spine.

Color Pattern.—Lateral spot round to slightly oval, extending from

Chetodon robustus juvenile. This may be the first known photo of a juvenile specimen of this species. Photo by Roger Lubbock, Ghana.

Chaetodon robustus adult. One of the characteristics of this species is the first dark band not touching the opercle as it does in *C. hoefleri.*

Chaetodon ocellicaudus juvenile. This species has white plevic fins. Photo by F. Earl Kennedy, Philippine Islands.

The caudal marking in the adult *Chaetodon ocellicaudus* is an ocellated spot. Photo by Aaron Norman.

Chaetodon zanzibariensis, juvenile, 36.5 mm S.L. Seychelles.

level of about ninth or tenth dorsal fin spine to first to third dorsal fin ray; in alcohol eyeband chestnut brown with dark brown to black edges; connection of eyebands at nape and isthmus weak; each scale on body with dark central bar giving rise to horizontal lines (less distinct above lateral line).

Juvenile color pattern similar to that of adults. Connection of eyeband on nape and isthmus stronger; almost two-thirds of caudal fin hyaline; dorsal and anal fin edges hyaline (36 mm S.L. specimen). Young specimens of 20-30 mm S.L. have a proportionately much larger side spot and a very narrow black intramarginal line in the anal fin (Ahl, 1923, Seychelles).

Remarks.—*Chaetodon luctuosus* Cuvier (1831) may be this species. The description is brief and the color is apparently lost ("je ne puis indiquer les couleurs, parce qu' il est devenu entierement noir"—Cuvier, 1831), but the 14 dorsal fin spines, 16 anal rays, and 15 pectoral rays place it very close to *C. zanzibariensis,* if not identical with it. In addition, the locality of *C. luctuosus* is unknown, placing some doubt as to whether or not it might be *C. speculum,* a species with similar characteristics. On the basis of the similarity of *C. zanzibariensis* and *C. speculum,* I have not replaced either name with *C. luctuosus,* which predates them both. I have not seen the type specimen, although Mme. Bauchot kindly provided me with a photograph of the type, and will withhold any further action until I do, in the hope that I may be able to place the species with more certainty.

Chaetodon zanzibariensis appears to be the Indian Ocean replacement species of *C. speculum*. *Chaetodon speculum*, however, has been reported from the Indian Ocean along the western coast of Australia. Since specimens smaller than 35 mm S.L. were not available, I cannot say whether this species exhibits a dark edge to the anal fin as do early juveniles of *Chaetodon speculum*.

Distribution.—Zanzibar, Mombasa, Mauritius, Aldabra, Seychelles, and Chagas Archipelago (new record). This species probably has a distribution covering the tropical western Indian Ocean.

Material Examined.—(16 spec.: 35-105 mm S.L.) MCZ 5999, 5745, and 1153 (3: 69-97), Mauritius; ANSP 108388, 108409, and 108549 (3: 70-105), Seychelles; ANSP 108357 (2: 37-93), Seychelles; SOSC HA 67-18 and HA 67-36 (6: 35-67), Chagas Archipelago; JLBS Z.246 and Z.902 (2: 43-98), Zanzibar.

CHAETODON BENNETTI Cuvier
Bennett's butterflyfish

Chaetodon Bennetti Cuvier, 1831: p. 84 (type locality Sumatra).

Chaetodon vinctus Bennett, *in* Lay and Bennett, 1839: p. 62, pl. 17, fig. 1 (type locality Byam Martin Island, Paumotus).

Coradion Bennetti, Kaup, 1860: p. 147 (Sumatra, new combination).

Sarothroedus bennetti, Bleeker, 1863: p. 156 (Halmahera; new combination).

Tetragonoptrus bennetti, Bleeker, 1865: p. 286 (new combination).

Tetragonoptrus (Rabdophorus) bennetti, Bleeker, 1877: p. 34, pl. 376, fig. 2 (Sumatra, Java, Halmahera, Amboina).

Rabdophorus bennetti, Whitley, 1932: p. 288 (new combination).

Chaetodon (Rabdophorus) bennetti, Weber and de Beaufort, 1936: p. 62 (various localities).

Diagnosis.—D. XIV (rarely XIII), 16-17 (occasionally 15); A. III, 15-16 (rarely 14); pectoral rays 15 (one with 14, one with 16); two dark (blue in life) lines, one on either side of pectoral fin, extending from origin of lateral line to vicinity of anal base; ocellated spot (often lost in larger blackish area) straddling lateral line below dorsal fin.

Largest species in this subgenus. Immediately recognizable by the above-mentioned color characteristics.

Newly transformed tholichthys of *Chaetodon melannotus*. Photo by Allan Power, New Hebrides.

Juvenile *Chaetodon melannotus* resemble *C. ocellicaudus* greatly, but *melannotus* has yellow pelvic fins. Photo by K.H. Choo, Taiwan.

Adult *Chaetodon melannotus* with broken caudal peduncle band. Photo by K.H. Choo, Taiwan.

Chaetodon melannotus in its natural habitat. Photo by Michio Goto, Marine Life Documents.

Chaetodon bennettii Cuvier. 155 mm S.L. Enewetak, Marshall Islands.

Ratios	10-39	Standard Length (mm) 40-69(8)	above 69(17)
Depth/S.L.............	---	1.6-1.8	1.4-1.8
Head/S.L..............	---	3.0-3.3	3.4-3.8
Eye/Head.............	---	2.7-3.1	2.9-3.4
Snout/Head...........	---	3.0-3.6	2.8-3.9
Interorb. W./Head......	---	2.6-2.9	2.3-2.9
Maxillary/Head........	---	3.7-4.4	3.8-5.1
Caud. Ped./S.L........	---	8.6-9.5	7.7-9.6
Pect. Fin/S.L..........	---	3.8-4.0	3.6-4.2
Pelvic Sp./S.L.........	---	4.4-4.6	4.1-5.4
Predorsal L./S.L.......	---	2.2-2.4	2.3-2.8
Prepelvic L./S.L.......	---	2.2-2.6	2.5-2.9
Dorsal Sp. No. 1/S.L....	---	9.2-10.9	9.3-15.8
Dorsal Sp. No. 2/S.L....	---	6.6-8.1	7.1-12.8
Dorsal Sp. No. 3/S.L....	---	5.1-5.6	5.5-8.7
Dorsal Sp. No. 4/S.L....	---	4.3-4.9	4.8-7.5
Dorsal Sp. No. 5/S.L....	---	---	4.2-5.9
Dorsal Sp. No. 6/S.L....	---	---	4.3-5.5
Anal Sp. No. 1/S.L......	---	6.2-7.6	6.5-9.2
Anal Sp. No. 2/S.L......	---	4.5-4.8	4.5-5.5
Anal Sp. No. 3/S.L......	---	4.4-5.7	4.5-6.4

Meristics.—D. XIV (rarely XIII), 16-17 (occasionally 15); A. III, 15-16 (rarely 14); pectoral rays 15 (one with 14/14, one with 16/16, and three with 14/15); L.l. scales 36-40; L.l. pores 29-37 (usually 31-36); scales above L.l. 8-11 (usually 10 or 11); scales below L.l. 17-19 (occasionally 20); gill rakers 15-20.

Description.—Body oval; dorsal spines strong, evenly graduated, fifth to eighth longest; second and third anal spines approximately equal, first about three-fourths second; pelvic fins very short, falling short of anal opening by half their length; base of spinous dorsal fin approximately twice that of soft portion (1.9-2.0 and 3.7-4.1 in standard length respectively).

Preopercle right-angled to slightly obtuse-angled, serrate, a notch above angle; supraorbital smooth to toothed; lachrymal short, rounded, smooth on lower edge; teeth in about 8-9 rows in lower jaw, about 7-8 rows in upper jaw, the anterior rows more compact; caudal peduncle greater than or equal to interorbital width; interorbital width greater than eye and eye greater than snout.

Lateral line about 5 to 6 scale rows distant from base of dorsal fin; scales rounded to slightly angular; scales cover less than half of third anal spine.

Color Pattern.—Lateral spot varies from a large blackish area indefinite in outline to a discrete round black spot ocellated with a light colored ring. This ocellated spot can often be seen within the blackish area. In alcohol the lateral stripes vary from solid brown to bluish with dark borders. Eyeband light with dark borders (in life blue), blackish on nape and not always connected with one from opposite side, extends to lower edge

Chaetodon bennettii is rather uncommon and very shy, therefore difficult to photograph. Photo by Rodney Jonklaas, Sri Lanka.

Juvenile *Chaetodon striatus* with well-defined ocellated dorsal fin spot. Photo by Dr. P. Colin, Aguadilla, Puerto Rico.

Defensive posture of *Chaetodon striatus* with fins raised and eye on supposed source of danger. Photo by Dr. Walter A. Starck II.

Subadult *Chaetodon striatus* with dorsal fin spot almost gone. Photo by Douglas Faulkner.

Adult *Chaetodon striatus* from the Virgin Islands. Photo by Ken Lucas, Steinhart Aquarium.

of interopercle, the posterior dark edge sometimes evident on isthmus. Pale band across caudal peduncle darker bordered, extending into posterior rays of dorsal and anal fins; two short vertical stripes on snout.

Juvenile color pattern similar to that of adult. Eyeband connection on nape more solid; caudal peduncle band more distinct; outer portion of caudal fin hyaline, the width becoming narrower with increase in size.

Remarks.—*Chaetodon bennetti* was reported by Cuvier (1831) to have nine dorsal spines. This error was noticed by Bleeker (1853), who gave the proper number as XIV. Kaup (1860), on the basis of Cuvier's count of nine spines, placed *C. bennetti* in genus *Coradion*, but later (1863) he replaced it in *Chaetodon*. Although widely distributed, the species does not appear to be common at any locality. Herre and Montalban (1927) found ripe females in the Philippines in March.

Distribution.—Tropical Pacific and Indian Oceans. From the Society and Tuamotu Islands throughout most of Polynesia (except the Hawaiian Islands), Micronesia (including Eniwetok, Marshall Islands—new record), Melanesia to New Caledonia and the Great Barrier Reef of Australia. The East Indies and Philippine Islands to southern Japan (Osaka). Across the Indian Ocean (including the Laccadive Islands and Cocos-Keeling Islands) to the east coast of Africa as far south as Delagoa Bay. Not yet recorded from the Red Sea.

Material Examined.—(25 spec.: 42-155 mm S.L.) BPBM 5877 (3: 104-130), Tahiti, Society Islands; BPBM (uncatalogued) (2: 151-155), Eniwetok, Marshall Islands; CAS 37777 (1: 133), Ifaluk Atoll, Caroline Islands; CAS 37778 (1: 116), Palau Islands; CAS 37779 (1: 129), Palau Islands; CAS 37780 (1: 150), Moorea, Society Islands; CAS 37776 (1: 119), Palau Islands; CAS 37781 (1: 118), Palau Islands; CAS 37782 (1: 75), Palau Islands; CAS 37783 (1: 121), Palau Islands; CAS Reg. 1976 Sta. 715 (1: 108), Palau Islands; CAS 37784 (1: 46), Yap I., Western Caroline Islands; CAS 37785 (4: 42-58), Koror I., Palau Islands; CAS 37786 (2: 111-126), Kapingamarangi Atoll, Caroline Islands; CAS 37787 (1: 50), Palau Islands; SOSC Te Vega Sta. 314 (3: 109-118), Canton I., Phoenix Islands.

CORALLOCHAETODON Burgess,
NEW SUBGENUS

Type-species.—*Chaetodon trifasciatus* Park, 1794, by original designation.

Diagnosis.—Body elongate-oval; spinous dorsal fin evenly graduated; dorsal and anal fins with blunt angles; snout short, blunt, 3.1-4.1 in head length; teeth grouped in indistinguishable rows in front of jaws; lachrymal almost completely hidden by scales; lateral line in high, angular arc; exposed parts of scales on body vertically elongate; eyeband with additional band on either side; D. XIII, 20-21; A. III, 19; pect. 14; L.l. scales 34-42.

Description.—Body oval to elongate; snout short, blunt, 3.1-4.1 in head length; predorsal contour slightly convex to almost straight; mouth small, gape horizontal to slightly oblique; teeth in a band of closely packed rows in each jaw; preopercle right-angled, the angle rounded and with light serrations (particularly at angle); supraorbital smooth; lachrymal almost hidden, covered with scales.

Dorsal spines increasing in height until sixth or seventh, then approximately equal or slightly shorter until last; first two dorsal spines short, approximately equal or second could be shorter than first; second and third anal spines subequal, first not much shorter than second; soft portions of dorsal and anal fins equal, with rounded angle or very blunt angle; vertical fins, when spread, form an almost continuous margin, though the caudal exceeds edge of dorsal and anal fins with its transparent edging; base of spinous portion of dorsal fin longer (2.1-2.4 in S.L.) than that of soft portion (3.2-3.6 in S.L.); caudal fin truncate, edges rounded; pectoral fins normal; pelvic fins short, not reaching anus in adults.

Lateral line describing a high, angular, skewed arc on body, highest point at about last three spines or first rays, and following base of rayed portion of dorsal fin for a short distance before ending high above area of caudal peduncle; scales large, rounded, exposed portions vertically elongate; scales in horizontal rows on body, slightly ascending rows above lateral line; scaled part of dorsal spines normal to high, starting at base of first spine and reaching past middle of seventh before covering almost all of last few.

Juveniles similar to adults in form, dorsal and anal fins more rounded, but different somewhat in color pattern.

Widely distributed in tropical areas of Pacific and Indian Oceans, Red Sea included. Absent from East Pacific and Atlantic Ocean.

Three species recognized and distinguishable by the following key.

Key to the Species of the Subgenus Corallochaetodon

1. Caudal and anal fins solid black, at most with light edging; confined to western Indian Ocean and Red Sea 2
   Caudal and anal fins not solid black; widely distributed in Pacific and Indian Oceans........................*Chaetodon trifasciatus*
2. Dorsal fin solid black except for spines not covered with scales; depth of caudal peduncle 8.7-9.5.....................*C. melapterus*
   Dorsal fin not solid black but posteriorly edged with black; depth of caudal peduncle 9.5-10.0........................*C. austriacus*

Remarks.—Nalbant (1971) placed the above three species into the same subgenus as *Chaetodon meyeri*, *C. ornatissimus* and *C. reticulatus* (sub-

Tholichthys stage of *Chaetodon capistratus*. The first elements of the color pattern are just appearing. Photo by Dr. Warren E. Burgess.

Newly metamorphosed or very early juvenile *Chaetodon capistratus*. The dorsal fin spot is evident for only a short time. Photo by Aaron Norman.

Very young juvenile *Chaetodon capistratus* that has lost the dorsal fin spot already. Photo by Aaron Norman.

Normal juvenile *Chaetodon capistratus* with full pattern. The dark bars may come and go with the mood of the fish, the darker the bars the more "unhappy" the fish. Photo by Dr. Herbert R. Axelrod.

genus *Citharoedus*). I hesitate to follow this classification on the basis of the scales and scale pattern. The scales of this subgenus are vertically elongate and arranged in horizontal rows over most of body, becoming inclined only above the lateral line. In *Citharoedus* the scales are rounded and, except for the lowermost portion of the body, are arranged in ascending rows. In addition, the vertical fins of *Corallochaetodon* form an almost continuous line when spread, the species of *Citharoedus* less so.

Subgenus *Corallochaetodon* has a typical tholichthys larva, and metamorphosis occurs at a relatively small size. Subgenus *Citharoedus* has a specialized tholichthys larva with supraorbital processes, and metamorphosis occurs at a larger than usual size.

The two groups are almost certainly related, but to place them together at this point is not warranted.

CHAETODON TRIFASCIATUS Mungo Park
Melon butterflyfish
(Lineated butterflyfish)

Chaetodon trifasciatus Mungo Park, 1797: p. 34 (type locality Sumatra).

Chaetodon vittatus Bloch & Schneider, 1801: p. 227 (type locality Sumatra; on Mungo Park).

Chaetodon lunulatus Quoy & Gaimard, 1824: p. 381 (type locality Guam; juvenile).

Chaetodon tau-nigrum Cuvier, 1831: p. 38 (type locality Guam; juvenile).

Chaetodon bellus Lay & Bennett, 1839: p. 61 (after Solander; name in synonymy).

Chaetodon Layardi Blyth, 1852: p. 50 (type locality Ceylon).

Chaetodon ovalis Thiolliere, 1857: p. 164 (type locality Woodlark Island).

Chaetodon pepek (Montrouzier) Thiolliere, 1857: p. 164 (type locality Woodlark Island).

Citharoedus vittatus, Kaup, 1860: p. 142 (new combination).

Citharoedus taunigrum, Kaup, 1860: p. 142 (new combination).

Sarothrodus vittatus, Bleeker, 1863: p. 156 (new combination).

Tetragonoptrus (*Rabdophorus*) *trifasciatus*, Bleeker, 1877a: p. 35, pl. 377, fig. 1 (East Indies; new combination). Bleeker, 1877b: p. 63 (Mauritius).

Chaetodon (*Tetragonoptrus*) *trifasciatus*, Sauvage, 1891: p. 254 (Madagascar).

Chaetodon spp. (part), Jordan & Seale, 1906: p. 344 (foot-

note, second paragraph, beginning "Life colors. . .
young."; Samoa; juvenile).
Chaetodon punctato-fasciatus (not of Cuvier), Fowler,
1918: p. 64 (Philippine Islands).
Chaetodon trifasciatus caudifasciatus Ahl, 1923: p. 57 (type
locality Pedang, Siporab, Madagascar, Mozambique,
German East Africa).
Chaetodon (Rhabdophorus) trifasciatus, Weber & de Beau-
fort, 1936: p. 66 (Malay, Batavia).
Rhabdophorus trifasciatus, Fowler, 1946: p. 137 (Riu Kiu
Islands).

Chaetodon trifasciatus Mungo Park. 65 mm S.L. Mentawai Island, off western
coast of Sumatra, Indian Ocean.

Diagnosis.—D. XIII-XIV, 20-22 (usually 21); A. III, 18-21 (usually 19);
pectoral rays 13-15 (usually 14); L.l. scales 30-39 (usually 34-39); black
stripes at base of dorsal and anal fins and across middle of caudal fin, the
entire fins not black.

Meristics.—D. XIII (three with XIV), 20-22 (usually 21); A. III, 18-21
(usually 19); pectoral rays 14 (two with 13, two with 15, three with
13/14, four with 15/14); L.l. scales 30-39 (normally 34-39); L.l. pores
27-36 (normally 30-32); scales above L.l. 4-6 (usually 5); scales below L.l.
13-15; gill rakers 15-23.

Chaetodon capistratus adult in its natural habitat. The eye band in this individual has faded but can become very black with a change in the mood of the fish. Photo by Dr. P. Colin, Grand Bahama Bank.

Chaetodon capistratus adult from the Virgin Islands. This species is very common in the Caribbean. Photo by Ken Lucas, Steinhart Aquarium.

Chaetodon ocellatus adult. The two characteristic black dorsal fin spots are evident in this individual. Photo by R. Straughan.

Ratios	Standard Length (mm)		
	20-50(3)	51-79(7)	above 79(15)
Depth/S.L............	1.7	1.5-1.7	1.5-1.8
Head/S.L.............	2.5-3.0	3.4-3.7	3.5-4.0
Eye/Head............	2.4-2.5	2.6-2.9	2.7-3.4
Snout/Head	3.1-3.8	3.3-4.5	3.1-4.4
Interorb. W./Head......	2.8-3.4	2.5-2.9	2.3-3.1
Maxillary/Head	3.6-6.2	3.3-5.1	3.7-5.3
Caud. Ped./S.L.........	8.4-9.5	9.1-10.3	9.4-11.3
Pect. Fin/S.L..........	3.4-3.5	3.2-3.7	3.4-4.1
Pelvic Sp./S.L..........	4.5-5.3	4.4-5.3	4.9-6.3
Predorsal L./S.L........	2.0-2.1	2.2-2.4	2.2-2.5
Prepelvic L./S.L........	2.2-2.6	2.5-2.8	2.6-2.9
Dorsal Sp. No. 1/S.L.....	9.3-12.5	10.3-12.7	9.6-13.5
Dorsal Sp. No. 2/S.L.....	5.6-8.0	7.8-10.9	8.7-14.6
Dorsal Sp. No. 3/S.L.....	3.9-5.5	6.4-8.3	6.5-11.3
Dorsal Sp. No. 4/S.L.....	3.5-4.3	5.1-6.5	5.6-8.3
Anal Sp. No. 1/S.L.......	6.7-8.6	7.0-8.1	7.0-9.2
Anal Sp. No. 2/S.L.......	5.0-6.8	4.6-6.0	5.2-6.6
Anal Sp. No. 3/S.L.......	5.0-5.9	4.6-6.7	5.1-7.2

Description.—Light serrations on preopercle; teeth in a band of rows in anterior part of jaws; interorbital width greater than caudal peduncle depth, which is greater than eye diameter; eye diameter greater than snout length.

Sixth or seventh dorsal spine longest; second and third anal spines longest, about equal, first not much shorter; base of spinous portion of dorsal fin longer (2.1-2.3 in S.L.) than soft portion (3.2-3.5 in S.L.); pelvic fins short, reaching a point somewhat short of the anus.

Lateral line with peak of angle at about end of spinous portion of dorsal fin; it either ends shortly after angle or continues along base of soft portion of dorsal fin a short distance, ending normally a moderate distance from last rays of dorsal fin; scaly covering of anal spines extending halfway or more up third spine.

Color Pattern.—Subspecies *lunulatus:* About 16 horizontal stripes on body, usually 4 above lateral line, the rest below, becoming perceptibly faded below level of pectoral fin; uppermost stripe connects with dark stripe which runs along ascending limb of preopercle; light anterior border to this stripe as it descends; eyeband connects with opposite member at nape and chest, dark bordered, the dark borders themselves bordered with light (sometimes not visible); chin dark; interorbital area dusky; caudal peduncle body color; edge of caudal fin hyaline; vertical caudal fin bar dark and light bordered as eyeband; spinous portion of dorsal fin with several narrow horizontal lines; soft portion of dorsal fin with two lines (extending forward on spinous portion).

Subspecies *trifasciatus:* Similar to the above with the following exceptions. Band posterior to eyeband slightly wider; eyebands do not connect on nape; anal fin dark, stripe slightly narrower, the lighter section of the fin almost yellowish. The greatest difference is that the area from the dark band on the caudal fin to and including most of the caudal peduncle is yellow.

Juveniles of both forms with body and eyebands much the same as adult pattern. Band posterior to eyeband and dark chin color absent; dorsal fin leaving broader hyaline edge to fin; anal fin without dark band, mostly light but with broad dark edge from angle to base of first anal spine; base of caudal fin grayish brown in Pacific subspecies and yellow in Indian Ocean subspecies; caudal peduncle dark brown except for two light spots, one above and one below; dark areas extend around upper spot to last rays of dorsal fin; light area anterior to this dark brown area; dusky margin to soft dorsal fin. (From a 23 mm S.L. specimen.)

By a size of 31 mm S.L., the caudal fin band has moved outward, the band behind the eye is faintly visible, and the pattern of the dorsal and anal fins is starting to become visible; anal fin dark with yellow line at base.

A 44 mm S.L. specimen has the center of the anal fin becoming lighter, the interior portion forming the dark band; dark area of caudal peduncle now only brown vertical spot, the portion on the dorsal fin extending into the dark band at its base; brownish dusky area at outer edge of soft dorsal still visible; chin dark.

Remarks.—There appears to be an abrupt change from one subspecies to the other in the area of Sumatra, Java, and the other islands of the archipelago. On the eastern coasts of these islands *Chaetodon trifasciatus lunulatus* is the form found, whereas on the western coasts of these same islands the range of *C. trifasciatus trifasciatus* begins. The meristics and proportional measurements overlap considerably, if not exactly identical. A slight difference may be found in the lateral line scale counts. *Chaetodon t. lunulatus* has a range of 34-37 scales, *C. t. trifasciatus* has 36-38. The pores follow this pattern, with a peak number of 30 in the former subspecies and 31 or 32 in the latter. Scales below the lateral line show a very slight difference, with 13 or 14 in the Pacific form and normally only 14 in the Indian Ocean form. Gill rakers show more differentiation, with 15 to 17 in *C. t. lunulatus* and 15 to 23 in *C. t. trifasciatus,* but more usually 19 to 21 in this latter form.

The color differences are slight, with a field character being the bright orange caudal base in the Indian Ocean subspecies.

Park's original specimen is preserved as a dry skin in the British Museum (Natural History). I have seen this skin and the original color illustration taken from it, and there is little doubt that the orange caudal base is present. The type therefore is the Indian Ocean form. Since *Chae-*

Chaetodon ocellatus juvenile, probably not too long after metamorphosis although tholichthys plates are already gone. Photo by Aaron Norman.

A pair of adult *Chaetodon ocellatus* in their natural habitat. This pair lacks the large black spot at the base of the dorsal fin (although it may appear at any time). Photo by Dr. P. Colin.

Small juvenile (above) and the juveniles (below) of *Chaetodon ocellatus* may be found in temperate waters during the summer months. Photos by Aaron Norman at Shark River, New Jersey.

todon vittatus Bloch and Schneider (1801) was based on the description of Park, this name must be placed in synonymy with Park. *Chaetodon lunulatus* Quoy and Gaimard (1824) is the first description of the true Pacific form, and this name is now used by me for the subspecies from that area. Ahl (1923) also recognized the difference as subspecific, but gave a new name, *caudifasciatus*, to the Indian Ocean form. This of course was a mistake since the Indian Ocean form is the original form described and must take the name *Chaetodon trifasciatus trifasciatus*. In addition there was another name available (*layardi* Blyth, 1852) that would take precedence over Ahl's name if the original form proved to be the Pacific Ocean subspecies.

Chaetodon trifasciatus, aside from having one of the widest distributions of the genus *Chaetodon*, is perhaps one of the most common species of this large genus. It was very common in the Hawaiian Islands in certain high coral density areas, the juveniles and adults inhabiting the same areas. Harry (1953) reported that this species, "is the most abundant butterflyfish at Raroia, occurring in great numbers in the lagoon on coral heads, shore reefs, and also on outer reef flats."

Nothing is known about the spawning habits of this species, although Herre and Montalban (1927) reported on two specimens 90 and 101 mm in length which were ripe females ready to spawn. They were collected in January, 1921.

Distribution.—Widespread in the central and western Pacific Ocean and throughout the tropical Indian Ocean. This species is absent from the Red Sea and has not been reported from the Persian Gulf. It is present on the east African Coast to Sri Lanka and East Indies, to Japan and Australia (including Lord Howe Island), and across the Pacific Islands to the Hawaiian Islands.

The subspecies *lunulatus* is restricted to the Pacific side of Java, Sumatra, and the Lesser Sundra Archipelago; the subspecies *trifasciatus* is restricted to the Indian Ocean side of these islands (to western Australia), the dividing line between these subspecies being quite abrupt.

Material Examined.—(48 spec.: 19-118 mm S.L.).

Chaetodon trifasciatus trifasciatus (23 spec.: 36-118 mm S.L.) SOSC HA67-3 (8: 72-99), Chagas Archipelago, Indian Ocean; SOSC HA67-16 (5: 40-97), Chagas Archipelago; SOSC HA67-57, and HA67-74 (10: 36-118), Aldabra Atoll, Indian Ocean.

Chaetodon trifasciatus lunulatus (25 spec.: 19-113 mm S.L.) SOSC Te Vega Cr. #6 Sta. 216 (2: 92-95), Borneo; WEB (9: 19-106), Oahu, Hawaiian Islands; WEB (7: 38-110), Tahiti, Society Islands; WEB (5: 61-85), Heron Island, Queensland, Australia; HIMB (1: 53), Palmyra Island, Line Islands; UH (1: 113), Christmas Island.

CHAETODON MELAPTERUS Guichenot
Black-finned melon butterflyfish

Chaetodon melapterus Guichenot, 1862: p. 6 (type locality
Reunion (Bourbon)).
Chaetodon melanopterus Playfair, 1865: p. 34 (type locality
Aden).
Chaetodon (Tetragonoptrus) melanopterus, Sauvage, 1891:
p. 256, p. XXIX, fig. 4 (not 3 as indicated) (Reunion).
Chaetodon trifasciatus var. *arabica* Steindachner, 1902:
p. 16 (138), pl. 2, fig. 3 (type locality Makalla).
Chaetodon trifasciatus arabica, Ahl, 1923: p. 58.

Chaetodon melapterus Guichenot. 106 mm S.L. Persian gulf.

Diagnosis.—D. XIII, 19-20 (usually 20-21); A. III, 18-20 (usually 18 or
19); pectoral rays 14-15 (usually 14); vertical fins entirely black along
with peduncle and part of posterior of body near fins.

This is the only species of this subgenus with the dorsal and anal
spines black.

Meristics.—D. XIII, 19-21 (rarely 19); A. III, 18 or 19 (two specimens
have 20 rays, one has 14); pectoral rays 14 (four specimens with 15/15,
four with 14/15); L.l. scales 33-42 (usually 35-39); scales above L.l. 6 (one
with 7); scales below L.l. 12-15 (usually 13 or 14); gill rakers 17-22.

Chaetodon kleinii from the Hawaiian Islands. The Hawaiian form was, until this study, called *C. corallicola*. Photo by Dr. Herbert R. Axelrod.

Chaetodon kleinii from Sri Lanka. This form was once described as *C. cingulatus*. Photo by Rodney Jonklaas.

Chaetodon kleinii juvenile. There is no appreciable difference in the color pattern between juveniles and adults. Photo by H. Hansen.

Chaetodon kleinii adult. Photo by Dr. Gerald R. Allen, Hawaii.

| | | Standard Length (mm) | |
Ratios	20-50(6)	51-79(55)	above 79(7)
Depth/S.L..............	1.5-1.6	1.5-1.8	1.6-1.8
Head/S.L..............	2.7-2.9	3.0-3.5	3.4-3.6
Eye/Head.............	2.7-3.0	2.7-3.0	3.0-3.1
Snout/Head...........	3.4-4.0	3.5-4.5	3.5-4.1
Interorb. W./Head......	2.8-3.1	2.4-2.9	2.4-2.7
Maxillary/Head........	3.9-4.7	3.6-5.0	3.7-4.7
Caud. Ped./S.L........	8.5-9.1	8.6-9.5	8.7-9.5
Pect. Fin/S.L..........	3.0-3.8	3.1-4.1	3.5-3.9
Pelvic Sp./S.L.........	4.3-4.9	4.7-5.4	5.0-5.3
Predorsal L./S.L........	2.0-2.1	2.1-2.3	2.2-2.3
Prepelvic L./S.L........	2.3-2.5	2.5-2.7	2.6-2.8
Dorsal Sp. No. 1/S.L.....	8.9-12.1	8.4-14.1	11.9-16.8
Dorsal Sp. No. 2/S.L.....	6.5-9.1	6.6-11.1	10.7-13.1
Dorsal Sp. No. 3/S.L.....	4.5-6.8	5.1-8.8	7.9-10.4
Dorsal Sp. No. 4/S.L.....	3.7-4.6	4.7-7.5	6.3-9.3
Anal Sp. No. 1/S.L.......	5.7-6.4	6.0-8.0	7.3-9.5
Anal Sp. No. 2/S.L.......	4.8-5.5	4.4-5.5	5.1-5.9
Anal Sp. No. 3/S.L.......	4.2-5.1	4.4-5.5	4.9-6.2

Description.—Preopercle with light serrations; teeth grouped in band at front of jaws; interorbital width greater than depth of caudal peduncle, which is greater than eye diameter; eye diameter greater than snout length.

Sixth or seventh dorsal spine longest; second and third anal spines subequal, first not much shorter; base of spinous portion of dorsal fin longer (2.1-2.4 in S.L.) than base of soft portion (3.3-3.6 in S.L.).

Lateral line with peak under last two spines of dorsal fin, in many specimens ending at this height, in others it continues a short distance along base of dorsal rays, but always ending well before base of last rays of dorsal fin; scales on anal fin spines covering a small portion of second spine and about two-thirds of third spine.

Color Pattern.—About 15 lines following scale rows from behind head to black area; black area sharply defined and includes dorsal scaly sheath; spines light; narrow white edge to dorsal and anal fins (slightly lighter in dorsal fin); clear edge to caudal fin separated from black by white band; anal spines dark except for their tips; pectoral fins clear, pelvic fins light; eyebands join at nape and on throat broadly; chin and upper part of mouth black (as a band around mouth but with chin area much larger); black stripe across interorbital area with variable design above this.

Juveniles, at about 30-35 mm, somewhat differently colored. The body stripes, eyeband, and posterior head band as in adults, although posterior head band very faded in some specimens (probably absent in smaller specimens). Some examples have upper mouth area dusky, others with no markings on face. Anal fin, caudal peduncle, and base of caudal fin black, a white line crossing the caudal fin about one-third distance from the fin base and bordered on its outer edge with a black line, remaining portion of fin clear. This light stripe variable, but usually slightly curved, the bow pointing posteriorly, the two ends also pointing posteriorly a short distance, sometimes connecting with the clear portion. Blackish area extends into dorsal fin for varying amounts, becoming blotchy and indistinct there, the entire fin base sometimes covered, other times just the posterior portion. Edges of dorsal and anal fins light, a submarginal dark stripe in the dorsal fin which is usually lighter inside this stripe. This dark posterior area of juveniles is not as well defined as in adults. Smaller specimens not available.

Remarks.—This species is common in the Gulf of Aden and therefore is located between the other two species of this complex in that area. Ahl's record of *Chaetodon melapterus* from the Seychelles is of a juvenile which was originally described by Guichenot (1862). A comparison between a photograph of the type specimen supplied by Bauchot and the juveniles I have seen exhibit no differences whatever. I cannot surmise whether the adults have not yet been found in the more southern localities or whether the juveniles were carried away from their center of distribution in the Gulf of Aden, as has been reported for some species of butterflyfishes. It appears that *Chaetodon trifasciatus* and *C. melapterus* could be sympatric in this area. *Chaetodon melapterus* has been reported from the Red Sea and therefore could also be sympatric over part of the range with *C. austriacus*.

It is also interesting to note that the extent of the black color in *C. trifasciatus* (no black fins) to *C. austriacus* (caudal and anal fins black) to *C. melapterus* (dorsal, anal, and caudal fins black) does not correspond with their ranges if one suspects a transition in color from one species to the next, the greatest extent of black being found in a species located *between the two others.*

The identification of the juveniles was first made through color pattern, but a juvenile specimen was brought from the Persian Gulf by Mr. Enfield and confirmation of the juvenile identity was made.

Distribution.—Gulf of Aden, Seychelles, Reunion, Muscat, Red Sea (Br. Mus.)?, Persian Gulf.

Material Examined.—(68 spec.: 30-93 mm S.L.) SOSC Anton Bruun Cr. 9, FT-26 (59: 30-76), Gold Mohur Bay (12°46'S, 44°59'15"E), Aden; USNM 147890 (6: 77-87), Saudi Arabia; USNM 147891 (3: 81-93), Persian Gulf.

Chaetodon kleinii in its defensive posture (dorsal spines raised). Photo in Japan by Michio Goto, Marine Life Documents.

The clear light area behind the pectoral fins may become darker (body color) depending on the mood of the fish. Photo by K.H. Choo, Taiwan.

The upper part of the eyeband of *Chaetodon kleinii* is bluish in life as can be seen here. Photo by Dr. Fujio Yasuda.

Chaetodon kleinii is one of the more common species of butterflyfishes, but in some areas it is found only in deep water. Photo by Dr. Gerald R. Allen, New Hebrides.

CHAETODON AUSTRIACUS Ruppell
Red Sea melon butterflyfish

Chaetodon austriacus Ruppell, 1835: p. 30, pl. 9, fig. 2 (type locality Red Sea).

Citharoedus austriacus, Kaup, 1860: p. 142 (Red Sea; new combination).

Chaetodon vittatus (not of Bloch), Klunzinger, 1870: p. 782 (Red Sea).

Chaetodon Klunzingeri Kossman and Rauber, 1876: p. 19 (type locality Red Sea).

Chaetodon trifasciatus var. *Klunzingeri*, Kossman and Rauber, 1877: p. 13 (Red Sea).

Chaetodon trifasciatus var. *austriacus*, Klunzinger, 1884: p. 55 (Red Sea).

Chaetodon trifasciatus austriacus, Ahl, 1923: p. 57 (Red sea).

Chaetodon austriacus Ruppell. 113 mm S.L. Red Sea.

Diagnosis.—D. XIII, 20-21; A. III, 19; pectoral rays (13) 14; L.l. scales 39-42; caudal and anal fins entirely black, dorsal fin with black edge only, never solid black; usually an enlarged spot in the center or posterior center of the fourth horizontal body line.

Ratios	20-50	Standard Length (mm) 51-79(1)	above 79(4)
Depth/S.L............	---	1.7	1.7
Head/S.L.............	---	3.5	3.6-3.9
Eye/Head............	---	3.0	3.0-3.4
Snout/Head..........	---	4.0	3.3-4.1
Interorb. W./Head......	---	2.8	2.5-2.6
Maxillary/Head........	---	3.9	4.0-4.1
Caud. Ped./S.L.........	---	9.3	9.5-10.0
Pect. Fin/S.L...........	---	3.8	3.7-4.2
Pelvic Sp./S.L..........	---	4.8	5.6-5.8
Predorsal L./S.L........	---	2.2	2.3-2.5
Prepelvic L./S.L........	---	2.6	2.7-2.9
Dorsal Sp. No. 1/S.L.....	---	11.5	10.6-15.5
Dorsal Sp. No. 2/S.L.....	---	10.5	10.1-12.4
Dorsal Sp. No. 3/S.L.....	---	8.7	7.3-8.8
Dorsal Sp. No. 4/S.L.....	---	6.0	7.2-7.3
Anal Sp. No. 1/S.L.......	---	6.8	7.9-9.1
Anal Sp. No. 2/S.L.......	---	5.2	5.2-6.4
Anal Sp. No. 3/S.L.......	---	5.2	4.6-6.0

Meristics.—D. XIII, 20-21; A. III, 19; pectoral rays 14 (one 13/13, one 13/14); L.l. scales 39-42; L.l. pores 24-29; scales above L.l. 4-5; scales below Ll. 12-14; gill rakers 20 (one with 17).

Description.—Teeth in a single band of closely packed rows, possibly about 9-10 rows in the lower jaw, only 5 rows in the upper jaw; inter-orbital width and depth of caudal peduncle about equal, both greater than eye diameter, which is greater than snout length; lachrymal covered with scales, hidden from view.

Sixth or seventh dorsal spine longest, rest approximately equal to last; first two dorsal spines usually significantly shorter than others; second and third anal spines about equal, first not much shorter; base of spinous portion of dorsal fin longer (about 2.3 in S.L.) than that of soft portion (3.3 in S.L.).

Peak of lateral line under about first rays of dorsal fin, after which it follows base of dorsal fin (almost on fin itself), ending far above caudal peduncle (in some specimens it does not reach point of curvature); scaly covering of anal fin reaches, at most, midpoint of third spine.

Color Pattern.—About 14 horizontal body lines following scale rows, the last six or seven fading or faded; fourth or fifth line with lens-shaped thickening just below peak of lateral line; eyeband connected at nape and throat, forming a complete band around head; eyeband dark, with darker borders; mouth and chin area black; interorbital area with vary-ing patterns of lines, dots, triangles, etc.; dark posterior area sharply

Chaetodon trichrous has a rather restricted range in the southeastern corner of the central Pacific. Photo by Dr. J.E. Randall, Tahiti.

Chaetodon litus is found only around Easter Island. Photo by Dr. J.E. Randall.

Chaetodon hemichrysus is very closely related to *C. litus* but differs immediately in color pattern. Photo by Dr. J.E. Randall.

Chaetodon hemichrysus occurs only around Pitcairn Island. Photo by Dr. J. E. Randall.

defined; light line extends along base of anal fin, and edge is narrowly pale; edge of caudal fin pale or clear with submarginal white or yellow line; narrow light border to black band on dorsal fin rays; pectoral fins hyaline, pelvic fins body color.

Remarks.—Clearly distinct from the other closely related species of this group, *Chaetodon austriacus* is apparently restricted to the Red Sea. It seems to be in the "wrong" area geographically if there is to be a smooth color transformation from the *Chaetodon trifasciatus* form to the highly melanistic *C. melapterus: Chaetodon melapterus* is found between the former species in the Gulf of Aden.

Chaetodon austriacus is rather abundant along the coral slopes (Klunzinger, 1870). It frequents the lower parts of corals, rarely deeper than below the coralline barrier, and prefers clear water (Baschieri-Salvatore, 1954). It is found in the northern sector of the Red Sea (Sudanese coast, Egypt) but is absent in the southern sector (Dahlak, near Massaua) (Baschieri-Salvatore, 1954).

Also according to Baschieri-Salvatore (1954), this species frequently occurs in pairs, never as individuals.

Distribution.—Apparently endemic to the Red Sea.

Material Examined.—(5 spec.: 72-113 mm S.L.) USNM 166959-60 (2: 72-92), Ghardaqa, Red Sea; USNM 191664 (1: 106), Red Sea; CAS 37817 (1: 113), Red Sea; WEB (1: 106), Red Sea.

Subgenus CITHAROEDUS Kaup

Citharoedus Kaup, 1860: pp. 136, 141. (Type-species *Chaetodon meyeri* Schneider, 1801, by subsequent designation of Bleeker, 1876: p. 305.)

Diagnosis.—Body rounded to oval; dorsal spines evenly graduated; dorsal and anal fins with blunt angles; snout short, blunt, 3.0-4.0 in head length; teeth grouped in indistinguishable rows in front of jaws; lachrymal almost hidden by scales; lateral line high and angular; scales moderate to small, rounded; eyeband with additional band on either side; D. XII, 23-28; A. III, 19-23; pectoral 16; L.l. scales 45-55.

Description.—Body oval to nearing rounded; snout short, blunt, robust, 3.0-4.0 in head length; predorsal contour approximately straight; mouth small, gape horizontal to slightly oblique; teeth in band of closely packed rows in each jaw; preopercle right-angled, the angle rounded, crenulate; supraorbital serrate; lachrymal hidden, covered by scales.

Dorsal spines evenly graduated, first two sometimes significantly smaller or first slightly smaller than second; fifth to eighth dorsal spines longest; second and third anal spines subequal, although second sometimes longer; first anal spine half to two-thirds of second; soft portions of dorsal and anal fins, when spread, not forming complete edge; base of spinous portion of dorsal fin longer (2.1-2.5 in S.L.) than that of soft por-

Chaetodon meyeri has a very distinctive color pattern of curved black lines. Photo by W. Deas.

tion (2.5-3.0 in S.L.); pectoral fins normal; pelvic fins short, not reaching level of anal opening; caudal fin rounded, corners angled.

Lateral line describing a high, angular arc, its peak under the last spines or first rays of the dorsal fin, following the base of the soft dorsal fin to the level of the last dorsal rays; scales moderate to small, rounded, in horizontal rows in lower half of body and increasingly ascending rows in upper portions; scaly covering of dorsal fin normal, reaching midpoint of sixth or seventh dorsal spine.

Juveniles similar to adults in both form and color pattern.

Widely distributed in tropical areas of the Pacific and Indian Oceans, Red Sea and Hawaiian Islands included. Absent from the East Pacific region and Atlantic Ocean.

Three species recognized and distinguishable by the following key.

Key to the Species of Subgenus Citharoedus

1. Body color pattern consisting of lines or stripes, not reticulated or spotted; caudal peduncle not black; no broad light band from anterior dorsal spines to pelvic base; pelvic fins light 2
   Body color pattern reticulated, composed of a large light spot on each scale; caudal peduncle black; broad light band from anterior dorsal spines to pelvic fin base; pelvic fins black (Pacific) . . . .
   . . . .*Chaetodon reticulatus*

2. Several curved black lines on body; D. XII, 23-24; A. III, 19-20 (Indo-Pacific) . . . .*C. meyeri*
   Six diagonal dark bordered orange stripes crossing body; D. XII, 26-28; A. III, 21-23 (Pacific) . . . .*C. ornatissimus*

499

Juvenile and adult *Chaetodon quadrimaculatus*. There is essentially no difference in color pattern with age. Photo by Dr. Warren E. Burgess.

Two white spots of *Chaetodon quarimaculatus* stand out quite distinctly. Photo by Dr. Fujio Yasuda.

Chaetodon quadrimaculatus, nighttime coloration. Photo by Scott Johnson, Hawaii.

Remarks.—*Citharoedus* appears to fall between *Corallochaetodon* and *Chaetodontops*, showing affinities to both groups. One species, *Chaetodon collare*, has been a problem and it is difficult for me to determine its proper placement. It falls very close to this subgenus and perhaps should be placed here, but I finally determined that it rightfully belongs to subgenus *Chaetodontops*. The peculiar larval stage of both *Chaetodon meyeri* and *C. ornatissimus* (larval stage not known in *C. reticulatus*), which is absent in *C. collare*, helped me make this decision.

This larval stage is a typical tholichthys with plates as in most other species, but in addition there are "horns" extending from the supraorbital area. No other tholichthys larva has this type of development. It should be noted here that subgenus *Corallochaetodon* does not have this type larvae but has a typical tholichthys, and all species are much smaller at time of metamorphosis than any species of *Citharoedus*.

CHAETODON MEYERI Schneider
Meyer's butterflyfish

Chaetodon meyeri Schneider, 1801: p. 223 (type locality Moluccas).

Holacanthus flavo-niger Lacepede, 1802: pp. 529, 535, pl. 13, fig. 2 (no locality).

Citharoedus meyeri, Kaup, 1860: p. 141 (Moluccas; new combination).

Tetragonoptrus meyeri, Bleeker, 1863: p. 234 (Ternate; new combination).

Tetragonoptrus (Citharoedus) meyeri, Bleeker, 1877: p. 32, pl. 378, fig. 5 (Java, Celebes, Amboina, Ceram, New Guinea).

Chaetodon (Citharoedus) meyeri, Weber and de Beaufort, 1936: p. 69 (various localities).

Diagnosis.—D. XII (one with XIII), 23-25 (rarely 25); A. III, 18-20 (rarely 18); pectoral rays 15-16 (usually 16); L.l. scales 47-55; several curved and looping black lines on body.

Closely related to *Chaetodon ornatissimus*, but easily distinguishable on the basis of color. In addition *C. meyeri* has fewer dorsal and anal fin rays.

Meristics.—D. XII (one with XIII), 23-25 (rarely 25); A. III, 18-20 (rarely 18); pectoral rays 16 (three with 15/16, two with 15/15); L.l. scales 47-55; L.l. pores 37-49 (usually 40-47); scales above L.l. 9-11 (rarely 11); scales below L.l. 25-28; gill rakers 21-29.

Description.—Teeth in about 9-12 rows in each jaw; caudal peduncle approximately equal to or slightly greater than interorbital width, which is greater than eye diameter; eye diameter equal to snout.

Chaetodon meyeri Schneider. 118 mm S.L. Kapingamaringi Atoll, Caroline Islands.

Ratios	30-59	Standard Length (mm) 60-89(6)	above 89(22)
Depth/S.L.............	---	1.4-1.5	1.3-1.6
Head/S.L..............	---	3.1-3.4	3.2-3.7
Eye/Head.............	---	2.7-3.0	2.9-3.7
Snout/Head...........	---	3.2-4.1	2.6-4.2
Interorb. W./Head.....	---	2.1-2.5	2.1-2.5
Maxillary/Head........	---	4.1-4.4	3.1-5.8
Caud. Ped./S.L........	---	7.8-8.5	7.8-8.8
Pect. Fin/S.L..........	---	3.1-3.3	3.2-4.0
Pelvic Sp./S.L.........	---	4.6-4.7	4.5-5.9
Predorsal L./S.L.......	---	2.2-2.3	2.2-2.5
Prepelvic L./S.L.......	---	2.2-2.6	2.5-2.9
Dorsal Sp. No. 1/S.L....	---	8.3-10.0	7.4-11.2
Dorsal Sp. No. 2/S.L....	---	8.2-10.3	8.4-12.1
Dorsal Sp. No. 3/S.L....	---	6.6-8.6	7.5-10.3
Dorsal Sp. No. 4/S.L....	---	5.9-6.4	6.1-8.3
Anal Sp. No. 1/S.L......	---	7.0-9.1	7.5-10.1
Anal Sp. No. 2/S.L......	---	5.1-5.3	5.2-6.7
Anal Sp. No. 3/S.L......	---	5.1-5.2	5.4-7.7

Chaetodon quadrimaculatus occurs only in the tropical Pacific. Photo by Dr. Herbert R. Axelrod.

Chaetodon quadrimaculatus in its natural habitat in Hawaii. Photo by Paul Allen.

The pattern of the anal fin makes this easily identifiable as *Chaetodon citrinellus*. Photo by Dr. Herbert R. Axelrod, Maldives.

A juvenile *Chaetodon meyeri* in an aquarium along with two young *Heniochus acuminatus*. Photo by Wilhelm Hoppe.

First two dorsal spines often equal, first sometimes longer than second; fifth to seventh dorsal spines longest; pelvic fins moderately short, reaching just short of the anal opening; base of the spinous portion of dorsal fin longer (2.1-2.5 in S.L.) than that of soft portion (2.8-2.9 in S.L.).

Peak of flattened portion of lateral line at last spines or first rays of dorsal fin; scales cover about three-fourths of third anal spine.

Color Pattern.—Eyeband narrowly connected across nape, more broadly connected on isthmus, where it extends part way toward pelvic fins; a dark isolated spot between pelvic fins; dark band surrounds snout; chin dark; interorbital grayish; submarginal dark bands on dorsal and anal fins with lighter centers.

Juveniles similar in pattern but with some differences. Body stripes less curved, steeply descending anteriorly; dark band crossing caudal fin at about its center, outer portion hyaline; edges of dorsal and anal fins dusky to dark.

Remarks.—Although widely distributed, *Chaetodon meyeri* does not seem to be common.

The similarity between the juvenile of this species and that of *C. ornatissimus* indicates perhaps a closer relationship than one would infer from a comparison of the adults.

At Palau, *Chaetodon meyeri* was "often found swimming with *C. ornatissimus*" (De Witt, unpublished MS). De Witt reported on two such occasions, the first in which a specimen of each species stayed together "for some time," the second when four *C. ornatissimus* specimens and one of *C. meyeri* were seen swimming together, "the latter was larger than and at times, chased the former."

Distribution.—Tropical Pacific and Indian Oceans. Micronesia, Polynesia (exclusive of the Hawaiian Islands), and Melanesia, to the East Indies and Philippine Islands. Indian Ocean including the Mentawai Islands, Cocos-Keeling Island, Laccadive Islands, Maldives, Sri Lanka, Chagas Archipelago, Aldabra, Mauritius, Madagascar, Seychelles, and Comoro Islands to the coast of East Afria as far south as Durban.

Material Examined.—(28 spec.: 65-132 mm S.L.) USNM 171030 (1: 84), Madagascar; USNM 182197 (3: 104-113), Tidore Islands, East Indies; CAS 37788 (2: 101-102), Palau Islands; CAS 37789 (2: 87-93), Palau Islands; CAS 37790 (2: 67-101), Kapingamarangi Atoll, Caroline Islands; CAS "No Data" (1: 132); CAS 37791 (2: 104-111), Palau Islands; CAS 37792 (2: 115-121), Kapingamarangi Atoll, Caroline Islands; CAS G.V.F. Sta. 59-692 Reg. 1953 (1: 86), Palau Islands; CAS Sta. 5 1956 (1: 109), Palau Islands; CAS 37793 (1: 119), Kapingamarangi Atoll, Western Caroline Islands; CAS 37794 (2: 109-113), Palau Islands; SOSC HA 67-8 (1: 124), Chagas Archipelago; SOSC HA 67-45 (1: 116), Chagas Archipelago; SOSC HA 67-14 (2: 117-121), Chagas Archipelago; SOSC Te Vega Sta. 179 (1: 65), Comoro Islands; SOSC HA-14 (1: 72), Comoro Islands; SOSC Te Vega Sta. 249 (1: 115), Solomon Islands; SOSC Te Vega Sta. 112 (1: 99), Mentewai Island, off western coast of Sumatra, Indian Ocean.

CHAETODON ORNATISSIMUS Cuvier
Ornate butterflyfish
(Clown butterflyfish)

Chaetodon ornatissimus Cuvier, 1831: p. 22 (type locality Tahiti (after Solander)).

Chaetodon ornatus Gray, 1831: p. 33 (type locality Hawaiian Islands).

Citharoedus ornatissimus, Kaup, 1860: p. 142 (Tahiti; new combination).

Tetragonoptrus ornatissimus, Bleeker, 1865: p. 286 (Amboina; new combination).

Tetragonoptrus (Citharoedus) ornatissimus, Bleeker, 1877: p. 32, pl. 375, fig. 2 (Amboina, New Guinea).

Chaetodon ornatissimus var. Kaupi Ahl, 1923: p. 52 (no locality).

Chaetodon (Citharoedus) ornatissimus, Weber and de Beaufort, 1936: p. 71 (various localities).

Chaetodon lydiae Curtiss, 1938: p. 118 (type locality Tahiti).

Diagnosis.—D. XII (one with XIII), 24-28 (usually 26-28); A. III, 20-23 (rarely 20); pectoral rays (15) 16; L.l. scales 47-52; six to seven dark bordered orange stripes crossing body, ascending posteriorly.

The lateral spotting of *Chaetodon citrinellus* varies from blue to violet to orange. Photo by K.H. Choo, Taiwan.

Chaetodon citrinellus photographed at night. There are usually two white lateral spots (the anterior spot is indistinct here). Photo by R. O'Conner.

Chaetodon citrinellus photographed in its natural habitat at Kenn Reef, Great Barrier Reef. Photo by W. Deas.

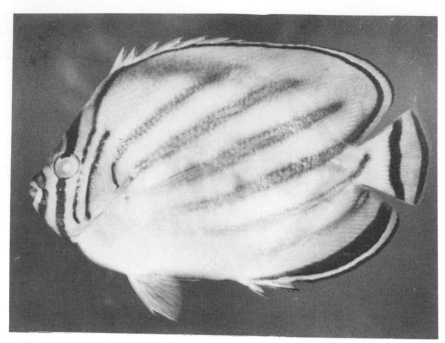

Chaetodon ornatissimus Cuvier. 115 mm S.L. Oahu, Hawaiian Islands.

Ratios	Standard Length (mm)		
	30-59(4)	60-89(5)	above 89(5)
Depth/S.L.	1.4-1.5	1.3-1.6	1.4-1.6
Head/S.L.	2.5-3.1	3.1-3.5	3.5-4.1
Eye/Head	2.6-2.7	2.7-3.5	2.7-3.6
Snout/Head	3.6-6.1	2.6-4.4	3.0-4.2
Interorb. W./Head.	2.3-2.7	2.2-2.7	2.1-2.4
Maxillary/Head	3.9-5.5	3.9-5.0	3.4-4.5
Caud. Ped./S.L.	6.8-9.2	7.5-8.7	8.3-9.1
Pect. Fin/S.L.	2.9-3.0	2.9-3.2	3.4-4.1
Pelvic Sp./S.L.	3.9-4.9	4.6-4.9	5.0-5.7
Predorsal L./S.L.	1.8-2.0	2.0-2.3	2.2-2.5
Prepelvic L./S.L.	2.1-2.5	2.3-2.7	2.6-2.8
Dorsal Sp. No. 1/S.L.	6.5-10.1	8.6-12.1	8.9-11.2
Dorsal Sp. No. 2/S.L.	4.3-7.2	8.4-10.0	8.9-13.2
Dorsal Sp. No. 3/S.L.	3.6-5.1	6.2-7.5	7.2-13.7
Dorsal Sp. No. 4/S.L.	3.7-5.1	4.1-6.7	6.0-10.2
Anal Sp. No. 1/S.L.	5.8-7.8	7.2-7.8	8.0-9.2
Anal Sp. No. 2/S.L.	4.6-7.4	4.8-6.0	5.5-6.8
Anal Sp. No. 3/S.L.	4.9-8.2	4.5-7.6	4.7-9.0

Similar in shape and meristics to the other members of this subgenus but easily recognizable by the color pattern. The ascending orange stripes are unique among the butterflyfishes.

Meristics.—D. XII (one with XIII), 24-28 (usually 26-28); A. III, 20-23 (usually 21-23); pectoral rays 16 (one with 15/15, one with 15/16, two with 17/16; L.l. scales 47-52; L.l. pores 36-51; scales above L.l. 8-11 (usually 9 or 10); scales below L.l. 23-29 (usually 26-28); gill rakers 21-23.

Description.—Dorsal spines one and two sometimes equal or first even longer than second; sixth to eighth dorsal spines longest; pelvic fins moderately short, just short of or barely reaching anal opening; base of spinous portion of dorsal fin longer than that of soft portion (2.1-2.5 and 2.7-3.0 in standard length respectively).

Teeth in about 9-12 rows in each jaw; interorbital greater than or approximately equal to caudal peduncle which is greater than eye, eye greater than or equal to snout.

Scales cover about three-fourths of third anal spine.

Color Pattern.—Diagonal body stripes light brown with darker brown borders in alcohol; two of the stripes faintly evident on chest below gill opening; lower lip and chin dark brown; dark band encircles snout; eyebands broadly connected on nape, narrowing toward eye, joined again at isthmus; interorbital area grayish brown, leaving snout band and anterior edge of eyeband bordered with lighter color.

Juveniles similar to adults, with the inclined orange stripes; vertical head stripe immediately posterior to eye absent; stripe on preopercle edge present.

Remarks.—Closely related to *Chaetodon meyeri* but easily distinguishable by color pattern. The juveniles are closer in appearance, although the stripes of *Chaetodon meyeri* are narrow, blackish, and more vertical whereas those of *C. ornatissimus* are dusky, wider, and more inclined.

Chaetodon ornatissimus var. *Kaupi* Ahl 1923 could be *C. trifasciatus* according to the description (horizontal stripes, eyeband, counts, etc.), but it is retained here for convenience until the type can be examined.

Chaetodon ornatissimus was almost always seen in pairs. At Johnston Island a pair of about five inches total length was seen by the author. It is not known how much earlier a pair bond may form.

Distribution.—Tropical Pacific Ocean, extending a short distance into the Indian Ocean, Polynesia (including the Hawaiian Islands), Micronesia, and Melanesia to the East Indies; south to the Great Barrier Reef, north through the Philippine Islands to China and the Ryu Kyu Islands; west to Christmas Island (Indian Ocean off west coast of Java) and Cocos-Keeling Islands.

Material Examined.—(14 spec.: 31-143 mm) SOSC Te Vega 247 (2: 88-111), Solomon Islands; WAM P. 5979 (1: 67), Christmas Island, Indian Ocean; NMFS-H CHG 55-109 (1: 31), "Hawaiian waters" (in stomach contents of yellowfin tuna); HIMB (uncatalogued) (2: 78-135), Oahu, Hawaiian Islands; UH 2639 (1: 51), Palmyra Island, Line Islands;

Juvenile *Chaetodon assarius* look very much like adults. Photo by Dr. Gerald R. Allen.

Adult *Chaetodon assarius.* This species occurs only in Western Australia. Photo by Dr. Gerald R. Allen.

Chaetodon assarius looks very much like other species in the *miliaris*-complex except in anal fin pattern. Photo by Roger Steene and Rudie Kuiter.

WEB (1: 85), Tahiti, Society Islands; BPBM (uncatalogued) (2: 111-115), Hawaiian Islands; WEB (4: 71-143), Oahu, Hawaiian Islands.

CHAETODON RETICULATUS Cuvier
Mailed butterflyfish
(Black butterflyfish; reticulated butterflyfish)

Chaetodon reticulatus Cuvier, 1831: p. 32, pl. 171 (type locality Tahiti).

Chaetodon superbus Cuvier, 1831: p. 32 (type locality Ulea, Caroline Islands; on Broussonet; in synonymy of Cuvier's *C. reticulatus*, no description given).

Citharoedus collaris (not of Bloch), Kaup, 1860: p. 144 (Tahiti).

Chaetodon collaris (not of Bloch), Gunther, 1874: p. 40. Seale 1901: p. 99 (Guam). Fowler, 1923: p. 384 (Honolulu). Fowler, 1925: p. 34 (Samoa). Fowler and Ball, 1926: p. 18 (Wake Island).

Chaetodon reticulatus Cuvier. 97 mm S.L. Hitiaa, Tahiti, Society Islands.

Diagnosis.—D. XII, 26-29 (usually 27-28); A. III, 20-22 (usually 21); pectoral rays 16; L.l. scales 45-48; broad pale band behind eyeband from first three or four dorsal fin spines to, but not including, pectoral fins; body blackish, each scale with light center.

Ratios	Standard Length (mm)		
	30-59(3)	60-89(2)	above 89(6)
Depth/S.L..............	1.3-1.4	1.3-1.4	1.4-1.6
Head/S.L..............	2.9-3.2	3.1-3.5	3.4-3.7
Eye/Head.............	2.3-2.9	2.9	3.0-3.7
Snout/Head...........	2.8-3.6	3.2-4.2	2.8-3.4
Interorb. W./Head......	2.5	2.3-2.4	2.1-2.5
Maxillary/Head........	3.4-3.6	3.6-4.0	3.4-4.0
Caud. Ped./S.L.........	7.4-7.8	7.9-8.2	8.1-8.4
Pect. Fin/S.L...........	2.6-2.8	2.8-3.1	3.0-3.5
Pelvic Sp./S.L..........	3.5-4.2	4.3-4.9	4.8-5.2
Predorsal L./S.L........	1.9-2.0	2.0-2.2	2.3-2.4
Prepelvic L./S.L........	2.3-2.4	2.5-2.6	2.7-2.9
Dorsal Sp. No. 1/S.L.....	7.5-7.9	8.8	8.2-8.7
Dorsal Sp. No. 2/S.L.....	4.4-5.6	6.5-8.8	7.7-8.7
Dorsal Sp. No. 3/S.L.....	3.8-4.2	4.6-5.8	6.7-7.5
Dorsal Sp. No. 4/S.L.....	3.5-3.9	4.1-5.5	5.7-6.4
Dorsal Sp. No. 5/S.L.....	3.2-3.4	3.7	4.9-5.5
Dorsal Sp. No. 6/S.L.....	3.3-3.7	3.5	4.7-5.2
Anal Sp. No. 1/S.L.......	6.0-6.5	6.7-6.9	6.9-8.8
Anal Sp. No. 2/S.L.......	4.6-5.8	4.7-5.3	5.0-5.7
Anal Sp. No. 3/S.L.......	4.5-5.5	4.8-6.7	4.7-6.0

Often confused with *Chaetodon collare* and *C. auripes*, but easily distinguishable from those species by color pattern.

Meristics.—D. XII, 26-29 (usually 27 or 28); A. III, 20-22 (usually 21); pectoral rays 16 (two with 15/16, one with 16/17); L.l. scales 45-48; L.l. pores 40-46; scales above L.l. 7-9; scales below L.l. 17-20; gill rakers 18-28.

Description.—First two dorsal spines often equal, first sometimes longer than second; sixth to seventh dorsal spines longest; pelvic fins moderate, reaching beyond level of anus but not to anal spines; base of spinous portion of dorsal fin longer than that of soft portion (2.2-2.3 and 2.5-2.7 in standard length respectively).

Teeth in about 10 rows in upper jaw and about 12 rows in lower jaw; interorbital greater than caudal peduncle, which is greater than eye; eye equal to snout.

Scales cover about one-half of third anal spine.

Color Pattern.—Eyeband broadly joining across nape and also on chest, the black extending posteriorly on the chest to include the pelvic fins and ventral edge of body; narrow yellowish streak separating eyeband from broad whitish band from anterior dorsal spines to pelvic fins; interorbital area gray, bordered above and below by light streaks; very

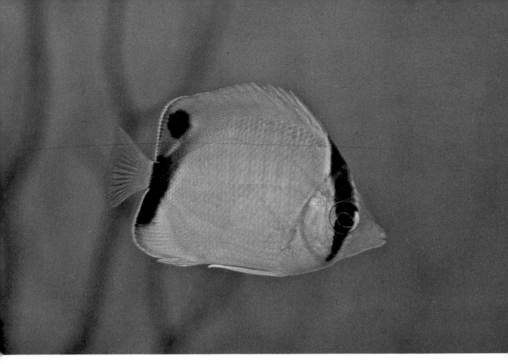

Chaetodon sedentarius juvenile with a well-defined dorsal fin spot. Photo by Aaron Norman.

Subadult *Chaetodon sedentarius* without a dark spot in the dorsal fin. Photo by Dr. Herbert R. Axelrod.

Larval (tholichthys) stage of *Chaetodon sedentarius* with silvery body color.

Chaetodon sedentarius in its natural habitat in Bermuda. Photo by Dr. P. Colin.

narrow hyaline edge to dorsal fin and submarginal dark line; edge of caudal fin hyaline, a submarginal dark stripe present.

Juvenile similar in color pattern to adult. The caudal fin with broader hyaline edge; a single instead of two dark lines crossing caudal fin; hyaline edge of dorsal fin wider.

Remarks.—*Chaetodon reticulatus*, as can be seen from the above synonymy, has often been called *C. collare*. *Chaetodon collare* in turn has been incorrectly identified with *C. auripes*. The three species are quite distinct as can be seen from the descriptions and photographs. Only those synonyms that included a description which enabled positive identification have been included.

Chaetodon Bellicosus, mentioned by Quoy and Gaimard, is a *nomen nudum* but placed in the synonymy of *C. reticulatus* by Ahl. According to the descriptions of the behavior of the fish by Quoy and Gaimard it appears to be more like a pomacentrid than a species of *Chaetodon*.

Chaetodon reticulatus is usually paired and found in the clearer waters of the reef. It is one of the less common Hawaiian chaetodonts.

Distribution.—Tropical Pacific Ocean. Polynesia (including the Hawaiian Island), Micronesia, and Melanesia to the East Indies; Philippine Islands north to the Ryu Kyu Islands.

Material Examined.—(11 spec.: 38-132 mm) BPBM 8472 (1: 129), Hawaiian Islands; EMBL (4: 38-65), Eniwetok, Marshall Islands; WEB (1: 88), Tahiti, Society Islands; WEB (2: 105-108), Johnston Island; WEB (3: 118-132), Oahu, Hawaiian Islands.

Subgenus CHAETODONTOPS Bleeker

Chaetodontops Bleeker, 1876: p. 305. (Type-species *Chaetodon collaris* Bloch, 1787, by original designation.)

Diagnosis.—Body oval; snout short, 2.8-3.5 in head length; dorsal and anal fins with blunt angles; teeth in spaced rows in each jaw; lateral line in high, angular arc; scales rounded; lachrymal not hidden by scales; eyeband variable, usually not a simple band; juveniles usually differently patterned, almost always with dorsal fin spot and normal eyeband; D. XII, 23-26; A. III, 17-22; pectoral fin rays usually 15; lateral line scales usually 37-44 (one species with 24-30).

Description.—Body oval; snout short, pointed, 2.8-3.5 in head length; predorsal contour straight, slightly concave, or gibbous; gape slightly oblique; teeth in spaced rows in each jaw; preopercle right-angled to slightly oblique-angled, corner rounded, crenulate; lachrymal smooth; supraorbital smooth to lightly serrate.

Dorsal spines graduated, fourth to sixth normally longest; dorsal fin continuous, no notch present; second and third anal spines equal or second slightly longer, first about half to two-thirds of second; dorsal and anal fins with rounded angles posteriorly; base of spinous portion of dorsal fin longer (equal in one species) than that of soft portion (2.1-2.8 and 2.4-3.3 in S.L. respectively); pectoral fins normal; pelvic fins moderate to long, in some species reaching first anal fin spine, in most falling between anus and first anal fin spine, and in at least one species falling short of anal opening; caudal fin truncate-rounded.

Lateral line ascending in a high flattened arc, posteriorly higher and peaking about the 9th or 10th dorsal fin spines, then following base of soft portion of dorsal fin to near base of last rays; scales moderate to large, rounded to vertically elongate (exposed portion); scales arranged in ascending rows (horizontal in lower portion and ascending in upper portion in one species); scale covering of dorsal fin normally to midpoint of sixth dorsal spine; scale covering of anal fin also normal, reaching past midpoint and usually to two-thirds of third anal spine.

Juveniles resemble adults in form, dorsal and anal fins more rounded, however, and differ considerably in color pattern. Normally a dark spot is present in dorsal fin of juvenile and the eyeband is normal. Other differences are described under species headings.

Color pattern variable, usually browns and yellows with black markings (but with exceptions). Eyeband in all but one species not a simple band but a broad belt or patch.

Widely distributed in tropical areas of the Pacific and Indian Oceans, Red Sea and Hawaiian Islands included. Absent from the East Pacific region and Atlantic Ocean.

Eight species are included in this subgenus, distinguishable by the following key.

Key to the Species of the Subgenus Chaetodontops (Adults)

1. Caudal peduncle with dark color on at least part of its length, usually anteriorly 2
   Caudal peduncle and its anterior base not dark colored, usually similar to body color 3

2. Eyeband broad, wider than eye, broadly connected across interorbital; spot on caudal peduncle extends dorsally along base of soft dorsal fin as narrowing stripe; large dark triangle-shaped marks in anterodorsal section of body (Indo-Pacific) . . . . . *Chaetodon lunula*
   Eyeband obscure, more distinct below eye, not evident on interorbital; anterior portion of caudal peduncle crossed by wide dark band which extends along bases of soft dorsal and anal fins; entire body usually dark, sometimes obscuring the band (Melanesia to Queensland) . . . . *C. flavirostris*

3. Lines crossing body vertical; eyeband a large patch, no separate spot or marking at nape (Red Sea and Gulf of Aden) . . . *C. semilarvatus*
   Lines crossing body diagonal or horizontal, never vertical; eyeband various 4

519

Chaetodon guentheri from Japan. The dorsal fin spot is very evident. Photo by Dr. Fujio Yasuda.

Chaetodon guentheri juvenile collected off Tsian-Shan at the southern tip of Taiwan. Photo by Dr. Shih-chieh Shen.

Chaetodon guentheri subadult from the Great Barrier Reef of Australia. Photo by Roger Steene.

This adult *Chaetodon guentheri* lacks the dorsal fin spot. It was photographed in its natural habitat at Lord Howe Island by Dr. Gerald R. Allen.

4. Lines on body definitely horizontal, above lateral line anteriorly reduced to rows of ascending spots; eyeband normal, a band narrower than eye extending from nape to isthmus (western Pacific) . . . .*C. auripes*
Lines on body inclined, higher posteriorly; eyeband various, usually with some peculiarity 5

5. Eyeband usually a patch, much broader than eye, not normally connected across nape; caudal fin pattern of various colors but not with blackish band; snout end usually color of head or dusky 6
Eyeband extending from interopercle to nape, connecting there or not, only slightly broader than eye; caudal fin with dark vertical band; snout end dark brown to blackish 7

6. Separate dark spot at nape; lines on body steeply ascending, not connected along base of soft dorsal fin (southern Japan to western Australia). . . . .*C. adiergastos*
Large triangular dark area from nape to middle of dorsal fin; lines on body gradually ascending, connected by a line running along base of dorsal fin (Red Sea) . . . .*C. fasciatus*

7. Head divided into dark bands by light stripes; broad white band from first dorsal spine to throat; no separate dark marking crossing nape from gill cover to gill cover (Indian Ocean and Western Pacific) . . . .*C. collare*
Eyeband wide, crossing nape (though sometimes not connected across nape); separate dark marking crossing nape above eyeband from corner of one gill cover to the other; tip of snout black, chin light (eastern Indian Ocean and western Pacific) . . . .*C. wiebeli*

Remarks.—Subgenus *Chaetodontops* contains species which undergo a color metamorphosis with growth. The species typically have a dark spot in the soft dorsal fin which disappears as the fish reaches subadulthood. The one exception is *Chaetodon semilarvatus* of the Red Sea. The eyebands of species in this subgenus are quite variable, some being isolated spots, some bordered with a broad white band posteriorly, etc., but those of the juveniles are quite normal, being a simple band through the eye.

CHAETODON COLLARE Bloch
Red-tailed butterflyfish

Chaetodon collare Bloch, 1787: p. 116, pl. 216, fig. 1 (type locality Japan?).
Chaetodon viridis Bleeker, 1845: p. 520 (type locality Batavia).
Chaetodon praetextatus Cantor, 1850: p. 1138, pl. III (type locality Sea of Penang). Gunther, 1860: p. 22 (Sea of Penang; on type specimen). Day, 1865: p. 31 (Malabar).

Chaetodon collaris, Kaup, 1863: p. 126.
Tetragonoptrus collaris, Bleeker, 1872: p. 140 (new combination).
Tetragonoptrus (Chaetodontops) collaris, Bleeker, 1877: p. 42 (various localities).
Chaetodon collare var. *praetextatus,* Ahl, 1923: p. 136 (Sea of Penang).
Chaetodon collare var. *duplicollis* Ahl, 1923: p. 137 (type locality coast of India).
Chaetodon collare var. *parallelus* Ahl, 1923: p. 138 (type localities Sumatra, Nias, Penang, Java, Celebes).
Chaetodon fowleri Klausewitz, 1955: p. 313, fig. 2 (type locality Java Sea near Djakarta).

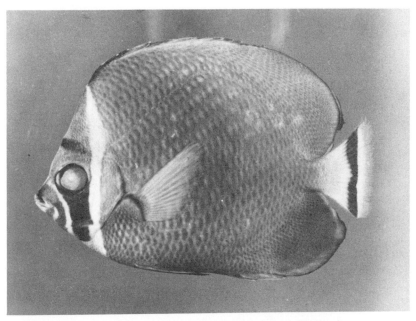

Chaetodon collare Bloch. 126 mm S.L. Similan Island, Thailand.

Diagnosis.—D. XII, 25-28 (usually 26-27); A. III, 20-22 (usually 20 or 21); pectoral rays (14) 15; L.l. scales 37-40; the broad head band bordered posteriorly by a white band and anteriorly by a white stripe, and the white chin stripes, as well as the dark band crossing the caudal fin, are distinctive for this subgenus.

Chaetodon miliaris subadult in an aquarium. Photo by Douglas Faulkner.

Chaetodon miliaris in its yellow phase. Photo by Dr. Gerald R. Allen, Hawaii.

Chaetodon miliaris juvenile in its natural habitat. Photo by Scott Johnson, Hawaii.

Chaetodon miliaris in its nighttime coloration. Photo by Scott Johnson, Hawaii.

| | Standard Length (mm) | | |
Ratios	20-49(5)	50-79(16)	above 79(7)
Depth/S.L.	1.5-1.6	1.4-1.6	1.4-1.5
Head/S.L.	2.7-2.9	2.9-3.2	3.1-3.5
Eye/Head	2.4-2.8	2.4-2.7	2.4-2.8
Snout/Head	3.0-3.9	3.3-4.1	3.3-4.2
Interorb. W./Head	2.7-3.0	2.8-3.0	2.7-3.0
Maxillary/Head	3.5-4.5	3.7-4.4	3.6-4.5
Caud. Ped./S.L.	7.9-8.8	8.5-8.9	8.4-9.3
Pect. Fin/S.L.	3.0-3.3	3.1-3.3	3.2-4.5
Pelvic Sp./S.L.	4.1-4.5	4.4-4.8	4.6-5.5
Predorsal L./S.L.	1.9-2.1	2.0-2.2	2.1-2.3
Prepelvic L./S.L.	2.1-2.3	2.2-2.4	2.4-2.6
Dorsal Sp. No. 1/S.L.	9.1-9.7	8.4-13.1	8.2-10.9
Dorsal Sp. No. 2/S.L.	5.6-6.0	5.6-7.3	6.6-9.6
Dorsal Sp. No. 3/S.L.	3.5-4.3	3.9-5.0	4.5-7.6
Dorsal Sp. No. 4/S.L.	3.3-4.2	3.5-4.4	4.1-5.2
Anal Sp. No. 1/S.L.	6.2-7.6	6.1-7.2	7.0-8.2
Anal Sp. No. 2/S.L.	4.8-5.4	4.1-4.8	4.2-5.0
Anal Sp. No. 3/S.L.	4.3-5.4	4.3-5.7	4.5-6.1

The head pattern approaches that of the members of the subgenus *Citharoedus*. The characteristics of the subgenera can serve to distinguish this species from that group.

Meristics.—D. XII, 25-28 (usually 26 or 27); A. III, 20-22 (usually 20 or 21); pectoral rays 15 (two with 14/14, four with 14/15); L.l. scales 37-40; L.l. pores 33-39; scales above the L.l. 7-8 (mostly 7); scales below the L.l. 15-18 (rarely 18); gill rakers 16-19.

Description.—Predorsal contour relatively straight, a concavity just above snout; gape horizontal to slightly oblique; teeth in 10-11 rows in each jaw; supraorbital smooth to lightly serrate; eye diameter greater than depth of caudal peduncle, which is greater than or equal to interorbital width; interorbital width greater than snout length.

Fourth to sixth dorsal spine longest; second anal spine slightly longer than third, first about two-thirds of second; pelvic fins short, not reaching level of anus; base of spinous portion of dorsal fin longer (2.1-2.2 in S.L.) than that of soft portion (2.7-2.9 in S.L.).

Lateral line peak under bases of ninth to tenth dorsal fin spines; scales moderately large, rounded, in steeply ascending rows on body; scaly portion of anal fin extending up to two-thirds length of third anal spine.

Color Pattern.—Body with each scale exhibiting a light center, formed in steeply ascending rows; anal fin with very narrow light or clear edge and submarginal dark line; pelvic fins brownish black.

Chaetodon collare juvenile, 37 mm S.L. Sri Lanka.

White band crossing opercle joined with opposite member at nape and across chest to form complete band around head; isthmus anterior to this band is body color; white stripe extends from one set of nostrils down across lower part of head to other set; second white stripe from one corner of mouth, across chin, to other corner of mouth; upper lip dark, lower lip white; spaces between white markings dark, lighter across nape; a blackish horizontal streak above eyes crossing nape.

Juvenile color pattern similar but with distinct differences. Dark band of caudal fin narrower and closer to base of the fin, outer portion of fin hyaline. A more normal, complete eyeband encircles head, broadly connected across nape, about equal or slightly narrower than eye diameter at eye; white band behind eyeband present; portion of eyeband below eye bordered anteriorly with white stripe; rest of markings on face absent. Juveniles from Sri Lanka had a dark lens- or crescent-shaped blackish spot in the soft dorsal fin at about the angle; this spot was separated from the dark edge of the fin by a white submarginal stripe.

Herre and Montalban, 1927 (after Bleeker, 1878) refer to the body as violaceous to yellowish green, head bands as violet-brown and white, deep green or violet-green stripes on body, spots golden; dorsal and pectoral yellowish to rosy, ventrals purple to blackish, free parts of soft dorsal and anal fins and basal half of caudal fin carmine; posterior margin of caudal fin yellowish, etc.

Remarks.—There has been a great deal of confusion concerning this species. It has often been synonymized with *Chaetodon aureus* Schlegel (= *C. auripes*), an entirely different species. A comparison of the accompanying photographs of these two species will clearly separate them. The

Chaetodon sanctaehelenae with a pattern of vertical spotted rows similar to those of other members of this same species complex. Photo by Ken Jourdan.

Chaetodon dolosus is the East African representative of the *miliaris*-group. Photo by Roger Lubbock.

A school of *Chaetodon sanctaehelenae* photographed in St. Helena at a depth of 40-50 feet. In the upper photo is a pair of *Chaetodon dichrous*. Photos by Ken Jourdan.

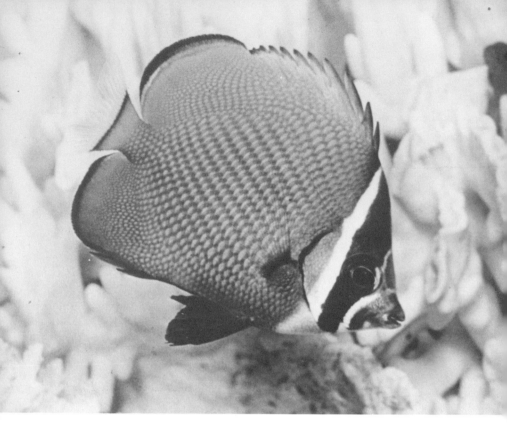

Chaetodon collare. Photo by Klaus Paysan.

figure of Bloch (1787), although leaving much to be desired, definitely shows the head coloration of *collare* and not *auripes*. The fin formulae also indicate *collare* (XII, 28 and III, 21 in Bloch) as compared to *auripes* (XII, 23-24, and III, 18-20). The caudal fin band is indicated as wide in Bloch's figure as it is in *collare*, compared with a narrower stripe in *auripes*.

Fowler's description of *Chaetodon collaris* in 1953 is that of *C. auripes*, but the figure (98) is more like *C. collare* (though quite poor).

Cantor (1850) reported this fish as being esteemed as food in Pinang.

Distribution.—Arabian Gulf (Muscat) to Sri Lanka, India, and East Indies; Philippine Islands north to China and southern Japan; Taiwan; Maldive Islands.

Material Examined.—(18 spec.: 24-126 mm S.L.) AMNH 14823 (1: 64), Singapore; ANSP 90438, 90435, and 96479 (3: 90-120), Batavia; MCZ 41718 and 41738 (3: 24-37), Colombo, Sri Lanka; SMF 3358 (1: 58), Java (holotype of *Chaetodon fowleri* Klausewitz); FMNH (no catalogue nos.) (8: 39-86), Musal Tivu; SOSC Te Vega Sta. 78 (2: 126-127), Similan Island, Thailand.

CHAETODON AURIPES Jordan and Snyder
Golden butterflyfish
(White collared butterflyfish)

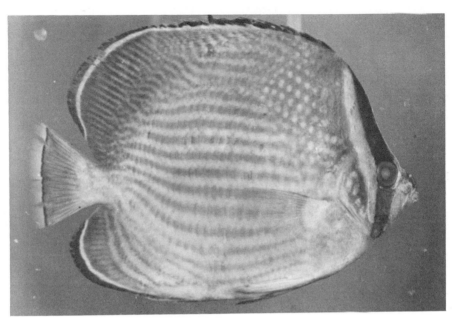

Chaetodon auripes Schlegel. 149 mm S.L. Riukiu Islands.

Chaetodon aureus Schlegel *In* Temminck & Schlegel, 1842: p. 81, pl. 42, fig. 1 (type locality "Seas of Japan;" preoccupied by *Chaetodon aureus* Bloch, 1787, an angelfish).

Chaetodon auripes Jordan and Snyder, 1901: p. 90 (substitute name for *Chaetodon aureus* Schlegel).

Chaetodon collaris (not of Bloch), Jordan & Fowler, 1902: p. 354, fig. 3 (Ikune, Tokyo). Jordan, Tanaka, & Snyder, 1913: p. 209, fig. 152. Kamohara, 1957: p. 32. Kamohara, 1964: p. 3. Okada, 1966: p. 292, fig. 265.

Chaetodon modestus (not of Schlegel), Jordan & Fowler, 1902: p. 535.

Chaetodon fallax Ahl, 1923: p. 64 (type locality Misaki; original description based on *Chaetodon modestus* Jordan & Fowler, 1902).

?*Chaetodon dorsiocellatus* Ahl, 1923: p. 111, pl. 2, fig. 1 (type locality Takao, Formosa).

Chaetodon sanctaehelenae juvenile, with a well-defined dorsal fin spot. Photo by Roger Lubbock.

Chaetodon sanctaehelenae adult. Ascension Island form with more yellow on vertical fins and caudal peduncle. Photo by Roger Lubbock.

Chaetodon sanctaehelenae adult. St. Helena form with less yellow posteriorly. Photo by Roger Lubbock.

Both forms of *Chaetodon sanctaehelenae* in an aquarium. The differences
can easily be seen. Photo by Ken Jourdan.

Chaetodon collare (not of Bloch), Fowler & Bean, 1929: p. 104 (Japan, Philippines, China). Aoyagi, 1943: 224 pp., pls. 1-37 (Japan). Liang, 1948: p. 59 (Pescadores, Taiwan).

Chaetodon (Rabdophorus) modestus (not of Schlegel), Fowler, 1953: p. 24 (China, Hong Kong, Canton, Amoy; juvenile).

Chaetodon (Chaetodontops) colloris Fowler, 1953: p. 34, fig. 98 (China, Hong Kong, Canton, Hokuko, Su Wan, Formosa, Yaeyama, Amami Oshima, Okinawa, Riu Kiu; misspelling only once).

Diagnosis.—D. XII, 23-24; A. III, 18-20 (usually 19); pectoral rays (14) 15; L.l. scales 37-45 (usually 40-43); stripes on body mostly horizontal; eyeband normal, about eye width, extending as a band from nape to throat.

This is the only species of this subgenus with more or less horizontal stripes.

Meristics.—D. XII, 23-24; A. III, 18-20 (usually 19); pectoral rays 15 (one with 14/14, four with 15/14, and one with 16/15); L.l. scales 37-45 (usually 40-43); L.l. pores 35-43 (usually 36-40); scales above L.l. 7; scales below L.l. 13/14; gill rakers 17-22.

Ratios	Standard Length (mm)		
	20-59(8)	50-79(3)	above 79(13)
Depth/S.L.	1.4-1.6	1.5	1.4-1.7
Head/S.L.	2.6-2.9	2.9-3.3	3.2-3.7
Eye/Head	2.5-2.8	2.6-2.7	2.8-3.2
Snout/Head	2.6-3.7	2.8-3.2	2.7-3.4
Interorb. W./Head	3.1-3.3	2.9-3.2	2.6-3.0
Maxillary/Head	3.7-4.5	3.9-4.2	3.4-4.7
Caud. Ped./S.L.	8.4-9.4	8.8-9.1	8.7-9.6
Pect. Fin/S.L.	3.1-3.7	2.9-3.4	3.2-3.9
Pelvic Sp./S.L.	4.1-5.2	4.4-5.1	4.9-5.6
Predorsal L./S.L.	2.0-2.2	2.0-2.2	2.1-2.3
Prepelvic L./S.L.	1.9-2.2	2.2-2.5	2.4-2.6
Dorsal Sp. No. 1/S.L.	8.0-10.4	9.2-10.9	8.7-11.4
Dorsal Sp. No. 2/S.L.	5.6-8.1	7.1-8.4	7.4-10.5
Dorsal Sp. No. 3/S.L.	4.1-5.3	5.3-6.4	5.7-7.4
Dorsal Sp. No. 4/S.L.	3.7-4.7	4.8-5.2	4.4-6.2
Anal Sp. No. 1/S.L.	6.0-7.7	7.5-7.6	6.8-9.4
Anal Sp. No. 2/S.L.	4.5-6.4	4.7-5.4	4.8-6.4
Anal Sp. No. 3/S.L.	4.9-6.6	5.2-6.4	5.5-7.1

Description.—Predorsal contour relatively straight to slightly convex; gape of mouth slightly oblique; teeth in 7-9 rows in each jaw; lachrymal short, smooth; supraorbital smooth; caudal peduncle depth greater than interorbital width, which is greater than eye diameter; eye diameter greater than snout length.

Fifth or sixth dorsal spines greatest; second anal spine greater than or equal to third, first about half of second; base of spinous portion of dorsal fin longer (2.3-2.4 in S.L.) than that of soft portion (2.4-2.7 in S.L.); pelvic fins moderate, extending beyond anus but not reaching anal fin base.

Peak of lateral line under last dorsal fin spines, though somewhat remote from them; scales moderate, rounded angular to elongate, in horizontal series in lower part of body and ascending rows in upper portion; dorsal spine scales reaching midpoint at about fifth or sixth spine; anal spine scales covering half to three-fourths of third.

Juveniles similar to adult.

Color Pattern.—Horizontal stripes of darker color passing through centers of scales below lateral line; above lateral line darker color on edges of scales leaving center a light spot; eyeband broadly connected with opposite member at nape, ending at edge of interopercle; face dusky, upper lip blackish; pectoral fins hyaline to grayish; pelvic fins chest color with dusky outer half or tips.

Juveniles with some differences in color pattern. There is a large blackish spot in the soft dorsal fin at about the "angle" but separated from the dark margin of that fin by a space. The horizontal stripes are present, serving as a good character for identification. The dorsal and anal fin edges are brown, the color continuing almost to the last rays, and submarginal white stripes. In very small specimens this white stripe includes the dorsal spot as an ocellus ring. Caudal peduncle with a dark band (22 mm S.L. specimen) that disappears early (at about 40-42 mm standard length). Caudal fin with a light dusky crossband near its base, separated from the caudal peduncle band by a light band. In the 40 mm specimen the caudal peduncle band is very faded but the caudal fin band is darker. Smaller specimens have a dark base to anal fin with light area between this and brown edge. The dark base stripe continues pattern across caudal peduncle as that band. In larger specimens light portion is just inside brown edge and quickly fades into darker area covering most of fin. White band noticeable in 40 mm specimen.

The dorsal spot is lost between the sizes of 45 and 80 mm standard length.

Remarks.—The confusion between the original descriptions of this species and *Chaetodon collare* still exists in recent literature. *Chaetodon collare* is a distinct and quite different species as can be seen by comparison of the photographs accompanying the two species. The broad white band behind the eyeband in both species no doubt contributed much to the confusion.

Chaetodon daedalma is more common in the area of southern Japan but does not extend further south. Photo by Dr. Fujio Yasuda.

Chaetodon daedalma juvenile. The color pattern of this fish gives a distinctly prehistoric impression. Photo by Dr. Fujio Yasuda.

Chaetodon punctatofasciatus in its natural habitat at Enewetak, Marshall Islands. Photo by Scott Johnson.

Chaetodon punctatofasciatus photographed at night by Scott Johnson, Enewetak.

Chaetodon aureus Temminck & Schlegel was preoccupied by *Chaetodon aureus* Bloch, a species now placed in the genus *Pomacanthus* of family Pomacanthidae. Jordan & Snyder (1901) recognized this and proposed a new name, *Chaetodon auripes*, as a substitute.

The juvenile color pattern is somewhat different from that of the adult, causing confusion in the identification of the juveniles of this subgenus. The horizontal nature of the body stripes is distinctive even to a very small size, and specimens still with the tholichthys-plates were identifiable in this manner.

This species reaches a length of about 170 mm.

Juveniles were frequently found in tidal pools in Japan (Okada, 1966). According to Okada (1966), this species is a food fish.

Distribution.—East Indies and Philippine Islands through the China Sea as far as Tokyo, Japan. Reported from the Maldive Islands, but this may be confusion with *Chaetodon collare*.

Material Examined.—(24 spec.: 22-142 mm S.L.) USNM 71487 (2: 38-49), Tanegashima, Japan; USNM 88059 (1: 33), Misaki, Japan; CAS 37796 (1: 80), Hong Kong; CAS 37797 (2: 75-80), Nha Trang, South Vietnam; CAS 37798 (1: 87), South Vietnam; CAS 37799 and 37795 (4: 96-129), Pratas Reef, South China Sea; CAS 37816 (2: 32-56), Japan; SMF (1: 54), Java; SOSC VGS 68-2 and 68-12 (2: 100-126), Taiwan; Yasuda (Univ. of Tokyo) (3: 109-142), Japan; BPBM 8662 (1: 45), Taiwan; CAS HK-78 (4: 22-44), Hong Kong.

CHAETODON WIEBELI Kaup
Pocket butterflyfish
(Sea beauty butterflyfish)

Chaetodon wiebeli Kaup, 1863: p. 127 (type locality Canton, China).

Chaetodon collaris (not of Bloch), Kner, 1865: p. 99.

Chaetodon bella-maris Seale, 1914: p. 72, pl. 1, fig. 1 (type locality Hong Kong Market). Ahl, 1923: p. 111, pl. 1, fig. 1. Rofen, 1963: p. 76-77 (Gulf of Thailand).

Chaetodon collare var. *Kneri* (not *collare* of Bloch) Ahl, 1923: p. 137 (Java, Hong Kong).

Chaetodon frenatus Fowler, 1934: p. 154, fig. 123 (type locality Bangkok).

Chaetodon (Chaetodontops) bella-maris, Weber & de Beaufort, 1936: p. 93 (various localities).

Chaetodon lunula (not of Lacepede), Okada & Matsubara, 1938: p. 269, pl. 61, fig. 2 (Japan).

Chaetodon (Chaetodontops) wiebeli, Fowler, 1953: p. 35, fig. 99 (China, Hong Kong, Canton, Tinghai Chusan Island, Takao, Taiwan).

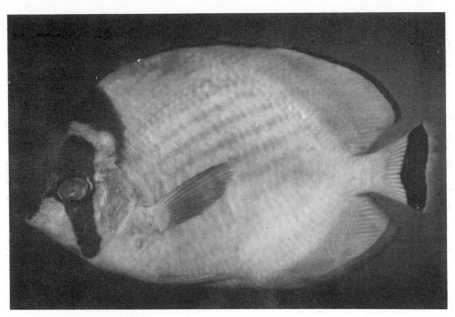

Chaetodon wiebeli Kaup. 139 mm S.L. Gulf of Thailand.

Ratios	Standard Length (mm)		
	20-49(1)	50-79(5)	above 79(16)
Depth/S.L.............	1.7	1.4-1.5	1.3-1.5
Head/S.L..............	2.7	2.9-3.1	3.0-3.5
Eye/Head	2.9	2.6-2.8	2.7-3.3
Snout/Head	3.2	2.9-3.2	3.0-3.4
Interorb. W./Head......	3.2	2.7-3.0	2.4-3.2
Maxillary/Head	3.7	3.7-4.1	3.8-4.8
Caud. Ped./S.L........	8.8	8.6-8.8	8.4-9.3
Pect. Fin/S.L..........	3.3	3.2-3.4	3.1-3.8
Pelvic Sp./S.L.........	4.4	5.0-5.3	4.6-5.7
Predorsal L./S.L.......	2.2	2.1	2.1-2.4
Prepelvic L./S.L.......	2.3	2.2-2.4	2.3-2.6
Dorsal Sp. No. 1/S.L.....	9.4	9.9-11.8	9.0-11.7
Dorsal Sp. No. 2/S.L.....	6.3	7.5-9.9	8.1-14.3
Dorsal Sp. No. 3/S.L.....	4.4	5.7-6.1	6.4-10.3
Dorsal Sp. No. 4/S.L.....	4.0	4.6-5.1	5.3-9.7
Anal Sp. No. 1/S.L......	6.4	7.2-7.9	7.3-9.2
Anal Sp. No. 2/S.L......	4.6	4.9-5.5	5.2-7.4
Anal Sp. No. 3/S.L......	4.9	5.1-5.7	5.0-7.5

Chaetodon punctatofasciatus juvenile. The eye band of this individual is still connected to the eventual nape spot. Photo by Dr. Warren E. Burgess, Philippines.

Chaetodon punctatofasciatus adult with separate nape spot. A similar development of nape spots occurs in subgenus *Rhombochaetodon*. Photo by Dr. Fujio Yasuda.

Chaetodon punctatofasciatus adult. Photo by Dr. Shih-chieh Shen.

Diagnosis.—D. XII (one with XIII), 22-25 (usually 23-24); A. III, 18-20 (usually 19); pectoral rays (14) 15; L.l. scales 38-46 (usually 42-44); stripes on body ascending posteriorly; large black blotch crossing nape from edge of one gill cover to the other; eyeband broad, partially or not connected across interorbital; snout tip variously dark pigmented; broad black bar crossing caudal fin.

Meristics.—D. XII (one with XIII), 22-25 (usually 23 or 24); A. III, 18-20 (usually 19); pectoral rays 15 (two with 14/14, three with 14/15); L.l. scales 38-46 (normally 42-44); L.l. pores 35-44 (usually 39-42); scales above L.l. 6-9 (usually 7 or 8); scales below L.l. 12 or 13; gill rakers 15-19 (usually 16-18).

Description.—Predorsal contour approximately straight, a concavity above snout; gape of mouth slightly oblique; teeth in 10-11 rows in each jaw; preopercle slightly obliquely angled; lachrymal and supraorbital smooth; interorbital space greater than depth of caudal peduncle; caudal peduncle greater than eye diameter, which is equal to or greater than snout.

Fifth or sixth dorsal spines longest; second and third anal spines about equal, first two-thirds second; base of spinous portion of dorsal fin slightly longer (2.5 in S.L.) than that of soft portion (2.6-2.9 in S.L.); pelvic fins moderate to long, reaching past anus and in one specimen to base of anal spine.

Peak of lateral line at about base of last dorsal fin spine or first ray; scales large, exposed portion vertically elongate, edge flattened, in ascending series; scaly covering of anal fin extending to midpoint of third anal fin spine or slightly beyond.

Juveniles similar to adults.

Color Pattern.—Ascending stripes sometimes very light, barely discernible; eyeband only partly connected with opposite member at nape or no connection at all; upper lip and part of snout adjacent black, at times with connecting stripe to orbit; a black spot on each side of lower lip; black patch across nape continuous, but separated from eyeband by light area; black bar of caudal fin margined with white on both sides; dark edges to dorsal and anal fins including lighter area within dark stripe, wider in anal fin; pectoral fins hyaline; pelvic fins body color.

Juveniles with differences in color pattern. Eyeband a complete band around head, connected with nape marking. The nape marking still evident as a notch in the eyeband even in specimens of 29 mm S.L. The separation of this part is complete at about 65-75 mm S.L., and the eyeband begins to fuse across its upper end, just above the interorbital area, at this size (or even smaller). The nape mark is almost triangular in shape at this point. A whitish color surrounds the eyeband and this marking but does not include the opercular bone or snout. A slightly darker color than body color can be seen along the posterior edge of this light color from the base of the first dorsal spine to the origin of the lateral line. This becomes darker and fuses with the nape spot to form the adult pattern. Edges of

Chaetodon
wiebeli 32 mm
S.L. (Taiwan) and
139 mm S.L.
(Hong Kong).

dorsal and anal fins hyaline, submarginal dark stripe present, and streak of light below it. Large dark spot on dorsal fin in vicinity of angle, adjacent to light stripe and ocellated with the same light color. A broad black band encircling caudal peduncle, though usually not connected ventrally; in smallest specimen (35 mm) it reaches almost to lower edge. A yellow band adjacent to this at base of caudal fin and a narrow dark stripe across its outer edge. Remainder of caudal fin hyaline. Snout tip light. Pelvics dusky, almost black in smallest specimens.

With growth the narrow caudal fin stripe becomes wider and darker as the caudal peduncle bar disappears. The spot in the dorsal fin disappears (a 42 mm S.L. specimen had only a trace of the spot). Caudal peduncle band was all but gone in the 68 mm S.L. specimen. The 42 mm S.L. specimen had the eyeband connected broadly with the mark above and barely touching the opposite band at one spot, above the interorbital area. Both the caudal fin and peduncular bands were present.

Remarks.—Although this species is currently known under the name *Chaetodon bellamaris*, Fowler in 1938 correctly identified this species as the same as that described by Kaup (1863) under the name *Chaetodon wiebeli*. It is a very distinctive species but has often been misidentified, usually confused with the foregoing two species, *Chaetodon auripes* and *C. collare*. The cotypes of *Chaetodon frenatus* are no doubt this species.

The change in color pattern from juvenile to adult leads to more confusion, and the juveniles are very often confused with other species in this

Chaetodon pelewensis with an almost normally developed color pattern. Photo by Dr. Dwayne Reed.

Chaetodon pelewensis (with disrupted color pattern) in its natural habitat. Photo by Keiko Bleher, Marau, Solomon Islands.

Chaetodon pelewensis (also with disrupted color pattern) feeding on one of the corals of the reef. Photo by Dr. Gerald R. Allen, Great Barrier Reef.

Chaetodon pelewensis. Photo by Roger Steene.

subgenus, particularly *Chaetodon auripes* and *C. adiergastos.* Similarly to *C. adiergastos,* this species is restricted to Southeast Asia, its range being centered around the Hong Kong area.

Distribution.—East Indies northward to the Gulf of Thailand and southern Japan. Common off the coast of China.

Material Examined.—(22 spec.: 31-153 mm S.L.) CAS 37800, CAS 37801, CAS 37802, CAS 37803, CAS 37804, CAS 37818, CAS 37805, and CAS 37806 (15: 96-153), Gulf of Thailand; CAS 37819 (4: 68-75), Hong Kong; CAS 37820 (1: 42), Hong Kong; ANSP 62658 (1: 143), Bangkok, Thailand (cotype of *Chaetodon frenatus*); BPBM 8669 (1: 31), Taiwan.

CHAETODON ADIERGASTOS Seale
Bantayan butterflyfish

Chaetodon adiergastos Seale, 1910: p. 116, pl. 1, fig. 2 (type
locality Bantayan Island, Philippine Islands).
Chaetodon fasciatus (not of Forsskal), Fowler, 1918: p. 64
(Philippines).

Chaetodon adiergastos Seale. 126 mm S.L. Philippine Islands.

Ratios	Standard Length (mm)		
	20-49(2)	50-89(3)	above 90(10)
Depth/S.L.	1.5-1.6	1.5-1.6	1.3-1.5
Head/S.L.	2.5-2.6	2.8-3.1	3.1-3.3
Eye/Head	2.8-2.9	2.6-3.1	2.6-3.1
Snout/Head	3.4-4.0	2.8-3.2	2.9-3.4
Interorb. W./Head.	2.9-3.0	3.3-3.7	2.5-2.9
Maxillary/Head	4.5-?	3.9-4.3	4.0-4.4
Caud. Ped./S.L.	7.5-9.2	8.1-8.8	8.3-8.8
Pect. Fin/S.L.	3.5-3.6	3.1-3.2	3.4-4.0
Pelvic Sp./S.L.	4.6-5.5	4.2-4.7	4.9-5.4
Predorsal L./S.L.	1.9	2.0-2.2	2.1-2.3
Prepelvic L./S.L.	2.2	2.1-2.3	2.2-2.5
Dorsal Sp. No. 1/S.L.	8.7	8.1-9.2	8.5-10.8
Dorsal Sp. No. 2/S.L.	5.6	5.4-6.0	7.5-9.6
Dorsal Sp. No. 3/S.L.	4.5	4.0-4.4	6.0-7.5
Dorsal Sp. No. 4/S.L.	4.2	3.2-4.0	5.0-6.4
Anal Sp. No. 1/S.L.	9.6	5.4-6.4	7.7-8.9
Anal Sp. No. 2/S.L.	7.3	4.4-4.5	5.3-6.2
Anal Sp. No. 3/S.L.	6.3	4.3-4.4	5.6-6.0

Diagnosis.—D. XII, 23-26 (usually 24-25); A. III, 18-21 (usually 19-20); pectoral rays 14; L.l. scales 35-43 (usually 38-40); black spot on gibbous nape is distinctive; stripes very steeply ascending on sides of body; broad, unconnected eyebands.

Meristics.—D. XII, 23-26 (usually 24 or 25); A. III, 18-21 (usually 19-20); pectoral rays 14 (two with 13/14, one with 15/14); L.l. scales 35-43 (normally 38-40); scales above L.l. 7; scales below L.l. 14-15; gill rakers 14-18 (usually 17).

Description.—Body deep, 1.4 in S.L., almost rounded; profile steep, "S"-shaped, a small hump at the nape accented by the black marking; preopercle slightly oblique, toothed at angle, dentate on horizontal and ascending limbs; supraorbital and lachrymal smooth; gape approximately horizontal; teeth in about 9-11 rows in each jaw; interorbital width equal to depth of caudal peduncle, both greater than eye diameter (see remarks about eye size), which is greater than snout length.

Fifth dorsal spine longest; angle of fins at about 18th or 19th rays in dorsal and 14th or 15th rays in anal; second and third anal fin spines equal in length (though second more robust), first about two-thirds of second; base of spinous portion of dorsal fin slightly longer (2.1-2.3 in S.L.) than that of soft portion (2.5-2.6 in S.L.); pelvic fins moderate to long, some reaching base of first anal fin spine.

Steeply ascending lateral line (40°) reaches peak at base of ninth dorsal fin spine; scales large, exposed portion vertically elongate, flattened at

Chaetodon pelewensis adult with a typical color pattern. Photo by W. Deas.

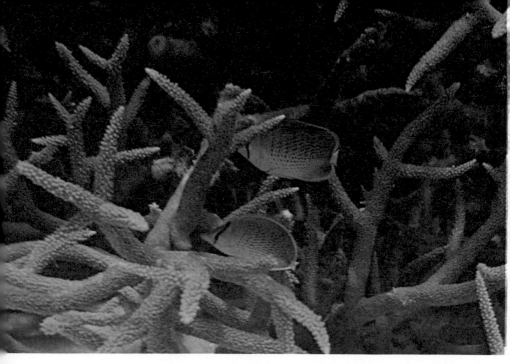

A pair of *Chaetodon guttatissimus* feeding among a stand of the reef coral *Acropora*. Photo by Dr. Herbert R. Axelrod, Maldives.

Chaetodon guttatissimus, another member of the *punctatofasciatus*-group. Photo by Dr. P. Colin, Cocos-Keeling Island, Indian Ocean.

3

Chaetodon adiergastos,
juvenile series showing
development of nape spot and
loss of dorsal fin spot.
1.   28 mm S.L.
2.   54 mm S.L.
3.   80 mm S.L.

edges, arranged in steeply ascending series; scaly portion of anal spines reaches to two-thirds of third spine.

Juveniles similar to adults, though some changes can be noted. Pelvic fins proportionately longer, dorsal and anal fins more rounded. The hump or gibbosity of the nape is not evident in the smaller specimen.

The 20 mm S.L. specimen still bears the plates characteristic of the tholichthys larva. The 28 mm specimen has lost these plates.

Color Pattern.—Thirteen or fourteen steeply ascending stripes crossing body, following scale rows (none bifurcate); chest plain or lightly spotted; black hoof-shaped spot (not ocellated) on nape completely separated from the ocular band; eyeband blackish, wide, approaching shape of patch in some examples, extends to edge of interoperculum and is separate from that of the opposite side; pelvic fins body color.

The color pattern of juveniles undergoes significant changes with age. The ocular band in a 20 mm specimen connects with the opposite one on the nape shortly before the origin of the spinous dorsal fin. It passes through the eye, but is not as wide as the eye, and ends at the edge of the interopercle. The eyeband widens with growth; the area above the eye but below the nape fades with growth, finally disappearing, leaving the hoof-shaped mark on the nape. A 60 mm specimen had the connection still fairly strong, while that of an 80 mm specimen had disappeared. There is a dark band crossing the caudal fin about one-third of the distance from the caudal peduncle. This band in the adult is more curved and approximately one-third the distance from the outer edge of the fin. This band also fades with growth but doesn't disappear. A dark band encircles the caudal peduncle in the 20 mm specimen. By 28 mm, the band is still evident but lighter in color. The 60 mm specimen has no trace of this band. The 20 mm specimen has a pale vertical streak just anterior to this peduncular band. The soft dorsal fin has a relatively large blackish oval spot in the soft dorsal fin on the 10th to 18th rays, at least in the very small individuals. This spot, at least in the 28 mm specimen, is ocellated. The aquarium specimens (2-3") had vestiges of the spot and were in the process of losing it. There is a clear marginal border to the soft dorsal and anal fins outside of the dark band. This clear edge either disappears in the older specimens or was not visible in the preserved material.

Remarks.—*Chaetodon fasciatus* Fowler was included in the synonymy on the basis of Fowler's own corrections; he included this entry in his 1929 work (Fowler & Bean, 1929).

The specimens I have seen agree quite closely with the original description and figure (Seale, 1910). Most specimens examined came from the original area, the Philippine Islands. According to Herre & Montalban (1934), Seale's specimens, including the type, had disappeared.

This species is often confused with other members of this subgenus, particularly as juveniles. Reference to the photographs and diagnoses of the various species should permit this species to be identified properly at all stages. The most difficult comparison is perhaps with *Chaetodon wiebeli* juveniles. The spot in *C. adiergastos*, however, is more vertically elongate, whereas that of *C. wiebeli* is more round.

The eye diameter is approximately equal to snout length in some specimens (both 2.9-3.1 in head length) but significantly larger in others (2.6-2.9 in head length), causing the snout length to be smaller in comparison to head length (3.2-3.4 in head length). This difference may possibly be due to sexual dimorphism. Unfortunately not enough specimens were available for dissection to prove this hypothesis.

Distribution—Apparently occurs from southern Japan southward throughthe East Indies to western Australia. The center of distribution appears to be the Philippine Islands. The specimen from Vietnam constitutes a new record, as does the one from Borneo. Also reported from the Celebes Sea. Also reported from the Celebes Sea.

Material Examined.—(15 spec.: 20-152 mm S.L.) USNM 181152-181172 (8: 99-152), Philippine Islands; ANSP 48692 and 98257 (2: 104-126) (as *C. bella-maris*), Philippine Islands; CAS 37821 (1: 59), Vietnam; CAS 37822 (1: 20), Philippine Islands; CAS 37823 (1: 28), Philippine Islands; SOSC Te Vega Sta. 213 (1: 52), Borneo; WEB (1: 61), Philippine Islands.

Chaetodon multicinctus adult showing distinct nape spot. Photo by Douglas Faulkner.

Chaetodon multicinctus juvenile with the eye band and nape spot still connected. Photo by Dr. Gerald R. Allen, Hawaii.

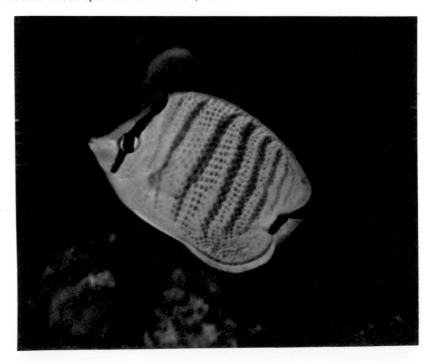

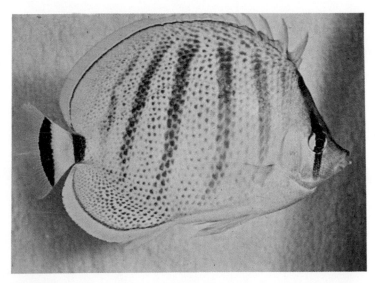

Chaetodon multicinctus subadult. The nape spot at this stage is weakly connected with the eye band. Photo by Dr. Herbert R. Axelrod.

Chaetodon multicinctus, 74 mm S.L. from Oahu, Hawaiian Islands. Photo by Dr. John E. Randall.

CHAETODON SEMILARVATUS Cuvier
Red-lined butterflyfish

Chaetodon semilarvatus Cuvier, 1831: p. 39 (type locality Red Sea; ex. Ehrenberg MS).
Chaetodon (*Anisochaetodon*) *semilarvatus*, Klunzinger, 1881: p. 57, pl. 11, fig. 1 (Red Sea).
Chaetodon melanopoma Playfair, 1866: p. 35, pl. 6, fig. 2 (type locality Aden). Ahl, 1923: p. 147 (Aden; Playfair).

Chaetodon semilarvatus Cuvier. 89 mm S.L. Massaua, Red Sea.

Diagnosis.—D. XII, 25-27; A. III, 20-22; pectoral rays 15; L.l. scales 28-32; body deep, 1.4-1.5 in S.L.; eyeband patch-like, extending from eye to lower posterior edge of gill opening; narrow vertical stripes (15 or more) crossing body.

Meristics.—D. XII, 25-27; A. III, 20-22; pectoral rays 15; L.l. scales 28-32; L.l. pores 20-28; scales above L.l. 5-6; scales below L.l. 13-15; gill rakers 17-20.

Description.—Body rounded, deep (1.4-1.5 in S.L.); predorsal contour straight to slightly concave; gape horizontal to slightly oblique; teeth in 12 to 13 rows in each jaw; lachrymal smooth, supraorbital lightly serrate; depth of caudal peduncle greater than interorbital width, which is greater than eye diameter; eye diameter greater than snout length.

Ratios	Standard Length (mm)		
	20-49(2)	50-69	above 69(8)
Depth/S.L.............	1.5-1.6	---	1.4-1.5
Head/S.L..............	2.4-2.7	---	3.0-3.2
Eye/Head	2.7-2.9	---	2.7-3.1
Snout/Head	2.8-2.9	---	2.9-3.5
Interorb. W./Head......	3.0-3.1	---	2.7-3.2
Maxillary/Head	3.9-4.1	---	3.6-4.5
Caud. Ped./S.L.........	8.1-8.3	---	8.0-8.8
Pect. Fin/S.L..........	3.3-3.5	---	3.4-4.3
Pelvic Sp./S.L.........	4.6-5.1	---	4.3-5.3
Predorsal L./S.L........	1.8-2.0	---	2.0-2.3
Prepelvic L./S.L........	1.9-2.1	---	2.2-2.4
Dorsal Sp. No. 1/S.L.....	8.9-11.0	---	8.1-12.0
Dorsal Sp. No. 2/S.L.....	5.7-6.1	---	6.5-8.7
Dorsal Sp. No. 3/S.L.....	4.1-4.1	---	5.1-7.0
Dorsal Sp. No. 4/S.L.....	3.5-3.7	---	4.4-6.0
Anal Sp. No. 1/S.L.......	6.8-7.7	---	6.5-7.9
Anal Sp. No. 2/S.L.......	5.1-5.2	---	4.7-5.8
Anal Sp. No. 3/S.L.......	4.7-5.2	---	4.3-5.4

Fifth to eighth dorsal spines longest; second and third anal spines equal, first not much shorter than second; outer edges of dorsal, anal, and caudal fins combined present an almost continuous edge; base of spinous portion of dorsal fin equal to or slightly longer (2.3-2.8 in S.L.) than that of soft portion (2.4-2.8 in S.L.); pelvic fins long, reaching base of anal spines.

Peak of lateral line under anterior dorsal rays; scales large, angular, in chevron pattern; scaly portion of dorsal fin reaching midpoint of sixth dorsal spine; scaly portion of anal fin covering two-thirds to three-fourths of third spine.

Juveniles similar to adults.

Color Pattern.—Usually about 15 vertical stripes crossing body following scale rows; nape, chest, and caudal peduncle area clear; upper part of snout to nape dusky.

The color pattern of juveniles is similar to that of the adults but with certain differences. The body is colored much the same as in the adult, with the same number of vertical stripes. The eyeband is close to normal, extending from the nape, where it connects with the one from the opposite side, to the lower edge of the interopercle. It is not as wide as the eye and passes through the posterior two-thirds of it. In addition, the caudal peduncle has a large dark spot on either side, connected narrowly

Chaetodon fremblii juvenile. The juvenile differs little from the adult. Photo by Douglas Faulkner.

Chaetodon fremblii feeding on one of the Hawiian corals. Photo by Dr. Gerald R. Allen.

Chaetodon fremblii is endemic to the Hawaiian Islands. Photo by Dr. Herbert R. Axelrod.

Chaetodon blackburnii occurs only on the eastern coast of Africa. Photo by Dr. Warren E. Burgess.

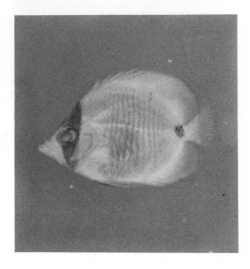

Chaetodon semilarvatus Cuvier.
39 mm S.L. Aden.

above but not reaching the lower edge of the peduncle. Submarginal dark lines are not visible on the fins in the smallest specimen (31 mm), and the fins are broadly hyaline-edged. The 39 mm S.L. specimen has one in the dorsal fin but not yet in the anal fin.

Remarks.—*Chaetodon semilarvatus* is a very distinctive fish from the Red Sea - Gulf of Aden area. Juveniles have been collected in depths of only two to five feet. The adults also are not deep water, many underwater photographs having been taken of this species.

Baschieri-Salvatore (1954) noted it as being very common in both the northern and southern sectors of the Red Sea. He saw mostly isolated individuals or pairs. They were around the lower portions of the madreporarians, rarely in the deeper waters.

Distribution.—Red Sea and Gulf of Aden (Aden, Kossier).

Material Examined.—(10 spec.: 31-140 mm S.L.) BPBM 7848 (6: 84-91), Massaua, Red Sea; SOSC Anton Bruun Cr. 9, Sta. FT-26 (2: 31-39), Gold Mahur Bay, Aden; BPBM 10513 (1: 108), Red Sea; SU 20481 (1: 140), Red Sea.

CHAETODON FLAVIROSTRIS Gunther
Yellow-face butterflyfish

Chaetodon flavirostris Gunther, 1874: p. 41, pl. 32, fig. A (type locality Vavau, Friendly Islands (Tonga)).

Chaetodon aphrodite Ogilby, 1889: p. 55, pl. 3, fig. 2 (type locality Lord Howe Island).

Chaetodon dorsiocellatus Ahl, 1923: p. 111, pl. 1, fig. 1 (type locality Takao).

Chaetodon flavirostris Goldman, 1967: p. 45, pl. VII-IX.

Ratios	Standard Length (mm)		
	20-59(5)	60-89(5)	above 89(10)
Depth/S.L.............	1.5	1.4-1.6	1.4-1.5
Head/S.L..............	2.5-2.9	2.9-3.1	3.0-3.2
Eye/Head.............	2.6-2.7	2.6-2.8	2.7-2.9
Snout/Head	3.0-3.3	2.9-3.2	3.0-3.7
Interorb. W./Head......	3.0-3.4	2.9-3.4	2.7-3.1
Maxillary/Head	3.7-4.5	4.0-4.7	3.7-4.8
Caud. Ped./S.L........	8.5-9.1	8.8-9.1	8.5-9.1
Pect. Fin/S.L..........	3.1-3.7	2.9-3.7	3.1-3.7
Pelvic Sp./S.L.........	4.1-4.6	4.3-4.8	4.4-5.0
Predorsal L./S.L.......	1.9-2.1	2.1	2.1-2.2
Prepelvic L./S.L.......	2.0-2.3	2.2-2.4	2.2-2.5
Dorsal Sp. No. 1/S.L....	7.9-11.2	8.0-10.0	7.6-10.5
Dorsal Sp. No. 2/S.L....	5.6-7.4	5.9-7.7	6.8-9.0
Dorsal Sp. No. 3/S.L....	4.2-5.1	4.6-5.2	5.2-6.8
Dorsal Sp. No. 4/S.L....	3.7-4.3	3.6-5.1	4.5-5.4
Anal Sp. No. 1/S.L......	5.7-7.6	6.0-6.5	6.5-8.7
Anal Sp. No. 2/S.L......	4.1-5.2	4.3-5.0	4.7-5.6
Anal Sp. No. 3/S.L......	4.5-5.3	5.0-5.5	4.5-6.2

Chaetodon flavirostris Gunther. 115 mm S.L. Heron Island, Queensland, Australia.

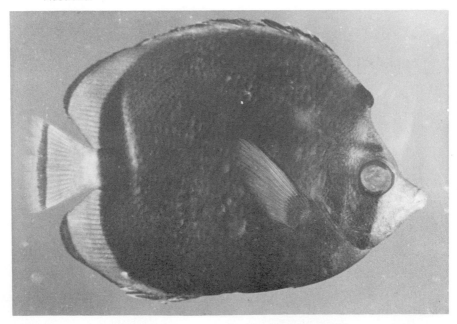

Heniochus acuminatus with a very elongate dorsal fin filament. Photo by W. Deas.

Heniochus intermedius with a divided or double fourth dorsal fin spine. Photo by Dr. Gerald R. Allen, Eilat.

An aberrant *Heniochus acuminatus* in which the fifth as well as the fourth dorsal fin spine has become elongated. Photo by Dr. Fujio Yasuda.

Chaetodon flavirostris in a pale phase. Photo by W. Deas.

Diagnosis.—D. XII-XIII (usually XII), 24-27 (usually 25-26); A. III, 20-21 (usually 20); pectoral rays 15 or 16; L.l. scales 40-46 (usually 41-44); dark brown with light streak crossing posterior end of body; nape gibbous; eyeband indistinct, not usually evident above eye; a horizontal dash above eye like eyebrow.

Meristics.—D. XII (two with XIII), 24-27 (usually 25 or 26); A. III, 20-21 (usually 20); pectoral rays 15 or 16 (five with 15/16, two with 14/15); L.l. scales 40-46 (usually 41-44); L.l. pores 35-43; scales above L.l. 7 or 8; scales below L.l. 17-19; gill rakers 16-21 (usually 19).

Description.—Predorsal contour gibbous, a prominence at nape reminiscent of the genus *Heniochus;* gape horizontal to slightly oblique; teeth in 8-10 rows in each jaw; preopercle oblique; lachrymal smooth; supraorbital smooth to lightly serrate; eye diameter greater than caudal peduncle depth, which is greater than interorbital width; interorbital width greater than snout length.

Fifth dorsal spine longest; second anal spine equal to or larger than third, first about two-thirds second; base of spinous portion of dorsal fin longer (2.1-2.3 in S.L.) than that of soft portion (2.9-3.2 in S.L.); pelvic fins moderately long, reaching beyond anus possibly to first anal spine.

Lateral line flattened above; scales moderate, rounded, in horizontal series in lowest portion of body, ascending series in remainder of body; scales on spinous dorsal fin reaching halfway up sixth or seventh dorsal spines; anal scaly covering reaching to two-thirds or three-fourths of third spine.

Juveniles lack the prominent hump at nape.

Color Pattern.—Yellow streak on body separates black band from dark brownish black of body color (sometimes very obscure); blackish horseshoe-shaped mark on nape hump, faintly connected with body color; pectoral fins hyaline; pelvic fins brownish-black.

Juveniles differ from adults in several aspects of the color pattern. Body color similar to that of adult; large black ocellated spot in soft portion of dorsal fin at angle (7-16th rays); edges of dorsal and anal fins dark with lighter soft portions; light color surrounds spot and extends from front of spot down across posterior portion of body to near midpoint of anal fin base (this becomes the light bordering streak for the black posterior band); base of caudal peduncle yellowish with brown stripe across fin about ⅓ from its base; posterior two-thirds hyaline. Juveniles to about 35 mm S.L. have normal eyeband extending from nape, where it joins opposite member, to lower edge of interopercle; it is not as wide as eye, and its posterior margin coincides with posterior margin of eye. Dorsal and anal fins with hyaline edge and submarginal dark stripe; with growth, stripe moves to edge of fin. At 70 mm S.L. or thereabouts dorsal spot becomes lost in posterior black band and caudal fin band moves toward outer edge.

In some specimens light spots, one per scale, follow scale rows. Adult pattern evident, and only traces of dorsal spot remained in 52 mm S.L. specimen.

Remarks.—*Chaetodon flavirostris* is a rather distinctive species due in part to the peculiar hump at the nape end and its somber coloration. The hump reminds one of that common in the genus *Heniochus*.

Changes in color pattern with age caused problems in nomenclature. Goldman (1967) treated this species in some detail, relegating *Chaetodon aphrodite* to its synonymy. *Chaetodon dorsiocellatus* also appears to be this species.

Chaetodon flavirostris has a relatively restricted range, being known only from Melanesia and the east coast of Australia. It probably exists in New Guinea and is expected to be reported from there with further collecting.

Ogilby (1889) reported it to be found in pools at low water (juveniles) at Lord Howe Island. Goldman (1967) said it was found on the reef crest and in deeper water at the edge of the reef to about 10 fathoms. Young were recorded along the coast of New South Wales as far south as Woolongong (34°25'S) in moderately shallow water (to about 7 fathoms) in protected bays and inlets. He said the young possibly arrived in spring and survive the summer, dying off when the cool winter temperatures arrived. No adults were recorded from New South Wales (Goldman, 1967).

Distribution.—Mostly throughout Melanesia and the Great Barrier Reef of Australia to New South Wales. Norfolk and Lord Howe Islands, New Caledonia, New Hebrides, Cook Islands, Tonga Islands, and a questionable record from Samoa. Not yet reported from New Guinea, Northern Australia, East Indies, or the Philippines.

Chelmon rostratus in which the anterior portion of the dorsal fin and part of the body are missing. Photo by Rudie Kuiter, south Queensland.

Opposite:
Chaetodon ephippium with a notch behind the first dorsal spine. Photo by Dr. Shih-chieh Shen.

Chaetodon reticulatus with a similar deformity. Photo by Scott Johnson, Enewetak.

Material Examined.—(19 spec.: 35-125 mm S.L.) SOSC 397 (8: 54-125), One Tree Island, Queensland, Australia; SOSC (Choat Coll.) (5: 65-110), Heron Island, Queensland, Australia; USNM 1823-6 (2: 35-53), New Caledonia; CAS 37807 (1: 99), Cook Islands; BPBM 598 (1: 70), New Hebrides; WEB (2: 54-93), Heron Island, Queensland, Australia.

CHAETODON LUNULA (Lacepede)
Raccoon butterflyfish
(Red striped butterflyfish)

Pomacentrus lunula Lacepede 1803: pp. 507, 511, 513 (no locality; Commerson MS).

Chaetodon lunula, Cuvier, 1831: p. 59, pl. 173 (Isle de France; new combination).

Chaetodon biocellatus Cuvier, 1831: p. 62 (type locality Oualan). Lesson, 1830 (=1831): p. 176 (Oualan).

Chaetodon ocellatus (not of Bloch), Bleeker, 1854: p. 212 (Timor).

Chaetodon fasciatus (not of Forsskal), Kaup, 1860: p. 150. Gunther, 1860: p. 24 (China, Red Sea; part). Herre and Montalban, 1927: p. 52 (Philippine Islands). Okada and Ikeda, 1936: p. 259, pl. 14, fig. 2 (Miyako Islands). Abe, 1939: p. 547 (Palau).

Sarothrodus lunula, Bleeker, 1863: p. 156 (new combination).

Tetragonoptrus fasciatus (not of Forsskal), Bleeker, 1863: p. 234 (new combination).

Tetragonoptrus biocellatus, Bleeker, 1863: p. 269 (new combination).

Chaetodon lunulatus Jouan, 1873: p. 90 (type locality Hawaiian Islands).

Tetragonoptrus lunula, Bleeker, 1875: p. 95 (Madagascar; new combination).

Tetragonoptrus (Chaetodontops) fasciatus (not of Forsskal), Bleeker, 1877: p. 77 (various localities).

Chaetodon (Chaetodontops) lunula, Weber and de Beaufort, 1936: p. 83 (various localities).

Chaetodontops lunula, Fowler, 1946: p. 138 (Riu Kiu Islands; new combination).

Diagnosis.—D. XI-XIII (usually XII), 22-25 (usually 24); A. III, 17-19 (usually 18); pectoral rays 15 or 16; L.l. scales 35-44 (usually 37-43); two large black areas on upper anterior part of body, one along base of anterior dorsal spines, the other from gill cover above pectoral fin to about sixth and seventh dorsal spine bases; both dark areas bordered with light stripes; eyeband broadly continuous across interorbital area.

Chaetodon lunula (Lacepede). 120 mm S.L. Hawaiian Islands.

Ratios	Standard Length (mm) 20-49(8)	50-79(6)	above 79(20)
Depth/S.L..............	1.6-1.8	1.5-1.7	1.4-1.8
Head/S.L..............	2.2-2.8	2.3-3.0	2.9-3.5
Eye/Head.............	2.2-3.0	2.4-3.0	2.8-3.3
Snout/Head...........	2.9-4.1	2.8-3.4	2.4-3.2
Interorb. W./Head......	2.5-3.6	2.8-3.6	2.4-3.2
Maxillary/Head........	3.6-5.0	3.7-4.4	3.1-4.6
Caud. Ped./S.L........	7.6-9.8	7.8-9.3	8.0-9.6
Pect. Fin/S.L..........	3.1-3.7	3.1-3.5	3.3-4.0
Pelvic Sp./S.L.........	4.0-4.4	4.2-4.9	4.5-5.8
Predorsal L./S.L.......	1.8-2.0	2.0-2.2	2.1-2.5
Prepelvic L./S.L.......	2.0-2.3	2.1-2.4	2.3-2.7
Dorsal Sp. No. 1/S.L.....	8.0-12.1	8.2-11.3	8.8-13.1
Dorsal Sp. No. 2/S.L.....	5.0-7.4	6.2-7.6	7.0-11.5
Dorsal Sp. No. 3/S.L.....	3.9-5.6	4.2-5.4	5.5-9.2
Dorsal Sp. No. 4/S.L.....	3.6-4.3	3.8-5.2	5.0-7.1
Anal Sp. No. 1/S.L.......	6.1-8.2	5.8-7.5	6.7-10.0
Anal Sp. No. 2/S.L.......	4.4-7.1	4.0-5.8	4.3-6.3·
Anal Sp. No. 3/S.L.......	4.8-7.8	4.5-7.5	4.2-7.8

Possible hybrid of unknown origin. Most likely parents are *Chaetodon auriga* and *C. lunula.* Photo by Roger Steene, Australia.

Aberrant *Chaetodon rafflesi* or hybrid between that species and possibly *vagabundus.* Photo by Roger Steene, Australia.

Apparent hybrid between *Chaetodon ephippium* and its closest relative, *C. xanthocephalus.* Photo by Dr. D. Terver, Nancy Aquarium, France.

Series of specimens showing color pattern changes between juvenile and adult *Chaetodon lunula.*

Meristics.—D. XII (two with XI, one with XIII), 22-25 (mostly 24); A. III, 17-19 (mostly 18, one with 20); pectoral rays 15 or 16 (two with 15/16, one with 15/14); L.l. scales 35-44 (usually 37-43); pores in L.l. 31-41; scales above L.l. 7-9; scales below L.l. 14-18; gill rakers 17-19.

Description.—Predorsal contour relatively straight; gape slightly oblique; teeth in 5-7 rows in each jaw; preopercle oblique-angled; lachrymal smooth, supraorbital smooth to lightly serrate; depth of caudal peduncle greater than snout length, which is greater than interorbital width; interorbital width greater than eye diameter.

Fifth dorsal spine longest; second anal spine longer than third, first half to two-thirds of second; base of spinous portion of dorsal fin longer (2.4-2.5 in S.L.) than that of soft portion (2.8-2.9 in S.L.); pelvic fins moderate, extending to area between anus and first anal spine base.

Highest point of lateral line at about ninth dorsal spine base; scales moderate, rounded to flattened, in horizontal series in lowest portion of body and ascending series in upper portion; scales of spinous dorsal fin reaching midpoint at about sixth or seventh dorsal spines; scaly portion of anal fin reaching halfway to ⅔ up third spine.

Juveniles similar to adults.

Color Pattern.—Eyeband connected broadly across interorbital and lower portion of nape; black area at base of dorsal fin continuous around front of first spine; posterior black spot continuous across upper part of caudal peduncle.

Color pattern of juveniles quite different from that of adults. In small juveniles there is a conspicuous black spot in the soft dorsal fin. In addition there is a black band surrounding the caudal peduncle. A dark streak crosses the caudal fin near its base, enclosing between it and the peduncle bar a white band. Anterior to the caudal peduncle bar a light streak; dorsal fin spot ocellated with light ring; eyeband continuous across nape, bordered its whole length posteriorly by a broad white band from nape to isthmus; a dark, indefinite area posterior to this from the anterior dorsal spines to below the pectoral fin.

With growth the dorsal fin spot eventually disappears; a dark streak appears along the base of the fin anteriorly, bordered with a light color; the caudal streak moves outward until only one-third or less distance from the edge; the eye bar connection across the nape moves down until it is crossing mostly the interorbital region; the fins become more angular; and the dark shoulder marking becomes resolved into a triangular patch bordered with lighter. A separate dark area appears at the base of the anterior spines, also light bordered; the white broad band behind the eye bar remains as its posterior border and also becomes more distant from the anterior dorsal spines.

Remarks.—*Chaetodon lunula* is relatively common throughout its range and undergoes a very distinct color change with growth. These facts help to explain why the synonymy of this species is remarkably long. Its closest relative, *Chaetodon fasciatus* from the Red Sea, is another cause for confusion. The closeness of color pattern has prompted various workers to synonymize the two species.

Juvenile *Chaetodon lunula* appear in Hawaiian waters in fair numbers in late spring and early summer.

Distribution.—Widely distributed in the tropical Indo-Pacific from the Hawaiian Islands to the east coast of Africa; from southern Japan to northern Australia, and the Great Barrier Reef off Queensland.

Material Examined.—(34 spec.: 18-159 mm S.L.) HIMB (uncatalogued) (1: 76), Hawaiian Islands; HIMB (uncatalogued) (1: 148), Gilbert Islands; UH (2: 134-156), Christmas Island; UH (1: 107), Gilbert Islands; WEB (9: 22-134), Oahu, Hawaiian Islands; NMFA-H 1065 (3: 24-54), Rose Island; BPBM (uncatalogued) (1: 26), Tonga Islands; USNM 53534 (1: 18), Japan; NMFS-H TC-32, Sta. 4 (1: 20), Oahu, Hawaiian Islands; ANSP 108561 and 108366 (2: 91-149), Seychelles; SOSC HA 67-60, HA 67-61, HA 67-22, HA 67-65, HA 67-66, HA 67-75, and HA 67-35 (11: 74-159), Aldabra; SOSC HA 67-2 (1: 39), Chagas Archipelago.

Possible hybrids between *Chaetodon miliaris* and *C. multicinctus*. These are periodically taken in deep water off the Hawaiian Islands. Photo above by Dr. Warren E. Burgess; photo below by Aaron Norman.

Possible hybrid between *Chaetodon auriga* and *C. lunula.* Photo by Scott Johnson, Hawaii.

An apparently aberrant *Chaetodon multicinctus* or hybrid between *multicinctus* and some species like *quadrimaculatus.* Photo by James H. O'Neill, Hawaii.

CHAETODON FASCIATUS Forsskal
Red Sea raccoon butterflyfish

Chaetodon fasciatus Forsskal, 1775: pp XII, 59 (type locality
Djedda, Red Sea).
Chaetodon flavus Schneider, 1801: p. 225 (type locality Red
Sea). Ruppell, 1828: p. 40, pl. 9, fig. 1 (Red Sea).
Chaetodon fasciatus (part), Gunther, 1860: p. 24 (Red Sea,
China)).
Tetragonoptrus (*Chaetodontops*) *fasciatus* (part), Bleeker,
1877: p. 41 (various localities).

Chaetodon fasciatus Forsskal . 142 mm S.L. Eilat, Red Sea.

Diagnosis.—D. XII, 23 or 24 (one with 20); A. III, 18 (one with 17);
pectoral rays 15 (16); L.l. scales 34-41 (usually 37-40); one large blackish
marking, triangular in shape, below anterior dorsal fin spines; eyeband
only narrowly connected across nape; no dark spot or band on caudal
peduncle; body stripes more prominent.
Meristics.—D. XII, 23 or 24 (one with 20); A. III, 18 (one with 17);
pectoral rays 15 (two with 16/16, two with 15/16, one with 13/15, two

Ratios	Standard Length (mm)		
	20-49(1)	50-79(7)	above 79(9)
Depth/S.L.	1.6	1.6-1.7	1.7-1.8
Head/S.L.	2.8	2.7-3.0	2.9-3.3
Eye/Head	3.0	2.9-3.3	3.2-4.0
Snout/Head	2.8	2.6-3.0	2.5-2.8
Interorb. W./Head	3.2	3.3-3.8	2.9-3.7
Maxillary/Head	4.0	3.6-4.1	3.8-4.1
Caud. Ped./S.L.	9.1	8.8-9.6	8.9-9.8
Pect. Fin/S.L.	3.4	3.3-3.7	3.3-3.9
Pelvic Sp./S.L.	4.4	4.4-4.9	4.4-6.5
Predorsal L./S.L.	2.1	2.0-2.4	2.2-2.5
Prepelvic L./S.L.	2.3	2.2-2.5	2.1-2.6
Dorsal Sp. No. 1/S.L.	8.6	8.5-12.1	9.1-13.0
Dorsal Sp. No. 2/S.L.	6.2	6.4-8.1	7.5-12.9
Dorsal Sp. No. 3/S.L.	5.6	4.8-5.6	5.5-9.6
Dorsal Sp. No. 4/S.L.	4.0	4.0-4.8	4.8-8.1
Anal Sp. No. 1/S.L.	6.3	6.1-7.6	6.1-10.3
Anal Sp. No. 2/S.L.	4.3	3.8-4.8	4.3-6.2
Anal Sp. No. 3/S.L.	5.1	3.9-5.3	4.6-6.3

with 14/15); L.l. scales 34-41 (usually 37-40); L.l. pores 29-38 (usually 32-35); scales above L.l. 6-8; scales below L.l. 10-14; gill rakers 16-18 (mostly 17).

Description.—Predorsal contour straight to slightly concave; gape oblique; teeth in 8-11 rows in each jaw (usually 8 or 9 in upper jaw); preopercle obtuse-angled, edge smooth; lachrymal rounded, smooth; supraorbital smooth; snout length greater than caudal peduncle depth, which is greater than eye diameter; eye diameter greater than or equal to interorbital width.

Fifth or sixth dorsal spine longest; second anal spine equal to or longer than third, first slightly more than half second; base of spinous portion of dorsal fin longer (2.3-2.6 in S.L.) than that of soft portion (2.9-3.3 in S.L.); pelvic fins moderate, reaching past anus.

Lateral line flattened on top, ending near last rays of dorsal fin; scales large, exposed portions vertically elongate, in ascending rows corresponding to the stripes across body, rounded or with flattened edge; scaly portion of dorsal fin reaching midpoint of sixth dorsal spine, that of anal fin reaching midpoint of third anal spine.

Color Pattern.—Upper corner of dark triangular patch connected with opposite member across nape; posterior extension of triangle to about base of ninth dorsal fin spine; eyeband reduced to a patch on each side con-

Hybrid between *Chaetodon unimaculatus* and *C. kleinii*. This hybrid is the only one that has crossed subgeneric lines. Photo by Dr. Gerald R. Allen.

Hybrid between *Chaetodon ephippium* and possibly *C. auriga*. Photo by Roger Steene, Great Barrier Reef.

Chaetodon fasciatus 49 mm S.L. Djidda, Red Sea.

nected narrowly across upper interorbital area; snout dusky; vertical fin color extends partially onto edge of body; pelvic fins body color.

Juvenile color pattern differs from that of the adult. A specimen of 49 mm S.L. had a large dark ocellated spot at the angle of the soft dorsal fin; edges of dorsal and anal fins with hyaline margin and submarginal black and white stripes continuing around angle to edge of last rays; white stripe separates the spot in the dorsal fin from the black stripe; remainder of anal fin brown, remainder of dorsal fin merging into dark brown triangular spot which is proportionately larger, the anterior corner extending down past the upper corner of the opercle; a light streak extends from the light ring of the dorsal spot across the anterior end of the caudal peduncle to the base of the caudal fin; caudal peduncle brown, with another light streak forming the posterior border at the base of the caudal peduncle to the base of the anal fin; caudal peduncle brown, crossing middle of fin, and the outer half clear to light yellowish; pectoral fins hyaline; pelvic fins colored like body; head light brown with eyeband about as wide as eye but only including posterior two-thirds of it; eyeband is widest in the middle, narrowing above and below, above broadly joining with the one from the opposite side, below reaching to the lower edge of the interopercle, the portion on the interopercle much faded.

With age the spot disappears, the band on the caudal fin moves outward closer to the posterior edge, and the eyeband decreases slightly above and below.

Remarks.—*Chaetodon fasciatus* is another of those species which have been synonymized with *Chaetodon lunula* on the basis of the descriptions but have been considered a separate species by those who apparently had access to specimens. The color patterns are similar, but a comparison of the photographs will show that they can easily be separated. This confusion with *Chaetodon lunula* has caused the two names to be interchanged with one another. Those references referring to *Chaetodon fasciatus* outside of the Red Sea area undoubtedly belong to *Chaetodon lunula* and vice versa.

The figure of *Chaetodon flavus* by Ruppell leaves no doubt that it is *C. fasciatus*. He lists the species as *C. flavus* (Schneider), but under the synonymy he has *Chaetodon fasciatus* Forsskal.

According to Baschieri-Salvatore (1954), *Chaetodon fasciatus* is frequently caught in the northern and southern sectors of the Red Sea but is not abundant. Generally it was seen in pairs and rarely as single specimens or as groups. It did not appear to descend to the depths beyond the precipice of the barrier and was found at the lower parts of the coralline or upper limit of the barrier. According to Klunzinger (1870), it was common at the coral slope.

Distribution.—Reported only from the Red Sea (Gulf of Aqaba, Eylath, Sanifer Island).

Material Examined.—(17 spec.: 49-153 mm S.L.) CAS 37824 and 37880 (2: 143-153), Red Sea; USNM 166962 (6: 69-135), Ghardaqa, Red Sea; USNM 147509 (4: 71-100), Jidda, Red Sea; USNM 147511 (3: 49-79), Saudi Arabia, Red Sea; USNM (1: 67), Saudi Arabia, Red Sea; BPBM 10511 (1: 98), Red Sea.

Subgenus RABDOPHORUS Swainson

Rabdophorus Swainson, 1839: pp. 170, 211. (Type-species *Chaetodon ephippium* Cuvier, 1831, by monotypy.)

Linophora Kaup, 1860: pp. 137 and 155. (Type-species *Chaetodon auriga* Forsskal, 1775, by subsequent designation of Bleeker, 1876: p. 306.)

Oxychaetodon Bleeker, 1876: p. 306. (Type-species *Chaetodon lineolatus* Cuvier, 1831, by original designation).

Anisochaetodon Klunzinger, 1884: p. 54. (Type-species *Chaetodon auriga* Forsskal, 1775, by subsequent designation of Jordan, 1920: p. 429.)

Diagnosis.—Body oval; snout pointed, moderate, 1.9-2.8 in head length; dorsal and anal fins with blunt angles; lateral line in high angular arc; teeth in spaced rows in jaws; lachrymal not hidden by scales; eyeband variable, usually a wide black band, but sometimes absent; scales angular; juveniles sometimes undergo a change in color, usually loss of caudal peduncle band with age, rarely with dorsal fin spot; D. XII-XIV, 20-25; A. III, 19-22; pectoral fin rays 14-16 (usually 15); L.l. scales 22-41 (usually 33-39).

Description.—Body oval; snout moderate, 1.9-2.8 in head length, pointed; predorsal contour various, concave above snout; gape horizontal to oblique; teeth in spaced rows in each jaw; preopercle obtuse-angled; lachrymal slightly elongate, smooth; supraorbital smooth to lightly serrate.

Dorsal spines graduated, middle spines longest; dorsal fin continuous, no notch present; second anal spine longer than or equal to third, first about half to two-thirds of second; dorsal and anal fins various, with blunt angles, or anal rounded and dorsal angular or with one or more rays elongated into a filament; base of spinous portion of dorsal fin longer (2.1-2.7 in S.L.) than that of soft portion (2.7-3.8 in S.L.); pectoral fins normal; pelvic fins short to moderately long, in some species not reaching anus, in others reaching beyond it as far as to the base of the first anal fin spines; caudal fin truncate-rounded.

Lateral line rising in a high, angular arc across body, ending in vicinity of last rays of dorsal fin; scales usually large, angular, in slightly ascending rows crossing body, more horizontal near ventral portion; scaly covering of dorsal fin normal, midpoint of middle spines covered; scale covering of anal spines also normal, covering half to two-thirds of third anal fin spine.

Juveniles resemble adults in form, though dorsal and anal fins more rounded, without filaments, and differ in several species in color pattern. Juveniles in many cases possess a caudal peduncular band which is lost with age. Eyeband in some species becomes lost in adults or otherwise modified, but usually eyeband is broad and black from nape to isthmus.

Color patterns of adults various, no common pattern discernible.

Widely distributed in tropical areas of the Pacific and Indian Oceans, Red Sea and Hawaiian Islands included. Absent from the eastern Pacific region and Atlantic Ocean.

Sixteen species included in this subgenus, distinguished by the following key.

Key to the Species of the Subgenus Rabdophorus (Adults)

1. Eyeband absent or reduced to a short dark line above and below each
   eye 2
   Eyeband present, usually a broad dark band, especially above eye . . 4

2. Nape with prominent hump, leaving predorsal contour concave;
   mostly brown, each scale with dark spot (Persian Gulf, Gulf of
   Oman) . . . . *Chaetodon nigropunctatus*
   Predorsal contour straight to slightly convex at nape; mostly light
   colored; eyeband reduced to dark lines above and below eyes . . . 3

3. Dorsal fin with filament; large black saddle covering dorsal fin and
   adjacent part of body; XIII dorsal spines (Pacific and eastern
   Indian Oceans) . . . . *C. ephippium*
   Dorsal fin without filament; dorsal fin dark but without prominent
   saddle; XIV dorsal spines (Indian Ocean) . . . . . *C. xanthocephalus*

579

4. Dorsal fin with one or more rays elongated into a filament 5
   Dorsal fin without filament 6
5. Body with slanting lines, about five in upper anterior portion of body, seven or eight extending from last line at right angle toward anal fin; dorsal fin with XIII spines (Indo-Pacific) .....*C. auriga*
   Body with slightly inclined rows of dots, one per scale; dorsal fin with XIV spines (Pacific) ....*C. semeion*
6. Body with thin vertical lines, usually 12 or more, extending from scaly sheath of dorsal to near ventral margin of fish 7
   Body without 12 or more thin vertical lines 11
7. Large black marking along base of soft dorsal fin, extending across caudal peduncle; no abrupt change of color either anteriorly or posteriorly 8
   No large black marking along base of soft dorsal fin; an abrupt change of color either anteriorly (to gray) or posteriorly (to yellow) 9
8. Large black mark along base of dorsal fin extends well into anal fin base; eyeband connected across nape, leaving light spot enclosed within it; D. XII, 25-27; A. III, 20-22; pect. 16 (Indo-Pacific)....
   ....*C. lineolatus*
   Large black mark along soft dorsal base stops at lower edge of caudal peduncle or only slightly indicated into anal fin; separate horse-shoe-shaped mark on nape, separated from eyeband by narrow band of body color; D. XII, 23-24; A. III, 19; pect. 15 (western Pacific and eastern Indian Oceans) ....*C. oxycephalus*
9. Anterior portion of fish abruptly gray, separated from posterior lined portion by narrow white line; no black markings extending down from dorsal edge; XII dorsal spines (Red Sea) .....*C. mesoleucos*
   Posterior portion of fish abruptly yellow; large black markings extending down from dorsal surface; caudal peduncle with black marking; XII dorsal spines 10
10. Large black markings extending to midpoint of body or beyond, broad; caudal peduncle marking a spot on either side, connected either above or below, usually not both; A. III, 19; snout length 2.2-2.5 in head (Pacific Ocean)..................*C. ulietensis*
    Large black markings smaller than above, not usually reaching mid-point of body; caudal peduncle with a black band; A. III, 20-21; snout length 1.9-2.2 in head (Indian Ocean).........*C. falcula*
11. Black band crossing caudal fin; body pattern either narrow lines slanting upward in upper anterior part of body and slanting toward anal fin and at right angles to the others at lower posterior part of body, or a crosshatched pattern, each scale outlined with orange 12
    No black band crossing caudal fin (though some lighter pattern may

exist); body pattern usually ascending lines or rows of dots, or
horizontal lines in lower portion of body 14

12. Caudal peduncle colored like body; body with crosshatched pattern;
D. XII, 22-23; dorsal fin with broad dark submarginal band past
angle (Pacific and northeastern Indian Oceans) . . . .*C. rafflesi*
Caudal peduncle with black color; body with slanting line pattern;
D. XII, 24-25; dorsal fin solid black or, if not black, without black
band broader past angle 13

13. Dorsal and anal fins, caudal peduncle, and adjacent part of body
black; yellow streak in anal fin (Indian Ocean) . . . .*C. decussatus*
Dorsal and anal fins not entirely black; a broad black band crossing
soft dorsal fin and caudal peduncle and ending in midbase of anal
fin (Indo-Pacific). . . . .*C. vagabundus*

14. Semilunar crescent-shaped black marking along base of dorsal fin,
crossing caudal peduncle, and ending along base of anal fin at
about its middle; ascending spotted lines in upper anterior portion
of body (Western Pacific) . . . .*C. selene*
Dorsal fin entirely dark, or with obscure black area along base of
dorsal fin, caudal peduncle, and anterior portion of anal fin base;
last rays of dorsal fin entirely black. .15

15. Dorsal fin entirely blackish (Gulfs of Aden, Oman, and Mannar) . . . .
. . . .*C. gardneri*
Only last rays of dorsal fin entirely black; base of other rays black
(Eastern Africa and Red Sea) . . . .*C. leucopleura*

Remarks.—Since not all juveniles were available, a key to the juveniles
is not possible. A photograph of the known younger stage for each species
is included wherever possible.

The scale size and shape as well as aspects of the color pattern remind
one of the subgenus *Rhombochaetodon*, for example *C. auriga* with the
posterior yellow coloration, diagonal lines forming chevrons posteriorly,
and the eyeband fading above the eye, almost, but not quite, leaving a
black nape spot.

CHAETODON AURIGA Forsskal
Threadfin butterflyfish
(Whip butterflyfish)

Chaetodon auriga Forsskal, 1775: pp. XII, 60 (type locality
Djedda, Red Sea).

Chaetodon setifer Bloch, 1793: p. 100, pl. 426, fig. 1 (locality not known, Coromandel according to checklist of
McCulloch, 1929).

Pomacentrus filamentosus Lacepede, 1802: pp. 506, 511,
and 572.

Pomacentrus setifer Lacepede, 1802: pp. 506, 511, and 512.
Chaetodon sebanus Cuvier, 1831: p. 74 (type localities Timor, Tongatabu, Isle de France, Oualan, Guam).
?*Chaetodon lunaris* Gray, 1854: p. 70.
Linophora auriga, Kaup, 1860: p. 156 (new combination).
Sarothrodus auriga, Bleeker, 1863: p. 144 (new combination).
Tetragonoptrus auriga, Bleeker, 1863: p. 234 (Ternate; new combination).
Tetragonoptrus setifer, Bleeker, 1868: p. 287.
Chaetodon auriga var. *setifer*, Day, 1875: p. 106, pl. 27, fig. 3 (India).
Tetragonoptrus (Linophora) auriga, Bleeker, 1877: p. 92.
Chaetodon (Anisochaetodon) auriga, Klunzinger, 1884: p. 56 (Red Sea).
Chaetodon satifer, Seale, 1901: p. 58 (Guam; misspelling of *setifer*).
Chaetodon auriga setifer, Ahl, 1923: p. 147.
Anisochaetodon (Linophora) auriga, Weber & de Beaufort, 1936: p. 103 (various localities).
Chaetodon (Linophora) auriga, Fowler, 1953: p. 42 (China, Taiwan, Riu Kiu, Tsingtau, Nafa, Yaeyama, Okinawa).

Chaetodon auriga Forsskal. 105 mm S.L. Red Sea.

Ratios	Standard Length (mm)		
	20-49(3)	41-70(4)	above 70(43)
Depth/S.L.	1.6-1.7	1.5-1.7	1.5-1.8
Head/S.L.	2.4-2.7	2.7-2.8	2.8-3.3
Eye/Head	2.7-2.8	2.9-3.3	3.0-3.9
Snout/Head	2.8-2.9	2.5-2.7	2.2-2.9
Interorb. W./Head	3.4-3.8	3.3-3.4	3.0-3.8
Maxillary/Head	3.8-4.5	3.6-3.8	3.1-4.4
Caud. Ped./S.L.	8.3-9.2	8.4-9.2	8.6-9.5
Pect. Fin/S.L.	3.1-3.4	3.3-3.6	3.3-4.0
Pelvic Sp./S.L.	3.7-4.1	4.3-4.6	4.4-6.2
Predorsal L./S.L.	1.9-2.0	2.0-2.1	2.0-2.5
Prepelvic L./S.L.	2.1-2.2	2.2-2.4	2.2-2.6
Dorsal Sp. No. 1/S.L.	10.6-11.8	8.6-13.4	9.9-14.5
Dorsal Sp. No. 2/S.L.	5.9-7.1	7.5-9.6	8.3-14.3
Dorsal Sp. No. 3/S.L.	4.1-4.6	5.5-7.4	6.0-10.4
Dorsal Sp. No. 4/S.L.	3.5-3.7	4.5-6.1	4.6-8.6
Anal Sp. No. 1/S.L.	7.0-7.8	7.2-8.2	7.7-12.3
Anal Sp. No. 2/S.L.	4.3-4.9	4.5-5.3	4.5-7.1
Anal Sp. No. 3/S.L.	4.1-4.7	4.0-5.2	4.3-7.4

Diagnosis.—D. XIII (two with XII), 22-25 (mostly 23); A. III, 19-21; pectoral rays (14) 15; L.l. scales 33-43 (usually 34-40); one or more dorsal rays extended into a filament; slanting gray stripes meeting at right angles on side of body with other slanting gray stripes.

Meristics.—D. XIII (two with XII), 22-25 (mostly 23); A. III, 19-21; pectoral rays 15 (four with 14/14, two with 16/16, four with 14/15, one with 14/16); L.l. scales 33-43 (usually 34-40); L.l. pores 29-40 (usually 30-37); scales above L.l. 5 or 6; scales below L.l. 13-17 (usually 14-16); gill rakers 16-20.

Description.—Predorsal contour approximately straight, concave above nostrils; snout moderate, 2.2-2.9 in head length, pointed; gape horizontal, teeth in about 7 rows in upper jaw and about 9-11 rows in lower jaw; teeth in jaws typical, those in lower jaw long, slender, curved mostly at their tips; an additional five rows are present along sides of jaw, the rows decreasing in width posteriorly; anterior rows in lower jaw longest, those along the side of the jaw gradually shorter posteriorly; upper jaw with evenly curved teeth, outer two rows long, succeeding rows much shorter, additional teeth on side of jaws very short; preopercle obtuse-angled, smooth to lightly serrate; lachrymal and supraorbital smooth; snout length greater than depth of caudal peduncle, which is greater than eye diameter and interorbital width, which are equal.

Fifth dorsal spine longest, succeeding spines about equal; second and third anal spines equal in length, first just more than half second; soft

Three specimens of *Chaetodon auriga* from the Red Sea, one without a dorsal fin spot, one with, and one intermediate between the other two.

dorsal filament composed of fifth and sixth rays, either one being longest (in one specimen the fourth was longest, and this ray sometimes, but not often, is included in the filament); filament usually extends beyond caudal fin; angle of anal fin at about twelfth or thirteenth ray; base of spinous portion of dorsal fin longer (2.3-2.6 in S.L.) than that of soft portion (2.9-3.1 in S.L.); pelvic fins short, the longest ray barely reaching anus.

Lateral line peak at about level of ninth dorsal spine base; scales large, angular, arranged in ascending rows almost in chevron pattern; scaly portion of dorsal fin reaching midpoint of fifth or sixth dorsal fin spine; anal scales to one-half to two-thirds of third spine.

Gas bladder with "horns" extending anteriorly.

Juveniles with differences in form; the dorsal fin filament is conspicuously absent in juvenile specimens. The filament is variable in length in adults (a 133 mm S.L. specimen had one 23 mm long, a specimen of 98 mm S.L. had one over 40 mm long) and makes its first appearance in specimens over 50 mm S.L., starting as a small spike and gradually increasing with the age of the fish. The pelvic fin is proportionately longer in small specimens, the longest ray reaching base of anal fin spines. Other proportional changes are incorporated into the table of measurements.

Color Pattern.—About five lines are present in the upper anterior part of the body, eight to ten in the lower posterior part; these lines become more diffuse distally; posteriorly the chevron-shaped markings are variable as to number and completeness; pelvic fins dusky to body colored; eyeband fades somewhat above eye, dark on nape, narrowly joined to one opposite (sometimes lateral connection is weak or absent); face dusky; a large black spot sometimes present (usually in all but Red Sea specimens) in soft dorsal fin near angle; spot variable from very large to absent with all gradations in between; when present it usually extends from 6-11 soft dorsal fin rays, separated from the edge of the fin by a narrow yellow stripe (in specimens without the spot this stripe is still present); in both types of specimens this stripe forms the lower edge of the dorsal filament.

Juveniles similar to adults, black spot when present is present throughout life.

Remarks.—The original description of Chaetodon auriga was of specimens from the Red Sea (Forsskal, 1775). In the Red Sea, Chaetodon auriga normally occurs without the dorsal fin spot. When specimens from other parts of the range of C. auriga were discovered with a dorsal fin spot, they were considered a new species and described under the name C. setifer. Although various authors chose one or the other of the two names and Ahl (1923) called setifer a subspecies of auriga, most modern authors have accepted C. auriga as the name and refer to the spotless specimens as a simple color variety. In a collection from the Red Sea I have observed specimens without the spot in the dorsal fin as well as others which had a spot and still others which were intermediate. Also, there appeared to be some specimens from Kaneohe Bay, Hawaiian

Islands which lacked the spot. The late Dr. Herald of the Steinhart Aquarium sent a color slide of a spotless *C. auriga* that he received in a shipment of fishes from the Hawaiian Islands from Mr. Lester Zukeran. Mr. Zukeran, of the Hawaii Institute of Marine Biology, reported that other references to these spotless *Chaetodon auriga* were made from reliable sources, also referring to Kaneohe Bay specimens. Close inspection of hundreds of Kaneohe Bay specimens of *C. auriga* revealed no further fishes which lacked the spot.

Chaetodon sebanus Cuvier is simply a juvenile form which lacks the dorsal filament.

Baschieri-Salvatore (1954) reports that *C. auriga* was not found in the southern sector of the Red Sea and only rarely in the northern sector. Klunzinger (1870), however, had stated that it was common on the coral slopes in the Red Sea. Harry (1953) reported it as the most abundant species of butterflyfish at Raroia, occurring in great numbers on the lagoon coral heads, shore reefs, and outer reef flats. I have found it to be common in the Hawaiian Islands and present in fair numbers in the Marshall Islands, Johnston Island, and the Philippine Islands.

Baschieri-Salvatore (1954) found isolated individuals, rarely in pairs, frequenting the lower parts of coral formations to the upper limit of the barrier. DeWitt (MS) found it in pairs at Palau, although groups of three or four were not uncommon. I have seen individuals, pairs, and small schools of 15 or more individuals in the Hawaiian Islands and Johnston Island. Although also found on the reefs, *C. auriga* was found at Johnston Island in sandy areas where coral heads and rocks were infrequent.

Weber (1913) referred to a 23 mm specimen which still retained the tholichthys plates. I have seen such small individuals, still with tholichthys plates, which have been collected night-lighting; this seems to be the size at which the color metamorphosis and settling take place.

Distribution.—Widespread throughout the tropical Indo-Pacific from the Hawaiian Islands to the Red Sea, and southern Japan to the Great Barrier Reef of Australia (possibly as far south as Sydney).

Material Examined.—(50 spec.: 32-143 mm S.L.) USNM 147508 (6: 95-120), five miles from Djidda, Red Sea; SOSC HA 67-2, HA 67-11, HA 67-16, HA 67-17 (14: 50-133), Chagas Archipelago, Indian Ocean; SOSC HA 67-59, HA 67-69 (11: 84-135), Aldabra Atoll, Indian Ocean; SOSC Cr. 9 RS-40 FT-19 (1: 112), Amirante Islands, Indian Ocean; SOSC Cr. 7 Sta. 295 (1: 122), Fiji Islands; ANSP 97480 (1: 60), East Africa; ANSP 108356 (1: 103), Seychelles Islands, Indian Ocean; AMS IB 8166 (3: 31-98), Heron Island, Queensland, Australia; UH (1: 109), Christmas Island, Pacific Ocean; HIMB (uncatalogued) (2: 85-143), Gilbert Islands; WEB (6: 32-131), Hawaiian Islands; WEB (3: 131-141), Johnston Atoll, Pacific Ocean.

CHAETODON VAGABUNDUS Linnaeus
Vagabond butterflyfish
(Crisscross butterflyfish)

Chaetodon vagabundus Linnaeus. 126 mm S.L. Aldabra, Indian Ocean.

Chaetodon vagabundus Linnaeus, 1758: p. 276 (type locality "Indiis").

Chaetodon pictus Forsskal, 1775: p. 65 (type locality Mokka). Schneider, 1801: p. 226. Cuvier, 1831: p. 55 (on Forsskal, 1775; Mokka).

Chaetodon nesogallicus Cuvier, 1831: p. 63 (type locality Isle de France).

Sarothrodus vagabundus, Bleeker, 1863: p. 152 (new combination).

Tetragonoptrus nesogallicus, Bleeker, 1863: p. 234 (new combination).

Tetragonoptrus vagabundus, Bleeker, 1863: p. 234 (new combination).

Tetragonoptrus (Linophora) vagabundus, Bleeker, 1877: p. 48 (various localities).

??*Chaetodon vagabundus* var. *pictus*, Ahl, 1923: p. 154.
Chaetodon setifer var. *hawaiiensis* (not *setifer* of Bleeker) Borodin, 1930: p. 55, pl. 1, fig. 2 (Hawaiian Islands).
Anisochaetodon (Linophora) vagabundus, Weber & de Beaufort, 1936: p. 107 (various localities).
Linophora vagabunda, Fowler, 1946: p. 147 (Riu Kiu Islands; new combination).
Anisochaetodon (Linophora) vagabundus pictus, Fraser-Brunner, 1949: pp. 43-48, 2 pls., 1 text fig.
Anisochaetodon vagabundus, Marshall, 1950: pp. 166-205 (Cocos-Keeling Islands).
Chaetodon (Linophora) vagabundus, Fowler, 1953: p. 40 (China, Soowan, Nan Wan, Takao, Taiwan, Yaeyama, Amami Oshima, Formosa, Aguni Shima, Riu Kiu).

Diagnosis.—D. XIII, 23-25 (one with 22); A. III (one with II), 19-22 (usually 19-20); pectoral rays 15 (16); L.l. scales 34-40; six diagonal lines running from head to spinous dorsal fin, 11 or 12 running at right angles from the last of these to the anal fin and caudal peduncle; a black band originates in spinous dorsal fin, crosses that fin and soft portion to caudal peduncle, extending into anal fin (entire dorsal, anal, and base of caudal fins not black).

Ratios	Standard Length (mm)		
	20-59(4)	60-89(7)	above 89(9)
Depth/S.L.	1.5-1.6	1.5-1.7	1.5-1.7
Head/S.L.	2.6-3.0	3.0-3.3	3.0-3.4
Eye/Head	2.7-3.3	2.9-3.3	3.0-3.5
Snout/Head	2.7-2.9	2.7-3.0	2.5-3.2
Interorb. W./Head	3.4-3.7	3.2-3.6	2.9-3.4
Maxillary/Head	3.9-4.1	3.4-4.2	3.7-5.1
Caud. Ped./S.L.	8.6-9.2	8.7-9.7	9.0-9.8
Pect. Fin/S.L.	2.9-3.6	3.2-3.6	3.5-3.7
Pelvic Sp./S.L.	4.3-4.9	4.7-5.4	5.0-5.9
Predorsal L./S.L.	2.1-2.2	2.1-2.3	2.2-2.4
Prepelvic L./S.L.	2.2-2.4	2.4-2.6	2.5-2.8
Dorsal Sp. No. 1/S.L.	8.4-10.6	8.9-11.1	9.7-12.6
Dorsal Sp. No. 2/S.L.	6.0-7.4	6.8-10.4	8.2-12.2
Dorsal Sp. No. 3/S.L.	3.6-5.2	5.0-6.7	5.8-9.1
Dorsal Sp. No. 4/S.L.	3.2-4.3	4.3-5.4	4.5-7.8
Anal Sp. No. 1/S.L.	6.6-7.5	7.1-8.4	8.2-9.9
Anal Sp. No. 2/S.L.	4.1-4.5	4.2-5.5	4.6-6.1
Anal Sp. No. 3/S.L.	4.0-4.4	4.0-5.7	4.6-6.5

Meristics.—D. XIII, 23-25 (one with 22 rays); A. III, (one with II), 19-20 (one with 21, another with 22 rays); pectoral rays 15 (two with 16/16, two with 14/15); L.l. scales 34-40; L.l. pores 30-37; scales above L.l. 4-6 (usually 5); scales below L.l. 13-18; gill rakers 15-18.

Description.—Snout moderate to short, 2.5-3.2 in head, pointed; predorsal contour straight, concave above snout; gape oblique; teeth in 7-9 rows in each jaw; preopercle obtuse-angled, edge crenulate; lachrymal smooth; snout greater than caudal peduncle, which is greater than eye diameter; eye diameter greater than interorbital width.

Sixth dorsal spine longest; second and third anal spines about equal, first about two-thirds of second; dorsal and anal fins with blunt angles; spinous portion of dorsal fin longer (2.4-2.7 in S.L.) than soft portion (2.7-3.1 in S.L.); pelvic fins moderate, reaching to or beyond anus.

Lateral line flattened on top; scales moderate, angular to rhomboid, in descending rows from upper edge of opercle to anal base or ascending above lateral line (approaching chevron pattern); scale covering of dorsal fin spines reaching midpoint of fifth spine, that of anal spines covering about three-fourths of the third spine.

Juveniles similar to adult in form.

Color Pattern.—Eyebands broadly joined at nape, slightly faded between nape and eye; eyeband with light edge; pelvic fins body color; face dusky.

Two different color forms have been observed, one widespread throughout the tropical Indo-Pacific, the other restricted to the area of southern Arabia. They possibly constitute subspecies, that of the Arabian waters being *Chaetodon vagabundus pictus*. The *pictus* pattern has the ends of the dorsal spines entirely black, the bordering blackish band of the soft dorsal fin with a light center, the band crossing caudal peduncle broader as it enters the anal fin, a different caudal fin pattern, a broader eyeband below the eye, the middle dorsal soft rays longer (producing a broader yellow area in the fin), and the submarginal black bands of dorsal and anal fins closer to the edge.

Color pattern of juveniles is somewhat different from that of adults. Eyeband and body stripes similar. The posterior body band indistinct, extending from last spines of dorsal fin across space in front of caudal peduncle and into anal fin; rest of anal fin dusky, edge hyaline; edge of dorsal fin hyaline with submarginal dark brown line, rest of fin light yellowish; large black spot in soft dorsal fin juxtaposed to submarginal line; caudal fin mostly hyaline, a faint line crossing base (specimens of 27-39 mm S.L.).

A 55 mm S.L. individual had the black dorsal fin spot almost completely absorbed into the band, the band in both dorsal and anal fins still extending around angle of fin; caudal fin half hyaline, rest of color pattern near base, moving out.

Remarks.—Fraser-Brunner (1949) was correct in assuming the species described by Forsskal (1775) as *Chaetodon pictus* was the subspecies of

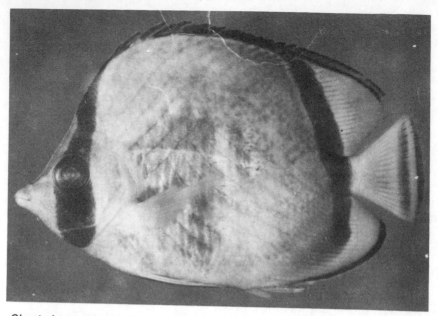

Chaetodon vagabundus pictus. 86 mm S.L. Gold Mohur Bay, Aden.

C. vagabundus and not the following species (*C. decussatus*). Forsskal's description is not good but he does refer to a stripe or fascia and omits any mention of the extensive black region of *C. decussatus* with which his species has been confused. His reference to spines in front of dorsal black could refer to the dorsal spines themselves. In addition the type locality is not within the known present range of *C. decussatus* but coincides exactly with the collections of *C. vagabundus pictus*.

Although Borodin's description of *Chaetodon setifer* var. *hawaiiensis* (1930) is rather confused and nondiagnostic the figure provided leaves no doubt that it is *C. vagabundus*. Whether this constitutes a new Hawaiian record for *C. vagabundus*, a mislabelled specimen, or a stray cannot be determined.

Distribution.—Widespread throughout the Indo-Pacific (possibly also the Hawaiian Islands—see remarks above) possibly including the Red Sea proper. Subspecies *pictus* restricted to southern Arabia.

Material Examined.—(20 spec.: 37-121 mm S.L.) SOSC TV-236 (2: 37-74), Rabaul, New Britain; SOSC (1: 56), "off Fort Washington", Indian Ocean?; WEB (1: 84), Tonga Islands; BPBM 5181 (1: 100), Savai, Samoa; WEB (1: 105), Tahiti; BPBM 5878 (1: 111), Tahiti; ANSP 77872 (1: 78), Natal; SOSC HA 67-55 (1: 121), Aldabra; SOSC 103 (1: 81), Mentawei Islands; SOSC Te Vega 259 (1: 103), Vanikoro; SOSC Te Vega-247 (3: 92-104), Solomon Islands; SOSC VGS 68-2 (1: 59), Taiwan; SOSC VGS 68-19, 68-3, and 68-6 (3: 41-110), Taiwan.

Subspecies *pictus*: SOSC FT-26 (2: 80-85), Gold Mohur Bay, Aden.

CHAETODON DECUSSATUS Cuvier
Black-finned vagabond

Chaetodon decussatus Cuvier, 1831: p. 54 (type locality Pondichery).

Chaetodon vagabundus (not of Linnaeus) Bennett, 1851: page numbers absent, fig. #6 (Ceylon).

Chaetodon pictus (not of Forsskal), Bleeker, 1852: p. 177 (Sumatra). Gunther, 1860: p. 24 (Madras). Kaup, 1860: p. 154. Day, 1878-1888: p. 105, pl. 26, fig. 6 (India). Ahl, 1923: p. 182, Addenda (Ceylon).

Chaetodon decussatus, Kner, 1865: p. 101.

?*Chaetodon vagabundus* (not of Linnaeus), Day, 1889: p. 4 (India).

Chaetodon vagabundus var. *jordani* Ahl, 1923: p. 181 (Ceylon).

Anisochaetodon (*Linophora*) *pictus* (not of Linnaeus), Klausewitz, 1957: p. 1, fig. 1, pl. 1.

Chaetodon decussatus Cuvier. 120 mm S.L. Sri Lanka.

Diagnosis.—D. XIII, 24-25; A. III, 20-21; pectoral rays (14) 15; L.l. scales 36-41; about six diagonal lines extending from upper posterior part.

Ratios	Standard Length (mm)		
	20-59(7)	60-89(5)	above 89(2)
Depth/S.L.............	1.4-1.6	1.5-1.7	1.5-1.6
Head/S.L..............	2.6-2.9	2.8-3.2	3.3-3.7
Eye/Head	2.5-3.0	2.5-3.0	2.9-3.0
Snout/Head	2.9-3.7	3.0-3.8	3.0-4.1
Interorb. W./Head......	3.1-3.7	3.0-3.5	2.8-3.0
Maxillary/Head	3.2-4.6	3.7-4.6	4.3
Caud. Ped./S.L.........	7.7-8.8	8.1-9.1	8.7-9.2
Pect. Fin/S.L...........	3.0-3.4	3.3-4.3	3.2-3.8
Pelvic Sp./S.L..........	4.2-4.6	4.6-5.4	5.3-5.8
Predorsal L./S.L........	1.9-2.1	2.1-2.2	2.2-2.5
Prepelvic L./S.L........	2.2-2.4	2.2-2.5	2.6, 2.6
Dorsal Sp. No. 1/S.L.....	8.8-13.9	9.9-12.6	10.4-12.6
Dorsal Sp. No. 2/S.L.....	5.3-8.3	6.4-7.9	8.6-10.4
Dorsal Sp. No. 3/S.L.....	3.8-5.3	4.9-6.1	6.3-6.9
Dorsal Sp. No. 4/S.L.....	3.6-4.8	4.2-5.3	4.9-6.3
Anal Sp. No. 1/S.L......	5.8-7.2	6.2-7.8	7.1-8.7
Anal Sp. No. 2/S.L......	4.2-4.8	4.3-4.8	4.7-5.5
Anal Sp. No. 3/S.L......	4.0-5.0	4.1-5.4	4.7-6.3

of head to base of dorsal spines; 11 or 12 similar lines extending at right angles from last of previous lines toward anal fin; dorsal and anal fins, caudal peduncle, and adjacent areas black, with yellow stripe through anal fin. Its closest relative, C. vagabundus, has a black band posteriorly, not completely black fins as in this species.

Meristics.—D. XIII, 24-25; A. III, 20-21; pectoral fin 15 (one with 14/14, one with 14/15); L.l. scales 36-41; L.l. pores 33-40; scales above L.l. 6 (occasionally 5); scales below L.l. 17-18; gill rakers 17-20.

Description.—Snout moderate to short, 3.0-4.1 in head length; gape oblique, teeth in 8-10 rows in each jaw; predorsal contour approximately straight, a slight convexity at nape and a slight concavity at level of nostrils; preopercle obtuse-angled, edge serrate; lachrymal smooth; caudal peduncle depth greater than eye diameter, which is greater than interorbital width; interorbital width greater than snout length.

Fifth or sixth dorsal spine longest; second and third anal spines equal, first about half second; dorsal and anal fins with blunt angle; base of spinous portion of dorsal fin longer (2.2-2.4 in S.L.) than that of soft portion (2.8-3.2 in S.L.); pelvic fins moderate, longest ray extending past anus but not as far as first anal spine base.

Lateral line describing high arc, flattened on top from eighth or ninth dorsal spine base to first few dorsal rays; scales moderate, angular to rhomboidal, in descending rows from upper anterior portion of body (lower half of chevron pattern), ascending above lateral line; scale covering of dorsal spines reaching midpoint of sixth spine, that of anal spines reaching beyond midpoint of third.

Juveniles similar to adults.

Color Pattern.—Ascending lines about five or six in number, descending lines about 10-12; eyeband connected at nape; upper lip and adjacent part of snout dusky; tips of dorsal spines white, anal spines gray; pelvic fins body color.

Juveniles similar in color pattern but with some distinctions. Dorsal and anal fins with hyaline edges; posterior portion of body dark, but bases of dorsal and anal fins with darker blotches; caudal fin mostly hyaline, base pale.

Juveniles white with yellowish cast; base of caudal fin, posterior edge of anal fin, and edge of last dorsal fin rays orange-yellow; remainder of caudal fin hyaline; rest of dorsal fin edge hyaline.

Remarks.—There has been a great deal of confusion surrounding this species and the subspecies of *Chaetodon vagabundus* (*C. vagabundus pictus*) from the area of southern Arabia. Forsskal's description of *Chaetodon pictus* states "P.D. nigra ante radios spinosas." This has been interpreted as (1) dorsal fin black after spinous rays, which would indicate the *decussatus*-form, and as (2) anterior dorsal spines black, which is the case in the *pictus* subspecies. Klausewitz (1957) ascribed to the former definition, whereas Fraser-Brunner (1949) interpreted it as the latter. I agree

Chaetodon decussatus in an aquarium. This species is closely related to *C. vagabundus.* Photo by Klaus Paysan.

with Fraser-Brunner since the dark posterior portion of the body including the caudal peduncle and anal fin are so striking I cannot see why Forsskal would not have mentioned a black anal fin rather than just a black dorsal fin in his description. In addition, the type locality of Forsskal's *pictus* is identical with that of the subspecies of *vagabundus*. I therefore am calling the posteriorly dark form *Chaetodon decussatus*, the next available name for this species, and the *pictus* of Forsskal a subspecies of *C. vagabundus*.

Klunzinger (1870) adds *Chaetodon pictus* to the Red Sea fauna, but his description appears to be a composite of Forsskal's description and that of other authors of the *decussatus* form. I do not believe he had specimens to refer to and based his description on previous lists and descriptions.

Distribution.—India, Sri Lanka, and Andaman Islands to the East Indies, at least as far as Singapore and Thailand.

Material Examined.—(14 spec.: 29-120 mm S.L.) AMNH 14792 (1: 35), Bali; AMNH 14821 (3: 63-84), Singapore; USNM 197604 (2: 56-67), coast of Sri Lanka; SOSC PCH 69-256 (1: 120), Colombo, Sri Lanka; SOSC #4 Anton Bruun Cr. #1 (1: 95), Patong Bay, Thailand; SOSC SV 69-120 (1: 35), Sri Lanka; SOSC SV 69-121 (3: 29-60), Sri Lanka; SOSC SV 69-119 (2: 37-50), Sri Lanka.

CHAETODON RAFFLESI Bennett
Raffles butterflyfish
(Latticed butterflyfish)

Chaetodon Rafflesi Bennett, 1830: p. 689 (type locality Sumatra).

Chaetodon princeps Cuvier, 1831: p. 33 (type locality New Ireland).

Chaetodon Sebae Cuvier, 1831: p. 52 (type locality Nouvelle Guinee).

Sarothrodus princeps, Bleeker, 1863: p. 156 (new combination).

Tetragonoptrus Rafflesi, Bleeker, 1863: p. 234 (Ternate; new locality).

Chaetodon dahli Ahl, 1923: p. 143, pl. 1, fig. 3 (Ralum, Bismark Arch.).

Anisochaetodon (Linophora) rafflesi, Weber & de Beaufort, 1936: p. 109 (various localities, new combination). Marshall, 1950: pp. 166-205 (Cocos-Keeling Islands).

Diagnosis.—D. XII-XIII (usually XIII), 21-23; A. III, 18-20; pectoral rays (14) 15; L.l. scales 30-37 (usually 33-35); each scale outlined by darker color, producing crosshatched pattern; dark submarginal stripe of dorsal fin continuing as broad band around angle of fin.

Chaetodon rafflesi Bennett. 92 mm S.L. Vanikolo Island, Solomons.

		Standard Length (mm)	
Ratios	**20-49**	**50-89(2)**	**above 89(15)**
Depth/S.L..............	---	1.6-1.7	1.4-1.8
Head/S.L..............	---	2.9-3.0	2.9-3.2
Eye/Head	---	3.1-3.5	3.3-3.6
Snout/Head	---	2.5-2.6	2.3-3.0
Interorb. W./Head......	---	3.5	3.1-3.6
Maxillary/Head	---	3.9-4.2	3.7-5.2
Caud. Ped./S.L.........	---	9.1-9.7	8.7-10.0
Pect. Fin/S.L...........	---	3.6-3.8	3.4-4.9
Pelvic Sp./S.L..........	---	4.7-4.9	4.5-6.1
Predorsal L./S.L........	---	2.1-2.2	2.3-2.5
Prepelvic L./S.L........	---	2.4-2.5	2.3-2.6
Dorsal Sp. No. 1/S.L.....	---	9.3-11.9	8.8-13.4
Dorsal Sp. No. 2/S.L.....	---	8.1-9.8	8.7-12.9
Dorsal Sp. No. 3/S.L.....	---	6.7-7.1	7.1-10.0
Dorsal Sp. No. 4/S.L.....	---	5.3-6.0	5.3-7.5
Anal Sp. No. 1/S.L......	---	6.9-7.5	7.1-9.7
Anal Sp. No. 2/S.L......	---	4.9-5.2	4.7-5.9
Anal Sp. No. 3/S.L......	---	5.1-5.5	5.4-6.7

Meristics.—D. XII-XIII (usually XIII), 21-23; A. III, 18-20; pectoral fin 15 (one with 14/14, five with 14/15); L.l. scales 30-37 (usually 33-35); L.l. pores 25-35 (usually 27-32); scales above L.l. 4 or 5; scales below L.l. 12-14 (usually 13 or 14); gill rakers 15-19.

Description.—Predorsal contour straight, concave above nostrils; snout projecting, 2.3-3.0 in head length, pointed; gape oblique, teeth in 7-8 rows in each jaw; preopercle right-angled to slightly oblique, edge crenulate; lachrymal and supraorbital smooth; snout greater than depth of caudal peduncle, which is greater than interorbital width; interorbital width greater than or equal to eye diameter.

Fifth dorsal spine longest; second and third anal spines approximately equal, first between half and two-thirds second; dorsal and anal fins with rounded angles, dorsal angle sharper; base of spinous portion of dorsal fin longer (2.4 in S.L.) than that of soft portion (3.5 in S.L.); pelvic fins short, longest ray not reaching level of anus.

Lateral line describing a high arc, flattening out about eighth dorsal spine level, following dorsal fin base curvature until its last rays; scales moderately large, mostly angular (though some scales rounded), in diagonal rows; dorsal fin scales reach midpoint of about sixth or seventh spine, that of anal fin reaching just past midpoint of third spine.

Juveniles similar to adults, dorsal and anal fins more rounded and equal.

Color Pattern.—Crosshatched pattern sometimes very faded so as to be indistinguishable; a large dark spot sometimes present under spinous portion of dorsal fin and straddling lateral line (this spot may also be faded beyond perception); eyeband connected across nape; face below light, above dusky to dark except for lighter portion at interorbital space; upper lip dark, darkish marks on upper and lower edges of caudal peduncle; pelvic fins body color.

Juvenile with slightly different color pattern. A black spot is contained in the soft dorsal fin positioned against the posterior edge of the fin just past the angle. A clear border separates this from the extreme edge of the fin; a submarginal black stripe extends from each end of the spot and follows the curvature of the fin; black band crosses caudal fin near base, rear of fin hyaline; anal fin dusky with broad light colored border; eyeband narrower than that of adult; crosshatched pattern not as vivid (28 mm S.L. specimen).

At a size of 48 mm S.L. the spot in dorsal fin spreads into the submarginal band of adults; eyeband wider (but still not as wide as in adults); caudal fin band has moved out to center of fin; yellowish border of anal fin narrower, with evidence of submarginal line.

Remarks.—Thanks to Mme. Bauchot supplying a photograph of the holotype of *Chaetodon sebae* Cuvier, there is no doubt that it is synonymous with *Chaetodon rafflesi*.

The dark blotch in the upper anterior portion of the body of some specimens represents the stress or night coloration. This is commonly seen

Chaetodon rafflesi has a distinctive cross-hatched pattern. Photo by G. Marcuse.

in aquaria where conditions have not been made suitable for this species.

Chaetodon rafflesi has been reported to occur in pairs. I have seen such pairs in the Philippines.

Herre and Montalban have reported a female in spawning condition in the month of December in the Philippines.

Distribution.—Widely distributed in the Pacific Ocean from the Society Islands and Tuamotus to the East Indies; islands of Melanesia and Micronesia, the Philippines to China and Japan; south to Queensland; extends into the Indian Ocean to the offshore islands of the Malay Archipelago, Cocos-Keeling Islands, and Sri Lanka.

Material Examined.—(17 spec.: 78-114 mm S.L.) (Additional specimens from 28 mm S.L. and up were examined but not measured). CAS 37808 (10: 78-103), Angaur I., Palau Islands; SOSC Te Vega Cr. #7 Sta. 259 (2: both 94), Vanikoro Island; BPBM 6189 (2: 107-110), Samoa; CAS 37809 (1: 114), Palau Islands; CAS 37810 (1: 94), Palau Islands; CAS 37811 (1: 71), Palau Islands.

CHAETODON EPHIPPIUM Cuvier
Saddle-back butterflyfish
(Blackblotched butterflyfish)

Chaetodon ephippium Cuvier. 138 mm S.L. Christmas Island, Line Islands.

Chaetodon ephippium Cuvier, 1831: p. 80, pl. 174 (type localities Moluccas, Bora Bora (Society Islands)).
Chaetodon principalis Cuvier, 1831: p. 81 (type locality East Indies; on Renard's figure and Valentyn).
Chaetodon Garnotii Lesson, 1835: p. 174, pl. 29, fig. 1 (name in synonymy—Lesson MS).
Rhabdophorus ephippium, Swainson, 1839: p. 211 (new combination).
Chaetodon Mulsanti Thiolliere, 1857: p. 163 (type locality Woodlark Island; on Montrouzier MS; juvenile).
Chaetodon pepek (part) Thiolliere, 1857: p. 163 (name in synonymy—Montrouzier MS).
Linophora ephippium, Kaup, 1860: p. 156 (Moluccas, Tahiti; new combination).

Linophora principalis, Kaup, 1860: p. 156 (new combination).
Tetragonoptrus ephippium, Bleeker, 1863: p. 234 (Ternate; new combination).
Tetragonoptrus (Rhabdophorus) ephippium, Bleeker, 1877: p. 36, pl. 378, fig. 2 (new localities).
Chaetodon ephippium var. *principalis*, Ahl, 1923: p. 66.
?*Chaetodon lunula* (not of Lacepede), Whitley, 1932: p. 286.

Diagnosis.—D. XII-XIV (usually XIII), 21-24 (usually 23-24); A. III, 20-22 (usually 21); pectoral rays 15 (16); L.l. scales 33-40 (usually 36-39); closely related to *Chaetodon xanthocephalus* but easily distinguishable by a large black saddle at the upper posterior portion of the body and including the soft dorsal fin, and the presence in adults of a filament in the soft dorsal fin.

Meristics.—D. XIII (one with XII, one with XIV), 21-24 (usually 23-24); A. III, 20-22 (usually 21) pectoral rays 15 (one with 16/16, one with 15/16, two with 14/15); L.l. scales 33-40 (usually 36-39); L.l. pores 31-37; scales above L.l. 8-9; scales below L.l. 13-16; gill rakers 14-17.

Ratios	20-49(2)	Standard Length (mm) 50-89(5)	above 89(9)
Depth/S.L............	1.4-1.5	1.6-1.7	1.6-1.8
Head/S.L.............	2.4-2.5	3.0-3.1	3.0-3.4
Eye/Head............	2.4-2.6	3.4-3.6	3.3-4.1
Snout/Head..........	3.7	2.5-2.8	2.3-2.8
Interorb. W./Head......	3.6-3.9	3.3-3.6	2.9-3.7
Maxillary/Head........	3.9-4.1	3.3-3.7	3.1-4.5
Caud. Ped./S.L........	7.3-7.6	9.0-9.4	8.9-11.2
Pect. Fin/S.L..........	3.4-3.5	3.6-4.0	3.6-5.3
Pelvic Sp./S.L.........	3.5-3.8	4.6-5.0	5.1-5.9
Predorsal L./S.L.......	1.9-2.0	2.4-2.6	2.5-2.9
Prepelvic L./S.L.......	2.1, 2.1	2.4	2.4-2.7
Dorsal Sp. No. 1/S.L....	7.9-9.6	9.1-11.0	9.1-13.8
Dorsal Sp. No. 2/S.L....	4.9-5.3	7.7-10.5	8.1-10.7
Dorsal Sp. No. 3/S.L....	3.6-3.7	6.0-8.2	7.0-10.2
Dorsal Sp. No. 4/S.L....	3.1-3.3	5.1-6.5	5.3-8.4
Anal Sp. No. 1/S.L.....	6.6-8.6	6.8-8.4	8.1-11.0
Anal Sp. No. 2/S.L.....	5.3-6.8	4.9-5.9	5.3-7.2
Anal Sp. No. 3/S.L.....	5.4-7.0	4.5-7.4	4.8-7.3

Description.—Predorsal contour straight, concave above nostrils; gape oblique, teeth in 6-8 rows in upper jaw and 7-10 rows in lower jaw; snout projecting, 2.3-2.8 in head length; preopercle obtuse-angled, edge crenulate; lachrymal long, smooth; snout length greater than depth of caudal peduncle, which is greater than interorbital; interorbital width greater than eye diameter.

Fifth or sixth dorsal spine longest; third anal spine equal to or greater in length than second, first about half to two-thirds second; anal fin rounded; dorsal fin with fourth ray produced into a filament (that can include third and fifth rays), edge of fin below filament rounded, above it horizontal; base of spinous portion of dorsal fin longer (2.3-2.6 in S.L.) than that of soft portion (2.9-3.6 in S.L.); pelvic fins short, sometimes barely reaching level of anus.

Lateral line describing moderately high arc crossing body; scales moderate, angular, in horizontal rows along lower portion of body and slightly ascending rows in upper portion; scale covering of dorsal spines reaching midpoint of fifth spine, that of anal fin covering half to three-fourths of third anal spine.

Juveniles differ somewhat in form from the adults. The filament is absent, the dorsal fin almost right-angled.

Color Pattern.—Black saddle extends from seventh dorsal fin spine posteriorly; dorsal filament receives its color from the upper edge of the dorsal fin, a bit of dark line from the saddle, and a narrow stripe from the broad posterior band (there may also be a lower border as a continuation of the dark line); caudal fin with upper and lower edges yellowish, membranes hyaline, and rays blackish bordered; a dusky to gray streak or line, vertical or slightly inclined, between base of dorsal fin and pectoral base; pelvic fins body colored.

Juveniles undergo some color changes with growth. A 19 mm S.L. specimen had the following color pattern: eyeband complete, united at nape just before dorsal spines and extending to lower edge of interopercle, not as wide as eye but almost so; black band surrounds caudal peduncle, wide in center and narrower above and below, the midportion resembling a spot; caudal fin hyaline, a light stripe bordering peduncle band; saddle present but not well differentiated, the lower edge with a dusky extension reaching the anal fin; edge of dorsal fin hyaline, a submarginal stripe present within which is another light stripe which borders the saddle. By 31 mm S.L. the eyeband is narrower and the saddle extension is absent. In many specimens the anal fin is dark grayish (entirely or partly); saddle better differentiated and with the light zone appearing. At 45 mm S.L. the caudal peduncle band shows signs of fading and the eyeband below the eye is showing similar signs, as the eyeband itself is narrower; posterior pattern of saddle approaching that of adult. A 72 mm S.L. specimen shows the beginnings of a dorsal fin spike; caudal peduncle band definitely faded; eyeband much faded, especially at upper and lower areas.

Remarks.—*Chaetodon ephippium* is one of the few species that loses the eyeband with age. It also possesses a caudal peduncular band as a juvenile which is lost in the adult stage. The dorsal filament appears in specimens usually above 70 mm S.L. and consists of the fourth dorsal ray with the third and fifth sometimes as auxiliaries.

The closest relative of *C. ephippium* is *C. xanthocephalus* from the Indian Ocean, which perhaps is a geographic replacement species although *C. ephippium* has made inroads into the Indian Ocean. Color characteristics are strikingly similar, such as the yellow color pattern around the head and chest and the loss of the eyeband. The caudal fin pattern of dark lines along each ray is common to both species.

Chaetodon principalis was described as a new species by Cuvier (1831) on the basis of the blackish area, edged in white, on the anal fin. I have seen the dark anal fin in many specimens and believe this is simply an artifact of preservation. Normal specimens of *C. ephippium* collected in the field were noted to have this dark anal fin area after being preserved. Several collections had mixed dark anal fin and light anal fin specimens from the same station. They were of all sizes and could not represent a juvenile coloration as Jordan and Seale (1906) indicated. Perhaps the physiological state of the fish when preserved determines whether or not the dark anal fin will show up.

Although juveniles were not encountered very frequently around Oahu, they were seen in fair numbers when diving in the protected

A pair of *Chaetodon ephippium* being cleaned by a cleaner wrasse, *Labroides dimidiatus*. Photo by W. Deas.

lagoon waters around rocks and walls at Johnston Atoll. Adults were seen schooling with *Chaetodon auriga* in several areas, and a specimen closely resembling one that Dr. John E. Randall collected at Tahiti, a hybrid between these two species, was seen at Johnston Atoll, still schooling with *C. auriga*.

According to Harry (1953), at Raroia *C. ephippium* is a moderately rare species usually found in the lagoon. It normally occurred in small schools and very seldom as single individuals. I have seen it as pairs, individuals, small groups, and in one instance as seven animals all juveniles but of different sizes inhabiting one coral head about 5-8 feet in diameter.

A *C. ephippium* kept in an open-water aquarium was seen being cleaned by another juvenile butterflyfish, *C. miliaris*.

Distribution.—Widely distributed in the central and western Pacific Ocean from the Hawaiian Islands to the East Indies; from southern Japan to the Great Barrier Reef of Australia; and extending into the Indian Ocean at least as far as the Cocos-Keeling Islands.

Material Examined.—(16 spec.: 20-165 mm S.L.) HIMB (uncatalogued) (1: 132), Marakei, Gilbert Islands; WEB (3: 73-109), Gilbert Islands; WEB (2: 75-88), Honolulu Market; NMFS-H (uncatalogued) (2: 20-21), Gilbert Islands; SOSC Te Vega 295 (1: 162), Fiji Islands; SOSC Te Vega 255 (1: 165), Rennell Islands; SOSC Te Vega 308 (5: 86-130), Vava'u, Tonga Islands; SOSC TV 314 (1: 145), Phoenix Islands.

CHAETODON XANTHOCEPHALUS Bennett
Yellowhead butterflyfish

Chaetodon xanthocephalus Bennett, 1832: p. 182 (type locality Ceylon).

Chaetodon nigripinnatus Desjardins, 1836: p. 57 (type locality Mauritius). Ahl, 1923: p. 69.

Chaetodon nigripinnis Peters, 1855: p. 246 (=438) (type locality Mozambique; juvenile). Gunther, 1860: p. 32 (after Peters, 1855; Mozambique). Jastrow & Lenz, 1898: p. 503 (Zanzibar).

Chelmo pulcher Steindachner, 1875: p. 382 (type locality Mauritius).

Chaetodon "?" Day, 1875: Addenda, p. 109 (Tellicherry, India).

Chaetodon auromarginatus Bliss, 1883: pp. 48-49 (type locality Mauritius).

Chaetodon (Tetragonoptrus) nigripinnis, Sauvage, 1891: p. 260, pl. 29, fig. 3 (not 4, error in numbering).

Chaetodon dayi Ahl, 1923: p. 127 (type locality Tellicherry, India; on Day, 1875, *Chaetodon* "?").

Chelmon? pulcher, Ahl, 1923: p. 15 (Mauritius; after Steindachner, 1875).

Chaetodon xanthocephalus Bennett. 146 mm S.L. Seychelles.

Ratios	Standard Length (mm)		
	20-59(3)	60-99(6)	above 99(27)
Depth/S.L.	1.6-1.7	1.6-1.7	1.5-1.8
Head/S.L.	2.8	2.8-3.2	3.1-3.6
Eye/Head	3.1-3.4	3.1-3.7	3.3-4.2
Snout/Head	2.6-3.0	2.6-3.1	2.3-3.1
Interorb. W./Head	3.3-3.4	3.1-3.5	2.9-3.6
Maxillary/Head	3.7-4.4	3.3-3.5	3.0-3.7
Caud. Ped./S.L.	8.9	8.8-8.9	8.5-9.5
Pect. Fin/S.L.	3.3	3.4-3.9	3.6-4.2
Pelvic Sp./S.L.	4.5-4.8	4.6-5.3	5.2-6.6
Predorsal L./S.L.	2.2-2.4	2.3-2.6	2.4-2.8
Prepelvic L./S.L.	2.2-2.4	2.2-2.5	2.4-2.7
Dorsal Sp. No. 1/S.L.	10.2-11.9	9.2-11.7	8.7-13.6
Dorsal Sp. No. 2/S.L.	7.5-8.5	8.1-10.1	9.2-15.3
Dorsal Sp. No. 3/S.L.	5.4-6.5	6.2-8.5	7.5-11.4
Dorsal Sp. No. 4/S.L.	4.3-5.0	5.2-6.4	6.7-10.8
Anal Sp. No. 1/S.L.	6.4-7.0	7.2-8.1	7.6-11.8
Anal Sp. No. 2/S.L.	4.6-5.2	5.2-6.2	5.1-7.4
Anal Sp. No. 3/S.L.	4.5-5.0	4.9-6.3	5.0-8.2

Chaetodon xanthocephalus subadult. The eyeband is still evident and the caudal peduncle is barely visible. Photo by Klaus Paysan.

Diagnosis.—D. XIV (two with XIII), 21-26 (usually 23-25); A. III, 21-23 (usually 22); pectoral rays 15; L.l. scales 34-40; close to *C. ephippium* but with XIV dorsal spines; no filament in dorsal fin; eyeband reduced or absent; about 5 narrow angled lines crossing body; dorsal and anal fins dusky.

Meristics.—D. XIV (two with XIII), 21-26 (usually 23-25); A. III, 21-23 (usually 22); pectoral rays 15 (three with 14/15, one with 15/16); L.l. scales 34-40; L.l. pores 30-39; scales above L.l. 9-11; scales below L.l. 17-19; gill rakers 15-19.

Description.—Predorsal contour approximately straight, concave above nostrils; snout projecting, pointed, 2.3-3.1 in head length; gape oblique, teeth in about 7 rows in upper jaw and 8-9 in lower jaw; preopercle oblique-angled, edge crenulate; lachrymal smooth, supraorbital serrate; snout length and depth of caudal peduncle equal, both larger than interorbital width, which is greater than eye diameter.

Fifth to seventh dorsal spines longest or all succeeding spines after these about equal; second and third anal spines equal, first between half and two-thirds second; dorsal and anal fins rounded; base of spinous portion of dorsal fin longer (2.1-2.3 in S.L.) than that of soft portion (3.0-3.2 in S.L.); pelvic fins moderately short, barely reaching anus; caudal fin truncate, upper rays sometimes elongated into a short spike.

Lateral line describing a high arc crossing body; scales moderately large, rounded to angular, in horizontal series at lower portion of body, in ascending rows above this; scale covering of dorsal spines reaches midpoint of fifth or sixth spine; scale covering of anal spines reaching to about three-fourths of third anal spine.

Juveniles similar to adults.

Color Pattern.—Usually about five angled lines crossing body (though number may vary); face dusky, lower portion of head, entire snout, and ventral portion of body to anal spines yellow; pelvic fins also this color; the body color extends part way onto anal fin and is separated from the color of the anal fin by a stripe which continues at the lower edge of the caudal peduncle and caudal fin; border of dark area of dorsal fin extends on caudal peduncle upper border and upper edge of caudal fin in balance with the lower border; dark lines edging each caudal fin ray, on the upper edge of the upper rays and lower edge of the lower rays.

Juveniles with some differences from the adult color pattern. A distinct eyeband is present, very narrow, and extends from nape where the two sides join, to the lower edge of interopercle. With growth this band gradually diminishes until it virtually disappears in the adults. Juveniles also possess a black band encircling the caudal peduncle which disappears with age. In smaller specimens of 50 mm S.L. or thereabouts the dark of the dorsal fin may connect with the black peduncular band. At about 56 mm S.L. the dorsal fin dark area is more diffuse. By 67 mm S.L. the eyeband is no longer connected at nape, and by 82 mm S.L. the caudal peduncle band is indistinct and the eyeband extends only halfway to nape and down to the edge of the preoperculum.

Remarks.—The color changes that this species undergoes lead to a great deal of confusion. The loss of the caudal peduncular band occurs in many chaetodont species and by itself would not lead to too many problems. But this species also loses the eyeband, and the dorsal and anal fins change color with age. The dorsal and anal fins change from black or dark brown to shades of yellow. In preservation these fins appear dark, much like the *principalis* anal fin change in the closely related *Chaetodon ephippium*.

The yellow pattern on the head and chest is strikingly similar to that of *C. ephippium* and *C. semeion*. Both these Pacific species have a filament in the dorsal fin which *C. xanthocephalus* lacks.

The elongate snout has led to the naming of this fish *Chelmo pulcher* by Steindachner. The descriptions of *Chaetodon nigripinnis* and *C. nigripinnatus* are not diagnostic but do resemble this species. The redescription of *C. nigripinnis* by Sauvage (1891) with a figure of the type specimen supports placing this species in synonymy. Smith (1949) included these two species with *C. xanthocephalus*, and his figures of this species as juveniles and adult compare favorably with the descriptions given of *C. nigripinnatus*.

This species is one of the more common Indian Ocean butterflyfishes and reaches a fairly large size of up to 200 mm in length.

Distribution.—Widespread in the Indian Ocean from the Maldive Islands to the east coast of Africa and the offshore islands.

Material Examined.—(36 spec.: 49-162 mm S.L.) ANSP 108595, 108583, 108571, 108574, and 108389 (7: 81-151), Seychelles; MCZ 41738 (2: 50-59), Colombo, Sri Lanka; SOSC HA 67-16, HA 67-36, HA 67-14 (9: 67-139), Chagas Archipelago, Indian Ocean; SOSC HA 67-62, HA 67-59, HA 67-65, HA 67-66, HA 67-56, HA 67-60, HA 67-69, HA 67-74, and HA 67-57 (18: 49-162), Aldabra.

CHAETODON ULIETENSIS Cuvier
Saddled butterflyfish
(Double-barred butterflyfish)

Chaetodon ulietensis Cuvier. 138 mm S.L. Enewetak, Marshall Islands.

Chaetodon ulietensis Cuvier, 1831: p. 39 (type locality Ulietea; on a figure by Parkinson in the Library of Banks).

Tetragonoptrus ulietensis, Bleeker, 1863: p. 234 (Ternate; new combination).

Chaetodon falcula (not of Bloch), Gunther, 1874: p. 39, pl. 27, fig. e (Tuamotu Is., Society Is., Hawaiian Is., Samoa, Kings Mills Is.).

Tetragonoptrus (Oxychaetodon) falcula (not of Bloch), Bleeker, 1877: p. 52, pl. 373, fig. 1 (Batu, Ternate, Amboina).

Chaetodon aurora De Vis, 1885: p. 453 (type locality Queensland coast).

Chaetodon fulcula Seale, 1901: p. 101 (Guam; misspelling of *falcula*, not *C. falcula*, Bloch).

Chaetodon ulietensis var. *confluens* Ahl, 1923: p. 172 (South Seas).

Chaetodon ulietensis var. *aurora*, Ahl, 1923: p. 172 (coast of Queensland).

Anisochaetodon (Oxychaetodon) falcula (not of Bloch), Weber & de Beaufort, 1936: p. 116 (East Indies).

Chaetodon facula Schultz, 1943: p. 151 (misspelling of *falcula*, not *C. falcula* Bloch).

Chaetodon (Oxychaetodon) falcula (not of Bloch), Fowler, 1953: p. 45, fig. 103 (China, Nafa, Okinawa, Aguni Shima).

Anisochaetodon falcula (not of Bloch), Munro, 1967: p. 368 (New Guinea; color plate #3 is *Chaetodon falcula* Bloch).

Diagnosis.—D. XII, 23-24 (one with 25); A. III (one with IV), 19-21 (usually 19); pectoral rays (14) 15; L.l. scales 32-37; close to *Chaetodon falcula*, but black bars extend to and below midpoint of body and are wider and less triangular than that species; snout shorter than in *C. falcula* (2.3-2.7 in head length as compared with 1.9-2.1 in *C. falcula*); *C. ulietensis* has fewer dorsal and anal fin rays than *C. falcula*; narrow vertical lines, black bars, and posterior abrupt yellow coloration distinguish this species from most other chaetodonts.

Meristics.—D. XII, 23-24 (one with 25); A. III (one with IV), 19-21 (usually 19); pectoral rays 15 (one with 14/14, three with 14/15, one with 15/16); L.l. scales 32-37; L.l. pores 23-30; scales above L.l. 5-6; scales below L.l. 12-14; gill rakers 14-20.

Description.—Predorsal contour straight, concave above nostrils; snout moderately projecting, pointed, 2.1-2.5 in head length; gape slightly oblique, teeth in 7-9 rows in each jaw; preopercle oblique-angled, edge smooth to crenulate; lachrymal smooth, supraorbital smooth; snout length greater than depth of caudal peduncle, which is greater than eye diameter; eye diameter greater than or equal to interorbital width.

Fifth or sixth dorsal spine longest; second anal spine equal to or longer than third, first just over half length of second; dorsal and anal fins with blunt angles; base of spinous portion of dorsal fin longer (2.2-2.7 in

Ratios	Standard Length (mm)		
	20-49	50-89(7)	above 89(13)
Depth/S.L.	---	1.6-1.9	1.6-1.9
Head/S.L.	---	2.7-3.1	2.8-3.1
Eye/Head	---	3.1-3.5	3.4-3.6
Snout/Head	---	2.3-2.7	2.1-2.5
Interorb. W./Head.	---	3.6-3.9	3.2-3.8
Maxillary/Head	---	3.3-3.7	3.3-3.8
Caud. Ped./S.L.	---	9.2-11.3	9.2-10.0
Pelvic Sp./S.L.	---	4.4-4.9	4.3-5.3
Predorsal L./S.L.	---	2.1-2.3	2.1-2.4
Prepelvic L./S.L.	---	2.1-2.5	2.1-2.5
Dorsal Sp. No. 1/S.L.	---	9.4-11.0	8.5-14.8
Dorsal Sp. No. 2/S.L.	---	7.4-9.1	7.6-12.7
Dorsal Sp. No. 3/S.L.	---	5.4-7.7	5.8-8.8
Dorsal Sp. No. 4/S.L.	---	4.7-6.8	4.7-7.9
Anal Sp. No. 1/S.L.	---	6.7-8.5	7.7-9.6
Anal Sp. No. 2/S.L.	---	4.2-5.5	4.7-6.2
Anal Sp. No. 3/S.L.	---	4.3-7.1	4.9-6.7

S.L.) than that of soft portion (3.1-3.8 in S.L.); pelvic fins moderate, longest ray reaching to and beyond anus.

Lateral line describing moderately high, smooth arc across body; scales large, rhomboidal, in slightly ascending series across body; scales covering dorsal spines extending to midpoint of fifth spine, those of anal fin reaching midpoint of third spine.

Juveniles similar to adults.

Color Pattern.—First black bar includes from fourth to seventh dorsal spines, second includes last spines and first rays; 16 to 17 vertical lines are present; black spot on caudal peduncle sometimes connected with one on opposite side, at least ventrally; eyebands join at nape in almost a horseshoe-shaped mark as in the *mertensi* group, but continue to eye, widening close to eye but quite weak at side of head; pelvic fins body color.

Juveniles similar in pattern to adults although the eyeband is more solid and the black bars may extend further ventrally; caudal fin more than half hyaline, the edges of the dorsal and anal fins without adult markings (from a specimen 24 mm S.L.).

Remarks.—*Chaetodon ulietensis* has been consistently synonymized under a very closely related species, *C. falcula* from the Indian Ocean. *Chaetodon ulietensis* is apparently a geographic replacement for that species. The differences given in the diagnosis are of specific magnitude, and these two forms must be considered as separate species. All references to *Chaetodon falcula* from the Pacific Ocean are undoubtedly *Chaetodon ulietensis*. As these are very numerous, all have not been included in the synonymy.

The possible record of *C. ulietensis* in the Indian Ocean at Cocos-Keeling Islands may represent a reinvasion of the ocean. There is no evidence that these two closely related species occur sympatrically.

Harry (1953) reports *Chaetodon ulietensis* (as *C. falcula*) scattered over the lagoon area around coral heads. He did not find it common at any area. He did not find them in the surge channels, and only rarely were individuals seen on the outer reef flats. I found them, usually paired, at Eniwetok around luxuriant coral growth in the lagoon or in the deep channels between islands.

Distribution.—Widespread in the central and western Pacific from the Tuamotu and Society Islands to the Great Barrier Reef of Australia and southern Japan; Philippines, East Indies; no authenticated report from the Hawaiian Islands; listed as from the Cocos-Keeling Islands in the Indian Ocean.

Material Examined.—(20 spec.: 66-118 mm S.L.) WEB (10: 71-118), Tahiti; WEB (1: 66), Gilbert Islands; BPBM 6110 (1: 109), Tahiti; SOSC Te Vega Sta. 308 (3: 68-95), Tonga Islands; SOSC Te Vega 314 (5: 95-117), Phoenix Islands.

CHAETODON FALCULA Bloch
Sickle butterflyfish

Chaetodon falcula Bloch, 1793: p. 102, pl. 426, fig. 2 (no locality).

Pomacentrus falcula, Lacepede, 1802: pp. 506, 511, 513 (new combination).

Chaetodon dizoster Valenciennes, 1831: p. 527 (type locality Mauritius, Ile de France; from a figure by Theodore Delise). Valenciennes, 1839: pl. 39, fig. 2.

Diagnosis.—D. XII (one with XIII), 23-25; A. III, 20-21; pectoral rays 15; L.l. scales 29-34; two triangular black saddles dorsally, with narrow vertical lines between them crossing body; snout elongate, 1.9-2.1 in head length; caudal peduncular band present.

Closely related to *Chaetodon ulietensis*, but differs in having a longer snout, a higher dorsal and anal ray count, the black triangles not extending to or beyond midline of body, peduncular band a true band—not a spot, and minor differences in the eyeband and dorsal and anal fin pattern and number of vertical lines.

Meristics.—D. XII (one with XIII), 23-25; A. III, 20-21; pectoral rays 15 (three have 14/15, one has 16/15); L.l. scales 29-34; L.l. pores 23-31; scales below L.l. 12 or 13 (usually 13); scales above L.l. 6-7 (usually 6); gill rakers 17-21 (usually 19-21).

Ratios	Standard Length (mm)		
	20-49(1)	50-89(2)	above 89(6)
Depth/S.L.............	1.7	1.6-1.7	1.7-1.8
Head/S.L..............	2.6	2.7,2.8	2.9-3.2
Eye/Head	3.1	3.4,3.4	4.1-4.2
Snout/Head	2.4	2.2,2.3	1.9-2.1
Interorb. W./Head......	3.8	3.6-4.0	3.5-3.9
Maxillary/Head	3.5	3.7,4.2	3.2-3.4
Caud. Ped./S.L.........	9.6	9.1,10.0	8.9-10.2
Pect. Fin/S.L..........	3.3	3.4,3.4	3.7-4.1
Pelvic Sp./S.L.........	4.0	4.5,4.6	5.1-5.6
Predorsal L./S.L........	2.0	2.0,2.0	2.3-2.4
Prepelvic L./S.L........	2.3	2.2,2.3	2.3-2.6
Dorsal Sp. No. 1/S.L.....	8.3	9.3,10.9	10.9-12.0
Dorsal Sp. No. 2/S.L.....	6.1	7.7,9.4	9.8-11.7
Dorsal Sp. No. 3/S.L.....	4.4	5.4-6.6	8.1-9.4
Dorsal Sp. No. 4/S.L.....	3.4	4.2-5.5	6.2-8.5
Anal Sp. No. 1/S.L.......	6.4	7.1-7.7	8.7-10.0
Anal Sp. No. 2/S.L.......	4.4	4.6-4.6	5.4-6.1
Anal Sp. No. 3/S.L.......	4.4	4.2,4.5	5.3-6.5

Chaetodon falcula Bloch. 133 mm S.L. Chagas Archipelago, Indian Ocean.

Chaetodon
falcula. 65 and 38
mm S.L. Diego
Garcia Ar-
chipelago.

Description.—Predorsal contour slightly gibbous at nape in largest specimens, a concavity at level of nostrils to accommodate snout, otherwise straight; snout relatively elongate, 1.9-2.1 in head length, pointed; gape slightly oblique; teeth in 8-9 rows in each jaw; preopercle oblique-angled, edge smooth to crenulate; lachrymal long, smooth; supraorbital smooth; snout length greater than depth of caudal peduncle, which is greater than interorbital width; interorbital width greater than eye diameter.

Fifth or sixth dorsal spine longest; second anal spine about equal to third, first about half or more of second; dorsal and anal fins with blunt angles, that of anal fin more acute; base of spinous portion of dorsal fin longer (2.3-2.4 in S.L.) than that of soft portion (2.9-3.6 in S.L.); pelvic fins moderate, reaching to and beyond anal opening.

Lateral line describing a high, smooth arc reaching its peak below last spines of dorsal fin; scales large, rhomboidal, in diagonal rows across body (or even suggesting chevron pattern); dorsal spine scales reaching midpoint at about sixth spine; anal covering reaching to midpoint or beyond of third spine.

Juveniles similar to adults, snout proportionately shorter, 2.4 in standard length.

Color Pattern.—First black triangle at 2-5 dorsal fin spines, the "point" reaching to lateral line but not much, if any, beyond; second triangle covers last three dorsal spines and first rays of dorsal fin, extending below lateral line almost to upper level of caudal peduncle; black band surrounds caudal peduncle, sometimes not connected ventrally, and usually wider in the center; eyeband at nape horseshoe-shaped, the connection to the lower portion often lighter on each side; snout dusky; pelvic fins body color.

Juveniles similar in color pattern to adults. Caudal peduncle band complete, black triangles extend further ventrally but still not past midline of body, eyeband not faded at side of nape, edge of caudal fin broadly hyaline, edges of dorsal and anal rayed portions of fins hyaline, a narrow blackish stripe possibly at the upper portion of the dorsal fin.

Remarks.—*Chaetodon falcula* is quite distinct from *C. ulietensis* of the Pacific Ocean by the characters noted in the diagnosis. They can easily be distinguished in the field on the basis of color alone. This represents another case in which there are species-pairs, one from the Indian Ocean area and one from the Pacific Ocean.

Chaetodon falcula represents another species in which the snout has become more elongated than in most other species of *Chaetodon*. It is comparable with the snout length of *C. aculeatus* of the western Atlantic Ocean, which had previously been included in its own genus, *Prognathodes*, on that basis.

Distribution.—Indian Ocean: east coast of Africa to India and Sri Lanka with possible records from western Sumatra and Doworra of the East Indies.

Material Examined.—(9 spec.: 38-151 mm S.L.) ANSP 108546 and 108373 (2: 76-151), Seychelles Islands; SOSC HA 67-11, HA 67-14, and HA 67-3 (4: 128-140), Chagas Archipelago; SOSC HA 67-36 (2: 38-63), Diego Garcia Atoll; SOSC HA-17 (1: 143), Aldabra Atoll.

CHAETODON LINEOLATUS Cuvier
Lined butterflyfish

Chaetodon lineolatus Cuvier, 1831: p. 40 (type locality Isle de France (Mauritius); after Quoy & Gaimard, MS).

Chaetodon lunatus Cuvier, 1831: p. 57 (ex Ehrenberg MS; type locality Mer Rouge).

Chaetodon Tallii Bleeker, 1854: p. 97 (type locality Banda Neira; juvenile).

Tetragonoptrus (*Oxychaetodon*) *lineolatus*, Bleeker, 1877: p. 51, pl. 377, fig. 2 (part).

Chaetodon (*Anisochaetodon*) *lineolatus*, Klunzinger, 1884: p. 57 (Red Sea).

Anisochaetodon (*Oxychaetodon*) *lineolatus* (part), Weber and de Beaufort, 1936: p. 114 (new combination).

Anisochaetodon lineolatus, Marshall, 1950: pp. 166-205 (Cocos-Keeling).

Chaetodon (*Oxychaetodon*) *lineolatus*, Fowler, 1953: p. 43, fig. 102 (China, Hokoto, Pescadores Is.).

Chaetodon lineolatus Cuvier. 234 mm S.L. Enewetak, Marshall Islands.

Ratios	Standard Length (mm)		
	20-49(6)	50-89(4)	above 89(8)
Depth/S.L............	1.6-1.7	1.5-1.7	1.5-1.8
Head/S.L.............	2.5-2.7	2.7-2.9	3.0-3.5
Eye/Head	2.8-3.1	3.0-3.2	3.5-5.4
Snout/Head	2.6-3.3	2.4-2.7	2.1-2.8
Interorb. W./Head......	2.7-3.3	3.1-3.4	2.7-3.3
Maxillary/Head	3.8-4.4	3.7-4.0	3.4-4.1
Caud. Ped./S.L........	8.1-8.4	8.6-9.1	8.7-9.4
Pect. Fin/S.L..........	3.3-3.4	3.4-4.0	3.7-4.4
Pelvic Sp./S.L.........	4.5-6.4	4.3-5.1	5.1-6.5
Predorsal L./S.L.......	1.9-2.1	2.1	2.2-2.6
Prepelvic L./S.L.......	2.2- 2.3	2.2-2.4	2.3-2.7
Dorsal Sp. No. 1/S.L.....	8.8-10.6	10.0-13.2	11.5-16.8
Dorsal Sp. No. 2/S.L.....	6.5-7.1	7.2-10.7	9.1-13.2
Dorsal Sp. No. 3/S.L.....	4.7	5.3-7.0	7.4-10.9
Dorsal Sp. No. 4/S.L.....	3.9-4.1	4.5-5.9	5.1-8.9
Anal Sp. No. 1/S.L.......	8.0-8.8	7.0-9.4	9.1-11.0
Anal Sp. No. 2/S.L.......	5.0-5.5	4.8-5.8	6.1-8.3
Anal Sp. No. 3/S.L.......	4.8	4.4-6.5	6.3-7.3

Diagnosis.—D. XII, 24-27 (rarely 24); A. III, 20-22; pectoral rays 15-17 (usually 16); L.l. scales 26-33; 16 to 17 parallel vertical lines crossing body; large black lunate band from base of posterior dorsal spines to base of anal fin rays, including caudal peduncle; eyeband extends from nape to interopercle, leaving light spot on space between nape and interorbital; grows to large size, 12 inches or more.

Close to *C. oxycephalus* but differs from that species in the following characters: lunate band of *C. oxycephalus* ends at base of caudal peduncle; separate nuchal spot in *C. oxycephalus* (not connected with lower portion of eyeband); fewer dorsal, anal, and pectoral fin rays in *C. oxycephalus*; snout of *C. oxycephalus* is longer than that of *C. lineolatus*.

Meristics.—D. XII, 24-27 (rarely 24); A. III, 20-22; pectoral rays 16 (one with 15/15, one with 17/17, four with 15/16, and one with 17/16); L.l. scales 26-33; L.l. pores 21-30; scales above L.l. 5-7; scales below L.l. 12-15 (usually 14 or 15); gill rakers 15-18.

Description.—Predorsal contour convex at nape, concave at nostrils, straight in between; snout projecting, 2.1-2.8 in head length; gape slightly oblique; teeth in about 12 rows in each jaw; preopercle oblique-angled, edge serrate; lachrymal and supraorbital smooth; snout length greater than depth of caudal peduncle, which is greater than interorbital width; interorbital width greater than eye diameter.

First and second dorsal fin spines thick and short; fifth or sixth dorsal spine longest; second and third anal spines subequal, first about two-thirds of second; dorsal and anal fins with blunt angles; base of spinous portion of dorsal fin longer (2.2-2.4 in S.L.) than soft portion (2.8-3.1 in S.L.); pelvic fins short, not extending beyond anal opening.

Lateral line describing moderately high arc, peaking under last spine and first rays of dorsal fin; scales large, angular, in horizontal rows in lower portion of body and ascending in upper portion (although chevron pattern is noticeable); scales reaching midpoint of sixth dorsal spine and midpoint to ¾ of third anal spine.

Juveniles similar to adults.

Color Pattern.—About 16 to 17 vertical lines across body; eyeband broadly connected across nape and again across interorbital, leaving light patch isolated; snout tip dusky; pelvic fins body color; a paler lunate band (yellow in life) sometimes evident, sometimes faded in preserved specimens, following inner edge of black lunate mark.

Juveniles with some differences in color pattern: eyeband lacks light spot on nape and is somewhat narrower; lunate band very diffuse, appearing more like a smudge than discrete band; dorsal and anal fins with narrow blackish edge, a clear band beneath this, otherwise uniformly colored; caudal fin about half or more hyaline; black band surrounds caudal peduncle, bordered on both sides by light stripes.

Remarks.—Although closely related to *Chaetodon oxycephalus*, this species is quite distinct as indicated in the diagnosis. The two species appear to be sympatric over the entire range of *C. oxycephalus* but with

C. *lineolatus* having a much broader range.

Chaetodon lineolatus is probably the largest species in the genus *Chaetodon* and is rivaled in the family only by *Heniochus acuminatus.*

I have never seen a specimen with the lines as oblique as those depicted by Gunther (1874), although one specimen from the Line Islands did approach it somewhat. I believe it may be a case of artist's license, or if an accurate representation, an abberant specimen in which the lines followed the alternate angle of the scale edges. Gunther's description says the lines are "mit feinen verticalen schwarzen linien."; Jordan and Evermann (1905), who include Gunther's figure, also mention the "narrow blackish vertical lines."

Chaetodon lineolatus appears to occur in pairs in most areas I have visited. Baschieri-Salvatore (1954) found them in the Red Sea in about 4 to 20 meters of depth near shelter of the coral reef barrier.

Herre and Montalban (1927) reported ripe males and females in the Philippine Islands in August of 1925.

Distribution.—Widely distributed in the Indo-Pacific region from the Hawaiian Islands to the eastern African coast and Red Sea; also found in southern Japan to the Great Barrier Reef of Australia.

Material Examined.—(18 spec.: 33-240 mm S.L.) WEB (4: 98-126), Hawaiian Islands; BPBM (uncatalogued) (1: 76), Tonga Islands; WEB (2: 153-234), Eniwetok, Marshall Islands; Yasuda, Univ. of Tokyo (uncatalogued) (1: 64), Japan; FMNH 73964 (5: 33-34), Maldive Islands; SOSC HA 67-57 (2: 235-240), Aldabra Atoll; SOSC HA 67-36 (1: 75), Chagas Archipelago; CAS 37825 (1:40), Palau Islands; BPBM (uncatalogued) (1:200), Ryu Kyu Islands.

CHAETODON OXYCEPHALUS Bleeker

Chaetodon oxycephalus Bleeker, 1853: p. 603 (type locality Ternate).

Tetragonoptrus (Oxychaetodon) lineolatus var. *oxycephalus,* Bleeker, 1877: p. 51 (Ternate).

Anisochaetodon (Oxychaetodon) lineolatus (part), Weber & de Beaufort, 1936: p. 114, fig. 29 (new combination).

Chaetodon lineolatus var. *oxycephalus,* Ahl, 1923: p. 169 (New Guinea, New Pomerania, Ternate).

Diagnosis.—D. XII (one with XI), 22-24 (usually 23-24); A. III, 18-20 (usually 19); pectoral rays 14-16 (usually 15); L.l. scales 26-34; large black lunate band extending from last spines of dorsal fin to lower edge of caudal peduncle (extension below this only as narrow stripe, a continuation of dorsal fin pattern); separate horseshoe-shaped mark on nape.

Very closely related to *Chaetodon lineolatus* and distinguished from that species as noted in diagnosis. In addition, depth of body less in C. *oxycephalus* than in C. *lineolatus.*

Chaetodon oxycephalus Bleeker. 79 mm S.L. Philippine Islands.

Ratios	20-69	Standard Length (mm) 70-99(3)	above 99(15)
Depth/S.L.	---	1.7-1.8	1.8-2.0
Head/S.L.	---	2.8-3.0	2.9-3.3
Eye/Head	---	3.3-3.5	3.8-4.2
Snout/Head	---	2.4-2.6	2.1-2.6
Interorb. W./Head	---	3.5-3.8	2.9-3.9
Maxillary/Head	---	3.5-3.8	3.2-3.9
Caud. Ped./S.L.	---	9.0-9.4	9.1-10.5
Pect. Fin/S.L.	---	3.5-3.7	3.7-4.6
Pelvic Sp./S.L.	---	4.2-4.7	5.0-6.2
Predorsal L./S.L.	---	2.3-2.4	2.3-2.5
Prepelvic L./S.L.	---	2.4	2.3-2.5
Dorsal Sp. No. 1/S.L.	---	10.1-14.1	10.7-17.5
Dorsal Sp. No. 2/S.L.	---	7.7-9.9	9.4-13.9
Dorsal Sp. No. 3/S.L.	---	5.8-7.2	7.8-11.3
Dorsal Sp. No. 4/S.L.	---	4.6-5.8	6.2-9.8
Anal Sp. No. 1/S.L.	---	7.9	8.4-11.1
Anal Sp. No. 2/S.L.	---	5.3-5.6	5.8-7.9
Anal Sp. No. 3/S.L.	---	4.8-5.6	5.7-8.5

Meristics.—D. XII (one with XI), 22-24 (rarely 22); A. III, 18-20 (rarely 18 or 20); pectoral rays 15 (one with 14/14, one with 16/16, three with 14/15, and two with 16/15); L.l. scales 26-34; L.l. pores 24-30; scales above L.l. 5-6; scales below L.l. 13-15 (usually 14); gill rakers 13-15 (usually 15).

Description.—Predorsal contour concave at level of nostrils, approximately straight above them; snout robust, projecting, pointed, 2.1-2.6 in head length; gape horizontal to slightly oblique; teeth in about 8 rows in each jaw; preopercle oblique-angled, edge crenulate; lachrymal and supraorbital smooth; snout length greater than depth of caudal peduncle, which is greater than interorbital width; interorbital width greater than eye diameter.

Sixth or seventh dorsal spines longest; first two dorsal spines subequal; second anal spine only slightly longer than third, first about half to two-thirds second; dorsal and anal fins with blunt angles; base of spinous dorsal fin longer (2.4 in S.L.) than that of soft portion (3.3-3.4 in S.L.); pelvic fins short, just failing to reach anal opening.

Lateral line a moderately high arc peaked under last spine and first rays of dorsal fin; scales large, angular, in ascending series; scaly covering of dorsal spines reaching midpoint of fifth or sixth dorsal spines; anal covering to the midpoint of the third anal spine.

Juveniles not known but should be similar to the adults as in the case of *Chaetodon lineolatus.*

Color Pattern.—Sixteen to 18 vertical lines across body; lunate black marking originates from about the ninth or tenth dorsal spine base; black hoof-shaped mark on nape, completely separate from eyebands; eyebands connect across upper interorbital space; upper part of snout dusky; pelvic fins body color.

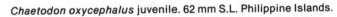
Chaetodon oxycephalus juvenile. 62 mm S.L. Philippine Islands.

Juvenile specimens not known. The 80 mm S.L. specimen is very much like the adults, the inner line of the anal fin, however, very faint to absent. The juveniles may be included with specimens identified as *Chaetodon lineolatus* if the similarity is very close.

Remarks.—*Chaetodon oxycephalus* can easily be identified by the hoof-shaped marking on the nape. The true extent of the range, however, is probably overshadowed by that of *C. lineolatus*, and only reexamination of the museum material can help delineate the boundaries. The distribution of both species appears to overlap in the Philippines, East Indies, New Guinea, and Palau Islands and associated areas.

Although juveniles are not known for *Chaetodon oxycephalus*, they should be quite similar to those of *C. lineolatus*. In addition, it is expected that the nape marking would be confluent with the eyeband proper in the smaller specimens as this is the case in other species (ex. *C. adiergastos*) of this genus. Fortunately, the meristics are sufficiently different to enable one to correctly identify the two species.

It perhaps should be noted here that Copely (1944) gives an illustration which resembles *C. oxycephalus* moreso than it does *C. lineolatus*. This could mean the range extends to the African coast.

Distribution.—East Indies and adjacent areas such as the Philippine Islands, Palau Islands, and New Guinea. Also known from the Indian Ocean side of the Malay Archipelago and Sri Lanka.

Material Examined.—(18 spec.: 80-171 mm S.L.) USNM 181021-181032 (17: 80-171), Philippine Islands; SOSC Te Vega Sta. 104 (1: 158), Mentewai Island, western coast of Sumatra (new record). Photographed at Sri Lanka (new record).

CHAETODON SEMEION Bleeker
Decorated butterflyfish

Chaetodon semeion Bleeker, 1855: p. 450 (type locality Cocos-Keeling Islands, Indian Ocean).

Tetragonoptrus (Rhabdophorus) semeion, Bleeker, 1877: p. 37, pl. 374, fig. 5 (various localities; new combination).

Chaetodon decoratus Ahl, 1923: p. 71, pl. 1, fig. 6. Fowler & Bean, 1929: p. 79 (type locality Yokohama, Japan; Juvenile).

Chaetodon (Rhabdophorus) semeion, Weber & de Beaufort, 1936: p. 61 (various localities).

Diagnosis.—D. XIV (two with XIII), 23-26 (usually 24 or 25); A. III, 19-22 (usually 21); pectoral rays (14) 15; L.l. scales 33-39; dorsal fin rounded but with filament composed of first few rays; black bands along bases or through middle of rayed portions of dorsal and anal fins; small black spots form horizontal rows across body.

Chaetodon semeion Bleeker. 151 mm S.L. Bora Bora, Society Islands.

Ratios	Standard Length (mm)		
	15-59(4)	60-99(5)	above 99(15)
Depth/S.L.	1.6-1.7	1.6-1.8	1.7-1.9
Head/S.L.	2.9-3.0	2.9-3.1	3.2-3.7
Eye/Head	3.0-3.2	3.1-3.4	3.5-4.1
Snout/Head	2.5-2.6	2.5-2.8	2.4-3.1
Interorb. W./Head	3.1-3.5	3.1-3.4	2.8-3.6
Maxillary/Head	3.3-3.5	3.5-3.7	3.3-4.1
Caud. Ped./S.L.	9.3-9.5	9.0-9.8	9.1-10.1
Pect. Fin/S.L.	3.9	3.6-5.0	4.0-4.4
Pelvic Sp./S.L.	4.6-4.8	4.8-5.3	5.6-6.7
Predorsal L./S.L.	2.0-2.4	2.4-2.6	2.6-3.0
Prepelvic L./S.L.	2.3-2.4	2.4-2.6	2.5-2.8
Dorsal Sp. No. 1/S.L.	9.3-12.5	9.3-11.4	8.8-12.2
Dorsal Sp. No. 2/S.L.	7.8-9.5	8.4-10.3	10.5-13.3
Dorsal Sp. No. 3/S.L.	5.7-6.5	6.4-8.7	8.9-12.7
Dorsal Sp. No. 4/S.L.	4.4-5.5	5.9-7.6	8.6-11.2
Anal Sp. No. 1/S.L.	6.7-7.9	7.5-9.2	9.4-12.7
Anal Sp. No. 2/S.L.	5.0-5.7	5.5-6.6	6.4-8.2
Anal Sp. No. 3/S.L.	4.8-4.9	5.2-6.6	6.2-8.0

Meristics.—D. XIV (two with XIII), 23-26 (usually 24 or 25); A. III, 19-22 (usually 21); pectoral rays 15 (one with 14/14, three with 14/15); L.l. scales 33-39; L.l. pores 28-35; scales above L.l. 6-8 (usually 7); scales below L.l. 13-16 (usually 14-15); gill rakers 12-17 (usually 16 or 17).

Description.—Predorsal contour slightly convex at nape and concave just above nostrils, otherwise straight; snout moderate, pointed, 2.4-3.1 in head length; gape oblique; teeth in 7-9 rows in each jaw; preopercle oblique-angled, edge smooth; lachrymal and supraorbital smooth; snout length greater than depth of caudal peduncle, which is greater than eye diameter.

Sixth or seventh dorsal spines longest; first dorsal spine shorter than, equal to, or even longer than second dorsal spine; second and third anal spines approximately equal, first just over half of second; dorsal and anal fins low, rounded, accenting curvature of body; soft dorsal fin with a filament composed of third ray or combination of second and third or third and fourth rays; in one specimen the first ray was involved; base of spinous portion of dorsal fin longer (2.5-2.6 in S.L.) than that of soft portion (2.9-3.2 in S.L.); pelvic fins short, failing to reach anal opening by a short distance.

Lateral line a high peaked arc, the peak at the base of the last spines and first rays of dorsal fin; scales large, rounded but with a flat edge, in ascending series on body, lowest rows almost horizontal; scales of dorsal

Chaetodon semeion juveniles. 28 and 48 mm S.L. Palau Islands.

Chaetodon semeion is one of the few species of butterflyfishes to have a filament in the dorsal fin. Photo by W. Deas.

fin reaching midpoint of sixth spine, those of anal fin covering half to two-
thirds of third spine.

Juveniles similar to adults but lack the dorsal fin filament.

Color Pattern.—Spots on side occur one per scale; eyebands joined
broadly at nape; interorbital area almost to edge of lachrymal and above
blending into the eyeband, dark brown and obscuring the forward edge
of the eyeband; pelvic fins body color; caudal fin with dark line or lines
outlining each ray (as in *Chaetodon ephippium* and *C. xanthocephalus*).

Juveniles differ from pattern of adults in certain aspects: black bands
at bases of dorsal and anal fins are absent; eyeband more "normal,"
extending from nape to interopercle; black caudal peduncle band present,
wider at center but connected above and below in 29 mm specimen; in a
50 mm specimen the band connects above but only slightly ventrally;
caudal fin mostly hyaline, as are edges of dorsal and anal fin. A 17.2 mm
specimen was similar to the 29 mm specimen but still retained the tholichthys plates.

By 55 mm (a specimen from Palau) the first traces of the dorsal and
anal fin markings appear and light traces of the submarginal dark line are
evident. The caudal peduncle band is present but as two spots, the dorsal
and ventral connections reduced to mere threads. The eyeband is still narrower than the eye, and there are no traces of the filament.

At 80 mm the filament is noticeable, the caudal peduncle band is
very faded (but still visible), and both dorsal and anal bands are present.

Color of living animals entirely rich lemon yellow to orange-yellow
with black markings and blue-black spots. Interorbital area blue; pectoral
fins hyaline and pelvic fins yellow; caudal fin hyaline with each ray out-

621

lined in violet; edges of dorsal spines yellow with submarginal blue-whitish stripe; rayed portion of fins with submarginal white to yellow-white stripes; filament yellow; forehead gray; black band margined with dark yellow, then light yellow, gray, and blackish.

Color of juveniles yellow with black markings.

Remarks.—*Chaetodon semeion* is a fairly distinctive butterflyfish, apparently uncommon throughout its range. Reports of sightings of this species at Eniwetok, Marshall Islands are not common in spite of intensive diving over a period of years by experienced divers and ichthyologists. It is easily recognizable by color pattern and dorsal fin shape with its filament.

The change with age in color pattern and form have led but once to alternative naming of this species, *C. decoratus* Ahl (1923).

The caudal fin pattern is similar to that of both *C. ephippium* (which also has a filament) and *C. xanthocephalus* (which does not).

E.K. Jordan (1925) lists *Chaetodon semeion* from the Hawaiian Islands: "A fine cast of this showy species is in the Bishop Museum."

Distribution.—Polynesia (? from the Hawaiian Islands), Melanesia and Micronesia to the East Indies, Philippine Islands, and north to the Ryu Kyu Islands and southern Japan. Extends into the Indian Ocean as far as the Cocos Keeling Islands. Not reported from Australia.

Material Examined.—(24 spec.: 17-166 mm S.L.) BPBM 4324 (1: 166), Shortland Islands, Solomons; BPBM 4130 (1: 166), Wake Island; BPBM 5872 (1: 151), Bora Bora, Society Islands; CAS 37812 (3: 135-141), Ifaluk Atoll, Caroline Islands; CAS 37813, CAS 37814, and Sta. 1955 113 Reg 619 (10: 67-123), Palau Islands, Western Caroline Islands; CAS 37826 (2: 29-50), Palau Islands; CAS 37827 (1: 55), Palau Islands; CAS 37815 (4: 123-142), Polim Reef, Kapingamarangi Atoll; CAS 38778 (1: 17.2), Palau Islands.

CHAETODON MESOLEUCOS Forsskal
Red Sea butterflyfish

Chaetodon mesoleucos Forsskal, 1775: pp. xii, 61 (type locality Red Sea).

Chaetodon hadjan Bloch, 1801: p. 227 (type locality Red Sea).

?*Holacanthus mesoleucus* (not of Bloch), Lacepede, 1802: p. 528, 535 (Red Sea; misspelling of *mesoleucos* Forsskal).

Chaetodon (*Anisochaetodon*) *mesoleucus* (not of Bloch), Klunzinger, 1884: p. 57 (Red Sea; misspelling of *C. mesoleucos* Forsskal).

Diagnosis.—D. XIII, 21-23 (rarely 21); A. III, 18-20 (usually 19); pectoral rays 14 (15); L.l. scales 22-25 (normally 22-23); anterior third gray, posterior two-thirds vertically striped, the two zones separated by a white stripe; eyeband present but weak; endemic to Red Sea area.

Chaetodon mesoleucos Forsskal . 90 mm S.L. Red Sea.

Ratios	Standard Length (mm)		
	20-50	51-79(2)	above 79(7)
Depth/S.L.............ccc	---	1.7, 1.9	1.6-1.8
Head/S.L..............	---	2.8, 2.8	2.9-3.1
Eye/Head	---	3.3, 3.5	3.4-3.6
Snout/Head	---	2.3, 2.4	2.3-2.7
Interorb. W./Head......	---	4.0, 4.3	3.5-3.9
Maxillary/Head	---	3.4, 3.7	3.4-3.8
Caud. Ped./S.L.........	---	8.2, 8.9	8.1-9.2
Pect. Fin/S.L...........	---	3.7, 3.8	3.7-4.2
Pelvic Sp./S.L..........	---	4.7, 4.9	4.7-5.5
Predorsal L./S.L........	---	2.1, 2.3	2.3-2.4
Prepelvic L./S.L........	---	2.4, 2.5	2.3-2.5
Dorsal Sp. No. 1/S.L.....	---	11.2, 12.5	9.7-11.5
Dorsal Sp. No. 2/S.L.....	---	8.6, 9.4	6.7-10.0
Dorsal Sp. No. 3/S.L.....	---	6.3, 6.7	5.2-6.9
Dorsal Sp. No. 4/S.L.....	---	5.3	4.7-6.1
Anal Sp. No. 1/S.L.......	---	7.6	6.7-9.3
Anal Sp. No. 2/S.L.......	---	4.8, 5.1	4.5-5.5
Anal Sp. No. 3/S.L.......	---	4.7, 5.1	4.5-6.3

Chaetodon mesoleucos occurs most often in small groups.

Meristics.—D. XIII, 21-23 (rarely 21); A. III, 18-20 (normally 19); pectoral rays 14 (one with 15/15, two with 14/15); L.l. scales 22-25 (normally 22 or 23); L.l. pores 15-20 (usually 15-18); scales above L.l. 7-8; scales below L.l. 13-14; gill rakers 14-16 (usually 16).

Description.—Predorsal contour approximately straight until level of eye, then concave; snout projecting, 2.3-2.7 in head length, pointed; gape horizontal to slightly oblique; teeth in six to seven rows in each jaw; preopercle oblique to very oblique, edge crenulate to serrate; lachrymal long, smooth; supraorbital smooth; snout length greater than depth of caudal peduncle, which is greater than eye diameter; eye diameter greater than interorbital width.

Fourth to sixth dorsal spines longest; second anal spine stronger, longer than or equal to third, first about ⅔ of second; dorsal fin very angular, posterior edge vertical, anal fin with rounded angle, edge also vertical or slanting back towards body; both fins about equal; base of spinous portion of dorsal fin longer (2.2-2.4 in S.L.) than that of soft portion (3.0-3.4 in S.L.); pelvic fins long, reaching bases of first or second anal fin spines.

Lateral line a high arc across body; scales large, rhomboidal, following a chevron-type pattern similar to chevron group; dorsal scales reaching midpoint of sixth dorsal spine; anal spine covering reaching midpoint of third spine.

Juveniles similar to adults.

624

Color Pattern.—Body with 15 or 16 dark vertical lines along edges of scale rows, another four to six on caudal peduncle; pelvic fins body color; dusky stripe from front edge of each eye to upper part of lachrymal edge, connecting across top of snout; eyeband faint, connected on nape and again on chest, although very faded (in one specimen eyeband was indiscernible).

Juveniles similar to adults.

Head and anterior portion of body white to pearl gray, posterior portion chestnut with black and white stripes; narrow edge of dorsal and anal fins white, submarginal lines black; caudal fin chestnut, semicircular band yellowish-white, posterior border of fin hyaline; eyeband dusky gray to blackish; line from eye to upper lip dusky; pectoral fins hyaline, pelvic fins grayish to white.

Remarks.—*Chaetodon mesoleucos* should not be confused with *Chaetodontoplus mesoleucus*, an angelfish. The names are very similar, and although the difference of one letter seems slight, it is enough to prevent invalidation of one of the species. Adding to the confusion is the fact that the angelfish was originally described by Bloch under the name *Chaetodon mesoleucus*.

Chaetodon mesoleucos is a very distinctive butterflyfish whose color pattern resembles no other chaetodontid. It is a Red Sea endemic and may be an offshoot of *Chaetodon falcula* or some related species.

Apparently it is found throughout the Red Sea, most often along the coralline barrier or around the bases of the corals. *Chaetodon mesoleucos* is a gregarious species, fairly common as small groups (Baschieri-Salvatore, 1954).

Distribution.—Red Sea.

Material Examined.—(9 spec.: 76-99 mm S.L.) AMNH 9457 (4: 82-99), Red Sea; BPBM 7846 (4: 76-90), Massaua, Red Sea; 20482 (1: 79), Red Sea.

CHAETODON SELENE Bleeker
Moon butterflyfish

Chaetodon selene Bleeker, 1853: p. 76 (type locality Lawajong, Solor).

Tetragonoptrus selene, Bleeker, 1865: p. 286 (new combination).

Tetragonoptrus (Chaetodontops) selene, Bleeker, 1877: p. 44, pl. 15 (377), fig. 5 (Celebes, Moluccas).

Chaetodon (Chaetodontops) selene, Weber & de Beaufort, 1936: p. 90 (various localities).

Diagnosis.—D. XII, 20-22; A. III, 18 (one with 19); pectoral rays 14; L.l. scales 31-36 (usually 32-34); gill rakers 17-20; black crescent-shaped marking along base of dorsal fin to mid-base of anal fin; 3-4 rows of light dots ascending from upper edge of gill cover to dorsal fin base; greater

Chaetodon selene Bleeker. 129 mm S.L. Philippine Islands.

Ratios	20-59	Standard Length (mm) 60-89(2)	above 89(10)
Depth/S.L.	---	1.6-1.7	1.6-1.8
Head/S.L.	---	2.9-3.0	2.9-3.2
Eye/Head	---	3.3-3.5	3.1-3.7
Snout/Head	---	2.3-2.4	2.2-2.7
Interorb. W./Head	---	3.8	3.3-4.0
Maxillary/Head	---	3.5-3.8	8.7-9.8
Caud. Ped./S.L.	---	8.8-9.2	8.7-9.8
Pect. Fin/S.L.	---	4.0-4.4	3.8-4.5
Pelvic Sp./S.L.	---	4.9-5.9	5.3-6.4
Predorsal L./S.L.	---	2.0-2.1	2.0-2.2
Prepelvic L./S.L.	---	2.4	2.2-2.7
Dorsal Sp. No. 1/S.L.	---	12.0-15.0	12.7-17.9
Dorsal Sp. No. 2/S.L.	---	8.0-11.3	7.7-11.9
Dorsal Sp. No. 3/S.L.	---	5.5-7.9	4.7-8.4
Dorsal Sp. No. 4/S.L.	---	4.3-6.9	5.1-6.6
Anal Sp. No. 1/S.L.	---	7.4-9.9	7.8-10.6
Anal Sp. No. 2/S.L.	---	5.2-6.2	5.7-7.0
Anal Sp. No. 3/S.L.	---	4.9-6.7	5.5-7.1

portion of dorsal and anal fins light colored; lower mean number of lateral line scales than *Chaetodon gardneri*; eyeband narrower than that of *C. gardneri* below eye, and posterior edge passes through eye (in *C. gardneri* it touches posterior rim of orbit).

Meristics.—D. XII, 20-22; A. III, 18 (one with 19); pectoral fin 14 (three with 13/14); L.l. scales 31-36 (usually 32-36); pores in L.l. 27-34 (usually 27-34); scales above L.l. 5 or 6; scales below L.l. 12 or 13; gill rakers 17-20.

Description.—Predorsal contour slightly convex at nape, concave at nostrils, otherwise straight; snout moderate, pointed, 2.2-2.7 in head length; gape horizontal; teeth in 10 to 11 rows in each jaw; preopercle obtuse-angled, edge crenulate; lachrymal and supraorbital smooth; snout length greater than depth of caudal peduncle, which is greater than eye diameter; eye greater than interorbital width.

Fifth dorsal spine longest; second and third anal spines subequal, first about two-thirds second; dorsal and anal fins with blunt angle at thirteenth to fifteenth rays in dorsal fin and eleventh ray in anal fin; base of spinous portion of dorsal fin longer (2.5-2.8 in S.L.) than that of soft portion (3.1-3.3 in S.L.); caudal fin truncate to slightly rounded, upper rays slightly extended; pelvic fins short, at most reaching anus.

Peak of lateral line at about eighth dorsal spine base; scales moderately large to large, exposed portion vertically elongate, rounded; scales in horizontal series in lower portions of body, ascending rows in middle and upper portions; scales cover about half of fifth dorsal spine and reach midpoint or less of third anal spine.

Juveniles similar to adults.

Color Pattern.—Three or four rows of light colored spots in upper anterior portion of body; black lunate-shaped marking at times connected narrowly with eyeband; light stripe bordering this also connects with posterior light stripe bordering eyeband; pelvic fins body color; eyebands connected before dorsal fin, cross through eye (though posterior edge of band does not extend to posterior edge of orbit), become silvery below eye to lower edge of preopercle, and possibly connected again on isthmus although this connection very faint if present; eyebands bordered posteriorly with white stripe and possibly also anteriorly (at least above eye).

Juveniles with black posterior mark that extends from base of spinous dorsal fin across soft dorsal fin and caudal peduncle to mid-base of anal fin; origin of this band expanded, almost a large spot (similar to that of *Chaetodon ocellatus* juvenile); anterodorsal spots not evident.

Remarks.—*Chaetodon selene* is a rather poorly known species with a restricted range compared with most other chaetodonts, including the East Indies and Philippine Islands to southern Japan.

It is closely related to *C. leucopleura* and *C. gardneri*, two species equally poorly known. The orange or yellow spots on the shoulder region seem to be unique for this species, although the violet or dusky lines on the lower portions of the body are found in all three. The eyeband in *C.*

selene appears to be more anterior than in the other two, the posterior edge not coinciding with the posterior edge of the orbit. The peculiarity of the silvery or yellow eye band below the eye (in preservative) is unique for these three species, no other such occurrence having been reported for any other chaetodont. This apparently is an adult trait, as subadults and juveniles of *C. selene* did not exhibit this characteristic. The dark posterior lunate band seems intermediate in extent between the other two species, although in *C. leucopleura* a dusky area also appears in the upper portion of the body as an extension of the blackish area near the caudal peduncle.

Distribution.—East Indies (Amboina, Java); Philippine Islands; southern Japan (Kashiwajima as far north as Yokahama).

Material Examined.—(12 spec.: 82-129 mm S.L.) USNM 182015-18, 182013-14 (9: 88-129), Philippine Islands; SU 25794 and 25797 (3: 82-121), Philippine Islands.

CHAETODON LEUCOPLEURA Playfair
Somali butterflyfish

Chaetodon leucopleura Playfair, 1866: p. 35, pl. 6, fig. 3 (type locality Zanzibar).

Chaetodon leucopygus Ahl, 1923: p. 72, pl. 2, fig. 12 (type locality Daressalem). Tortonese, 1936: p. 255 (Italian Somaliland).

Chaetodon Gardneri (not of Norman), Kotthaus, 1976: pp. 45-61, fig. 376.

Chaetodon leucopleura Playfair. 135 mm S.L. Somali Coast.

Ratios	Standard Length (mm)		
	20-50	60-89	above 89(11)
Depth/S.L.............	---	---	1.6-1.8
Head/S.L..............	---	---	3.0-3.3
Eye/Head.............	---	---	2.8-3.3
Snout/Head...........	---	---	2.3-2.8
Interorb. W./Head......	---	---	3.0-3.5
Maxillary/Head........	---	---	3.5-3.8
Caud. Ped./S.L.........	---	---	8.9-9.9
Pect. Fin/S.L...........	---	---	3.8-4.3
Pelvic Sp./S.L..........	---	---	5.9-6.9
Predorsal L./S.L........	---	----	2.1-2.4
Prepelvic L./S.L........	---	---	2.4-2.6
Dorsal Sp. No. 1/S.L.....	---	---	13.1-19.4
Dorsal Sp. No. 2/S.L.....	---	---	8.6-14.6
Dorsal Sp. No. 3/S.L.....	---	---	6.4-8.6
Dorsal Sp. No. 4/S.L.....	---	---	5.6-7.2
Anal Sp. No. 1/S.L.......	---	---	8.5-11.2
Anal Sp. No. 2/S.L.......	---	---	5.7-7.0
Anal Sp. No. 3/S.L.......	---	---	5.4-7.1

Diagnosis.—D. XII, 22 (occasionally 21 or 23); A. III, 18-19 (usually 19); pectoral rays 14; L.l. scales 31-37 (usually 32-34); gill rakers 17-20; anal fin light colored; dorsal fin mostly light colored but black at base and last few rays entirely black; 10 or 11 scales below lateral line.

Meristics.—D. XII, 22 (occasionally 21 or 23); A. III, 18 or 19 (usually 19); pectoral rays 14 (two with 13/14, one with 15/14); L.l. scales 31-37 (usually 32-34); L.l. pores 25-34 (usually 28-32); scales above L.l. 4 (occasionally 5); scales below L.l. 10 or 11; gill rakers 15-22 (usually 17-20).

Description.—Predorsal contour concave, a convexity just before dorsal fin; snout pointed, slightly extended, 2.3-2.8 in head length; gape horizontal to slightly oblique; teeth in 10 to 12 rows in each jaw; preopercle with obtuse angle, edge smooth to crenulate; lachrymal and supraorbital smooth; posterior nostril with groove to eye; snout length greater than depth of caudal peduncle, which is greater than eye diameter; eye diameter greater than interorbital width.

Sixth dorsal spine longest (occasionally fourth or fifth), first short, ⅔ of second, which is also short; second and third anal spines about equal, first approximately ⅔ of second; dorsal and anal fins with blunt angle at about fourteenth or fifteenth ray of dorsal fin and eleventh to twelfth rays of anal fin; base of spinous portion of dorsal fin longer (2.3-2.6 in S.L.)

than that of soft portion (2.9-3.4 in S.L.); caudal fin truncate, upper rays somewhat extended into a point; pelvic fins short, falling quite short of the anus.

Peak of lateral line at base of eighth or ninth dorsal spines (one or two scales from dorsal fin base); scales large, exposed portion vertically elongate, rounded to slightly flattened, in horizontal series on lower part of body, slightly to moderately ascending near and above lateral line; scaly covering of dorsal spines reaching midpoint of fifth to sixth dorsal fin spines, and that of anal fin extending over two-thirds to three-fourths of third anal spine.

Juveniles not seen.

Color Pattern.—About five to six horizontal lines crossing lower portion of body, running through broader but paler stripes; in some specimens narrow vertical stripes cross body following scale rows; pelvic fins approximately body color; eyebands broadly joined in front of nape and again on chest, where they extend back to the area between base of pelvic fins; eyeband below eye generally faded or blotchy; snout tip dark.

Juveniles not seen, but a photo of a small specimen (subadult?) had more hyaline edge to caudal fin and white dark bordered stripe about ⅓ in from caudal fin edge.

Remarks.—*Chaetodon leucopleura* is a rarely encountered species of the East African coast. It reaches the Arabian Sea and might possibly enter into the Gulf of Aden. The lack of adequate collections in the area of northeastern Africa and Arabia leaves the question open as to whether this species and *Chaetodon gardneri* are sympatric. The portion of the eyeband on the preopercle and cheek appears to be mostly dark colored. The light portion seen on *Chaetodon selene* and *C. gardneri* may be indicated on a couple of specimens. Playfair mentioned this character in his original description yet indicates a dark band in his figure. The color has been noted in the other closely related species and is most likely consistent in the three species. The yellow color apparently fades or is lost in preservation in some specimens but not in others.

The type specimen appears to agree well with the specimens on hand. The comparison was made thanks to a photograph of the type provided by Mr. Alwyne Wheeler of the British Museum (Natural History).

The eight specimens from the *Anton Bruun* were caught at a depth of from 62 to 72 meters. Like *Chaetodon tinkeri*, this species may be common below 30 meters.

The scales are normally large, vertically elongate, and, though mostly rounded, somewhat irregular on their posterior edges. In large portions of the side of most of the specimens examined smaller scales replaced the larger ones. There are too many to be expected due to natural losses and replacement, though no explanation is forthcoming at this time.

Distribution.—Eastern coast of Africa and adjacent islands from Dar Es Salaam, Zanzibar, and Shimomi in Tanzania to the northern Somali coast (new record) and Red Sea (new record). Listed by Smith (1955) from Aldabra.

Material Examined.—(11 spec.: 122-144 mm S.L.) JLBS M.244 (1: 123), Malindi; JLBS S.169 (1: 136), Shimomi; SOSC Anton Bruun Cr. 9, Sta. 25-29 (8: 122-133), Somali Coast (11°18′N 51°08′E); SOSC Anton Bruun Cr. 9, Sta. 465 (1: 134), Somali Coast (11°37′N 51°27′E).

CHAETODON GARDNERI Norman
Gardner's Butterflyfish

Chaetodon selene Boulenger, 1887: p. 657. (Muscat). (non *C. selene* Bleeker).
Chaetodon gardneri Norman, 1939: p. 65 (Gulf of Aden, Gulf of Oman).
Chaetodon [*Chaetodontops*] *gardneri* Fraser-Brunner, 1949: p. 45. (Aden).

Chaetodon gardneri Norman. 120 mm S.L. Muscat, Gulf of Oman. (Paratype).

Diagnosis.—D.XII, 20-22;, A.III, 18-19; pectoral rays 14 (one with 13/14);L.1. scales 33-36; gill rakers 15-20; dorsal fin mostly dark the color extending across posterior part of body to base of anal fin; broad eye band from nape to chest; close to *Chaetodon selene* and *C. leucopleura* but differing in color pattern; *Chaetodon leucopleura* has a higher dorsal ray count, lower scale count, and fewer scales below the L.l., and has only the last few dorsal fin rays black; *C. selene* has a lower mean scale count, and the dorsal fin is mostly light colored with a black marking along the base.

Meristics.—D.XII, 20-22; A. III, 18-19; pectoral rays 14 (one with 13/14 ; L.l. scales 33-36; L.l. pores 29-35; scales above L.l. 4-5; scales below L.l. 13; gill rakers 15-20.

Ratios	20-59	Standard Length (mm) 60-89(2)	above 89(5)
Depth/S.L.............	---	1.6	1.6-1.7
Head/S.L..............	---	2.9-3.0	3.1-3.4
Eye/Head	---	3.2	3.2-3.3
Snout/Head	---	2.5-2.7	2.5-2.8
Interorb. W./Head......	---	3.8-3.9	3.4-3.7
Maxillary/Head	---	3.8-3.9	3.7-4.0
Caud. Ped./S.L.........	---	9.6-9.7	8.7-9.8
Pect. Fin/S.L..........	---	3.9-4.0	4.1-4.3
Pelvic Sp./S.L.........	---	5.3-5.8	5.9-6.8
Predorsal L./S.L.......	---	2.1-2.2	2.3-2.7
Prepelvic L./S.L.......	---	2.5-2.6	2.4-2.7
Dorsal Sp. No. 1/S.L.....	---	10.6-11.8	11.7-19.0
Dorsal Sp. No. 2/S.L.....	---	7.4-8.1	8.1-11.2
Dorsal Sp. No. 3/S.L.....	---	4.9-5.2	5.7-8.5
Dorsal Sp. No. 4/S.L.....	---	4.4-4.9	5.8-6.4
Anal Sp. No. 1/S.L.......	---	7.1-7.4	8.3-9.5
Anal Sp. No. 2/S.L.......	---	5.0-5.5	5.4-6.5
Anal Sp. No. 3/S.L.......	---	4.7-5.2	5.0-6.4

Description.—Predorsal contour convex at nape, concave at nostrils, otherwise straight; snout moderately extended, 2.5-2.8 in head length, pointed; gape horizontal; teeth in nine to ten rows in upper and lower jaws; preopercle slightly obtuse-angled, edge crenulate; lacrymal and supraorbital smooth; snout length greater than caudal peduncle depth, the latter greater than eye diameter which is greater than interorbital width.

Fifth dorsal spine longest; second and third anal spines subequal, first about two-thirds of second; dorsal and anal fins with blunt angle at about 14th ray in dorsal fin and eleventh ray in anal fin; base of spinous portion of dorsal fin longer (2.4-2.8 in S.L.) than soft portion (3.0-3.4 in S.L.); caudal fin truncate to slightly emarginate, upper rays sometimes extended slightly; pelvic fins short, not reaching anus.

Lateral line peak at about seventh or eight dorsal spine bases, then descending in smooth arc along base of rayed portion of dorsal fin; scales moderately large, exposed portion slightly elongate vertically, rounded to slightly flattened, in horizontal series in lower part of body, slightly to moderately ascending near and above lateral line; scaly covering of dorsal spines reaching midpoint of fifth to sixth dorsal fin spines, and that of anal fin extending more than half of third anal spine. Juveniles not seen.

Color Pattern.—In preserved specimens horizontal lines present in lower portions of body; eye band silvery (black in life) below to lower edge of preopercle; eye bands joined on chest forming a blotch where they meet, and on nape before origin of dorsal fin; silvery stripe (yellow in life) extending from silver or lower eye band along posterior edge of upper eye band and along base of spinous dorsal fin, ending at about first ray. Juveniles not known.

Remarks.—This species is very closer to *Chaetodon selene* and *C. leucopleura* yet differentiated from them by color and meristics as noted under diagnosis. It apparently is a geographic replacement species of both *C. selene* (of the East Indies and Philippines) and of *C. leucopleura* (African coast) occurring in the vicinity of Arabian peninsula. The distribution appears similar to that of *C. trifasciatus* complex.

Distribution.—Known only from the Gulf of Aden and Gulf of Oman.

Material Examined.—(2 speci.: 101-120 mm S.L.) BMNH 1888.29.37-40 (2: 101-120), Muscat, Gulf of Oman. (PARATYPES).

CHAETODON NIGROPUNCTATUS Sauvage
Mystery butterflyfish

Chaetodon nigropunctatus Sauvage, 1880: p. 222 (type locality Muscat, Arabia).

Chaetodon obscurus Boulenger, 1887: p. 657 (type locality Muscat).

Chaetodon (Tetrachaetodon) nigropunctatus Sauvage, 1891: p. 257, pl. 29, fig. 2 (Madagascar).

Chaetodon obscurus, Blegvad, 1944: p. 148, fig. 83 (Iranian Gulf).

Diagnosis.—D. XIII, 21-23; A. III, 18-20; pectoral rays (14) 15; L.l. scales 36-39; overall brown with darker spot on each scale base; head, nape and breast lighter; broad yellow edge to caudal fin; nape prominent; eyeband absent.

Meristics.—D. XIII, 21-23; A. III, 18-20; pectoral rays 15 (one with 14/14, three with 14/15); L.l. scales 36-39; pores in L.l. 28-36 (usually 30-34); scales above L.l. 7-8; scales below L.l. 16-18; gill rakers 15 or 16.

Description.—Predorsal contour concave in largest specimen, almost straight in others; nape prominent; snout moderate, pointed, 3.0-3.3 in S.L.; gape slightly oblique; teeth in 9-10 rows in lower jaw and 8-9 rows in upper jaw; preopercle right-angled, edge smooth to slightly serrate; lachrymal and supraorbital smooth; depth of caudal peduncle greater

Chaetodon nigropunctatus Sauvage. 109 mm S.L. Muscat, Gulf of Oman. (Syntype).

| Ratios | Standard Length (mm) | | |
	20-59(2)	60-89(1)	above 89(4)
Depth/S.L.............	1.6-1.7	1.6	1.5-1.6
Head/S.L..............	2.6	3.1	3.1-3.3
Eye/Head	2.8-2.9	3.3	3.0-3.5
Snout/Head	2.8	2.6	3.0-3.3
Interorb. W./Head......	3.0-3.2	3.5	2.8-3.2
Maxillary/Head	3.6-4.6	4.1	3.8-4.3
Caud. Ped./S.L.........	7.9-8.2	8.9	8.2-9.1
Pect. Fin/S.L..........	3.4-3.6	3.9	3.8-4.0
Pelvic Sp./S.L.........	4.4-5.0	4.7	5.2-5.7
Predorsal L./S.L........	1.9-2.0	2.3-	2.3-2.4
Prepelvic L./S.L........	2.0-2.1	2.3	2.2-2.5
Dorsal Sp. No. 1/S.L.....	11.6	10.9	11.1-13.6
Dorsal Sp. No. 2/S.L.....	5.9	7.4	8.5-10.6
Dorsal Sp. No. 3/S.L.....	4.4	6.0	6.7-8.0
Dorsal Sp. No. 4/S.L.....	3.9	4.7	5.1-6.5
Anal Sp. No. 1/S.L.......	---	8.7	8.6-9.3
Anal Sp. No. 2/S.L.......	---	5.3	5.5-6.0
Anal Sp. No. 3/S.L.......	---	5.2	5.1-6.4

than snout length, which is equal to or greater than interorbital width; interorbital width greater than eye diameter.

Fifth or sixth dorsal spine longest; second and third anal spines about equal, first two-thirds second; dorsal and anal fins with blunt angle, dorsal sharper; base of spinous portion of dorsal fin longer (1.9-2.3 in S.L.) than that of soft portion (2.9-3.3 in S.L.); caudal fin truncate-rounded; pelvic fins moderate, reaching beyond anus but not to anal fin spines.

Peak of lateral line at about tenth dorsal spine base; scales moderate to large, angular, in slightly rising series on body, more rapidly ascending above lateral line; scaly covering of dorsal spines reaching midpoint of sixth spine, that of anal fin reaching midpoint of third anal spine.

Juveniles similar to adults but nape is less prominent.

Color Pattern.—Edge of caudal fin hyaline, a light band submarginally; face, nape, and throat to chest lighter brown to yellow; pectorals light brown, pelvic fins blackish brown; dark indistinct smudge on nape just anterior to first dorsal fin spine (on one specimen the color extends downward on both sides of head across opercle); opercular flap black-brown; spots on scales may be very faded to absent or lost in a darker background color.

Juveniles with some color distinctions. Two specimens of 25 mm and 35 mm S.L. had overall lighter color, the lighter anterior portion extending to origin of pelvic fins; eyeband poorly defined, extending from just anterior   dorsal fin to eye, not as wide as eye, and below eye, where it is very faded, to lower edge of preopercle; posterior edge of eyeband coincides with posterior rim of orbit; in 35 mm specimen a brown indistinct band across base of caudal fin fading into body color, leaving less of the fin yellowish than other specimen; in many cases this brown color extends further into fin with age; dorsal and anal fins with hyaline edges and submarginal dark brown band; in smaller specimen a dark brown spot in dorsal and anal fin, that of the dorsal fin more rounded and more distinct, both near edge of the fin just where angle will be (juvenile fins are rounded); in the 35 mm juvenile the spots are larger and less defined —they presumably will become larger and eventually include the entire fins.

Color of juveniles not known but should be yellowish brown to darker brown, with yellow face and black spots.

Remarks.—*Chaetodon nigropunctatus* is a rather poorly known species from the Persian Gulf and Gulf of Oman. A photograph of a cotype of *Chaetodon obscurus* kindly supplied by Mr. Alwyne Wheeler leaves no doubt that it is synonymous with this species.

Sauvage (1891) believed this species to be closely related to *C. collaris* Bloch. I think he meant *C. aureus* rather than the true *C. collaris* (see these species for discussion of confusion between them).

Distribution.—Known only from the Gulf of Oman and the Persian Gulf. There is a sight record from the Iranian Gulf near Kharg, and specimens in the British Museum (Nat. Hist.) are from the Jask-Mekran coast (Muscat) and Gwadar-Baluchistan.

Material Examined.—(7 spec.: 23-109 mm S.L.) MNHN A. 305, (3: 100-109), Muscat, Arabia (syntypes); FMNH 5754 (1: 96), Muscat, Arabia; SMF 10551 (1: 87), Persian Gulf (60 miles from Kuwait City); USNM 196507 (2: 23-35), Jaraid Island, Persian Gulf.

Subgenus LEPIDOCHAETODON Bleeker

Lepidochaetodon Bleeker, 1876: p. 306. (Type-species *Chaetodon unimaculatus* Bloch, 1787, by original designation).

Diagnosis.—Body oval to rounded; dorsal and anal fins rounded; snout short, robust, 2.5-3.2 in head length; lateral line a high smooth arc; lachrymal partially hidden by scales; teeth in rows, outer row noticeably stronger than inner rows; lateral black spot situated on lateral line; D. XIII, 21-23; A. III, 19; pectoral fin 14-15; L.l. scales 38-47.

Description.—Body oval to rounded; snout short, blunt, robust, 2.5-3.2 in head length; predorsal contour convex at nape, concave at level of nostrils, or completely straight; mouth small, wide, terminal, gape slightly oblique; teeth in several rows in each jaw, outermost row noticeably larger than inner rows; preopercle right-angled to slightly obtuse; lachrymal partially hidden by scales; supraorbital smooth to lightly serrate.

Dorsal spines increase in length until middle spines (fifth through seventh) then decrease gradually until last; anal spines strong, second and third approximately equal, first about two-thirds of second; soft portions of dorsal and anal fins approximately equal, rounded, the posterior edges in a vertical plane; base of spinous portion of dorsal fin longer (about 2.2 in S.L.) than that of rayed portion (3.1 in S.L.); caudal fin truncate-rounded; pectoral fins normal; pelvic fins short, not reaching anus by a short distance.

Lateral line describing a moderately high arc across body, ending near last rays of dorsal fin; scales moderate, rounded to nearly angular or rhomboidal, usually a mixture of the different types; scales smaller on head, chest, posterior third of body, caudal peduncle and vertical fins; scaly covering of dorsal spines normal, reaching midpoint of sixth dorsal spine; covering of anal spines extending to three-fourths length of third spine.

Juveniles similar to adults though the snout is comparatively more slender or less robust.

Widely distributed in Indo-Pacific region from the Hawaiian Islands to the eastern coast of Africa and from southern Japan to the Great Barrier Reef of Australia.

A single species with two subspecies is recognized.

Key to the Subspecies of *Chaetodon unimaculatus*

Eyeband broad, almost as wide as eye, continuing to chest and joining opposite band; lower portions of body whitish (Pacific Ocean) . . . .
. . . .*C. unimaculatus unimaculatus*
Eyeband narrow, considerably narrower than eye, ending at lower edge of interopercle; lower area of body yellow (Indian Ocean) . . . .
. . . .*C. unimaculatus interruptus*

Remarks.—The peculiarities of the snout and teeth are enough to warrant a separate subgenus for *Chaetodon unimaculatus*. Although quite normal in the younger stages, the snout is very robust (pig-like) in large adults. The teeth are normal except for an enlarged outer row which has not been found in any other species of butterflyfish.

CHAETODON UNIMACULATUS Bloch
Teardrop butterflyfish
(One-spot coralfish)

Chaetodon unimaculatus Bloch, 1787: p. 75, pl. 201, fig. 1 (East Indian collection).

Citharoedus unimaculatus, Kaup, 1860: p. 145 (no locality, but description coincides with Indian Ocean subspecies; new combination).

Tetragonoptrus unimaculatus, Bleeker, 1863: p. 234 (East Indies; new combination).

Tetragonoptrus (Lepidochaetodon) unimaculatus, Bleeker, 1877: p. 45 (various localities).

Chaetodon sphenospilus Jenkins, 1901: p. 395, fig. 8 (type locality Hawaiian Islands).

Chaetodon unimaculatus sphenospilus, Ahl, 1923: p. 140 (Hawaiian Islands).

Chaetodon unimaculatus interruptus Ahl, 1923: p. 142 (Malay Archipelago to African coast; Mauritius).

Anisochaetodon (Lepidochaetodon) unimaculatus, Weber and de Beaufort, 1936: p. 97 (East Indies; new combination).

Chaetodon (Lepidochaetodon) unimaculatus, Fowler, 1953: p. 37 (China, Amami Oshima, Riu Kiu, Formosa, Yaeyama, Okinawa).

Anisochaetodon unimaculatus, Munro, 1967: p. 369, pl. 50, #696, color pl. 3 (New Guinea).

Diagnosis.—D. XIII (one with XII), 21-23 (one with 19); A. III, 18-20; pectoral rays 14 or 15; L.l. scales 38-47 (usually 41-45); large black spot on side of body (sometimes with pointed extension from lower edge);

Chaetodon unimaculatus interruptus, 145 mm S.L. Seychelles Islands.

Ratios	Standard Length (mm)		
	20-49(3)	50-89(7)	above 89(8)
Depth/S.L.	1.5-1.6	1.4-1.6	1.5-1.6
Head/S.L.	3.0-3.1	3.2-3.3	3.1-3.4
Eye/Head	2.7-2.8	2.8-3.0	2.9-3.6
Snout/Head	2.7-3.1	2.6-3.3	2.5-3.2
Interorb. W./Head	3.1-3.3	2.9-3.3	2.5-2.8
Maxillary/Head	4.2-4.7	3.3-4.5	2.9-3.6
Caud. Ped./S.L.	8.6-9.6	8.8-9.2	9.1-9.8
Pect. Fin/S.L.	3.1-3.3	3.1-3.5	3.2-4.2
Pelvic Sp./S.L.	4.1	4.1-4.6	4.8-5.2
Predorsal L./S.L.	2.3	2.4-2.5	2.4-2.7
Prepelvic L./S.L.	2.2	2.3-2.5	2.2-2.4
Dorsal Sp. No. 1/S.L.	10.0-11.0	9.5-12.2	11.1-13.6
Dorsal Sp. No. 2/S.L.	4.0-4.4	5.0-6.2	5.8-8.0
Dorsal Sp. No. 3/S.L.	3.1-3.7	4.5-5.1	5.0-6.5
Dorsal Sp. No. 4/S.L.	2.9-3.2	3.9-4.7	4.7-5.6
Anal Sp. No. 1/S.L.	6.2-6.7	6.6-8.5	8.1-10.4
Anal Sp. No. 2/S.L.	4.3-4.6	4.4-5.2	4.8-5.9
Anal Sp. No. 3/S.L.	4.4-4.5	4.3-5.8	4.5-6.1

rounded dorsal and anal fins; posterior edges of dorsal and anal fins black, the color crossing caudal peduncle.

Two subspecies, *Chaetodon unimaculatus unimaculatus* of the Pacific with wide eyeband joining ventrally on chest, and *C. unimaculatus interruptus* of the Indian Ocean, in which the eyeband is narrow and fades rapidly below eye, reaching only to the lower edge of the interopercle; lower portions of the body more yellow in the Indian Ocean form, the Pacific Ocean form being more white.

Meristics.—D. XIII (one with XII), 21-23 (one with 19); A. III, 18-20; pectoral rays 14 or 15 (one with 16/15, one with 14/13, and three with 15/14); L.l. scales 38-47 (usually 41-45); L.l. pores 37-44 (usually 38-42); scales above L.l. 6-10; scales below L.l. 18-22; gill rakers 17-21.

Description.—Outer rows of teeth heavier than slender inner rows; edge of preopercle smooth to lightly serrate; *Chaetodon u. unimaculatus* with snout equal to or greater than interorbital width, which is greater than depth of caudal peduncle, and depth of caudal peduncle greater than eye diameter; *Chaetodon u. interruptus* with interorbital width greater than depth of caudal peduncle, which is greater than snout length, and snout length greater than eye diameter.

Fifth through seventh dorsal spines longest; base of spinous dorsal fin longer (about 2.2 in S.L.) than that of rayed portion (3.1 in S.L.).

Juveniles similar to adults.

Color Pattern.—Pelvic fins similar to body color; large black spot about level of 9-13 dorsal spine bases; some specimens have a round spot, others have one that is teardrop-shaped, the point being toward the ventral side and sometimes lighter in color; black band encircles caudal peduncle; some specimens with plain sides, others with a faint series of vertical, slanting, or chevron-shaped stripes following scale row edges, absent on posterior portion of body; face dusky.

Eyeband of *Chaetodon u. unimaculatus* black, almost as wide as eye, extending from nape, where it broadly joins with opposite member, to chest where they again join broadly. In *Chaetodon u. interruptus* the eyeband is much narrower than eye, extending from nape, where the two bands meet, to lower edge of interopercle, after fading perceptibly below cheek.

Juveniles very similar in pattern to adults. In the Indian Ocean form the eyeband appears slightly wider than adult eyeband and is black to edge of interopercle.

Remarks.—The two subspecies are easily distinguishable by the width and extent of the eyebands. They are apparently not sympatric, although possibly they may come together in the vicinity of the western part of the East Indies. However, the slight difference in pattern does not seem to merit specific status. There appears to be a difference in the number of gill rakers (18-20 in the Pacific form and 21 in the Indian Ocean form), but there are not enough counts to ascertain if this is a true distinguishing

Chaetodon unimaculatus unimaculatus, series from juvenile to adult. Enewetak, Marshall Islands.

character. Smith (1949) mentioned that he found 12 gill rakers in his Indian Ocean form, which certainly casts doubt as to a higher count for Indian Ocean *C. unimaculatus. Ch. sphenospilus* of Jenkins is not distinct enough for specific or subspecific separation.

The large, robust snout combined with the squamation of this species makes it stand apart from the other species of the genus *Chaetodon* enough to merit its being placed in a separate subgenus.

Herre & Montalban (1927) found a 95 mm female "ready to spawn" in the Philippines in April. The tholichthys larva grows quite large before metamorphosing, as exhibited by my collections of Hawaiian specimens. Fowler (1938) had a 50 mm specimen from Tahiti that still possessed the characteristic plates.

Chaetodon unimaculatus may be found in pairs in fair numbers throughout its range (though Harry, 1953, reported it as very rare) although nowhere abundant.

Distribution.—Widespread throughout the Indo-Pacific region. *Chaetodon unimaculatus unimaculatus* is found in the western and central Pacific Ocean from the Hawaiian Islands to the East Indies, north to Japan and south to the Great Barrier Reef of Australia. *Chaetodon u.*

interruptus is widely distributed in the Indian Ocean from the Maldives to the African coast and its offshore islands. It is also known from Sri Lanka and may possibly reach the Indo-Australian Archipelago.

Material Examined.—(18 spec.: 40-145 mm S.L.) EMBL (6: 43-96), Eniwetok, Marshall Islands; SIO 61-83 (1: 40), Tahiti (tholichthys); BPBM 5870 (1: 102), Tahiti; WEB (3: 64-68), Tahiti; SOSC TV-295 (2: 79-112), Fiji Islands; ANSP 108370 and 108596 (4: 114-145), Seychelle Islands; SOSC (1: 56), reef outside Port Louis, Mauritius.

Subgenus DISCOCHAETODON Nalbant

Discochaetodon Nalbant, 1971: p. 222. (Type-species *Chaetodon octofasciatus* Bloch by original designation.)

Diagnosis.—Body rounded, almost circular; snout short, 2.8-5.1 in head length; dorsal and anal fins strongly rounded; lateral line describing a low, smooth arc across body; scales small, rounded, in horizontal series on lower half of body, slightly ascending series on upper half; scale covering of dorsal spines normal; teeth in spaced rows in jaws; lachrymal partially hidden by scales; juveniles similar to adults, color changes, if any, minor; color usually vertical bars (in *C. aureofasciatus* reduced to weak pectoral stripes); D. XI-XII, 19-22; A. III, 15-18; pectoral rays 13-15; L.l. scales 35-45.

Description.—Body rounded, almost circular; snout short, blunt, 2.8-4.5 in head length; predorsal contour straight to slightly convex; gape oblique; teeth in spaced rows in each jaw; preopercle right-angled to obtuse-angled, edge smooth to lightly serrate; supraorbital smooth to lightly serrate; lachrymal partially hidden by scales.

Dorsal spines increase in length until middle ones, then become gradually shorter until last; dorsal fin continuous, no notch present; second anal spine equal to or slightly longer than third, first shorter; dorsal and anal fins strongly rounded, posterior edges in vertical plane; base of spinous portion of dorsal fin longer than (but sometimes very close to) that of rayed portion, 2.0-2.7 in S.L. compared to 2.2-3.1 in S.L.; pectoral fins normal; pelvic fins moderate to long, often reaching base of anal fin spines; caudal fin truncate-rounded.

Lateral line forming a low, smooth arc across body, ending in vicinity of last rays of dorsal fin; scales small, rounded, in horizontal series on lower half of body and slightly ascending rows on upper half; scaly covering of dorsal spines normal, extending to midpoint at about middle spines; scaly covering of anal spines normal.

Juveniles resemble adults in form and color pattern.

Color pattern usually vertical markings of some sort, whether broad bars or narrow stripes.

Distribution restricted to East Indies and Australia although one species (*C. octofasciatus*) reaches the Philippines, China, and across the Indian Ocean to Sri Lanka and India.

Four species are included in this subgenus, distinguished by the following key.

Key to the Species of the Subgenus Discochaetodon

1. Dorsal fin with XII spines; pectoral fin with 15 rays; body with broad solid bars; eye bar solid, dark (Norfolk and Lord Howe Is.) . . . .
. . . . *Chaetodon tricinctus*
Dorsal fin with XI spines; pectoral fin 13 or 14; body with narrow bars or if broad, not solid; eye bar light with dark edges 2

2. Dorsal fin with 19 rays, anal with 15-17; eight narrow black stripes crossing head, body, and fins, usually paired (Indo-West Pacific)
. . . . *C. octofasciatus*
Dorsal fin with 21-22 rays, anal with 17-18; body variously barred but not as above 3

3. Body barred with pattern of light and dark (Queensland, Australia)
. . . . *C. rainfordi*
Body mostly uniform color, bar present from about origin of L.l. through pectoral base (as in above), but lacking body markings of *rainfordi* (Australia and New Guinea). . . . . : . . *C. aureofasciatus*

Remarks.—*Discochaetodon* is a small group of butterflyfishes with their center of occurrence around Australia and the East Indies. The scaly covering of the lachrymal is shared by other subgenera, but other characteristics make it obvious that they form a natural and separate group of species.

CHAETODON AUREOFASCIATUS Macleay
Sunburst butterflyfish
(Goldenrod)

Chaetodon aureofasciatus Macleay, 1878: p. 351, plate 8,
fig. 3 (type locality Port Darwin, Australia).

Diagnosis.—D. XI (one with X), 20-22 (usually 21-22); A. III, 17-18 (usually 18); pectoral rays 14 (one with 15); L.l. scales 38-42 (mostly 39-40); eyeband light with dark borders; light streak from origin of lateral line through pectoral base to behind pelvic fins; no other bars on body.

Meristics.—D. XI (one had X), 20-22 (usually 21 or 22); A. III, 17-18 (usually 18); pectoral rays 14 (one with 15/15, three with 15/14); L.l. scales 38-42 (mostly 39-40); L.l. pores 33-39 (usually 34-37); scales above L.l. 12-14 (usually 13); scales below L.l. 22-25 (usually 23 or 24); gill rakers 12-17.

Chaetodon aureofasciatus Macleay. 77 mm S.L. Yirrkalla, Northern Territory, Australia.

Ratios	Standard Length (mm)		
	20-39(2)	40-59(6)	above 60(9)
Depth/S.L.	1.4-1.5	1.3-1.5	1.2-1.4
Head/S.L.	2.5-2.9	3.0-3.3	3.2-3.7
Eye/Head	2.7	2.5-2.8	2.4-2.9
Snout/Head	2.8-2.9	2.8-3.9	3.1-5.1
Interorb. W./Head	2.9	2.4-2.5	2.1-2.5
Maxillary/Head	3.6-4.0	3.8-5.2	3.8-5.4
Caud. Ped./S.L.	7.1-8.3	7.5-8.9	7.0-8.5
Pect. Fin/S.L.	3.1-3.4	3.1-3.9	3.2-3.8
Pelvic Sp./S.L.	4.0-4.7	4.1-4.7	3.8-4.5
Predorsal L./S.L.	1.9-2.2	1.9-2.1	2.0-2.3
Prepelvic L./S.L.	1.9-2.1	2.3-2.5	2.3-2.5
Dorsal Sp. No. 1/S.L.	8.9-9.7	9.9-12.3	9.6-13.7
Dorsal Sp. No. 2/S.L.	5.0-6.2	5.8-7.1	6.1-9.1
Dorsal Sp. No. 3/S.L.	3.5-4.5	3.9-5.2	4.1-6.8
Dorsal Sp. No. 4/S.L.	2.9-3.5	3.4-4.3	3.6-5.1
Anal Sp. No. 1/S.L.	4.8-6.0	5.4-7.9	5.7-7.3
Anal Sp. No. 2/S.L.	3.9-4.7	4.4-5.6	4.1-5.4
Anal Sp. No. 3/S.L.	3.8-4.5	4.7-5.8	4.0-5.2

Chaetodon
aureofasciatus
juveniles, 25 and
36 mm S.L.
Queensland.

Description.—Body nearly circular, snout projecting only slightly from frontal contour, 2.8-5.1 in head length; preopercle obtuse-angled, smooth to finely serrate; lachrymal rounded, partly hidden by scales; gape horizontal to slightly oblique; teeth in 8 rows in each jaw; depth of caudal peduncle greater than interorbital width, which is greater than eye diameter; eye diameter greater than snout length.

Fourth or fifth dorsal spine longest; second and third anal spines about equal or second longest, first more than half second; dorsal and anal fins strongly and equally rounded, no angle present; they do not appear confluent with caudal fin as in other chaetodonts; spinous portion of dorsal fin longer (2.5-2.7 in S.L.) than that of soft portion (2.8-3.1 in S.L.); caudal fin truncate-rounded; pelvic fins long, extending as far as second anal fin spine base.

Lateral line a low arc across body; scale covering of dorsal spines reach midpoint of about fifth or sixth spine, that of anal fin covers half to three-fourths of third spine.

Juveniles similar in shape to adults.

Color Pattern.—Eyebands join at nape and extend to chest as two indistinct lines, the anterior lines again joined; indistinct dark bordered light stripe in interorbital; color of pelvic fins similar to that of body; an almost obscure band surrounding caudal peduncle; very indistinct indication of dark spot laterally astride lateral lines.

Juveniles with similar pattern though lateral spot more distinct, as is band surrounding caudal peduncle; more of caudal fin hyaline.

Remarks.—*Chaetodon aureofasciatus* is very closely related to *C. rainfordi* and differs, as far as can be seen, by color pattern alone. The two species are sympatric over part of their ranges, but *C. aureofasciatus* is more widely distributed and is found in areas where *C. rainfordi* is apparently absent.

Distribution.—Australia, from the Great Barrier Reef across the northern coast to Western Australia; New Guinea and perhaps further into Melanesia.

Material Examined.—(17 spec.: 25-96 mm S.L.) USNM 173528 (8: 45-96), Yirrkalla, Northern Territory, Australia; USNM 177156 (2: 25-38), Green Island, Queensland, Australia; USNM Acc. 267599 (1: 69), One Tree Island, Great Barrier Reef, Queensland, Australia; MCZ 36946 (2: both 61), Gladstone, Queensland, Australia; W. Aust. Mus. P4674 (4: 44-51), Point Quobba, Western Australia, Australia.

CHAETODON RAINFORDI McCulloch
Rainford's butterflyfish

Chaetodon rainfordi McCulloch, 1923: p. 4, pl. ii, fig 1 (type locality Holbourne I., off Port Denison, Queensland).

Chaetodon rainfordi McCulloch. 94 mm S.L. Gladstone, Australia.

Chaetodon rain-
fordi juvenile and
adult, 44 and 74
mm S.L.,
Queensland,
Australia.

Diagnosis.—D. XI (one with X), 20-22 (rarely 20); A. III, 17-19 (usually 18); pectoral rays 14 (two with 15); L.l. scales 37-43; eyeband light with dark borders; very close to *C. aureofasciatus* but with a series of dark and light bars crossing body (body of *C. aureofasciatus* mostly uniformly colored); gill rakers 17-21 (usually 18-19) (in *C. aureofasciatus* they number 12-17).

Meristics.—D. XI (one with X), 20-22 (rarely 20); A. III, 17-19 (usually 18); pectoral rays 14 (two with 15/15, one with 15/14, two with 13/14); L.l. scales 37-43; L.l. pores 32-39; scales above L.l. 13 or 14; scales below L.l. 22-26; gill rakers 17-21 (usually 18-19).

Description.—Body nearly circular; snout short, 2.8-3.6 in head length; gape slightly oblique; teeth in 8-9 rows in each jaw; preopercle right-angled to slightly oblique, edge crenulate; lachrymal hidden by scales; supraorbital lightly serrate; depth of caudal peduncle greater than or equal to interorbital width, which is greater than eye diameter; eye diameter greater than snout length.

Fifth or sixth dorsal spine longest; second and third anal spines equal, first only little shorter; dorsal and anal fins strongly rounded, equal; spinous portion of dorsal fin longer (2.0-2.7 in S.L.) than base of rayed portion (2.2-2.8 in S.L.); pelvic fins long, reaching base of at least first anal spine.

Lateral line a low arc; scales small, rounded, in horizontal series in

Ratios	Standard Length (mm)		
	20-39(2)	40-59(6)	above 60(15)
Depth/S.L.............	1.4,1.4	1.3-1.5	1.2-1.5
Head/S.L..............	2.7,2.9	2.9-3.2	3.2-3.5
Eye/Head	2.7,2.7	2.4-2.9	2.6-3.0
Snout/Head	2.7,3.9	2.6-3.3	2.8-3.6
Interorb. W./Head......	2.5,3.0	2.5-3.0	2.4-2.9
Maxillary/Head	3.8-4.4	3.5-4.3	3.7-4.2
Caud. Ped./S.L.........	7.6,7.7	7.6-8.5	7.9-8.8
Pect. Fin/S.L...........	3.2,3.2	3.0-4.1	3.2-3.9
Pelvic Sp./S.L..........	3.9-4.1	3.6-4.5	3.6-4.6
Predorsal L./S.L........	1.8,1.9	1.8-2.0	1.9-2.1
Prepelvic L./S.L......:.	2.1,2.2	2.2-2.4	2.1-2.6
Dorsal Sp. No. 1/S.L.....	10.4,10.6	7.4-12.1	8.9-14.4
Dorsal Sp. No. 2/S.L.....	6.0-6.3	6.0-8.4	5.9-10.1
Dorsal Sp. No. 3/S.L.....	4.0,4.7	4.2-5.5	4.5-7.8
Dorsal Sp. No. 4/S.L.....	3.7,3.9	3.5-4.3	3.5-5.0
Anal Sp. No. 1/S.L.......	5.9,6.3	4.8-6.2	6.0-7.2
Anal Sp. No. 2/S.L.......	4.8-6.0	4.3-5.3	4.3-5.7
Anal Sp. No. 3/S.L.......	5.2	3.8-5.3	3.6-5.8

lower half of body; scaly portion of dorsal fin extending to midpoint of fifth dorsal spine, that of anal fin covering about three-fourths of third spine.

Juveniles quite similar to adults in form.

Color Pattern.—Stripe on middle of snout light with dark borders, yet solid color on upper lip, extending to level shortly above eyes; eyebands faintly connected on nape and again faintly on chest; dark band surrounds caudal peduncle; pelvic fins body color.

Juveniles similarly patterned. Caudal peduncle marking darker, more like ocellus, the upper and lower connections very narrow; caudal fin with two parallel dusky lines across center, the hyaline outer portion larger; interorbital stripe extends higher toward nape. Smallest specimen has darkish bar across caudal fin with dark edges; edge of soft dorsal and anal fins clear with submarginal dusky lines; yellowish area between the line and basic fin color.

According to McCulloch (1923) the body bars are deep lilac bordered with rich orange; dark basal spots to each scale; all fins bright yellow, caudal with broad pale lavender border. Grant (1965) reports the species brilliant yellow with orange crossbands; broad lilac band edged with orange across midbody with similar but less distinct one behind and parallel to it; large orange-yellow spot at caudal base; caudal fin bordered pale purple.

Remarks.—The two species *Chaetodon rainfordi* and *C. aureofasciatus* are closely related and share most of the meristic and proportional characteristics. The color patterns are different enough to easily distinguish the species but show remarkable similarities as well. The gill raker difference may not hold up when more specimens are examined. It may indicate a slightly different feeding behavior or selection of different food types. *Chaetodon rainfordi* has a more restricted range than does *C. aureofasciatus*, but it is relatively common within its range.

Chaetodon rainfordi reaches a length of 140 mm standard length. Grant (1965) reports it rarely exceeds five inches and is quite common in northern Queensland waters, but small individuals can be seen in the vicinity of wharf piles in the lower reaches of the Noosa River (southern Queensland). This may also indicate a wider salinity tolerance than thought for butterflyfishes.

Distribution.—So far reported only from the area of the Great Barrier Reef off Queensland.

Material Examined.—(23 spec.: 31-94 mm S.L.) USNM Acc. 267599 (5: 51-84), One Tree Island, Queensland, Australia; MCZ 36946 (5: 55-94), Gladstone, Queensland, Australia; AMS IB. 8165 (1: 36), Heron Island, Queensland, Australia; WEB (3: 60-70), Heron Island, Queensland, Australia; USNM Acc. 285012 (4: 42-71), Heron Island, Queensland, Australia; SOSC #397 (5: 31-70), One Tree Island, Queensland, Australia.

CHAETODON TRICINCTUS Waite
Three-banded butterflyfish
(Lord Howe butterflyfish)

Chaetodon tricinctus Waite, 1901: p. 45, fig. 12. (Type locality Lord Howe Island.)

Chaetodon tricinctus Waite. 37 mm S.L. Lord Howe Island.

648

Ratios	Standard Length (mm)		
	20-39(1)	40-59	above 59(2)
Depth/S.L.	1.4	---	1.3-1.4
Head/S.L.	2.8	---	3.4-3.5
Eye/Head	2.5	---	3.0-3.1
Snout/Head	3.3	---	3.0
Interorb. W./Head.	2.6	---	2.5-2.7
Maxillary/Head	3.9	---	3.5-3.8
Caud. Ped./S.L.	7.0	---	7.6-7.8
Pect. Fin/S.L.	3.4	---	3.4-3.8
Pelvic Sp./S.L.	4.2	---	4.0-4.4
Predorsal L./S.L.	1.8	---	2.1
Prepelvic L./S.L.	2.1	---	2.3-2.5
Dorsal Sp. No. 1/S.L.	8.6	---	12.5
Dorsal Sp. No. 2/S.L.	5.0	---	8.7
Dorsal Sp. No. 3/S.L.	3.7	---	5.9
Dorsal Sp. No. 4/S.L.	3.4	---	5.3
Anal Sp. No. 1/S.L.	7.4	---	8.1
Anal Sp. No. 2/S.L.	6.1	---	6.1
Anal Sp. No. 3/S.L.	Bkn	---	6.7

Diagnosis.—D. XII, 21; A. III, 17-18; pectoral rays 15; L.l. scales 43-46; three broad black bars, two on body and one through eye, crossing body and head; gill rakers 21-22.

Meristics.—D. XII, 21; A. III, 17-18; pectoral rays 15; L.l. scales 43-46; L.l. pores 40-44; scales above L.l. 14; scales below L.l. 26-30; gill rakers 21-22.

Description.—Body circular; snout short, blunt, 3.0 in head length; gape horizontal; teeth in about 9 rows in each jaw; preopercle right-angled, edge lightly serrate; lachrymal scaled; depth of caudal peduncle greater than interorbital width, which is greater than eye diameter; eye diameter greater than or equal to snout length.

Fifth or sixth dorsal spine longest; second anal spine equal to or longer than third, first two-thirds or more of second; dorsal and anal fins strongly rounded; pelvic fins long, extending to base of anal fin spines; base of spinous portion of dorsal fin longer (about 2.1 in S.L.) than that of rayed portion (2.7 in S.L.)

Scales and lateral line as in previous species of this subgenus; scaly covering of dorsal spines reaching midpoint of sixth dorsal spine and up to two-thirds of third anal spine.

Juveniles similar to adults.

Color Pattern.—Eyebands connect broadly in front of dorsal fin insertion and again across chest (weakly) (in a painting by James Stuart, No. 134 in Whitley (1955), the band ends high on chest and is not connected); second band connects across abdomen, extending from the anus to behind the pelvic fins; pelvic fins light colored; dark stripe on upper lip, not noticeable on snout.

Juvenile and adult patterns do not seem to differ significantly.

Remarks.—*Chaetodon tricinctus* appears to be an insular representative of its two closest relatives, *C. rainfordi* and *C. aureofasciatus.* The broad bars are distinctive, however, and the solid color of the eyeband distinguishes it from the other members of this subgenus.

Distribution.—Known only from Norfolk and Lord Howe Islands.

Material Examined.—(3 spec.: 37-148 mm S.L.) AMS IB. 5677 (1: 37), Lord Howe Island; AMS IB. 5356 (2: 120-148), Lord Howe Island.

CHAETODON OCTOFASCIATUS Bloch
Eight-striped butterflyfish

Chaetodon octofasciatus Bloch. 75 mm S.L. Philippine Islands.

Chaetodon octofasciatus Bloch, 1787: p. 113, pl. 215, fig. 1 (type locality East Indies).
Chaetodon octolineatus Gray, 1854: p. 69.
Citharoedus octofasciatus, Kaup, 1860: p. 142 (new combination).

Tetragonoptrus octofasciatus, Bleeker, 1865: pp. 182-193
(Ceram; new combination).
Tetragonoptrus (Tetragonoptrus) octofasciatus, Bleeker,
1877: p. 38, pl. 376, fig. 3 (various localities).
Chaetodon (Tetragonoptrus) octofasciatus, Weber & de
Beaufort, 1936: p. 72, figs. 21 & 22 (various localities).
Chaetodon (Chaetodon) octofasciatus, Fowler, 1953: p. 28
(China, Hong Kong).

Diagnosis.—D. X-XII (usually XI), 17-19 (usually 18-19); A. III (one
with IV), 14-17 (usually 15-16); pectoral rays 12-14 (usually 13-14); L.l.
scales 36-42 (usually 39 or 40); eyeband dark bordered; eight stripes,
including eyeband and stripes crossing dorsal and anal fins, on head and
body, usually paired.

Meristics.—D. XI (two with XII, one with X), 17-19 (usually 18 or 19);
A. III (one with IV), 14-17 (usually 15 or 16); pectoral rays 12-14 (usually
13 or 14) (one with 13/14); L.l. scales 36-42 (usually 39 or 40); L.l. pores
27-38; scales above L.l. 10-13 (usually 11 or 12); scales below L.l. 19-24
(usually 21 or 22); gill rakers 11-19 (usually 14-16).

Description.—Gape slightly oblique; teeth (like *trifasciatus*) bunched
into 4 rows (three behind these) in upper jaw and 5 rows (three rows
behind these) in lower jaw; preopercle right-angled, edge crenulate;

Ratios	20-39	Standard Length (mm) 40-59(9)	above 59(15)
Depth/S.L.	---	1.4-1.5	1.4-1.6
Head/S.L.	---	3.1-3.3	3.2-3.5
Eye/Head	---	2.5-2.9	2.5-2.9
Snout/Head	---	3.2-3.9	3.0-4.1
Interorb. W./Head	---	2.3-2.7	2.3-2.6
Maxillary/Head	---	3.5-4.7	3.5-5.6
Caud. Ped./S.L.	---	7.5-8.3	7.9-9.5
Pect. Fin/S.L.	---	3.3-3.6	3.4-4.2
Pelvic Sp./S.L.	---	3.9-4.5	3.7-4.6
Predorsal L./S.L.	---	2.1-2.2	2.1-2.4
Prepelvic L./S.L.	---	2.3-2.6	2.4-2.7
Dorsal Sp. No. 1/S.L.	---	9.8-16.3	9.8-17.3
Dorsal Sp. No. 2/S.L.	---	5.8-8.4	6.0-10.9
Dorsal Sp. No. 3/S.L.	---	4.2-5.8	4.0-6.4
Dorsal Sp. No. 4/S.L.	---	3.3-4.3	3.4-4.7
Anal Sp. No. 1/S.L.	---	6.1-7.7	5.3-8.7
Anal Sp. No. 2/S.L.	---	4.4-5.4	3.7-4.7
Anal Sp. No. 3/S.L.	---	4.3-5.4	3.5-4.9

*Chaetodon oc-
tofasciatus* 14.5
and 16.0 mm S.L.
Palawan, Philip-
pine Islands.

supraorbital serrate, lachrymal restricted by scales; interorbital width greater than or sometimes equal to depth of caudal peduncle, which is equal to or greater than eye diameter; eye diameter greater than snout length.

Fifth or sixth dorsal spine longest, first very short (up to 17.3 in S.L.); second anal spine equal to or longer than third, first little over half second; dorsal and anal fins rounded, equal; base of spinous portion of dorsal fin longer (2.3-2.5 in S.L.) than that of soft portion (2.9-3.1 in S.L.); pelvic fins moderate, extending past anus but not reaching anal spine bases.

Scales small, rounded, in horizontal series over most of body and slightly ascending series above lateral line; scaly covering of dorsal fin extending to midpoint of sixth dorsal spine; scales covering almost three-fourths of third anal spine.

Juveniles similar to adults.

Color Pattern.—Eyebands join at nape and again weakly on chest; interorbital stripe present from nape to and including upper lip; band encircles caudal peduncle, white-bordered; pelvic fins light colored; darkish blotch sometimes present between the two pairs of body bands.

Juveniles similar to adults. Peduncle band more like spots, widened in center (28 mm). By 61 mm the band was evident (de Witt MS).

Remarks.—There appears to be some slight differences between the specimens from Thailand (CAS 37925) and those from Palau (CAS

37890). The Thai specimens have the central body stripes closer together, the stripes heavier, the stripe associated with the caudal peduncle band reaching further into the fins, and a different shape to the caudal peduncle band (the band in the Thai specimens is more vertically elongate and less bulging in the center than the Palau specimens). The spot in the center of the body tends to be larger in the Thai specimens. These differences are certainly not specific in magnitude, and it is very doubtful whether they are subspecific.

Chaetodon octofasciatus is a common shore butterflyfish and can tolerate lessened salinity. It usually occurs in pairs or groups of four to five individuals.

Distribution.—East Indies and the Philippine Islands through New Guinea to the Solomon Islands, Palau Islands, and north to China; extends into the Indian Ocean at least to the Maldive Islands, India and Sri Lanka; south to the Great Barrier Reef of Queensland, Australia.

Material Examined.—(24 spec.: 44-74 mm S.L.) CAS 37890 (8: 61-74), Koror Is., Palau Islands; SOSC Te Vega Exped. Cr. #6 (6: 64-72), east end of Borneo; CAS 37925 (6: 44-64), Gulf of Thailand; FMNH 73093 (4: 44-46), Maldive Islands, Indian Ocean.

Subgenus CHAETODON Linnaeus

Chaetodon Linnaeus, 1758: p. 272. (Type-species *Chaetodon capistratus* Linnaeus, by subsequent designation of Jordan & Gilbert, 1883: p. 614.) Ex. Artedi, 1738: p. 51.

Tetragonoptrus Klein, 1776: p. 153. (Type-species *Chaetodon striatus* Linnaeus, 1758, by subsequent designation of Bleeker, 1876: p. 305).

Sarothrodus Gill, 1861: p. 99. (Substitute name for *Chaetodon* Linnaeus, 1758, and therefore taking the same type-species, *Chaetodon capistratus* Linnaeus, 1758.)

Hemichaetodon Bleeker, 1876: p. 305. (Type-species *Chaetodon capistratus* Linnaeus, 1758, by original designation.)

Tifia Jordan and Jordan, 1922: p. 60. (Type-species *Chaetodon corallicola* Snyder, 1904, by original designation.)

Exornator Nalbant, 1971: p. 215. (Type-species *Chaetodon punctatofasciatus* Cuvier, 1831, by original designation.)

Diagnosis.—Body oval; snout short, pointed, 2.9-3.5 in head length; dorsal fins various, rounded, with blunt angles or with posterior edge nearly vertical; dorsal spines graduated, first short, middle one usually longest; lateral line moderately high, angular; lachrymal free; teeth in discrete rows; scales small to moderate, usually mixed rounded and angular; color pattern various; D. XI-XVI, 18-25; A. III, 16-20; pectoral fin 13-16 (usually 14); L.l. scales 33-55 (usually 33-46).

Description.—Body oval; snout short, pointed, 2.9-3.5 in head length; predorsal contour mostly straight, sometimes slightly concave, other times convex at nape and straight or concave below; mouth small, terminal, gape horizontal; teeth in several rows in each jaw, spaced; preopercle right-angled to slightly oblique; lachrymal not partly obstructed by scales, free; supraorbital smooth to lightly serrate.

Dorsal spines graduated, first very small (11.3-16.3 in standard length), middle spines longest; anal spines strong, second and third approximately equal; soft portions of dorsal and anal fins rounded to bluntly angled or with posterior edge nearly vertical, never with a filament; base of spinous portion of dorsal fin longer (1.6-3.0, though usually 2.1-2.6, in standard length) than that of soft portion (2.5-3.7, more usually 2.9-3.4, in standard length); caudal fin truncate-rounded; pectoral fins normal; pelvic fins short to moderate, not reaching base of anal fin.

Lateral line describing a moderately high arc crossing body, angular, usually flattened on top, ending near last rays of dorsal fin; scales small to moderate, usually mixed rounded and slightly angular; scaly covering of dorsal and anal spines normal, reaching midpoint of middle spines in dorsal fin and covering half or more of third anal spine.

Juveniles similar to adults though minor color changes occur in some species.

Color pattern various.

Widely distributed throughout the tropical oceans of the world, some species venturing into temperate waters to a greater or lesser degree.

Some 28 species recognized as distinguished by the following key.

Key to the Species of the Subgenus Chaetodon

1. Dorsal fin with XVI spines (East Africa)......*Chaetodon blackburni*
   Dorsal fin with XI-XIV spines 2
2. Dorsal fin with XI spines 3
   Dorsal fin with XII-XIV dorsal spines........................4
3. Dorsal fin XI, 23-24, anal fin III, 18-19; subadults with two black spots in the dorsal fin (southern and southeastern Africa)........
   ....*C. marleyi*
   Dorsal fin XI, 22-23, anal fin III, 17; subadults with only one dorsal fin spot (tropical western Africa)...................*C. hoefleri*
4. Eyeband absent, no trace remaining in adult if present in juvenile
  5
   Eyeband present either as black band or as light band with dark borders 8
5. Horizontal to inclined stripes (blue in life) from head (radiating from eye) to posterior end of fish; black spot on nape and another at

17. Black spot or ocellus either at base of dorsal rays or below base of posterior dorsal rays 18
    Black spot absent, or, if present, at angle of dorsal fin, never both at angle and base of dorsal fin 19
18. Black spot at base of last rays of dorsal fin, ocellated; body with narrow dark lines converging at about center of body (Caribbean) . . . . C. capistratus
    Black spot at base of dorsal rays and another small black spot at angle of dorsal fin; body without lines (Caribbean) . . . . C. ocellatus
19. Dorsal fin XIII, 19; anal III, 16; pectoral rays 15-16 (Eastern Pacific) . . . . C. humeralis
    Dorsal XIII, 21-25; anal III, 17-19; pectoral rays usually 14 (occasionally 15) 20
20. Body plain; eyeband broad, faintly indicated (Saint Helena and Ascension Islands) . . . . C. sanctaehelene
    Body with dark marking of some kind present; eyeband various . . . 21
21. Eyeband broad, dark, broader above eye and joined across nape . . 22
    Eyeband narrow, light with dark edges, rarely extending to nape or connecting at nape 26
22. Broad black band surrounding caudal peduncle, not continued extensively on dorsal or anal fins (Hawaiian Islands) . . C. miliaris
    Caudal peduncle plain or, if dark band present, it is continued on dorsal and/or anal fins as dark band 23
23. Caudal peduncle body color; anal fin body color; dorsal fin with or without dark spot at angle (Japan to Australia) . . . . . C. guentheri
    Caudal peduncle dark; anal fin with dark band or totally dark; dorsal fin dark, with dark spot at angle or with dark band extending on it from caudal peduncle 24
24. Dark spot at angle of dorsal fin; caudal peduncle band extended as band across anal fin to anal spines (Western Australia) . . . . C. assarius
    No dark spot at angle of dorsal fin; caudal peduncle band extending onto dorsal and anal fins to various degrees 25
25. Rayed portion of dorsal and anal fins blackish (East Africa) . . . . C. dolosus
    Dark band of caudal peduncle extending along edge of anal fin and into dorsal fin a short distance or to angle, entire rayed portions never darkish (Caribbean) . . . . C. sedentarius
26. Black stripes on body strongly angled from lower anterior to upper posterior margins (Tahiti to Australia) . . . . C. pelewensis
    Stripes on body, if present, vertical or slightly inclined from spinous dorsal fin to anal fin 27
27. Caudal peduncle without band; stripes not usually extending far beyond center of body, more evident posteriorly (Pacific Ocean)

.................................*C. punctatofasciatus*
Caudal peduncle with band; vertical bands, when evident, extending below center of body 28
28. Eyeband separated from nuchal spot; bands evident on body
(Hawaiian Islands and Johnston Atoll).........*C. multicinctus*
Eyeband continuous with nuchal spot; spots on body not in distinct
solid bands (Indian Ocean)..................*C. guttatissimus*

Remarks.—This subgenus is the base group of genus *Chaetodon*. It
contains several distinct groups of species which have been considered
subgenera by other workers but which I do not believe are distinct enough
to be rated as such. One species group includes *Chaetodon capistratus*,
C. striatus, *C. humeralis*, *C. hoefleri*, *C. marleyi*, *C. ocellatus*, and probably *C. robustus*, *C. melannotus*, and *C. ocellicaudus*. These species
together comprise the subgenus *Chaetodon* of some authors (with a few
additions by me). These species are worldwide in distribution and usually
have a lower dorsal spine count (XI or XII), although three of them have
XIII spines. The dorsal fin ray count is generally lower, usually 19-21, as
compared to the rest of the species in the subgenus *Chaetodon* sensu latu
(21-25). Most of the other meristics are very similar.

A second species group, including *Chaetodon miliaris*, *C. guentheri*,
C. dolosus, *C. sedentarius*, *C. assarius*, and *C. sanctaehelene*, are
extremely close with almost identical meristics and similar color patterns.
In no case, however, do the geographic ranges of any two of these species
overlap. *Chaetodon citrinellus* could belong to this group but has XIV
dorsal fin spines as compared to XIII for all the others. These species
together with *C. litus*, *C. hemichrysus*, and possibly *C. daedalma*, *C.
fremblii*, and *C. blackburnii* comprise a group of species which stands
slightly apart from the others but have never been given a name. For convenience of referral I will call this section "heterochaetodons." Nalbant
(1971) erected a subgenus, *Exornator*, with the type-species being *C.
punctatofasciatus*. I agree with him in that the species group in which
C. punctatofasciatus belongs is partially distinguishable from the above
groups, but I disagree in the composition of this group. I include *C. punctatofasciatus*, *C. multicinctus*, *C. pelewensis*, and *C. guttatissimus*, with
the possible addition of *C. citrinellus* (rather than it being in the above
group) and *C. quadrimaculatus*. Nalbant includes both the *punctatofasciatus* group, comprising that species plus *multicinctus* and *pelewensis*,
and the *miliaris* group including that species (*miliaris*) as well as *assarius*,
punctulatus, *dixoni*, and *citrinellus*. I believe *C. dixoni* Regan from the
New Hebrides to be a synonym of *C. mertensii* rather than a member of
this group from East Africa as Nalbant suggests. *Chaetodon punctulatus*
Ahl I consider as a synonym of *C. guentheri*. *Chaetodon guttatissimus* is
considered by Nalbant as intermediate between the latter two groups
whereas I believe it is very closely allied with *punctatofasciatus*, *pelewensis*, and *multicinctus* and distinct enough from the "heterochaetodon"

complex to be able to distinguish the two groups.

A final species pair had been given its own generic name, *Tifia*, by Jordan & Jordan (1922), with *C. corallicola*, which I have placed in synonymy with *C. kleinii*, as type-species. *Chaetodon trichrous*, the other member of this pair, may be parapatric with *C. kleinii*. This will be discussed in more detail under those species.

As can be seen, the species grouped under subgenus *Chaetodon* are a mixed lot with intermediates between each section. There are few distinguishing characteristics that would allow the above groups to stand as separate subgenera without causing considerable confusion as to where certain species would fall. I have therefore placed all these species under the single subgenus.

CHAETODON CAPISTRATUS Linnaeus
Four-eyed butterflyfish

Chaetodon capistratus Linnaeus, 1758: p. 275 (type locality "Habitat in Indiis").

Sarothrodus capistratus, Poey, 1868: p. 352 (new combination).

Chaetodon bricei Smith, 1897: p. 102, fig. p. 103 (type locality Woods Hole Mass; juvenile). Jordan & Evermann, 1898: p. 1678. Evermann & Marsh, 1902: p. 250, pl. 35 (Fajardo, Puerto Rico).

Chaetodon capistratus Linnaeus. 78.1 mm S.L. Florida. Photo by Dr. Henry A. Feddern.

Ratios	Standard Length (mm)		
	20-39(6)	40-69(7)	above 69(4)
Depth/S.L............	1.6-1.8	1.6-1.7	1.5-1.6⁻
Head/S.L.............	2.4-3.0	3.0-3.3	3.1-3.3
Eye/Head	2.3-2.4	2.6-2.9	2.7-2.8
Snout/Head	3.3-4.7	2.7-3.3	3.0-3.5
Interorb. W./Head......	2.8-3.5	2.8-3.0	2.7-2.8
Maxillary/Head	3.9-4.7	3.9-4.9	4.6-5.2
Caud. Ped./S.L.........	7.3-9.5	8.5-9.7	8.8-9.5
Pect. Fin/S.L..........	3.6-3.9	3.5-4.0	3.4-4.0
Pelvic Sp./S.L..........	3.9-4.2	4.3-4.6	4.4-4.7
Predorsal L./S.L........	1.8-2.1	2.1-2.4	2.1-2.3
Prepelvic L./S.L........	1.8-2.3	2.3-2.6	2.4-2.5
Dorsal Sp. No. 1/S.L.....	11.2-13.7	10.4-15.7	10.7-15.6
Dorsal Sp. No. 2/S.L.....	5.6-8.1	6.3-8.1	6.5-8.2
Dorsal Sp. No. 3/S.L.....	3.8-4.4	4.2-4.9	4.3-5.8
Dorsal Sp. No. 4/S.L.....	3.3-4.2	3.7-4.1	3.5-4.2
Anal Sp. No. 1/S.L.......	7.0-8.6	6.9-9.0	6.9-8.2
Anal Sp. No. 2/S.L.......	4.1-5.9	4.3-4.9	4.4-4.6
Anal Sp. No. 3/S.L.......	4.4-6.2	4.6-5.6	4.2-4.8

Diagnosis.—D. XIII, 17-20 (rarely 17); A. III, 16-17; pectoral rays 13-15 (mostly 14); L.l. scales 35-41 (usually 38-40); large black ocellated spot below last rays of dorsal fin; black lines converging at midline of body forming anteriorly directed angles.

Meristics.—D. XIII, 17-20 (rarely 17); A. III, 16-17; pectoral rays 14 (two with 13/13, one with 15/15, and four with 13/14); L.l. scales 35-41 (usually 38-40); L.l. pores 30-37 (usually 33-35); scales above L.l. 6-7; scales below L.l. 16-17; gill rakers 17-21.

Description.—Snout short, pointed, 3.0-3.5 in head length; predorsal contour straight to slightly concave; gape horizontal; teeth in 6-7 rows in each jaw; preopercle right-angled, edge crenulate; lachrymal smooth; eye equal to or sometimes greater than interorbital width, which is greater than depth of caudal peduncle; caudal peduncle depth greater than snout length.

Fifth dorsal spine longest; second anal spine longer than third, first about half second; dorsal and anal fins with blunt angle; base of spinous portion of dorsal fin longer (2.4 in S.L.) than that of soft portion (3.7 in S.L.); pelvic fins moderate, extending past anus but not as far as anal fin.

Lateral line a moderately high, smooth arc; scales small, rounded and angular, in horizontal series on lower portion of body and ascending series on upper; scaly covering of dorsal spines normally reaching midpoint of about fifth or sixth dorsal spine; anal covering reaching to half or more of third anal spine.

Chaetodon capistratus juvenile, 15 mm S.L. Bahama Islands.

Juveniles similar to adults.

Color Pattern.—Eyebands join at nape just before dorsal fin origin; eyeband with dark edges; dusky area on chest may be remnants of ventral eyeband connection; pelvic fins light; snout and face dusky; dark bands may appear on body though present pattern still obvious.

Juveniles with some pattern differences; 28 mm specimen with second spot, fading in 32 mm specimen and gone in 35 mm specimen, in soft dorsal fin above body spot; caudal fin with band near base, outer portion hyaline, hyaline portion becoming narrower with age; anal fin dusky, with a narrow clear edge and submarginal dark line; dorsal fin colored as anal fin, both fins having the adult stripe represented as an indistinct brownish line or stripe, with a light streak just anterior to it in the dorsal fin.

Remarks.—This butterflyfish, type species of the genus *Chaetodon*, is common in the Caribbean. Meek & Hildebrand (1923-1926) reported it as common at Panama, Evermann & Marsh (1902) said it was the most abundant chaetodont at Puerto Rico, and Boehlke & Chaplin (1968) describe it as the most common Bahaman butterflyfish, "often occurring in large numbers." Longley & Hildebrand (1941) report it as occasional, singly, in pairs, and rarely more.

Chaetodon capistratus can be found in rocky and reef areas as well as in grass beds such as *Thalassia*. According to Longley & Hildebrand (1941) the young were more apt to be taken in grass flats, the adults being reef fishes. They report that the dark humeral band is occasionally evident (more regularly in young), the adults displaying it over "dark, muddy bottom." This dark-barred pattern appears to be a night or fright pattern.

This species is closely related to the banded butterflyfish, *Chaetodon striatus*, and resembles it in form. The banded phase of *C. capistratus* is somewhat similar to the regular pattern of *C. striatus*.

Distribution.—Tropical western Atlantic from Brazil to the Carolinas; also Bermuda and straggling north to Massachusetts.

Material Examined.—(17 spec.: 15-80 mm S.L.) USNM 178211 (7: 50-69), Haiti; UMML 10929 (1: 20), Puerto Rico; UMML 12648 (4: 15-26), Exuma, Bahama Islands; USNM 194076 and 194081 (3: 74-80), Los Roques, Venezuela; USNM 48526 (1: 25), Woods Hole, Mass. (holotype of *Chaetodon bricei*); SIO 60-333 (1: 54), Haiti.

CHAETODON STRIATUS Linnaeus
Banded butterflyfish

Chaetodon striatus Linnaeus. 95 mm S.L. San Juan, Puerto Rico.

Chaetodon striatus Linnaeus, 1758: p. 275 (type locality "Habitat in Indiis").

Sarothrodus striatus Poey, 1868: p. 352 (Cuba; new combination).

Chaetodon consuelae Mowbray, 1928: p. 23, pl. 4 (type locality Cay Sal Banks, Bahama Islands).

Anisochaetodon (Lepidochaetodon) trivirgatus Weber & de
Beaufort, 1936: p. 101, fig. 27 (type locality Ambon).
Chaetodon ocellatus (not of Bloch), Fowler, 1944: p. 137.
Chaetodon striatus var. *albipinnis* Ahl, 1923: p. 91.
Chaetodon striatus var. *dorsimacula* Ahl, 1923: p. 91.

Diagnosis.—D. XII, 19-20 (rarely 19); A. III 16-17 (one with 15); pectoral rays 14-15 (usually 14); L.l. scales 37-42; two broad dark vertical bands crossing body, a third lighter band extending from the dorsal fin base to the anal fin base, crossing the caudal peduncle.

Chaetodon striatus is close to *C. capistratus* but differs in color pattern and number of dorsal fin spines, XIII in *C. capistratus* and XII in *C. striatus*.

Meristics.—D. XII, 19-21 (rarely 19); A. III, 16-17 (one with 15; usually 17); pectoral rays 14-15 (usually 14; one with 14/15, one with 13/14); L.l. scales 37-42; L.l. pores 32-42 (usually 35-38); scales above L.l. 7-8; scales below L.l. 15-16 (occasionally 14); gill rakers 15-21 (usually 17-20).

Description.—Snout short, pointed, 2.9-3.8 in head length; predorsal contour straight; gape slightly oblique; teeth in 9-10 rows in each jaw; preopercle right-angled to slightly oblique-angled, edge crenulate to serrate; lachrymal smooth; supraorbital lightly serrate; depth of caudal

Ratios	Standard Length (mm)		
	20-40(1)	41-69(2)	above 69(13)
Depth/S.L.	1.8	1.6-1.7	1.4-1.8
Head/S.L.	2.6	2.9-3.2	3.0-3.3
Eye/Head	2.6	2.6-2.9	2.7-3.2
Snout/Head	3.1	2.9-4.1	2.9-3.8
Interorb. W./Head.	2.9	2.9-3.4	3.0-3.4
Maxillary/Head	4.7	4.3-4.6	3.7-4.8
Caud. Ped./S.L.	7.3	7.9-8.5	7.2-8.5
Pect. Fin/S.L.	4.2	3.4-3.7	3.4-3.8
Pelvic Sp./S.L.	4.5	4.1-4.8	4.1-4.7
Predorsal L./S.L.	2.0	2.0-2.1	2.0-2.4
Prepelvic L./S.L.	2.0	2.3-2.4	2.3-2.5
Dorsal Sp. No. 1/S.L.	12.0	13.1-17.1	10.6-15.6
Dorsal Sp. No. 2/S.L.	6.6	7.7-9.2	7.0-9.8
Dorsal Sp. No. 3/S.L.	5.0	4.6-5.6	4.9-5.8
Dorsal Sp. No. 4/S.L.	4.1	3.5-3.8	3.3-4.0
Anal Sp. No. 1/S.L.	9.7	7.3-8.3	6.7-8.5
Anal Sp. No. 2/S.L.	7.9	4.0-4.5	4.0-4.5
Anal Sp. No. 3/S.L.	10.2	4.8-5.7	4.3-4.9

Chaetodon
striatus juvenile,
27 mm S.L.
Florida.

peduncle greater than eye diameter, which is greater than snout length; snout length greater than or equal to interorbital width.

Fourth or fifth dorsal spines longest; second anal spine longest, not much longer than third, first about half or slightly more than half of second; dorsal and anal fins equal, with blunt angle at about 13th-14th ray of dorsal fin and 11th ray of anal fin; base of spinous portion of dorsal fin longer (about 2.5-2.6 in S.L.) than that of soft portion (3.4-3.5 in S.L.); pelvic fins moderate, reaching anus.

Lateral line a moderately high, peaked arc; peak about under last spines of dorsal fin; scales small, rounded and angular, in horizontal series on lower portion of body and ascending rows on upper portion; scaly covering of dorsal spines reaches midpoint of sixth dorsal spine, that of anal fin covering but one-third of third anal spine.

Juveniles similar to adults though dorsal fin has proportionately higher peak and a notch.

Color Pattern.—Eyebands joined a short distance in front of dorsal fin origin; first band from dorsal spines 2-4 to belly, where it is continuous to opposite side; second band originates at last four dorsal fin spines; pelvic fins blackish-brown on posterior two-thirds and yellowish to white near base; snout and face dusky.

Juveniles depart from the basic adult color pattern in several respects. There is a large ocellated dark spot in the dorsal fin at its base covering the last spine and first few rays; eyeband and two body bands similar to adults; the second band not differentiated in dorsal and anal fins, the dark color of dorsal fin almost including the entire ocellated spot but extending only along the base after the spot; anal fin with similar pattern but without spot; posterior portions of both fins clear; caudal peduncle with dark band; caudal fin with outer part hyaline, inner portion yellowish, no markings evident. Description from a 20 mm S.L. specimen still retaining the tholichthys plates.

Remarks.—*Chaetodon trivirgatus*, described from a specimen supposedly from Ambon, apparently was based on a mislabeled specimen. Fowler (1939) corrected this mistake and referred it to the proper synonymy.

According to Meek & Hildebrand (1928) this species was found in tidal pools and seined in eel grass. The dark stripes made this fish difficult to see among the blades of grass, and the barred pattern therefore affords it some protective coloration. Longley & Hildebrand (1941) reported its preferred habitat to be coral rubble bottom only sparsely covered with algae.

Distribution.—Western Atlantic Ocean from Brazil to Bermuda, straggling north to Woods Hole, Massachusetts.

Material Examined.—(16 spec.: 20-94 mm S.L.) USNM 104223 (4: 62-72), Brazil; USNM 249582 (2: 78-82), Dominica, B.W.I.; CAS 37891 (2: 70-81), St. Croix, Virgin Islands; USNM Acc. 249592 (5: 85-88), Dominica, B.W.I.; USNM Acc. 254747 (2: 20-94), San Juan, Puerto Rico; SIO 60-333 (1: 82), Haiti.

CHAETODON HOEFLERI Steindachner
Canario

Chaetodon hoefleri Steindachner. 122 mm S.L. Lobito, West Africa.

Chaetodon hoefleri Steindachner, 1881: p. 14, pl. 5, fig. 1
(type locality Goree).
Chaetodon luciae (not of Rochebrune), Fowler, 1936: p.
906 (Ashantee). Jordano & Muruve, 1959: p. 122 (Spanish markets).
?*Chaetodon luciae*, Cadenat & Roux, 1960: pp. 81-102.

Diagnosis.—D. XI, 21-23 (usually 22-23); A. III, 16-17 (usually 17); pectoral rays 15 or 16; L.l. scales 39-43 (usually 42-43); two bands crossing body, one just passing behind pectoral fin, other from last spines of dorsal fin to anal fin; second darkish band with black spot at upper end. Closely related to *C. marleyi* but differing in dorsal and anal ray counts, 22-23 and 16-17 in *C. hoefleri* and 23-24 and 18-19 in *C. marleyi*. Other differences are noted under *C. marleyi*.

Meristics.—D. XI, 21-24 (usually 22-23); A. III, 16-17 (usually 17); pectoral rays 15 or 16 (one with 14/15); L.l. scales 39-44 (usually 42-43); L.l. pores 31-44 (usually 40-43); scales above L.l. 6-7; scales below L.l. 17-18; gill rakers 13-15.

Description.—Snout short, pointed, 3.8-4.1 in head length; predorsal contour approximately straight; gape of mouth slightly oblique; teeth in 10-11 rows in each jaw; preopercle right-angled, edge crenulate; lachrymal smooth, supraorbital smooth; depth of caudal peduncle greater

| | | Standard Length (mm) | |
Ratios	20-49(1)	50-79(1)	above 79(3)
Depth/S.L.	1.6	1.6	1.5
Head/S.L.	2.7	2.9	3.1-3.2
Eye/Head	2.9	2.8	2.9-3.1
Snout/Head	3.4	4.1	3.8-4.1
Interorb. W./Head.	4.0	3.6	3.2-3.4
Maxillary/Head	4.4	3.8	4.3-4.4
Caud. Ped./S.L.	7.3	8.0	7.7-7.9
Pect. Fin/S.L.	3.4	3.3	3.4-3.5
Pelvic Sp./S.L.	4.6	4.8	4.8-5.2
Predorsal L./S.L.	2.1	2.2	2.1-2.2
Prepelvic L./S.L.	2.1	2.1	2.4-2.5
Dorsal Sp. No. 1/S.L.	10.9	13.2	13.8-15.0
Dorsal Sp. No. 2/S.L.	6.9	7.4	7.8-8.9
Dorsal Sp. No. 3/S.L.	5.1	5.3	5.4-5.9
Dorsal Sp. No. 4/S.L.	4.4	4.3	4.6-5.0
Anal Sp. No. 1/S.L.	6.5	7.8	7.7-8.8
Anal Sp. No. 2/S.L.	4.2	5.4	4.7-5.2
Anal Sp. No. 3/S.L.	4.8	5.2	5.2-5.9

Chaetodon
hoefleri juvenile
53 mm S.L.
Elmina, Gold
Coast.

than eye diameter, which is greater than interorbital width; interorbital width greater than snout length.

Fourth to fifth dorsal spines longest; second anal spine slightly longer than or equal to third, first more than half second; dorsal and anal fins smoothly rounded; base of spinous portion of dorsal fin longer (2.2-2.5 in S.L.) than that of rayed portion (2.5-3.0 in S.L.); pelvic fins long, barely reaching base of first anal spine.

Lateral line a moderately high arc, flattened on top from the sixth to last dorsal spines; scales moderate, rounded to angular, in horizontal rows on lower portion of body, ascending rows on upper; scaly covering of dorsal fin reaching midpoint of fifth or sixth dorsal spine; anal covering reaching to midpoint of third anal spine.

Juveniles similar to adults.

Color Pattern.—Short median stripe present on interorbital from just below eye level to upper lip; upper lip entirely dark; eyebands joined at nape just before origin of dorsal fin; second bar including black spot, originating from last three spines and first dorsal ray; dark band surrounds caudal peduncle; pelvic fins dusky.

Juveniles similar to adults. The bars (including that surrounding caudal peduncle) light bordered; caudal fin similar to adults except that the brownish band is closer to fin base; dorsal fin spot not very distinct and still included in second body bar, as if the upper end of the bar were darkened; dorsal fin spot not ocellated; grayish lines follow centers of scale rows on lower portion of body, reduced to dark spots at base of scales in ascending rows (adult).

Remarks.—Chaetodon hoefleri is closely related to C. marleyi and is separated from that species geographically by only 15-20° of latitude along the west African coastline. The relationship seems to extend via

C. striatus in the Caribbean to *C. humeralis* of the East Pacific. None of the Indo-Pacific species bears too close of a resemblance to *Chaetodon hoefleri*, though *C. melannotus* comes closest. Variations in meristic counts as well as color pattern separate these species, the African forms with XI dorsal spines, the Caribbean species with XII dorsal spines, and the east Pacific species with XIII dorsal spines; *Chaetodon melannotus* has XII spines.

Poll (1949) considered *C. hoefleri* a common species along the coast of Africa, frequenting various depths from 20-150 meters, but more commonly at 20-75 meters. Bottom types estimated from trawl hauls were brown sand, coral, greenish-brown mud, black sand mud, and rocks.

Attains a length of about 140 mm (Bauchot & Blanc, 1962).

Distribution.—Western coast of Africa from Angola to Cape Blanc and possibly the Canary Islands. A record from the Mediterranean (Torchio, 1968) is possible but unsubstantiated.

Material Examined.—(5 spec.: 49-125 mm S.L.) USNM 42230 (2: 49-54), Elmina, Ashantee (Ghana); SOSC Sta. 68-278 (3: 123-125), Lobito, Angola.

CHAETODON MARLEYI Regan
Marley's butterflyfish
(Bontvis)

Chaetodon marleryi Regan. 91 mm S.L. Algoa Bay, South Africa.

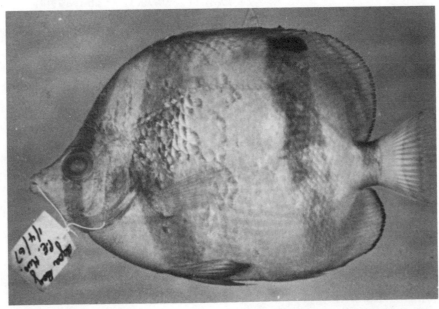

Chaetodon marleyi Regan, 1921: p. 1 (type locality East
London, South Africa).
Chaetodon notophthalmus Ahl, 1923: p. 81, pl. 2, fig. 10
(locality unknown).

Diagnosis.—D. XI, 23-24; A. III, 18-19; pectoral rays 14-15; L.l. scales
39-47; two bars on body, second with black spot at upper end; closely
related to *C. hoefleri* but differing in dorsal and anal ray count and color
pattern of juveniles—second dorsal fin spot present in *C. marleyi*, absent
in *C. hoefleri*, the spot located posteriorly to second bar eventually being
replaced by spot included in bar, the two being present together only
during this change-over period.

Meristics.—D. XI, 23-24; A. III, 18-19; pectoral rays 14-15 (one with
14/15); L.l. scales 39-47; L.l. pores 37-43; scales above L.l. 7 or 8; scales
below L.l. 19-20; gill rakers 11-14.

Description.—Snout about 3.3 in head length; gape horizontal to
slightly oblique; teeth in 8-10 rows in each jaw; preopercle right-angled,
edge smooth to crenulate; lachrymal and supraorbital smooth; depth of
caudal peduncle greater than eye diameter, which is greater than snout
length; snout length greater than interorbital width.

Fifth to seventh dorsal spines longest; second and third anal spines
about equal, first approximately half second; dorsal and anal fins smoothly rounded; base of spinous portion of dorsal fin approximately equal in

Ratios	Standard Length (mm)		
	20-49(4)	50-79(1)	above 79(4)
Depth/S.L.	1.5-1.7	1.5	1.4-1.6
Head/S.L.	2.8-3.0	3.1	2.9-3.2
Eye/Head	2.7-2.9	3.0	3.2
Snout/Head	3.3-3.5	3.2	3.3
Interorb. W./Head.	3.3-3.4	3.4	3.5
Maxillary/Head	3.7-3.8	4.3	4.1-4.2
Caud. Ped./S.L.	7.3-8.2	8.1	7.9-8.5
Pect. Fin/S.L.	3.2-2.7	3.5	3.7-4.0
Pelvic Sp./S.L.	4.7-4.8	5.0	5.0-5.8
Predorsal L./S.L.	2.1-2.2	2.2	2.1-2.3
Prepelvic L./S.L.	2.2-2.3	2.1	2.1-2.3
Dorsal Sp. No. 1/S.L.	8.8-9.9	11.9	12.8-14.0
Dorsal Sp. No. 2/S.L.	5.7-6.4	7.7	8.1-10.1
Dorsal Sp. No. 3/S.L.	4.4-4.8	5.6	6.3-8.2
Dorsal Sp. No. 4/S.L.	3.7-4.3	5.2	6.1-6.4
Anal Sp. No. 1/S.L.	6.4-7.4	8.9	8.9-11.2
Anal Sp. No. 2/S.L.	4.9-5.5	6.1	5.7-6.6
Anal Sp. No. 3/S.L.	4.7-5.3	6.3	5.8-7.0

length to that of rayed portion (both 3.0 in standard length); pelvic fins moderate, extending to area between anus and origin of anal fin.

Lateral line a moderately high arc flattened on top; scales moderate, rounded, in horizontal rows on lower portion of body and ascending rows on upper portion; scaly portion of dorsal spines reaching midpoint of fourth or fifth dorsal spine; anal scaly covering reaching to about midpoint of third anal spine.

Juveniles similar to adult.

Color Pattern.—Median stripe present on interorbital from nape just above level of eyes to tip of upper lip; eyebands joined at nape; second bar includes black spot starting from bases of last two or three spines (9th-11th) and first three or four rays; dark band surrounding caudal peduncle, bordered by pale lines; pelvic fins dusky; second dorsal fin spine with black flap.

Chaetodon marleyi juvenile, 44 mm S.L. Knysna, South Africa.

Juveniles similar to adults but with one important difference. A black ocellated spot is present in the dorsal fin between rays three or four to eight or nine and is not included within second body bar; dorsal and anal fins light dusky with white to hyaline edges and submarginal black stripes; color of fins "connects" with dark band of caudal peduncle; caudal fin with band across middle or basal third, outer portion hyaline or very pale; pelvic fins dark brown. The juvenile spot disappears as the adult dorsal fin spot appears. In specimens 65 to 95 mm standard length both spots are present at the same time.

Remarks.—*Chaetodon marleyi* is patterned similarly to the closely related *C. hoefleri* of West Africa, though distinguishable by characters given in the key and diagnosis. The juveniles provide the most dramatic difference between the two species, with *Chaetodon marleyi* having an ocellated spot in the soft dorsal fin which fades with growth and is replaced with a second, more anteriorly placed, non-ocellated spot. *Chaetodon hoefleri* does not undergo such replacement of dorsal fin spots, its single black, non-ocellated spot remaining in place (within the upper end of the second body bar) throughout life.

According to Smith (1953), this species enters estuaries, living in the weeds. The barred pattern most likely aids in concealment of this species much as has been indicated for *Chaetodon striatus* of the Caribbean. Smith (1953) also states that *C. marleyi* occurs down to depths of 60 fathoms.

Earlier Smith (1953) reported of *Chaetodon marleyi* ". . . at Knysna, in summer it is not uncommon for very cold water to appear suddenly. The presence of *Chaetodon marleyi* in the river is an infallible sign that such an onset is imminent and when the cold water actually enters the river dead specimens of this species are generally thrown ashore."

Smith & Smith (1966) report *Chaetodon marleyi* from shallow water among rocks and weeds. It was said to favor estuaries. The type specimen of this species, however, was taken at 40 fathoms.

Grows to 225 mm.

Distribution.—Southern Africa from Delagoa Bay to the Cape and around it to Lamberts Bay; also reported to be present near Madagascar.

Material Examined.—(9 spec.: 33-111 mm S.L.) USNM 103112 (2: 73-85), Durban, Natal, South Africa; USNM 153513 (3: 44-48), Knysna, South Africa; JLBS 1119220 (1: 111), Algoa Bay, South Africa; JLBS 591 (1: 33), Port Elizabeth, South Africa; JLBS (uncatalogued) (1: 90), Algoa Bay, South Africa; JLBS (uncatalogued) (1: 108), East London, South Africa.

CHAETODON HUMERALIS Gunther
East Pacific banded butterflyfish

Chaetodon humeralis Gunther, 1860: p. 19 (type locality "Sandwich Islands").

Diagnosis.—D. XIII (one with XII), 18-20 (usually 19); A. III, 15-17 (usually 16); pectoral rays 15-16; L.l. scales 34-39; two dark bars crossing body, first to and including pectoral base, second near bases of dorsal and anal fins; three dark bars crossing caudal fin. Closely related to the previous two species but easily separated by dorsal spine number and color pattern.

Meristics.—D. XIII (one with XII), 18-20 (usually 19); A. III, 15-17 (usually 16); pectoral fin 15-16 (one with 14/15, five with 15/16); L.l. scales 34-39; L.l. pores 29-38 (normally 32-36); scales above L.l. 5-8; scales below L.l. 16 or 17; gill rakers 16-20.

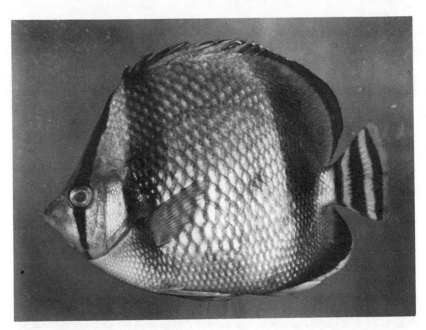

Chaetodon humeralis Gunther. 134 mm S.L. Coast of Mexico.

Ratios	Standard Length (mm)		
	20-49(5)	50-79(11)	above 79(16)
Depth/S.L.............	1.5-1.6	1.4-1.5	1.2-1.5
Head/S.L..............	2.3-2.7	2.8-3.1	2.6-3.0
Eye/Head	2.6-2.9	2.8-3.1	2.8-3.3
Snout/Head	2.8-3.6	2.7-3.4	3.1-3.3
Interorb. W./Head......	2.8-3.7	3.1-3.6	2.9-3.3
Maxillary/Head	3.1-5.1	3.8-5.2	3.9-5.0
Caud. Ped./S.L.........	6.9-7.6	7.4-8.3	6.4-8.5
Pect. Fin/S.L...........	2.9-3.3	3.2-3.7	2.8-3.6
Pelvic Sp./S.L..........	4.0-4.3	4.0-4.6	3.8-4.9
Predorsal L./S.L........	1.9-2.1	1.9-2.0	1.7-2.2
Prepelvic L./S.L........	2.0-2.3	2.1-2.5	1.8-2.4
Dorsal Sp. No. 1/S.L.....	6.6-15.1	10.5-16.5	10.7-16.8
Dorsal Sp. No. 2/S.L.....	3.2-5.0	5.5-7.5	6.2-9.2
Dorsal Sp. No. 3/S.L.....	2.7-3.6	3.5-4.2	3.6-4.8
Dorsal Sp. No. 4/S.L.....	2.9-3.2	3.0-3.7	3.0-3.9
Anal Sp. No. 1/S.L.......	5.4-6.3	5.7-6.8	5.7-7.4
Anal Sp. No. 2/S.L.......	4.2-5.3	4.1-5.5	3.6-4.8
Anal Sp. No. 3/S.L.......	4.6-6.2	5.0-6.2	3.9-5.8

Description.—Snout about 3.1-3.3 in head length; predorsal contour straight; gape slightly oblique; teeth in 8-10 rows in each jaw; preopercle right-angled, edge serrate; lachrymal and supraorbital smooth; depth of caudal peduncle greater than eye diameter, which is greater than or equal to interorbital width; interorbital width greater than or equal to snout length.

Fourth or fifth dorsal spines longest, first spine short; second anal spine longest, first about two-thirds of second and only slightly shorter than third; dorsal and anal fins rounded; base of spinous portion of dorsal fin longer (1.6-2.1 in S.L.) than that of soft portion (2.0-3.2, though usually 2.5-2.6 in S.L.); pelvic fins moderate, barely reaching to anus.

Lateral line a moderately high arc; scales moderate to large, rounded but with flattened edge, in moderately ascending rows becoming more strongly inclined on upper portions of body; scale covering of dorsal spines low, reaching midpoint of about eighth dorsal spine; anal spines with scale covering reaching midpoint of third spine.

Juveniles similar to adults.

Color Pattern.—Each scale with silvery to white center, edge darker; eyebands joined on nape; face dusky, upper lip dark; pelvic fins dusky.

Juveniles like adults; eyebands extend to isthmus, where they join; first body bar more distinct below pectoral base; posterior body bar with dark mark in upper portion similar to spots in previous two species; stripe across base of caudal fin infringes on the caudal peduncle, a dusky band

Chaetodon humeralis juvenile and subadult, 36 and 60 mm S.L. Sinaloa, Mexico.

crosses just inside midpoint of fin, the area between these bands white to light yellowish; remainder of fin dusky hyaline; no third band present.

Remarks.—The original description by Gunther (1860) indicated the type locality as the Sandwich Islands. This apparently was a mistake as has been reported in earlier literature (Jordan & Gilbert 1883: p. 51, footnote). Gunther (1869) reported on this species again. He at that time had specimens from Panama and probably Guatamala. He stated that these areas were its true home but, "I have no doubt that the statement of the species extending to the Sandwich Islands is correct. The Panama examples differ from the typical specimens only in having an additional black crossband near the hind margin of the caudal fin."

The tholichthys larva of this species was presented by Fowler (1944) in an outline drawing. A 36 mm S.L. specimen at hand has almost completely resorbed the plates characteristic of these larvae. The size at metamorphosis is therefore probably about 28-35 mm in standard length.

Chaetodon humeralis is common in rocky tide pools and on the shores of the small islands near Panama City. It is rarer in the mid-Peruvian coast.

Distribution.—Eastern Pacific Ocean from Ecuador to Mexico; offshore islands including the Galapagos Islands.

Material Examined.—(32 spec.: 25-134 mm S.L.) CAS 37903 (2: 100-114), Mazatlan, Sinaloa, Mexico; CAS 18506 (1: 100), Colima, Mexico; CAS 37904 (8: 55-77), Acapulco, Mexico; CAS 37905 (1: 86), Gulf of California; CAS 37096 (6: 35-91), Mazatlan, Sinaloa, Mexico; USNM 144840 (3: 31-47), Panama; WEB (6: 110-134), Baja California; SIO (3: 100-110), Baja California Sur, Mexico; SIO 60-305 and W51-58 (2: 25-35), west coast Mexico.

CHAETODON MELANNOTUS Schneider
Black back butterflyfish

Chaetodon melannotus Schneider, 1801: p. 224 (type locality Tranquebar).

Chaetodon dorsalis Ruppell, 1828: p. 41, pl. 9, fig. 2 (type locality Mohila, Red Sea). Cuvier, 1831: p. 70 (Moluccas, Reinwardt MS). Kner & Steindachner, 1867: footnote, p. 361 (on Cuvier 1831, color variety; Mauritius).

Chaetodon marginatus Cuvier, 1831: p. 57 (type locality Massowah, Red Sea; Ehrenberg MS). Ruppell, 1835: p. 28 (Red Sea).

Chaetodon Abhortani Cuvier, 1831: p. 58 (type locality Ile-de-France (=Mauritius)).

Chaetodon melanotus, Cuvier, 1831: p. 71 (Tranquebar, Reinwardt MS).

Chaetodon reinwardti Gunther, 1860: p. 23 (on Cuvier, 1831, *C. melanotus,* Molucca Sea; on the authority of Bauchot with the help of Boeseman).

Tetragonoptrus melanotus, Bleeker, 1863: p. 228 (Ternate; new combination).
?*Chaetodon ocellicauda* (not of Cuvier), Playfair, 1865: p. 35 (Zanzibar).
Tetragonoptrus (Chaetodontops) melanotus, Bleeker, 1877: p. 43, pl. 376, fig. 1 (various localities).
Chaetodon sp., Jordan & Seale, 1906: p. 344 (footnote, in part: paragraph beginning "Another species. . ."; juvenile; Samoa).
Chaetodon plebejus (not of Cuvier), Meinken, 1935: p. 172 (Darassalam).
Chaetodon (Chaetodontops) melanotus, Weber & de Beaufort, 1936: p. 87 (various localities).
Chaetodon (Chaetodontops) melannotus, Fowler, 1953: p. 36 (Riu Kiu, China, Aguni-Oshima).

Chaetodon melannotus Schneider. 85 mm S.L. Ponape, Caroline Islands.

Diagnosis.—D. XII (two with XIII), 18-20 (usually 19-20); A. III, 16-18 (usually 17); pectoral rays 14 (15); L.l. scales 33-39; narrow dark lines following scale rows across body ascending posteriorly; caudal peduncle with black interrupted band; close to *Chaetodon ocellicaudus* but has a higher pectoral ray count (*C. ocellicaudus* has 13) and differs in

Ratios	Standard Length (mm)		
	20-49(4)	50-89(19)	above 89(8)
Depth/S.L.............	1.6-1.7	1.6-1.8	1.6-1.8
Head/S.L..............	2.8-3.0	3.0-3.4	3.2-3.5
Eye/Head	2.4-2.8	2.6-3.0	2.8-3.1
Snout/Head	3.1	2.8-3.6	2.8-3.6
Interorb. W./Head......	2.7-3.1	2.6-3.3	2.6-2.9
Maxillary/Head	3.8-4.5	3.9-6.4	3.4-5.5
Caud. Ped./S.L.........	8.7-9.7	8.7-10.0	8.9-10.2
Pect. Fin/S.L...........	3.4-3.9	3.3-4.0	3.4-3.9
Pelvic Sp./S.L..........	4.2-5.0	4.2-4.7	4.4-5.0
Predorsal L./S.L........	2.1-2.3	2.1-2.4	2.3-2.5
Prepelvic L./S.L........	2.3-2.5	2.3-2.6	2.4-2.6
Dorsal Sp. No. 1/S.L.....	12.3-17.7	10.6-14.4	10.9-13.2
Dorsal Sp. No. 2/S.L.....	6.9-8.2	6.1-9.1	7.1-9.4
Dorsal Sp. No. 3/S.L.....	4.3-4.7	4.4	4.8-6.1
Dorsal Sp. No. 4/S.L.....	3.5-4.0	3.6-5.0	4.1-4.9
Anal Sp. No. 1/S.L.......	7.0-7.3	5.6-7.4	6.7-8.5
Anal Sp. No. 2/S.L.......	4.6-4.9	3.9-4.7	4.2-4.9
Anal Sp. No. 3/S.L.......	5.0-5.2	4.5-6.2	4.6-6.0

color pattern (caudal peduncle band differs and *C. melannotus* has a black spot on its chest that *C. ocellicaudus* lacks; in life *C. ocellicaudus* has white pelvic fins, *C. melannotus* has yellow).

Meristics.—D. XII (two with XIII), 18-20 (usually 19-20); A. III, 17-18 (usually 17); pectoral fin 14 (one with 15/15, one with 12/14, one with 14/15, and two with 13/14); L.l. scales 33-39; L.l. pores 29-36; scales above L.l. 6-7; scales below L.l. 15-17; gill rakers 13-16 (usually 14 or 15).

Description.—Snout short, 2.8-3.6 in head length; predorsal profile straight; gape oblique; teeth in 6 to 7 rows in each jaw; preopercle right-angled to slightly oblique, edge smooth to crenulate; lachrymal and supraorbital smooth; interorbital width greater than or equal to eye diameter, which is greater than depth of caudal peduncle; peduncle depth greater than snout length.

Fifth dorsal spine longest; second anal spine slightly longer than third, first about half or slightly more than half second; dorsal and anal fins rounded or with slight blunt angle; base of spinous portion longer (2.1-2.4 in S.L.) than that of rayed portion (3.3-4.0 in S.L.); pelvic fins short, not reaching anus.

Lateral line a high arc, angular on top under base of ninth dorsal spine; scales moderate, rounded, in ascending series; scaly portion of dorsal fin reaching midpoint of fifth dorsal spine, that of anal fin covering about ⅔ of third anal spine.

Juveniles similar to adults.

Chaetodon melannotus juvenile and subadult, 40 and 68 mm S.L. Japan.

Color Pattern.—About 21-22 dark narrow oblique lines; back black-ish, the black area extending to cover much of back, except for two light spots, under adverse conditions or at night; chest with round black spot in center; eyebands join at nape (chest spot is possible continuation of eye-bands); black band surrounds caudal peduncle, usually broken on one or both sides; face dusky; pelvic fins light.

Juveniles with variations from adult pattern. Spot on chest connected with eyebands and extends closer to pelvic fins; black mark on caudal peduncle much wider in center, resembling a spot, though still connected above and below and bordered with white stripe anteriorly and whitish band posteriorly; more of caudal fin hyaline; dorsal and anal fin markings not evident.

Remarks.—*Chaetodon melannotus* is very close to *C. ocellicaudus* and is often confused with that species. The range of *C. ocellicaudus* is not completely known for that reason. The two species can easily be separated by the characters given in the diagnosis.

Chaetodon reinwardti has been included in the synonymy on the basis of the explanation in Bauchot (1963).

Herre & Montalban (1927) reported ripe females in the Philippines in March.

According to Baschieri-Salvatore (1954), this species prefers clear waters and occurs either as pairs or as isolated individuals in the Red Sea.

Distribution.—Widespread in the Pacific and Indian Oceans: islands of the central and western Pacific exclusive of the Hawaiian Islands and possibly the Society and Tuamotu Islands; across Melanesia to the Great Barrier Reef, New Guinea, Philippine Islands, East Indies to China and Japan; across the Indian Ocean to Sri Lanka, southern India, Africa, and offshore islands; Red Sea.

Material Examined.—(31 spec.: 34-121 mm S.L.) CAS 37892 (12: 34-88), Palau Islands; CAS 37893 (1: 106), Guam; BPBM 6192 (1: 78), Samoa; BPBM 5842 (1: 103), Guam; WEB (1: 63), Tonga Islands; WEB (4: 66-71), Heron Island, Queensland, Australia; AMS IB. 8161 (3: 66-95), Heron Island, Queensland, Australia; Yasuda (Univ. of Tokyo) (5: 39-100), Japan; USNM 147512 (1: 49), Red Sea; SOSC RS-40 Ft-19 (1: 121), Amirantes Islands; SOSC Anton Bruun (1: 73), off Port Louis Harbor, Mauritius.

CHAETODON OCELLICAUDUS Cuvier
Spot-tail butterflyfish

Chaetodon ocellicaudus Cuvier. 80 mm S.L. New Ireland, New Guinea.

Chaetodon ocellicaudus Cuvier, 1831: p. 69. (No locality; Timor according to Bauchot, 1963).
Chaetodon melannotus (not of Schneider), Munro, 1967: Fig. 693 (part, description of true *C. melannotus*).

677

Diagnosis.—D. XII, 19-20; A. III, 17 (one with 18); pectoral rays 13 (14); L.l. scales 29-34; about 22 slanting black stripes crossing body; large black spot on side of caudal peduncle; no black spot on chest; pelvics white. Close to *Chaetodon melannotus* but differing from that species in pectoral fin ray count and color pattern as described under that species.

Meristics.—D. XII, 19-20; A. III, 17 (one with 18); pectoral fin 13 (one with 14/14); L.l. scales 29-34; scales above L.l. 5 or 6; scales below L.l. 14 (one with 13); gill rakers 12-15.

Description.—Predorsal contour straight; snout short, 2.6-3.3 in S.L.; gape horizontal to slightly oblique; teeth in 5-6 rows in each jaw; preopercle right-angled, edge crenulate; lachrymal and supraorbital smooth; eye diameter greater than or equal to snout length, which is greater than interorbital width; interorbital width greater than depth of caudal peduncle.

Fifth or sixth (occasionally seventh) dorsal spine longest; second and third anal spines equal, first between ½ and ⅔ second; dorsal and anal fins rounded or with slight blunt angle; base of spinous portion of dorsal fin longer (2.4-2.5 in S.L.) than that of soft portion (3.7-4.0 in S.L.); pelvic fins short, barely reaching anus.

Lateral line a high arc, angled under base of eighth dorsal fin spine; scales moderate, rounded in steeply ascending series; scaly covering of dorsal spines low, reaching midpoint of seventh or eighth dorsal spine, that of anal spines extending to midpoint of third anal spine.

Ratios	Standard Length (mm)		
	20-49(6)	50-89(2)	above 89
Depth/S.L.	1.8-1.9	1.6-1.8	---
Head/S.L.	2.6-2.8	3.0-3.3	---
Eye/Head	2.6-2.7	2.9-3.0	
Snout/Head	2.6-3.0	2.6-3.3	---
Interorb. W./Head.	3.3-3.7	2.7-3.1	---
Maxillary/Head	3.7-4.3	3.1-4.4	---
Caud. Ped./S.L.	9.0-10.0	9.9-10.0	---
Pect. Fin/S.L.	3.4-3.7	3.7-4.0	---
Pelvic Sp./S.L.	3.4-4.2	4.4-4.5	---
Predorsal L./S.L.	2.1-2.2	2.2-2.3	---
Prepelvic L./S.L.	2.2-2.5	2.5-2.6	---
Dorsal Sp. No. 1/S.L.	10.8-13.9	11.4-12.7	---
Dorsal Sp. No. 2/S.L.	6.1-7.3	7.0-7.3	---
Dorsal Sp. No. 3/S.L.	3.7-4.8	4.7-5.2	---
Dorsal Sp. No. 4/S.L.	3.0-3.7	3.7-4.2	---
Anal Sp. No. 1/S.L.	7.3-8.7	7.4-8.0	---
Anal Sp. No. 2/S.L.	4.8-5.4	5.0	---
Anal Sp. No. 3/S.L.	4.8-5.6	5.0-5.1	---

Color Pattern.—Body with about 22 stripes; black spots near base of anterior anal rays sometimes overlap to form single larger spot; no black spot on chest; eyebands join at nape; face dusky; pelvic fins light; large black spot on side of caudal peduncle surrounded by white ring; dorsal area where stripes broader sometimes becomes completely blackish except for two light spots (usually a distress or nocturnal pattern).

Juveniles with peduncular spot more centrally located (adults with spot near upper border) and lack of patterns in vertical fins (edges of fins hyaline).

Chaetodon ocellicaudus, series showing juvenile, subadult and adult.

Remarks.—There has been a great deal of confusion between the two closely related and very similar appearing species *Chaetodon ocellicaudus* and *C. melannotus*. They are separable as indicated in the diagnoses. Most of the nominal species can be relegated to *C. melannotus*, but some are too poorly described to ascertain their position with any certainty. *Chaetodon ocellicaudus* has a smaller geographic range than does *C. melannotus*, although the true extent of the range may be obscured by misidentifications. The two species are sympatric over the entire known range of *Chaetodon ocellicaudus*.

Distribution.—Melanesia through East Indies and Philippine Islands to Sri Lanka and Zanzibar. Possibly reaches African coast.

Material Examined.—(8 spec.: 27-80 mm S.L.) SOSC Te Vega Cr. 6 Sta. 234 (4° 14'S 152° 26'E) (8: 27-80), New Ireland.

CHAETODON MILIARIS Quoy & Gaimard
Millet-seed butterflyfish

Chaetodon miliaris Quoy & Gaimard, 1824: p. 380, pl. 62, fig. 6 (type locality Iles Sandwich).
Chaetodon miliaris (part), Gunther, 1874: p. 46, pl. 35, fig. A.
Chaetodon mantelliger Jenkins, 1901: p. 394, fig. 7 (type locality Hawaiian Islands).
?*Chaetodon Garretti* Ahl (part), 1923: p. 96 (Hawaiian Islands only).

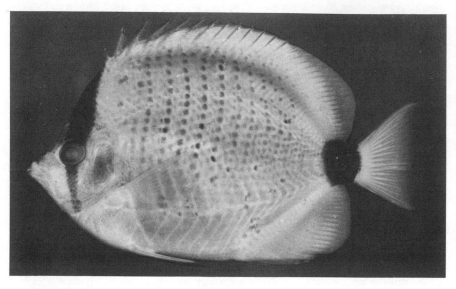

Chaetodon miliaris Quoy and Gaimard. 108 mm S.L. Hawaiian Islands.

Diagnosis.—D. XIII (two with XIV), 20-23 (usually 22 or 23); A. III (one with II), 17-20 (usually 19); pectoral rays 14 (15); L.l. scales 38-53 (usually 40-45); black band surrounding caudal peduncle; narrow vertical rows of spots crossing body; no black spot in dorsal fin. Close to other species in this species group, especially *C. guentheri*, from which it differs in lacking a black dorsal fin spot and possessing a wide black band surrounding caudal peduncle. Endemic to Hawaiian Islands.

Meristics.—D. XIII (two with XIV), 20-23 (usually 22 or 23); A. III (one had II), 17-20 (usually 19); pectoral rays 14 (four with 15/15, one with 14/15, one with 13/14); L.l. scales 38-53 (usually 40-45); L.l. pores 34-43; scales above L.l. 7-9 (rarely 7); scales below L.l. 19-24 (usually 23 or 24); gill rakers 17-19.

Ratios	Standard Length (mm)		
	10-39(9)	40-69(6)	above 69(15)
Depth/S.L............	1.6-1.8	1.6-1.7	1.5-1.8
Head/S.L.............	2.5-3.0	2.8-3.2	3.2-3.8
Eye/Head............	2.5-3.0	2.8-3.1	2.7-3.5
Snout/Head..........	2.7-3.4	2.8-3.1	2.7-3.4
Interorb. W./Head......	2.9-4.0	3.2-3.6	3.1-3.5
Maxillary/Head........	3.9-5.3	3.9-5.0	3.8-4.8
Caud. Ped./S.L........·..	8.1-10.1	9.2-10.3	8.8-10.5
Pect. Fin/S.L..........	3.2-4.1	3.0-4.0	3.5-4.6
Pelvic Sp./S.L..........	3.1-4.4	4.1-5.0	4.4-5.6
Predorsal L./S.L........	2.0-2.2	2.0-2.4	2.3-2.6
Prepelvic L./S.L........	2.0-2.4	2.1-2.5	2.3-2.6
Dorsal Sp. No. 1/S.L.....	8.8-10.7	9.3-13.7	11.8-18.8
Dorsal Sp. No. 2/S.L.....	3.2-4.6	4.3-6.5	5.5-10.5
Dorsal Sp. No. 3/S.L.....	3.0-4.1	4.0-5.6	4.7-8.0
Dorsal Sp. No. 4/S.L.....	3.8-4.5	3.8-4.9	4.3-6.4
Anal Sp. No. 1/S.L.......	6.6-8.9	7.5-9.7	8.3-11.9
Anal Sp. No. 2/S.L.......	4.6-6.8	4.8-5.3	4.7-6.3
Anal Sp. No. 3/S.L.......	4.9-9.8	4.7-5.1	4.5-6.1

Description.—Snout short, 2.7-3.4 in head length; predorsal contour straight; gape horizontal to slightly oblique; teeth in about 4 rows in each jaw; preopercle right-angled, edge crenulate; lachrymal and supraorbital smooth; depth of caudal peduncle greater than snout length, which is greater than eye diameter; eye diameter greater than or equal to interorbital width.

Fifth to seventh dorsal spines longest; second and third anal spines equal, first about half to ⅔ second; dorsal and anal fins rounded; base of spinous portion of dorsal fin longer (2.1 in S.L.) than that of rayed portion (about 3.0 in S.L.); pelvic fins short, failing to reach level of anus; caudal fin truncate, upper rays sometimes extended.

Lateral line a moderately high arc; scales moderate, rounded, in horizontal series in lower portion of body and slightly ascending series in upper portion; scaly portion of dorsal spines reaching midpoint of fifth spine; anal covering reaching just past halfway mark of third anal spine.

Juveniles similar to adults.

Color Pattern.—Second series of gray spots on body "behind" and between darker vertical line spots; usually 8-10 spot-rows, one spot per scale, parallel and separated by two scale rows; second pattern forming lines of spots following scale rows and disposed similarly to those of *Chaetodon citrinellus* or others of the spotted butterflyfish complex; eyebands joined at nape; tip of snout dusky; black band surrounding caudal peduncle; pelvic fins light.

Juveniles similar to adults.

Remarks.—*Chaetodon miliaris* belongs to a complex of species occurring circumtropically but as geographic replacement species, no two species occurring sympatrically. These species are mostly wide ranging in depth, found at various depths to or beyond 600 feet and, at least in the Hawaiian Islands and Caribbean, in shallower water as well. Others of this complex are collected by trawling in deeper waters, although in the case of *C. dolosus* the juveniles are collected from shallow water.

Reports of *Chaetodon miliaris* outside of the Hawaiian Islands are probably due to the close physical resemblance of the species in this complex to each other. The two specimens identified by Gunther (1871) as *C. miliaris* were redescribed as a new species, *C. guentheri*, by Ahl (1923). Gunther (1874) records *C. miliaris*, but his description appears to be a composite of both *C. miliaris* and *C. guentheri* (he mentions the two specimens from Manado.)

Jenkins reports XII dorsal spines for his *C. mantelliger*, although the figure appears to have XIII. He distinguishes his species from *C. miliaris* by the arrangement of spots on the body, a rather poor characteristic.

Longley (1918) mentions that the colors fade when individuals leave the protection of the reef and move over pale sand. He also states, "The same is true when it rises a yard or more from the bottom."

In dissections of adult specimens from the Hawaiian Islands I found the peritoneum to be silvery; the stomach was thin-walled with seven pyloric caecae. In one specimen the length of the testis was 26 mm, width 6.5 mm.

Young *Chaetodon miliaris* appear inshore in April and May, transforming at about a size of 25-30 mm S.L.

Distribution.—Endemic to the Hawaiian Islands.

Material Examined.—(30 spec.: 26-119 mm S.L.) HIMB (uncatalogued (7: 36-110), Oahu, Hawaiian Islands; WEB (18: 26-119), Oahu, Hawaiian Islands; NMFS-H TC 32-4 (1: 28) (tholichthys) Oahu, Hawaiian Islands; UH (4: 29-79), Oahu, Hawaiian Islands.

CHAETODON ASSARIUS Waite
Assarius butterflyfish

Chaetodon assarius Waite, 1905: p. 66, pl. xi, fig. 1 (type locality between Fremantle and Houtman's Abrolhos, Western Australia).

Diagnosis.—D. XIII (one with XII), 21 (one with 22); A. III, 19 (one with 18); pectoral rays 14 (15); L.l. scales 37-43 (usually 40-42); four to five vertical lines of spots in upper anterior section of body; caudal peduncle band continued as band through anal fin to anal spines; black ocellated spot in angle of dorsal fin.

Chaetodon assarius Waite. 88 mm S.L. Sharks Bay, Western Australia.

Ratios	Standard Length (mm)		
	20-40	**41-60**	**61 and above (5)**
Depth/S.L.	---	---	1.6-1.7
Head/S.L.	---	---	3.2-3.3
Eye/Head	---	---	2.8-2.9
Snout/Head	---	---	2.8-3.1
Interorb. W./Head	---	---	2.8.3.1
Maxillary/Head	---	---	3.3-3.4
Caud. Ped./S.L.	---	---	3.8-4.4
Pect. Fin/S.L.	---	---	9.4-10.8
Pelvic Sp./S.L.	---	---	4.5-5.6
Predorsal L./S.L.	---	---	2.4-2.6
Prepelvic L./S.L.	---	---	2.1-2.3
Dorsal Sp. No. 1/S.L.	---	---	15.0-17.5
Dorsal Sp. No. 2/S.L.	---	---	7.0-8.4
Dorsal Sp. No. 3/S.L.	---	---	5.0-6.0
Dorsal Sp. No. 4/S.L.	---	---	4.7-6.0
Anal Sp. No. 1/S.L.	---	---	8.0-9.2
Anal Sp. No. 2/S.L.	---	---	4.9-5.4
Anal Sp. No. 3/S.L.	---	---	5.2-5.3

Meristics.—D. XIII (one with XII), 21 (one with 22); A. III, 19 (one with 18); pectoral rays 14 (one with 15/15); L.l. scales 37-43 (usually 40-42); L.l. pores 35-41; scales above L.l. 8-9; scales below L.l. 21-24; gill rakers 15-16.

Description.—Antero-dorsal profile concave; snout short, pointed, 2.8-3.1 in head length; preopercle right-angled, edge smooth; lachrymal and supraorbital smooth; gape horizontal; teeth in 5 rows in each jaw; eye diameter greater than or equal to snout length, which is greater than or equal to depth of caudal peduncle; caudal peduncle depth greater than interorbital width.

Fourth to sixth dorsal spines longest, last one or two slightly longer than previous spines; second and third anal spines equal, first more than half second; soft dorsal fin with an obtuse angle at its center, soft anal evenly rounded; base of spinous portion of dorsal fin longer (2.3 in S.L.) than that of soft portion (3.2 in S.L.); pelvic fins short to moderate, barely reaching level of anus.

Lateral line a moderately high, smooth arc; scales moderate, in horizontal series on lower portion of body, ascending series in upper portion; scaly sheath of dorsal fin high, fifth spine ¾ covered; scaly portion of anal fin spines covering ¾ of third spine.

Juveniles not seen but are expected to closely resemble adults.

Color Pattern.—Spot in dorsal fin is ocellated with white; brownish band surrounding caudal peduncle bordered anteriorly with white, band extending obscurely into dorsal fin for a short distance; eyeband with dark borders below eye; body pale posterior to eyebands; eyebands connected at nape; head dusky, snout darkish.

Remarks.—There are no particular problems evident in the nomenclature of this species. It is very closely related to the species located on either side of it geographically, *Chaetodon guentheri* of the western Pacific and *C. dolosus* of the African coast.

The original description records the dorsal fin counts as XIII, 21, the anal fin count as III, 17, and pectoral fin as 16. These are slightly different from my counts. In addition, the band of the caudal peduncle is paler in the type specimen. There is no doubt, however, as to the identity of this species.

Greatest size recorded was 122 mm standard length.

Distribution.—Restricted to the western coast of Australia; Exmouth Gulf to Houtman's Abrolhos, Western Australia (Wallabi Group, Abrolhos; between Fremantle and Shark's Bay).

Material Examined.—(5 spec.: 61-89 mm S.L.) WAM P. 13792-5 (4: 61-89), Shark's Bay, Western Australia, Australia (line haul 72-75); WAM P. 15579 (1: 81), between Shark's Bay and Onslow, Western Australia, Australia.

CHAETODON GUENTHERI Ahl
Gunther's butterflyfish
(Crochet butterflyfish)

Chaetodon guentheri Ahl. 85 mm S.L. Manado, Celebes (Cotype)

Chaetodon miliaris (not of Quoy and Gaimard), Gunther, 1871: p. 658 (Manado, Celebes).
Chaetodon miliaris (part), Gunther, 1874: p. 46, pl. 35, fig. A (Manado, Celebes; Hawaiian Islands).
Chaetodon guntheri Ahl, 1923: p. 99 (on Gunther, 1871; type locality Manado, Celebes).
Chaetodon Garretti Ahl, (part), 1923: p. 96 (Samoa only).
Chaetodon punctulatus Ahl, 1923: p. 97 (type localities Amboina, New Guinea).
Chaetodon miliaris (not of Quoy and Gaimard), Kamohara, 1935: p. 734. Munro, 1967: p. 367, pl. 3 (Plate adapted from Jordan & Evermann of Hawaiian specimen of true *C. miliaris*).

Diagnosis.—D. XIII, 21-22; A. III, 18; pectoral rays 14; L.l. scales 39-40; vertical dotted lines anterodorsally; black spot in angle of dorsal fin; no caudal peduncle band or bands in dorsal or anal fins; close to other

685

species in this complex but differing in color pattern; in addition differs from *C. miliaris* by scale count (39-40 as opposed to 42-47 in *C. miliaris*).

Meristics.—D. XIII, 21-22; A. III, 18; pectoral rays 14; L.l. scales 39-40; L.l. pores 36-38; scales above L.l. 7-8; scales below L.l. 19; gill rakers 16-17.

Description.—Predorsal contour straight; snout short, 3.3-3.4 in head length; gape oblique; teeth in 4-5 rows in lower jaw, 5-6 rows in upper jaw; preopercle right-angled to slightly oblique-angled, edge smooth to lightly crenulate; lachrymal and supraorbital smooth; eye diameter greater than depth of caudal peduncle, which is greater than or equal to interorbital width; interorbital width greater than snout length.

Fourth or fifth dorsal spine longest; second anal spine longest, first half or slightly longer than half third; dorsal and anal fins rounded; base of spinous portion of dorsal fin longer (2.1-2.2 in S.L.) than that of soft portion (3.1-3.6 in S.L.); pelvic fins moderate, reaching level of anus.

Lateral line a high arc, flattened on top; scales moderate, rounded-angular, in horizontal series on lower portion of body and ascending rows on upper portion; scaly covering of dorsal spines reaching midpoint of fifth spine, that of anal spines covering half of third spine.

Juveniles similar to adults.

Color Pattern.—Suggestion of spotted pattern similar to *Chaetodon miliaris*, vertical dotted rows overlying a horizontal spotted pattern; edges of dorsal and anal fins pale with submarginal black line; black spot at

Ratios	Standard Length (mm)		
	10-39	40-69	above 69
Depth/S.L.	---	---	1.5,1.7
Head/S.L.	---	---	3.4,3.4
Eye/Head	---	---	2.3,2.6
Snout/Head	---	---	3.3,3.4
Interorb. W./Head	---	---	2.9,3.0
Maxillary/Head	---	---	4.7,4.8
Caud. Ped./S.L.	---	---	9.9,10.1
Pect. Fin/S.L.	---	---	3.7,3.7
Pelvic Sp./S.L.	---	---	4.9,5.1
Predorsal L./S.L.	---	---	2.4,2.7
Prepelvic L./S.L.	---	---	2.2,2.3
Dorsal Sp. No. 1/S.L.	---	---	11.3,13.7
Dorsal Sp. No. 2/S.L.	---	---	7.3,7.6
Dorsal Sp. No. 3/S.L.	---	---	5.7,6.2
Dorsal Sp. No. 4/S.L.	---	---	4.6,5.0
Anal Sp. No. 1/S.L.	---	---	8.9,9.0
Anal Sp. No. 2/S.L.	---	---	4.6,5.0
Anal Sp. No. 3/S.L.	---	---	4.8,4.9

dorsal fin angle adjacent to black line, covering about six rays and non-ocellated; eyebands joined at nape; snout and upper lip dark; eyeband with light posterior bordering stripe; pelvic fins pale.

Juveniles similarly colored.

Remarks.—Gunther (1871) identified the two specimens from Manado, Celebes as *Chaetodon miliaris*. Ahl (1923) recognized that the description was different from that of *Chaetodon miliaris* and called it *C. guentheri.* The original specimens are then the cotypes.

The juvenile to adult color pattern is not totally known. The indication of a dark saddle on the caudal peduncle may be a remnant of a juvenile band surrounding the caudal peduncle, and the spot may fade with age. More material is needed to settle these questions.

This species is apparently a deep-water butterflyfish. In Japan it is found closer to the surface, but in New South Wales it was captured at a depth of 20 fathoms (Whitley, 1965).

Distribution.—Southern Japan to Byron Bay, New South Wales, Australia; possibly Samoa (on Steindachner, 1906).

Material Examined.—(2 spec.: 85-100 mm S.L.) BM(NH) 1871.7.19.22 & 58 (2: 85-100), Manado, Celebes (cotypes).

CHAETODON DOLOSUS Ahl
African butterflyfish

Chaetodon chrysurus (not of Bloch & Schneider) Lienard, 1835: p. 30 (Mauritius).

Chaetodon (Tetragonoptrus) miliaris (not of Quoy & Gaimard), Sauvage, 1891: p. 259 (on Lienard, 1835; Madagascar).

Chaetodon dolosus Ahl, 1923: p. 99 (type locality Mauritius).

Chaetodon guntheri (not of Ahl), Smith, 1946: p. 800 (S. Mozambique). Smith, 1953: p. 239, fig. 604 (S. Mozambique).

Chaetodon mendoncae Smith, 1953: p. 9 (type locality Mozambique Channel).

Chaetodon Guntheri (not of Ahl), Fourmanoir, 1957: p. 28, fig. 21 (Mozambique Channel, 80 meters depth).

Chaetodon miliaris (not of Quoy & Gainard), Fourmanoir, 1957: p. 28 (fig. 22 is of *C. kleinii*, not *miliaris* or *dolosus*, probably a mistake; Mutsamudu (Anjouan)).

Diagnosis.—D. XIII, 22; A. III, 18-19; pectoral rays 14; L.l. scales 40-42; typical of *C. miliaris* complex species but with large dark area at posterior end of body including dorsal and anal fins; *C. dolosus* possesses black spot in dorsal fin which is absent in *C. sedentarius*, the other species with dark posterior area.

Chaetodon dolosus Ahl. 99 mm S.L. Mozambique Channel.

Ratios		Standard Length (mm)	
	10-39	40-69(1)	above 69(3)
Depth/S.L..............	---	1.9	1.7-1.8
Head/S.L..............	---	3.0	3.4-3.5
Eye/Head	---	2.7	2.8-3.0
Snout/Head	---	3.3	2.8-3.0
Interorb. W./Head......	---	3.1	3.0-3.2
Maxillary/Head	---	4.8	4.6-4.7
Caud. Ped./S.L.........	---	10.2	9.6-10.2
Pect. Fin/S.L..........	---	3.7	4.0-4.1
Pelvic Sp./S.L.........	---	4.0	5.2-5.5
Predorsal L./S.L.......	---	2.4	2.6
Prepelvic L./S.L.......	---	2.2	2.3-2.5
Dorsal Sp. No. 1/S.L.....	---	12.7	12.8(27.5)
Dorsal Sp. No. 2/S.L.....	---	5.4	7.4-9.2
Dorsal Sp. No. 3/S.L.....	---	4.1	5.6-7.6
Dorsal Sp. No. 4/S.L.....	---	4.0	4.7-6.3
Anal Sp. No. 1/S.L.......	---	7.5	9.5-11.0
Anal Sp. No. 2/S.L.......	---	5.5	5.0-5.2
Anal Sp. No. 3/S.L.......	---	5.6	5.2-5.3

Meristics.—D. XIII, 22; A. III, 18-19; pectoral rays 14; L.l. scales 40-42; L.l. pores 37-40; scales above L.l. 9-10; scales below L.l. about 20; gill rakers 17-18.

Description.—Predorsal contour straight; snout short, 2.8-3.0 in head length; gape horizontal to slightly oblique; teeth in 7-8 rows in upper jaw; preopercle right-angled to slightly oblique-angled, edge smooth; lachrymal and supraorbital smooth; eye diameter equal to snout length, both greater than depth of caudal peduncle, which is greater than interorbital width.

Fourth to sixth dorsal spines longest; second anal spine slightly longer than third, first half or more of second; dorsal and anal fins rounded (dorsal less so); base of spinous portion of dorsal fin longer (2.1-2.4 in S.L.) than that of soft portion (3.3-3.5 in S.L.); pelvic fins short, falling short of anus.

Lateral line a moderate arc, slightly flattened on top; scales moderate, rounded-angular, in horizontal series on lower portion of body, ascending series on upper portion; scales of dorsal spines reaching midpoint of about fifth dorsal spine; anal spine scales covering more than half of third anal spine.

Juveniles similar to adults.

Color Pattern.—Caudal fin abruptly yellow; posterior section of body (including fins) blackish; pelvic fins dusky; edges of dorsal and anal fins white, a submarginal dark line present; eyebands connected at nape; predorsal area sometimes blackish from eyeband to nostrils; spotted pattern of other species of the complex faintly present.

Juveniles similar but with large dark brown ocellated spot at angle of dorsal fin (8th-12th rays in medium sized specimens, 9th-15th in smaller ones); several (6-8) vertical spotted lines as in other species; dark posterior

Chaetodon dolosus juvenile 42 mm S.L. Mazeppa Bay.

area much reduced, including area just anterior to caudal peduncle and above it to the dorsal spot; eyeband with white stripe at posterior edge (after Smith, 1966).

Posterior dark area becomes darker with age, while the dorsal spot fades; vertical rows of spots fade also with growth, and the spots on the scales become more prominent (after Smith, 1966, and 35 mm color transparency).

Remarks.—*Chaetodon dolosus* is a poorly known species apparently endemic to the eastern African coast. Most specimens are in poor condition because of their collection by trawling. The adults are found in deep water (Smith, 1966); the Somali specimens were taken by trawl at a depth of 59-61 meters. The juveniles, however, are captured in shallow water. The type specimens of C. *mendoncae* were taken in 60 fathoms in the Mozambique Channel.

Smith contrasted this species with Ahl's (1923) and Gunther's (1871) descriptions of *Chaetodon guentheri* and Weber & de Beaufort's (1936) description of C. *guentheri*. Fourmanoir reported capturing this species at 80 fathoms.

Distribution.—East coast of Africa from Delagoa Bay to the Somali Coast. Probably also from the islands near the African coast.

Material Examined.—(4 spec.: 43-99 mm S.L.) JLBS Aug. 1950 (2: 76-99), Mozambique Channel; JLBS 3-1-52 (1: 43) Mazeppa Bay; SOSC Anton Bruun, Cr. 9 Sta. 447 (1: 94), Somali Coast, 10°00'N, 51°15'E.

CHAETODON SANCTAHELENAE Gunther
Saint Helena butterflyfish

Chaetodon Sanctae Helenae Gunther, 1868: pp. 225, 227
(type locality St. Helena).
Chaetodon Sanctae Helenae var. *uniformis* Ahl, 1923: p. 93
(on Gunther, 1868).

Diagnosis.—D. XIII, 21-23; A. III, 19; pectoral rays 14 or 15; L.l. scales 42-46; plain colored with only ocular band as marking; endemic to Ascension Island and St. Helena Island, Atlantic Ocean.

Meristics.—D. XIII, 21-23; A. III, 19; pectoral rays with 14 or 15 rays; L.l. scales 42-46; L.l. pores 41-45; scales above L.l. 10; scales below L.l. 23; gill rakers 18.

Description.—Predorsal contour slightly convex at nape, concave at nostrils, straight between; snout short, 2.6-3.4 in head length; gape slightly oblique; teeth in close bunch in front of jaws; preopercle right-angled, edge smooth; lachrymal angular anteriorly, smooth; supraorbital smooth; depth of caudal peduncle greater than interorbital width, which is greater than eye diameter; eye diameter greater than snout length.

Fifth dorsal spine longest; second anal spine slightly larger than third, first about half second; dorsal and anal fins well rounded; base of spinous portion of dorsal fin longer (2.1-2.3 in S.L.) than that of soft por-

Chaetodon sanctaehelenae Gunther. 123 mm S.L. Ascension Island.

Ratios	10-49	50-89	Standard Length (mm) above 89 (3)
Depth/S.L............	---	---	1.7
Head/S.L.............	---	---	3.7-4.2
Eye/Head............	---	---	3.0-3.1
Snout/Head..........	---	---	2.6-3.4
Interorb. W./Head.....	---	---	2.9
Maxillary/Head.......	---	---	3.9-4.0
Caud. Ped./S.L........	---	---	9.4-10.1
Pect. Fin/S.L..........	---	---	4.0-4.2
Pelvic Sp./S.L.........	---	---	5.5-5.8
Predorsal L./S.L.......	---	---	2.6-2.7
Prepelvic L./S.L.......	---	---	2.5-2.6
Dorsal Sp. No. 1/S.L....	---	---	13.5-13.7
Dorsal Sp. No. 2/S.L....	---	---	7.9-8.4
Dorsal Sp. No. 3/S.L....	---	---	6.1-7.1
Dorsal Sp. No. 4/S.L....	---	---	5.2-5.7
Anal Sp. No. 1/S.L......	---	---	9.6-10.5
Anal Sp. No. 2/S.L......	---	---	5.2
Anal Sp. No. 3/S.L......	---	---	5.4-5.8

tion (3.0-3.4 in S.L.); pelvic fins short, not reaching anus.

Lateral line moderately low arc; scales small, angular, in horizontal series in lower part of body and increasingly ascending rows in upper portion; scaly portion of dorsal spines reaching midpoint of fifth dorsal spine; anal scaly covering reaching just past midpoint of third spine.

Color Pattern.—Eyebands connected at nape, becoming very weak below eye; dusky triangular spot between eyes to snout tip in one of the preserved specimens, reduced to crossband plus spot in same area of second; pelvics dusky; no other conspicuous markings visible.

Color of living animals white with violet or light purple above (Cunningham, 1910; Cadenat and Marchal, 1963). There is a yellow edge to the dorsal and anal fins, the color crossing the caudal peduncle. At Ascension Island this yellow includes most of soft dorsal fin, entire anal fin and entire caudal peduncle including the caudal fin base; at St. Helena the yellow is more restricted, covering only about half soft dorsal and anal fins and about half caudal peduncle but also including caudal fin base. In the correct light some vertical spotted lines can be seen that agree with the patterns of most of the other members of this species group.

Juveniles similar to adults but possess a dark half-spot along edge of soft dorsal fin and a fairly broad dark stripe along length of anal fin just within bordering white line. Juvenile eyeband darker, more complete.

Remarks.—The variety named by Ahl *(uniformis)* does not appear to be valid. Nor does there appear to be any significant difference between the two color forms of this species from the two islands. Gunther stated that the eyeband is much narrower than the eye. This does not appear to be true in the adults although in juveniles the eyeband appears less broad.

Chaetodon sanctaehelenae is a very abundant species at both St. Helena and Ascension Islands. According to Ken Jourdan there were "thousands" at Ascension and "billions" at St. Helena. He further stated that, "they were so abundant that I observed them swimming upside down eating on the underside of our boat [an old fishing boat with marine growths] in 15 feet of water!" They were abundant at all depths that Jourdan and his diving partner "Mac" Macdowell dove at, from 5 to 80 feet. Cunningham (1910) states dozens or hundreds appeared when refuse was thrown into the water at St. Helena. He was able to capture "more than a hundred at one haul" of the net. Some of the specimens were running ripe, the eggs being about 1 mm in diameter and with a single yellowish oil globule.

Distribution.—Known only from Ascension and St. Helena.

Material examined.—(3 spec.: 106-123 mm S.L.) USNM 42311 and 42312 (2: 115-123), Ascension Island; (1: 106), St. Helena Island.

CHAETODON SEDENTARIUS Poey
Bank butterflyfish

Chaetodon sedentarius Poey, 1858: p. 203 (type locality Cuba).

Chaetodon gracilis Gunther, 1860: p. 20 (type locality Caribbean Sea).

Sarothrodus sedentarius, Poey, 1868: p. 364 (Cuba; new combination). Cope, 1870: p. 474 (St. Martins).

Chaetodon sedentarius Poey. 63 mm S.L. "off Brazil".

Ratios	Standard Length (mm)		
	10-39(4)	40-69(12)	above 69(15)
Depth/S.L............	1.6-1.7	1.7-1.8	1.6-1.8
Head/S.L.............	2.5-2.7	2.9-3.3	3.2-3.6
Eye/Head............	2.4-2.6	2.4-2.9	2.6-3.2
Snout/Head	3.1-3.2	2.7-3.3	3.0-3.6
Interorb. W./Head......	2.9-3.4	3.0-3.6	2.8-3.4
Maxillary/Head	4.1-4.3	4.1-5.1	4.2-5.0
Caud. Ped./S.L........	8.1-9.1	8.5-10.0	9.3-9.8
Pect. Fin/S.L..........	3.5-4.3	3.5-4.0	3.7-4.7
Pelvic Sp./S.L.........	3.6-4.4	4.4-5.2	4.8-5.5
Predorsal L./S.L.......	2.1	2.3-2.6	2.4-2.6
Prepelvic L./S.L.......	2.0-2.1	2.2-2.5	2.4-2.5
Dorsal Sp. No. 1/S.L.....	8.8-9.4	9.9-14.7	11.2-15.7
Dorsal Sp. No. 2/S.L.....	3.8-4.6	5.2-7.5	7.6-9.5
Dorsal Sp. No. 3/S.L.....	3.9-4.7	4.3-5.4	5.4-7.4
Dorsal Sp. No. 4/S.L.....	4.0-5.0	4.1-5.0	4.9-6.5
Anal Sp. No. 1/S.L.......	6.9-7.6	6.9-8.5	8.7-10.2
Anal Sp. No. 2/S.L.......	4.9-7.1	4.5-5.4	4.8-5.5
Anal Sp. No. 3/S.L.......	4.8-9.6	4.4-5.9	4.4-5.9

Chaetodon sedentarius newly metamorphosed, 24 mm S.L. Florida.

Diagnosis.—D. XIII (XIV), 20-22 (usually 21-22); A. III, 17-19 (usually 18); pectoral rays (13) 14; L.l. scales 36-44 (usually 36-40); similar to other members of the *miliaris* complex but with a dark area including caudal peduncle and adjacent area plus parts of dorsal and anal fins; differs from *C. dolosus* in extent of dark color and in lacking dorsal fin spot; Caribbean species.

Meristics.—D. XIII (two with XIV), 20-22 (normally 21 or 22); A. III, 17-19 (mostly 18); pectoral rays 14 (one with 13/13, one with 13/14, one with 14/15); L.l. scales 36-44 (usually 36-40); L.l. pores 33-41; scales above L.l. 7-9; scales below L.l. 17-20 (normally 18 or 19); gill rakers 14-18 (usually 16-17).

Description.—Predorsal contour straight; snout short, 3.0-3.6 in head length; gape horizontal to slightly oblique; teeth in 5-6 rows in each jaw; preopercle right-angled, edge smooth to crenulate; lachrymal and supraorbital smooth; eye diameter greater than depth of caudal peduncle, which is greater than snout length; snout length greater than interorbital width.

Fifth or sixth dorsal spine longest, first short; second and third anal spines equal, first about half second; dorsal and anal fins rounded; base of spinous portion of dorsal fin longer (2.0-2.4 in S.L.) than that of soft portion (3.3-3.6 in S.L.); pelvic fins moderate, reaching to anus or slightly beyond.

Lateral line a moderately high arc, slightly flattened on top; scales moderate, rounded to slightly angular, in horizontal series only along very lowest portion of body; scaly covering of dorsal spines reaching midpoint of sixth dorsal spine; scaly covering of anal spines covering about one-third of third spine.

Color Pattern.—Dark posterior color variously represented in rayed portion of dorsal fin, sometimes covering most of it, other times just last few rays are black; caudal peduncle is black, sometimes with a small portion of adjacent body black as well; extension onto anal fin variable also, sometimes covering posterior section of rays and not reaching angle except for extension along edge of fin, other times the black area extending vertically from anterior edge of caudal peduncle to edge of fin, the extension reaching spines and running along scale covering to base of first spine as indistinct gray-brown color; eyebands broadly joined before nape; narrow edges of dorsal and anal fins white, submarginal lines black; pelvic fins body color; vertical spotted lines, as in other species of this complex, present.

Juveniles with some differences in color pattern; dark posterior area may be faded, revealing two vertically oval to rounded spots, one in dorsal fin fairly distinct, close to the posterior edge of the fin; second less distinct and occupying a similar place in anal fin (this latter spot more likely to remain obscured by blackish posterior part of the fin).

Remarks.—There seems to be very little problem with *Chaetodon sedentarius*. The smallest specimens do exhibit slight color changes, but apparently they have not been mistaken for other species. The variation of the color pattern in the posterior portion of the body does not follow any geographic pattern. The dark area of the dorsal fin apparently can be a strong black to a dusky color. The spots of the juveniles are not evident in faded adult specimens.

This species is obviously related to the other species of the *miliaris* complex through meristics and color pattern. It appears very close to *Chaetodon dolosus* from the East African coast. The mid-Atlantic *C. sanctaehelene* also is close to this group but is too poorly known to consider its relationships.

According to Bohlke and Chaplin (1968), *Chaetodon sedentarius* is the least common Bahamanian butterflyfish with the possible exception of *Chaetodon aculeatus*. In the Florida Keys it is perhaps more common in deeper water, a trait it shares with several other members of the complex. Briggs, et al (1964) reports it from 31 fathoms off the coast of Texas. Durand (1960) had previously recorded *C. sedentarius* in depths of 40 meters to more than 100 meters, but Longley and Hildebrand (1941) found one at 2.5 fathoms, others at 40 fathoms.

Distribution.—Western Atlantic Ocean from Brazil to off the North Carolina coast; Bermuda; Gulf of Mexico.

Material Examined.—(31 spec.: 25-116 mm S.L.) USNM 20062 (14: 49-87), off Brazil, 02°40'N, 48°39'W'; USNM 159266 (1: 45), Surinam; USNM 152071 (1: 116), North Carolina coast; UMML 17187 (3: 26-28),

Alligator Reef, Florida; UMML 11382 (1: 25), Bahama Islands; MCZ 16198 (1: 88), Cuba (holotype); NMFS-M Oregon 5034 (1: 64), Venezuela; NMFS-M Oregon 4884 (2: 71-84), Columbia; NMFS-M Oregon 3589 (4: 68-89), Panama; NMFS-M Oregon 3640 (1: 90), Yucatan; NMFS-M SB 5650 (2: both 72), North Carolina.

CHAETODON CITRINELLUS Cuvier
Citron butterflyfish
(Speckled butterflyfish)

Chaetodon citrinellus Cuvier. 72 mm S.L. Oahu, Hawaii.

Chaetodon citrinellus Cuvier, 1831: p. 27 (type localities Guam, Tahiti; on Broussonet, MS).

Chaetodon punctatus (not of Linnaeus), Cuvier, 1831: p. 28 (noted in discussion of *C. citrinellus*); (on Parkinson; ex. Banks and Solander, MS; Tahiti).

Tetragonoptrus citrinellus Bleeker, 1863: p. 234 (new combination).

Chaetodon nigripes De Vis, 1885: p. 453 (Queensland; see Ogilby, 1892).

Chaetodon miliaris (not of Quoy and Gaimard), Fowler & Silvester, 1922: p. 123.
Chaetodon citrinellus var. *semipunctatus* Ahl, 1923: p. 104 (on Gunther, 1874).
Chaetodon citrinellus nigripes Ahl, 1923: p. 105 (Queensland). Whitley, 1930: p. 17 (coast of S. Queensland).
Chaetodon (Tetragonoptrus) citrinellus, Weber & de Beaufort, 1936: p. 76, fig. 23 (various localities).
?*Chaetodon miliaris* (not of Quoy & Gaimard), Fowler & Silvester, 1944: p. 123.
Chaetodon (Chaetodon) citrinellus, Fowler, 1953: p. 30 (China, Nafa, Formosa, Okinawa, Aguni Shima, Kotosho).

Diagnosis.—D. XIV (one with XIII), 20-22 (usually 21-22); A. III, 16-17; pectoral rays (13) 14; L.l. scales 36-42 (usually 39-41); body with horizontal and ascending rows of spots, one per scale; anal fin with broad black edge and submarginal whitish band. Easily distinguished from other spotted *Chaetodon* species by dorsal count and color pattern of anal fin.

Meristics.—D. XIV (one with XIII), 20-22 (usually 21 or 22); A. III, 16 or 17; pectoral rays 14 (one with 13/13, one with 14/15, one with 13/14); scales in L.l. 36-42 (usually 39-41); L.l. pores 35-41 (usually 37-40); scales above L.l. 7 or 8; scales below L.l. 15-17; gill rakers 20-22.

Ratios	Standard Length (mm)		
	10-49(8)	50-69(7)	above 69(10)
Depth/S.L.	1.7-1.9	1.8-1.9	1.7-1.9
Head/S.L.	2.5-3.1	3.2-3.4	3.3-3.6
Eye/Head	2.4-3.0	2.8-3.0	2.9-3.3
Snout/Head	2.5-3.2	2.6-2.9	2.7-3.1
Interorb. W./Head	3.3-3.8	3.1-3.5	3.1-3.4
Maxillary/Head	3.9-5.1	4.1-4.5	4.2-4.7
Caud. Ped./S.L.	8.0-9.3	8.9-10.1	9.2-10.2
Pect. Fin/S.L.	3.1-3.8	3.3-3.8	3.3-4.1
Pelvic Sp./S.L.	3.4-4.5	4.0-4.7	4.4-5.4
Predorsal L./S.L.	2.0-2.4	2.2-2.6	2.3-2.6
Prepelvic L./S.L.	2.1-2.5	2.5-2.7	2.2-2.7
Dorsal Sp. No. 1/S.L.	7.6-10.5	9.8-12.3	10.9-15.9
Dorsal Sp. No. 2/S.L.	4.1-5.1	5.3-7.3	5.9-9.1
Dorsal Sp. No. 3/S.L.	3.6-4.0	4.5-5.5	4.8-6.6
Dorsal Sp. No. 4/S.L.	3.5-4.1	3.9-4.7	4.2-5.2
Anal Sp. No. 1/S.L.	6.0-7.7	6.5-8.4	7.5-9.6
Anal Sp. No. 2/S.L.	3.7-5.3	3.5-4.2	3.7-4.6
Anal Sp. No. 3/S.L.	3.8-6.4	3.8-4.4	4.1-5.2

Chaetodon citrinellus juvenile, 26 mm S.L. Enewetak, Marshall Islands.

Description.—Predorsal contour straight to slightly concave; gape horizontal to slightly oblique; teeth in 6-7 rows in each jaw; snout short, 2.7-3.1 in head length; preopercle right-angled, edge crenulate to lightly serrate; lachrymal and supraorbital smooth; snout length and depth of caudal peduncle equal, both greater than eye diameter, which is greater than interorbital width.

Fourth to sixth dorsal spines longest, first very small; second anal spine longest, first about half of second; dorsal and anal fins with blunt angle, about equal in size; spinous portion of dorsal fin longer (2.1-2.3 in S.L.) than that of rayed portion (3.1-3.4 in S.L.); pelvic fins moderate, barely reaching to anus.

Lateral line a moderately high arc, slightly flattened on top but with peak at last dorsal spines; scales moderate, rounded, in horizontal series on lower portion of body and ascending rows on upper portions; scales covering dorsal spines reaching midpoint at fifth to sixth dorsal spines, anal covering reaching midpoint of third anal fin spine.

Juveniles similar to adults.

Color Pattern.—Spots approximately one to a scale; eyebands joining at nape, including first dorsal spine; top of snout, including upper lip, dusky; dorsal fin with narrow hyaline border; pelvic fins pale.

Juveniles similar to adults; black anal band extending on more anal fin rays (14 as opposed to 11 in adult) and reaches around fin angle; eyeband relatively wider, being almost as wide as eye and touching posterior border of orbit; dark line of dorsal fin also extends around angle of fin (absent in newly transformed individuals).

Remarks.—*Chaetodon citrinellus* is a fairly common and widely distributed species. The spots are variable in intensity and may show different patterns. The lower edge of the anal fin may be damaged and the dark band gone. These two facts may help to explain the synonyms of this species. *Chaetodon citrinellus* belongs to the spotted butterflyfish species complex of Ahl (1923). He could not distinguish the various species included and left the problem to future investigators. The anal fin band is distinctive and serves to identify this species immediately. It also has XIV dorsal fin spines, one more than the other members of the complex. *Chaetodon citrinellus* is most often confused with *C. miliaris*, a species which differs considerably in color pattern, lacking the anal fin band, having a caudal peduncle band, and having the spots of the body blackish and differently arranged.

Okada & Ikeda (1936) reported XVI dorsal spines for this species, probably a reversal of XIV.

Ogilby (1912), who saw the type specimen of *C. nigripes*, reported it could not be distinguished from *C. citrinellus*.

Harry (1953) reported seeing it at Raroia but noted it was rare. He said pairs were occasionally seen on the western shore reef in the lagoon.

Distribution.—Widely distributed in the Pacific and Indian Oceans, including Hawaiian Islands, but not reported from the Red Sea.

Material Examined.—(25 spec.: 24-84 mm S.L.) EMBL (15: 28-83), Eniwetok, Marshall Islands; FMNH 75045 (1: 28), Sri Lanka; SOSC HA 67-20 (1: 72), Chagas Archipelago; WEB (1: 24) Queensland, Australia; BPBM 6171 (3: 61-71), Tahiti, Society Islands; BPBM 1075 (1: 84), New Hebrides; BPBM 5176 (1: 84), American Samoa; SOSC Te Vega Cr. 1 Sta. 21 (2: 40-70), American Samoa.

CHAETODON KLEINII Bloch
Klein's butterflyfish
(Whitespotted butterflyfish)

Chaetodon Kleinii Bloch, 1790: p. 7, pl. 218, fig. 2 (type locality East Indies).

Chaetodon melastomus Schneider, 1801: p. 224 (type locality Tranquebar).

Chaetodon melammystax Schneider, 1801: p. 225 (no locality).

Chaetodon virescens Cuvier, 1831: p. 30 (type locality Timor).

Chaetodon flavescens Bennett, 1831: p. 61 (type locality Mauritius).

?*Chaetodon bellulus* Thiolliere (in Montrouzier), 1857: p. 443 (type locality Woodlark Island).

Citharoedus melastomus, Kaup, 1860: p. 144 (Moluccas and Mozambique; new combination).

Tetragonoptrus kleini, Bleeker, 1868: p. 287 (new combination).

Tetragonoptrus (Lepidochaetodon) kleini, Bleeker, 1877: p. 45, pl. 11 (East Indies, New Guinea).

Chaetodon (Tetragonoptrus) kleinii, Sauvage, 1891: p. 258 (Madagascar).
Chaetodon corallicola Snyder, 1904: p. 531, pl. 11, fig. 20 (type locality off Oahu, Hawaiian Islands).
Tifia corallicola, Jordan & Jordan, 1922: p. 60 (Hawaiian Islands; new combination).
Chaetodon melanomystax Ahl, 1923: p. 144 (in synonymy— misspelled version of *C. melammystax* Schneider, 1801).
Chaetodon cingulatus Fowler, 1934: p. 480, fig. 45 (type locality Durban, Natal).
Chaetodon (Lepidochaetodon) kleini, Fowler, 1953: p. 38, fig. 100 (China, Formosa, Yaeyama, Itoman, Okinawa, Riukiu).
?*Chaetodon miliaris* (not of Quoy and Gaimard), Four-manoir, 1957: p. 28, fig. 22 (Mutsamudu (Anjouan), Africa; part, figure is *kleinii*, text is not!).
Anisochaetodon kleini, Munro, 1967: p. 369, pl. 50 (new combination; New Guinea).

Chaetodon kleinii Bloch. 89.5 mm S.L. Enewetak, Marshall Islands.

Diagnosis.—D. XIII (four with XIV), 20-23 (usually 21-22); A. III, 17-20 (usually 18-19); pectoral rays 13-15 (usually 14); L.l. scales 33-41 (usually 36-40); eyebands united on chest and continuing to or near pelvic fin insertion; pelvic fins black; close to *Chaetodon trichrous* but distinguishable by color pattern and pectoral ray count (*C. trichrous* with 15

| | Standard Length (mm) | | |
Ratios	10-39(1)	40-69(11)	above 69(55)
Depth/S.L.............	1.6	1.4-1.6	1.4-1.7
Head/S.L..............	3.1	3.0-3.7	3.4-4.0
Eye/Head.............	2.6	2.1-2.9	2.2-3.1
Snout/Head...........	3.1	2.8-3.6	3.0-4.1
Interorb. W./Head......	3.3	2.9-3.2	2.5-3.1
Maxillary/Head........	4.2	3.5-4.6	3.9-6.0
Caud. Ped./S.L........	9.1	8.3-10.3	9.5-10.9
Pect. Fin/S.L..........	3.3	3.1-3.6	3.2-4.3
Pelvic Sp./S.L.........	3.9	4.2-5.0	4.5-5.4
Predorsal L./S.L........	2.4	2.2-2.5	2.4-2.9
Prepelvic L./S.L........	2.2	2.1-2.5	2.3-2.7
Dorsal Sp. No. 1/S.L....	13.0	11.8-22.9	10.3-32.7
Dorsal Sp. No. 2/S.L....	5.0	5.9-7.9	5.8-11.9
Dorsal Sp. No. 3/S.L....	4.4	4.7-6.0	4.7-7.5
Dorsal Sp. No. 4/S.L....	4.3	4.3-5.4	4.3-6.7
Anal Sp. No. 1/S.L.......	5.8	6.3-9.1	6.8-11.1
Anal Sp. No. 2/S.L.......	4.6	4.2-5.5	4.3-7.0
Anal Sp. No. 3/S.L.......	5.4	4.0-5.6	4.2-6.0

rays and dark brown in life, *C. kleini* more orange and with 14 rays).

Meristics.—D. XIII (four with XIV), 20-23 (usually 21 or 22); A. III, 17-20 (usually 18-19); pectoral rays 14 (five with 13/13, two with 15/15, two with 13/14, three with 14/15); L.l. scales 33-41 (usually 36-40); L.l. pores 29-39 (usually 32-38); scales above L.l. 5-7; scales below L.l. 12-14; gill rakers 18-23.

Description.—Snout short, 3.0-4.1 in head length; predorsal contour straight; gape horizontal to slightly oblique; teeth in few rows in front of jaws (4-6?); preopercle right-angled, edge crenulate; lachrymal and supraorbital smooth; depth of caudal peduncle equal to or greater than interorbital width, which is equal to or greater than eye diameter; eye diameter greater than snout length.

Sixth dorsal spine longest, first very small, to 32.7 in S.L.; second and third anal spines equal, first between half and ⅔ second; dorsal and anal fins rounded; base of spinous portion of dorsal fin longer (1.8-2.1 in S.L.) than that of rayed portion (2.8-2.9 in S.L.); pelvic fins short, not quite reaching anal opening.

Lateral line moderately high arc, peak under last spine and first rays of dorsal fin; scales moderate, mixed rounded and slightly angular, in horizontal series on body converging towards caudal peduncle, above L.l. in arched series from dorsal base to L.l.; scaly portion of dorsal spine slightly high, reaching midpoint at fifth dorsal spine, that of anal fin reaching just beyond midpoint of third anal spine.

Juveniles similar to adults.

Color Pattern.—Eyebands joined at nape, sometimes including first dorsal spine, continued on chest where they join again; in most cases in the Indian Ocean and most of the Pacific specimens the dark bands continued to the pelvic fins; in some Indian Ocean specimens the joined bands do not reach pelvic base, and pelvic fins are lighter at base, darker on edges—a single collection sometimes showing all intergrades between the two extremes; pelvic fins blackish; dark and light pattern of body often faded, being completely light; spotted rows on sides usually 10-11 below L.l.; snout tip and lips blackish; pectoral fins hyaline.

Juveniles similar to adults, caudal fin edge broader hyaline; pale band around caudal peduncle.

According to Copley (1944), live African specimens were pale yellow merging into yellow-brown posteriorly; white spots on body; shoulder band reddish-brown; caudal fin bright yellow edged with pale blue; snout and eyeband black; pelvic fins jet black; pale blue and black edging to dorsal and anal fins; pectoral fin plain, with a blackish band at base.

Remarks.—*Chaetodon kleinii* is perhaps the most difficult species to reliably establish an identity for. Other than the eyeband reaching the pelvic fins, there is not much color pattern to distinguish this species from others of similar shape and meristics. In addition, the life color pattern fades in preservative, leaving a very plainly colored fish.

The original description leaves much to be desired and gives XVII dorsal spines, four more than are present. Perhaps the error is a replacement of the first "I" with "V". It has been accepted as this species because *Chaetodon vagabundus*, a more distinctive fish with its description also copied from a previous work (Klein, 1754), was also given XVII dorsal spines in the figure of Klein.

Kaup (1860) refers to a correspondence with Peters in which the latter maintains that *Chaetodon kleinii* is identical with *C. melastomas* Bloch. He apparently was able to see the specimens in Bloch's collection, one of which was labelled *C. kleinii*. Kaup believed that in illustrating the specimen Bloch fabricated an additional four spines in conformity with Klein's illustration. Although seventeen spines were mentioned in Klein's description, it is possible that the description was made after an erroneous figure and not vice versa. To support this figure one may notice that *C. vagabundus* was illustrated with a total of seventeen dorsal spines and that figure was similarly given in the description. It was Kaup's contention that Peter s was correct in his belief that *C. kleinii* and *C. melastomas* were one and the same species. The complete lateral line as shown in Bloch's figure, in contrast to the properly incomplete lateral line, was written off as poor draftsmanship, and Kaup believed that the more correctly described *C. melastomas* should take preference over the poorly described *C. kleinii*.

Snyder (1904) failed to compare his *C. corallicola* with other closely related species. A comparison with *C. kleinii* would have shown that these two species were identical. Minor points of color differences would at most cause *Chaetodon corallicola* to be considered a subspecies of *C.*

kleinii. Chaetodon flavescens, C. virescens, and *C. cingulatus* are all synonyms of *C. kleinii* based on comparison with the type specimens I have seen or have photographs of. *Chaetodon* "orangee" of Desjardins (1836) (Septieme Rapp.) from Mauritius is probably this species, but the name is not admissible under the present international rules. In Fourmanoir (1957), figure 22 is *C. kleinii,* but the description mentions the black peduncular bar of *C. miliaris.* He lists this species as *C. miliaris.* In the same work, p. 31, *C. kleinii* is present. The reference of Steindachner (1893) to a dorsal ocellus in *C. kleinii* (under the description of *C. vagabundus*) is erroneous. He probably was referring to the juveniles of *C. vagabundus* which do have the dorsal ocellated spot near the edge of the fin.

Herre & Montalban (1927) found ripe females in April.

Ahl (1923) claims a juvenile of 36 mm still in the tholichthys stage has an eye-spot in the soft dorsal fin. I find no such spot in any of the juveniles examined. I have seen the species metamorphose from the oceanic larvae to the juvenile. The apparent transformation size is 30-40 mm standard length.

In Hawaii, *C. kleinii* is usually found in deeper water than most of the common butterflyfish species. Gilbert (1905), in Jordan & Evermann, reports collections of this species in Hawaii at depths of about 15-30 fathoms. It does appear in shallower water, juveniles being collected in waters less than 20 feet deep. In the Philippines I have seen adult *C. kleinii* in water less than ten feet deep.

Distribution.—Widespread in Pacific and Indian Oceans, including the Hawaiian Islands and Red Sea. Not, however, found in the Society Islands!

Material Examined.—(68 spec.: 30-109 mm S.L.) USNM 43933 (3: 78-95), Mauritius; USNM 45090 (2: 70-79), Samoa; USNM 196654 (1: 73), Amami Islands, Japan; USNM 18044-18070 (26: 64-109), Philippine Islands; USNM 167292 (2: 39-79), Onotoa, Gilbert Islands; Yasuda (Univ. of Tokyo) (4: 58-89), Japan; WEB (7: 68-92), Honolulu Fish Market; WEB (1: 30), night-light, Hawaiian Islands; BPBM 6010 (2: 48-87), Oahu, Hawaiian Islands; USNM 50880 (2: 48-49), Hawaiian Islands (types of *Chaetodon corallicola*); SOSC HA 67-56, HA 67-60, HA 67-55, HA 67-65 (13: 57-101), Aldabra; SOSC HA 67-16 (1: 59), Chagas Archipelago; ANSP 63791 (1: 100), Natal; ANSP 55264 (1: 92) Natal (holotype of *C. cingulatus*); USNM 133829 (1: 55), Tuamotus.

CHAETODON TRICHROUS Gunther
Tahitian butterflyfish

Chaetodon trichrous Gunther, 1874: p. 40, pl. 36, fig. A
(type locality Society Islands). Jordan & Snyder, 1905:
p. 355, fig. 2 (Tahiti, Society Islands).

Chaetodon trichrous Gunther. 85 mm S.L. Tahiti, Society Islands.

Diagnosis.—D. XIII, 21-23; A. III, 17-19; pectoral rays 15 (two with 14); L.l. scales 36-42; close to *Chaetodon kleinii* and has the extended black eyebands to the pelvic fins; body dark brown with light spots on side, one per scale; 15 pectoral rays as compared to 14 for *C. kleinii*.

Meristics.—D. XIII, 21-23; A. III, 17-19; pectoral rays 15 (two with 14/14); L.l. scales 36-42; L.l. pores 35-41; scales above L.l. 4-7 (usually 5 or 6); scales below L.l. 12 or 13; gill rakers 22-25.

Description.—Snout short, 3.0-4.4 in head length; predorsal contour slightly concave; gape horizontal to slightly oblique; teeth in 5-6 rows in each jaw; preopercle right-angled, smooth to slightly serrate; lachrymal and supraorbital smooth; eye diameter greater than or equal to depth of caudal peduncle, which is equal to or greater than interorbital width; interorbital width greater than snout length.

Fifth to seventh dorsal spines longest, first very small (to 16.5 in S.L.); second and third anal spines about equal, first slightly more than half second; dorsal and anal fins rounded; base of spinous portion of dorsal fin longer (2.1-2.3 in S.L.) than that of rayed portion (2.9-3.2 in S.L.); pelvic fins moderate, reaching past anus but not to anal spines.

Lateral line a moderately high peaked arc, flat on top, peak under eleventh dorsal spine or first two dorsal fin rays; scales moderate, rounded to slightly angular, in horizontal series on lower portion of body and slightly descending rows nearing lateral line due to the anterior scales being larger than those posteriorly; above L.l., scales form diagonal rows from anterior dorsal fin to L.l.; scaly portion of dorsal spines reaching midpoint at about fifth or sixth spines, that of anal fin reaching midpoint

Ratios	Standard Length (mm)		
	10-39	40-69(2)	above 69(19)
Depth/S.L.............	---	1.4-1.6	1.5-1.7
Head/S.L.............	---	3.3-3.8	3.4-3.8
Eye/Head	---	2.5-2.9	2.5-2.9
Snout/Head	---	3.4-3.8	3.0-4.4
Interorb. W./Head......	---	2.7-3.0	2.6-3.0
Maxillary/Head	---	3.8-3.9	3.3-5.2
Caud. Ped./S.L.........	---	10.0	9.4-10.7
Pect. Fin./S.L..........	---	3.6	3.4-3.9
Pelvic Spine/S.L........	---	4.8	4.4-5.0
Predorsal L./S.L........	---	2.5	2.3-2.8
Prepelvic L./S.L........	---	2.4-2.6	2.4-2.5
Dorsal Sp. No. 1/S.L.....	---	12.3-12.5	10.9-16.5
Dorsal Sp. No. 2/S.L.....	---	6.9-7.0	6.4-8.9
Dorsal Sp. No. 3/S.L.....	---	4.7-5.5	4.7-6.4
Dorsal Sp. No. 4/S.L.....	---	4.7-4.9	4.0-5.8
Anal Sp. No. 1/S.L.......	---	7.9-8.3	6.9-9.4
Anal Sp. No. 2/S.L.......	---	4.5	4.2-5.5
Anal Sp. No. 3/S.L.......	---	5.0-5.4	3.9-5.2

of third anal spine.

Juveniles similar to adults.

Color Pattern.—Light anterior area variable in extent, sometimes extending back as far as end of the pectoral fin; sometimes central or upper central portion of body darker than posterior section; caudal fin with hyaline border; dorsal and anal fins with narrow or white hyaline border with black submarginal line; anal fin spines brown with white tips; pelvic fins black; eyebands joined at nape and at chest, where they extend to base of pelvic fins and join same color on rayed portion of fins; snout, including lips, black.

Juveniles similar to adults.

Remarks.—*Chaetodon trichrous* is one of the more somber-colored species of butterflyfish. It is closely related to *Chaetodon kleinii* and is a geographic replacement in the area of the Society Islands. It is quite common at Tahiti.

The original description is quite poor and leaves a slight doubt as to the correct identity of this fish. The figure is poor and the dorsal spine count was given as XII instead of the proper XIII for this species.

Distribution.—Restricted to the area of the Pacific Ocean around the Society Islands and Tuamotus.

Material Examined.—(21 spec.: 41-92 mm S.L.) CAS 37926 (14: 69-86), Raiatea, off Iruru Island, Society Islands; CAS 37894 (Moorea) and CAS 37895 (Tahiti) (2: 70-82), Society Islands; BPBM 6107 and 6046 (3: 82-92), Tahiti; WEB (1: 77), Tahiti; UH (1: 41), Onotoa (?).

CHAETODON BLACKBURNII Desjardins
Blackburn's butterflyfish
Chaetodon blackburnii Desjardins, 1836: p. 58 (type locality Mauritius). Fowler, 1935: p. 394, fig. 27 (Durban, Natal).

Chaetodon blackburnii Desjardins. 86 mm S.L. Natal, Africa.

Diagnosis.—D. XVI, 21-23; A. III, 17-18; pectoral rays 14; L.l. scales 38-41; six or more diagonal brownish lines crossing body; easily distinguishable from all other chaetodonts by the XVI dorsal fin spines, highest in the genus.

Meristics.—D. XVI, 21-23; A. III, 17-18; pectoral rays 14; L.l. scales 38-41; L.l. pores 36-40; scales above L.l. 8-9; scales below L.l. 21-22; gill rakers 16.

Description.—Snout short, about 3.3 in head length; predorsal contour straight; gape horizontal; teeth in 6-7 rows in each jaw; preopercle right-angled to slightly obtuse-angled; edge denticulate; lachrymal and supraorbital smooth; depth of caudal peduncle greater than interorbital width, which is greater than eye diameter; eye diameter greater than or equal to snout length.

Fifth dorsal spine longest; first dorsal spine very short, to 22.0 in S.L.; second and third anal spines about equal or third longest, first short,

Ratios	Standard Length (mm)		
	10-39(1)	40-69(2)	above 69(1)
Depth/S.L.............	1.8	1.9	1.9
Head/S.L.............	2.7	3.3	3.6
Eye/Head.............	2.9	2.9-3.0	3.2
Snout/Head...........	3.1	3.0-3.3	3.3
Interorb. W./Head......	3.1	3.2-3.3	3.1
Maxillary/Head........	4.3	3.9-5.2	4.1
Caud. Ped./S.L.........	9.6	10.2-11.3	10.9
Pect. Fin./S.L..........	3.7	4.1	4.6
Pelvic Spine/S.L........	3.7	5.0-5.3	5.6
Predorsal L./S.L........	2.2	2.6-2.7	3.1
Prepelvic L./S.L........	2.2	2.4	2.4
Dorsal Sp. No. 1/S.L.....	10.0	12.0-13.0	22.0
Dorsal Sp. No. 2/S.L.....	4.2	6.5-7.5	9.6
Dorsal Sp. No. 3/S.L.....	4.0	6.0-6.7	7.8
Dorsal Sp. No. 4/S.L.....	4.5	5.6-6.1	6.9
Anal Sp. No. 1/S.L.......	7.1	9.8-11.7	12.9
Anal Sp. No. 2/S.L.......	5.9	5.1-5.3	5.7
Anal Sp. No. 3/S.L.......	5.4	4.9-5.0	5.2

at most half second; dorsal fin squarish; anal fin with blunt angle at about sixth or seventh rays; base of spinous portion of dorsal fin longer (2.2 in S.L.) than that of soft portion (3.7 in S.L.); pelvic fins short, separated from anus by short distance.

Lateral line a moderate arc, flattened on top, peak at 14th or 15th dorsal spine bases; scales moderate, rounded to angular; scaly covering of dorsal spines moderate to high, covering half of sixth spine, that of anal spines reaching midpoint of third spine.

Juveniles similar to adults.

Color Pattern.—About seven dark stripes (usually faded or obscure); pelvic fins body color; eyebands joined at nape, a small dark spot at isthmus possibly representing remnant of eyeband; in faded specimens dark edge noticeable on dorsal and anal fins.

Juveniles similarly patterned.

Color of living animals yellowish, quickly changing to brown posteriorly; stripes dark brown to black; dorsal fin stripe and base of caudal fin yellow; rest of caudal fin hyaline; pectoral fins hyaline; pelvic fins yellowish; eyeband dark brown to black; edge of dorsal fin hyaline to yellowish white.

According to Fowler (1935), the body color is uniform olive brown with faint cross-stripes of the same color; some yellow in pectoral fin area and through dorsal spines.

Juveniles similarly colored.

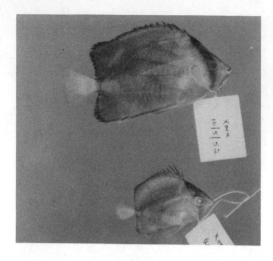

Chaetodon blackburnii
newly transformed
tholichthys, 23.5 mm
S.L. and subadult 40.0
mm S.L. Xora, South
Africa.

Remarks.—*Chaetodon blackburnii* is distinctive in having XVI dorsal fin spines, highest number in the genus *Chaetodon*. It appears to resemble *C. fremblii* in some ways, i.e. the pattern of stripes, squamation, and general shape.

This species is poorly known and still not abundant in collections.

Distribution.—Endemic to the African coast and nearby islands, from Mauritius to the Xora River and Bashee. (Durban, Natal; Mozambique Channel.)

Material Examined.—(4 spec.: 27-86 mm S.L.) JLBS 8735 (1: 59 mm) Durban, South Africa; JLBS 10.5.52 April 1951 (2: 27-57), Xora; ANSP 63854 (1: 86;), Natal.

CHAETODON FREMBLII Bennett
Blue-striped butterflyfish

Chaetodon fremblii Bennett, 1828: p. 42 (type locality Hawaiian Islands).

Chaetodon frehmlii, Cuvier, 1831: p. 18 (Hawaiian Islands).

Chaetodon Frehmli Bennetti, Kaup, 1860: p. 16 (Sandwich Islands).

Chaetodon bleekeri Seale, 1902: p. 16 (Honolulu).

Chaetodon fremblyi, Jordan, 1925: p. 21 (Hawaiian Islands).

Diagnosis.—D. XIII (one with XII, one with XIV), 20-21; A. III, 17 (occasionally 16 or 18); pectoral rays 15; L.l. scales 41-55; yellow with seven diagonal blue stripes rising posteriorly and with large black blotch on last dorsal fin rays and caudal peduncle; no ocular band.

Chaetodon fremblii Bennett. 99 mm S.L. Kahe Point, Oahu, Hawaiian Islands.

Ratios	10-30	Standard Length (mm) 31-60(11)	above 60(9)
Depth/S.L.	---	1.8-1.9	1.7-2.0
Head/S.L.	---	2.8-3.1	3.0-3.6
Eye/Head	---	2.6-3.0	2.6-3.4
Snout/Head	---	2.5-2.9	2.7-3.1
Interorb. W./Head	---	3.4-3.9	2.9-4.0
Maxillary/Head	---	3.7-4.5	3.7-4.5
Caud. Ped./S.L.	---	9.1-10.5	9.1-10.3
Pect. Fin./S.L.	---	3.0-3.8	3.2-3.9
Pelvic Spine/S.L.	---	3.6-4.4	4.1-5.4
Predorsal L./S.L.	---	2.2-2.5	2.5-2.7
Prepelvic L./S.L.	---	2.1-2.4	2.4-2.6
Dorsal Sp. No. 1/S.L.	---	8.5-11.0	10.4-17.8
Dorsal Sp. No. 2/S.L.	---	4.0-5.2	5.1-10.3
Dorsal Sp. No. 3/S.L.	---	3.2-4.4	4.0-7.7
Dorsal Sp. No. 4/S.L.	---	3.2-4.8	3.8-5.5
Anal Sp. No. 1/S.L.	---	6.1-7.3	7.0-10.0
Anal Sp. No. 2/S.L.	---	4.3-5.3	4.6-5.6
Anal Sp. No. 3/S.L.	---	4.4-6.0	4.2-6.3

Chaetodon fremblii
juvenile, 31.6 mm
S.L. Hawaiian
Islands.

Meristics.—D. XIII (one with XII, one with XIV), 20-21; A. III, 17 (occasionally 16 or 18); pectoral rays 15 (one with 14/15); L.l. scales 41-55; L.l. pores 39-49; scales above L.l. 8-11; scales below L.l. 23-26 (usually 24 or 25); gill rakers 16-19.

Description.—Snout short, 2.7-3.1 in head length; predorsal contour straight; gape slightly oblique; teeth in 6-8 rows in each jaw; preopercle slightly obtuse-angled, edge crenulate or slightly denticulate; snout length greater than or equal to depth of caudal peduncle, which is greater than eye diameter; eye diameter greater than interorbital width.

Fifth or sixth dorsal spine longest; first dorsal spine very short, to 17.8 in S.L.; dorsal and anal fins rounded, posterior edge near vertical; second and third anal spines about equal, first about half second; base of spinous portion of dorsal fin longer (1.9-2.3 in S.L.) than that of soft portion (3.2-3.7 in S.L.); pelvic fins moderate, reaching past anal opening and almost to first anal spine base.

Lateral line a moderate arc, flattened on top, peak at about 12th dorsal spine; scales small, angular; scaly portion of dorsal fin slightly high, reaching midpoint of fourth or fifth dorsal spine, that of anal fin covering half of third spine.

Juveniles similar to adults.

Color Pattern.—About seven diagonal blue lines; blackish spot on nape just in front of dorsal fin; face dusky; eyeband absent; blue body stripes may, when reaching black posterior spot, form part of its border; pelvic fins dusky.

Juvenile similar in color pattern but the caudal fin is almost all hyaline, a dark line dividing this from basal dusky yellowish color.

Remarks.—Chaetodon fremblii is endemic to the Hawaiian Islands. The scales are small, up to 55 in the lateral line; scales angular, approaching the rhomboid shape of the subgenus Rhombochaetodon. Also reminiscent of that subgenus are the nape and posterior black areas. This species definitely forms a connection between the basic Chaetodon stock and the subgenus Rhombochaetodon.

Chaetodon fremblii has a wide depth range in the Hawaiian Islands, being found from tidal pools to depths of more than 600 feet.

This species is one of the few butterflyfishes that have completely lost the eyeband. Even in the juveniles it is not present. *Chaetodon argentatus* of the subgenus *Rhombochaetodon* has lost the eyeband below the eye.

According to Tilden (1929), *C. fremblii* is a herbivore, living on a diet consisting of certain kinds of seaweed. Bits of algae were found in the digestive tract.

Distribution.—Found only in the Hawaiian Islands.

Material Examined.—(20 spec.: 39-136 mm S.L.) WEB (17: 39-103), Oahu, Hawaiian Islands; NMFS-H TC-36, Sta. 32 and Sta. 14 (3: 44-136) Hawaiian Islands (100 fathoms).

CHAETODON LITUS Randall & Caldwell
White-tip butterflyfish

Chaetodon litus Randall & Caldwell, 1973: p. 1-11 (type locality Easter Island).

Chaetodon litus Randall and Caldwell. 99 mm S.L. Easter Island.

Ratios	Standard Length (mm) 20-59(2)	60-89	above 89(6)
Depth/S.L.............	1.6, 1.7	---	1.6-1.7
Head/S.L..............	2.9, 2.9	---	3.3-3.8
Eye/Head	2.5, 2.6	---	2.9-3.2
Snout/Head	2.9, 3.1	---	2.5-3.0
Interorb. W./Head......	3.4, 3.7	---	2.8-3.2
Maxillary/Head	4.7, 5.2	---	3.7-4.8
Caud. Ped./S.L.........	9.0, 9.2	---	9.9-10.8
Pect. Fin/S.L..........	3.2, 3.3	---	3.5-3.7
Pelvic Sp./S.L.........	3.6, 4.1	---	4.4-4.9
Predorsal L./S.L........	2.5, 2.6	---	2.5-2.7
Prepelvic L./S.L........	2.2, 2.2	---	2.3-2.5
Dorsal Sp. No. 1/S.L.....	6.9, 7.6	---	11.5-12.9
Dorsal Sp. No. 2/S.L.....	3.5, 4.1	---	6.0-8.1
Dorsal Sp. No. 3/S.L.....	3.2, 3.9	---	5.1-5.9
Dorsal Sp. No. 4/S.L.....	3.4, 3.7	---	4.6-5.5
Anal Sp. No. 1/S.L.......	6.3, 6.6	---	7.5-8.6
Anal Sp. No. 2/S.L.......	4.3-4.7	---	4.4-4.9
Anal Sp. No. 3/S.L.......	4.3-4.7	---	4.5-5.4

Diagnosis.—D. XIII, 23-25 (one with 25); A. III, 19-20; pectoral rays 14 or 15 (more often 14); L.l. scales 39-46 (usually 40-44); overall dark brown with white border to anal fin and hyaline edge to caudal fin; close to *Chaetodon hemichrysus* but differing in color, and to *C. nigropunctatus* in color but differing in characteristics listed under the subgenera from that species.

Meristics.—D. XIII, 23-25 (one with 25); A. III, 19-20; pectoral rays 14 or 15 (more often 14; two with 14/15); L.l. scales 39-46 (usually 40-44); L.l. pores 37-45; scales above L.l. 9-11; scales below L.l. 24-26; gill rakers 16-21.

Description.—Snout short, 2.5-3.0 in head length; predorsal contour straight; gape slightly oblique, teeth in 7-8 rows in each jaw; preopercle right-angled to slightly oblique, lightly serrated at edge; lachrymal and supraorbital smooth; depth of caudal peduncle greater than snout length and eye diameter, which are equal; both greater than interorbital width.

Fourth or fifth dorsal spine longest, first very short, to 12.9 in S.L.; second anal spine slightly longer than or equal to third, first a little more than half second; dorsal and anal fins rounded; base of spinous portion of dorsal fin longer (2.1 in S.L.) than that of soft portion (3.0-3.1 in S.L.); pelvic fins moderate, reaching beyond anus but not as far as first anal spine.

Lateral line a moderate arc across body, slightly flattened on top, posterior peak at about last two dorsal spines; scales moderate, rounded,

Chaetodon litus, newly transformed tholichthys, 40 mm S.L. Easter Island.

in slightly ascending series on most of body, horizontal on lowermost portion; dorsal fin scale covering reaching midpoint of fifth or sixth spine; anal scale covering reaching midpoint of third spine.

Juveniles similar to adults.

Color Pattern.—Edges of dorsal and anal fins white with submarginal black lines, white of anal fin including spines (yellowish-white); dorsal spines brown with yellowish white tips; pelvic fins brownish black.

In faded specimens each scale is seen to have a light center; nape to upper edge of opercle darker; head and breast uniform; dorsal and anal fins dark.

Juveniles similarly colored; lighter specimens pale brown on lower portion of head, breast yellowish brown; edge of dorsal and anal fins hyaline with submarginal stripes of dark brown, fins brown; dark smudge on soft portion of dorsal fin at about its center; dark brown smudge at nape; caudal peduncle half body color, then abruptly light, caudal fin itself hyaline with dusky upper and lower edges and base, each ray outlined with brown.

Remarks.—*Chaetodon litus* is the only chaetodon thus far found at Easter Island. It is a somber-colored species that resembles *Chaetodon nigropunctatus* somewhat in color but is not very close to that species. *Chaetodon litus* is close to *Chaetodon hemichrysus* of Pitcairn and Rapa Islands but differs markedly in color pattern.

Distribution.—Apparently endemic to Easter Island.

Material Examined.—(8 spec.: 40-113 mm S.L.) BPBM 6656-6657 (2: 97-113), Easter Island; BPBM 6659 and 6660 (4: 90-108), Easter Island; BPBM 6663 (2: 40-43), Easter Island.

CHAETODON HEMICHRYSUS Burgess and Randall
NEW SPECIES *
Half-yellow butterflyfish

Chaetodon hemichrysus Burgess and Randall. 90 mm S.L. Rapa Islands.

Diagnosis.—D. XIII, 21-24 (usually 23-24); A. III, 18-20 (usually 19-20); pectoral rays 14; L.l. scales 41-47 (usually 42-45); anterior half blackish, posterior half white or yellow; close to *Chaetodon litus* but differing in color pattern.

Meristics.—D. XIII, 21-24 (usually 23 or 24); A. III, 18-20 (usually 19 or 20); pectoral rays 14; L.l. scales 41-47; L.l. pores 37-46; scales above L.l. 9 or 10; scales below L.l. 24-30; gill rakers 17-20.

Description.—Snout short, 3.0-3.1 in head length; predorsal contour straight; gape slightly oblique; teeth in 5-7 rows in each jaw; preopercle right-angled to slightly oblique, edge crenulate; lachrymal and supraorbital smooth; eye diameter greater than snout length, which is greater than both interorbital width and depth of caudal peduncle, which are equal.

Fourth to sixth dorsal spines longest, first short; second anal spine slightly longer than third, first about half second; dorsal and anal fins rounded; base of spinous portion of dorsal fin longer (2.1-2.2 in S.L.) than

*Completed manuscript sent to Dr.Randall in Summer, 1974 for joint publication.

Ratios	Standard Length (mm)		
	20-59(5)	60-79(1)	above 79(14)
Depth/S.L.	1.6-1.8	1.6	1.7-1.9
Head/S.L.	2.7-2.8	3.3	3.2-3.7
Eye/Head	2.7-2.8	2.9	2.7-3.2
Snout/Head	2.9-3.1	2.7	2.8-3.1
Interorb. W./Head.	3.2-3.6	3.4	2.6-3.1
Maxillary/Head	3.9-4.9	4.0	4.1-4.7
Caud. Ped./S.L.	9.1-9.7	10.6	10.2-11.8
Pect. Fin/S.L.	3.2-3.6	3.4	3.3-4.1
Pelvic Sp./S.L.	3.4-4.5	4.8	4.1-5.6
Predorsal L./S.L.	2.1-2.3	2.6	2.5-2.8
Prepelvic L./S.L.	2.2-2.3	2.4	2.3-2.7
Dorsal Sp. No. 1/S.L.	6.9-9.4	15.0	9.6-12.5
Dorsal Sp. No. 2/S.L.	3.3-3.7	6.5	6.2-9.8
Dorsal Sp. No. 3/S.L.	3.3-3.7	5.1	4.9-6.8
Dorsal Sp. No. 4/S.L.	3.4-3.8	4.8	4.4-5.5
Anal Sp. No. 1/S.L.	6.0-6.6	7.7	7.2-9.3
Anal Sp. No. 2/S.L.	5.0-5.5	4.1	3.6-4.8
Anal Sp. No. 3/S.L.	4.9-6.6	4.3	3.8-5.0

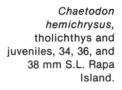

Chaetodon hemichrysus, tholichthys and juveniles, 34, 36, and 38 mm S.L. Rapa Island.

that of soft portion (3.0-3.2 in S.L.); pelvic fins moderate, extending past anus but not reaching first anal spine.

Lateral line a moderate arc, peak at about last dorsal fin spines; scales moderate, rounded, in slightly ascending series on most of body, horizontal on lower portion; dorsal scales covering to midpoint of fifth or sixth dorsal spine; scaly portion of anal fins to ⅔ of third anal spine. Juveniles similar to adults.

Color Pattern.—Edges of dorsal and anal fins hyaline, with a submarginal black line; pelvic fins body color; eyeband absent; extent of each color somewhat variable.

Juveniles similar to adults, in some specimens a grayish to blackish spot or smudge in dorsal fin near or below angle (not evident in all specimens); caudal fin mostly hyaline; black submarginal line wider.

Remarks.—*Chaetodon hemichrysus* is closely related to *Chaetodon litus* of Easter Island, but apparently the two species are mutually exclusive geographically. If the color differences were not present the two species would be almost impossible to separate.

Smaller specimens still have tholichthys plates.

Distribution.—Known only from Pitcairn and Rapa Islands.

Material Examined.—(10 spec.: 33-140 mm S.L.) AMNH (uncatalogued) (8: 33-88), Rapa Island; BPBM 13219 (2: 138-140), Pitcairn Island.

CHAETODON PUNCTATOFASCIATUS Cuvier
Spot-band butterflyfish
(Seven band butterflyfish)

Chaetodon punctato-fasciatus Cuvier, 1831: p. 28 (no locality).

Chaetodon punctato-lineatus Gray, 1854: p. 70 (no locality).

Citharoedus punctatofasciatus, Kaup, 1860: p. 144 (Amboina; new combination).

Tetragonoptrus punctato-fasciatus, Bleeker, 1863: p. 242 (new combination).

Tetragonoptrus (Tetragonoptrus) punctato-fasciatus, Bleeker, 1877: p. 40, pl. 374, fig. 3 (various localities).

Chaetodon (Tetragonoptrus) punctatofasciatus, Weber & de Beaufort, 1936: p. 75 (various localities).

Chaetodon (Chaetodon) punctatofasciatus, Fowler, 1953: p. 29 (Okinawa, China, Kominato, Riu Kiu).

Diagnosis.—D. XIII (one with XIV), 22-25 (usually 23-24); A. III, 17-18; pectoral rays (13) 14; L.l. scales 37-44 (usually 39-42); several bands of dark color made up of spots partially in upper posterior section of body, oriented vertically or slightly slanting anteriorly; close to *Chae-*

Chaetodon punctatofasciatus Cuvier. 77 mm S.L. Enewetak, Marshall Islands.

| | Standard Length (mm) | | |
Ratios	20-39(3)	40-59(2)	above 59(15)
Depth/S.L............	1.6-1.7	1.6	1.6-1.8
Head/S.L.............	2.8-3.0	3.2-3.4	3.4-3.7
Eye/Head.............	2.7-3.1	2.7	2.7-3.1
Snout/Head...........	2.5-3.1	3.1-3.3	2.7-4.1
Interorb. W./Head......	3.4-3.7	3.3	2.8-3.3
Maxillary/Head........	4.2-4.4	4.9-5.8	4.4-5.6
Caud. Ped./S.L........	9.6-9.9	10.1-10.9	10.0-11.2
Pect. Fin/S.L..........	3.1-3.4	3.2-3.3	3.2-3.7
Pelvic Sp./S.L.........	3.8-4.2	4.1-4.5	4.2-4.9
Predorsal L./S.L.......	2.1-2.2	2.2-2.5	2.3-2.5
Prepelvic L./S.L.......	2.3-2.5	2.4-2.5	2.5-2.7
Dorsal Sp. No. 1/S.L....	8.7-13.6	9.9-11.0	9.8-12.7
Dorsal Sp. No. 2/S.L....	4.2-5.4	5.1-5.2	5.0-7.1
Dorsal Sp. No. 3/S.L....	3.8-4.2	4.5	4.8-5.8
Dorsal Sp. No. 4/S.L....	3.4-4.2	4.4-4.8	4.4-5.4
Anal Sp. No. 1/S.L......	6.7-8.0	7.4-7.9	7.0-9.3
Anal Sp. No. 2/S.L......	4.0-4.3	3.8-4.1	3.7-4.4
Anal Sp. No. 3/S.L......	4.1-4.5	3.9-4.7	4.1-4.9

Chaetodon punc-
tatofasciatus, recent-
ly transformed
tholichthys, 28 and
30 mm S.L.
Enewetak, Marshal
Islands.

todon pelewensis but that species has its bands strongly inclined posteriorly (the reverse of *C. punctatofasciatus*); *C. punctatofasciatus* lacks
the caudal peduncle band of both *C. multicinctus* and *C. guttatissimus*,
other closely related species.

Meristics.—D. XIII (one has XIV), 22-25 (usually 23 or 24); A. III, 17
or 18; pectoral rays 14 (three with 13/13, two with 13/14); L.l. scales
37-44 (usually 39-42); L.l. pores 34-42; scales above L.l. 7 or 8; scales
below L.l. 15-16; gill rakers 15-19 (usually 17).

Description.—Snout short, 2.7-4.1 in head length; predorsal contour
straight; gape oblique; teeth in 6-7 rows in each jaw; preopercle right-
angled, edge crenulate; lachrymal smooth, supraorbital smooth to lightly
serrate; eye diameter greater than or equal to depth of caudal peduncle,
which is greater than or equal to interorbital width; interorbital width
equal to or greater than snout length.

Fourth or fifth dorsal spine longest, first small, to 12.7 in S.L.;
second anal spine slightly longer than or equal to third, first less than half
second; dorsal and anal fins rounded; spinous dorsal fin base longer (2.1-
2.3 in S.L.) than rayed dorsal fin base (2.7-3.0 in S.L.); pelvic fins moderate, reaching beyond anus but not to anal spine base.

Lateral line a moderately high arc; scales moderate, rounded to
slightly angular, in horizontal rows along ventral area, ascending rows
above; scales covering dorsal spines reaching midpoint of sixth dorsal

spine, scales covering slightly more than half of third anal fin spine. Juveniles similar to adults. 28 mm S.L. juvenile not a tholichthys.

Color Pattern.—Eyeband reduced; black horseshoe-shaped mark on nape above which a pale area extends to and includes first dorsal spine; upper lip dusky.

Juveniles generally like adults but with slight differences; dorsal and anal fins with broader hyaline edges; eyeband connected with horseshoe-shaped mark on nape; faded indication of band surrounding caudal peduncle; broad edge of caudal fin hyaline.

Remarks.—*Chaetodon punctatofasciatus* belongs to a complex of closely related species from the Indo-Pacific region. The other species concerned are *C. pelewensis, C. multicinctus,* and *C. guttatissimus.* Except for color they are almost identical, and they are also geographically exclusive. However, they all have different color patterns which hold true over large geographic areas, except for *C. multicinctus,* a Hawaiian endemic.

Abe's (1939) record from Palau of *C. pelewensis* is most likely this species.

Distribution.—Micronesia, Philippine Islands, East Indies, New Guinea, Taiwan to southern Japan; Marshall and Caroline Islands as well as Palau.

Material Examined.—(20 spec.: 33-78 mm S.L.) BPBM 6245 (3: 71-78), Eniwetok, Marshall Islands; BPBM 6298 (3: 51-67), Eniwetok, Marshall Islands; WEB (7: 33-77), Eniwetok, Marshall Islands; CAS 37896 (2: 74-76), Palau Islands; CAS 37897 (3: 71-75), Palau Islands; CAS 37898 (2: 35-54), Ifaluk Atoll.

CHAETODON PELEWENSIS Kner
Sunset butterflyfish

Chaetodon pelewensis Kner, 1968: p. 306 (type locality Pellew Islands).
Chaetodon germanus De Vis, 1884: p. 454 (Queensland).
Chaetodon punctato-fasciatus var., Gunther, 1860: p. 515 (New Hebrides).
Chaetodon pelewensis germanus, Ahl, 1923: p. 103 (Queensland).

Diagnosis.—D. XIII (one with XIV), 22-25 (usually 24-25); A. III, 17-18; pectoral rays 14 (15); L.l. scales 39-47 (usually 39-44); eyeband orange, dark bordered; several dark stripes extending diagonally from rayed dorsal fin toward pectoral fin, turning into dots near pectoral fin; very close to *Chaetodon punctatofasciatus* but differing in color pattern, that species having the stripes vertical or nearly so.

Chaetodon pelewensis Kner. 83 mm S.L. Paparaa, Tahiti.

Ratios	20-39(1)	Standard Length (mm) 40-59(1)	above 59(11)
Depth/S.L.	1.5	1.6	1.6-1.7
Head/S.L.	---	3.5	3.5-3.9
Eye/Head	---	2.7	2.5-3.1
Snout/Head	---	3.3	2.9-4.1
Interorb. W./Head	---	3.3	2.8-3.8
Maxillary/Head	---	5.9	4.3-5.5
Caud. Ped./S.L.	10.1	10.8	10.7-11.5
Pect. Fin/S.L.	3.1	3.2	3.1-3.6
Pelvic Sp./S.L.	4.1	4.3	4.3-5.1
Predorsal L./S.L.	2.3	2.3	2.4-2.8
Prepelvic L./S.L.	2.4	2.5	2.5-2.8
Dorsal Sp. No. 1/S.L.	8.3	11.2	10.6-12.6
Dorsal Sp. No. 2/S.L.	4.6	5.7	5.3-6.9
Dorsal Sp. No. 3/S.L.	4.4	5.1	4.6-6.7
Dorsal Sp. No. 4/S.L.	4.1	4.6	4.6-6.7
Anal Sp. No. 1/S.L.	6.7	6.2	8.0-10.3
Anal Sp. No. 2/S.L.	4.1	3.8	3.7-5.2
Anal Sp. No. 3/S.L.	4.7	4.1	3.8-4.9

Meristics.—D. XIII (one with XIV), 22-25 (usually 24 or 25); A. III, 17 or 18; pectoral rays 14 (one with 15/15, one with 13/14); L.l. scales 39-47 (usually 39-44); L.l. pores 38-42; scales above L.l. 7 or 8; scales below L.l. 15-18 (usually 17); gill rakers 16-18.

Description.—Snout short, 2.9-4.1 in head length; predorsal contour straight; gape horizontal to slightly oblique; teeth in about 6 rows in both jaws; preopercle right-angled, edge crenulate; lachrymal smooth, supraorbital smooth to serrate; eye diameter greater than both interorbital width and depth of caudal peduncle, which are equal; all greater than snout length.

Fourth to sixth dorsal spines longest, first small, to 12.6 in S.L.; second anal spine slightly longer than third, first less than half second; dorsal and anal fins rounded; spinous dorsal fin base longer (about 2.3 in S.L.) than that of rayed portion (3.0 in S.L.); pelvic fins short, not reaching anus.

Lateral line a high arc, slightly flattened on top; scales moderate, rounded, in horizontal rows on lower part of body, ascending rows on upper portion; dorsal spine scaly covering reaching midpoint of fifth or sixth dorsal spine, that of anal fin covering half to ¾ of third spine.

Juveniles similar to adults.

Color Pattern.—Dark spot on nape horseshoe-shaped; light streak just above this to dorsal fin spines, including at least first spine; face dusky, upper lip black; pelvic fins body color to dusky.

Juveniles with similar pattern but with eyeband connected with nape spot.

Remarks.—Apparently there has been some confusion concerning the distribution of *Chaetodon pelewensis*. The name 'pelewensis' was taken to mean the Palau Islands. This was not within the normal range of this species, which was never recorded from there other than through the inference from the name. There are islands in Northern Australia that bear the name Pellew Islands, and this might be the proper type locality. The description mentions diagonal lines, which fits this species rather than the closely related *C. punctatofasciatus*. *C. punctatofasciatus* has been collected in the Palau Islands, as well as the Philippine Islands and as far south as New Guinea. Further south it is replaced by *C. pelewensis*.

Distribution.—Restricted to the southern portions of the tropical Pacific Ocean from the Society Islands and Tuamotu Islands through Samoa, Fiji, to Queensland, Australia, and around the northern coast of Australia to the northwestern part of that continent.

Material Examined.—(13 spec.: 38-84 mm S.L.) BPBM 6070 (1: 84), Tahiti; BPBM 6053 (2: 56-83), Tahiti; BPBM 6120 (2: 73-74), Tahiti; CAS 37899 (1: 77), Bora Bora, Society Islands; CAS 37900 (1: 38), Moorea, Society Islands; CAS 37901 (3: all 71), Teavaraa Pass, Tahiti; CAS 37902 (2: 75-84), Takaroa, Tuamotu Arch.; SOSC Te Vega 308 (1: 72), Tonga Islands.

CHAETODON GUTTATISSIMUS Bennett
Peppered butterflyfish

Chaetodon guttatissimus Bennett, 1832: p. 183 (type locality Ceylon).
Chaetodon miliaris (part), Day, 1889: vol. 2, p. 170.
Chaetodon (*Tetragonoptrus*) *maculatus* Sauvage, 1891: p. 259 (on *Chaetodon tachete;* Mauritius).
Chaetodon maculatus, Ahl, 1923: p. 94 (Mauritius).

Chaetodon guttatissimus Bennett. 68 mm S.L. Seychelles Islands.

Diagnosis.—D. XIII (one with XII), 22-23 (24); A. III, 16-18 (rarely 16); pectoral rays 14 (one with 13); L.l. scales 34-43 (usually 37-40); many small spots covering body and dorsal and anal fins, arranged in weak pattern of vertical and horizontal lines; dusky band around caudal peduncle; eyeband extends to nape, not a separate nape spot.

Meristics.—D. XIII, 22-23 (one with XII, 24); A. III, 16-18 (rarely 16); pectoral rays 14 (one with 13/13, one with 13/14); L.l. scales 34-43 (usually 37-40); L.l. pores 33-41; scales above L.l. 5-7; scales below L.l. 13-15; gill rakers 16-19.

| | | Standard Length (mm) | |
Ratios	2-39	40-59(2)	above 59(18)
Depth/S.L............	---	1.6	1.4-1.8
Head/S.L.............	---	3.2-3.3	3.2-3.7
Eye/Head............	---	2.7,2.7	2.6-3.2
Snout/Head..........	---	3.0,3.0	2.8-4.0
Interorb. W./Head......	---	3.6,3.6	2.4-3.7
Maxillary/Head........	---	4.1,4.6	4.3-5.7
Caud. Ped./S.L........	---	10.5,10.5	8.7-11.6
Pect. Fin/S.L..........	---	3.1,3.3	3.0-3.6
Pelvic Sp./S.L..........	---	4.4,4.5	4.1-5.2
Predorsal L./S.L........	---	2.4,2.6	2.3-2.8
Prepelvic L./S.L........	---	2.6,2.7	2.3-2.8
Dorsal Sp. No. 1/S.L.....	---	---	9.3,10.2
Dorsal Sp. No. 2/S.L.....	---	4.7,5.4	5.5-8.0
Dorsal Sp. No. 3/S.L.....	---	4.0,4.2	4.7-6.0
Dorsal Sp. No. 4/S.L.....	---	3.7,4.0	4.5-5.6
Anal Sp. No. 1/S.L......	---	7.1,7.3	7.3-9.2
Anal Sp. No. 2/S.L......	---	3.8,4.4	3.6-4.5
Anal Sp. No. 3/S.L......	---	3.8,4.0	3.9-4.6

Description.—Snout short, 2.8-4.0 in head length; predorsal contour straight; gape oblique; teeth in 6-7 rows in each jaw; preopercle right-angled, edge smooth to lightly crenulate; lachrymal smooth, supraorbital serrate; eye diameter greater than depth of caudal peduncle, which is greater than or equal to interorbital width; interorbital width greater than snout length.

Fourth or fifth dorsal spine longest, first small, to 15.7 in S.L.; second anal spine longer than or equal to third, first less than half second; dorsal and anal fins rounded; base of spinous portion of dorsal fin longer (1.9-2.3 in S.L.) than soft portion (2.9-3.1 in S.L.); pelvic fins moderate, usually reaching anus.

Lateral line a moderately high arc, smooth; scales moderate, rounded-angular, in horizontal series on lower portions of body and ascending series on upper portions; dorsal spine scales reaching midpoint at fifth spine, that of anal spines covering less than half third spine.

Juveniles similar to adults.

Color Pattern.—Eyeband joined at nape, darkish above eyes (although sometimes with a lighter center); scales each have one spot; chest clear or with very faint horizontal lines; pelvic fins pale toward base, dusky on outer half; head brownish in alcohol, darker above, the face abruptly brown, including upper lip; eyeband separated from face color by narrow light line.

Juveniles similar to adults.

Remarks.—The red color seen in an adult was not seen in juveniles. It is not known whether this was a true color or whether the largest specimen was damaged and the red color was due to blood.

This is a fairly distinctive species of butterflyfish of the Indian Ocean. It definitely belongs to the *Chaetodon punctatofasciatus* species group mentioned earlier. The eyebands connect at the nape, a characteristic not evident in the other species of this group.

Distribution.—Indian Ocean and Red Sea, from Sri Lanka and Cocos Keeling to the east coast of Africa, including most of the islands of the tropical Indian Ocean.

Material Examined.—(20 spec.: 47-91 mm S.L.) USNM 171996 (1: 68), Mauritius; ANSP 108560 and 108548 (3: 73-87), Seychelles; ANSP 108540, 108359, 108384, 108362 (7: 67-91), Seychelles; SOSC Anton Bruun RS-41 KA-39 (2: 74-78), Amirantes Islands; SOSC HA-14 (2: 48-71), Comoros Islands; SOSC Sta. 179 (5: 47-81), Comoros Islands.

CHAETODON MULTICINCTUS Garrett
Pebbled butterflyfish

Chaětodon multicinctus Garrett. 75 mm S.L. Oahu, Hawaiian Islands.

Chaetodon multicinctus Garrett, 1863: p. 65 (type locality Hawaiian Islands).
Chaetodon punctato-fasciatus (not of Cuvier), Jordan & Seale, 1906: p. 343 (based on Hawaiian material). Jordan & Evermann, 1906: p. 369, fig. 162 (based on Hawaiian material). Fowler, 1925: p. 27. Fowler, 1928: p. 248. Fowler, 1938: p. 288.
Chaetodon punctato-fasciatus multicinctus, Ahl, 1923: p. 101 (Hawaiian Islands).

Diagnosis.—D. XIII (one with XIV), 23-26; A. III, 18-20 (rarely 20); pectoral rays 14 (one with 15); L.l. scales 35-44; a member of the *Chaetodon punctatofasciatus* group and very closely related to them; vertical spotted bands extending almost to ventral regions, tan, not blackish; body white, not yellowish; dark band (orange with black edging and spotting) surrounds caudal peduncle; eyeband ending before reaching black nape spot; endemic to the Hawaiian Islands.

Meristics.—D. XIII (one with XIV), 23-26; A. III, 18-20 (rarely 20); pectoral rays 14 (one with 15/15, two with 14/15); L.l. scales 35-44 (usually 37-42); L.l. pores 34-42 (usually 36-40); scales above L.l. 6-8; scales below L.l. 15-20 (usually 16-19); gill rakers 15-20.

Description.—Snout short, 3.0-3.6 in head length; predorsal contour straight; gape horizontal to slightly oblique; teeth in 4-6 rows in each jaw

Ratios	Standard Length (mm)		
	20-39(3)	40-59(3)	above 59(9)
Depth/S.L.	1.7-1.8	1.6-1.7	1.5-1.7
Head/S.L.	2.9-3.0	3.0-3.2	3.2-3.8
Eye/Head	2.5-2.8	2.6-3.2	2.8-3.5
Snout/Head	2.6-3.1	2.7-2.8	3.0-3.6
Interorb. W./Head	3.8-3.9	3.5-3.9	2.7-3.7
Maxillary/Head	3.9-4.3	4.0-4.7	3.9-6.3
Caud. Ped./S.L.	9.3-10.4	8.8-10.6	9.4-12.9
Pect. Fin/S.L.	2.9-3.3	2.9-3.1	3.2-3.5
Pelvic Sp./S.L.	3.8-4.3	4.1-5.3	4.6-5.5
Predorsal L./S.L.	2.2-2.4	2.2-2.4	2.3-2.6
Prepelvic L./S.L.	2.3-2.4	2.3-2.4	2.4-2.7
Dorsal Sp. No. 1/S.L.	9.4-9.9	10.3-11.1	10.7-14.7
Dorsal Sp. No. 2/S.L.	3.8-4.0	4.6-5.2	5.9-7.7
Dorsal Sp. No. 3/S.L.	3.6	3.7-4.5	5.1-6.9
Dorsal Sp. No. 4/S.L.	3.7-4.2	3.7-4.5	4.9-6.0
Anal Sp. No. 1/S.L.	6.3-6.6	6.9-9.4	9.2-11.5
Anal Sp. No. 2/S.L.	4.2-4.5	4.0-4.5	4.7-5.5
Anal Sp. No. 3/S.L.	4.3-4.8	4.1-4.6	4.5-5.8

(?); preopercle right-angled, edge crenulate; eye diameter greater than or equal to depth of caudal peduncle, which is greater than snout length; snout length greater than or equal to interorbital width.

Fourth to sixth dorsal spines longest, first short, to 14.7 in S.L.; second anal spine equal to or slightly longer than third, first not half length of second; dorsal and anal fins rounded; base of spinous portion of dorsal fin longer (2.7-2.9 in S.L.) than that of rayed portion (3.0-3.3 in S.L.); pelvic fins moderate, reaching anus but not extending as far as base of anal spines.

Lateral line a moderately high arc, somewhat flattened on top; scales moderate, rounded to angular, in horizontal series on lower portion of body, increasingly ascending rows on upper portions; scales covering base of dorsal spines reaching to midpoint of about sixth spine, that of anal spines covering half or slightly more of third anal spine.

Juveniles similar to adults.

Color Pattern.—Spots usually one per scale; chestnut band, dark edged, surrounding caudal peduncle; eyeband abbreviated, a small triangle left above eye; dark horseshoe-shaped spot on nape; face sooty, upper lip dark; pelvic fins pale to dusky.

Juvenile color pattern very close to adults but with eyeband connected to nape spot.

Remarks.—*Chaetodon multicinctus* is the Hawaiian representative of the *C. punctatofasciatus* species group.

Distribution.—Found only in the Hawaiian Islands and Johnston Atoll.

Material Examined.—(15 spec.: 32-90 mm S.L.) WEB (6: 69-90), Oahu, Hawaiian Islands; BPBM (uncatalogued) (5: 42-75), Oahu, Hawaiian Islands; BPBM (uncatalogued) (4: 32-41), Waimea Bay, Oahu, Hawaiian Islands.

CHAETODON DAEDALMA Jordan & Fowler
Wrought-iron butterflyfish
(Work-of-art butterflyfish)

Chaetodon daedalma Jordan & Fowler, 1903: p. 538, fig. 4 (type locality Nafa, Okinawa).

Chaetodon (Rabdophorus) daedalma, Fowler, 1953: p. 21, fig. 92 (China, Riukiu, Okinawa, Formosa, Aguni Shima, Taiwan).

Diagnosis.—D. XIII (one with XII), 22; A. III, 16; pectoral rays 14; L.l. scales 38-43; each scale outlined with brown, giving distinctive appearance to fish, almost reptilian in aspect; edges of vertical fins pale; eyeband absent.

Meristics.—D. XIII (one with XII), 22; A. III, 16; pectoral rays 14; L.l. scales 38-43; L.l. pores 38-41; scales above L.l. 7 or 8; scales below L.l. 17-19; gill rakers 16.

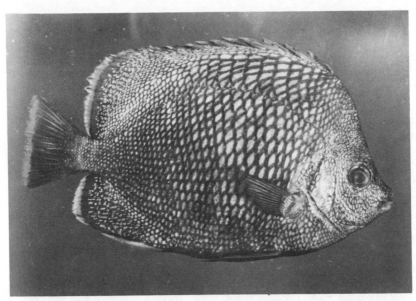

Chaetodon daedalma Jordan and Fowler. 138 mm S.L. Wakanoura, Japan.

| Ratios | Standard Length (mm) | | |
	20-39	40-59	above 59(3)
Depth/S.L..............	---	---	1.4-2.6
Head/S.L..............	---	---	3.6-3.9
Eye/Head	---	---	3.1-3.4
Snout/Head	---	---	2.9-3.1
Interorb. W./Head......	---	---	2.8-2.9
Maxillary/Head	---	---	3.9-5.5
Caud. Ped./S.L.........	---	---	9.3-9.6
Pect. Fin/S.L..........	---	---	3.7-4.2
Pelvic Sp./S.L.........	---	---	4.8-5.2
Predorsal L./S.L........	---	---	2.5-2.7
Prepelvic L./S.L........	---	---	2.5-2.6
Dorsal Sp. No. 1/S.L.....	---	---	11.7-12.5
Dorsal Sp. No. 2/S.L.....	---	---	7.4-7.6
Dorsal Sp. No. 3/S.L.....	---	---	5.6-6.1
Dorsal Sp. No. 4/S.L.....	---	---	4.5-5.1
Anal Sp. No. 1/S.L......	---	---	9.6-9.9
Anal Sp. No. 2/S.L......	---	---	4.2-4.3
Anal Sp. No. 3/S.L......	---	---	4.5-5.1

Description.—Snout short, 2.9-3.1 in head length; predorsal contour straight to slightly concave; gape oblique; teeth in about seven rows in each jaw; preopercle right-angled, edge crenulate to lightly serrate; lachrymal smooth, supraorbital smooth; depth of caudal peduncle greater than eye diameter, which is greater than snout length; snout length less than to greater than interorbital.

Fourth dorsal spine longest; second and third anal spines long and strong, second slightly longer than third, first less than half second; dorsal and anal fins rounded, posterior edges nearly vertical; base of spinous portion of dorsal fin longer (about 2.0 in S.L.) than that of soft portion (about 2.9 in S.L.); pelvic fins short, failing to reach anus.

Lateral line a high arc, flattened on top; scales mostly angular, large anteriorly, decreasing in size posteriorly, in horizontal series below lateral line, those close to the lateral line with the posterior portions descending toward caudal peduncle due to the larger size of the scales in the anterior section of the body; scales above lateral line in curved series both vertically from base of dorsal spines to lateral line and diagonally from anterior end of dorsal fin to lateral line; scaly portion of dorsal fin base low, reaching midpoint of ninth and tenth dorsal spines, that of anal fins crossing only lower third of third spine, leaving parts of the first and second fin rays unscaled.

Juveniles similar to adults, the snout perhaps more projecting.

Color Pattern.—Eyeband absent; pectoral fins tan to brown; pelvic fins blackish; flaps of dorsal and anal spines brown; slight extensions of some rays of dorsal fin noticeable, including brown spots.

Juveniles similarly patterned.

Remarks.—*Chaetodon daedalma* is quite distinctive in its color pattern. It lacks the eyeband, a situation not common in this genus. The scales and their light centers are larger anteriorly and smaller posteriorly, giving the posterior end of the fish a darker hue.

Chaetodon daedalma is the only species of *Chaetodon* in which some of the dorsal fin rays extend a slight distance beyond the edge of the fin.

This species is apparently endemic to the area of southern Japan.

Distribution.—Okinawa, Ryukyu Islands, Bonin Islands, Taiwan, to Japan (Yonekichi, Koneyama).

Material Examined.—(3 spec.: 113-138 mm S.L.) SU 7190 (1: 113), Nafa, Okinawa (holotype); USNM 51390 (1: 119), Nafa, Okinawa (paratype); SU 7159 (1: 138), Wakanoura, Japan.

CHAETODON QUADRIMACULATUS Gray
Four-spot butterflyfish

Chaetodon quadrimaculatus Gray, 1831: p. 53 (type locality Sandwich Islands; as *C. 4-maculatus*).

Chaetodon quadrimaculatus Gray. 91 mm S.L. Oahu, Hawaiian Islands.

Ratios	Standard Length (mm)		
	2-49(1)	50-79	above 79(8)
Depth/S.L..............	1.7	---	1.7-1.8
Head/S.L..............	3.1	---	3.4-3.7
Eye/Head.............	2.6	---	2.9-3.4
Snout/Head...........	3.1	---	2.5-3.1
Interorb. W./Head......	3.2	---	2.6-3.2
Maxillary/Head........	---	---	3.7-4.2
Caud. Ped./S.L.........	8.9	---	8.4-9.8
Pect. Fin/S.L...........	---	---	3.3-3.4
Pelvic Sp./S.L..........	4.6	---	4.7-5.3
Predorsal L./S.L........	2.2	---	2.3-2.5
Prepelvic L./S.L........	2.3	---	2.5-2.6
Dorsal Sp. No. 1/S.L....	12.4	---	9.9-14.4
Dorsal Sp. No. 2/S.L....	5.4	---	5.8-7.4
Dorsal Sp. No. 3/S.L....	4.6	---	4.2-5.3
Dorsal Sp. No. 4/S.L....	4.2	---	3.7-4.8
Anal Sp. No. 1/S.L......	7.1	---	6.8-8.6
Anal Sp. No. 2/S.L......	3.9	---	3.8-4.4
Anal Sp. No. 3/S.L......	4.5	---	4.1-4.4

Diagnosis.—D. XIV (one with XIII), 20-23; A. III, 16-18; pectoral rays 15 (one with 16); L.l. scales 38-45; upper portion of body blackish, lower half yellow; two large white spots in dark section; eyeband broad, light, dark bordered.

Meristics.—D. XIV (one with XIII), 20-23; A. III, 16-18; pectoral rays 15 (one with 16/16); L.l. scales 38-45; L.l. pores 38-43; scales above L.l. 9-11; scales below L.l. 15-19; gill rakers 15-19.

Description.—Snout short, 2.5-3.1 in head length; predorsal contour straight; gape slightly oblique; teeth in 7-9 rows in each jaw; preopercle slightly oblique-angled; lachrymal smooth; depth of caudal peduncle and snout length equal, both greater than interorbital width, which is greater than eye diameter.

Fifth dorsal spine longest; second anal spine longest, first about half second; dorsal and anal fins with blunt angles; base of spinous portion of dorsal fin longer (1.9-2.2 in S.L.) than that of rayed portion (3.0-3.3 in S.L.); pelvic fins moderate, reaching to level of anus.

Lateral line a moderately high, smooth arc; scales moderate, rounded to slightly angular, in horizontal series on lower portion of body, slightly ascending rows on upper portion; scaly portion of dorsal spines extends to midpoint of sixth dorsal spine, that of anal fin reaching barely to midpoint of third anal spine.

Juveniles similar to adults.

Color Pattern.—Spots on body one per scale; dark band of caudal peduncle encircling it; white border behind eyebands connected at first dorsal spine; eyebands faintly joining at nape; upper lip and part of snout dusky.

Juvenile pattern similar to adults; single line on dorsal and anal fins instead of a stripe.

Remarks.—*Chaetodon quadrimaculatus* apparently has permanently adopted the nighttime color pattern of many of the butterflyfishes, where the dorsal area darkens and two white spots are noticeable.

This species is found mostly in the clearer waters of the reef. In personal observations it was seen either on the reef itself or to the oceanside, never behind the reef in the quieter waters of the lagoon. It was not common and usually was seen as pairs, though single specimens were observed. Harry (1953) regarded it as rare at Raroia. It occurred in the lagoon and surge channels of the outer reef. He never saw more than two individuals at the same locality.

Distribution.—Islands of Oceania including the Hawaiian Islands.

Material Examined.—(9 spec.: 47-108 mm S.L.) BPBM 2034-36 (3: 91-106), Hawaiian Islands; BPBM 7758 (3: 91-100), Washington Island, Line Islands; HIMB (uncatalogued) (1: 108), Waianae, Oahu, Hawaiian Islands; BPBM 6105 (1: 91), Tahiti; WEB (1: 47), Oahu, Hawaiian Islands.

CHAETODON ROBUSTUS Gunther
Ghana butterflyfish

Chaetodon robustus Gunther, 1860: p. 18 (no locality, Hasler Collection).
Chaetodon luciae Rochebrune, 1880: p. 160 (type locality Sainte Luciae (Cape Verde)).

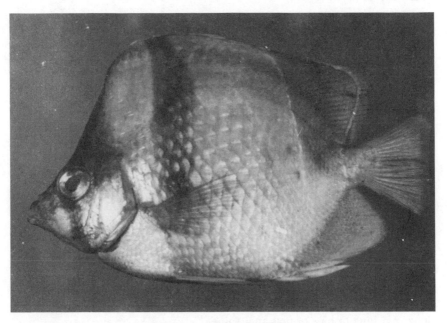

Chaetodon robustus Gunther. 113 mm S.L. Ghana.

Diagnosis.—D. XII, 20-22; A. III, 17-19; pectoral rays 15 (one had 14); L.l. scales 33-39; dark band present from base of anterior portion of dorsal fin to area just behind pectoral fin base, where it stops; soft dorsal fin and posterior end of body dark, the border between this color and body color a narrow white line.

Meristics.—D. XII, 20-22; A. III, 17-19; pectoral rays 15 (one with 14/14, one with 14/15); L.l. scales 33-39; L.l. pores 33-39; scales above L.l. 5; scales below L.l. 16-18; gill rakers 13-15.

Description.—Snout short, 3.3 in head length; predorsal contour straight to concave, nape prominent; gape horizontal; teeth in 9-11 rows in upper jaw, 10-12 rows in lower jaw; preopercle right-angled, edge crenulate; lachrymal and supraorbital smooth; depth of caudal peduncle greater than or equal to eye diameter, which is greater than or equal to snout length; snout length greater than interorbital width.

Ratios	Standard Length (mm)		
	20-49	50-79(3)	above 79(3)
Depth/S.L.............	---	1.4-1.6	1.4-1.5
Head/S.L.............	---	2.7-2.8	2.7-2.9
Eye/Head.............	---	2.6-2.7	2.9
Snout/Head...........	---	3.1-3.3	3.3
Interorb. W./Head......	---	3.4-3.5	3.4-3.8
Maxillary/Head........	---	3.9-4.1	4.1
Caud. Ped./S.L........	---	7.5-8.1	8.1-8.7
Pect. Fin/S.L..........	---	3.1-3.2	3.4-3.6
Pelvic Sp./S.L.........	---	4.2-4.4	4.5-5.1
Predorsal L./S.L........	---	1.9-2.1	2.2
Prepelvic L./S.L........	---	1.9-2.1	2.2
Dorsal Sp. No. 1/S.L.....	---	9.8-10.7	11.3
Dorsal Sp. No. 2/S.L.....	---	5.4-6.8	8.1
Dorsal Sp. No. 3/S.L.....	---	3.9-4.4	4.9
Dorsal Sp. No. 4/S.L.....	---	6.2-7.4	8.1
Anal Sp. No. 1/S.L......	---	3.9-4.3	4.2-4.9
Anal Sp. No. 2/S.L......	--	3.9-4.3	4.2-4.9
Anal Sp. No. 3/S.L......	---	4.4-4.8	4.9

Fourth dorsal spine longest; anal spines strong, second longest, first about half second; dorsal and anal fins with well rounded angle; spinous dorsal fin roughly triangular; base of spinous portion of dorsal fin longer (2.0-2.2 in S.L.) than that of soft portion (3.2-3.6 in S.L.); pelvic fins long, reaching to base of first anal spine.

Lateral line a moderately high, smooth arc; scales moderately large, rounded-angular, in slightly ascending series on body, increasingly ascending near upper part of body; scaly covering of dorsal spines low, reaching midpoint of eighth spine, that of anal spines covering less than half of third spine.

Juveniles with a dark ocellated spot in the dorsal fin.

Color Pattern.—Dark band originates about the third and fourth dorsal fin spines; pectoral fin base not included in this band; possible band surrounding caudal peduncle, light edged anteriorly; pelvic fins light to dusky; face brownish; eyebands join at nape; interorbital stripe above eye level, to and including upper lip.

Color of living animals white to silvery, each scale bordered with yellow; eyeband, body band, and posterior area including soft dorsal fin brown to orange-brown, posterior area bordered anteriorly with narrow white stripe;.snout stripe brownish orange; head body color, snout yellowish orange; eyeband white bordered, point on nape where the eyebands join bright orange to orange-red; dorsal spines orange to red-orange; pectoral fins hyaline, base orange; body band red-orange bordered, the band quickly turning red-orange at level of pectoral, the red orange color connecting across abdomen; pelvic fins orange to red-orange; brownish-orange posterior area becoming more orange ventrally; posterior ⅔ or more of anal fin orange, anterior third or less body color; edges of dorsal and anal fins hyaline, submarginal blue-white stripe in dorsal fin bordered with blackish stripes; blue-white stripe continues across caudal peduncle and a short distance onto anal fin; this cuts section of orange to brownish orange off as caudal peduncle band; whitish border posteriorly to this band weak; caudal fin mostly hyaline or whitish, posterior edge with orange tint; anal spines orange.

Remarks.—The type of *Chaetodon robustus* is undoubtedly the same as *Chaetodon luciae* Rochebrune and has priority over that name.

Chaetodon robustus has been confused with another west African chaetodont, *Chaetodon hoefleri*. They are easily distinguishable by meristics and color pattern. The color pattern of *Chaetodon robustus* is close to that of *C. humeralis* as are some other characteristics. *Chaetodon hoefleri* has XI dorsal spines and *C. humeralis* XIII, compared with XII for *C. robustus*. In addition, *C. robustus* has 20-21 dorsal fin rays, *C. hoefleri* has 22-23, and *C. humeralis* has 19-20.

Distribution.—Tropical western Africa to the Cape Verde Islands and Senegambia.

Material Examined.—(6 spec.: 64-117 mm S.L.) USNM Acc. 272618 (1: 70), Tema, Ghana; BMNH 1866-4-10-29 (1: 64), Cape Verde; UMML (uncatalogued) (2: 101-117), Gulf of Guinea; USNM Field 824, Cornell Univ. Fish Coll. (2: 74-117), Shama Bay, Ghana.

CHAETODON OCELLATUS Bloch
Spotfin butterflyfish

Chaetodon ocellatus Bloch, 1781: p. 105, pl. 211, fig. 2 (type locality "Ostindien").

Chaetodon bimaculatus Bloch, 1790: p. 9, pl. 219, fig. 1 (type locality "Ostindien").

Sarothrodus maculo-cinctus Gill, 1861: p. 99 (type locality Newport, Rhode Island).

Sarothrodus ataeniatus Poey, 1868: p. 353 (type locality Havana).

Sarothrodus bimaculatus, Cope, 1870: p. 474 (St. Croix; new combination).

?*Sarothrodus amplexicollis* Poey, 1875: p. 63 (type locality Cuba; tholichthys larva).

Chaetodon maculocinctus, Jordan & Gilbert, 1883: p. 615 (new combination).

Chaetodon ataeniatus, Jordan & Evermann, 1898: p. 1676 (tholichthys stage; new combination).

Chaetodon ocellatus Bloch. 99.0 mm S.L. Florida. Photo by Dr. Henry A. Feddern.

Ratios	Standard Length (mm)		
	20-49(16)	50-79(4)	above 79(10)
Depth/S.L.	1.6-1.7	1.5-1.7	1.4-1.7
Head/S.L.	2.4-2.7	2.7-2.9	3.0-3.3
Eye/Head	2.4-3.1	3.0-3.1	3.0-3.4
Snout/Head	2.7	2.8-2.9	2.7-3.3
Interorb. W./Head.	2.7-3.6	3.4	2.9-3.6
Maxillary/Head	3.4-4.5	4.0-4.1	3.7-4.3
Caud. Ped./S.L.	6.6-8.3	7.9-8.2	7.7-8.4
Pect. Fin/S.L.	3.2-3.6	3.4-3.7	3.5-4.2
Pelvic Sp./S.L.	3.2-4.5	4.6-4.7	4.4-5.3
Predorsal L./S.L.	1.7-2.1	2.0	2.1-2.3
Prepelvic L./S.L.	2.0-2.5	2.4	2.3-2.5
Dorsal Sp. No. 1/S.L.	7.1-11.7	13.7-14.3	13.7-19.8
Dorsal Sp. No. 2/S.L.	4.3-5.9	7.3-7.8	7.4-11.7
Dorsal Sp. No. 3/S.L.	3.1-4.0	4.4-4.7	4.4-6.7
Dorsal Sp. No. 4/S.L.	2.9-3.4	3.7-3.8	3.7-4.8
Anal Sp. No. 1/S.L.	6.1-8.4	7.1-8.1	7.7-8.8
Anal Sp. No. 2/S.L.	4.4-5.9	4.9-5.2	4.6-5.5
Anal Sp. No. 3/S.L.	4.9-7.1	5.0-5.5	5.0-6.1

Diagnosis.—D. XII-XIII (one with XIV), 18-21 (rarely 21); A. III, 15-17 (usually 16 or 17); pectoral rays 14 or 15 (rarely 16); L.l. scales 33-40 (usually 35-39); western Atlantic species distinguished by a small dark spot at angle of dorsal fin and another (sometimes faded) at base of dorsal fin rays.

Meristics.—D. XII-XIII (one with XIV), 18-21 (rarely 21); A. III, 15-17 (usually 16 or 17); pectoral rays 14 or 15 (rarely 16, two with 14/15); L.l. scales 33-40 (usually 35-39); L.l. pores 30-38; scales above L.l. 6-8 (usually 7); scales below L.l. 15-18 (usually 16-17); gill rakers 14-17 (usually 16).

Description.—Snout short, 2.7-3.3 in head length; predorsal contour straight; gape horizontal; teeth in 8-9 rows in upper jaw and 6-9 rows in lower jaw; preopercle right-angled, edge slightly serrate; lachrymal smooth; depth of caudal peduncle greater than snout length, which is equal to or greater than both interorbital width and eye diameter, which are equal.

Fourth to sixth dorsal spines longest (?); anal spines with second slightly longer than third, first about ⅔ of second; dorsal and anal fins with blunt angles; base of spinous portion of dorsal fin longer (2.6-2.9 in S.L.) than that of rayed portion (3.6-3.9 in S.L.); pelvic fins moderate, reaching level of anus.

Lateral line a high, posteriorly peaked arc; scales moderate, angular to rounded (?), in horizontal rows on lower portion of body, slightly ascending rows on upper portion; scales covering dorsal spines reaching midpoint of sixth spine, that of anal fin covering to midpoint of third spine.

Juveniles similar to adults.

Color Pattern.—Pelvic fins body color to dusky; eyebands dark edged, joining at nape (sometimes including first dorsal fin spine); large spot at base of dorsal fin may be very dark or very faded, almost absent, spot at angle of fin always black.

Juvenile color pattern differing from adults somewhat; the pattern appears similar to adults in some specimens, but others have a dark spot, indistinct at the edges, at base of anal fin rays, with dark streak extending from dorsal spot to anal spot (dorsal spot usually darker than anal spot); dorsal, anal, and caudal fins hyaline in smallest specimens; in some juveniles a dark submarginal streak in dorsal and anal fins following around curve of fins, later broadening on longest rays to give rise to the black spot at the fin angle (the fins are not angular in juveniles).

Remarks.—The *Chaetodon ocellatus* accepted today as Bloch's species does not fully agree with his description. Bloch shows an ocellated spot at the base of the soft dorsal fin, which in the true *C. ocellatus* is not ocellated. Secondly there is no indication of the second spot at the fin angle. Also the locality given is the East Indies rather than the proper locality, the West Indies. His counts are XII/XXXIV (=XII,22) and III,XXII (=III,19) both rather high for *C. ocellatus*. In his later species *C. bimac-*

Chaetodon ocellatus, series of juveniles showing variations in color pattern.

ulatus both black spots are present and the figure closely resembles the *C. ocellatus* as known today. The spots are, however, ocellated and the locality given is East Indies. The counts are slightly different (XII,22 and III,15).

This species has been taken as juveniles by seining through eel grass at Wood's Hole (H.M. Smith, 1897), and I have captured juveniles on the New Jersey coast in late summer. They are fairly common at that time but are absent the rest of the year.

Durand (1960) reports that this species was encountered rather frequently at depths of 40-80 meters. According to Longley & Hildebrand (1941) they are frequently in pairs and sometimes small groups of four or five. They were said to be more apt to swim and feed over comparatively bare and sandy areas than other species of chaetodonts.

Longley and Hildebrand (1941) report the posterior band of the young specimens disappears at about 40 mm or before.

Night coloration varies somewhat from the daytime color pattern. The eyeband is black with white edges. The dorsal spot is sharp, clear, and dark black; the angle spot is dark black. A conspicuous black area, not well-defined, in center of body, is roughly lens-shaped, from about 4-5th dorsal fin spines, and extends toward anal fin spines. Boehlke and Chaplin (1968) give night coloration as "large dusky spot becomes black. Broad but diffuse dark bands appear on the body and sometimes there is a lightening of the characteristic small dark mark at the edge of the dorsal fin." Longley & Hildebrand (1941) have also noted the nighttime color pattern of this species. They report the dorsal spot sharp and distinct, as well as a dark humeral band which varies "from moment to moment" when light is played on the fish and is broad and diffused or clearly defined. The young also exhibit a night pattern according to Longley & Hildebrand (1941). They lose the posterior black bar, retaining only the spot. White spots were seen on the side.

This species reaches a length of about 150 mm S.L.

Distribution.—Western Atlantic Ocean from Brazil to the Carolinas and possibly northward to Massachusetts in summer months.

Material Examined.—(30 spec.: 18-143 mm S.L.) USNM 159278 (2: 80-84), Florida; USNM 159277 (1: 105), Florida; USNM 68574 (1: 50), Florida; UMML 12150 (1: 48), Lake Worth, Florida; USNM 185257 (2: 103-104), Surinam; USNM 159272 (4: 132-143), coast of North Carolina; USNM 68065 (9: 18-38), Massachusetts (Martha's Vineyard); NMFS-M Gulfarium (1: 34), Florida; NMFS-M SB 1208 (2: 43-51), North Carolina; NMFS-M Oregon 4849 (1: 101), Columbia; NMFS-M Oregon 4865 (1: 77), Columbia; NMFS-M (2: 18-39), Panama City, Florida; NMFS-M Ft. Walton (1: 29), Florida; NMFS-M Destin (1: 33), Florida; NMFS-M SB 1364 (1: 51), South Carolina.

Anomalies and Hybrids

At disturbingly frequent intervals supposed hybrids of various species of butterflyfishes have been brought to my attention. Also very common are specimens which do not conform to the "normal" definition of the species. This may be in the form of pattern anomalies or meristic differences. It is often very difficult to decide where one begins and the other leaves off, i.e., whether a particular specimen is anomalous, a hybrid or, for that matter, a possible new species. Unfortunately, by looking through the systematic portion of this book these specimens cannot be identified with certainty. It is therefore considered useful to add a section on anomalies and hybrids to help place these specimens.

Anomalous specimens may result from mutations or from injuries. One common conditon is the occurrence of specimens that have lost two or three anterior dorsal fin spines, often leaving a "notch" in the back at that point. These fish look odd (see photos) but are easily recognized since the rest of the fish appears normal. There does not seem to be any systematic pattern and the precise reason for this deformity is not known. It could be the result of a genetic disturbance or due to the fish's defensive behavioral posture presenting the dorsal fin to its enemies and simply being bitten off. I have not seen juveniles with this deformity although such problems might cause them to become easier prey. On the other hand, several species have a tendency towards a reduction in the first two or three dorsal fin spines disproportionate to the following spines.

Odd spine counts occur from time to time but do not usually make identification difficult. Most often extra spines will appear in the anal fin, but since there is a strong tendency toward four or even five anal fin spines this should not be considered too unusual. In several species five is even the normal number of anal fin spines. Again there is no apparent systematic pattern to these extra anal fin spines.

More common are the specimens which have an extreme variation in color or pattern. With much of the basic pattern remaining the species can, with a bit of logic, be determined. Most obvious pattern alterations are in the banded and striped or lined species such as *Chaetodon lineolatus, C. auriga, C. meyeri, C. trifasciatus, C. auripes*, etc. The stripes, lines, and bands may be broken, forked, or even wander in obscure patterns. The branches may even fork again and some lines may anastomose. Spots rarely vary except perhaps in *C. auriga*, where the dorsal fin spot is normally missing in Red Sea forms and present in Indo-Pacific individuals. But there

Hybrid between *Chaetodon auriga* and *C. ephippium* from Tahiti. The author saw a similar hybrid at Johnston Atoll.

are Red Sea *C. auriga* with a spot (or even part of one) and there are reports of specimens from the Pacific lacking spots.

When the pattern is so different as to preclude placing the specimen with any particular species, chances are it is a hybrid. In such a case a calculated guess as to the parentage will usually explain the combination of patterns, for in butterflyfishes a hybrid will show a blending of characters of the parents. The photos at the end of the color section of this book depict most of the known hybrids of butterflyfishes.

CLASSIFICATION SYSTEMS AND COMPARISONS

A comparison between Ahl's classification of 1923 and my system is included so that the reader may see the changes, in list form, that were
necessary. My listing here represents taxa corresponding to Ahl's species
and is not complete, the species described since 1923 are not being included.

Ahl Subfamily Chaetodontinae	Burgess Family Chaetodontidae
Genus *Forcipiger*	Genus *Forcipiger*
flavissimus	*flavissimus*
longirostris	*longirostris*
Genus *Prognathodes*	Subgenus Prognathodes of Genus *Chaetodon*
aculeatus	*aculeatus*
Genus *Chelmon*	Genus *Chelmon*
rostratus rostratus	*rostratus*
rostratus marginalis	*marginalis*
Mülleri	*muelleri*
?pulcher	*(= Chaetodon xanthocephalus)*
Genus *Chelmonops*	Genus *Chelmonops*
truncatus	*truncatus*
trochilus	*(= truncatus)*
Genus *Parachaetodon*	Genus *Parachaetodon*
ocellatus	*ocellatus*
townleyi	*(= ocellatus)*
Genus *Vinculum*	(removed to Family Kyphosidae)
Genus *Microcanthus*	(removed to Family Kyphosidae)
Genus *Heniochus*	Genus *Heniochus*
varius	*varius*
pleurotaenia	*pleurotaenia*
singularius	*singularius*
monoceros	*monoceros*
chrysostomus	*chrysostomus*
intermedius	*intermedius*
macrolepidotus	*= acuminatus*
Genus *Hemitaurichthys*	Genus *Hemitaurichthys*
polylepis	*polylepis*
zoster	*zoster*
Genus *Coradion*	Genus *Coradion*
chrysozonus	*chrysozonus*
melanopus	*melanopus*
Genus *Chaetodon*	Genus *Chaetodon*
Section *Citharoedus*	Subgenus *Citharoedus*
meyeri	*meyeri*
ornatissimus	*ornatissimus*
Section *Rabdophorus*	Subgenus *Rabdophorus*
blackburnii	(placed in S.G. *Chaetodon*)
luctuosus	(placed in S.G. *Tetrachaetodon*)
plebeius	(placed in S.G. *Tetrachaetodon*)
maculiceps	*(= plebeius)*
trifasciatus	(placed in S.G. *Corallochaetodon*)
trifasciatus austriacus	*(= austriacus* and placed in S.G. *Cor-allochaetodon)*
trifasciatus arabica	*(= melapterus)*
lunulatus	*(= trifasciatus)*
melanopterus	*(= melapterus* and placed in S.G. *Cor-allochaetodon)*
fallax	*(= auripes)*
ephippium	*ephippium*
xanthocephalus	*xanthocephalus*
nigripinnatus	*(= xanthocephalus)*
semeion	*semeion*
decoratus	*(= semeion)*
leucopleura	*leucopleura*
leucopygus	*(= leucopleura)*
fremblii	(placed in S.G. *Chaetodon*)
Bennetti	*(bennettii* placed in S.G. *Tetrachaetodon)*

Ahl	Burgess
speculum	*(placed in S.G. Tetrachaetodon)*
zanzibariensis	*(placed in S.G. Tetrachaetodon)*
ocellifer	*(= speculum)*
carens	*(= nippon)*
nippon	(placed in S.G. *Roa*)
daedalma	(placed in S.G. *Chaetodon*)
decipiens	*(= nippon)*
howensis	(placed in genus *Amphichaetodon*)
Section *Chaetodon*	Subgenus *Chaetodon*
notophthalmus	*(= marleyi)*
modestus	(placed in S.G. *Roa*)
aureofasciatus	(placed in S.G. *Discochaetodon*)
octofasciatus	(placed in S.G. *Discochaetodon*)
flavirostris	(placed in S.G. *Chaetodontops*)
corallicola	*(= kleinii)*
mitratus	(placed in S.G. *Roa*)
sedentarius	*sedentarius*
robustus	*robustus*
tricinctus	(placed in S.G. *Discochaetodon*)
striatus	*striatus*
hoefleri	*hoefleri*
luciae	*(= robustus)*
Sanctae Helenae	*sanctaehelenae*
trichrous	*trichrous*
maculatus	*(= guttatissimus)*
miliaris	*miliaris*
garretti	*(= guentheri* (part), *miliaris* (part))
punctulatus	*(= guentheri*)
Güntheri	*guentheri*
dolosus	*dolosus*
guttatissimus	*guttatissimus*
punctatofasciatus	*punctatofasciatus*
punctatofasciatus multicinctus	*multicinctus*
pelewensis	*pelewensis*
pelewensis germanus	= *pelewensis*
citrinellus	*citrinellus*
citrinellus nigripes	= *citrinellus*
quadrimaculatus	*quadrimaculatus*
Section *Paracoradion*	(to Genus *Vinculum* which is placed in Fam. Kyphosidae)
Section *Hemichaetodon*	Subgenus *Chaetodon* (part)
capistratus	*capistratus*
Section *Chaetodontops*	Subgenus *Chaetodontops*
dorsiocellatus	*(= flavirostris)* or *(= auripes)*
adiergastos	*adiergastos*
bella-maris	*(= wiebeli)*
lunula	*lunula*
fasciatus	*fasciatus*
selene	(placed in S.G. *Rabdophorus*)
humeralis	(placed in S.G. *Chaetodon*)
aya	(placed in S.G. *Prognathodes*)
eques	*(= aya)*
nigrirostris	(placed in Genus *Pseudochaetodon*)
dichrous	(placed in S.G. *Prognathodes*)
ocellatus	(placed in S.G. *Chaetodon*)
ataeniatus	*(= ocellatus)*
unicolor	*(= aculeatus)*
dayi	*(= xanthocephalus)*
obscurus	*(= nigropunctatus)*
melannotus	(placed in S.G. *Chaetodon*)
ocellicauda	(placed in S.G. *Chaetodon*)
Reinwardti	*(= melannotus)*
auripes	*auripes*
nigropunctatus	(placed in S.G. *Rabdophorus*)
collare	*collare*
unifasciatus	*(= xanthocephalus?)*
reticulatus	(placed in S.G. *Citharoedus*)
Section *Lepidochaetodon*	Subgenus *Lepidochaetodon*
unimaculatus	*unimaculatus unimaculatus*
u. sphenospilus	*(= unimaculatus unimaculatus)*
u. interruptus	*u. interruptus*
dahli	*(= rafflesi)*

741

Ahl	Burgess
Kleinii	*(kleinii* moved to S.G. *Chaetodon)*
melanopoma	*(= semilarvatus)*
Section *Linophora*	Subgenus *Linophora*
auriga	*auriga*
auriga setifer	*(= auriga)*
decussatus	*decussatus*
vagabundus	*vagabundus vagabundus*
vagabundus var. *pictus*	*vagabundus pictus*
rafflesi	*rafflesi*
assarius	(moved to S.G. *Chaetodon)*
dixoni	*(= mertensii)*
chrysurus	*(= madagascariensis)*
chrysurus paucifasciatus	*(= paucifasciatus)*
chrysurus madagascariensis	*(= madagascariensis* and placed in S.G. *Rhombochaetodon)*
chrysurus xanturus	*(= xanthurus* and placed in S.G. *Rhombochaetodon)*
Mertensii	*(= mertensii* and placed in S.G. *Rhombochaetodon*
argentatus	(placed in S.G. *Rhombochaetodon)*
Section *Oxychaetodon*	= Subgenus *Chaetodontops* (part)
semilarvatus	*semilarvatus*
lineolatus	*lineolatus*
lineolatus var. *oxycephalus*	*oxycephalus*
dizoster	*(= falcula)*
falcula	*falcula*
ulietensis	*ulietensis*
ulietensis aurora	*(= ulietensis)*
mesoleucus	*mesoleucos*
Subgenus *Gonochaetodon*	Subgenus *Gonochaetodon*
triangulum	*triangulum*
triangulum baronessa	*baronessa*
larvatus	*larvatus*
Subgenus *Megaprotodon*	Subgenus *Megaprotodon*
strigangulus	= *trifascialis*
Incertae Sedis	
Chaetodon aphrodite	*(= Chaetodon (Chaetodontops) flavirostris)*
Chaetodon vagabundus var *jordani*	*(= decussatus)*
C. excelsus	(placed in S.G. *Roa)*

While working on the new classification of the butterflyfishes I had to decide whether to lump many species, split them, or follow some middle road. It is this last course that I followed, perhaps leaning toward splitting a bit. But thoughts of what the classification would look like if a "lumper" got hold of it constantly cropped up, and I decided to add such a scheme to this book as a comparison and to show where I think the various species would fall.

Present Classification Family Chaetodontidae	Alternate Classification Family Chaetodontidae
Genus *Chelmon*	Genus *Chelmon*
rostratus	*rostratus rostratus*
marginalis	*rostratus marginalis*
muelleri	*muelleri*
Genus *Chelmonops*	Genus *Chelmonops* (or included in Genus *Chelmon)*
truncatus	*truncatus*
Genus *Coradion*	Genus *Coradion*
chrysozonus	*chrysozonus*
melanopus	*melanopus*
altivelis	*altivelis*
Genus *Forcipiger*	Genus *Forcipiger*
flavissimus	*flavissimus*
longirostris	*longirostris*

Present Classification	Alternate Classification
Genus *Hemitaurichthys*	Genus *Hemitaurichthys*
zoster	zoster zoster
polylepis	zoster polylepis
thompsoni	thompsoni
multispinis	multispinis
Genus *Heniochus*	Genus *Heniochus*
acuminatus	acuminatus
intermedius	intermedius
monoceros	monoceros
singularius	singularius
varius	varius varius
pleurotaenia	varius pleurotaenia
chrysostomus	chrysostomus
Genus *Parachaetodon*	Genus *Parachaetodon*
ocellatus	ocellatus
Genus *Amphichaetodon*	Genus *Amphichaetodon*
howensis	howensis howensis
melbae	howensis melbae
Genus *Pseudochaetodon*	Genus *Pseudochaetodon*
nigrirostris	nigrirostris
Genus *Chaetodon*	Genus *Chaetodon*
Subgenus *Prognathodes*	Subgenus *Prognathodes*
aculeatus	aculeatus
marcellae	marcellae
aya	aya aya
guyanensis	aya guyanensis
falcifer	falcifer
dichrous	dichrous
Subgenus *Roa*	Subgenus *Roa* (possibly incl. with *Prognathodes*)
modestus	modestus modestus
jayakari	modestus jayakari
excelsa	modestus excelsa
tinkeri	tinkeri tinkeri
declevis	tinkeri declevis
mitratus	mitratus mitratus
burgessi	mitratus burgessi
nippon	nippon
Subgenus *Rhombochaetodon*	Subgenus *Rhombochaetodon*
mertensii	mertensii mertensii
madagascariensis	mertensii madagascariensis
paucifasciatus	paucifasciatus (or subsp. of *mertensii*)
xanthurus	xanthurus
argentatus	argentatus
Subgenus *Megaprotodon*	Subgenus *Megaprotodon*
trifascialis	trifascialis
Subgenus *Gonochaetodon*	Subgenus *Gonochaetodon*
triangulum	triangulum triangulum
baronessa	triangulum baronessa
larvatus	larvatus
Subgenus *Tetrachaetodon*	Subgenus *Tetrachaetodon*
plebeius	plebeius
speculum	speculum speculum
zanzibariensis	speculum zanzibariensis
bennetti	bennetti
Subgenus *Corallochaetodon*	Subgenus *Corallochaetodon*
trifasciatus trifasciatus	trifasciatus trifasciatus
trifasciatus lunulatus	trifasciatus lunulatus (or color var.)
austriacus	trifasciatus austriacus
melapterus	melapterus
Subgenus *Citharoedus*	Subgenus *Citharoedus*
meyeri	meyeri
ornatissimus	ornatissimus
reticulatus	reticulatus
Subgenus *Chaetodontops*	Subgenus *Chaetodontops*
collare	collare
auripes	auripes
wiebeli	wiebeli
adiergastos	adiergastos
semilarvatus	semilarvatus
flavirostris	flavirostris
lunula	lunula (or subsp. of *fasciatus*)
fasciatus	fasciatus

Present Classification	Alternate Classification
Subgenus *Rabdophorus*	Subgenus *Rabdophorus*
auriga	auriga
vagabundus vagabundus	vagabundus
vagabundus pictus	(color var. of *vagabundus*)
decussatus	decussatus
rafflesi	rafflesi
ephippium	ephippium
xanthocephalus	xanthocephalus (or subs p. of *ephippium*)
ulietensis	falcula ulietensis
falcula	falcula falcula
lineolatus	lineolatus
oxycephalus	oxycephalus (or subs p. of *lineolatus*)
semeion	semeion
mesoleucos	mesoleucos
selene	selene selene
leucopleura	selene leucopleura
gardneri	selene gardneri
nigropunctatus	nigropunctatus
Subgenus *Lepidochaetodon*	Subgenus *Lepidochaetodon*
unimaculatus unimaculatus	unimaculatus
unimaculatus interruptus	(color var.)
Subgenus *Discochaetodon*	Subgenus *Discochaetodon*
aureofasciatus	aureofasciatus
rainfordi	rainfordi
tricinctus	tricinctus
octofasciatus	octofasciatus
Subgenus *Chaetodon*	Subgenus *Chaetodon*
capistratus	capistratus
striatus	striatus
hoefleri	hoefleri hoefleri
marleyi	hoefleri marleyi
humeralis	humeralis
robustus	robustus
melannotus	melannotus
ocellicaudus	ocellicaudus (close to *melannotus*)
miliaris	miliaris miliaris
assarius	miliaris assarius
guentheri	miliaris guentheri
dolosus	miliaris dolosus
sedentarius	miliaris sedentarius
sanctaehelenae	miliaris sanctaehelenae
citrinellus	citrinellus
kleinii	kleinii kleinii
trichrous	kleinii trichrous
blackburnii	blackburnii
fremblii	fremblii
litus	litus litus
hemichrysus	litus hemichrysus
punctatofasciatus	punctatofasciatus punctatofasciatus
pelewensis	punctatofasciatus pelewensis
guttatissimus	punctatofasciatus guttatissimus
multicinctus	punctatofasciatus multicinctus
daedalma	daedalma
quadrimaculatus	quadrimaculatus
ocellatus	ocellatus

The following names are to be considered *incertae sedis* in my classification until such time that more information is available and they can be classified with more certainty.

Chaetodon festivus Desjardins
Chaetodon luctuosus Quoy and Gaimard
Chaetodon bellicosus Quoy and Giamard (nomen nudem)
Tholichthys osseus Gunther
Chaetodon modestus of Jordan & Fowler
Osteochromis larvatus Franz
Chaetodon miliaris of Weber

Familial Relationships

Most authors have classified the butterflyfishes and angelfishes as two subfamilies, Chaetodontinae and Pomacanthinae, of the family Chaetodontidae (Woods and Schultz *in* Schultz *et al*, 1953; Greenwood *et al*, 1966; and Bohlke and Chaplin, 1968). Ahl (1923), Weber and de Beaufort (1936), and Marshall (1964) used the same division but included additional subfamilies, such as Scatophaginae, Drepaninae, etc., as well. These additional subfamilies, for the most part, are presently considered as families. Smith (1953, 1955) and Munro (1955, 1967) preferred to use family Chaetodontidae and family Pomacanthidae. None of the above authors gave sufficient supporting evidence to justify their use of a particular classification.

Fraser-Brunner (1945) recognized some of the distinguishing characteristics of the angelfishes (frontal bones forming a concavity between the orbits; the presence of a strong spine at the angle of the preoperculum; the absence of the pelvic axillary process; the distal portions of the ribs normally formed; a forward ventral expansion of the first interhaemal bone) but continued to use the subfamilies Chaetodontinae and Pomacanthinae.

A few workers dealing with specific aspects of the anatomy of fishes have mentioned particular differences between the two groups. Some of them, such as Cockerell (1915, 1916) and Freihofer (1963), were of the opinion that the differences might be enough to warrant full family distinction.

On the basis of the following anatomical and life history differences the two subfamilies should be considered as separate and distinct families.

SCALES

Cockerell (1915, 1916) investigated the form of the scales in the genera *Chaetodon, Heniochus, Chelmon, Chaetodontoplus, Pomacanthus, Centropyge* (*Holacanthus bicolor = Centropyge bicolor*), and *Microcanthus*. In his analysis of scale structure these fishes fell into three distinct groups which happen to correspond to the currently accepted families Chaetodontidae, Pomacanthidae, and Scorpididae (or Kyphosidae (Greenwood, *et al*, 1966)).

Cockerell (1915) found the scales of the butterflyfish genera similar and remarked, "It is impossible to find satisfactory characters for the separation of the species of *Chaetodon, Chelmon* and *Heniochus*. The ctenoid elements of *Chelmon* are coarser than those of *Heniochus*, but the structure is the same." I have examined scales from all genera and subgenera of the Chaetodontidae and found that, although the scales are variable in size and shape, the basic structure is the same. The chaetodontids have scales in which the ctenii extend in a band along the apical margin with the elements separate and striated (Fig. 1B).

Pomacanthids have scales in which the median ribs of apical teeth extend as continuing rods to the base of the apical field (Fig. 1A). Cockerell (1915) reported this for the genera *Chaetodontoplus, Pomacanthus,* and *Centropyge*. I have examined scales from the other genera of the family Pomacanthidae and found all of them to be similarly structured.

Cockerell also reported that the scales of *Microcanthus* were similar to those of *Chaetodon, Heniochus,* and *Chelmon*. They differed however in general shape and the genus was placed in a third group apart from the pomacanthids and chaetodontids mentioned above. Although *Microcanthus* was considered a genus of the family Chaetodontidae in Cockerell's time, it was placed in the family Scorpididae by Fraser-Brunner in 1945.

FIG. 1. Body scales. **A,** *Centropyge* (Pomacanthidae); **B,** *Chaetodon* (Chaetodontidae).

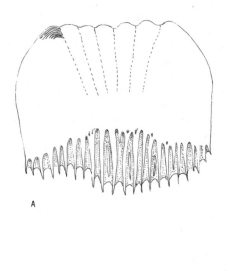

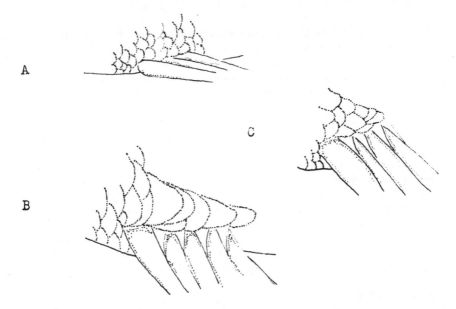

FIG. 2. **A,** Base of pelvic fin of *Pomacanthus* (Pomacanthidae); **B,** base of pelvic fin showing axillary scaly process of *Chaetodon* (Chaetodontidae); **C,** base of pelvic fin showing axillary scaly process of *Heniochus* (Chaetodontidae).

AXILLARY SCALES

Regan (1913) and Norman (1957) made their primary division of percoid families on the basis of the presence or absence of a scaly process in the axil of the pelvic fins. They placed the Chaetodontidae (including Pomacanthidae) with the families that have this feature. Gosline (1966) discusses this character and points out that the "axillary process is not an all or none character; it can be and frequently is rudimentary or practically transitional between a ridge and a process."

However, Gosline says that the scaly axillary process in the great majority of percoid families is either consistently absent or consistently present. I have examined all genera of both families and found as Fraser-Brunner (1945) reported that, although variable in size and shape, the axillary process is consistently present in the Chaetodontidae but consistently absent in the Pomacanthidae (Fig. 2 A-C).

RAMUS LATERALIS ACCESSORIUS NERVE

Freihofer (1963), in dealing with the patterns exhibited by the *ramus lateralis accessorius*, discovered that the arrangement of these nerves in genera of the family Chaetodontidae was different from that of the pomacanthid genera. He stated, "Although still incomplete, the survey for RLA

747

in chaetodontid (*sensu lato*) genera indicates that pattern 8 is characteristic of the Chaetodontinae (two genera examined) and pattern 9 the Pomacanthinae (three genera examined). Judging from the apparent significance RLA has in other groups, such a distribution in the Chaetodontidae raises serious doubts that the two subfamilies are correctly classified."

AUXILIARY SCALES

Auxiliary scales (small scales at the base of the larger ones) occur in adult specimens of all pomacanthid genera and are absent in all genera of chaetodontids (personal observations).

Fraser-Brunner (1933) used the presence or absence of these scales in his generic keys to the angelfishes to help separate various groups of species. I have examined several of the species which were reported by him as lacking auxiliary scales (e.g. *Chaetodontoplus melanosoma, Pomacanthus imperator, Apolemichthys xanthurus*) and found that these small scales were present in large individuals, particularly in the areas below the anterior dorsal fin spines and on the chest.

OSTEOLOGY

Skeletons of the following species were examined in an attempt to determine differences between the families Chaetodontidae and Pomacanthidae: *Chaetodon ornatissimus, C. multicinctus, C. trifasciatus, C. auriga, C. lunula, C. lineolatus, Chelmon rostratus, Forcipiger flavissimus, Hemitaurichthys polylepis,* and *Heniochus acuminatus* of the family Chaetodontidae; *Pomacanthus imperator, Apolemichthys arcuatus, Pygoplites diacanthus,* and *Centropyge potteri* of the family Pomacanthidae. Some of the above species were represented by articulated skeletons. Abbreviations used in the illustrations are as follows:

FR — frontal	PF — prefrontal
V — vomer	SO — supraoccipital
PS — parasphenoid	ME — mesethmoid
OP — opercle	BO — basioccipital
IO — interopercle	PO — preopercle
EX — exoccipital	SO — subopercle
EP — entopterygoid	P — palatine
HY — hyomandibular	MP — metapterygoid
Q — quadrate	PT — pterygoid
CLT — cleithrum	S — symplectic
SCA — scapula	COR — coracoid
AR — articular	DN — dentary
FM — foramen magnum	

Within each family the skeletons are essentially similar, although variations do exist, e.g. greater or lesser spination of certain bones (both chaetodontids and pomacanthids), proportional differences due to prolongation of the snout (chaetodontids) and varying body depths (both

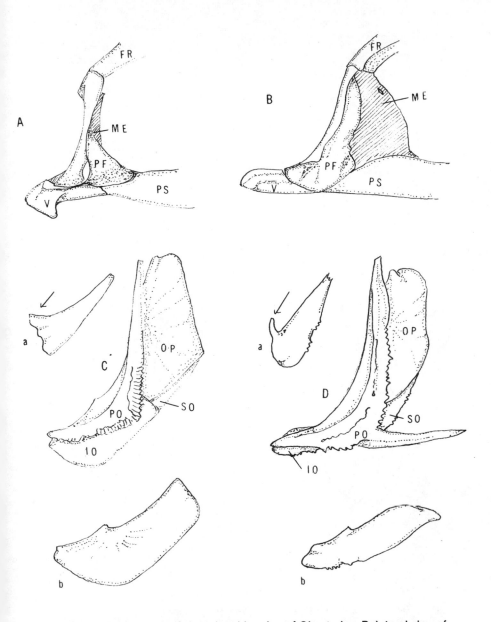

FIG. 3. **A,** lateral view of the ethmoid region of *Chaetodon:* **B,** lateral view of the ethmoid region of *Pomacanthus:* **C,** opercular bones of *Chaetodon:* **a,** subopercle of *Chaetodon;* **b,** interopercle of *Chaetodon:***D,** opercular bones of *Holacanthus:* **a,** subopercle of *Holacanthus:* **b,** interopercle of *Holocanthus.* See page **748** for definitions and symbols.

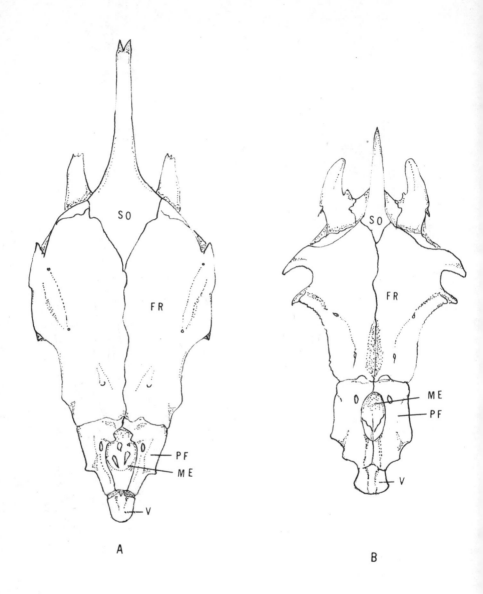

FIG. 4. Dorsal view of skulls. **A**, *Chaetodon*, **B**, *Holacanthus*.

families). The differences between the families, however, are much more extensive.

The form of the preopercle has served as the most useful and distinctive character to differentiate between the two groups. In pomacanthids there is a large spine at the angle of the preopercle and smaller spines on the preopercle, lachrymal, and interopercle (Fig. 3D). The chaetodontids lack the spine at the angle and have, at most, small serrations on the preopercle and lachrymal; the interopercle is smooth (Fig. 3C).

The opercles, although somewhat variable within the two families, are similar. This is also true of the subopercles with but one major exception. The process on the upper edge of the subopercle in the chaetodontid genera is perpendicular to the long axis of the bone but forms an acute angle with the long axis in the pomacanthids (Fig. 3 Ca & Da). The interopercles are not only shaped differently, but their relative position is not the same in the two families. In the chaetodontids the long axis of the interopercle is set at about an angle of 45 with the horizontal. The broad anterior end of the bone is curved inward toward the mid-ventral line where it meets the one from the opposite side (Fig. 9A). The interopercle of the pomacanthids is relatively flat, the longest axis almost horizontal or only slightly inclined; the narrow anterior ends of the right and left interopercle approach each other but do not meet midventrally (Fig. 9B).

Except for differences in spination, the lachrymal and orbital bones are similar. A subocular shelf is present in both families.

The supraoccipital crest is comparatively shorter and not as well developed in the pomacanthids as it is in the chaetodontids (Fig. 4). This is true even when comparing such deep-bodied angelfishes as *Pomacanthus imperator* with shallow-bodied butterflyfishes such as *Chaetodon trifascialis*. In addition, the tip of the supraoccipital crest of the chaetodontids has a distinct bifurcation (Fig. 4A). By contrast, in the pomacanthids, it has a single point (Fig. 4B). The bifurcation of the tip in chaetodontids accepts the first predorsal bone (Fig. 5C). The first predorsal bone just touches the point of the occipital crest in the pomacanthids (Fig. 5D).

The urohyals of the two families are similarly shaped (Fig. 7 C & D), that of *Hemitaurichthys*, although distinctly chaetodontid, resembling the pomacanthid type more than any of the other chaetodontid genera do. The pomacanthids have a peculiar double-pronged arrangement at the end of the ventral process of the urohyal (Fig. 7D). The forward edge of the cleithrum fits into the fork and is braced by it. Chaetodontids have no such connections. The bracing between head and axial skeleton in the chaetodontids is between the supraoccipital and predorsals. The brace in the pomacanthids is between the urohyal and the pectoral girdle.

The shape of the vomer is quite different in the two families. That of the pomacanthids is depressed with the anterior end wider than the posterior (Fig. 4B). The vomer of the chaetodontids is not depressed but hoof-shaped, the anterior end narrower than the posterior (Fig. 4A).

The bones of the ethmoid region were discussed by Starks (1926).

The specimens of angelfishes he examined (*Angelichthys ciliaris, Hola-canthus tricolor*, and *Pomacanthus paru*) were found to be "strikingly similar to *Drepane.*" According to Starks, and confirmed by me on speci-mens of additional genera, "the inner edges of the prefrontals are turned backward [not visible in illustration (Fig. 4B)] and attached to the side walls of the mesethmoid, which is in the form of two converging walls enclosing a wedge-shaped cavity between them." In the butterflyfishes, the prefrontals are not turned back, but "there is a deep cavity that occupies the greater part of the mesethmoid and extends back somewhat into the interorbital region behind the prefrontals. It is more or less com-pletely walled behind by very open, lace-like bone, that occasionally is nearly absent, and the cavity becomes simply a large foramen through the mesethmoid." The cavity, instead of being wedge-shaped as in *Holacan-thus et al*, is cup-shaped (Fig. 4A).

There is a depression or groove at the anterior half of the median suture of the frontals in the pomacanthids which is absent in the chaeto-dontids (Fig. 4A & B). The anterior wedge of the supraoccipital that ex-tends between the posterior part of the frontal is much more developed in the butterflyfishes, being a pointed wedge; that of the angelfishes is short and sometimes irregular (Fig. 4A & B).

The posterior ventral section of the skull in the Chaetodontidae is narrower than in most pomacanthids, where it is slightly inflated. The basioccipital has a more-or-less rounded area for attachment of the lower edge of the vertebral centrum in the chaetodontids (Fig. 5A); in the pomacanthids this area is triangular (Fig. 5B). The butterflyfishes, in addition to the foramen magnum, have an opening or canal immediately below the basioccipital (Fig. 5A). This canal is pinched off in the angel-fishes (Fig. 5B). The first vertebra is firmly wedged into the skull of the pomacanthids; that of the chaetodontids is not.

No important differences were seen between the posttemporal and supracleithral bones of the two families.

The hyomandibular bones are somewhat different. The pomacan-thids have a hyomandibular that is laterally flared in the upper portion, becoming abruptly a strut which is sometimes flattened below (Fig. 6B). The condyles are low and almost continuous. In the Chaetodontidae the flared portion of the hyomandibular reaches to, or almost to, the lower end of the bone (Fig. 6A). The condyles are better differentiated and well separated.

Starks (1930) studied the shoulder girdle in several species of butter-flyfishes and angelfishes and pointed out that the pomacanthids, as opposed to the genus *Chaetodon*, "do not have the interosseus space (between the coracoid and the cleithra) divided, and in the latter genus (*Angelichthys*) the cleithrum does not send a process back to meet the tip of the coracoid." The coracoid in the pomacanthids has a lesser amount of thin bone filling the space between the coracoid and scapula. The lower tip of the cleithrum is curved posteriorly to meet the tip of the coracoid in

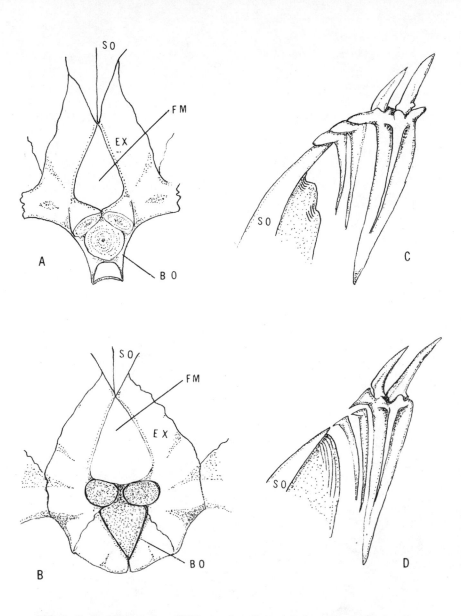

FIG. 5. **A,** occipital region of *Chaetodon:* **B,** occipital region of *Holacanthus:* **C,** predorsal and first interneural of *Chaetodon:* **D,** predorsal and first interneural of *Pomacanthus.*

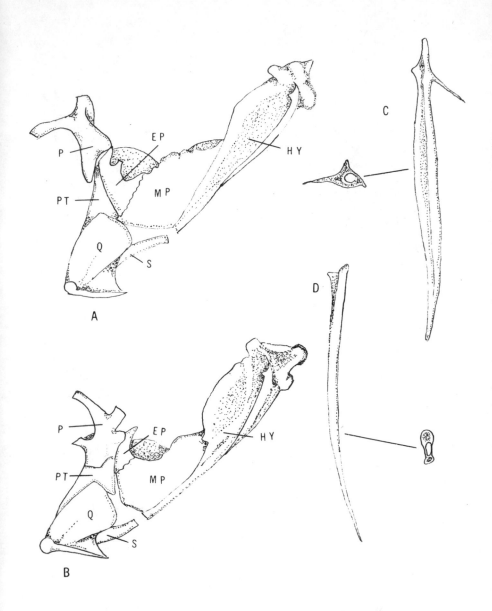

FIG. 6. **A,** suspensorium of *Chaetodon;* **B,** suspensorium of *Pomacanthus:* **C,** lateral view and cross section of rib of *Chaetodon:* **D,** lateral view and cross section of rib of *Pomacanthus.*

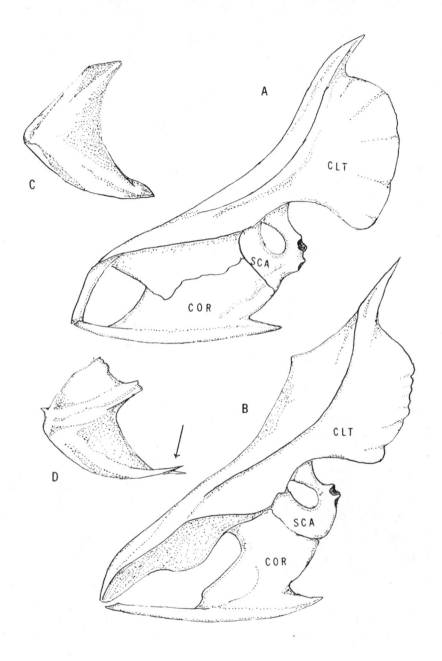

FIG. 7. **A,** pectoral girdle of *Chaetodon:* **B,** pectoral girdle of *Holacanthus:* **C,** urohyal of *Chaetodon:* **D,** urohyal of *Holacanthus.*

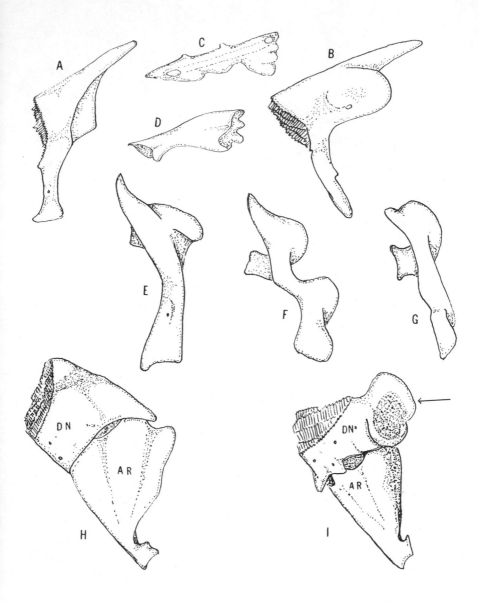

FIG. 8. **A**, premaxilla of *Chaetodon:* **B**, premaxilla of *Holacanthus:* **C**, nasal of *Chaetodon:* **D**, nasal of *Holacanthus:* **E, F**, maxillae of *Chaetodon:* **G**, maxillae of *Holacanthus:* **H**, lower jaw of *Chaetodon:* **I**, lower jaw of *Holacanthus*.

the chaetodontids but is almost straight in the pomacanthids, the coracoid extending forward to meet it (Fig. 7A & B).

The suspensorium is similar in both families except for minor differences in the shapes of the various bones and the differences mentioned above pertaining to the hyomandibular.

The maxillaries of both the chaetodontids and pomacanthids are twisted and irregularly shaped (Fig. 8E-G). Although most butterflyfishes have an extra flared portion, some species (ex. *Chaetodon ornatissimus, C. trifasciatus*) do not. The premaxilla of the chaetodontids has a long, slender median ascending process; that of the pomacanthids has a broader base to the median ascending process and a straight, pointed lateral process (Fig. 8A & B).

The nasal bones of the butterflyfishes are irregular in shape but heavier than those of the pomacanthids and have a slender tube through their center (Fig. 8C). The angelfish have a shorter, stubbier nasal bone which is practically hollow, the tube being much wider (Fig. 8D).

The lachrymal bone is irregular in both families, a comparison not revealing anything that can be construed as important as a family distinction.

The dentary and articular bones are similar when using a short-snouted chaetodontid such as *Chaetodon ornatissimus* for the comparison. The pomacanthids have an extra process which the chaetodontids lack (Fig. 8H & I).

No important differences were noted in the pelvic girdles of these families.

The first interneural has an anteriorly-directed spine (procumbent spine at the base of the first dorsal fin spine) in the pomacanthids (Fig. 5D), whereas in the chaetodontids this was a blunt, flattened, spade-shaped process (Fig. 5C). The predorsals in the chaetodontids are incorporated into the connection between the supraoccipital crest and the first interneural (Fig. 5C); those of the pomacanthids are separate (Fig. 5D). The first interhaemal of the pomacanthids has a prominent anteriorly-directed process at the base of the first anal fin spine (Fig. 9D); in the chaetodontids this process is blunt (Fig. 9C).

The ribs of butterflyfishes are distinctive in having flattened, expanded medial and distal portions, giving extra protection to the visceral area (Fig. 6C). The ribs of angelfishes are without these expansions (Fig. 6D). In both families the ribs are attached to the transverse processes.

OTOLITHS

Mr. John Fitch, California Department of Fish and Game, California State Fisheries Laboratory, examined the otoliths of various genera of butterflyfishes and angelfishes at my request. He found significant differences in size and configuration between those of the chaetodontids and pomacanthids and considers the otolith as a "good tool at the family level" (personal communication). Mr. Fitch has indicated he will report on the specific differences in his own papers.

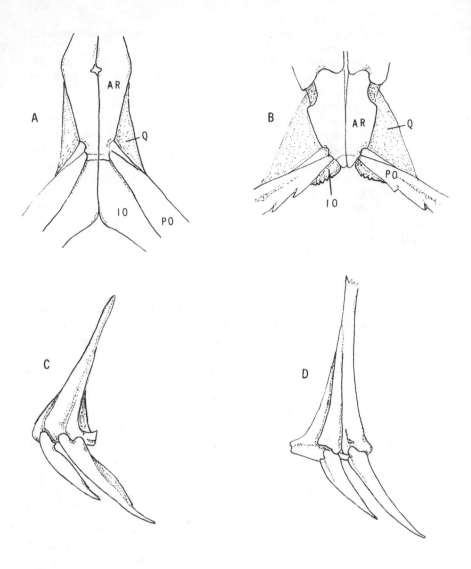

FIG. 9. **A,** ventral view of opercular region of *Chaetodon:* **B,** ventral view of opercular region of *Holacanthus:* **C,** first interhaemal of *Chaetodon:* **D,** first interhaemal of *Pomacanthus.*

SWIM BLADDER

The swim bladder in the Chaetodontidae has two anteriorly-directed processes, or "horns." The swim bladder of the pomacanthids lacks such anterior horns but may possess posteriorly-directed extensions.

NUMBER OF VERTEBRAE

Both chaetodontids and pomacanthids have 24 vertebrae. The angelfishes, however, have a formula of 10+14; the butterflyfishes 11+13. Scorpidids, on the other hand, have 10+15, and scatophagids have 11+12 (Weber & de Beaufort, 1936).

LARVAE

One of the main arguments for retaining the angelfishes as a subfamily of the Chaetodontidae is that it is considered to have a "tholichthys" stage similar to that of the butterflyfishes (Lutken, 1880; Fraser-Brunner, 1933). The tholichthys larva is highly modified with large bony plates extending from the posterior portion of the head; the head itself is encased in bony armor (Fig. 10). Lutken (1880) described and figured several of these forms. One of them he identified as a larval stage of *Pomacanthus*. This specimen, reported as coming from the South Atlantic, is even more peculiarly developed. In addition to the bony development of the head it has two "horns" projecting from the supraorbital region. Fraser-Brunner (1933) followed Lutken in referring this type of tholichthys to the Pomacanthidae.

FIG. 10. Larval stage (tholichthys) of a 10-mm chaetodontid.

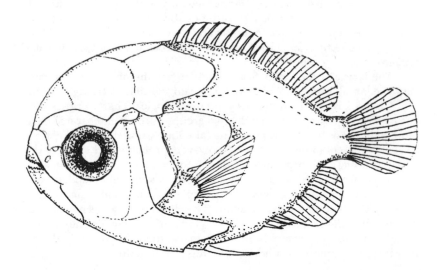

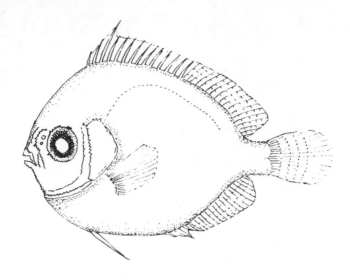

FIG. 11. Larval stage of a 12-mm pomacanthid.

I have studied many larvae of both the Pomacanthidae and Chaetodontidae, including most of the Atlantic species. The larvae of the pomacanthids (Fig. 11), including those of the Atlantic species of the genus *Pomacanthus*, do not pass through a tholichthys stage. They are compressed, round to oval, and lack the characterstic head armature.

The form illustrated by Lutken and Fraser-Brunner as belonging to the genus *Pomacanthus* is typical of that occurring in *Chaetodon ornatissimus* and *C. meyeri*. It is not a pomacanthid larva and apparently was erroneously recorded from the Atlantic Ocean. Gunther (1871) illustrated a larger specimen of the same type of tholichthys and correctly identified it as a chaetodontid. I have found several specimens of this horned tholichthys in collections and identified them all as belonging to the subgenus *Citharoedus*.

The larvae of the family Scatophagidae are the only other tholichthys-like larval form (see Weber and de Beaufort, 1936, VII, Fig. 3A-D).

On the basis of the differences in morphological characteristics discussed above it is surprising that the two groups were never separated on a more stable basis before this time. The false impression that a tholichthys stage was present in the angelfishes, however, probably had much to do with repressing any further investigation into the matter. Although major differences were noted in such things as otoliths and swim bladders, the most interesting finding was the completely different relationship between the skull and axial skeleton. The dissimilar basioccipitals and atlas combination, together with the two types of bracing, dorsally in the Chaetodontidae and ventrally in the Pomacanthidae, leave little doubt that these two groups of fishes deserve full family status.

Patterns of Distribution of the Family Chaetodontidae

The butterflyfishes, with 114 species, lend themselves well to zoogeographic analysis. Their distinctive color patterns make identification easy and relatively accurate. A brief description or an illustration in a reference is usually sufficient for recognition of the species and subspecies. The color patterns are uniform over large geographic areas and can be used to define or characterize the different geographic regions. Faunal reports almost always include a good representation of the chaetodontid species. Therefore, the large number of papers dealing in part or entirely with the chaetodontids confirm and reconfirm the various distributional records of each species. Checklists, although more reliable when dealing with chaetodontids than with most other fishes, have not been used to any great extent in this treatment.

It is anticipated that the patterns of distribution exhibited by the family Chaetodontidae will lend themselves readily to computer analysis, and such a project in collaboration with another worker is planned for the future. There are practically no up-to-date monographic studies such as this one in which the data are reliable enough to be used for such an undertaking, and it is hoped that the resulting analysis will aid zoogeographers in the future.

One disadvantage in analyzing the distribution patterns of this group of fishes is that several species (or groups of species) have become adapted to deep-water (60 meters or more) habitats near or beyond the present limits of SCUBA equipment. Since trawling over reef or rocky areas, the typical habitats of butterflyfishes, is difficult and chances of losing nets and catch are great, the capture of such chaetodontid species has been sporadic. Most of the recently described butterflyfish species were captured either in this deep-water habitat or in outlying areas that had never been collected (e.g., remote oceanic islands) or had been poorly collected. Thus the representation of the family from these remote areas and from deep water is not comparable to that of readily visited localities and shallow water.

The family Chaetodontidae is essentially a circumtropical family of fishes with the vast majority of species included within the boundaries of the 70°F isotherm of the Southern Hemisphere in January.

A few species of butterflyfishes do have normal ranges in subtropical or even temperate regions. The genus *Amphichaetodon*, including two species, occurs in the southern Pacific. One species, *A. howensis*, is found in southeastern Australia (New South Wales), Lord Howe Island, and northern New Zealand. The second species occurs only at the San Felix Islands off the coast of Chile, despite the close proximity to South America. This seemingly unusual pattern is seen in other groups (see Eschmeyer, 1976, for a recent discussion of this pattern). A second genus entirely distributed in a temperate area is *Chelmonops*. The single species, *Chelmonops truncatus*, occurs along the southern coast of continental Australia. This genus is closely related to, and apparently derived from, the tropical genus *Chelmon,* whose major speciation appears to have occurred along the northern, northeastern and northwestern shores of Australia. The two genera have a slight degree of overlap in their distributions at the southern tip of the Great Barrier Reef, *Chelmon* in shallow water and *Chelmonops* deeper, cooler, water.

The only other non-tropical species of butterflyfish is *Chaetodon marleyi,* from the southern tip of Africa.

There are reports of some species of butterflyfishes in temperate areas, but only as juvenile stragglers. The normal and reproductive ranges are only within the tropical zones. I have collected or have seen *Chaetodon ocellatus, C. striatus, C. capistratus,* and *C. sedentarius* in New Jersey, but only as juveniles when they appear in late summer and early fall. They are not rare and are usually accompanied by other 'tropical' fishes such as pomacentrids, lutjanids, and serranids which normally are found no further north than Florida and the Bahamas or Bermuda.

The basic pattern of distribution for most of the butterflyfishes is tropical and warm temperate Indo-West Pacific. That is, the species occur within the area from the East African coast to the central Pacific Islands. Of the 114 species of butterflyfishes, 16 (14%) of them occur over this area. Six of the 16 species have distributions including both the Red Sea and the Hawaiian Islands, five extend to the Hawaiian Islands but not the Red Sea, and two include the Red Sea and not the Hawaiian Islands. Several of the Indo-West Pacific species that do not reach the Red Sea themselves have close relatives there. *Chaetodon lunula,* for example, is a wide-ranging species that is apparently replaced in the Red Sea with a species it is often synonymized with, *C. fasciatus; Heniochus acuminatus* has a similar type distribution, with *H. intermedius* the Red Sea form. *Chaetodon auriga* is an unusual case wherein its range includes the Red Sea but the Red Sea forms have a tendency to lack the dorsal fin spot, indicating that there has been some divergence within the species. *Chaetodon trifasciatus* is replaced in the Red Sea by *C. austricus,* though a third species, *C. melapterus,* occurs between them in the Arabian Sea. If the species pair of *C. triangulum* and *C. baronessa* are combined they show a similar distribution with a replacement species in the Red Sea, *C. larvatus;* similarly, the *mertensii* group, including the Indian Ocean *C. madagascariensis,* shows the same type distribution with *C. paucifasciatus,* the Red Sea representative.

There are several other species pairs in which closely related species occur on the Pacific side of the Malay-Australian Archipelago and on the

A pair of *Chaetodon trifasciatus* on the reef at Heron Island. This is a widely distributed species in the tropical Indo-Pacific. Photo by Dr. E. Reese, Great Barrier Reef.

Indian Ocean side of the Malay Archipelago, the combined ranges giving an Indo-West Pacific type distribution. These are *Heniochus varius* (Pacific Ocean side) and *H. pleurotaenia* (Indian Ocean side), *Hemitaurichthys polylepis* (Pacific Ocean side) and *H. zoster* (Indian Ocean side), *Chaetodon ephippium* (Pacific Ocean side) and *C. xanthocephalus* (Indian Ocean side), etc. Two subspecies pairs, *Chaetodon trifasciatus trifasciatus* (Indian Ocean side) and *C. t. lunulatus* (Pacific Ocean side), and *C. unimaculatus unimaculatus* (Pacific Ocean side) and *C. u. interruptus* (Indian Ocean side), show similar distributions. *Chaetodon trifasciatus* is an especially good example since better collecting and locality data are available. Of the specimens I have been able to examine the one subspecies occurs right up to the western coast of Java and Sumatra whereas the other occurs right up to the eastern side.

The trend is therefore to a broad Indo-West Pacific distribution for species, species pairs, or even closely related species groups. There is also a trend for some differentiation between the Indian Ocean and Pacific Ocean (including the East Indies) forms at a specific or subspecific level, as well as differentiation between the Indo-West Pacific forms and the Red Sea form, usually however, at the specific level.

It was mentioned that *Chaetodon trifasciatus* was a wide-ranging Indo-West Pacific species with a replacement species in the Red Sea. There is another species, *C. melapterus*, in this complex that occurs in the Arabian Sea (along the coast of Saudi Arabia) between these two. One *other species*, *C. vagabundus*, shows a similar pattern at the sub-specific level. *Chaetodon vagabundus pictus* occurs only in the Arabian Sea area. A closely related species, *C. decussatus* (often referred to erroneously as *C. pictus* in much of the literature), occurs along the Indian coast and Sri Lanka to Singapore and vicinity. This species is, however, sympatric with *C. vagabundus vagabundus*.

There are several groups of species, sometimes equivalent to an entire subgenus, that include closely related species which, when considering their combined ranges, possibly indicate the range of an ancestral species (or series of species) that has fragmented into the currently accepted species. The *punctatofasciatus*-group for example has a typical Indo-West Pacific distribution when the individual species *(guttatissimus—* Indian Ocean; *pelewensis*—tropical south Pacific Ocean; *punctatofasciatus*—tropical north Pacific Ocean; and *C. multicinctus*—Hawaiian Islands) are considered as one. Two groups show a southeast Asian distribution; they are the *gardneri* group of genus *Chaetodon*, subgenus *Rabdophorus* (*C. selene*—southern Japan to and including the East Indies; *C. gardneri*—Sri Lanka to the Arabian Sea; *C. leucopleura*—eastern coast of Africa to Red Sea) and the *modestus* group of genus *Chaetodon*, subgenus *Roa* (*C. excelsa*—Hawaiian Islands; *C. modestus*—southern Japan to the East Indies; *C. jayakari*—Arabian Sea to Sri Lanka and perhaps to Nicobars or Java).

A pair of *Chaetodon vagabundus* feeding along the reef top at Heron Island, Great Barrier Reef. Photo by Dr. E. Reese.

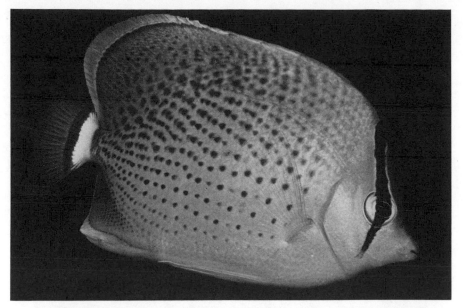

Chaetodon guttatissimus is the Indian Ocean representative of the *punctatofasciatus group. Photo by Klaus Paysan.*

The second group within the subgenus *Roa* of the genus *Chaetodon*, the *tinkeri* group, involves species that do not have ranges which are as closely related as the previously mentioned groups, indicating that the collections are not adequate enough to show the complete boundaries of the respective distributions (they are deep-water forms and difficult to collect) or that the intermediates have been eliminated by some biological or physical force. The species are *C. tinkeri*—Hawaiian Islands, *C. burgessi*—Palau Islands, *C. declevis*—Marquesas Islands, and *C. mitratus*—Cocos Keeling Islands and Mauritius(?).

The *miliaris* group of the subgenus *Chaetodon*, when all the species are considered together, has a much greater distribution than any other group of butterflyfishes. Together they may be considered circumtropical (*C. miliaris*—Hawaiian Islands; *C. guentheri*—southern Japan to Australia (eastern side); *C. assarius*—Western Australia; *C. dolosus*—eastern Africa; *C. sanctaehelenae*—St. Helena and Ascension Islands; *C. sedentarius*—tropical western Atlantic). Note the absence of representatives from the eastern Atlantic Ocean and eastern Pacific Ocean, both depauperate areas.

The subgenus *Prognathodes*, genus *Chaetodon*, must be considered in this group of fragmented distributions. The area covered is from the East Pacific through the western Atlantic to the west African coast. The species involved are *C. falcifer* (East Pacific), *C. aya* (northern Caribbean), *C. guyanensis* (southern Caribbean), and *C. marcellae* (West Afri-

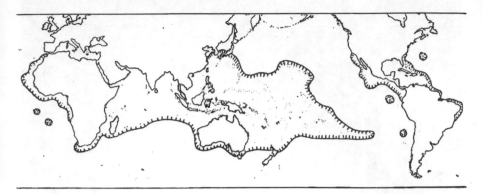

Distribution of the family Chaetodontidae.

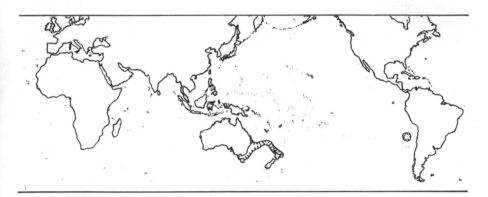

Distribution of genus *Amphichaetodon.*

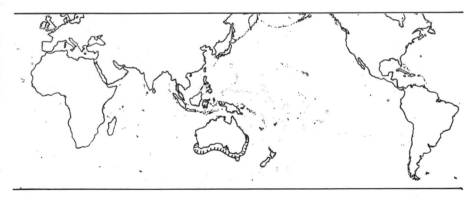

Distribution of genus *Chelmonops.*

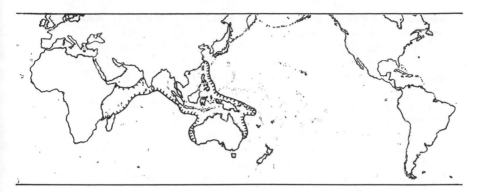

Distribution of genus *Chelmon.*

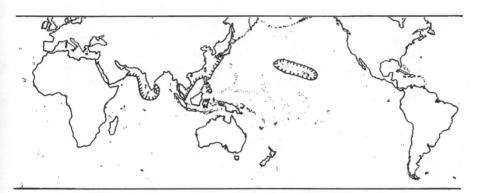

Distribution of *modestus*-group of subgenus *Roa.*

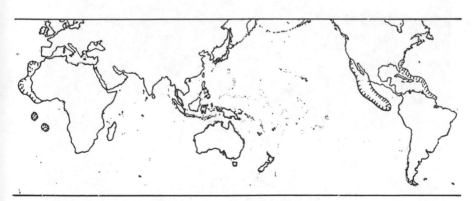

Distribution of the subgenus *Prognathodes.*

can coast). Another species that may be added to this group is *C. dichrous* from Saint Helena and Ascension Islands in the mid-Atlantic.

Others that might be considered fragmented or fragmenting groups but at a lower level are *Hemitaurichthys* with *H. thompsoni* and *H. multispinus*, from the Hawaiian Islands to Guam and the Marquesas Islands respectively, and the species pair of *H. polylepis* (Pacific Ocean) and *H. zoster* (Indian Ocean). *Hemitaurichthys polylepis* and *H. thompsoni* are, however, sympatric in the area of the Hawaiian Islands.

Chelmon has two species along the northern coast of Australia, one (*C. muelleri*) to the east of Torres Straits and the other (*C. marginalis*) to the west, that might be considered fragmenting species, with *Chelmonops* (*C. truncatus*) a closely related or derived genus, occurring along the southern Australian coast.

The butterflyfishes can be seen then to have several levels of differentiation: (1) a broad Indo-West Pacific distribution where species are not variable over a broad geographic area; (2) some differentiation where subspecies are formed between the Pacific and Indian Oceans; (3) more differentiation where the Pacific and Indian Ocean forms are full species; (4) further fragmentation of species where several species combined make up the larger distributions but where they are allopatric or nearly so; and (5) well fragmented groups of species where there are obvious gaps between the species.

A pair of *Chaetodon baronessa*. This is a Pacific Ocean species, its counterpart in the Indian Ocean being *C. triangulum*.

Most butterflyfishes can be found around the coral reefs of the world. This is a group of *Chaetodon lineolatus* feeding around a stand of *Acropora*. Photo by Rodney Jonklaas.

There are some closely related species with gaps that might be considered as relict or disjunct species. The two species of *Amphichaetodon*, for instance, are very closely related but one (*A. howensis*) occurs in the western Pacific at New South Wales, Lord Howe Island, and New Zealand, whereas the second species (*A. melbae*) occurs in the eastern Pacific at the San Felix Islands off the coast of Chile. A second pair of species that are very closely related occur in Africa, one (*C. marleyi*) along the coast of South Africa, the second (*C. hoefleri*) from tropical West Africa. These two species are particularly interesting in that one (*C. marleyi*) is temperate in distribution while the other is tropical, yet they are so similar as to be difficult to distinguish.

The recent discovery of *Chaetodon mitratus* at Cocos Keeling extends its range considerably since it was originally described from Mauritius. The distribution as it now stands is Mauritius and Cocos Keeling, islands on the opposite sides of the Indian Ocean. Perhaps it will be discovered in some intermediate area, thus solidifying the range, or perhaps there will be evidence that the original specimen was incorrectly designated as coming from Mauritius. It is also possible that the populations in the intervening area have been obliterated.

There is also a pattern in butterflyfishes in which very closely related species are found sympatrically, one with a considerably smaller distribution than the other. *Chaetodon oxycephalus*, for instance, is very similar to *C. lineolatus*, so much so that they have been synonymized with

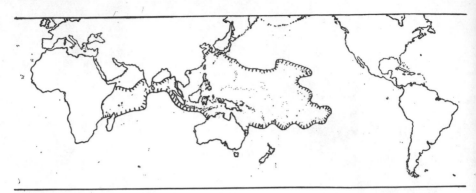

Distribution of genus *Hemitaurichthys.*

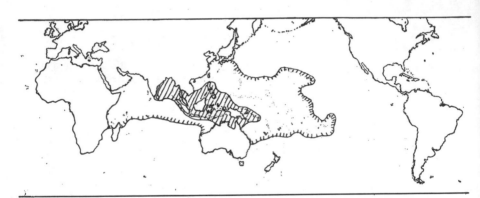

Distribution of *C. oxycephalus* and *C. lineolatus.*

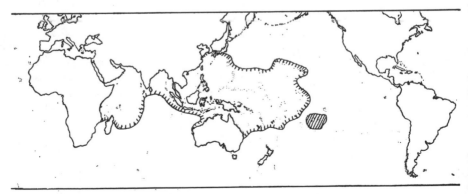

Distribution of *C. kleinii* and *C. trichrous.*

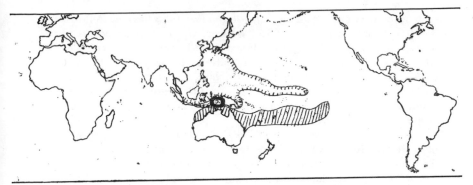

Distribution of *C. punctatofasciatus* and *C. pelewensis.*

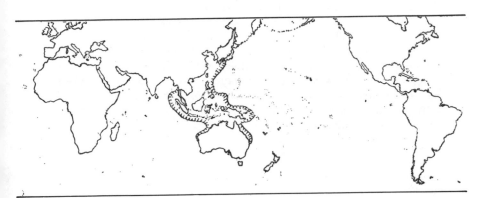

Distribution of genus *Coradion.*

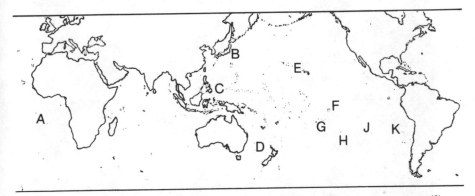

Distribution of Island Endemics: A. Saint Helena and Ascension Islands (2); B. Japan and Riu Kiu Islands (3); C. Palau (1); D. Lord Howe Island (1); E. Hawaiian Islands (6); F. Marquesas (1); G. Society and Tuamotu Islands (1); H. Pitcairn and Rapa Islands (1 each); J. Easter Island (1); K. San Felix Island (1).

771

each other more often than not. *Chaetodon lineolatus* has a wide distribution (Hawaiian Islands to Red Sea) whereas *C. oxycephalus* occurs from New Guinea and the Philippine Islands to Sri Lanka, a range completely within that of *lineolatus*. Similar distributions can be found in the species *C. melannotus* and *C. ocellicaudus* (*melannotus* with the wider distribution), *C. aureofasciatus* and *C. rainfordi* (*C. aureofasciatus* with the wider distribution), and *Forcipiger flavissimus* and *F. longirostris* (*F. flavissimus* with the broad distribution).

    Forcipiger flavissimus in fact has the widest range of any species of butterflyfish. It occurs from the eastern African coast and the Red Sea to the Gulf of California. Its range includes the Hawaiian Islands as well as Easter Island, being the only non-endemic species to have reached any of the outlying Pacific islands as Easter, Pitcairn or Rapa. It is thus the only member of the family to have bridged the broad expanse of open water in the eastern Pacific called the East Pacific Barrier.

    Two other rather unusual distribution patterns occur in the family Chaetodontidae. The first involves *Chaetodon kleinii* and its close relative, *C. trichrous*. *C. kleinii* is a wide-ranging species that occurs from the Hawaiian Islands to the eastern African coast. There are some minor differences that show some differentiation between the Pacific Ocean populations and the Indian Ocean populations (but not enough to justify calling them subspecies), and between the Pacific Ocean populations and those in the Hawaiian and Johnston Atoll area (where it was described as

Chaetodon kleinii is common and widespread from Hawaii to the African coast but apparently is replaced in the area of the Pacific around the Society and Tuamotu Islands by *C. trichrous*. Photo by Klaus Paysan.

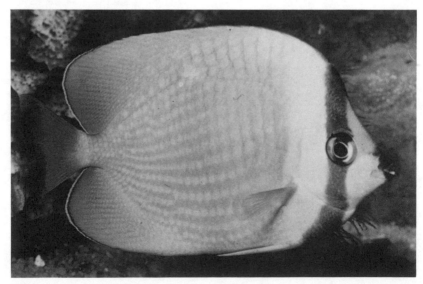

Parachaetodon ocellatus has a more restricted distribution in the western Pacific Ocean.

C. corallicola). The unusual aspect of this form is that in the southeastern corner of the Pacific Ocean (the Society Islands and Tuamotus) it is replaced by a closely related species called *C. trichrous*. No other pair of butterflyfishes shows this type of distribution pattern.

The second pattern involves *Chaetodon punctatofasciatus* and *C. pelewensis*. *Chaetodon punctatofasciatus* occurs in the northern part of the tropical Pacific (exclusive of the Hawaiian Islands) from the Marshall and Marianas Islands to Japan, the Philippines, and the East Indies to New Guinea. *C. pelewensis* occurs along the southern part of the tropical Pacific from the Society and Tuamotu Islands to Australia and southern New Guinea. Records are not accurate, and confusion between the two species makes it impossible to determine whether there is any area around New Guinea where the two forms meet. No other chaetodontids have this type of distribution pattern.

Certain species and species groups (even genera) are almost exclusively found in the vicinity of the East Indies or extend north to perhaps the RyuKyu Islands and south to the northern coast of Australia. These forms generally have not extended into the Pacific Island chains or into the Indian Ocean to any extent. The three species of *Coradion* for instance, are basically within this range, as is the single species of *Parachaetodon*. The species of subgenus *Discochaetodon* are basically northeastern Australia with an endemic at Lord Howe Island, but the most widespread species of the group, *C. octofasciatus*, occurs from southern Japan to Aus-

Chaetodon collare school or aggregation on a reef off Sri Lanka. This species is basically distributed around southeast Asia. Photo by Rodney Jonklaas.

tralia and westward to Sri Lanka and the Maldives. It extends eastward into the Pacific only as far as the Solomon Islands. *Chelmon* has a similar pattern with two species occurring in northeastern and northwestern Australia respectively, but the species with the widest distribution, *Chelmon rostratus*, occurs from southern Japan to Australia and westward to Sri Lanka and across to the African coast. This species has not extended its range into the Pacific Island arcs.

A group of related species, *C. wiebeli*, *C. adiergastos*, *C. auripes*, and perhaps even *C. collare*, all in the subgenus *Chaetodontops*, have similar distributions but, rather than being more concentrated in the Australian region, they are more northerly (Philippines, China, and Japan) species.

The area including the eastern Pacific, western Atlantic, central Atlantic, and western Africa is comparatively depauperate of chaetodontid species. Only four species are present in the East Pacific (not including the temperate *Amphichaetodon melbae*): *Pseudochaetodon nigrirostris*, *Chaetodon humeralis*, *C. falcifer*, and *Forcipiger flavissimus*. This last species is basically Indo-Pacific in distribution. Three species, *Chaetodon marcellae, C. robustus,* and *C. hoefleri* occur in the West African region, and seven, *Chaetodon ocellatus, C. capistratus, C. sedentarius, C. striatus, C. aculeatus, C. aya,* and *C. guyanensis,* are found in the western Atlantic.

The remaining two species, *Chaetodon dichrous* and *C. sanctaehelenae,* are endemic to the islands of Saint Helena and Ascension in the central Atlantic. *Pseudochaetodon* and the subgenus *Prognathodes* (genus *Chaetodon*) are entirely restricted to this eastern Pacific-Atlantic region.

There are 16 island endemics, six of which occur only in the Hawaiian Island area (including Johnston Island). Pitcairn and Rapa Islands each have one species, and two species are endemic to Saint Helena and Ascension Islands (mid-Atlantic). The remaining island endemics are found at San Felix Island (1 species), Palau Islands (1), Society Islands (1), Lord Howe Island (1), the Marquesas Islands (1), and Easter Island (1).

Species occurring in deep water usually correspond to phylogenetic relationships. All members of the subgenus *Prognathodes* are deep-water chaetodontids, as are most members of the *miliaris* group of subgenus *Chaetodon*. The distributions of these two groups were mentioned above. All species of the subgenus *Roa* are deep-water except one, *Chaetodon modestus* from southern Japan and China. This is interesting as *modestus* is part of a three-species complex; the other two species, *C. excelsa* from the Hawaiian Islands and *C. jayakari* from the eastern Arabian Sea, are both deep-water species. *Amphichaetodon howensis* is not only temperate in distribution but is also a deep-water species, as is the monotypic *Chelmonops truncatus* (temperate Australia).

The family Chaetodontidae, like many perciform families, shows extensive radiation in the tropical Indo-West Pacific region, but with several patterns of distribution within this region such as endemism, related species on both sides of the Malayan Archipelago, species groups exhibiting normal broad Indo-West Pacific ranges when considered as a single entity, difficulty in crossing the East Pacific Barrier, few species in East Pacific and West African regions (and limited number of species in the tropical West Atlantic), etc. The movement of species into cold water habitats (temperate regions or deep water) is very restricted.

Acknowledgments

In any work of this size there is bound to be a great number of people who have given aid in one way or another. It is impossible for me to be able to give credit to all those who have contributed to the successful completion of this work. For those whom I have inadvertently omitted please accept not only my thanks for your contribution but also my sincerest apologies for the omission of your name.

I am grateful to the following people who provided me with financial support while I was attending the University of Hawaii: Mr. Vernon Brock (deceased), Dr. Garth Murphy, and Dr. Philip Helfrich, formerly of the Hawaii Institute of Marine Biology, provided employment for me in the form of research assistantships with the aquaculture program.

A grant of $500 was awarded by the TFH Fund of the Smithsonian Institution, a grant of $150 was awarded by the Society of Sigma Xi, and a grant of $300 was awarded by Dr. Herbert R. Axelrod of T.F.H. Publications, Inc. for the purpose of traveling to various museums and other institutions within the United States so that I might study the butterflyfish and angelfish types as well as other specimens. Funds for studying the chaetodontid and pomacanthid collections while at the California Academy of Sciences, San Francisco, were arranged for by Dr. W. N. Eschmeyer.

Two expeditions to Enewetak Atoll, Marshall Islands, and one to Johnston Atoll were made through the aid of the Atomic Energy Commission and arranged through the Hawaii Institute of Marine Biology.

I wish to thank the following people for providing specimens, photographs, museum assistance, and loans of specimens: Dr. Gerald R. Allen, Dr. Herbert R. Axelrod, Mr. Wayne Baldwin, Dr. Marie-Louise Bauchot, Dr. James Boehlke, Dr. M. Boeseman, Mr. Victor Bota, Dr. David K. Caldwell, Dr. Thomas Clark, Mr. Ben Cropp, Dr. William P. Davis, Mr. Walter Deas, Mr. Helmut Debelius, Mrs. Lillian Dempster, Dr. Myvanwy Dick, Mr. Peter Enfield, Dr. William N. Eschmeyer, Mr. Douglas Faulkner, Dr. Henry A. Feddern, Dr. John E. Fitch, Dr. Warren C. Freihofer, Mr. Nate Gamblin, Mr. Barry Goldman, Mr. James Gordon, Mr. Robert Gornichec, Mr. Noel Gray, Mr. Herman Gruhl, Dr. Philip Heemstra, Dr. W. Herkner, Dr. Bruce Higgens, Mr. Arthur Hine, Mrs. G. Hirsch, Dr. Douglas Hoese, Dr. Tomio Iwamoto, Mr. Scott Johnson, Mr. E. C. Jones, Dr. Robert Jones, Mr. Rodney Jonklaas, Mr. Ken Jourdan, Mr. Earl Kennedy, Mr. Alex Kerstitch, Mr. Horst Kipper, Dr. Wolfgang Klausewitz, Dr. Leslie Knapp, Mrs. Edith Korthaus, Dr. Robert Lavenberg, Mr. Roger Lubbock, Mr. Hans Mayland, Dr. George

Miller, Mr. Jerry Neumann, Mr. Aaron Norman, Mr. James H. O'Neill, Dr. John Paxton, Mr. Allan Power, Dr. John E. Randall, Dr. Ernst Reese, Dr. C. Richard Robins, Dr. Richard H. Rosenblatt, Mrs. Margaret M. Smith, Dr. William Smith-Vaniz, Mrs. Pearl Sonoda, Dr. Victor G. Springer, Mr. Roger Steene, Dr. W. Ralph Taylor, Dr. F. Terofal, Mr. Spencer Tinker, Dr. Walter Van den Bergh, Dr. Richard Wass, Mr. Murray Wiener, Mr. Alwyne Wheeler, Dr. Loren P. Woods, Dr. Fujio Yasuda, and Mr. Lester Zukeran.

Thanks are due to Dr. Alan Ziegler, Bernice P. Bishop Museum, Honolulu, for his help in preparing the skeletons and to my wife, Lourdes, who prepared the osteological drawings.

My initial committee consisted of Dr. John E. Randall, Dr. William A. Gosline, Dr. Philip Helfrich, Dr. E. Alison Kay, and Dr. Garth Murphy. Through replacements the final committee included Dr. Sidney Townsley, Dr. E. Alison Kay, Dr. Julie Bailey, Dr. John Maciolek, and Dr. Robert May. Dr. William N. Eschmeyer served as the ichthyological advisor during the preparation of the final draft. I wish to thank all of them for their patience, advice, and encouragement during my doctoral program. Drs. Townsley and Kay were particularly helpful in the forming of the second committee and guiding me through the final stages in preparation for graduation, and Dr. Eschmeyer was also particularly helpful in providing advice, encouragement, and other aid during my stay at the California Academy of Sciences, San Francisco. I am particularly grateful to them for this help.

Thanks are also due to Mr. Jerry Walls, Dr. Richard H. Rosenblatt, Mrs. Lillian Dempster, Dr. Victor G. Springer, and Dr. Gerald R. Allen for reading this large thesis (or parts of it) and for making very useful and pertinent suggestions.

I am particularly grateful for the help and understanding of all the people at TFH Publications who suffered through the last stages of the completion of this dissertation with me. The typists who made the various drafts, including the final typing, deserve medals for successfully completing this difficult job. Mrs. Evelyn Axelrod was particularly helpful in seeing to it that everything ran as smoothly as possible and gave me encouragement throughout.

Special thanks go to Dr. Herbert R. Axelrod, who provided help and encouragement through a very difficult period, and a very special thanks to my wife, Lourdes, without whose love and understanding I could never have completed this dissertation.

BIBLIOGRAPHY

Abe, T. 1939. A list of the fishes of the Palao Islands. *Palao Trop. Biol. Sta., Stud. (Tokyo), 1*(4): 523-583.

Abel, E.F. 1960. Zur Kenntnis des verhaltens und der Okologie von Fischen an Korallenriffen bei Ghardaga (rotes Meer). *Z. Morphol. Okol. Tiere, 49:* 430-503.

Ahl, E. 1923. Zur Kenntnis der Knochenfischfamilie Chaetodontidae, insbesondere der Unterfamilie Chaetodontinae. *Archiv für Naturg.,* Abth. A, *89* (5): 1-205, pls. 1-3.

——————. 1926. Neue oder selten importierte Fische, IV. *Bl. Aquarienkunde Stuttgart, 37*(15): 1-4.

——————. 1933. Neue oder selten eingeführte Fische, Lurche und Kriechtiere. *Aquar. Berlin:* 37-39.

Albrecht, H. 1965. Color signals as a dynamic means of demarcating territory. Pp. 114-117. *In:* Burkhardt, Schleidt, and Altner (Ed.). *Signals in the Animal World.* Allen & Unwin, London.

Albuquerque, M.P. 1956. Peixes de Portugal e Ilhas Adjacentes. Claves para sua determinacao. *Port. Acta Biol.,* Ser. B, *5:* 1-1164.

Alcock, A.W. 1896. Natural history notes from H.M. Indian Marine Survey Steamer "Investigator". Ser. II, No. 23. A supplemental list of the marine fishes of India, with descriptions of two new genera and eight new species. *J. Asiat. Soc. Bengal, 65:* 301-338.

Alfred, E.R. 1961. The Javanese fishes described by Kuhl and van Hasselt. *Bull. Natl. Mus. Singapore,* December 1961, (30):80-88.

Allen, G.R., and W.A. Starck II. 1973. A new species of butterflyfish (Chaetodontidae) from the Palau Islands. *Trop. Fish Hobbyist,* March 1973, *21*(7): 17-28.

Alleyne, H.G., and W. Macleay. 1877. The ichthyology of the Chevert Expedition *Proc. Linn. Soc. N.S.W.:* 261-281, 321-359, pls. I-IX, X-XVII.

Anderson, J. 1878. *Anatomical and zoological researches; comprising an account of the zoological results of the two expeditions to Western Yunnan in 1868 and 1875.* Pisces: *1:* 863-869. Anat. Res., London.

——————. 1904. Algues marines du Quang Binh (Les). *Bull. Econ. Indochine, Hanoi-Haiphong,* No. 24: 343.

Anderson, W.D. 1964. New records of fishes for South Carolina and the occurrence of *Chaetodipterus faber* in fresh water. *Copeia,* 1964 (1): 243—244.

—————— and E.J. Gutherz. 1965. New Atlantic coast ranges for fishes. *Q. J. Fla. Acad. Sci., 27*(4): 299-306.

Angot, M. 1950. Poissons de récifs. *Nat. Malgache, 2*(2): 135-142, pl.

Aoyagi, H. 1943. *Coral Fishes.* Maruzen Co. Ltd., Tokyo. 224 pp., 37 pls.

Arambourg, C. 1927. Les poissons fossile d'Oran. Matériaux carte géologique d'Algérie Algerm, Sér. 1. *Palaeont. Bull. Serv. carte Géol. Algér.,* No. 6. 298 pp., 46 pls.

Artedi, 1738. *Ichthyologia, sive opera omnia de piscibus scilicet: Biblioteca ichthyologica. Philosphia ichthyologica. Generum piscium. Synonymia specierum. Descriptiones specierum. Omnia in hoc opere perfectiora, quam antea ulla. Post-*

huma vindicavit, recognovit, coeptavit et edidit Carolus Linnaeus. 5 parts. Lugduni Batavorum. Leyden.

Asano, N. 1936. List of the fishes of the Palau region. *J. Fish. Res.,* 31 (7): 414-420.

Atz, J.W. 1949. They proved it—the fish shoots. *Anim. Kingdom, New York,* 52: 44-47.

_____ and G. Pickford. 1959. The use of pituitary hormones in fish culture. *Endeavour, 18*(71): 125-129.

Bailey, R.M. 1951. Ichthyological notes: the authorship of names proposed in Cuvier and Valenciennes' "Histoire Naturelle des Poissons." *Copeia,* 1951 (3): 249-251.

_____ and others. 1970. A list of common and scientific names of fishes from the United States and Canada (Third Edition). *Amer. Fish. Soc., Spec. Pub., No. 6:* 1-150.

Baird, S.F. 1884. On the specimens received by the Smithsonian Institution from the United States lifesaving service. *Bull. U.S. Fish Comm.,* 4: 177-178.

Bakus, G.J. 1967. The feeding habits of fishes and primary production at Eniwetok, Marshall Islands. *Micronesica, 3* (2): 135-149.

Balan, V. 1958. Notes on a visit to certain islands of the Laccadive Archipelago, with special reference to fisheries. *J. Bombay Nat. Hist. Soc.,* 55(2): 297-306.

Baldwin, W.J. 1963. A new chaetodont fish, *Holacanthus limbaughi,* from the eastern Pacific. *Los Ang. Cty. Mus., Contrib. Sci.,* No. 74: 1-8.

Bardach, J.E. 1958. On the movements of certain reef fishes. *Ecology, 39*(1): 139-146.

Barnard, J.E. 1925. *A pictorial guide to South African fishes, marine and freshwater.* Maskew Miller Limited, Cape Town. 226 pp, 25 pls.

_____. 1925-27. A monograph of the marine fishes of South Africa. *Ann. S. Afr. Mus., 21*:1-1065.

_____. 1937. Further notes on South African marine fishes. *Ann. S. Afr. Mus., 32:* 41-67.

Barnhart, P.S. 1936. *Marine fishes of Southern California.* University of California Press, Berkely.

Bartlett, J. & D. Bartlett. 1967. (They Live in Africa.) *Nature's Paradise.* Collins, St. James' Place, London.

Baschieri-Salvadori. F, 1954. Spedizione subacquea italiana nel mar rosso recerche zoologiche. VII. Chetodonti. *Riv. Biol. Colon, 14:*87-110, pls. I-VIII.

Bassani, F. 1889. Richerche sui pesce fossili di Chiavon (Strati di Sotzka, Miocene inferiore). *Atti Accad. Sci. Napoli,* 2nd ser., *3*(6): 104 pp., 18 pls.

Bauchot, M.L. 1963. Catalogue critique des types de poissons du Muséum nationale d'Histoire Naturelle. II. Familles du Chaetodontidae, Toxotidae, Scatophagidae, Monodactylidae, Ephippidae, Scorpididae, Pempheridae, Kyophosidae, Girellidae. *Publ. Mus. Natl. Hist. Nat.,* No. 20: 115-179.

_____. 1969a. Les poissons de la collection de Broussonet au Muséum Nationale d'Histoire Naturelle de Paris. *Bull. Mus. Natl. Hist. Nat., 41 (1):* 125-143.

—————————. 1969b. Étude de une collection récolte au cours des campagnes de chalutage dans le golfe de Guinée (G.T.S. 1963-64). *Bull. Mus. Natl. Hist. Nat.*, *41*(1): 410-425.

—————————— and M. Blanc. 1961. Poissons marins de l'Est Atlantique Tropical. II. Percoidei (Teleosteens Perciformes). *Atlantide Repts.*, No. 6: 65-100.

Baughman, J.L. 1947. Fishes not previously reported from Texas, with miscellaneous notes on other species. *Copeia*, 1947 (4): 280.

Bayer, F.M., and R.R. Harry. 1957. Project coral-fish looks at Palau. *Smithson. Inst. Ann. Rep. for 1956*: 481-508.

Bean, B.A., and A.C. Weed. 1912. Notes on a collection of fishes from Java, made by Owen Bryant and William Palmer in 1909, with description of a new species. *Proc. U.S. Natl. Mus.*, *42*: 587-611, pls. lxxiii-lxxv.

Bean, T.H. 1879. A list of European fishes in the collection of the United States National Museum. *Proc. U.S. Natl. Mus.*, 2: 10-44.

—————————. 1880. Checklist of duplicates of North American fishes distributed by the Smithsonian Institution in behalf of the United States National Museum, 1877-1880. *Proc. U. S. Natl. Mus.*, *3*: 75-116.

—————————. 1890. Notes on fishes collected at Cozumel, Yucatan, by the U.S. Fish Commission, with descriptions of new species. *Bull. U.S. Fish. Comm.*, 1888, *8*(4): 193-206, 1 pl.

—————————. 1906. A catalogue of the fishes of Bermuda, with notes on a collection made in 1905 for the Field Museum. *Field Columbian Mus.*, Pub. 108, Zool. ser. 2nd ser., 7: 21-89.

—————————— and H.G. Dresel. 1885. A catalogue of fishes received from the public museum of the Institute of Jamaica, with descriptions of *Pristipoma approximus* and *Tylosurus euryops*, two new species. *Proc. U.S. Natl. Mus.*, 7: 151-170.

Beaufort, L.F. de. 1913. Fishes of the eastern part of the Indo-Australian Archipelago, with remarks on its zoogeography. *Bijdr. Nederl. Dierk. Ver. Amster.*: 95-163, 1 pl.

—————————. 1926. On a collection of marine fishes from the Miocene of southern Celebes. *Jaarb. Mijnwezen Nederl.-Ost. Indie Weltefreden, Java, 1*,: 117-148, 9 pls.

Beebe, W. and G. Hollister. 1935. The fishes of the Union Islands, Grenadines, British West Indies, with the description of a new species of stargazer. *Zoologica, (N.Y.), 19*(6): 209-224.

Bennett, E.T. 1828. Observations on the fishes contained in the collection of the Zoological Society. Art. No. 3. On some fishes from the Sandwich Islands. *Zool. J.*, *4*: 31-43, 1 pl.

—————————. 1830. Catalogue of the fishes of Sumatra. *In: Memoir of the life and public services of Sir Thomas Stamford Raffles*, ed. by his widow (Lady Sophia Hull Raffles). London.

—————————. 1831. Observations on a collection of fishes from the Mauritius, with characters of new genera and species. *Proc. Zool. Soc. London*, Part 1: 32; 59-61; 126-128; 165-169. Part 2: 182-184.

—————————. 1839. Fishes. *In:* Lay, G.T. and E.T. Bennett. *The Zoology of*

Captain Beechey's voyage. London. Pp. 41-75, pls. xv-xxiii.

Bennett, J.W. 1851. *A selection of rare and curious fishes found upon the coast of Ceylon: from drawings made in that island, and coloured from life.* London. Printed for the author. 3rd ed., 30 pls.

Bennett, Q. 1969. Colour Bar. Why are bright fish bright? *Dive Mag.*, *9*(1): 22 pp, photos.

Ben-Tuvia, A., and H. Steinitz. 1952. Report on a collection of fishes from Eylath (Gulf of Aqaba), Red Sea. *Bull. Sea fish. Res. Stn. Haifa*, No. 2: 1-12.

Berg, L. 1947. *Classification of fishes both recent and fossil.* English & Russian edition, Ann Arbor Michigan. 517 pp.

Birdsong, R. and A.R. Emery 1968. New Records of fishes from the western Caribbean. *Q.J. Fla. Acad. Sci.*, *30*(3): 187-196.

Blache, J. 1962. Liste des poissons signalés dans l'Atlantique Tropico-Oriental Sud du Cap des Palmes (4° Lat. N) a Mossamedes (15° Lat. S) (Province Guinea-Equatoriale). *Cah. O.R.S.T.O.M.* océanogr. No. 2: 1-178.

Blanc, M. & P. Fourmanoir. 1964. Étude préliminaire des poissons de la côte Cambodgienne. *Cah. Pac.*, (6): 33-46.

Blanco, G.J. and D.V. Villadolid. 1951. The young of some fishes of Luzon. *Philipp. J. Fish.*, *1*: 67-93, 35 figs.

_____ and H.R. Montalban, 1956. A bibliography of Philippine fishes and fisheries. *Philipp. J. Fish.*, *1*: 107-130.

Bleeker, P. 1845. Bijdragen tot de geneeskundige Topographie van Batavia. Generisch overzicht der Fauna. *Nat. en. Geneeskd. Arch. Nederl. Ind.*, *2(3)*: 505-528.

_____. 1848. A contribution of the Ichthyology of Sumbawa. *J. Indian Arch.*, *2*(9): 632-639.

_____. 1850. Bijdrage tot de kennis der Chaetodontoiden van den Soenda-Molukschen Archipel. *Verh. Batav. Gen.*, *23:* 1-31.

_____. 1851a. Faune ichthyologicae, Javae insularumque adjacentium, genera et species novae (1). *Nat. Tijdschr. Nederl. Ind.*, *1*: 98-108.

_____. 1851b. Nieuwe Bijdrage tot de kennis der Percoidei, Scleroparei, Sparoidei, Maenoidei, Chaetodontoidei en Scomberoidei van den Soenda-Molukschen Archipel. *Nat. Tijdschr. Nederl. Indie*, *2*: 163-179.

_____. 1851c. Bijdrage tot de kennis de ichtyologische fauna van de Banda-eilanden. *Nat. Tijdschr. Nederl. Ind.*, *2*: 225-261.

_____. 1852a. Bijdrage tot de kennis der ichthyologische fauna van de Moluksche eilanden. Vischen van Amboina en Ceram. *Nat. Tijdschr. Nederl. Ind.*, *3*:229-309.

_____. 1852b. Bijdrage tot de kennis de ichthyologische fauna van het eiland Banka. *Nat. Tijdschr. Nederl. Ind.*, *3*: 443-460.

_____. 1852c. Derde bidrage tot de kennis der ichthyologische fauna van Celebes. *Nat. Tijdschr. Nederl. Ind.*, *3*: 739-782.

_____. 1853a. Diagnostische beschrijvingen van nieuwe of weinig bekende vischsoorten van Batavia. Tiental I-VI. *Nat. Tijdschr. Nederl. Ind.*, *4*: 451-516.

_____. 1853b. Nieuwe bijdrage tot de kennis der ichthologische fauna van Ternate en Halamaheira (Gilolo). *Nat. Tijdschr. Nederl. Ind.,* 4: 595-610.

_____. 1853c. Bijdrage tot de kennis de ichthyologische fauna van Solor. *Nat. Tijdschr. Nederl. Ind.,* 5: 67-96.

_____. 1853d. Vierde bijdrage tot de kennis der ichtyologische fauna van Celebes. *Nat. Tijdschr. Nederl. Ind.,* 5: 153-174.

_____. 1853e. Vierde bijdrage tot de kennis der ichtyologische fauna van Amboina. *Nat. Tijdschr. Nederl. Ind.,* 5: 317-352.

_____. 1853f. Nieuwe tientalen diagnostische beschrijvingen van niewe of weinig bekende vischsoorten van Sumatra. *Nat. Tijdschr. Nederl. Ind.,* 5: 495-534.

_____. 1854a. Bijdrage tot de kennis de ichthyologische fauna van Halmaheira (Gilolo). *Nat. Tijdschr. Nederl. Ind.,* 6: 49-62.

_____. 1854b. Derde bijdrage tot de kennis der ichthyologische fauna van de Banda-eilanden. *Nat. Tijdschr. Nederl. Ind.,* 6: 89-114.

_____. 1854c. Nieuwe bijdrage tot de kennis der ichthyologische fuana van Timor. *Nat. Tiijdschr. Nederl. Ind.,* 6: 203-214.

_____. 1854d. Bijdrage tot dekennis der ichthyologische fauna het eilande Flores. *Nat. Tijdschr. Nederl. Ind.,* 6: 309-338.

_____. 1854e. Vijfde bijdrage tot de kennis de ichthyologische fauna van Amboina. *Nat. Tijdschr. Nederl. Ind.,* 6: 455-508.

_____. 1854f. Overzicht der ichthyologische fauna van Sumatra, met beschrijving van eenige nieuwe soorten. *Nat. Tijdschr. Nederl. Ind.,* 7: 49-108.

_____. 1854g. Specierum piscium javanesium novarus vel minus cognitarum diagnoses adumbratae. *Nat. Tijdschr. Nederl. Ind.,* 7: 415-448.

_____. 1854h. Nalezingen op de ichthyologische fauna van Bengalen en Hindostan. *Verh. Batav. Gen.,* 26: 165-166.

_____. 1855a. Bijdrage tot de kennis de ichthyologische fauna van de Batoe-eilanden. *Nat. Tijdschr. Nederl. Ind.,* 8: 305-328.

_____. 1855b. Zesde bijdrage tot de kennis der ichthyologische fauna van Amboina. *Nat. Tijdschr. Nederl. Ind.,* 8: 391-434.

_____. 1855c. Vierde Bijdrage tot de kennis der ichthyologische fauna van de Kokos-eilanden. *Nat. Tijdschr. Nederl. Ind.,* 8: 445-460.

_____. 1856. Bijdrage tot de kennis der ichthyologische fauna van det eiland Boero. *Nat. Tijdschr. Nederl. Ind.,* 11: 383-414.

_____. 1857a. Descriptiones specierum piscium javanesium novarum vel minus cognitarum diagnosticae. *Nat. Tijdschr. Nederl. Ind.,* 13: 323-368.

_____. 1857b. Achtste bijdrage tot de kennis der vischfauna van Amboina. *Act. Soc. Sci. Indo-Neerl.,* 2: 1-102.

_____. 1859. Over eenige vischsoorten van de zuidkust-wateren van Java. *Nat. Tijdschr. Nederl. Ind.,* 19: 329-352.

_____. 1860. Elfde bijdrage de kennis der visch-fauna van Amboina. *Act. Soc. Sci. Indo-Neerl.,* 8: 1-14.

_____. 1861a. Mededeeling omtrent vischsoorten, nieuwe voor de kennis der fauna van Singapoera. *Versl. Akad. Amst.,* 12: 28-63.

_____. 1861b. Iets over de vischfauna van het eiland Pinang. *Versl. Akad. Amst.,* 12: 64-80.

_____. 1863a. Troisième mémoire sur la faune ichthyologique de l'île de Batjan. *Nederl. Tijdschr. Dierk.*, *1*: 153-159.

_____. 1863b. Onzième notice sur la faune ichthyologique de l'île de Ternate. *Nederl. Tijdschr. Dierk.*, *1*: 228-238.

_____. 1865a. Énumération des espèces de poissons actuellement connues de l'île de Ceram. *Nederl. Tijdschr. Dierk.*, *2*: 182-193.

_____. 1865b. Enumération des espèces de poissons actuellement connues de l'île d'Amboine. *Nederl. Tijdschr. Dierk.*, *2*: 270-293.

_____. 1868a. Douzième notice sur la faune ichthyologique de l'île de Batjan. *Versl. Akad. Amst.*, sér. 2, *2*: 273-274.

_____. 1868b. Huitième notice sur la fauna ichthyologique d'île de Baitian. *Versl. Akad. Amst.*, sér. 2, *2*: 276-277.

_____. 1868c. Cinquième notice sur la fauna ichthyologique de l'île de Solor. *Versl. Akad. Amst.*, sér. 2, *2*: 283-288.

_____. 1868d. Sixième notice sur la faune ichthyologique de l'île de Bintang. *Vers. Akad. Amst.*, sér. 2, *2*: 289-294.

_____. 1868e. Notice sur la fauna ichthyologique d'île de Waigiou. *Versl. Akad. Amst.*, sér. 2, *2*: 295-301.

_____. 1868f. Deuxième notice sur la faune ichthyologique de l'île de Sangir. *Versl. Akad. Amst.*, sér. 2, *2*: 302-304.

_____. 1873. Description de quelques espèces de poissons de l'île de la Réunion et de Madagascar. *Nederl. Tijdschr. Dierk. 4*: 92-105.

_____. 1874. Typi nonnulli generici piscium neglecti. *Versl. Akad. Amst.*, sér. 3, *8*: 367-371.

_____. 1875. Recherches sur a faune de Madagascar et de ses dépendances d'àpres le découvertes de François P.L. Pollen et D.C. van Dam. Part 4. *Poissons de Madagascar et de l'île de la Réunion.* Leiden.

_____. 1876a. Systema Percarum revisum. *Arch. Neerl. Sci. Nat.*, *11*, (part 1): 247-288; (part 2): 289-340.

_____. 1876b. Notice sur les genres et les espèces des Chetodontoides de la sousfamille des Taurichthyiformes. *Versl. Akad. Amst.*, Ser. 2, *10*: 308-320.

_____. 1876c. Notice sur le genre *Chaetodon* Art. (*Pomacanthus* Lac. Cuv.) et sur la pluralité de ses espèces vivantes. *Arch. Neerl. Sci. Nat.*, *11*: 178-185.

_____. 1877a. *Atlas Ichthyologique des Indes Orintales Neerlandaises publie sous les auspices du Governement colonia neerlandais. 9*: 1-80 , pls. 361-382.

_____. 1877b. Revision des espèces insulindiennes de la famille des Chaetodontoides. *Verh. Akad. Amst.*, *17*: 1-174.

_____. 1877c. Notice sur la sousfamille de Holacanthiformes et description de quelques espèces insufissament conues. *Arch. Neerl. Sci. Nat.*, *12*: 17-37. pls.

_____. 1879. Contribution a la faune ichthologique de l'île Maurice. *Verh. Akad. Amst.*, *18*: 1-23.

Blegvad, H. 1944. Fishes of the Iranian Gulf. *Danish Scientific Investigations in*

Iran, Copenhagen, 3: 5-247.

Bliss, R. 1883. Descriptions of new species of Mauritian fishes. *Trans. R. Soc. Artes Sci. Maurice,* n.s., *13:* 45-63.

Bloch, M. 1787. *Naturgeschichte der Ausländischen Fische. Dritter Theil.* Vol. 4-6: 46-117, pls.

——————. 1793 *Naturgeschichte der Ausländischen Fische.* Vol. 7-9: 1-104, pls.

—————— and J.G. Schneider. 1801. *M.E. Blochii . . . Systema Ichthyologiae iconibus ex illustratum.* Post obitum aucoris opus inchoatum absolvit, correxit, interpolavit Jo. Gottlob Schneider, Saxo. Berolini. 1x and 584 pp., 110 col. pls.

Blosser, C.B. 1909. Reports on the expedition to British Guiana of the Indiana University and the Carnegie Museum, 1908. Report No. 3. The Marine Fishes. *Ann. Carnegie Mus., Pitts., 6* (1): 295-300, 3 pls.

Blyth, E. 1852. Report on Ceylon mammals, birds, reptiles and fishes. Pp. 37-50. *In:* E.F. Kelaert, *Prodromus faunae Zeylanicae.* Ceylon.

Boddaert, P. 1782. Auszug eines Briefes des herrn Doct. Boddaert zu Utrecht an herrn D. Bloch, vom ersten Mai 1781. *Gesell. Naturf. Fr.* Berlin.

Boeseman, M. 1947. *Revision of the fishes collected by Burger and von Siebold in Japan.* E.F. Brill, Leiden. 240 pp.

Bogatchev. V.V. 1938. A new genus and species of fish from the Paleogen of Abkhasia. *Bull. Mus. Georgie. Tiflis, 9A:* 2-5.

Böhlke, J. 1953. A catalogue of the type specimens of recent fishes in the natural history museum of Stanford University. *Stanford Ichthyol. Bull., 5:* 1-168.

—————— & C.C.G. Chaplin.1968. *Fishes of the Bahamas and adjacent tropical waters.* Livingston Publishing Co., Wynnewood, Pa. 771 pp, 36 pls.

Bonnaterre, J.P. 1788. *Tableau encyclopédique et méthodique des trois règnes de la nature . . . Ichthyologie.* Paris, 1788. vi, 215 pp., 102 pls.

Borodin, N.A. 1928. Scientific results of the yacht "Ara" expetition during the years 1926 to 1928 while in command of William K. Vanderbilt. Fishes. *Bull. Vanderbilt Ocean. Mus., 1*(1): 1-37.

——————. 1930. Scientific results of the yacht "Ara" expedition during the years 1926-1930, while in command of William K. Vanderbilt. Fishes collected in 1929. *Bull. Vanderbilt. Mar. Mus., 1 (2):* 39-64.

——————. 1932a. Scientific results of the yacht "Alva" world cruise. July 1931-March 1932 in command of William K. Vanderbilt. Fishes. *Bull. Vanderbilt Mar. Mus., 1*(3): 65-101.

——————. 1932b. Scientific results of the yacht "Alva" Mediterranean Cruise, 1933, in command of William K. Vanderbilt. Fishes. *Bull. Vanderbilt Mar. Mus., 1*(4): 103-123, 2 pls.

——————. 1934. About the types of fishes from Mauritius Isl., Indian Ocean, in the Museum of Comparative Zoology. *Copeia,* 1934 (1): 44.

Boulenger, G.A. 1887. An account of the fishes obtained by Surgeon-Major A.S.G. Jayakar at Muscat, east coast of Arabia. *Proc. Zool. Soc. Lond.,* No. 63: 653-667, pl.

——————. 1897. A list of the fishes obtained by Mr. J. Stanley Gardiner at Rotuma, South Pacific ocean. *Ann. Mag. Nat. Hist.*, Ser. 6, *20*: 371-374.

Breder, C.M. Jr. 1927. Scientific results of the first Oceangraphic Expedition of the "Pawnee" 1925. Fishes. *Bingham Oceanog. Coll., 1*(1): 1-90.

—————. 1928. Fish notes for 1927 from Sandy Hook Bay. *Copeia,* 1928 (166): 5-7.

—————. 1931. Fish notes for 1929 & 1930 from Sandy Hook Bay. *Copeia,* 1931 (2): 39-40.

—————. 1932. Fish notes for 1931 & 1932 from Sandy Hook Bay. *Copeia,* 1932 (4): 180.

—————. 1948. Observation on coloration in reference to behavior in tide pool and other marine shore fishes. *Bull. Am. Mus. Nat. Hist., 92*:285-311, 4 pls., 5 text figs.

————— and D.E. Rosen. 1966. *Modes of Reproduction in Fishes,* Am. Mus. Nat. Hist., The Natural History Press, Barden City, N.Y. 941 pp.

Brevoort, J.C. 1856. Notes on some of Japanese fishes taken from recent specimens by the artists of the U.S. Japan Expedition. *In: Narrative of the Expedition of an Amer. Squadron to the China Seas and Japan, performed in the years 1852-53-54, under the command of Commodore M.C. Perry, U.S. Navy, by order of the Gov't of the U.S. Wash. Ex. Doc. No. 97, 2:* 253-288, pl. III-XII.

—————. 1864. Enumeration of the fishes described and figured by Parra, scientifically named by Felipe Poey. (Translated and edited by J.C. Brevoort). *Proc. Acad. Nat. Sci. Phila., 1863, 15:* 174-180.

Briggs, J.C. 1955. A list of Florida fishes and their distribution. *Bull. Fla. State Mus., Biol. Sci., 2*(8): 223-318.

—————, H.D. Hoese, W. Hadley, and R.S. Jones. 1964. Twenty-two new marine fish records from the northwestern Gulf of Mexico. *Tex. J. Sci., 16*(1): 113-116.

Brock, V.E. 1938. Notes on the ranges of fishes from Lower California and the west coast of Mexico; with a discussion on the use of diving apparatus in making collections. *Copeia,* 1938 (3): 128-131.

—————. 1950. Keys to Hawaiian Fishes. *Fish and Game Special Bulletin,* No. 4: 128-134.

—————, R.S. Jones, & P. Helfrich. 1965. An ecological reconnaissance of Johnston Island and the effects of dredging. *University of Hawaii, Hawaii Mar. Lab. Tech. Rept.,* No. 5: 1-91.

Brock, V.E. & T.C. Chamberlain. 1968. A geological and ecological reconnaissance off Western Oahu, Hawaii, principally by means of the research submarine "Asherah". *Pac. Sci., 22:* 373-394.

Broussonet, P.M.A. 1782. *Ichthyologia, sistens piscium descriptiones et icones.* Decas i. London, iv + 41 pp., 11 pls.

Browne, P. 1756. *The civil and natural history of Jamaica. In three parts. Containing . . . A history of the natural productions including the various sorts of native fossils . . .* London.viii + 503 pp., 49 pls.

Buen, F. de. 1961. Los peces de la isla de Pascua. *Bol. Soc. Biol. Concepcion, Chile, 35-36:* 3-80.

Cadenat, J. 1951. Poissons de Mer du Sénégal. *Inst. Fr. Afr. Noire (I.F.A.N.), Dakar. 3:* 1-345.

_____. 1960. Notes d'Ichthyologie ouest-Africaine. XXX. Poissons de mer oest-Africaines observes du Sénégal au Cameroun et plus spécialement large des côtes de Sierra Léone et de Ghana. *Bull. I.F.A.N.* sér. A, *22*(4): 1358-1420.

_____ and E. Marchal. 1963. Résultats des campagnes océanographique de la Reine-Pokou aux îles Sainte-Hélène et Ascension. Poissons. *Bull. I.F.A.N.,* sér. A, *25*(4): 1235-1315.

_____ and C. Roux. 1964. Résultats scientifiques des campagnes de la "Calypso." Îsles du Cap Vert III. Poissons Teleostéens. *Ann. Inst. Océanogr., 41:* 81-102.

Caldwell, D.K. 1959. Observations on tropical marine fishes from the northeastern Gulf of Mexico. *Q.J. Fla. Acad. Sci., 22*(1): 69-74.

_____. 1963a. Tropical marine fishes in the Gulf of Mexico. *Q.J. Fla. Acad. Sci., 26* (2): 188-191.

_____. 1963b. Marine shore fishes from near Puerto Rico Limon, Caribbean Costa Rica. *Nat. Hist. Mus. Los Ang. Cty., Contrib. Sci.,* No. 67: 3-11.

_____ and J.C. Briggs. 1957. Range extensions of western North Atlantic fishes with notes on some soles of the genus *Gymnachirus. Bull. Fla. Acad. Sci., 2*(1): 1-11.

Cantor, T.E. 1849. Catalogue of Malayan fishes. *J. Roy. Asiat. Soc. Bengal., 18:* 983-1155, pls. (Reprint A. Asher & Co., Amsterdam. 1966).

Castelnau, F.L. de L. 1855. *Animaux nouveaux ou rares recueilles pendant l'Expédition dans les parties centrales de l'Amérique du sud. Poissons. Part vii,* Zoologie. Tom. iii, *Poissons.* xii + 112 pp., 50 col. pls.

_____. 1861. *Mémoire sur les poissons de l'Afrique australe.* Paris. vii + 78 pp.

_____. 1875. Researches on the fishes of Australia. *Intercol. Exhib. Essays, Victorian Dept.,* No. 2.

_____. 1878. Essay on the ichthyology of Port Jackson. *Proc. Linn. Soc. N.S.W., 3:* 347-402.

Catala, R. 1949. Sur un cas tératologique remarquable chez un Chaetodontidae du genre *Heniochus. Bull. Soc. Zool. Fr., 74:* 108-111.

_____. 1964. *Carnival Under the Sea.* Edited by R. Sicard, Paris. 141 pp., 27 color pls.

Catesby, M. 1731. *The natural history of Carolina, Florida and the Bahama islands; containing the figures of birds, beasts, fishes, serpents, insects and plants; Together with their descriptions in English and French . . . To the whole is prefixed a new and correct map of the countries treated of . . .* 2 vols. London. 43 color pls. (2nd ed. 1754 London, 3rd ed. 1771 London. Both edited and revised by George Edwards.)

Cervigon, F.M. 1966. Los peces marinos de Venezuela. Tome II. *Estación de Investigaciónes Marinas de Margarita, Caracas, Monografia,* No. 12: 1-951.

Chaine, J. 1958. Reserches sur les otoliths des poissons. *Bull. Cent. Étud. Rech.*

Sci. Biarritz, 2(2): 141-233. 8 pls.

Chave, E.H. and D. Echert. 1972. Distribution of fishes at Fanning Island. *Final Rept. of the Fanning Island Exped. HIG-73-13. Univ. of Hawaii:* 135-171.

_____ and P.S. Lobel. 1974. Marine and freshwater aquarium systems for tropical animals. *Sea Grant Advisory Report UNIHI-SEAGRANT-AR-74-01:* 1-88.

Chen, J.T.F. 1953. Checklist of the species of fishes known from Taiwan. (Formosa) (Concluded). *Q.J. Taiwan Mus. (Tai Pei),* 6 (2): 102-140.

_____ & L.N. Chao. 1971. A review of the Chaetodontidae of Taiwan. *Biol. Bull. 39, Dept. Biol. College Sci. Tunghai Univ. (Ichthyol. Ser.),* 9:1-69

Chevey, P. 1932. Poissons des campagnes du "de Lanessan" (1925-1929). *Trav. Inst. Océanogr. Indochine, 4th Mémoire., Icon. Icty. de l'Indochine:* 1-155, 50 col. pls.

Chhapgar, B.F. and J.K. Jatar. 1968. Records of rare fishes the family Chaetodontidae from Bombay. *J. Bombay Nat. Hist. Soc.,* 65(1): 58-63, illustr.

Chlupaty, P. 1962. About the butterflyfishes of the genus *Chaetodon. Trop. Fish Hobbyist, 11* (3): 42-47.

_____. 1964. *Schmetterlingsfische. Kleine DATZ-Bucher,* No. 18: 1-48,

Chu, K.Y. 1957. List of fishes from Pescadores Id. *Rept. Inst. Fish Biol. Minist. Econ. Aff. Natl. Taiwan Univ.,* 1 (2): 14-23.

Clemens, H.B. 1954. Fishes collected in the tropical Eastern Pacific, 1952-53. *Calif. Fish Game, 41* (2): 161-166.

_____ and J.C. Howell. 1963. Fishes collected in the eastern Pacific during tuna cruises, 1952 through 1959. *Calif. Fish. Game, 49* (4): 240-264.

Cloquet, H. 1817. *Dictionnaire des Sciences Naturelles.* vol. *8:* 369 pp.

Cockerell, T.D.A. 1915. The scales of some Australian fishes. *Mem. Queensl. Mus., 3:* 35-46.

_____. 1916. Some Australian fish scales. *Mem. Queensl. Mus., 5:* 52-57.

Colin, P. 1971. The other reef. *Sea Frontiers, 17:* 160-170.

Collette, B.B. and F.H. Talbot. 1972. Activity patterns of coral reef fishes with emphasis on nocturnal-diurnal changeover. *In:* B.B. Collette and S.A. Earle. *Results of the Tektite Program: Ecology of coral reef fishes. Nat. Hist. Mus. Los Ang. Cty., Sci. Bull., 4:* 98-124.

Collins, R.A. and R.E. Smith. 1959. Occurrence of butterflyfish in Mississippi Sound. *Copeia,* 1959 (3): 252.

Cooke, E. 1712. *A voyage to the South Seas, and round the world, performed in the years 1708, 1709, 1710, and 1711.* 2 vols. London, 1712: vol. I, 456 pp; vol, II, 318 pp.

Cope, E.D. 1870. Observations on some fishes new to the American fauna, found at Newport, R.I. by Samuel Powell. *Proc. Acad. Nat. Sci. Phila., 22:* 118-121.

_____. 1871. Contribution to the ichthyology of the Lesser Antilles. *Trans. Amer. Philos. Soc., 14:* 445-483.

Copley, H. 1944. A popular guide to some fishes of the coral reef. *J. East Afr. Ug. Nat. Hist. Soc., 17:* 295-307, 16 pls.

Cousteau, J-Y. 1952. Fish men explore a new world undersea. *Natl. Geogr. Mag.,*

Oct. 1952, *102* (4): 423-439

Cunningham, J.T. 1910. 2. On the marine fishes and invertebrates of St. Helena. *Proc. Zool. Soc. Lond.,* Jan.-Mar. 1910: 86-131, 4 pls.

Curtiss, A. 1938. *A short zoology of Tahiti.* Privately printed (Fishes on pp. 32-139)

Cuvier, G.L.C.D.F. 1817. *Le règne animal distribue d'après son organisation, pour servir de base à l'histoire naturelle des animaux et d'introduction à l'anatomie comparee.* 4 vols. Paris. Poissons, vol. 2, 532 pp. (2nd ed. 1829)

———————— and A. Valenciennes. 1831. *Histoire naturelle des poissons.* Paris. Vol. 7.

Day, Francis. 1865. *The Fishes of Malabar.* London. 293 pp., 20 col. pls.

————————. 1869. Remarks on some of the fishes in the Calcutta museum. *Proc. Zool. Soc. Lond.:* 511-527; 548-560; 611-623.

————————. 1870. On the fishes of the Andaman islands. *Proc. Zool. Soc. Lond.:* 677-705.

————————. 1873. On new or imperfectly known Fishes of India and Burmah. *J. Linn. Soc. Lond.,* 11: 524-529.

————————. 1875. *The Fishes of India . . . being a natural history of the fishes known to inhabit the seas and fresh waters of India, Burma, and Ceylon.* Text and atlas in 4 parts, x + 778 pp., 198 pls. (Reprinted by: William Dawson & Sons Ltd., London, 1958. Vol. 1 text, vol. 2 plates.)

————————. 1881. On Asiatic blowpipe fishes. *Zoologist,* 3rd ser., *5:* 91-96.

————————. 1889. Fishes. *In: The fauna of British India including Ceylon and Burma,* ed. by W.T. Blanford. 2 vols. Lond. 341 pp.

Day, J.H. and J.F.C. Morgans. 1956. The ecology of South African estuaries. Part 8. The biology of Durban Bay. *Ann. Natal Mus., 13* (part 3): 259-312, pl. IV.

Delsman, H.C. and J.D.F. Hardenberg. 1934. VI. De Indische Zeevesschen en Zeevisscherij. *Bibliotheek van den Nederlandsch-Indische Natuurhistorische Vereeniging.* N.V. Boekhandel en Drukkerij Visser & Co., Bâtavia Centrum. 388 pp., col. plates.

Desjardins, M.J. 1833. (No title.) *Proc. Zool. Soc. Lond.* Part 1, *11:* 117.

————————. 1836. Septième rapport annuel sur les traveaux de la société d'histoire naturelle de l'île Maurice. *Ann. Soc. Hist. Nat. Maurice:* 1-64.

Desmarest, A.G. 1831. Ouvres du Compte de Lacépède. *Histoire Naturelle des Poissons.* A. Paris. Tome V (pp. 356-457).

De Vis, C. 1885. New Australian fishes in the Queensland Museum. *Proc Linn. Soc. N.S.W., 9* (2): 453-462.

Doak, W. 1972. *Fishes of the New Zealand Region.* Hodder & Stoughton, Auckland, Sydney, and London. 132 pp., 48 pls.

Domm, S. and A. Domm. 1973. The sequence of appearance at dawn and disappearance at dusk of some coral reef fishes. *Pac. Sci., 27* (2): 128-135.

Dragovich, A. 1969. Review of studies of tuna food in the Atlantic Ocean. *U.S. Fish & Wildlife Serv. Spec. Sci. Rept.,* No. 593: 1-21.

————————. 1970. The food of skipjack and yellowfin tuna in the Atlantic Ocean. *Fish. Bull., 68* (3): 445-460.

Duncker, G. 1904. Die Fische der malayischen Halbinsel. *Mitth. Natur. Hist. Mus. Hamburg,* 1904, *21:* 133-207. 2 pls.

Durand, J. 1960. Chaetodontidae (Poissons Teleostéens Percoidei) récoltes au large de la Guyane. Description d'une espèce nouvelle. *Bull. Mus. Natl. Hist. nat. Paris,* Sér. 2, *32*(3): 209-213.

Eibl-Eibesfeldt, I. 1962. Freiwasserbeobachtungen zur Deutung des Schwarmverhaltens verschiedener Fische. *Z. Tierpsychol. Beit.,* 19 (2): 165-182.

——————. 1964. *Land of a Thousand Atolls.* MacGibbon & Kee, London. 195 pp.

Eigenmann, C.H. 1893. The fishes of San Diego, California. *Proc. U.S. Natl. Mus., 15:* 123-178, 9 pls.

—————— and J.E. Horning. 1887. A review of the Chaetodontidae of North America. *Ann. N.Y. Acad. Sci. 4:* 1-18.

Elera, R.P. 1895. *Catalogo sistematico de toda la fauna de Filipinas.* Vol. 1. Vertebrados. Manila, Imprenta del Colegio de Santo Tomas. 510 pp.

Erdman, D.S. 1957. Recent records from Puerto Rico. *Bull. Mar. Sci. Gulf & Caribb.,* 6(4): 315-340.

Erhardt, H. and B. Werding. 1973. Peces Chaetodontidae en las Bahias Orientales de Santa Marta. *Museo del Mar, Boletin,* No. 5: 8-17.

Evermann, B.W. and O.P. Jenkins. 1891. Report upon a collection of fishes made at Guaymas, Sonora, Mexico, with descriptions of new species. *Proc. U.S. Natl. Mus., 14:* 121-165, 2 pls.

—————— and M.C. Marsh. 1902. The fishes of Porto Rico. *Bull. U.S. Fish Comm.,* 1900, (1902), *20* (part 1): 51-350, pls. i-xlix.

—————— and A. Seale. 1923. Note on fishes from Guadalcanal, Solomon Islands. *Copeia,* 1923 (120): 77-78.

Eyiuzo, E.N.C. 1963. The identification of otoliths from west African demersal fishes. *Bull. I.F.A.N., 25A:* 488-512.

Fitch, J.E. & R.J. Lavenberg. 1975. *Tide Pool Fishes of California.* Calif. Nat. Hist. Guides, No. 38. Univ. of Calif. Press. Pp. 1-156.

Forsskål, P. 1775. *Descriptiones Animalium Avium, Amphibiorum, Piscium, Insectorum, Vermium; Quae in Itinere Orientali Observavit.* Post Mortem Auctoris Edidit Carsten Nie Buhr. Havniae, 1775. 164 pp., 43 pls., map.

Forster, J.R. 1781. *Zoologia Indica, Sistens Descriptiones Animalium Selectorum. Observationes de Finiaus et Indole Aeris, Soli, Marisque Indici; Denique Faunam Indicam.* Halae, 1781. Fol. (2nd ed. 1795)

Fourmanoir, P. 1955. Icthyologie et peche aux Comores. *Mém. Inst. Sci. Madagascar, 9A:* 187-239.

——————. 1957. Poisson teleostéens de eaux malgaches du Canal de Mozambique. *Mém. Inst. Sci. Madagascar Océanogr.,* Sér. F, *1:* 1-316, pls. 1-17.

——————. 1961. Liste complimentaire des poissons du Canal de Mozambique. *Mém. Inst. Sci. Madagascar,* Sér. F, *4:* 83-107.

——————. 1965. Liste complimentaire des poissons marins de Nha-Thrang. *Cah. O.R.S.T.O.M., No. Special,* July, 1965: 15-63.

—————— and A. Mauge. 1962. Poissons teleostéens de l'île de Sainte Marie. *Nat. Malgache, 13:* 257-264.

Fowler, H.W. 1899. Observations on fishes from the Caroline Islands. *Proc. Acad. Nat. Sci. Phila., 51:* 482-496, pls 17-18.

_____. 1900. Contribution to the ichthyology of the tropical Pacific. *Proc. Acad. Nat. Sci. Phila., 52:* 493-528, pls 18-20.

_____. 1903. Descriptions of several fishes from Zanzibar Island, two of which are new. *Proc. Acad. Nat. Sci. Phila., 55:* 161-176, pls 6-8.

_____. 1904. A collection of fishes from Sumatra. *J. Acad. Nat. Sci. Phila.,* Ser. 2, *12*(4): 497-560, pls 7-28.

_____. 1906. Some cold-blooded vertebrates of the Florida Keys. *Proc. Acad. Nat. Sci. Phila., 58:* 77-113; pls. 3-4.

_____. 1915a. A list of Santo Domingo fishes. *Copeia,* 1915 (24): 49-50.

_____. 1915b. Cold-blooded vertebrates from Florida, the West Indies, Costa Rica, and eastern Brazil. *Proc. Acad. Nat. Sci. Phila., 67:* 244-269.

_____. 1915c. The fishes of Trinidad, Grenada, and St. Lucia, British West Indies. *Proc. Acad. Nat. Sci. Phila., 67:* 520-546.

_____. 1916. Cold-blooded vertebrates from Costa Rica and the Canal Zone. *Proc. Acad. Nat. Sci. Phila. 68:* 389-414.

_____. 1917. A second collection of fishes from the Panama Canal Zone. *Proc. Acad. Nat. Sci. Phila., 69:* 127-136.

_____. 1918. A list of Philippine fishes. *Copeia,* 1918 (58): 62-65.

_____. 1919a. Notes on tropical American fishes. *Proc. Acad. Nat. Sci. Phila., 71:* 128-155.

_____. 1919b. The fishes of the United States Eclipse Expedition to West Africa. *Proc. U.S. Natl. Mus., 56:* 195-292.

_____. 1922a. Record of fishes for the southern and eastern United States. *Proc. Acad. Nat. Sci. Phila. 74:* 1-27, pls. 1-2.

_____. 1922b. A list of Hawaiian fishes. *Copeia,* 1922 (112): 82-84.

_____. 1923. New or little known Hawaiian fishes. *Occas. Pap. Bernice P. Bishop Mus., 8*(7): 373-392.

_____. 1924. Fishes from Madeira, Syria, Madagascar, and Victoria, Australia. *Proc. Acad. Nat. Sci. Phila., 75:* 33-45.

_____. 1925a. Fishes from Natal, Zululand, and Portuguese East Africa. *Proc. Acad. Nat. Sci. Phila., 77:* 187-268.

_____. 1925b. Fishes of Guam, Hawaii, Samoa, and Tahiti. *Bull. Bernice P. Bishop Mus.,* No. 22: 1-38.

_____. 1926a. Records of fishes in New Jersey. 1925. *Copeia,* 1926 (156): 146-150.

_____. 1926b. Fishes from Florida, Brazil, Bolivia, Argentina, and Chile. *Proc. Acad. Nat. Sci. Phila., 78:* 249-285.

_____. 1927a. Fishes of the tropical central Pacific. *Bull. Bernice P. Bishop Mus.,* Publ. No. 1: 38: 1-32, 1 pl.

_____. 1927b. Notes on the Philippine fishes in the collection of the Academy. *Proc. Acad. Nat. Sci. Phila., 79:* 255-297.

_____. 1928a. The fishes of Oceania. *Mem. Bernice P. Bishop Mus.,*

10: 1-540; pls 1-49.

_____. 1928b. Fishes from Florida and the West Indies. *Proc. Acad. Nat. Sci. Phila., 80:* 451-473.

_____. 1929. Notes on New Jersey fishes. *Proc. Acad. Nat. Sci. Phila., 80:* 607-614, pl. 31.

_____. 1930a. Notes on Japanese and Chinese fishes. *Proc. Acad. Nat. Sci. Phila., 81:* 589-616.

_____. 1930b. The fishes obtained by Mr. James Bond at Granada, British West Indies, in 1929. *Proc. Acad. Nat. Sci. Phila., 82:* 269-277.

_____. 1931a. Studies of Hong Kong Fishes - No. 2. *Hong Kong Nat., 2*(4): 287-317.

_____. 1931b. The fishes of Oceania. Suppl. 1. *Mem. Bernice P. Bishop Mus., 11*(5): 311-381.

_____. 1932a. The fishes obtained by Lieut. H.C. Kellers of the United States Naval Eclipse Expedition of 1930, at Niuafoou Island, Tonga Group, in Oceania. *Proc. U.S. Natl. Mus., 81*(8): 1-9.

_____. 1932b. Fishes obtained at Samoa in 1929. *Occas. Pap. Bernice P. Bishop Mus., 9* (18): 1-16.

_____. 1932c. Fishes obtained at Fiji in 1929. *Occas. Pap. Bernice P. Bishop Mus., 9* (20): 1-13.

_____. 1934a. Fishes obtained by Mr. H.W. Bell-Marley chiefly in Natal and Zululand in 1929 to 1932. *Proc. Acad. Nat. Sci. Phila., 86:* 405-514.

_____. 1934b. The fishes of Oceania. Suppl. II. *Mem. Bernice P. Bishop Mus., 11*(6): 383-466.

_____. 1934c. Zoological results of the Schauensee Third Siamese Expedition. I. Fishes. *Proc. Acad. Nat. Sci. Phila., 86:* 67-163.

_____. 1935a. Zoological results of the Third de Schauensee Siamese Expedition. Part VI. Fishes obtained in 1934. *Proc. Acad. Nat. Sci. Phila., 87:* 89-163.

_____. 1935b. South African fishes from Mr. H.W. Bell-Marley in 1935. *Proc. Acad. Nat. Sci. Phila., 87:* 361-408.

_____. 1936. The marine fishes of West Africa. Part 2. *Bull. Am. Mus. Nat. Hist., 70:* 607-1493.

_____. 1937a. Zoological results of the Third de Schaunsee Siamese Expedition. Part VIII. Fishes obtained in 1936. *Proc. Acad. Nat. Sci. Phila., 89:* 125-264.

_____. 1937b. A collection of Haytian fishes obtained by Mr. Stanley Woodward. *Proc. Acad. Nat. Sci. Phila., 89:* 309-315.

_____. 1938a. The fishes of the George Vanderbilt South Pacific Expedition, 1937. *Acad. Nat. Sci. Phila., Monogr.,* No. 2: 1-349. pls I-XII.

_____. 1938b. Studies of Hong Kong fishes. No. 3. *Hong Kong Nat.,* Suppl. No. 6: 1-52.

_____. 1938c. A list of fishes known from Malaya. *Fish. Bull., Singapore.* No. 1: 268 Pp.

_____. 1939a. Ichthyol. Notes. No. 1. *Not. Nat., Phila.,* No. 3: 1-2.

_____. 1939b. Zoological results of the George Vanderbilt Sumatran Expedition, 1936-1939. Part II. The Fishes. *Proc. Acad. Nat. Sci. Phila., 91:* 369-398.

_____. 1940. The Fishes obtained by the Wilkes Expedition, 1838-1842. *Proc. Amer. Philos. Soc., 82* (5): 733-757.

_____. 1941a. A list of fishes known from the coast of Brazil. *Arch. de Zool., Estado Sao Paulo, 3*(6): 115-184.

_____. 1941b. The George Vanderbilt Oahu Survey—The fishes. *Proc. Acad. Nat. Sci. Phila., 93:* 247-279.

_____. 1941c. Notes on Florida fishes with descriptions of seven new species. *Proc. Acad. Nat. Sci. Phila., 93:* 81-106.

_____. 1944a. Fishes obtained in the New Hebrides by Dr. Edward L. Jackson. *Proc. Acad. Nat. Sci. Phila., 96:* 155-199.

_____. 1944b. Results of the fifth George Vanderbilt Expedition. (1941) (Bahamas, Caribbean Sea, Panama, Galapagos Archipelago and Mexican Pacific Islands). *Acad. Nat. Sci. Phila., Monogr.,* No. 6: 1-583, pls. I-XX.

_____. 1945a. A study of the fish of the Southern Piedmont and Coastal Plain. *Acad. Nat. Sci. Phila., Monogr.* 7, xiii + 408 pp.

_____. 1945b. The fishes of the Red Sea. *Sudan Notes Rec. (Khartoum), 26*(1): 113-137.

_____. 1946. A collection of fishes obtained in the Riu Kiu Islands by Captain Ernest R. Tinkham, A. U.S. *Proc. Acad. Nat. Sci. Phila., 98:* 123-218.

_____. 1949. The fishes of Oceania. Suppl. 3. *Mem. Bernice P. Bishop Mus., 12*(2): 1-186.

_____. 1952a. A list of the fishes of New Jersey, with off-shore species. *Proc. Acad. Nat. Sci. Phila., 104:* 89-151.

_____. 1952b. The fishes of Hispaniola. *Mem. Soc. Cuba Hist. Nat. "Felipe Poey," 21*(1): 83-115, pls. XX-XXVI.

_____. 1953. A synopsis of the fishes of China. Part VII. *Q.J. Taiwan Mus. (Taipei), 6*(1): 1-77.

_____. 1955. A collecton of coral reef fishes made by Dr. and Mrs. Marshall Laird at Fiji. *Trans. R. Soc. N. Z., 82*(2): 373-381.

_____. 1959. *Fishes of Fiji.* Printed by the Government of Fiji, Suva, Fiji. Pp. 1-670.

_____ & S.C. Ball. 1925. Fishes of Hawaii, Johnston Island and Wake Island. *Bull. Bernice P. Bishop Mus.,* No. 26: 1-31.

_____ & B.A. Bean. 1923. Fishes from Formosa and the Philippine Islands. *Proc. U.S. Natl. Mus., 62* (2448): 1-73.

_____ and _____. 1928. Notes on fishes obtained in Sumatra, Java, and Tahiti. *Proc. U.S. Natl. Mus. 71* (2682): 1-15.

_____ and _____. 1929. The fishes of the series Capriformes, Ephippiformes, and Squamipennes, collected by the US Bureau of Fisheries steamer "Albatross", chiefly in Philippine seas and adjacent waters. *U.S. Natl. Mus. Bull., 100* (8): 1-352.

_____ and C.F. Silverster. 1922. A collection of fishes from Samoa.

Carnegie Inst. Washington Publ. 18. (312): 109-126.

Franz, V. 1910. Die japanischen Knochenfische der Sammlungen Haberer und Doflein. *In:* Beitrage zur Naturgeschichte Ostasiens. Hrgs. von F. Doflein. *Abhand. Math.-Phys. Klasse K. Bayer. Akad. Wiss.*, Suppl. IV, No. 1: 135 pp., pls.

Fraser-Brünner, A. 1945. On the systematic position of a fish, *Microcanthus strigatus* (C. & V.) *Ann. Mag. Nat. Hist.* Ser. 11, *12:* 462.

—————. 1949. *Holacanthus xanthotis,* sp. n., and other chaetodont fishes from the Gulf of Aden. *Proc. Zool. Soc. Lond., 120:* 43-48, pls. I-II.

Freihofer, W.C. 1963. Patterns of the ramus lateralis accessorius and their systematic significance in Teleostean fishes. *Stanford Ichthyol. Bull., 8*(2): 80-189.

—————. 1966. New distributional records for the butterflyfish *Chaetodon falcifer. Standford Ichthyol. Bull., 8*(3): 207.

Fricke, H.W. 1965a. Zum verhalten des putzerfische *Labroides dimidiatus. Z. Tierpsychol., 23:* 1-3.

—————. 1965b. Attrappenversuche mit einigen plakatfarbigen Korallenfischen in Roten Meer. *Z. Tierpsychol., 23:* 4-7.

Galloway, J.C. 1941. Lethal effect of the cold winter of 1939-40 on the marine fishes at Key West, Florida. *Copeia,* 1941 (2): 118-119.

Galstoff, P.S. 1933. Pearl and Hermes Reef, Hawaii, hydrographical and biological observations. *Bull. Bernice P. Bishop Mus., 107:* 1-49.

Garret, A.J. 1863. Descriptions of new species of fishes. *Proc. Calif. Acad. Nat. Sci., 3:* 63-66, 103-107.

George, K.C., & M.G. Dayanandan. 1968. *Atrophacanthus danae* Fraser-Brünner and *Chaetodon jayakari* Norman, new records of fishes from the Arabian sea off the southwest coast of India. *J. Mar. Biol. Assoc. India, 8:* 220-222.

Gilbert, C. 1972. Characteristics of the Western Atlantic reef fish fauna. *Q.J. Fla. Acad. Sci., 35* (2/3): 103-104.

Gilbert, C.H. 1905. Section II. The deep-sea fishes of the Hawaiian islands. *In:* Jordan and Evermann. The Aquatic Resources of the Hawaiian Islands. *Bull. U.S. Fish Comm. for 1903 (1905), 23* (part 2): 575-713, 45 pls.

Gilbert, C.H., and E.C. Starks. 1904. The fishes of Panama Bay. *Mem. Calif. Acad. Sci., 4:* 1-304, pls. 1-33.

Gilchrist, J.F.D., and W.W. Thompson. 1908. Descriptions of fishes from the coast of Natal. *Ann. S. Afr. Mus., 6* (part 1, No. 3): 145-206; 213-279.

Gill. T. 1862. Descriptions of two new species of marine fishes. *Proc. Acad. Nat. Sci. Phila., 13:* 98-99.

—————. 1863a. Remarks on the relations of the genera and other groups of Cuban fishes. *Proc. Acad. Nat. Sci. Phila., 14:* 235-242.

—————. 1863b. Catalogue of the fishes of lower California in the Smithsonian Institution, collected by Mr. J. Xantus. Part II. *Proc. Acad. Nat. Sci. Phila., 14:* 242-246.

—————. 1864. Descriptive enumeration of a collection of fishes from the western coast of Central America, presented to the Smithsonian Institution by Capt. John M. Dow. *Proc. Acad. Nat. Sci. Phila., 15:* 162-180.

_____. 1882. Note on the affinities of the Ephippiids. *Proc. U.S. Natl. Mus.*, *5:* 557-560.

_____. 1891. The characteristics of the family of scatophagoid fishes. *Proc. U.S. Natl. Mus.*, *13:* 355-360.

_____. 1903. On some fish genera of the first edition of Cuvier's *Règne Animal* and Oken's names. *Proc. U.S. Natl. Mus.*, *26:* 965-967.

Giltay, L. 1937. Poissons. *In:* Résultats scientifiques du voyage aux Indes Orientales Néerlandaises. *Mém. Mus. R. Hist. Nat. Belg.*, *5* (fasc. 3): 1-129.

Gmelin, J.F. 1788. *Caroli a Linne . . . Systema Naturae per regna tria naturae, secundum classes, ordines, genera, species, cum characteribus, differentiis, synonymis, locis.* Tomus I (-) III. Edito decimo tertia, aucta, reformata, Cura Jo(annis) Fred(erico) Gmelin. *1* (part 3): 1240-1269.

Goldman, B. 1967. *Chaetodon aphrodite*, the juvenile of *Ch. flavirostris* (Teleostei, Chaetodontidae). *Proc. Roy. Zool. Soc. N.S.W., for the years 1965-66:* 45-51, pls. 8-9.

Golvan, Y.J. 1965. *Catalogue Systématique des noms de genres de poissons Actuels* . . . Masson et Cie., Editeurs, 120, bd. St.Germain, Paris.

Goode, G.B. 1876. Catalogue of the fishes of the Bermudas, based chiefly upon the collections of the United States National Museum. *Bull. U.S. Natl. Mus.*, *1* (5): 1-82.

_____. 1879a. A preliminary catalogue of the fishes of the St. John's river and the east coast of Florida, with descriptions of a new genus and three new species. *Proc. U.S. Natl. Mus.*, *2:* 108-121.

_____. 1880b. Catalogue of a collection of fishes sent from Pensacola, Florida, and vicinity, by Mr. Silas Stearns, with descriptions of six new species. *Proc. U.S. Natl. Mus.*, *2:* 121-156.

_____ and T.H. Bean.1882. A list of the species of fishes recorded as occurring in the Gulf of Mexico. *Proc. U.S. Natl. Mus.*, *5:* 234-240.

Gorjanovic-Kramberger, C. 1895. De piscibus fossilibus Comeni, Mrzleci, Lesinae et M. Libanonis, et appendix de piscibus oligocaenicis ad Tuffer, Sagor et Trifail. *Opera Acad. Sci. Art, Slav. Merid. Agram.*, *16:* 1-67, 12 pls.

_____. 1898. Ueber fossile Fische von tuffer in Steiermark und Jurjevcani in Kroatien. *Glasnik Naravosl. Druzt., Zagreb, 10:* 12-34, pls. 2-3.

Gosline, W.A. 1955. The inshore fish fauna of Johnston Island, a central Pacific atoll. *Pac. Sci.*, *9* (4): 442-480.

_____. 1958. The nature and evolution of the Hawaiian inshore fish fauna. *Eighth Pac. Sci. Congress*, *3:* 347-357.

_____. 1965. Vertical zonation of inshore fishes in the upper water layers of the Hawaiian Islands. *Ecology*, *46* (6): 823-831.

_____. 1968. Considerations regarding the evolution of Hawaiian animals. *Pac. Sci.*, *22*(2): 267-273.

_____. 1971. The zoogeographic relationships of Fanning Island inshore fishes. *Pacific. Sci.*, *25:* 282-289.

_____ and V. Brock. 1960. *Handbook of Hawaiian Fishes.* Univ. of Hawaii Press, Honolulu. ix + 372 pp.

Grant, E.M. 1965. *Guide to Fishes.* Department of Harbours and Marine,

Queensland. 267 pp.

Gray, J.E. 1831. Description of three new species of fish from the Sandwich Islands, in the British Museum. *Zool. Misc.:* 33.

_____(Ed.).' 1854. *Catalogue of fish collected and described by L.T. Gronow, now in the British Museum.* London. Vol. 2.

Greenwood, P.H., D.E. Rosen, S.H. Weitzman, and G. Myers. 1966. Phyletic studies of teleostean fishes, with a provisional classification of living forms. *Bull. Amer. Mus. Nat. Hist., 131* (4): 339-356.

Gregory, W.K. 1932. Some strange teleost skulls and their deviation from normal forms. *Copeia,* 1932 (2): 53-60.

_____. 1933. Fish Skulls. *Trans. Am. Philos. Soc. 23* (part 2): 481pp.

_____ & LaMonte.1947. *The world of fishes.* Amer. Mus. Nat. Hist., Sci. Guide, No. 122: 1-96.

Gronovius, L.T. 1754. *Museum Ichthyologicum, sistens et quorundum exoticorum, qui in Museo Laur. Theod. Gronovii, adservantur, descriptiones, ordine systematico; accedunt nonnullorum exoticorum piscium icones, aeri incisae. 2 vols. Lugduni, 1754-56. 70, 46 pp., 25 pls. fol. (Vol. 1, 1754, contains the fishes).*

Gruvel, A. 1925. *L'Indo-Chine—Ses Richesses Marines et Fluviales—Exploitation actuelle avenir.* Paris. Société D'éditions. 319 pp., 26 pls.

Gudger, E.W. 1929. Morphology and behavior of 70 Teleostean fishes of the Tortugas, Florida. *Pap. Tortugas Lab., Carnegie Inst. Wash.,* Publ. No. 391: 149-204, 4 pls.

Guichenot, A. 1848. Notice sur l'établissement d'un nouveau genre de Chétodons *(Megaprotodon). Rev. Zool., 11:* 12-14.

_____. 1863. Faune Ichthyologique. *In:* Maillard, L. *Notes sur l'île de la Réunion.* Appendix C. Paris, 32 pp.

Gunter, G. 1950. Correlation between temperature of water and size of marine fishes on the Atlantic and Gulf coasts of the United States. *Copeia,* 1950 (4): 298-304.

Günther, A. 1860. *Catalogue of the fishes of the British Museum.* Vol. 2, Acanthopterygii. xii + 548 pp.

_____. 1868a. Additions to the ichthyological fauna of Zanzibar. *Ann. Mag. Nat. Hist.,* 4th ser., *1:* 457-459.

_____. 1868b. 4. Report on a collection of fishes made at St. Helena by J.C. Mellis, Esq. *Proc. Zool. Soc. Lond.,* 1868: 225-228, pls. 18-19.

_____. 1869a. An account of the fishes of the states of Central America, based on collections made by Capt. J.M. Dow, F. Godman, and O. Salvin, Esq. *Trans. Zool. Soc. London, 6:* 377-494, 24 pls.

_____. 1869b. Report of a second collection of fishes made at St. Helena by J.C. Mellis, Esq. *Proc. Zool. Soc. Lond.,* 1869: 238-239, pl. 16.

_____. 1871a. On the young state of fishes belonging to the family Squamipinnes. *Ann. Mag. Nat. Hist; 4th ser., 8:* 318-320.

_____. 1871b. Report on several collections of fishes recently obtained for the British Museum. *Proc. Zool. Soc. Lond.,* 1871: 652-675, 18 pls.

_____. 1873. Reptiles and fishes of the South Sea Islands. *In:* Brenchley, J.L. *Jottings during cruise of H.M.S. "Curacoa" among the South Sea*

Islands in 1865, etc. London 1873, 487 pp. 59 pls.

_____. 1874a. Descriptions of new species of fishes in the British Museum. *Ann. Mag. Nat. Hist.,* 4th Ser., *14:* 368-371; 453-455.

_____. 1874b. Andrew Garrett's Fische der Sudsee, beschrieben und redigirt von A.C.L.G. Gunther. *J. Mus. Godeffroy, 2-3* (5-6): 25-96, pls. 21-29.

_____. 1880. *Report on the shore fishes procured during the voyage of the H.M.S. "Challenger" in the years 1873-1876.* (Reprint 1963, J. Cramer, Weinhein, pp. 1-82.)

_____. 1899. Complete catalogue of Linne's private collection of fishes, now in possession of the Linnaean Society. In: President's anniversary address, one hundred and eleventh session, 1898-99. *Proc. Linn. Soc. London for 1899:* 15-38.

Haburay, K., C.F. Crooke, and R. Hastings. 1969. Tropical marine fishes from Pensacola, Florida. *Q.J. Fla. Acad. Sci., 31:* 213-219.

Hamilton, W.J. III, and R.M. Petermann. 1971. Countershading in the colorful reef fish *Chaetodon lunula:* concealment, communication or both? *Anim. Beh., 19*(2): 357-364.

Hardenberg, J.D.F. 1939. Some new or rare fishes of the Indo-Australian Archipelago. VII. *Treubia, 17*(2): 113-122.

Halstead, B.W. & N.C. Bunker 1954. A survey of the poisonous fishes of the Phoenix Islands. *Copeia,* 1954 (1): 1-11.

Harry, R.R. 1940. A new species of goby and new records of fishes from the Solomon Islands. *J. Wash. Acad. Sci., 39* (4): 140-146.

_____. 1953. Ichthyological field data of Raroia Atoll, Tuamotu Archipelago. *Atoll Res. Bull.,* No. 18: 1-190.

Hay, O.P. 1903. On certain genera and species of North American Cretaceous actinopterous fishes. *Bull. Am. Mus. Nat. Hist., 19:* 1-95, pls. 1-5.

Helfman, G.S. and J.E. Randall. 1973. Palauan fish names. *Pac. Sci., 27* (2): 136-153.

Hennig, Willi. 1966. *Phylogenetic Systematics.* Univ. of Ill. Press. 263 pp.

Henshall, J.A. 1891. Report upon a collection of fishes made in southern Florida during 1889. *Bull. U.S. Fish Comm., 9:* 371-389.

Herald, Earl S. 1961. *Living Fishes of the World.* Doubleday & Co. Inc., Garden City, New York. 304 pp.

Herre. A.W.C.T. 1931a. A check-list of fishes from the Solomon Islands. *J. Pan-Pac. Res. Inst., 6* (4): 4-9.

_____. 1931b. A list of fishes collected at Moorea, one of the Society Islands, being the first record from this island. *J. Pan-Pac. Res. Inst., 6* (4): 10.

_____. 1931c. A checklist of the fishes recorded from the New Hebrides. *J. Pan-Pac. Res. Inst., 6* (4): 11-14.

_____. 1932. A check-list of the fishes recorded from Tahiti. *J. Pan-Pac. Res. Inst., 7* (1): 2-6.

_____. 1933a. A check-list of fishes from Sandakan, British North Borneo. *J. Pan-Pac. Res. Inst., 8 (4): 2-5.*

_____. 1933b. A check-list of fishes from Damaguete, Oriental Negros, P.I., and its immediate vicinity. *J. Pan-Pac. Res. Inst.*, *8*(4): 6-11.

_____. 1934a. *Notes on fishes in the Zool. Mus. of Stanford Univ. 1. The fishes of the Herre Philippine Exped. of 1931.* 106 pp. (Published by the author.)

_____. 1934b. Notes on fishes in the zoological museum of Stanford University. VI. New and rare Hong Kong fishes obtained in 1934. *Hong Kong Nat.*, *6* (3/4): 285-293.

_____. 1935. A check-list of the fishes of Pelew Islands. *J. Pan-Pac. Res. Inst.*, *10* (2): 161-176.

_____. 1936. Fishes of the Crane Pacific Expedition. *Field Mus. Nat. Hist. Publ.*, Zool. Ser., *21* (353): 1-31.

_____. 1939. On a collection of fishes from Nanyo, the Japanese mandated island. *Annot. Zool. Jpn.*, *18*(4): 298-307.

_____. 1941. A list of fishes known from the Andaman Isl. *Mem. Indian Mus.*, *15* (3): 331-403.

_____. 1942. Notes on a collection of fishes from Antigua and Barbados, B.W.I. *Stanford Univ. Pub. Biol. Soc.*, *7:* 289-305.

_____ and G.S. Meyers. 1938. A contribution to the ichthology of the Malay Peninsula. *Bull. Raffles Mus.*, *13:* 5-75.

_____ and H.R. Montalban. 1927. The Philippine butterflyfishes and their allies. *Phil. J. Sci.*, *34*(1): 1-113, pls 1-24.

Hiatt, R.W. and D.W. Strasburg. 1960. Ecological relationships of the fish fauna on coral reefs of the Marshall Islands. *Ecol. Monogr.*, *30:* 65-127.

Hildebrand, H.H., Chavez, H., & H. Compton, 1964. Aporte al conocimiento de los peces del arrecife Alacranes, Yucatan (Mexico). *Trabajo y Investigaciónes No. 5, Instituto Tecnológico de Vera Cruz, Estación de Biologia Marina.* 32 pp.

Hildebrand. S.F. 1946. A descriptive catalogue of the shore fishes of Peru. *Bull. U.S. Nat. Mus.*, *189:* 1-530.

_____ & L.E. Cable. 1938. Further notes on the development and life history of some teleosts at Beaufort, N.C. *Bull. U.S. Bur. of Fish.*, *48:* 505-642.

_____ and W.C. Schroeder. 1928. Fishes of Chesapeake Bay. *Bull. U.S. Bur. Fish.*, *43(1):* 1-388.

Hobson, E.S. 1965. A visit with el barbero. *Underwater Nat.*, *3*(3): 5-10, 5 figs.

_____. 1968. Coloration and activity of fishes, day and night. *Underwater Nat.*, *5* (3): 6-11, 4 figs.

_____. 1971. Cleaning symbiosis among California inshore fishes. *U.S. Fish & Wildlife Serv. Fish Bull.*, *69* (3): 491-523.

_____. 1972. Activity of Hawaiian reef fishes during the evening and morning transistions between daylight and darkness. *U.S. Natl. Mar. Fish. Serv. Fish. Bull.*, *70* (3): 715-740.

_____. 1974. Feeding relationships of Teleostean fishes on coral reefs in Kona, Hawaii. *U.S. Natl. Mar. Fish. Serv. Fish. Bull.*, *72* (4): 95-131.

Honma, Y. 1952. A list of the fishes collected in the Province of Echigo, incl.

Sado Island. *Jap. J. Ichthy.*, 2 (4/5): 220-229.

Hora, S.L. 1924. Zool. results of a tour in the Far East. Fish of the Tale Sap, Peninsular Siam. Parts I, II. *Mem. Asiat. Soc. Bengal, Calcutta, 6:* 463-476, 479-501.

Howell y Rivero, F. 1938. On the types of Poey's Fishes in the Museum of Comparative Zoology. *Bull. Mus. Comp. Zool., 82:* 169-227.

Hubbs, C.L.' 1943. Criteria for subspecies, species and genera as determined by researches on fishes. *Ann N.Y. Acad. Sci., 44* (art. 2): 109-121.

————. 1963. *Chaetodon aya* and related deep-living butterflyfishes: their variation, distribution and synonymy. *Bull. Mar. Sci. Gulf Caribb., 13*(1): 133-192.

———— and A.B. Rechnitzer. 1958. A new fish, *Chaetodon falcifer,* from Guadalupe Island, Baja California, with notes on related species. *Proc. Calif. Acad. Sci.,* (4th Ser.), *29* (8): 273-313, 3 pls.

Huntsman, G.R. and I.G. MacIntyre 1971. Tropical coral patches in Onslow Bay. *Underwater Naturalist,* 1 (2): 32-34.

Inger, Robert F. 1957. Report on a collection of marine fishes from North Borneo. *Fieldiana, Zool., 36* (3): 339-405.

Irvine, F.R. 1947. *The fishes and fisheries of the Gold Coast.*

Jatzow, R. and H. Lenz. 1898. Fische von Ost-Afrika, Madagaskar und Aldabra. *Abhand. Senckenb. Naturf. Gesel. Frankfurt, 21:* 497-531, pls. 34-36.

Jenkins, O.P. 1901. Description of fifteen new species of fishes from the Hawaiian Islands. *Bull. U.S. Fish Comm.* 1899, *19:* 387-404.

————. 1904. Report on collections of fishes made in the Hawaiian Islands, with descriptions of new species. *Bull. U.S. Fish Comm.,* 1902, *22:* 417-511, 4 pls.

Jones, R.S. and J.A. Chase. 1975. Community structure and distribution of fishes in an enclosed high island lagoon in Guam. *Micronesica, 11* (1): 127-148.

Jones, S. and M. Kumaran. 1967. New Records of fishes from the seas around India. Part 3. *J. Mar. Biol. Assoc. India, 7* (2): 381-400.

———— and ————. 1968. New records of fishes from the seas around India. Part 5. *J. Mar. Biol. Assoc. India, 9*(1): 1-12.

Jordan, D.S. 1884a. Notes on species of fishes improperly ascribed to the fauna of North America. *Proc. Acad. Nat. Sci. Phila., 36:* 97-103.

————. 1884b. The fishes of the Florida Keys. *Bull. U.S. Fish Comm., 4* (35): 77-80.

————. 1885. An identification of the figures of fishes in Catesby's "Natural History of Carolina, Florida, and the Bahama islands." *Proc. U.S. Nat. Mus., 7:* 190-199.

————. 1886. A list of the fishes known from the Pacific coast of tropical America, from the Tropic of Cancer to Panama. *Proc. U.S. Nat. Mus., 8:* 361-394.

————. 1887a. Notes on fishes collected at Beaufort, North Carolina with a revised list of the species known from that locality. *Proc. U.S. Nat. Mus., 9:* 25-30.

————. 1887b. List of fishes collected at Havana, Cuba, in December

1883, with notes and descriptions. *Proc. U.S. Nat. Mus., 9:* 31-55.

_____. 1887c. Notes on some fishes collected at Pensacola by Mr. Silas Stearns, with descriptions of one new species *(Chaetodon aya). Proc. U.S. Nat. Mus, 9:* 225-229.

_____. 1887d. A preliminary list of the fishes of the West Indies. *Proc. U.S. Natl. Mus, 9:* 554-608.

_____. 1890a. Scientific results of explorations by the U.S. Fish Comm. Steamer "Albatross". IX. A catalogue of fishes collected at Port Castries, Saint Lucia, by the steamer "Albatross," November 1888. *Proc. U.S. Natl. Mus, 12* (789): 645-652.

_____. 1890b. Scientific results of explorations by the U.S. Fish Comm. steamer "Albatross". XVIII. A list of fishes collected in the harbor of Bahia, Brazil, and in adjacent waters by the U.S. Fish Commission steamer "Albatross". *Proc. U.S. Natl. Mus., 13* (829): 313-316.

_____. 1895. The fishes of Sinaloa. *Hopkins Lab. Contrib. Biol., 1:* 377-514, pls. 27-55.

_____.1903. Supplemental note on *Bleekeria mitsukurii,* and on certain Japanese fishes. *Proc. U.S. Nat. Mus., 26* (1328): 693-696.

_____. 1918. Note on Gistel's genera of fishes. *Proc. Acad. Nat. Sci. Phila., 70:* 335-340.

_____. 1922. Descriptions of deep-sea fishes from the coast of Hawaii, killed by a lava flow from Mauna Loa. *Proc. U.S. Natl. Mus., 59* (2392): 643-656.

_____. 1923. *Roa.* - A genus of chaetodont fishes. *Copeia,* 1923 (118): 63.

_____. 1927. Fishes of the Pacific Ocean: Shore fishes of Sinaloa. *J. Pan-Pac. Res. Inst., 2* (4): 3-11.

_____ and C.H. Bollman 1889. List of fishes collected at Green Turtle Cay, in the Bahamas, by Charles L. Edwards, with descriptions of three new species. *Proc. U.S. Nat. Mus., 11:* 549-553.

_____ and M.C. Dickerson 1908. On a collection of fishes from Fiji, with notes on certain Hawaiian fishes. *Proc. U.S. Nat. Mus., 34* (1625): 603-617.

_____ and B.W. Evermann. 1898. The fishes of North and Middle America. A descriptive catalogue of the species of fish-like vertebrates found in the waters of North America, north of the isthmus of Panama. *Bull. U.S. Natl. Mus., 47* (2): 1241-2183.

_____ and _____. 1903. Notes on a collection of fishes from the island of Formosa. *Proc. U.S. Natl. Mus., 25* (1289) : 315-368.

_____ and _____. 1905. The aquatic resources of the Hawaiian Islands. Part. 1.-The Shore Fishes of the Hawaiian Islands, with a general account of the fish fauna. *Bull. U.S. Fish Comm., 23* (1): 1-574, 73 col. pls.

_____ and _____. 1926. A check list of the fishes of Hawaii. *J. Pan-Pac. Res. Inst., 1 (1): 3-15.*

_____, _____ and H.W. Clark. 1930. Check list of the fishes

and fish-like vertebrates of North and Middle America north of the northern boundary of Venezuela and Colombia. *Rept. U.S. Comm. Fish Fiscal Year 1928,* part 2: 670 pp.

——————, ——————, and S. Tanaka. 1927. Notes on new or rare fishes from Hawaii. *Proc. Calif. Acad. Sci.,* Ser. 4, *16* (20): 649-680, pls. 22-24.

—————— and H.W. Fowler. 1902. A review of the Chaetodonidae and related families of fishes found in the waters of Japan. *Proc. U.S. Natl. Mus., 25* (1296): 513-563.

—————— and C.H. Gilbert. 1883. A synopsis of the fishes of North America. *Bull. U.S. Natl. Mus., 16:*1-1018.

—————— and ——————. 1883. List of fishes collected at Mazatlan, Mexico, by Charles Henry Gilbert. *Bull. U.S. Fish. Comm.,* 1882, 2: 105-108.

—————— and ——————. 1883. Catalogue of the fishes collected by Mr. John Xantus at Cape San Lucas, which are now in the USNM, with descriptions of eight new species. *Proc. U.S. Natl. Mus.,* 1882 5: 353-371.

—————— and ——————. 1883. List of fishes collected at Panama by Capt. John M. Dow, now in the United States National Museum. *Proc. U.S. Natl. Mus., 5:* 373-378.

—————— and ——————. 1883. On certain neglected generic names of Lacépède. *Proc. U.S. Natl. Mus., 5:* 570-576.

—————— and ——————. 1883. List of fishes collected at Panama by Charles H. Gilbert. *Bull. U.S. Fish Comm., 2:* 109-111.

—————— and ——————. 1887. Lists of fishes collected at Havana, Cuba, in December 1883, with notes and descriptions. *Proc. U.S. Natl. Mus., 9:* 31-55.

—————— and C.L. Hubbs. 1925. Record of fishes obtained by David Starr Jordan in Japan, 1922. *Mem. Carnegie Mus., 10* (2): 93-346, pls. 5-12.

—————— and E.K. Jordan. 1922. A list of the fishes of Hawaii, with notes and descriptions of new species. *Mem. Carnegie Mus., 10* (1): 1-92.

—————— and R.C. McGregor. 1899. List of fishes collected at the Revillagigedo Archipelago and neighboring islands. *Rept. U.S. Fish Comm., 24:* 271-284, 2 pls.

—————— and R.E. Richardson. 1908. Fishes from islands of the Philippine Archipelago. *Bull. Bur. Fish., 27:* 233-287.

—————— and ——————. 1909. A catalogue of the fishes of Formosa, or Taiwan, based on the collections of Dr. Hans Sauter. *Mem. Carnegie Mus., 4* (4): 159-204, 11 pls.

—————— and ——————. 1910. Checklist of the species of fishes known from the Philippine Archipelago. *Manila Bur. Printing,* Publ. No. 1: 1-78.

—————— and C. Rutter. 1898. A collection of fishes made by Joseph Seed Roberts in Kingston, Jamaica. *Proc Acad. Nat. Sci. Phila., 49:* 91-133.

—————— and A. Seale. 1905. List of fishes collected by Dr. Bashford Dean on the island of Negros, Philippines. *Proc. U.S. Nat. Mus., 28:* 769-803.

_____ and _____. 1906. The Fishes of Samoa. Descriptions of the species found in the archipelago, with a provisional check-list of the fishes of Oceania. *Bull. Bur. Fish.*, *25:* 175-455. 20 pls.

_____ and _____. 1906. List of fishes collected in 1882-83 by Pierre Louis Jouy at Shanghai and Hong Kong, China. *Proc. U.S. Nat. Mus.*, *29* (1433): 517-529.

_____ and A. Seale. 1907. Fishes of the islands of Luzon and Panay. *Bull. Bur. Fisheries*, *26:* 1-48.

_____ and J.O. Snyder, 1901. A preliminary check-list of the fishes of Japan. *Annot. Zool. Jap.*, Tokyo, 1899, *3:* 1-159.

_____ and _____. 1901. List of fishes collected in 1883 and 1885 by Pierre Louis Jouy and preserved in the U.S. National Museum, with descriptions of six new species., *Proc. U.S. Natl. Mus.*, *23* (1235): 739-769, 6 pls.

_____ and _____. 1904. Notes on collections of fishes from Oahu island and Laysan island, Hawaii, with descriptions of four new species. *Proc. U.S. Natl. Mus.*, *27* (1377): 939-948.

_____ and _____. 1905. A list of fishes collected in Tahiti by Mr. Henry P. Bowie. *Proc. U.S. Natl. Mus.*, *29* (1422): 353-357.

_____ and E.C. Starks. 1906. List of fishes collected on Tanega and Yaku, offshore islands of southern Japan, by Robert van Vleck Anderson, with descriptions of seven new species. *Proc. U.S. Natl. Mus.*, *30* (1462): 695-706.

_____ and _____. 1907. List of fishes recorded from Okinawa or the Riu Kiu islands of Japan. *Proc. U.S. Natl. Mus.*, *32* (1541): 491-504.

_____, S. Tanaka, and J.O. Snyder. 1913. A catalogue of the fishes of Japan. *Journal of the College of Science*, Imperial University, Tokyo, 33 (1): 1-497.

_____ and J.C. Thompson. 1905. The fish-fauna of the Tortugas archipelago. *Bull. Bur. Fish. for 1904*, *24:* 229-256.

_____ and W.F. Thompson. 1914. Record of the fishes obtained in Japan in 1911. *Mem. Carnegie Mus.*, *6* (4): 205-313, 19 pls.

Jordan, E.K. 1925. Notes on the fishes of Hawaii with descriptions of six new species. *Proc. U.S. Nat. Mus.* 66 (2570): 1-43.

Jordano, D. and M. Muruve. 1959. Ocho pecas trópicales en mercados españoles y cuatro primeras citaciónes para las pesquerias canario-africanas. *Arch. Zootech.* 8 (30): 103-129.

Jouan, H. 1873. Notes sur l'archipel Hawaiien (Îles Sandwich). *Mém. soc. Nat. Sci. Nat. Cherbourg*, *17:* 5-104.

Kailola, P. 1975. A catalogue of the fish reference collection at the Kanudi Fisheries Research Laboratory, Port Moresby. *Dept. Agric., Stock and Fish., Port Moresby, Res. Bull.*, No. 16: 1-277.

Kami, H.T. 1971. Checklist of Guam fishes. Suppl. 1. *Micronesica*, *7:* 215-228.

_____, I.I. Ikehara, and F.P. DeLeon. 1968. Check-list of Guam fishes. *Micronesica*, *4* (1): 95-131.

Kamohara, T. 1935. Distribution of Chaetodontidae in Tosa. *Bot. and Zool., 3-4:* 730-736.

———. 1942. Twelve unrecorded species of fishes from Kii Peninsula. *Annot. Zool. Jap., 21* (3): 163-168.

———. 1952a. Additions to the fish fauna of Prov. Tosa, Japan. *Rep. Kochi Univ. Nat. Sci.,* No. 2: 1-10.

———. 1952b. Revised descriptions of the offshore bottom fish of Prov. Tosa, Shikoku, Japan. *Rep. Kochi Univ. Nat. Sci.,* No. 3: 1-122.

———. 1954. A list of fishes from the Tokara Islands. Kagoshima Prefecture, Japan. *Publ. Seto Marine Biol. Lab., 3* (3): 266-299.

———. 1955. The fishes from the Tokara Islands. *Res. Rep. Kochi Univ., 4 (8):* 1-11.

———. 1957a. List of fishes from Amami-Oshima and adjacent regions, Kagoshima Prefecture, Japan. *Rep. Usa Biol. Stn., Kochi Univ., Japan, 4* (1): 1-65.

———. 1957b. Some little known fishes from Kochi Prefecture (Prov. Tosa), Japan, including one new species of the Family Peristediidae. *Jpn. J. Ichthyol., 6:* 75-81.

———. 1958a. A catalogue of fishes of Kochi Prefecture (Province Tosa), Japan. *Rep. Usa Mar. Biol. Stn.,* 5(1): 1-76.

———. 1958b. The fishes of Urado Bay, Kochi Prefecture. *Res. Rep. Kochi Univ. Nat. Sci., 7* (13): 1-11.

———. 1960. On the shore fishes of Okinoshima and adjacent regions, Kochi Prefecture, Japan. *Res. Rep. Kochi Univ. Nat. Sci., 9* (3): 1-30.

———. 1961a. Notes on the type of specimens of fishes in my laboratory. *Rep. Usa Mar. Biol. Stn., 8* (2): 1-9, 7 pls.

———. 1961b. Additional records of marine fishes from Kochi Prefecture, Japan, including one new genus of the Parapercid. *Rep. Usa Mar. Biol Stn., 8 (1):* 1-8.

———. 1964a. On the fishes of the family Chaetodontidae obtained in the Okinawa and the Yaeyama Islands. *Rep. Usa Mar. Biol. Stn. 11* (2): 1-6, 3 pls.

———. 1964b. Revised catalogue of fishes of Kochi Prefecture Japan. *Rep. Usa Mar. Biol. Stn., 11* (1): 1-99.

———. 1965. Chaetodontidae. *In:* Okada, K., S. Uchida, and T. Uchida. Eds. *New Illustrated Enclyclopedia of the Fauna of Japan* (III). Hokura-Kan, Tokyo. Pp. 390-395.

——— and T. Yamakawa. 1968. Additional records of marine fishes from Amami. (II). *Rep. Usa Mar. Biol. Stn.,* 15(2): 1-x.

Kataoka, T., and S. Kitamura, M. Sehido, and K. Yamamoto. 1970. *Coral fishes of the Ogasawara (Bonin) Islands. Rept. on the marine biological expedition to the Ogasawara (Bonin) Islands, 1968.* Toba Aquarium and Asahi Shimbun Publ. Co. Pp. 7-40, 33 pls.

Katayama, M. 1957. On some rare fishes from Izu-Oshima, Japan. *Jpn. J. Ichthyol., 6* (4/5/6): 147-152.

——— & Y. Fujioka. 1958. Fishes of Oosima-gun, Yamaguti Prefecture. *Bull. Fac. Agric. Yamaguti Univ.*, No. 9: 1-16.

Kato, S. 1944. *(Oplegnathus fasciatus, Chaetodon nippon* and *Pomacentrus coelestis).* Collecting and Breeding, 6 (9): 209.

Kaup. J.J. 1860. Ueber die Chaetodontidae. *Archiv. fur Naturg.*, 26(part 1): 133-156.

——————. 1863. Ueber einige Arten der Gattung *Chaetodon. Nederl. Tijdschr. Dierk.*, 1: 125-129.

Kendall, W.C. and E.L. Goldsborough. 1911. The Shore Fishes. *In:* Reports of the scientific results of the expedition to the tropical Pacific, in charge of Alexander Agassiz, by the U.S. Fish Commission steamer "Albatross", from August, 1899, to March, 1900, Commander Jefferson F. Moser, U.S.N., commanding. *Mem. Mus. Comp. Zool. Harv. Univ.*, 26 (7): 239-343, 7 pls.

——————— and L. Radcliffe. 1912. The Shore Fishes. (of the "Albatross" Expedition, 1904-1905). *Mem. Mus. Comp. Zool. (Harvard. Univ.)*, 35 (3): 75-171, 8 pls.

Kiwala, R.S. and Ronald R. McConnaughey. 1971. A second record of the scythe butterflyfish, *Chaetodon falcifer*, from California. *Calif. Fish Game*, 57 (3): 217-218.

Klausewitz, W. 1955. See- und Susswasserfische von Sumatra und Java. *Senckenb. Biol.*, 36 (5/6): 309-323.

——————. 1957. *Anisochaetodon (Linophora) pictus* Forskål eine gute Art der Borstenzähner (Pisces, Chaetodontidàe). *Bull. Aquat. Biol. Amst.*, 1 (1) 1-4.

——————. 1958. Fische aus dem Atlantik und Pazific. Ergibnesse der Galapagos-Expedition 1953/54 des Institutes für Submarine Forschung, Vadiz (Leitung: Dr. H. Haas). *Senckenb. Biol.*, 39 (1/2) : 57-84, 7 figs.

——————. 1964. *Die Erforschung der Ichthyofauna des Roten Meeres.* Verlag von J. Kramer. I-XXXVI.

——————. 1969. Vergleichend-taxonomische Untersuchungen an Fischen der Gattung *Heniochus. Senckenb. Biol.*, 50 (1/2): 49-89.

——————. 1970. *Forcipiqer longirostris* und *Chaetodon leucopleura* (Pisces, Perciformes, Chaetodontidae), neue Achweise für das Rote Meer, und einiger zoogeographischen Probleme der Rotmeer Fische. *Meteor-Forsch. Ergeb.*, Berlin., No. 5D: 1-5, 3 pls.

——————. 1974. Vergleichende-taxonomische Untersuchungen an *Hemitaurichthys zoster* und *polylepis* (Pisces: Perciformes: Chetontidae). *Senckenb. Biol.*, 55 (4/6): 213-221.

—————— and J.G. Nielsen. 1965. XII. On Forsskal's collection of fishes in the Zoological Musei Hauniensis XXII. *Scrift. Redg. Univ. Zool. Mus. Kopen:* 30 pp., 38 pls.

Klein, J.T. 1744. *De piscibus per branchias apertas spirantibus ad justum numerum et ordinum redigendis. Horum series prima cum additamento as missum tertium. Historiae naturalis piscium promovendae missus V, cum praefatione de piscium auditu.* Part IV: 68 p., 15 pls.

Klunzinger, C.B. 1870. Synopsis der Fische des Rothen Meeres. I. Theil. Percoiden-Mugiloiden. *Verh. Zool-Bot. Ges. Wien*, 20: 669-834, 16 pls.

_____. 1880. Die von Müllerische Sammlung australischer Fische in Stuttgart. *Sitzb. Akad. Wiss. Wien, Math-Naturwiss. Kl. 80* (1): 325-430, pls. 1-9.

_____. 1884. *Die Fische des Roten Meeres: Eine Kritische Revision mit Bestimmungs-Tabellen. Teil I Acanthopteri veri* Owen. Stuttgart 133 pp., pls. 1-8.

Kner, R. 1859. Ueber *Trachypterus altivelis* und *Chaetodon truncatus,* n. sp. *Spitzber. Akad. Wiss. Wien., 34*:437-445, 2 pls.

_____. 1865. *Reise der Osterreichischen Fregatte "Novara" um die Erde in den Jahren 1857, 1858, 1859, unter den Befehlen des Commodore B. von Wüllerstorf-Urbain.* Zoologischer Theil. Fische. 1-3 Abth. Wien, 1865-1867. Pp. 433, 16 pls.

_____. 1868. IV. Folge. Ueber neue Fische aus dem Museum der Herren Johann Cäser Godeffroy und Sohn in Hamburg. *Sitzber. Akad. Wiss. Wien., 58:* 26-31; 293-356, 9 pls.

_____ and F. Steindachner. 1866. Neue Fische aus dem Museum der Herren Johann C. Godeffroy und Sohn in Hamburg. *Sitzber. Akad. Wiss. Wien, 54:* 356-395, 5 pls.

Koepcke, H.W. 1956. Beitrage zur Kenntnis der Fische Perus. II Beitr. *Neotrop. Fauna., 1* (3): 249-268.

Kossman, R.A. & H. Rauber. 1877. Zoologische Ergebnisse einer im Auftrage der königlichen akademie der Wissenshaften zu Berlin ausgeführten Reise in Küstengebiete des Rothen Meers. Pisces. *In:* Erste Halfte. Leipzig 1877-80: 4to. & *Verh. Nat. Med Verein Heidelb.* I. Pisces (34 pp.) by Kaussman & Kauber.

Kotthaus, A. 1973. Fische des Indeschen Ozeans: Ergebnisse der ichthyologischen Untersuchungen während der Exped. der Forschungsschiffes "Meteor" in dem Indischen Ozean, Okt. 1964 bis Mai 1965. A.Systematischen Teil, X. Percomorphi (3). *Meteor Forshungsergebnisse Reihe D biol., 16:* 17-32.

Koumans, F.P. 1947. Zool notes from Port Dickson. II. A small collection of fishes from Malaya. *Zool. Meded. Rijksms. Nat. Hist. Leiden., 27:* 309-311.

_____. 1953. XVI. The Pisces and Leptocardii of the Snellius Expedition. *Biol. Res. Snellius Exped., Temminckia, 9:* 177-275.

Kumada, T. and Y. Hiyama. 1937. *Marine fishes of the Pacific coast of Mexico.* The Nissan Fisheries Institute & Co., Ltd. Odawara, Japan. 75 pp., 102 pls.

Kuroda, N. 1971. New additions and corrections to the list of fishes of Suruga Bay, Japan. No. 21. *Zool. Mag. Tokyo, 80* (2): 52-57.

Kuronoma, K. 1961. *A checklist of fishes from Vietnam.* Division of Agric. & Nat. Resources, U.S. Operations Mission to Vietnam. 66 pp.

Lacépède, B.G.E. Du La V. 1802. *Histoire naturelle des Poissons. 4:* 1-498 + 517-539.

Ladiges, W. 1953. Über die Haltung der Chaetodonten. *Aquarien Terrarien Z., 6:* 94-97, 4 figs.

Lay, G.T. and E.T. Bennett. 1939. Fishes. *In:* Richardson, J. et al. *The zoology of Captain Beechey's voyage.* London. Pp. 41-75, pls. 15-23.

Lesson, R.P. 1830. *Voyage autour du monde, Exécute par Ordre du Roi, Sur la Corvette de Sa Majesté, "La Coquille," pendant les années 1822, 1823, 1824, et 1825.* Poissons. 2 (part 1, chapt. 10): 86-238; Atlas 58 pls.

Liang, Y.S. 1948. Notes on a collection of fishes from Pescadores Islands, Taiwan. *Q.J. Taiwan Mus.*, 1 (2): 1-20.

_____. 1951. A check-list of the fish specimens in the Taiwan Fisheries Research Institute. Published by the Taiwan Fisheries Research Institute, Taiwan, China. *Laboratory of Biology, Report,* No. 3: 1-35.

Lien, Wen-Kuang.1960. Study on the fishes from Ma-Kung, Pescadores Islands (Penghu), Taiwan. Published by the Taiwan Fisheries Research Institute, Taiwan, China. *Laboratory of Fishery Biology, Report,* No. 13: 1-20.

Lienard, E. 1835. Sixième rapport annuel sur les traveaux de la société d'histoire naturelle de l'île Maurice. *Ann. Soc. Hist. Nat. Maurice:* 1-64.

Limbaugh, C. 1961. Cleaning symbiosis. *Sci. Amer.*, Aug. 1961 (No. 135): 1-9.

Linnaeus, C. 1754. Pisces. *In: Museum S.R.M. Adolphi Friderici Regis Suecorum . . . in quo animalia rariora imprimis et exotica . . . describuntu et determinantur, latinae et Suecici, etc.* Holmiae, 1754, 133 pp., 32 pl.

_____. 1758. *Systema Naturae.* ed. *Decima. Systema naturae sive regna tria naturae, systematicae proposita per classes, ordines, genera et species, cum characteribus, differentiss, synonymis, locis, etc. Editio decima, reformata.* Holmiae, 1758. Regnum animale, ii, 842 pp.

_____. 1766. *Systema Naturae,* 12th edition.

Longley, W.H. 1918. Habits and coloration of Hawaiian Brachyura and fishes, with a note on the possibility of submarine color-photography. *Carnegie Inst. Wash. Year Book for 1918:* 158-163.

_____. 1933. Preparation of a monograph on the Tortugas fishes. Carnegie Inst. Wash. Year Book, 32: 293-295.

_____ and S.F. Hildebrand. 1941. Catalogue of the Fishes of Tortugas. *Pap. Tortugas Lab., 34:* 1-374.

Lonnberg, A.J.E. 1896. Linnaean type specimens of birds, reptiles, batrachians and fishes in the zoological museum of the Royal University in Upsala. *Bihang Till K. Svenska Vet.-Akad. Handlingar.*, Band 22, Afs. IV, No. 1, Part 4: 1-45.

Lord, C. 1924. *Vinculum sexfasciatus* Richardson, an addition to the fish fauna of Tasmania. *Pap. Proc. R. Soc. Tasmania, for 1923:* 43-44.

Lorenz, K. 1962. The function of color in coral reef fishes. *Proc. Royal Instit.*, 39 (178): 282-296.

_____. 1962. Naturschönheit und Daseinskampf. *Kosmos, Stuttgart,* 58: 340-348.

Lunel, G. 1881. Liste de quelques espèces de poissons, nouvelles pour la faune de l'île Maurice suivie de descriptions et de remarques. *Mem. Soc. Phys. Geneve,* 27: 266-303, pl.

Lütken, C.F. 1880. Spolia Atlantica. Bidrag til kundskab om formforandringer hos fiske under deres vaext og unvikling, saerlight hos nogle af Atlanterhavets hjsofiske. *Dansk. Vid. Selsk. Skrift Kjobenhaun,* 5th Ser., 12: 409-613, 5 pls.

Macleay, W.S. 1878. The fishes of Port Darwin. *Proc. Linn. Soc. N.S.W.*, 2 (4):

344-367, 4 pls.

————————. 1879. Descriptions of some new fishes from Port Jackson and King Georges Sound. *Proc. Linn. Soc. N.S.W., 3:* 33-37, 4 pls.

————————. 1880. Descriptive catalogue of the fishes of Australia. *Proc. Linn: Soc. N.S.W., 5:* 302-444.

Mahadevan, S., and Nagappan Nayer.1968. Underwater ecological observations in the Gulf of Mannar off Tuticorin. VII. General Topography and Ecology of the rocky bottom. *J. Mar. Biol. Assoc. India, 9* (1): 147-163.

Marcgrave, George. 1658. G. Marcgravii Historiae rerum naturalium Brasiliae. *In:* Piso, G. *De Indiae utriusque re naturali et medica libri quaturodecim.* Amsterdam, 1658.

Marshall, N.B. 1950. Fishes from Cocos-Keeling Islands. *Bull. Raffles Mus. Singapore,* No. 22: 166-205.

————————. 1952. IX. Fishes. *In:* the 'Manihine' Expedition to the Gulf of Aqaba 1948-1949. *Bull. Br. Mus. (Nat. Hist.) Zool., 1*(8): 221-252.

Marshall, T.C. 1957. Ichthyological Notes. *Ichthyological Notes, Queensland, 1* (3): 117-137, 1 plate.

————————. 1965. *Fishes of the Great Barrier Reef and Coastal Waters of Queensland.* Livingston Publishing Co. 566 pp., 72 col. pls., 64 bl. & w. pls.

————————, E.M. Grant, & N.M. Hayson. 1959. Know your fishes. (An illust. guide to the principal commercial fishes and Crustacea of Queensland). *Ichthyol. Notes, Queensland, 1* (4): 1-137.

Martin, M. & B. Winks 1956. A note on the algal food of three marine fish, Southern Queensland. *Queensland Nat., 15* (4/6): 79.

Martin, F.S. 1956. Ictiologia del archipelago de los Roques. *In:* Mendez, A. and others. *Archipelago de los Roques y la Orchila, Caracas (Soc. Cien. Nat. LaSalle),* 1956: 87-144, 16 pls.

————————. 1958. Nota sobre seis especes de peces de las costas de Venezuela. *Soc. Cien. Nat. LaSalle, Mem. 18* (50): 95-99.

Matsubara, K. 1955. *Fish Morphology and Hierarchy.* Part II: Ishizaki-shoten, Tokyo, Japan.

McCann, C. 1953. Ichthyological notes, with special reference to sexual dimorphism in some New Zealand fishes. *Rec. Dom. Mus. (Wellington), 2*(1): 1-17, 18 figs.

McCosker, J.E. and R.H. Rosenblatt. 1975. Fishes collected at Malpelo Island. *In:* The biological investigation of Malpelo Island, Colombia. *Smithsonian Contrib. Zool,* No. 176: 91-93.

McCulloch, A.R. 1914. III. Report on some fishes obtained by the F.I.S. "Endeavour" on the coasts of Queensland, New South Wales, Victoria, Tasmania, south and southwestern Australia. Part. II. *Biol. Res. "Endeavor",* 2 (part 3): 77-165, pls. XII-XXXIV, 15 figs.

————————. 1916. IV. Report on some fishes obtained by the F.I.S. "Endeavour" on the coasts of Queensland, New South Wales, Victoria, Tasmania, south and southwestern Australia. Part IV. *Biol. Res. "Endeavor",* 4 (part 4): 169-199, pls. 49-58.

————————. 1923. Notes on fishes from Australia and Lord Howe Island.

Rec. Aust. Mus., 14(1): 1-22, 14 pls.

_____. 1926. Studies in Australian fishes. No. 8. *Rec. Aust. Mus., 15* (1): 28-39. 1 pl.

_____. 1929. A checklist of the fishes recorded from Australia. *Mem. Aust. Mus.,* 5: 534 pp.

_____ and E.R. Waite 1916. Additions to the fish fauna of Lord Howe Id. No. 5. *Trans. R. Soc. S. Aust., 40:* 437-451, pls. 40-43.

_____ and G.P. Whitley 1925. A list of the fishes recorded from Queensland waters. *Mem. Queensl. Mus., 8* (2): 125-182.

Meek, S. and S.F. Hildebrand. 1928. The marine fishes of Panama. *Field Mus. Nat. Hist. Publ.,* Zool. Ser. 215, 226 and 249. *15.* Chicago.

Mees, G.F. 1959. Additions to the fish fauna of Western Australia - No. 1. *Fish. Bull. W. Aust.,* No. 9 (1): 5-11.

_____. 1960. Additons to the fish fauna of Western Australia. 2. *Fish. Bull. W. Aust.,* No. 9 (2): 13-21.

_____. 1964. Additions to the fish fauna of Western Australia - 4. *Fish. Bull. W. Aust.,* No. 9 (4) 31-55.

Meinken, H. 1935. Ueber einige Meeresfische sus Darressalam und Luderitz-bucht. *Veroff. aus dem Deutchen Kolonial -und Uebersee-Museum, Bremen, 2:* 170-175, pl. xi.

Mendis, A.S. 1954. Fishes of Ceylon (a catalogue, key & bibliography). *Bull. Fish. Res. Stn. Ceylon,* (2): 1-122.

Menzel, D.W. 1959. Utilization of algae for growth by the angelfish. *J. Conseil. Int. Explor. Mer, 24:* 308-313.

Metzelaar, J. 1919. *Report on the fishes collected by Dr. J. Boeke in the Dutch West Indies 1904-1905. With comparative notes on marine fishes of tropical West Africa.* A. Asher & Co. (Reprint 1967.) 314 pp.

Monkman, N. 1958. "From Queensland to the Great Barrier Reef." *A Naturalist's Adventures in Australia.* Doubleday & Co., Inc. New York. 182 pp.

Monod, Theodore. 1968. Le Complexe Urophore du Poissons Teleosteens. *Mem. Inst. I.F.A.N.,* No. 81.

Montrouzier, X. 1856. Suite de la faune de l'île de Woodlark où Moiou. Ichthyologie. *Société d'Agriculture sciences et industrie de Lyon, Annales,* Sér. 2, 8: 393-504.

Mori, T. 1952. *Check list of the fishes of Korea.* Zool. Dept. Hyogo Univ. Agric., Sasayama, Japan. 864 pp.

Morrow, J.E. 1954. Fishes from East Africa, with new records and descriptions of 2 new species. *Ann. Mag. Nat. Hist.,* Ser. 12, 7: 797-820, 2 pls.

_____ & G.S. Pisner. 1957. Studies in Ichthyology and Oceanography off Coastal Peru. *Bingham Oceanogr. Coll., 16* (Art. 2): 5-55.

Mortensen, T. 1917. Observations on protective adaptations and habits, mainly in marine animals. *Saentryuk Videns. Medd. Dansk. naturhist. Foren, 69:* 57-96.

Müllegger, S. 1906. Ringelbrasse und Schmetterlingfische im Seewassera-quarium und an ihnen beobachtete Lahmungserscheinungen. *Blatt. Aquar.*

Terrar. Kunde, 1906, *17.* Jahrg., 263-266; 276-278; 284-286. pl.

Müller, J. 1844. Ueber den Bau und die Grenzen der Ganoiden und über das naturliche System der Fische. *Abh. Akad. Wiss. Berlin:* 117-216.

Müller, A.H. 1966. *Lehrbuch der paläozoologie.* Band III. Vertebraten Teil I. Fische im weiteren Sinn und Amphibien. VEB Gustav Fisher Verlag, Jena i-xvi + 1-638 pp.

Munro, I.S.R. 1955. *The marine and fresh water fishes of Ceylon.* Dept. of External Affairs. Canberra. xvi + 352 pp, 56 pls.

——————. 1958. The fishes of the New Guinea region. *Papua & New Guinea Agricultural Journal, 10(4); Territory of Papua and New Guinea, Fisheries. Bull. No. 1.*

——————. 1967. *The fishes of New Guinea.* Port Moresby, New Guinea. 650 pp., 6 col pls., 78 bl. & w. pls.

Munro, J., V. Gant, R. Thompson, and P. Reeson. 1973. The spawning seasons of Caribbean reef fishes. *J. Fish. Biol., 5:* 69-84.

Murphy, R.C. 1918. *Chaetodon ocellatus* on the Long Island shore. *Copeia,* 1918 (55): 39-40.

Myers, G.S. 1940. The fish fauna of the Pacific Ocean, with especial reference to zoogeographical regions and distribution as they affect the international aspects of the fisheries. *Proc. 6th Pac. Sci. Congr., 3:* 201-215.

——————. 1959. A Caribbean chaetodont fish, *Chaetodon eques* Steindachner, now referred to *Chaetodon aya* Jordan. *Copeia,* 1959 (2): 158.

Nair, R.V. 1952. Studies on some post-larval fishes of the Madras plankton. *Proc. Indian Acad. Sci., 35,* Sect. B (6): 225-244, 1 pl.

Nalbant, T. 1964. Note on a small collection of fishes from the East Atlantik (Coast of Ghana). *Zool. Anz., 173.*(6): 444-448, 4 figs.

——————. 1965. Sur les Chaetodons de l'Atlantique avec la description d'un nouveau genre *Bauchotia* (Pisces, Chaetodontidae). *Bull. Mus. Natl. Hist. Nat., Ser. 2, 36* (5): 584-589.

——————. 1971. On butterflyfishes from the Atlantic, Indian and Pacific Oceans (Pisces, Perciformes, Chaetodontidae). *Steenstrupia, 1*(20): 207-228.

Neave, F. 1959. Records of fishes from waters off the British Columbia coast. *J. Fish. Res. Board Can., 16* (3): 383-384.

Norman, J.R. 1939. Fishes. No. I. *Sci. Repts. John Murray Exped.,* 1933-34, 7(1): 1-116.

——————. 1942. A photographic record of the Linnaean collection. *Proc. Linn. Soc. Lond., 154* (part 1, 6): 1441-42.

——————. 1953. *A draft synopsis of fishes.* Brit. Mus. (Nat. Hist.).

Ogilby, J.D. 1889. The reptiles and fishes of Lord Howe Island. *Mem. Aust. Mus., 2* (3): 49-74, 2 pls.

——————. 1890. Report on a zoological collection from the Solomons. *Rec. Aust. Mus., 1* (1): 5-7.

——————. 1892. On some undescribed reptiles and fishes from Australia. *Rec. Aust. Mus., 2* (1): 23-26.

——————. 1911. On new or insuffcently described fishes. *Proc. R. Soc. Queensl. (Brisbane), 23:* 1-55.

_____. 1912. On some Queensland fishes. *Mem. Queensl. Mus.,* *Brisbane,* *1:* 26-65, 3 pls.

Okada, Y. & I. Ikeda. 1936. Notes on the fishes of the Riu-Kiu Islands. I. Chaetodontidae. *Bull. Biogeogr. Soc. Jpn., 6* (28): 253-273, pls. xiv, xv.

_____ and K. Matsubara. 1938. *Keys to the fishes and fish-like animals of Japan (incl. Kuril Isl., Southern Sakhalin, Bonin Islands, Ryukyu Isl., Korea & Formosa).* The Sanseido Co., Ltd., Tokyo & Osaka. 584 pp., 113 pls.

_____. 1966. *Fishes of Japan. Illustrations and Descriptions of the Fishes of Japan.* Uno Shoten Co. Ltd., Tokyo, Japan.

Oken, L. 1817. *Isis.* VIII, part 148: 1779-1782.

Okuno, R. 1962. Intra- and interspecific relations of salt-water fishes in aquarium. I. Butterflyfishes. *Jpn. J. Ecol., 12* (4): 129-133.

_____. 1963. Observations and discussions on the social behavior of marine fishes. *Publ. Seto Mar. Biol. Lab., 11* (2): 281-336.

_____. 1964. On the reef fishes of Tanabe Bay compared with those on the coral reefs of the Marshall Islands reported by Hiatt and Strasburg (1960). *Physiol., 12* (1/2): 272-285.

_____, M. Nischiguchi & T. Kurio. 1962. Underwater observations of reef fishes with reference to their microhabitats and behaviors III. 5. Longnosed butterflyfish, *Forcipiger longirostris. J. Jpn. Assoc. Zool. Gardens & Aquariums, 4* (2/3): 50-53.

Palmer, G. 1950. Additions to the fish fauna of Christmas Island, Indian Ocean. *Bull. Raffles Mus. Singapore,* No. 23: 200-205.

_____. 1961. New records of fishes from the Monte Bello Isl., Western Australia. *Ann. Mag. Nat. Hist.,* Ser. 13, *4* (45): 545-551.

_____. 1963. New records of fishes from the Maldive Islands, Indian Ocean. *Ann. Mag. Nat. Hist.,* Ser. 13, *5:* 497-503.

Palmer, G. 1970. New records and one new species of teleost fishes from the Gilbert Islands. *Bull. Br. Mus. Nat. Hist. (Zool.), 19:* 213-234.

Paradice, W.E.J., and others.1927. Northern Territory fishes. *Mem. Aust. Mus., 9* (1): 76-106, pls.

Parish, S. 1969. Fish in Focus. *DIVE, South Pacific Underwater Mag., 8* (6): 15-17, 5 photos.

Park, M. 1797. Descriptions of eight new fishes from Sumatra. *Trans. Linn. Soc. London, 3:* 33-38. pl.

Paysan, K. 1959. Neues in der "Wilhelma" Stuttgart. *Aquar. Terrar. Z., 12:* 287, photo.

Patterson, C. 1964. A review of Mesozoic acanthopterygian fishes with special references to those of the English Chalk. *Philos. Trans. Roy Soc. London.* Ser. B, Biol. Sci., *247* (739):213-482.

Pellegrin, J. 1914. Missions Gruvel sur la Côte occidentale d'Afrique (1905-1912). Poissons. *Ann. Inst. Ocèanogr., Monaco, 6*(4): 1-100, 2 pls.

Peterman, R.M. 1971. A possible function of coloration in coral reef fishes. *Copeia,* 1971: 330-331.

Peters, W.C.H. 1855. Uebersicht der in Mossambique beobachteten Seefische. *Monatsber. Dtsch. Akad. Wiss., Berlin:* 428-466. (Also *Arch. Naturgesch., 21*

Jahrg., *1:* 234-282.)

—————. 1876. Uebersicht der von Hrv. Prof. Dr. K. Mobius in Mauritius und bei den Seychellen gesammelten Fische. *Monatsber. Dtsch. Akad. Wiss., Berlin:* 435-447.

Pietschmann, Victor. 1930. Remarks on Pacific fishes. *Bull. Bernice P. Bishop Mus., 73:* 1-24, pls. III & IV.

Playfair, R.L. 1866. Acanthopterygii. *In:* Playfair, R.L. and A. Günther. The fishes of Zanzibar, with a list of the fishes of the whole east coast of Africa. John van Voorst, Paternoster Row. London. 153 pp., 21 pls.

—————. 1867. The fishes of Seychelles. *Proc. Zool. Soc. Londd.* 1867: 846-872.

Plessis, Yves & Pierre Fourmanoir. 1966. Mission d'étude de récifs coralliens de Nouvelle-Caledonie. Liste des poissons récoltes par Yves Plessis en 1961. *Cah. Pac.,* No. 170, *9:* 122-147.

Poey, F. 1860. Poissons de Cuba, Espèces nouvelles. *In: Memorias sobre la historia natural de la Isla de Cuba, 2:* 115-356.

—————. 1865. Revista de los typos Cuvierianos y Valenciennianos correspondientes a los peces de la isla de Cuba. *Repert. Fis.-nat. de la isla de Cuba, 1:* 409-412.

—————. 1868. Synopsis piscium cubensium, etc. *In: Repertorio fisico-natural de la isla de Cuba, 2:* 279-468, pls.

—————. 1875. Enumeratio piscium cubensium. *Anal. Soc. Espanola Hist. Nat. Madrid, 4:* 75-161, 3 pls.

Poll, M. 1942. Les poissons de Tahiti recueilles par G.A. de Witte. *Bull. Mus. R. Hist. Nat. Belgique, 18* (61): 1-20.

—————. 1949. Poissons. IV. Résultat Scientifiques des Croisieres du Navire-École Belge Mercator. *Mem. Inst. R. Sci, nat. Belg.,* Ser. 2a, *33:* 181-262.

—————. 1950. Description de deux Poissons percomorphes nouveaux des eaux côtières africaines de l'Atlantique Sud (1948-1949). *Bull. Mus. nat. Hist. Belg., 26* (49): 1-14.

—————. 1954. Expedition océanographique belge dans les eaux côtières africaines de l'Atlantique Sud (1948-1949). Résultats scientifiques. Poissons. IV. -Teleostéens acanthopterygiens, lre partie. *Inst. R. Sci. Nat. Belg., 4* (3a): 1-107, pls 1-9.

Pollon, F. 1964. Énumeration des Animaux Vertébrates de L'Îsle de Madagascar. Poissons. *Nederl. Tijdschr. Dierk., 1:* 277-345.

Powell, A.W.B. 1938. A new *Cleidopus* and four other fishes new to New Zealand. *Rec. Auckl. Inst. Mus., 2* (3): 151-156.

Quiguer, J.-P. 1963. Compte rendu de mission en Nouvelle-Caledonie (étude ichthyologique). *Cah. Pac.,* No. 5: 37-39, color plate.

—————. 1966. Poissons des recifs coralliens (Nouvelle-Caledonie). *Cah. Pac.,* No. 9: 70-75.

—————. 1967. Poissons de récifs coralliens de Nouvelle-Caledonie (Collection B. Salvat - Premier Liste). *Cah. Pac.,* No. 10: 79-84.

Quoy, J.R.C. & Gaimard, P. 1824. *Voyage autour du monde . . . execute sur les cor-*

810

vettes de S.M. "l'Uranie" et "La Physicienne," (under Capt. Louis de Freycenet) pendant les années 1817-1820. Paris. (Poissons. Chapt. 9: 192-401).

Ralston, S. 1975. Aspects of the age and growth, reproduction, and diet of the millet-seed butterflyfish, *Chaetodon miliaris* (Pisces, Chaetodontidae), a Hawaiian endemic. Unpublished masters thesis, University of Hawaii, 1975.

Randall, J.E. 1955. Fishes of the Gilbert Islands. *Atoll Res. Bull.,* No. 47: 1-243.

_____. 1961a. Two new butterflyfishes (Family Chaetodontidae) of the Indo-Pacific genus *Forcipiger. Copeia,* 1961 (1): 53-62.

_____. 1961b. Tagging reef fishes in the Virgin Islands. *Proc. Gulf & Caribbean Fish. Inst. 14th Annual Session:* 201-241.

_____. 1963. An analysis of the fish populations of artificial and natural reefs in the Virgin Islands. *Caribb. J. Sci., 3*(1): 31-47.

_____. 1973. Tahitian fish names and a preliminary checklist of the fishes of the Society Islands. *Occas. Pap. Bernice P. Bishop Mus., 24* (11): 167-214.

_____. 1974. The effect of fishes on coral reefs. *Proc. of the Second International Coral Reef Symposium. 1. Great Barrier Reef Committee, Brisbane.* October 1974: 159-166.

_____ and D.K. Caldwell. 1970. Clarification of the species of the butteflyfish genus *Forcipiger. Copeia,* 1970 (4): 727-731.

_____ and _____. 1973. A new butterflyfish of the genus *Chaetodon* and a new angelfish of the genus *Centropyge* from Easter Island. *Los. Ang. Cty. Mus., Contrib. Sci.,* No. 237: 1-11.

Reese, E.S. 1973. Duration of residence by coral reef fishes on "home" reefs. *Copeia,* 1973 (1): 145-149.

_____. 1975. A comparative field study of the social behavior and related ecology of reef fishes of the family Chaetodontidae. *Z. Tierpsychol., 37:* 37-61.

Reeves, C. 1927. A catalogue of the fishes of northeastern China and Korea. *J. Pan-Pac. Res. Inst., 2* (3): 3-16.

Regan, C.T. 1904. Description of a new fish of the genus *Chaetodon* from the New Hebrides. *Ann. Mag. Nat. Hist.,* Ser. 7, *13:* 276-277.

_____. 1905. On fishes from the Persian Gulf, the Sea of Oman and Karachi, collected by Mr. F.W. Townsend. *J. Bombay Nat. Hist. Soc., 16*(2): 318-393.

_____. 1909. A collection of fishes made by Dr. C.W. Andrews, F.R.S., at Christmas Island. *Proc. Zool. Soc. Lond.* 1909: 403-406, 2 pls.

_____. 1913. The classification of percoid fishes. XXX. *Ann. Mag. Nat. Hist.* Ser. 8, *12:* 111-145.

_____. 1921a. I. Three new fishes from South Africa, collected by Mr. H.W. Bell Marley. *Ann. Durban Mus., 3* (1): 1-2.

_____. 1921b. New fishes from deep water off the coast of Natal. *Ann. Mag. Nat. Hist.,* Ser. 9, *7:* 412-420.

Renard, L. 1718. *Poissons, écrevisses et crabes . . . que l'on trouvé autouor des îles Moluques, et sur les côtes des terres Australes . . . Ouvrage . . . qui contient un très grand nombre de poissons . . . de la mer des Indes: divise en*

*deux tomes, dont le premeir a été copie sur les originaux de M.B. Coyett . . .
Le second tome a été forme sur les recueils de M.A. Vander Stell . . . avec une
courte description de chaque poisson . . . Donne au public par . . .* L. Renard,
& c. 2 vols. (in 1), Amsterdam, 1718-1719. xviii, 100 col. pls.

Ribeiro, A. de M. 1915. Fauna brasiliense. Peixes. Tomo V. Eleutherobranchios
Aspiro Phoros (Physoclisti). *Arch. Mus. Nac. Rio de Janeiro*, 1915, *17:* 1-(c.
600), pls.

Richards, C.E. 1963. First record of four fishes from Chesapeake Bay, and observations of other fishes during 1962. *Copeia*, 1963: 584-585.

Richardson, J. 1842. VIII. Contributions to the Ichthyology of Australia. *Ann.
Mag. Nat: Hist.*, Ser. 2, *10:* 25-34.

Ricker, K.E. 1959. Mexican shore and pelagic fishes collected from Acapulco to
Cape San Lucas during the 1957 cruise of the "Marijean". *Mus. Cont. Inst.
Fish. Univ. British Columbia*, No. 3: 1-18.

——————. 1959. Fishes collected from the Revillagigedo Islands during
the 1954-1958 cruises of "Marijean". *Mus. Cont. Inst. Fish. Univ. British Columbia*, No. 4: 11 pp.

Rochebrune, A.T. de.1880. Descriptions de quelques espèces nouvelles de poissons propers a la Sénégambie. *Bull. Soc. Philom. Paris*, ser. 7, *4:* 159-169.

——————. 1883. Faune de la Sénégambie. Poissons. *Act. Soc. Linn.
Bordeaux*, *6:* 37-180, 6 pls.

Roessler, M. 1965. An analysis of the variability of fish population taken by ot-
ter trawl in Biscayne Bay, Florida. *Trans. Amer. Fish. Soc.*, *94* (4): 311-318.

Rofen, R.R. 1961. Identifications of fish collections from Kapingamarangi,
Eastern Caroline Islands, Ifaluk, Western Caroline Islands, Raroia, Tuamotu
Archipelago. *Biological Investigations in the Pacific Area, Pac. Sci. Bd., Nat.
Acad. Res. Council.* 32 pp.

——————. 1963. Handbook of the food fishes of the Gulf of Thailand.
*The George Vanderbilt Foundation and the University of Calif. Scripps Instit. of
Oceanography.* SIO Ref. No. 63-18: 1-238.

Roghi, G. and F. Baschieri, 1957. *Dahlak (With the Italian National Underwater
Expedition in the Red Sea).* Essential Books, Inc., Fair Lawn, N.J. 280 pp., 42
plates, 1 map.

Rosen, N. 1911. Contributions to the fauna of the Bahamas. I. A general account
of the fauna, with remarks on the physiography of the islands. II. The Reptiles. III. The Fishes. *Lunds Universitets Arsskrift*, N.F. Afd. 2. Bd. 7 (5): 1-
72, 1 pl., 2 maps.

Rosenblatt, R.H. & B.W. Walker 1963. The Marine Shore-Fishes of the
Galapagos Islands. *Occas. Pap. Calif. Acad. Sci.*, No. 44: 97-106.

——————, J.E. McCosker, and I. Rubinoff. 1972. Indo-west Pacific fishes
from the Gulf of Chiriqui, Panama. *Los. Ang. Cty. Nat. Hist. Mus., Contrib.
Sci.*, No. 234: 1-18.

Rosenthal, F.C. 1812. Ichthyotomische Tafeln. Berlin, 1812-25. *Arch. Physiol.*,
10: 393-414.

Roux, C. 1957. Poissons marins. *In:* Collignon, J., M. Rossigno and C. Roux:
Mollusques, Crustaces et Poissons marins des cotes de A.E.F. en collection au Cen-

tre d'Océanographique de l'Institut de Études Centraficaines de Pointe-Noire, Office de la Recherche Scientifique et Technique Outre-Mer, France: 137-368, 1 pl.

Roux-Esteve, & P. Formanoir, 1955. Poissons captures par la mission de la "Calypso" en Mer Rouge. Ann. Inst. Oceanogr. Paris, New Ser., 30 (part 7): 195-203.

Roxas, H.A. & C. Martin.1937. A check list of Philippine fishes. A check list of the fishes recorded from the Philippine Islands. Tech. Bull. 6, Commonwealth of the Philippines, Dept. of Agric. and Commerce, Manila. 314 pp.

Rüppell, E. 1828. Fische des Rothen Meers. In: Atlas zu der Reise im nordlichen Afrika. Zoologie. Frankfurt am Main. 4 vols. 1826-28 119 pls. fol.

_____. 1835. Neue Wirbelthiere zu Fauna von Abyssinien gehörig: Fische aus dem Rothen Meers. Frankfurt- a. - M. 1835-1840: 1-148.

Russell, B.C. 1971. A preliminary annotated checklist of fishes of the Poor Knight Islands. Tane, 17: 81-90.

Ruysch, H. 1718. Collectio nova piscium Amboinensium partim ibi ad vivum delineatorum, partim ex museo Henri Ruysch M.D. xx tabulis comprehensa. In: Theatrum unuversale omnium animalium etc. Amstelodami, 1718. 40 pp. 20 pls.

Ryder, J.A. 1887. On the development of osseous fishes, including marine and freshwater forms. Rept. U.S. Fish Comm., 1885, 13: 488-604, 30 pls.

Sanders, M. 1934. Die fossilen Fische des Alttertiaren Susswasserablagerungen aus Mittel Sumatra. Verh. Geol. Mijomb. Gen., 11 (1): 1-143, 9 pls.

Sauvage, H.E. 1880. Descriptions de quelques poissons d'espèces nouvelles de la collection du Muséum d'Histoire Naturelle. Bull. Soc. Philom. Paris, Sér. 7. 4:220-228.

_____. 1882. Note sur quelques poissons de la Martinique. Le Naturaliste, année 5, 2 (38): 292-293; 299-300.

_____. 1891. Histoire Naturelle des Poissons. (Vol. xvi of A. Grandidier, Histoire physique, naturelle, et politique de Madagascar.) Paris, 1891, 4to, 543 pp., 60 pls. (pls. issued in 1887-1888).

Saville-Kent, W. 1889. Preliminary observations on a natural history collection -made in connection with the surveying cruise of H.M.S. "Myrmidos", at Port Darwin and Cambridge Gulf - September to November 1888 by W. Saville-Kent, F.L.S., F.Z.S. & C., Commissioner of Fisheries, Queensland. Proc. R. Soc. Queensl., 6: 235.

Schlosser, J.A. 1764. An account of a fish from Batavia, called Jaculator: In a letter to Mr. Peter Collinson, F.R.S. from John Albert Schlosser, M.D. F.R.S. Philos. Trans. R. Soc. London, 54: 89-91, pl. 54.

_____. 1777. Some further intelligence relating to the jaculator fish mentioned in the Philosophical Transactions for 1764, Art. XIV. from Mr. Hommel, at Batavia, together with the description of another species, by Dr. Pallas, F.R.S. in a letter to Mr. Peter Collinson, F.R.S. Philos. Trans. R. Soc. London, 56: 186-188.

Schmidt, P.J. 1930a. Fishes of the Riu-Kiu Islands. Trudy Tikhookeankogo Kom. Akad. Nauk. SSSR (Trans. Pac. Committee Acad. Sci. USSR) 1: 19-156.

—————————. 1930b. A checklist of the fishes of the Riu-Kiu Islands. *J. Pan-Pac. Res. Inst.*, 5 (4): 2-6.

Schmidt, P. and G. Lindberg. 1930. On a new Japanese fish, *Paracanthochaetodon modestus* n. gen. et sp. (Chaetodontidae). *C.R. Acad. Sci. URSS.*, Ser. A., (17): 468-470.

————————— and —————————. 1930. A list of fishes, collected in Tsuruga (Japan) by W. Roszkowski. *Bull. Akad. Nauk. SSSR, Leningrad:* 1135-1150.

Schmidt, Waldo L. 1938. Annotated list of fishes, Presidential Cruise, 1938: Appendix to the "Log (of) the Cruise 1938," by Capt. D.J. Callaghan, U.S.N. Naval Aide to the President, with following title page: "The Inspection Cruise and Fishing Expedition of President Franklin D. Roosevelt on Board U.S.S. Houston, 16 July 1938-9 August 1938."

Schultz, L.P. 1943. Fishes of the Phoenix and Samoan Islands coll. in 1939 during the expedition of the U.S.S. *Bushnell. Bull. U.S. Natl. Mus., 180:* i + 316 pp.

—————————. 1948. The use of rotenone for collecting reef and lagoon fishes at Bikini. *Copeia,* 1948 (2): 94-98.

—————————. 1949. A further contribution to the ichthyology of Venezuela. *Proc. U.S. Natl. Mus., 99* (3235): 1-211, pls. 1-3.

—————————. 1951. *Chaetodon tinkeri,* a new species of butterflyfish (Chaetodontidae) from the Hawaiian Islands. *Proc. U.S. Natl. Mus., 101* (3285): 485-488.

————————— and Dunkle. 1948. Classification of fishes, Appendix *In* Schultz, L.P. & E.M. Stern. *The Ways of Fishes.* New York. Van Nostrand, 264 pp.

Scopoli, G.A. 1787. J.A. Scopoli . . . *Introductio ad historiam naturalem sistens genera lapidum, plantarum et animalium hactenus detecta, caracteribus essentialibus donata, in tribus divisa, subinde ad leges naturae.* Prague. x + 506 pp.

Scott, J.S. 1959. *An introduction to the Sea Fishes of Malaya.* Printed at the Gov't press by B.T. Fudge, Government Printer. Kuala Lumpur. 180 pp.

Scott, O.E.G. 1935. Observations on some Tasmanian fishes. Part 2, II *Pap. Proc. R. Soc. Tasmania,* 1934 (1935): 63-73.

—————————. 1975. Observations on some Tasmanian fishes. Part XXI. *Pap. Pro. R. Soc. Tasmania, 109:* 127-173.

Scott, T.D. 1959. Notes on Western Australian fishes. No. 1. *Trans. R. Soc. S. Aust., 82:* 73-91.

—————————. 1962. *The Marine and Fresh Water Fishes of South Australia.* Handbook of Flora and Fauna South Australia, South Australian Museum.

Scudder, S.H. 1882. Nomenclator Zoologicus. Part I. Supplemental List. *Bull. U.S. Natl. Mus., 19:* 1-716.

Seba, A. 1758. *Locuphetissimi rerum naturalium thesauri accurata descriptio et iconibus artificiosissimus expressio, per universam physicis historiam . . . Ex toto terarum orbe collegit, descripsit, et depingendum curavit Albertus Seba.* Amsteldami. Fishes. *3:* 58-109, pls. 23-24.

Seale, A. 1901. Report of a mission to Guam. Part II. Fishes. *Occas. Pap. Bernice P. Bishop Mus., 1* (3): 61-128.

——————. 1906. Fishes of the South Pacific. *Occas. Pap. Bernice P. Bishop Mus., 4* (1): 1-89, pl.

——————. 1910. Descriptions of four new species of fishes from Bantayan island, Philippine archipelago. *Philipp. J. Sci.,* Sec. D., *5* (2): 115-118, 2 pls.

——————. 1910. Fishes of Borneo, with descriptions of four new species. *Philipp. J. Sci.,* Ser. D, *5* (4): 263-288, 4 pls.

——————. 1914. Fishes of Hong Kong. *Philipp. J. Sci.,* Sec. D, *9:* 59-81.

——————. 1935. The Templeton Crocker Exped. to Western Polynesia and Melanesia Islands, 1933. No. 27. Fishes. *Proc. Calif. Acad. Sci., 21* (27): 337-378, pls. XX-XXIII.

——————. 1940. Report on fishes from Allan Hancock Exped. in the California Academy Sciences. *Allan Hancock Pac. Exped., 9* (1): 1-46.

Shen, S.C. 1973. Ecological and morphological study on fish fauna from the waters around Taiwan and its adjacent islands. 3. Study on the chaetodont fishes (Chaetodontidae) with description of a new species and its distribution. *Rep. Inst. Fish Biol. Min. Econ. Affairs Natl. Taiwan Univ., 3* (1): 1-75.

—————— and P.-C. Lim. 1975. An additional study on chaetodont fishes (Chaetodontidae) with descriptions of two new species. *Bull. Inst. Zool. Academia Sinica, 14* (2): 79-105.

Shaw, G. and F.P. Nodder. 1791. *The naturalist's miscellany, or coloured figures of the natural objects, drawn and described . . . from nature.* Vol. 2. pl. 67.

Shurcliff, S.N. 1930. *Jungle Islands. The Illyria in the South Seas, the record of the Crane Pac. Exped.* Field Mus. Nat. Hist., Chicago. G.P. Putnam Sons. 298 pp.

Slastenenko, E.P. 1957. A list of natural fish hybrids of the world. *Hidrobiologi, Istanbul, 4:* 76-97.

Smiley, C.W. 1884. Arrangement with the life-saving service and the light-house board for collecting whales, porpoises, sharks, and strange forms of marine life. *Bull. U.S. Fish Comm., 4:* 385-386.

Smith, Hugh M. 1898. The fishes found in the vicinity of Woods Hole. *Bull. U.S. Fish. Comm., 17:* 85-111.

—————— and T.C.B. Pope. 1906. List of fishes collected in Japan in 1903, with descriptions of new genera and species. *Proc. U.S. Natl. Mus., 31* (1489): 459-499.

—————— and L. Radcliffe. 1911. Descriptions of three new fishes of the Family Chaetodontidae from the Philippine Islands. Scientific results of the Philippine cruise of the Fisheries Steamer "Albatross," 1907-1910. No. 9. *Proc. U.S. Natl. Mus., 40* (1822): 319-326.

Smith, J.L.B. 1931. New and little known fishes from the south and east coasts of Africa. *Rec. Albany Mus., 4:* 145-160, pl. XVI.

——————. 1935. New and little known fishes from South Africa. *Rec. Albany Mus., 4:* 169-235, pls. 18-23.

——————. 1946. LXXVII. New species and new records of fishes from

South Africa. *Ann. Mag. Nat. Hist.,* Ser. 11, *13:* 793-821.

—————————. 1947. Brief revisions and new records of South African marine fishes. *Ann. Mag. Nat. Hist.,* Ser. 11, *15:* 335-346.

—————————. 1949. Forty-two fishes new to South Africa with notes on others. *Ann. Mag. Nat. Hist.,* Ser. 12, *2:* 97-111.

—————————. 1953. *The Sea Fishes of Southern Africa.* Central News Agency Ltd. (revised ed.). 564 pp. Grahamstown, South Africa. 111 pls.

—————————. 1953. Fishes taken in the Moçambique Channel by Mussolini P. Fajardo. *Mem. Mus. Dr. Alvaro de Castro, 2:* 5-20.

—————————. 1955. The Fishes of Aldabra. Part II. *Ann. Mag. Nat. Hist.,* Ser. 12, *8:* 689-697, 1 pl.

—————————. 1965. New records and new species of fishes from S. Africa, chiefly from Natal. *Occas. Pap. Dept. of Ichthyol. Rhodes Univ., Grahamstown,* No. 4: 27-42.

—————————. 1966. Interesting fishes from South Africa. *Occas. Pap, Dept. of Ichthyology, Rhodes University, Grahamstown,* No. 8: 83-94, pl. 15-17.

————————— and M.M. Smith. 1963. *The fishes of Seychelles.* The Dept. of Ichthyology, Rhodes Univ., Grahamstown. 215 pp., 98 pls.

————————— and —————————. 1966. *Fishes of the Tsitkikama Coastal National Park.* Swan Press Ltd., Johannesburg, S. Africa. 161 pp.

Smith, M.M. 1975. Common and scientific names of the fishes of Southern Africa. Part I. Marine Fishes. *J.L.B. Smith Institute of Ichthyology, Spec. Publ.,* No. 4: 1-178.

Smith, R. & J. Swain.1882. Notes on a collection of fishes from Johnston's island, including descriptions of five new species. *Proc. U.S. Natl. Mus.,* 5:119-143.

Snodgrass, R.E. and E.H. Heller. 1905. Papers from the Hopkins-Stanford Galapagos Exped., 1898-1899. Shore fishes of the Revillagigedo, Clipperton, Cocos and Galapagos islands. *Proc. Wash. Acad. Sci., 6:* 333-427.

Snyder, J.O. 1904. A catalogue of the shore fishes collected by the steamer "Albatross" about the Hawaiian Islands in 1902. *Bull. U.S. Fish.,* 1902 (1904), *22:* 513-538, 13 pls.

—————————. 1912. Japanese shore fishes collected by the United States Bureau of Fisheries steamer "Albatross" expedition of 1906. *Proc. U.S. Natl. Mus., 42:* 339-450, 11 pls.

—————————. 1912. The fishes of Okinawa, one of the Riu Kiu islands. *Proc. U.S. Natl. Mus., 42:* 487-519, 9 pls.

Sorenson, W.E. 1895. Are the extrinsic muscles of the air-bladder in some Siluridae and the "elastic spring" apparatus of others subordinate to the voluntary production of sounds?, etc. *J. Anat. Physiol., 29:* 109-139; 205-229; 399-423; 518-552. 14 figs.

Springer, V.G. and H.D. Hoese. 1958. Notes on records of marine fishes from the Texas coast. *Tex. J. Sci., 10:* 343-348.

Starck, W.A. II. 1968. A list of fishes from Alligator Reef, Florida with comments on the nature of the Florida reef fish fauna. *Undersea Biology, 1* (1): 5-36.

————————— and W.P. Davis. 1966. Night habits of fishes of Alligator Reef, Florida. *Ichthyol., Aquarium J., 38* (4): 313-356.

Starks, E.C. 1902. The relationship and osteology of the caproid fishes or Antigoniidae. *Proc. U.S. Natl. Mus., 25* (1297):567-572.

—————. 1906. On a collection of fishes made by P.O. Simons in Ecuador and Peru. *Proc. U.S. Natl. Mus., 30:* 761-800, 2 pls.

—————. 1926. Bones of the ethmoid region of the fish skull. *Stanford Univ. Publ.,* Univ. Ser. Biol., 4 (3): 141-338.

—————. 1930. The primary shoulder girdle of the bony fishes. *Stanford Univ. Publ.,* Univ. Ser. Biol., 6(2): 147-239.

Steindachner, F. 1866. Zur Fischfauna von Port Jackson in Australien. *Sitzgsber. Akad. Wiss. Wien, 53:* 424-481, 7 pls.

—————. 1868. Ichthyologische Notizen (VII). *Sitzgber. Akad. Wiss. Wien, 57:* 965-1008, 5 pls.

—————. 1870. Bericht über eine Sammlung von Fischen aus Singapore. *Sitzgsber. Akad. Wiss. Wien. 60:*557-571.

—————. 1874. Ichthyologische Beitrage. *Sitzgber. Akad. Wiss. Wien. 70.* (1 Abth.): 355-390, pl.

—————. 1879. Additions to the fauna of Southern Australia. *Denk. Akad. Berlin, 41* (Abth 1): 1-15, pl. 9.

—————. 1881. Beitrage zur Kenntniss der Fische Afrika's und Beschreibung einer neuen *Sargus*-Art von den Galapagos Inseln. *Denk. Akad. Math.-Naturw. Klasse, 44* (1): 19-58, 10 pls.

—————. 1883. Beitrage zur Kenntniss der Fische Afrikas. Part 2. *Denk. Akad. Wiss. Wien, 65:* 1-15.

—————. 1893. Ichthyologische Beitrage XVI. *Sitzber. Akad. Wiss. Wien., 102:* 215-243, 3 pls.

—————. 1895. Vorflaufige Mittheilung über einige neue Fischarten aus der ichthyologischen Sammlung des k. Naturhistorischen Hofmuseums in Wien. *Anz. Akad. Wiss. Wien, 32:* 180-183.

—————. 1901. Fische aus dem Stillen Ocean. Ergebnisse einer Reisse nach dem Pacific (Schauinsland, 1896-97). *Denk. Math-Natur. Kais. Akad. Wiss. Wien, 70:* 483-521, 6 pls.

—————. 1902a. Fische aus Sudarabien und Sokotra. *Denk. Math-Natur. Kais. Akad. Wiss. Wien, 71:* 123-168, 2 pls.

—————. 1902b. Wissenschaftliche Ergebnisse der sudarabischen Expedition in den Jahren 1898 bis 1899. Fische von Sudarabien und Sokotra. *Anz. Akad. Wiss. Wien, 1902, 39:* 316-318.

—————. 1903. Ueber einig neue Reptilien und Fischarten des Hofmuseums in Wien. *Sitzosbler. Akad. Wiss. Wien Mathem. - Natur. Klasse, I, 112:* 15-22, 1 pl.

—————. 1906. Zur Fischfauna der Samoa-Inseln. *Sitzgsber. Akad. Wiss. Wien, 115* (1): 1369-1425.

————— and L. Doderlein. 1883. Beitrage zur Kenntniss der Fische Japan's (II). parts 1-4. *Denk. Akad. Wiss. Wien Math. - Naturwiss-Klasse, 48* (1): 1-40, 7 pls.

Steinitz, H. & A. Ben-Tuvia.1955. Fishes from Eylath (Gulf of Aqaba), Red Sea, 2nd Report. State of Israel, Ministry of Agriculture, Div. of Fisheries. *Sea*

Fish. Res. Stn. Haifa, Bull., 11: 1-16.

Stinton, F.C. 1966. Fish otoliths from the London Clay. In: Cassier, E. Faune ichthyologique du London Clay. Brit. Mus. (Nat. Hist.) London: 404-496, 3 pls.

Strasburg, D.W. 1953. Fishes of the Southern Marshall Islands. Submitted as a report for Office of Naval Research. Contract 696 (00). pp. 267.

_____. 1962. Pelagic stages of Zanclus canescens from Hawaii. Copeia, 1962 (4): 844-845. 1 fig.

Streets, T.H. 1877. Contribution to the natural history of the Hawaiian and Fanning Islands and Lower California, made in connection with the U.S. North Pacific Surveying Expedition. 1873-75. Bull. U.S. Natl. Mus., 7: 43-102.

Suyehiro, Y. 1942. A study on the digestive system and feeding habits of fish. Jpn. J. Zool., 10 (1): 1-303, pls. X-XV.

Suzuki, K. 1964. Results of Amami-Expedition. 2. Fishes. Rept. Fac. Fish. Pref. Univ. MIE, 5 (1): 153-188.

Swain, J. 1882a. A review of Swainson's "Genera of fishes." Proc. Acad. Nat. Sci. Phila., 34: 278-284.

_____. 1882b. An identification of the species of fishes described in Shaw's "General Zoology". Proc. Acad. Nat. Sci. Phila., 34: 303-309.

Swainson, W. 1839. The natural history and classification of fishes, amphibians and reptiles or monocardian animals. 2 vols. London 1838-39.

Szajnocha, W. 1886. Ueber fossiel Fische von Monte Bolca bei Verona. (On fossil fish from Monte Bolca.) Pam. Ak. (Krakau), 12: 104-115. 4 pls.

Tanaka, S. 1918. Nihon San Gyorui no Juni Shinshu. (12 new species of Japanese fishes) Dobutsugaku zasshi (= Zool. Mag.) 30 (356): 223-227.

_____. 1930. Figures and Descr. of the fishes of Japan incl. Riu Kiu I. Bonin I., Formosa, Kurile I., Korea and southern Sakhalin. 47: 925-944, pls. CLXXXV-CLXXXVII.

Taylor, W.R. 1964a. Fishes of Arnhem Land. Records of the Amer-Australian Scientific Expedition to Arnhem Land, 4: 45-308.

_____. 1964b. Comment on the proposed rejection of Curimata Walbaum, 1792. Z.N. (S.) 1590. Bull. Zool. Nomencl., 21 (4): 260-261.

Temminck, C.J. and H. Schlegel. 1842. Pisces In: P.F. von Siebold. Fauna Japonica, sive descripto animalium quae in itinere per Japoniam suscepto annis 1823-30 collegit, etc. Lugduni Batavorum. 323 pp., 160 col. pls.

Thiollière, v.J. de I. 1856. Partie ichthyologique de la faune de l'île de Woodlark où Moiou (Mélanesie). Lyon. 89 pp.

Tilden, Josephine E. 1929. "Plant material and debris": The algal food of fishes. Trans. Amer. Fish. Soc., 59: 178-187.

Tinker, Spencer. 1953. Hawaiian Butterfly Fish. Paradise of the Pacific. 1953. Annual 4 pp.

Titcomb, M. and Mary Pukui. 1952. Native use of fish in Hawaii. Memoir no. 29. Supplement of the Journal of the Polynesian Society. New Plymouth, New Zealand. 162 pp.

Tomiyama, I. 1972. List of the fishes preserved in the Aitsu marine Bioligical Station, Kumanoto University, with notes on some interesting species and descriptions of two new species. *Publ. Amakusa Mar. Biol. Lab. Kyushu Univ.*, *3* (1): 1-21.

Torchio, M. 1968. Sulla eventuale presenza in acque mediterranee di individui dei generi *Cephalopholis* Bl. Schn. e *Chaetodon* L. (Pisces Osteichthyes). *"Natura" Riv. della Soc. Ital. di Sci. Nat. e del Mus. Civ. di Storia Nat. di Milano*, *59* (3/4): 210-212.

Tortonese, E. 1937. Due Squamipinni della Somalia italiana *(Chaetodon leucopygus* Ahl, *Zanclus canescens* (L.).) *Bol. Mus. Anat. Comp. Torino*, Ser. 3. *45* (65): 255-258.

_____. 1939. Resultati ittiologici del viaggio di circumnavigazione del globo della R.B. "Magenta" (1865-68). *Bol. Mus. Zool. Anat. Comp. Univ. Torino*, Ser. 3, *47* (100): 177-421 (1-245, double pagination).

_____. 1966. Contributo allo studio sistematico e biogeographico dei pesci della Nuova Guinea. *Annali Mus. civ. Stor. nat. Giacomo Doria*, 25 (1964-65): 13-98.

_____. 1968. Fishes of Eilat (Red Sea). *Sea Fish. Res. Sta. Haifa.*, *Bull.*, *51:* 6-30.

_____. 1975. Fishes of the Gulf of Aden. *Monit. Zool. Ital.*, *Suppl.*, *6* (8): 167-188.

Tweedie, M.W.F. 1936. A list of the fishes in the collection of Raffles Museum. *Bull. Raffles Mus.*, No. 12: 16-28.

Uchida, K. 1951. Notes on a few cases of mimicry in fishes. *Sci. Bull. Fac. Agric. Kyushu Univ.*, *13* (1-4): 294-296.

Vaillant, L. 1890. Zoologie. Sur quelques caracteres transitoires presentes par le *Chelmo rostratus* Linné, jeune. Note de M. Leon Vaillant, presentee par M.E. Blanchard. *Compte Rendu Acad. Sci. Paris.*, *111:* 756-757.

Valenciennes, A. 1835. *Cuvier's Règne Animal Illustre.* Pls.

_____.1839. *Regne Animal.* Poissons. vol. III. pls.

Visser, C. de 1912. Les poissons exotiques. *La Nature*, *40* (2): 401-403.

von Bonde, C. 1934. A collection of marine fishes from Zanzibar. *Ann. Natal Mus.*, *7* (3): 435-458, pl XXIII.

Waite, E.R. 1900. Additions to the fish fauna of Lord Howe Island. No. 1 *Rec. Aust. Mus.*, *3* (7): 193-209, 2 pls.

_____. 1901. Additions to the fish fauna of Lork Howe Island No. 2. *Rec. Aust. Mus.*, 4: 36-47, 4 pls.

_____. 1902. Notes on fishes from Western Australia. No. 2. *Rec. Aust. Mus.*, *4* (5): 179-190, pls.

_____. 1903. Additions to the fish fauna of Lord Howe Island, No. 3 *Rec. Aust. Mus.*, *5:* 20-45, 3 pls.

_____. 1904. Catalogue of the fishes of Lord Howe Islands. *Rec. Aust. Mus.*, *5* (3): 187-230, 24 pls.

_____. 1905. Notes on fishes from western Australia, No. 3. *Rec. Aust. Mus.*, *6:* 55-82, 6 pls.

_____.1921. Catalogue of the fishes of South Australia. *Rec. S. Aust. Mus.*, *2* (1): 332 pp.

_____. 1927. Supplement to the Catalogue of the Fishes of South

Australia. *Rec. S. Aust. Mus., 3* (3): 219-234, pl. 13.

Walbaum, J.J. 1779. Der Soldatenfisch, *Chaetodon capistratus. Hannov. Mag.,* p. 1570.

Walker, B.W. & K.S. Norris 1952. *Provisional checklist of the fishes of the Gulf of California.* Mimeograph 42.

Walls, J. 1975. *Fishes of the Northen Gulf of Mexico.* T.F.H. Publ. Inc. 432 pp.

Watanabe, M. 1949. Studies on the fishes of the Ryukyu Islands. I. Four unrecorded butterfly fishes. *Bull. Biogeogr. Soc. Jpn., 14* (8): 33-43.

Watson, S.W. 1953. Virus diseases of fish. *Trans. Am. Fish. Soc., 83:* 331-341.

Weber, M. 1910. Neue Fische aus niederlandisch Sud-Neu-Guinea. *Notes Leiden Mus. Jentink, 32* (4): 225-240. pl.

_____. 1913. Die Fische der Siboga-Expedition. *Siboga Expedition.* Leyden, 1913. *57:* 710 pp., 12 pls.

_____ and L.F. de Beaufort. 1936. *The Fishes of the Indo-Australian Archipelago.* Leiden. *7:* 1-566.

Wheeler, A.C. 1966. The Zoophylacium of Laurens Theodore Gronovius. *J. Soc. Bibliogr. Nat. Hist., 3* (3): 152-157.

_____. 1958. The Gronovius Fish Coll.: A catalogue and Historical account. *Bull. Br. Mus. (Nat. Hist),* Hist. Ser., *1* (5): 187-249.

_____. 1964. Rediscovery of the type specimen of *Forcipiger longirostris* (Broussonet) (Perciformes, Chaetodontidae). *Copeia,* 1964 (1): 165-169.

Whitehead, P.J.P. 1967. The dating of the 1st Edition of Cuvier's "Le Règne Animal distribue d'après son organization." *J. Soc. Bibliogr. Nat. Hist.,* 4(6): 300-301.

Whitley, G.P. 1926. The biology of north-west islet, Capricorn group. *Aust. Zool.,* 4 (4): 227-236.

_____. 1927. A check-list of the fishes recorded from Fijian waters. *J. Pan-Pac. Res. Inst., 2* (1): 3-8.

_____. 1928. Fishes from the Great Barrier Reef collected by Mr. Melbourne Ward. *Rec. Aust. Mus., 16* (6): 294-304.

_____. 1928. A check-list of the fishes of the Santa Cruz Archipelago, Melanesia. *J. Pan-Pac. Res. Inst., 3* (1): 11-13.

_____. 1929. Names of fishes in Meuschen's index to the "Zoolophylacium Gronovianum". *Rec. Aust. Mus., 17*(6): 297-307.

_____. 1930. Ichthyological Miscellanea. *Mem. Queensl. Mus.,* Brisbane, *10* (1): 8-31.

_____. 1931. New Names for Austral. fishes. *Aust. Zool., 6* (4): 310-334.

_____. 1932. Fishes. Great Barrier Reef Exped. 1928-29 *Sci. Rep. Br. Mus. (Nat. Hist.), 4* (9): 267-316.

_____. 1938. Fishes from Nauru, Gilbert Islands, Oceania. *Proc. Linn. Soc. N.S.W., 43* (3/4): 282-304, 1 pl.

_____. 1943. The fishes of New Guinea. *Aust. Mus. Mag., 8* (4): 141-144.

_____. 1944. Illust. of southwestern Australian fishes. *Proc. R. Zool. Soc. N.S.W.,* 1943-1944: 25-29.

——————. 1950. Studies in Ichthyology. No. 14. *Rec. Aust. Mus.,* *22* (3): 234-245, 1 pl.

——————. 1952. Some noteworthy fishes of Eastern Australia. *Proc. R. Zool. Soc. N.S.W.,* 1950-51: 27-32.

——————. 1954. New locality records for some Australian fishes. *Proc. R. Zool. Soc. N.S.W.,* 1952-1953: 23-30

——————. 1955. James Stewart - Ichthyologist. *In:* James Stewart: Artist Naturalist, by A. Musgrave. *Aust. Zool.,* *12* (2): 129-131, pls. 12-18.

——————. 1957. Ichthyological Illustrations. *Prov. R. Zool. Soc. N.S.W.,* 1955-56: 56-71.

——————. 1958. *List of type specimens of recent fishes in the Australian Museum.* Mimeo. 40 pp.

——————. 1961. Fishes from New Caledonia. *Proc. R. Zool. Soc. of N.S.W.,* 1958-1959: 60-65.

——————. 1964a. Presidential Address. A survey of Australian Ichthyology. *Proc. of the Linn. Soc. of N.S.W.* *89* (part 1, no. 404): 11-127.

——————. 1964b. Fishes from the Coral Sea and the Swain Reefs. *Rec. Aust. Mus.,* *26* (5): 145-195, pl. 8-10.

——————. 1964 c. New records of fishes from Australia. *Aust. Nat.,* *12* (4): 7-9, 1 pl.

——————. 1965. Illustrations and records of fishes. *Aust. Zool.,* *13* (2): 103-120.

——————. 1968a. A Checklist of the Fishes recorded from the New Zealand Region. *Aust. Zool.,* *15* (1): 1-102.

——————. 1968b. Some fishes from New South Wales. *Proc. R. Zool. Soc. N.S.W.,* 1966-67: 32-40, pl. VIII & IX.

Wickler, W. 1961. Funktionen der Farbmusterung bei Fischen. *Neptun,* 1 Jahrgang, Heft 3, September, 1961: 63-65.

——————. 1967. *The Marine Aquarium.* Aquarium Paperbacks. Studio Vista Ltd. Blue-Star House.

Wiegmann, W.H. and J.T. Nichols. 1915. Notes on fishes near New York. *Copeia,* 1915 (23): 43-45.

Willem, V. 1944. Contribution a l'étude des organes respiratoires chez les Teleostéens Plectognathes. 2 e Partie: Chaetodontiformes. *Bull. Mus. R. Hist. Nat. Belg.,* 20 (6): 21 pp.

Woodland, D.J. and R.J. Slack-Smith. 1963. Fishes of Heron Island, Capricorn Group, Great Barrier Reef. *Univ. Queensl. Pap.,* *2* (2): 1-69.

Woods, L.P. 1952. Fishes attracted to surface light at night in the Gulf of Mexico. *Copeia,* 1952 (1): 40-41.

——————. 1953. Subfamily Chaetodontinae. (Pp. 566-596). *In:* Schultz and others. Fishes of the Marshall & Marianas Islands. Vol. I. Families from Asymmetrontidae through Siganidae. *Bull. U.S. Natl. Mus.,* *202:* 1-685, pls 1-74.

——————. 1960. *Chaetodon goniodes,* a new butterfly fish from Puerto Rico. *Bull. Mar. Sci. Gulf & Caribb.,* *10* (4): 417-420.

—————— and L.P. Schultz. 1953. Subfamily Pomacanthinae. (Pp. 597-

608.) *In:* Schultz and others. Fishes of the Marshall and Marianas Islands. Vol. I. Families from Assymetrontidae through Siganidae. *Bull. U.S. Natl. Mus.,* 202: 1-685, pls. 1-74.

Woodward, A.S. 1942. Some new and little-known Upper Cretaceous fish from Mount Lebabon. *Ann. Mag. Nat. Hist.,* Ser. 11, *9:* 537-568.

Worrell, E. 1966. *The Great Barrier Reef.* Angus and Robertson. 128 pp.

Yamaguti, S. 1963. *Parasitic Copepoda and Branchiura of Fishes.* Interscience Publ., Division of John Wiley & Sons, New York. 1,104 pp, 333 pls.

Yamakawa, T. 1971. Additional records of marine fishes from Amami (4). *Rept. Usa Mar. Biol. Stn. Kochi Univ.,* 18 (2): 1-21.

Yamanouchi, T. 1956. The visual acuity of the coral fish *Microcanthus strigatus* (Cuv. & Val.). *Publ. Seto Mar. Biol. Lab.,* 5: 133-156, 10 figs.

Yusada, Fujio 1967. Some observations on the color of the young forms of *Chaetodontoplus septentrionalis* (T. & S.). *Sci. Rep. Yokosuka City Mus.,* *13:* 78-81, illus.

—————————, H. Masuda, and S. Takama. 1975. A butterflyfish, *Chaetodon selene,* from the Izu Peninsula, Japan, with a note on juvenile. *Jpn. J. Ichthyol.,* *22* (2): 97-99.

Zaneveld, J.S. 1961. The fishery resources and the fishery industries of the Netherlands Antilles. *Gulf & Caribb. Fisheries Institut., Proc. 14th Annual Session,* Nov. 1961: 137-171.

Zumpe, Doris 1963. *Chelmon rostratus* (Chaetodontidae) Kampfverhalten. *Encyclopedia Cinematographica,* E207/ 1963. Institut für Wissenschaftlichen Film; pp. 335-339.

—————————. 1964. Laboratory observations on the aggressive behaviour of some butterfly fishes. (Chaetodontidae). *Zeitschrift fur Tierpsychol.,* 22 (2): 226-236.

—————————. 1964. Kampfverhalten bei *Chelmon rostratus. Die Aquarien und Terrarien-Zeitschrift (D.A.T.Z.),* *17* (7): 210-212.

—————————. 1964. Das Kampfverhalten bei *Heniochus acuminatus. Die Aquarien und Terrarien Zeitschrift (D.A.T.Z.),* *17* (10): 303-305.

Index

Valid species, genera, subgenera and the pages where they are described are printed in **bold**. Page numbers in *italics* refer to photographs and illustrations.

823

distribution, *770*
paucifasciatus, *272, 273*, **402-3**, *403*,
 406
pelewensis, *543, 545, 548*, **719-21**,
 720
 distribution, *771*
p. *germanus*, *719*
pepek, *478, 598*
pictus, *587, 591*
plebeius, *33, 37, 88, 89, 304, 305,*
 307, 447, 450, **450-1**, *454*
plebeji, *447*
plebejus, *450, 674*
polylepis, *194, 199*
praetextatus, *522*
principalis, *598*
princeps, *594*
punctatofasciatus, *307, 537, 540, 541,*
 716-9, *717, 718*
 distribution, *771*
punctato-fasciatus, *479, 716, 719,*
 725
p. *multicinctus*, *725*
punctato-lineatus, *716*
punctatus, *696*
punctulatus, *685*
quadrimaculatus, *500, 501, 504,*
 728-30, *729*
rafflesi, *408, 409, 568*, **594-7**, *595,*
 597
rainfordi, *8, 36, 37, 444, 445, 645,*
 645-8, *646*
reinwardti, *673*
reticulatus, **324-5**, *514*, **514-5**, **518**,
 565
robustus, *461, 464*, **731-3**, *731*
rostratus, *114, 118*
Sanctae Helenae, *690*
Sanctae Helenae var. *uniformis*, *690*
sanctahelenae, *528, 529, 532, 533,*
 690-2, *691*
Sebae, *594*
sebanus, *582*
sedentarius, *34, 516, 517*, **692-6**,
 693, 694
selene, *428, 429*, **625-8**, *626, 631*
semilarvatus, *1, 77, 352, 353, 354,*
 554-5, *558, 558*
semeion, *105, 384, 385*, **618-22**,
 619, 620, 621
setifer, *581, 582*

s. var. *hawaiiensis*, *588*
speculum, *300, 301*, **454-5**, **458-9**,
 459, 462
sphenospilus, *637*
spilopleura, *454, 462*
striatus, *17, 472, 473, 661*, **661-4**,
 663
striganguli, *418*
strigangulus, *418*
superbus, *514*
Tallii, *612*
tau-nigrum, *478*
tearlachi, *418*
teatae, *234*
tinkeri, *240, 241, 370*, **370-1**, *374*
Townleyi, *278*
triangularis, *306, 418*
triangulum, *307, 418, 434*, **427**, *430,*
 430-1, *434*
t. baronessa, *434*
t. var. *larvatus*, *439*
trichrous, *496*, **703-5**, *704*
 distribution, *770*
tricinctus, *452, 453, 648*, **648-50**
trifascialis, *21, 76, 276, 277, 280,*
 281, **418-9**, *419*, **422-3**, *423, 426*
trifasciatis, *418*
trifasciatus, *25, 54, 88, 474*, **478-9**,
 479, **482-3**, **486**, *763*
t. arabica, *487*
t. austriacus, *494*
t. caudifasciatus, *479*
t. lunulatus, *312, 313*, **482-3**
t. trifasciatus, *316* **483**
t. var. *arabica*, *487*
t. var. *austriacus*, *494*
t. var. *Klunzingeri*, *494*
truncatus, *142, 143*
ulietensis, *52, 64, 400, 401, 606,*
 606-9
u. var. *aurora*, *607*
u. var. *confluens*, *607*
unicolor, *318*
unimaculatus, *306, 636*, **637-41**, *640*
u. unimaculatus, *432, 433, 436*
u. interruptus, *437, 637, 638*
u. sphenospilus, *637*
vagabundus, *13, 97, 412, 413, 587,*
 587-90, *591, 764*
v. pictus, *589, 590*
v. var. *jordani*, *591*